CW01236698

Financial Markets and Institutions
A Managerial Approach

Kenneth J. Thygerson

California State University, San Bernardino

**HarperCollins*CollegePublishers*

To my wife, Darlene, and

our sons, Keith and Kent

Acquisitions Editor: Kirsten D. Sandberg
Developmental Editor: Brown Editorial Service
Project Coordination, Text and Cover Design: Proof Positive/Farrowlyne
　Associates, Inc.
Cover Photo: Mitsugu Hara/Photonica
Production/Manufacturing: Michael Weinstein/Paula Keller
Compositor: Black Dot Graphics, Inc.
Printer and Binder: R.R. Donnelley & Sons Company
Cover Printer: The Lehigh Press, Inc.

FINANCIAL MARKETS AND INSTITUTIONS: A MANAGERIAL APPROACH
Copyright © 1993 by HarperCollins College Publishers

All rights reserved. Printed in the United States of America. No part of this book may be used or reproduced in any manner whatsoever without written permission, except in the case of brief quotations embodied in critical articles and reviews. For information address HarperCollins College Publishers, 10 East 53rd Street, New York, NY 10022.

Library of Congress Cataloging-in-Publication Data

Thygerson, Kenneth J. (Kenneth James)
　　Financial markets and institutions : a managerial approach /
　Kenneth J. Thygerson. — 1st ed.
　　　Includes bibliographical references and index.
　　　ISBN 0-06-501278-X
　　　1. Financial institutions—United States. 2. Financial
　　institutions—Government policy—United States. 3. Financial
　　instruments—United States. 4. Money market—United States.
　　I. Title.
HG2491.T49   1992   92-22258
332.1'0973–dc20   CIP

93 94 95   9 8 7 6 5 4 3 2

Brief Contents

Detailed Contents   v
Preface   xxv

Part 1 Financial Claims, Interest Rates, and Markets 1

Chapter 1   Overview: Claims, Markets, and Institutions   2
Chapter 2   Interest Rates and the Term Structure   19
Chapter 3   Financial Claims   51
Chapter 4   Valuation of Financial Claims   75
Chapter 5   Futures and Options   114
Chapter 6   Financial Markets   141

Part 2 Financial Intermediaries: Their Role in the Financial System 169

Chapter 7   The Theory of Intermediation and the Function of Intermediaries   170
Chapter 8   U.S. Financial Intermediary History   189
Appendix   The Objectives of an Efficient Payment System   211
Chapter 9   Commercial Banks   214
Chapter 10   Thrift Institutions   250
Appendix   The Thrift Debacle   273
Chapter 11   Life Insurance Companies and Pension Funds   284
Chapter 12   Other Financial Institutions   304

iii

Part 3 — Government's Role in the Financial Sector 331

Chapter 13 Federal Government Credit Activities 332

Chapter 14 Financial Institution Regulation, Insurers, and Regulators 349

Appendix A The Financial Institutions Reform, Recovery, and Enforcement Act of 1989: A Case Study in Regulatory Retribution 376

Appendix B Major Provisions of the Federal Deposit Insurance Corporation Improvement Act of 1991 382

Chapter 15 Structural Changes and the Performance of Financial Intermediaries 387

Part 4 — Managing Financial Intermediaries 411

Chapter 16 Basic Financial Management for Intermediaries 412

Appendix Financial Innovation: Theory and Practice 440

Chapter 17 Distribution Channels for Financial Products 448

Chapter 18 Measuring Interest Rate Risk 471

Chapter 19 Managing Interest Rate Risk 514

Chapter 20 Managing Credit Risk 547

Appendix Problem Loans and Investments 581

Chapter 21 Performance Analysis for Financial Institutions 590

Chapter 22 Asset Management and Pricing 613

Chapter 23 Liability Management and Pricing 645

Chapter 24 Foreign Exchange, Exchange Rates, and Managing Currency Risk 665

Financial Tables 690

Glossary 697

References 715

Index 727

Detailed Contents

Preface xxv

Part 1 Financial Claims, Interest Rates, and Markets 1

Chapter 1 Overview: Claims, Markets, and Institutions 2

Taking the Global Perspective 2
The Savings and Investment Process 4
Interest Rates as the Allocation Mechanism 6
Financial Claims 6
Financial Markets 7
Global Markets in Financial Claims 7
Financial Institutions 9
Agency Theory and Intermediaries 10
Government's Role in the Financial Process 11
The Flow of Funds 12
Managing Financial Institutions 13
Jobs in Financial Institutions 15

Summary 16
Questions 18

Chapter 2 Interest Rates and the Term Structure 19

Fluctuations in Interest Rates 19
    The Real Rate of Interest 19

Supply and Demand for Loanable Funds by Sector 21
    Income and Interest Rate Impact on Supply and Demand for Funds 22
    Interest Rate Impact on Supply and Demand for Funds 23
    Demand and Supply of Loanable Funds and the Business Cycle 24
    Federal Reserve's Impact on Interest Rates 26
Determinants of Market Interest Rates 28
    Inflation and Interest Rates: The "Fisher Effect" 28
    The Term Structure of Interest Rates 29
    Expectations Theory 31
    Implied Forward Interest Rate 33
    Demonstration Problem: Computing Implied Forward Rate 34
    Segmentation Theory 34
    Preferred Habitat Theory 36
    Liquidity Preference Theory 36
Specific Risk and Cost Factors Affecting Interest Rates 37
    Credit or Default Risk 38
    Marketability Risk 39
    Call or Prepayment Risk 39
    Servicing Cost 40
    Nominal Interest Rates on Taxable Debt 41
    Exchange Rate Risk 41
    Demonstration Problem: Nominal Interest Rate on Specific Type of Debt 42
    Taxability 43
    Reinvestment Risk 44

Summary 46
Questions 48
Problems 49

Chapter 3   Financial Claims   51

    Why Financial Claims Are Created 51
    The Debt Financial Claim as a Contract 52
    Who Creates Financial Claims? 53
    Household Holdings of Financial Claims 54
The Taxonomy of Financial Claims 55
    Primary and Secondary Claims 55
    Derivative Claims 55
    Asset-Backed Claims 56
    Hybrid Claims 56
Major Types and Issuers of Primary Financial Claims Outstanding 57
    Federal Government Claims 57
    Primary Debt Claims Issued by Nonfinancial Businesses 58
    Primary Claims Issued by Households 61

Detailed Contents **vii**

        Primary Claims Issued by State and Local Governments 62
        International Issuers of Claims 63
    Secondary Claims Issued by the Financial Sector 64
        International Focus International Investments Boom 64
        Secondary Claims Issued by Depositories 65
        Claims Issued by Government Agencies, Sponsored Enterprises, and International Institutions 67
        Mortgage-Backed Securities 71

Summary 72
Questions 73

Chapter 4 Valuation of Financial Claims 75

The Basics: Present and Future Values, Yields, and Compounding 75
        Present Value Theory 76
        Compounding 77
        Savings Certificate Compounding Wars 78
        Yield to Maturity 79
        Demonstration Problem: Yield to Maturity 80
        Equivalent Annual Yield 81
        Demonstration Problem: Equivalent Annual Yield 81
        Cash Flows 82
Valuation and Yields for Common Debt Claims 83
        Discounted Treasury Securities 83
        Bank Discount and Coupon Equivalent Yields on T-bills 84
        Yield to Maturity on a Bond and Yield to a Call 86
        Repurchase Agreements and Reverse Repurchase Agreements 87
        Perpetual Preferred and Consols 87
        Zero Coupon Bonds 88
Valuation and Yields on Fixed-Rate Mortgages and Hybrid Financial Claims 88
        Stripped Treasuries 89
        Reading the Financial Page Yields on Stripped Treasuries 91
        Fixed-Rate Mortgages and Mortgage-Backed Securities 92
        Prepayment Assumptions and Mortgage Yields 93
        Reading the Financial Page Yields on a Hypothetical Selection of Mortgage Securities 97
        Interest-Only and Principal-Only Strips on Mortgage Securities 98
        Servicing Income Contracts (Strips) 99
        Collateralized Mortgage Obligations and Real Estate Mortgage Investment Conduits 100
Senior-Subordinated Securities 102
Municipal Securities and Tax Exemption 104

Summary 105
Questions 109
Problems 109

Chapter 5 Futures and Options 114

Functions of Futures and Options Contracts   114
Using Futures and Options Contracts   115
Financial Futures   115
What Is a Financial Futures Contract?   116
Reading the Financial Page   Treasury Bond Futures Contract   116
Valuation of Financial Futures Contracts   117
Hedging   118
Mechanics of the Futures Market   119
Legal and Ethical Issues   Options and Futures Markets: Illegal Trading   120
Price Circuit Breaker—The Daily Limit   120
Options   121
International Focus   U.S. Domination of Derivatives Threatened   122
Common Options Found in Financial Intermediary Transactions and Claims   122
Understanding the Option Transaction   125
Reading the Financial Page   Stock Option Quotation   126
Option Payoffs   127
Intrinsic Value and Time Value   128
Factors That Influence the Value of an Option   128
Valuing Options: The Black-Scholes Option Pricing Model   129
Example of Option Valuation   131
Sensitivity Analysis and Option Values   133
Marketability and the Value of Options   134

Summary   134
Questions   136
Problems   136
Case 5.1   The Hot New Account   138

Chapter 6 Financial Markets   141

Functions of Financial Markets   141
The Taxonomy of Financial Markets   142
Types of Markets: Primary and Secondary   142
Types of Markets: Money Market and Capital Market   142
Types of Markets: Dealers and Organized Exchanges   143
Types of Markets: Spot and Forward   145
Types of Markets: Human Interface Versus Computers   146
Arbitrage   146
The Role of the Trader   149
Globalization of Financial Markets   150
Euromarkets   152

Legal and Ethical Issues   Michael Milken: Junk Bonds and Rigged Market?   153
The Efficiency of the Financial Claims Markets   154
    Why Efficiency Matters   154
Operational and Informational Efficiency   155
    Operational Efficiency   155
    Availability of Price Information   156
    Price Continuity   156
    Transaction Costs   157
    Circuit Breakers and Market Efficiency   158
    Informational Efficiency   159
    Weak-form Market Efficiency   159
    Semistrong-form Market Efficiency   160
    Strong-form Market Efficiency   161
    Legal and Ethical Issues   Ivan Boesky: Insider Trading   161
    Empirical Tests of Market Efficiency: Valuation Anomalies   162

Summary   163
Questions   165
Problems   166
Project 6.1   Analyzing a Market   167

Part 2   Financial Intermediaries: Their Role in the Financial System   169

Chapter 7   The Theory of Intermediation and the Function of Intermediaries   170

General Economic Rationale for Intermediaries   170
    Transaction Costs Reduction Rationale   171
    Operator of the Payment System Rationale   171
    Information Processing and Monitoring Rationale   171
    Asset and Liability Transformation Rationale   172
A Comprehensive Structure of the Functions of Intermediaries   174
    Financial Claim Origination   174
    Financial Claim Servicing   175
    Financial Claim Brokerage   175
    Market-Making   176
    Portfolio Risk Management Function   176
The Financial Claim/Function Matrix   177
    An Example of the Small Commercial Bank   179

Mission Insurance Company Financial Claim/Function Matrix   180

Summary   183
Questions   184
Case 7.1   Financial Functions: South Regional Bank   185

Chapter 8   U.S. Financial Intermediary History   189

Early Financial Intermediary History   189
    The Early History: 1620–1800   191
    Revolution and the Bank of North America   191
    Agrarian Interests Versus the Merchants and the Wealthy   191
    State Banks Fill Void   192
    The War of 1812 and the Second Bank of the United States   192
    Suffolk System and New York Safety Fund   192
    Second Bank Falls to Political Pressures   193
    State Banks Blossom and Then Bust   193
    Additional Efforts at State Banking Regulation   193
    Civil War Brings National Banking   194
Early History of Nonbank Intermediaries   194
    Insurance Companies   194
    The Thrift Institutions: The Banks' Missed Opportunities   195
    Pension Funds, Trusts, and Mutual Funds   195
    Lessons from History   196
The Federal Reserve System   196
    Safety and Soundness Responsibilities   197
    Implementing Monetary Policy   197
Modern Financial Intermediary History: Creating a Segmented Financial Structure   198
    McFadden Act of 1927: No Interstate Branching   198
    Deposit Insurance: The FDIC and FSLIC   199
    Federal Charters for Specialized Thrifts   199
    Glass-Steagall: The Wall Between Investment and Commercial Banking   200
    Federal Guarantee and Government Sponsored Credit Agencies   201
    Regulation Q: Interest Rate Price Controls   201
Modern Financial Institution History: On the Road to Deregulation   202
    A New Structure at Hand?   204

Summary   207
Questions   209
Appendix   The Objectives of an Efficient Payment System   211
   Electronic Payment Devices   211
      Check-Processing Improvements   212
      Paper to Electronic Transfers   213
      Consolidating the Banking System   213

Chapter 9 Commercial Banks 214

Asset and Liability Structure of Commercial Banks 214
    Asset Structure of Commercial Banks 215
    Liability Structure of the Banking System 217
    Asset Structure Differences by Size of Bank 219
    Liability Structure Differences by Size of Bank 220
    Regulation of Commercial Banks 220
    Financial Claim/Function Matrix 221
    Commercial Bank Financial Performance 222
    Management Highlights Special Management Concerns for Commercial Banks 225
    Bank Failures Climb 226
    Competition from Thrifts and Nonbanks 228
Bank Structure and Competition 229
    Size Structure 229
    Branching and Interstate Banking 230
    Efficiency Through Size: Economies of Scale and Scope 233
    Research Analyses and Limitations 235
    Entry and Exit 236
    Bank Holding Companies 236
International Banking 1960 to 1990 238
    Functions Performed by U.S. Banks Internationally 239
    How U.S. Banks Are Organized for International Banking 239
    Foreign Banks Operating in the United States 241
    Organizational Forms for Foreign Banks Operating in the United States 242
    Declining Relative Position of the United States in International Banking 243
    International Focus Japan Bank Capital and the Nikkei Average 244
    Reasons for the Changing Relative Position of International Banks 245

Summary 247
Questions 248

Chapter 10 Thrift Institutions 250

    Overview of Thrift Institutions 250
Savings and Loan Associations 252
    Mutual and Stock Institutions 252
    Regulation and Insurance of Accounts 253
    Size Structure of S&Ls 254
    Federal and State Charters 255
    Asset Structure of S&Ls 255

Liability Structure of S&Ls 257
Management Highlights Special Management Concerns for S&Ls and SBs 258
S&L Financial Performance 259
Failed Savings and Loans and the Resolution Trust Corporation 262
Legal and Ethical Issues Lincoln Savings: Security Fraud, Influence Peddling, and the Dual System of Chartering Financial Institutions 263
Financial Claim/Function Matrix 264

Savings Banks 264
Regulation and Insurance of Accounts 266
Asset Structure of Savings Banks 266
Liability Structure of Savings Banks 266
Recent Savings Bank Financial Performance 267

Credit Unions 267
Regulation and Insurance of Accounts 268
Common Bond 268
Credit Union Size and Ownership Structure 269
Asset Structure of Credit Unions 269
Liability Structure of Credit Unions 270
Management Highlights Special Management Concerns for Credit Unions 270
Recent Credit Union Financial Performance 271

Summary 271
Questions 272
Appendix The Thrift Debacle 273
  Overview 273
  Pre-1980 Protectionist Era 274
  Ineffective Regulation 275
    Legal and Ethical Issues Vernon Savings: Misuse of Corporate Resources and Political Influence Peddling 277
  Government Macroeconomic Policies and Induced Competition 278
  Who Gained from the Crisis and Who Pays for the Bailout? 279
  Proposed Solutions 281
  Questions 282

Chapter 11 Life Insurance Companies and Pension Funds 284

Life Insurance Companies 285
  Mortality Risk 286
  Basic Types of Life Insurance 287
  Types of Ordinary Life Policies 287
  Annuities 288
  New Policies Stress Investment Performance 290

Changing Pattern of Insurance Premiums   291
Asset Structure of Life Companies   292
Size and Ownership Structure of the Life Insurance Industry   293
Life Company State of Domicile   294
Pension Funds   294
Types of Pension Plans   295
Life Insurance Companies and Pension Programs   296
Asset Structure of Pension Funds   297
Growth of Pension Fund Assets   297
Putting Pension Obligations on the Balance Sheet   299

Summary   300
Questions   301
Problems   302

Chapter 12   Other Financial Institutions   304

Investment Banks   304
Types of Investment Bankers   305
Underwriting Debt and Equity Securities   306
Legal and Ethical Issues   Japanese Investment Banking Companies: Financial Guarantees for Customers and Influence Peddling   307
Mergers and Acquisitions   307
Market-Making and Trading   308
Legal and Ethical Issues   Salomon Brothers: Treasury Auction Irregularities   309
Assets and Liabilities of Investment Banks   310
Property and Casualty Companies   311
Operating or Underwriting Activities   311
Investment Performance   312
Recent P&C Company Financial Performance   312
Management Highlights   Special Management Concerns for Property and Casualty Companies   314
Finance Companies   314
Asset and Liability Structures of Finance Companies   315
Mortgage Banking Companies   316
Mortgage Loan Origination   317
Servicing   317
Warehousing and Interest Rate Risk Management   317
Size Structure of Mortgage Banking Companies   318
Diversified Financial Service Companies   318
Investment Intermediaries   320
Open-End Mutual Funds   320
Professional Asset Management   322
Organization and Administration   323

Limited Partnerships 324
Real Estate Investment Trusts 325
Trust Companies 326

Summary 328
Questions 329

Part 3 Government's Role in the Financial Sector 331

Chapter 13 Federal Government Credit Activities 332

Rationale for Federal Government Credit Activities 332
Types of Federal Government Lending Programs 333
Private Financial Institution Involvement with Government Credit Programs 336
Primary Federal Lending Organizations and Programs 338
Allocational Efficiency of Government Credit Programs 341
Impact of GSEs on Private Intermediaries 342
    Agency and Depository Pricing of Loans: The Agency Capital Advantage 342
    Agency and Depository Pricing of Loans: The Cost of Debt Advantage 344

Summary 346
Questions 348

Chapter 14 Financial Institution Regulation, Insurers, and Regulators 349

The Public Good Theory of Financial Regulation 350
    Achieve Competitive Financial Markets 351
    Reduce Information Imperfections and Asymmetries 351
    Eliminate Prejudice or Bias of Supply 352
    Achieve Equal Access 353
    Improve Implementation of Monetary Policy Goals 354
    Pursue Socially Desirable Credit Allocation 354
    Reduce Potential for Insider Abuse and Fraud 355
    Reduce Potential for Disruptive Impact of Financial Institutions' Failures 355
    Protect Taxpayers from Deposit Insurance Fund Failures 356
    Costs of Regulation 357
Issues Related to Deposit Insurance Programs 358

Deposit Insurance and Moral Hazard   358
Too Big to Fail   359
Protecting Deposit Insurance Fund Solvency   360
Constraints to Competition to Ensure Financial Soundness   362
How the Regulatory Process Works   363
Stigler Special Interest Theory   363
Kane Dialectical Theory of Regulation   363
Regulatory Procedures   364
Regulators' Impact on Financial Performance and Operations   365
Financial Institution Regulators and Insurers   366
Structure of the Regulatory System   366
Primary Regulators and Insurers   366
Office of the Comptroller of the Currency   367
Federal Reserve System   368
Legal and Ethical Issues   Bank of Credit and Commerce International: Money Laundering and International Influence Peddling   368
Federal Deposit Insurance Corporation   369
State Banking and Thrift Regulators   369
Office of Thrift Supervision   369
National Credit Union Administration   369
Department of Labor   370
Commodity Futures Trading Commission   370
Securities and Exchange Commission   370
State Insurance Commissions   371
Securities Investor Protection Corporation   372
Department of Housing and Urban Development   372
Pension Benefit Guarantee Corporation   372

Summary   373
Questions   374
Appendix A   The Financial Institutions Reform, Recovery, and Enforcement Act of 1989: A Case Study in Regulatory Retribution   376
Failure Due in Large Part to Early Economic Policies   376
Finding the Scapegoat(s)   377
Congress Reregulates and Weakens the Thrift Charter   377
Major Provisions Impacting Thrifts   378
Major Act Provisions Impacting Industry Structure   379
Resolution Trust Corporation   380
Appendix B   Major Provisions of the Federal Deposit Insurance Corporation Improvement Act of 1991   382
Safety and Soundness Reforms   382
Regulatory Powers for Dealing with Undercapitalized Depositories   383
Other Major Regulatory and Institutional Powers Changes   385
Questions   386

xvi   Detailed Contents

Chapter 15   Structural Changes and the Performance of Financial Intermediaries   387

Overview   388
Technologically Induced Changes   389
    Information Processing   389
    Communication Technology   390
Economically Induced Changes   390
    Inflation During Vietnam War Years   390
    October 1979 Federal Reserve Policy Change   391
    Oil Price Cycle   391
Governmentally Induced Changes   392
    Regulation Q and Delayed Deregulation   392
    Loss of Commercial Banks' Monopoly in the Payment System   393
    Government Sponsored Enterprises   394
    Inadequate Regulation and Supervision   395
    Expanded Deposit Insurance Coverage and Moral Hazard   396
    Constraints on Interstate Branching and Consolidation   397
    State Deregulation and Chartering Impact   397
    FIRREA Fallout   398
    1986 Tax Reform Act   399
Competitively Induced Changes   399
    Mutual Funds   399
    Money and Capital Market Access to High-Quality Borrowers   400
    Capital Market Access for Lower Quality Credits   400
    Growth in Foreign Banking Activities   400
    Competition from Investment Banks and Discount Brokers   401
    Nonbank Financial Competition   401
Overcapacity: An Industry Curse   401
Impact Assessment 1970–2000   402
Profits and Capital   404
Policy Options   406

Summary   407
Questions   408

Part 4   Managing Financial Intermediaries   411

Chapter 16   Basic Financial Management for Intermediaries   412

Primary Financial Management Duties   412
    Valuation of Financial Claims   413
    Interest Rate Risk Management   413
    Credit Risk Management   415

Pricing Loans and Liabilities and Selecting Distribution
    Channels   415
Capital Structure and Financial Leverage   417
    Financial Risk and Leverage   418
    Relative Capital Positions of the Major Financial Institutions   421
    Business Risks   422
Intermediary Profitability   423
    Net Origination Income   424
    Net Servicing Income   425
    Net Brokerage Income   425
    Net Portfolio Income   426
    Portfolio and Fee Income   427
Net Interest Margin and Spread   428
    Factors Influencing the Net Interest Spread and Net Interest Spread to
        Average Assets   429
Fee-Based Services of Financial Institutions   432
    Origination Sources of Fee Income   432
    Servicing Sources of Fee Income   433
    Servicing Fees That Are Transaction Related   434
    Brokerage Sources of Fee Income   435
Objectives of Mutual Institutions   435

Summary   437
Questions   439
Appendix   Financial Innovation: Theory and Practice   440
  Theories of Financial Innovation   440
      Silber's Constraint Theory of Innovation   441
      Kane's Market, Technology, and Political Theory of
          Innovation   441
      Miller's Regulation and Taxation Theory of Innovation   441
      Merton's Market Efficiency Theory of Innovation   441
      *Legal and Ethical Issues   Centrust Savings Bank: Patents on Financial
          Products*   442
      Technology and Financial Innovation   443
      Regulation and Financial Innovation   443
      Taxes and Financial Innovation   445
      New Products and Innovation   446
  Innovation and Monetary Policy   446
  Questions   447

Chapter 17   Distribution Channels for Financial Products   448

Alternative Channels of Distribution   448
Electronic Banking   451
    A Framework for Selecting Distribution Channels   454
A Model of Retail Depository Branch Profitability   455
    Why a Branch Profitability Model Is Needed   455

Model of Branch Functions and Activities 456
Measurement Model of Branch Profitability 456
Using the Model to Analyze Branch Purchases, Sales, Closures, and Swaps 463

Summary 463
Questions 464
Case 17.1 Case Study in Branch Profitability: To Keep or to Sell 466
Case 17.2 Determining the Appropriate Branch Premium to Pay for Acquisition 468

Chapter 18 Measuring Interest Rate Risk 471

An Example of Interest Rate Risk 472
Interest Rate Risk Is a Portfolio Concept 474
Periodic *GAP* 474
An Example of a Periodic *GAP* Report 475
GAP Buckets 479
Limitations of *GAP* Reports 479
What Is the Right *GAP*? 481
GAP and Forecasting Business Cycles 481
Duration 482
Calculating Duration 482
Properties of the Duration Measure 485
Duration and Interest Rate Elasticity 485
Portfolio Durations 486
Using Duration *GAP* for Interest Rate Risk Management 487
Duration and the Market Value of Equity 489
Problems and Limitations in Calculating Duration 490
Mark-to-Market 490
Mark-to-Market Equity Valuations 492
Mark-to-Market Valuation of Equity Sensitivity Analysis 492
Limitations of Mark-to-Market 495
Income Simulation 499
Example of an Income Simulation 500

Summary 502
Questions 505
Problems 506
Case 18.1 *GAP* Measurement of Interest Rate Risk for North Savings Bank 509

Chapter 19 Managing Interest Rate Risk 514

The Income and Interest Rate Risk Trade 514
Financial Futures and Forward Cash Markets 516
Futures and Forward Cash Market Hedges 516

Hedge Ratio   517
Demonstration Problem: Futures Hedge   521
Types of Risk-Reducing Hedging Transactions   522
Hazards of Futures Market Transactions   523
Basis Risk   523
Mixing Futures and Options   526
Accounting Issues   527
Futures Options   528
Futures Options: A Description   529
Reading the Financial Page   Futures Options   529
Intrinsic Value and Time Value   530
Using Traded Futures Options   530
Demonstration Problem: Futures Option Hedge   532
Interest Rate Swaps   533
The Typical Swap   534
Demonstration Problem: Interest Rate Swap   535
Commercial Bank Profit from the Swap   537
Risks in Managing Swap Portfolios   537
Interest Rate Swaps and Interest Rate Risk
   Management   538
Adjustable-Rate Lending   539
The Basic ARM Features   539
Other Adjustable Loans   542

Summary   542
Questions   544
Problems   545

Chapter 20   Managing Credit Risk   547

Overview of Credit Risk Trends   574
Major Types of Credit Risks   548
Pure Credit Risk   549
Underwriting Risk   549
Settlement Risk   549
Documentation Risk   550
Operating Risk   550
Political Risk   550
Event Risk   551
Techniques for Managing Credit Risks   551
Diversification of Credit Risk   551
Law of Large Numbers Diversification   552
Portfolio Diversification   555
The Law of Large Numbers/Portfolio Diversification
   Tradeoff   558

xx Detailed Contents

        The Large Loan Exposure: Risk-Sharing Through Participations and Reinsurance   560
Credit Analysis   560
        Cash Flow Analysis   561
        Altman's Z Score   562
        Argenti's Analysis   563
        Credit Analysis and Consumer Loans   563
Covenants in Financial Claims   564
        Typical Covenants Found in Car, Boat, or Recreational Vehicle Loans   564
        Typical Covenants in a Municipal Revenue Bond on an Electric-Generating Facility   565
        Typical Covenants in Noninvestment-Grade Corporate Bonds   565
        Fraud and Credit Losses   567
        Bankruptcy   567
        Collateral and Credit Risk   570
        Off-Balance Sheet Transactions   571

Summary   575
Questions   576
Problems   577
Project 20.1   Covenants   579
Appendix   Problem Loans and Investments   581
   Four Recent Waves of Problem Loans   581
        Risk Versus Return in Lending   583
   What Makes a Bad Loan?   584
   Problem Loan Management   584
        Loan Monitoring and Problem Loan Identification   584
        Collateral Protection and Workout   585
        Repossession and Foreclosure   586
        Bankruptcy   586
        Loan Loss Provisions, Charge-Offs, and Recoveries   587
        Legal and Ethical Issues   Shareholder Class Action Lawsuits   589

Chapter 21   Performance Analysis for Financial Institutions   590

        Time Series Analysis   591
        Cross-Sectional Analysis   591
Financial Ratios for Depositories   592
        Profitability: Overall Performance Measures   593
        Capital Adequacy/Financial Leverage   594
        Asset Credit Quality   596
        Interest Rate Risk Position   597
        Operating Efficiency   598
        Funding Risks   599
        Off-Balance Sheet Risks   600

Performance Criteria for Finance Companies, Property and Casualty
    Companies, Insurance Companies, and Pension Funds   600
Finance Companies   601
Property and Casualty Companies   601
        Profitability Ratios   601
Life Insurance Companies   602
        Funding Risk   602
Pension Funds   604
        Where to Obtain Financial Data   604

Summary   605
Questions   606
Case 21.1   Performance Evaluation: First Independent Bank of
    Boise   607

Chapter 22   Asset Management and Pricing   613

Determining the Asset Structure   613
        Laws and Regulations   614
        Diversification Options   614
        Market Demand Limitations and Pricing   615
        Economies of Scale   616
Liquidity Management   616
        Liquidity, Profitability, and Regulatory Requirements   616
        The Liquidity Management Process   617
        Developing Pro-Forma Cash Flow Statements   617
        Sources of Liquidity: Assets, Liabilities, and Collateral   618
        Liquidity and Regulatory Requirements   620
        Selecting the Liquidity Asset Portfolio   620
Financial Depository Pricing of Loans   622
        Capital Structure and Regulatory Capital Requirements   622
        Regulatory Capital Requirements   623
        *International Focus   Basle Committee Responds to New Bank
            Risks   625*
        Calculating the Weighted Average Cost of Capital   627
        Breakeven Risk Adjusted Asset Yield   628
        Using the BERAY   632
        The Prime Rate   633
Loan Participations and Syndications   633
        Profiting from Loan Participations and Syndications   634
        Demonstration Problem: Example of Participation Yield   637
Accounting for Loan Sales   638

Summary   639
Questions   641
Problems   642

Chapter 23 Liability Management and Pricing 645

Identifying Funding Sources: Wholesale and Retail 645
Costs of Alternative Depository Funding Sources 648
Picking the Optimal Funding Mix: The Funding Alternatives Matrix 651
The Marginal Cost of New Retail Deposits 652
Demonstration Problem: Calculating Marginal Cost of New Funds 653
Asset-Backed Financing 654
   Reasons for Securitization 655
   Types of Asset-Backed Securities 656
   Asset-Backed Collateral Attributes 656
Liability Management for Life Insurance Companies 657
   Liability Costs at Life Insurance Companies 658
   Demonstration Problem: Cost of Single Premium Annuity 661

Summary 661
Questions 663
Problems 663

Chapter 24 Foreign Exchange, Exchange Rates, and Managing Currency Risk 665

Changing Structure of Foreign Exchange Markets: Bretton Woods to Floating Rates 665
   Bretton Woods 666
   The Breakdown of Bretton Woods 667
   Floating Exchange Rates to the Present 668
Foreign Exchange Markets, Trading, and Exchange Rates 669
   Who Uses Foreign Exchange? 669
   Foreign Exchange Trading 670
   Foreign Exchange Rates 670
   Forward Foreign Exchange Market and Interest Rate Parity 672
   Reading the Financial Page   Spot and Forward Foreign Exchange Rates 672
   Why Exchange Rates Change 675
Managing Currency Risk 678
   The Volatility of Foreign Exchange Markets 678
   Forward Cash Markets 679
   Futures Markets in Foreign Currencies 680
   Reading the Financial Page   Exchange Futures Contracts 681
   Options on Foreign Exchange 682
   Reading the Financial Page   Exchange Options 683
   Currency Swaps 684

Summary 685
Questions 687
Problems 688

Financial Tables   690

Glossary   697

References   715

Index   727

Preface

If you want your students to get their hands dirty with real-world insight and experience, then this is the text for your classroom. Based upon years of observing, responding to, and anticipating rapid change in the U.S. financial system, this text represents one of the first major efforts to integrate three key components of the system: financial markets, financial institutions, and financial management of these institutions.

This text is not some catalog of institutional facts that students merely memorize for the upcoming test and then forget on the job. It does not list and describe the latest law, regulation, or financial innovation as so many existing texts do. Instead, it builds a framework for comprehending and thinking critically about financial markets and institutions and for applying the techniques of financial management. Founded upon sound coverage of concepts and theories, it becomes an engaging learning tool as well as a practical resource for students who want a deep understanding of, and profitable insights into, the relationships among markets, institutions, and management.

This text takes a new approach to the material: It maintains that, if students understand underlying principles, then they can apply their knowledge across the board to *all* intermediaries, past, present, and future. This means that the book considers topics relevant to *all* institutions—such as intermediation, arbitrage, financial innovation, regulation, asset and liability pricing, credit risk, interest rate risk, financial claim valuation, and efficiency in markets—first from a theoretical or conceptual perspective and then from a more practical point of view.

To be effective in the finance community today, students must also understand the market setting within which the institutions operate. However, too many texts present microeconomic optimization algorithms out of context; that is, they fail to explain the macroeconomic, regulatory, and competitive influences on institutions. In contrast, this book features an entire chapter on market structure and the competitive forces upon financial institution performance in the last decade.

Finally, the book includes a large number of decision-making algorithms—models for assets and liability pricing, interest rate risk management, credit risk management, branch profitability, and so forth—that financial managers have used successfully in a variety of financial institutions. By reviewing these key decision-making tools, students can effectively transfer and apply what they learned in prerequisite finance courses to their study of financial markets and institutions.

Innovative Features

1. *Financial Claim/Function Matrix:* Since financial intermediaries are becoming more alike in terms of the functions they perform and the services they provide, the theory of financial intermediation allows for the development of a financial claim/function matrix. Highlighting the similarities rather than the differences among financial intermediaries, this matrix or table visually explains and compares the financial claims created by, and the functions served by, particular institutions.

2. *Claim Origination and Credit Risk Management:* With so many problem loans plaguing financial institutions today, students should fully appreciate the essential tasks of intermediaries, specifically the origination of financial claims and the management of associated risks. The text features an early chapter on financial claims and a complete chapter on credit risk management that covers the theory and approach to diversification and the process of creating claims by focusing on the development of covenants.

3. *Valuation Techniques for Hybrid Financial Claims:* Chapter 4 on the valuation of financial claims extends valuation concepts in finance to more financial instruments and applies valuation techniques to such hybrid securities as stripped Treasury bills and mortgage securities. Chapter 18 on the measurement of interest rate risk stresses mark-to-market valuation techniques, which require broader knowledge of valuation.

4. *Theory and Practice of Regulation:* The savings and loan debacle of the 1980s revealed how inadequate regulation can affect the financial system. The book devotes a chapter to the theory of regulation, but focuses on those regulations common to all institutions because the system is so highly regulated.

5. *Theory and Applications of Options:* Since financial intermediaries write many financial contracts with options embedded in them, the

text also stresses option pricing theory so that students can learn how to identify and value options.

6. *Measurement and Management of Interest Rate Risk:* Since the tools that intermediaries use to measure and manage interest rate risks are the same for all financial institutions, two chapters devoted to interest rate risk treat these topics as general subjects with some reference to specific institutions where necessary. The chapters also incorporate more advanced valuation techniques, because more intermediaries are beginning to consider *GAP,* duration, and mark-to-market interest rate risk management techniques in order to remain profitable.

7. *Asset and Liability Pricing:* Several chapters treat asset and liability pricing with special care because financial managers of intermediaries must be able to perform this function.

8. *Theory of Innovation:* Keeping students up-to-date on the various financial instruments and institutional forms is quite a challenge given the last two decades of prolific financial innovation. To meet this challenge, the book focuses on the theory of innovation so that students can recognize the forces likely to motivate such innovation.

9. *Financial Product Distribution:* The continual blending of the U.S. financial system creates many new distribution channels for financial products and services. In a unique chapter on distribution channels, students examine the financial intermediary's role as distributor of financial products and services. This chapter also includes a model for assessing the profitability of retail branches for depository institutions.

10. *Macroeconomic and Structural Issues Affecting Intermediaries:* An entire chapter on the subject raises important macroeconomic and structural issues including the competitive forces that affect depositories. The appendix to this chapter takes a special look at the thrift crisis.

11. *International Activities:* The text gives students a sense of the international nature of financial institutions and markets in chapters on financial claims, markets, and commercial banks; in a separate chapter on foreign exchange, exchange rates, and currency risk management; and in international focus boxes throughout.

12. *Federal Government Credit Programs:* Since federal government credit programs now account for 25 percent of nonfederal borrowing, the text devotes an entire chapter to government credit agencies and programs. The chapter also discusses the impact of these programs on private sector intermediaries.

Possible Course Outlines

This book is designed to be used in various courses now included in many finance programs. These courses may have titles such as money and capital markets, financial institutions, financial markets and institutions, commercial bank management, and financial institution management. The following is a suggested order of presentation for three such courses:

Emphasis on Financial Institutions

Chapter 1	Overview: Claims, Markets, and Institutions
Part 2	Financial Intermediaries: Their Role in the Financial System
Part 3	Government's Role in the Financial Sector
Chapter 16	Basic Financial Management for Intermediaries
Chapter 18	Measuring Interest Rate Risk
Chapter 19	Managing Interest Rate Risk
Chapter 20	Managing Credit Risk
Chapter 24	Foreign Exchange, Exchange Rates, and Managing Currency Risk

Emphasis on Financial Markets

Part 1	Financial Claims, Interest Rates, and Markets
Chapter 1	Overview: Claims, Markets, and Institutions
Part 3	Government's Role in the Financial Sector
Chapter 24	Foreign Exchange, Exchange Rates, and Managing Currency Risk

Emphasis on Managing Financial Institutions

Chapter 1	Overview: Claims, Markets, and Institutions
Part 2	Financial Intermediaries: Their Role in the Financial System
Part 3	Government's Role in the Financial Sector
Part 4	Managing Financial Intermediaries

Key Features

- Each chapter concludes with a "Summary," which provides a review of each chapter.
- "Demonstration Problems" walk students through a realistic management problem and the financial tool used to solve it.
- Because of differences in teaching pedagogy, instructors will find questions, problems, projects, or case studies at the end of many chapters. Others may also include an Appendix if the text material requires more focus.

- "Management Highlights" summarize the major financial management issues that affect each institution.

- "Legal and Ethical Issues" summarize the legal and ethical issues that affect organized markets, regulatory institutions, and foreign financial institutions. The topics include profiles of Michael Milken and junk bond market rigging, Salomon Brothers' Treasury auction irregularities, and Lincoln Savings and Loan and Charles Keating.

- "Reading the Financial Page" features financial tables reprinted from various financial publications. Each of these tables includes an explanation of the data found in the table and a description of the abbreviations.

- "International Focus" gives worldwide perspective on investing, regulation, and financial markets.

Supplemental Materials

A number of additional materials have been prepared and class-tested to enrich students' learning experience and to enhance faculty efficiency.

Instructor's Manual and Transparency Masters

A comprehensive instructor's manual provides chapter-by-chapter outlines. Special references to the large number of transparency masters that accompany the instructor's manual are given. These are designed to outline the material for students and to provide important graphs, tables, and charts.

Over 200 transparency masters have been prepared from course lectures given by the author. These include conceptual talking outlines, graphs, charts, and tables. Examples of problems and solutions have been included on the transparencies to assist in those chapters that have significant problem content.

Printed and Computerized Test Bank

A test bank comprised of factual and conceptual problems in both true/false and multiple-choice format has also been developed. There are over 1,000 questions in the test bank. They have been tested by students to help ensure understandability and to eliminate ambiguity. The test bank is available in TestMaster, a program for IBM-PCs and compatibles.

Readings Book

A companion book, *Financial Markets and Institutions: Readings* by Kenneth J. Thygerson, is available from HarperCollins College Publishers, Inc. This book is designed specifically to accompany this text. It includes 29 readings that have been selected to complement various chapters in the text.

Acknowledgments

Textbooks are not written in a vacuum. Special acknowledgment must go to executives whom I had the pleasure to work with at several financial institutions. Kevin Villani provided much of the conceptual and operational framework for the managerial material found in the book. Kevin also assisted me greatly through his input acquired from teaching early versions of the text in his courses at the University of Southern California. Michael Lea also was responsible for a significant number of ideas that have found their way into the text. Mike's input was particularly useful in Chapters 17, 22, and 23.

Special acknowledgement must also go to H. Robert Bartell at the Center for Banking of East Tennessee State University. Dr. Bartell was a major contributor to Chapters 3, 4, 9, and 13. His close attention to detail and clear writing style greatly improved these chapters. Bob also used early versions of several chapters in his courses at East Tennessee State University.

The initial organization and early chapters benefitted greatly from the following reviewers: James C. Baker, Kent State University; Randall S. Billingsley, Virginia Polytechnic Institute and State University; Paul J. Bolster, Northeastern University; Elijah Brewer, Federal Reserve Bank of Chicago; Ivan T. Call, Brigham Young University; David B. Cox, University of Denver; Clifford L. Fry, University of Houston; John S. Jahera, Jr., Auburn University; Rauf Khan, California State University, San Bernardino; John Olieny, Colorado State University; Robert Schweitzer, University of Delaware; Charlene Sullivan, Purdue University; Haluk Unal, University of Maryland; and James A. Verbrugge, University of Georgia. The final reviews by David Cox and James Verbrugge were especially helpful.

I must also thank many of my undergraduate and graduate students at California State University, San Bernardino, who suffered the indignity of working through incomplete early versions of this text. They found numerous mathematical errors, tested the book's test bank, and provided ideas for problems. I must thank Eldon Lewis of California State University, San Bernardino, for providing a schedule that allowed me to take on this task.

I would also like to thank the team at and assembled by HarperCollins Publishers. This group includes Kirsten Sandberg, Evelyn Owens, Lynn Brown, Michael Weinstein, and Dennis Hamel. They all helped to improve the product and simplify the process.

Finally, to my wife, Darlene, thanks for proofing and typing, and, most of all, understanding.

Kenneth J. Thygerson

Financial Claims, Interest Rates, and Markets

Financial claims are the products created and held by financial intermediaries. Each firm's success relies on the proper valuation of these claims. Intermediaries operate in different financial markets for each type of claim. The chapters in Part 1 are mainly concerned with how financial markets work and how interest rates are set in a market economy.

This part opens with an overview of the savings and investment process, which includes a discussion of the role of financial claims, interest rates, and markets. Special attention is given to the structure of interest rates. After introducing financial claims, there is considerable discussion of the valuation of debt instruments and hybrid securities. Options and futures contracts are covered in a separate chapter, and a discussion of financial markets concludes Part 1.

Part Outline

Chapter 1:
Overview: Claims, Markets, and Institutions

Chapter 2:
Interest Rates and the Term Structure

Chapter 3:
Financial Claims

Chapter 4:
Valuation of Financial Claims

Chapter 5:
Futures and Options

Chapter 6:
Financial Markets

Overview: Claims, Markets, and Institutions

chapter 1

This chapter develops the basic concepts relating to the role of financial systems. It opens with a discussion about the savings and investment process. The motivation to both save and invest makes having financial claims, markets, and institutions worthwhile. The process of bringing savers and borrowers together and the role of financial intermediaries are also discussed. Finally, the chapter reviews the mechanisms and institutions that are available to governments to alter the allocation of savings. This topic is very much a global concern today. Consequently, a global perspective introduces the discussion.

Taking the Global Perspective

The 1990s is probably the most exciting time in history to be studying financial markets and institutions. In the United States, our system is undergoing its second decade of dynamic change—as dynamic as we experienced in the 1930s. The thrift crisis, bank failures, the junk bond controversy, and unprecedented innovation in the creation of new financial instruments has kept the most knowledgeable professionals in finance challenged.

However, as great as these changes have been, equally significant changes are occurring in the world financial markets. During the 1980s, the world's financial markets became integrated. Trading of financial instruments by financial institutions became a worldwide 24-hour occupation. The technological achievements in communication and data processing helped make globalization possible. But equally important was the tremendous growth in the world's economies outside the United States.

In the Pacific Basin, Japan took the lead and has become a financial powerhouse. Its financial institutions have become the largest measured in terms of assets in international banking markets. Europe is also witnessing a pace of change that could not have been forecast ten years ago. The integration of Europe and the United Kingdom economically has unleashed new forces that are impacting financial markets and institutions not only in Europe, but worldwide.

But, frankly, all that seems to be a sideshow compared to the changes in Eastern Europe and the new Republics of the former Soviet Union. The formerly closed economies and financial systems of these countries are being forced to integrate with the developed economies around the globe. This process is creating new challenges and opportunities for the rest of the world.

These changes raise a number of important questions that require answers. Consider this short list.

- What changes in law and financial structure will be needed to create an increased flow of capital from the developed countries to Eastern Europe and the former Soviet Union republics if these people are to be able to provide productive uses for the capital?
- What will be the new financial structure that evolves out of Western Europe's and the United Kingdom's economic unions?
- How will the U.S. financial system evolve in the wake of the thrift crisis and significant commercial bank and insurance company failures?
- How will the growing Pacific Basin economies, especially Japan, handle their growing asset accumulation? How will they invest these assets around the world? Which borrowers will be winners and which will be losers in the demand for capital?

While it is not presumptuous to ask questions of this significance, it is presumptuous to think that anyone can answer them. These questions can't be answered because they depend on political, social, and economic forces that defy prediction. What we can hope to do, however, is to begin to understand how we might best organize a financial system. That means starting from the beginning. First it is necessary to determine what it is that we need from a financial system. Then a system must be designed to provide these products and services most efficiently.

In this book, a conscious effort will be made to avoid referring to the U.S. financial system as a guide. Like all other countries, the U.S. system of financial institutions is the product of historical political decisions that were responses to immediate problems of the time. In fact, as everyone worldwide has learned in the last decade, the U.S. system of financial institutions is not a model to be exported around the world. The system has in many ways performed without distinction in the last decade or more.

The U.S. system of specialized financial institutions, government deposit insurance of accounts programs, government credit agencies, regulatory system, and ethical and legal framework have all required challenge during the last decade, and most of all, demanded major reform. As a result, you must be very leery of thinking about the United States as foremost in these matters. It is not. This introduction will look at the conceptual big picture. That way it is possible to avoid the more difficult job of actually designing a financial system.

The Savings and Investment Process

The function of financial claims, markets, and institutions is to facilitate the savings and investment process. This is the process of bringing savers, called *capital surplus units (CSUs),* together with borrowers, called *capital deficit units (CDUs).*

The process of saving begins with individuals who have to make a straightforward consumption choice. An individual with income can enjoy the benefits of the income by consuming it today or postponing the consumption until some later period. The choice to postpone consuming is affected by the options available to the individual to earn a profit on the savings during the period of postponed consumption. If the individual can earn a high return on invested savings, then the individual may be inclined to postpone more consumption into the future. The trade-off between consumption today and consumption in the future is known as *time preference.*

Why do people save? People save for a variety of reasons: They save in order to weather periods of financial distress when their incomes fall or expenses rise due to unemployment, illness, or other emergencies. They also save to obtain sufficient resources to make large purchases or to smooth out consumption over time. Typically a worker's earnings start low, rise in the middle-age years, and fall at retirement. This *life cycle* income pattern can be smoothed by borrowing in the early years, building savings in the middle years, and consuming these savings in the later years.

Another reason people save is to increase future consumption. This is accomplished by using some of their savings to invest in productive opportunities to increase future income. One approach involves *direct investment* in the creation of capital goods that create wealth. A farmer may save by investing in a tractor to increase the productivity of his farming profession, and an accountant may invest in a personal computer and software to increase the productivity of bookkeeping services.

Some people are compelled to save more if they can identify others who can invest their savings for them. They do this by lending to an entity that

Chapter 1 Overview: Claims, Markets, and Institutions

has demonstrated profitable investment and is willing to sell a claim against some portion of that expected income. This is a form of *indirect investment*. The saver is purchasing a claim against another individual or entity. This activity is called *intermediation*.

The *Flow of Funds Accounts* produced by the Federal Reserve Board provides an overview of how individuals hold their wealth. Table 1.1 provides a comprehensive view of the assets of households, personal trusts, and nonprofit organizations for year-end 1990. As a country that provides

Table 1.1

**Assets of Households, Personal Trusts, and Nonprofit Corporations
Year-end 1990
(dollars in billions)**

Tangible Assets	$ Amount
Residential structures	$3,420
Nonprofit plant and equipment	316
Consumer durables	2,024
Land	1,316
Total Tangible Assets	$7,076

Financial Assets	
Deposits	$3,429
U.S. government securities	1,142
Tax-exempt securities	343
Corp. and foreign bonds	138
Mortgages	248
Open-market paper	201
Corporate equities	2,355
Life insurance reserves	388
Pension fund reserves	2,945
Equity in personal businesses	2,634
Other	267
Total Financial Assets	$14,090
Total Assets	**$21,166**

Source: *Balance Sheets for the U.S. Economy 1945–90*. Board of Governors of the Federal Reserve System, Washington, DC (March 1991) p. 24.

for individual ownership of housing and the means of production, land and capital, a large percentage of household assets are invested in financial claims evidencing ownership of these assets. These data provide estimates for residential housing, consumer durable goods such as autos and appliances, and land. They also show investments in financial claims of financial institutions, corporations, and government units. Finally, they show investments held as reserves in life companies and pension funds. Many of these reserves are invested in credit market instruments of corporations and corporate equities.

The substantial assets held by households in the United States sharply contrasts to the Republics of the former Soviet Union and a number of Eastern European countries. Until recently, most of the assets in these countries were owned by government units and controlled by government bureaucrats. The challenge for these countries in the years ahead will be convincing or forcing government officials to give up the control they have over the means of production and the allocation of goods and services. The concept of private ownership is a major hurdle to be overcome.

In the case of either direct or indirect investment, a higher return in the form of future income, according to microeconomic theory, compels individuals to increase their savings.

Interest Rates as the Allocation Mechanism

In market-based economies, price is the allocating mechanism. When it is the market for allocating savings, interest rates become the price mechanism. Borrowers with unusually productive investment opportunities, as measured in terms of risk and return, can pay savers a higher income in the form of an interest rate on the savings they borrow than borrowers with less productive investments. The return may also be in the form of ownership in the business through the common stock of a company.

The major exception to the use of the interest rate allocation mechanism relates to governmental involvement in savings and investment markets. To the extent that federal government policymakers are not satisfied with the private sector's allocation of savings, government bureaucrats get involved. This involvement takes the form of direct investment by governments and the allocation of savings to governmentally identified purposes using various allocation devices.

The process of bringing all potential savers together with all potential investors is what our financial markets and institutions are all about. Let's bring them into the picture.

Financial Claims

As stated earlier, CSUs may invest indirectly by identifying CDUs that have identified profitable investments, but no resources to exploit them. The CDUs agree to borrow savings of CSUs by issuing financial claims. A *financial claim* is a contract or agreement between two parties, in which the borrowing party agrees to transmit income to the saver in order to obtain savings immediately.

The importance of the financial claim is easily seen when we consider the problems that have occurred in Eastern Europe and the Republics of the former Soviet Union as they move to reform their economies. Savers are not inclined to lend to CDUs without a financial claim contract. The probability that the contract will be honored involves such issues as *property rights, legally binding contracts,* and a *convertible currency*. McDonald's, the fast-food chain, opened up its very successful restaurant in Moscow. Still, a main issue is how will it ever take any profits it might earn out of Russia. Without clear title to the business they developed, the ability to transfer ownership of the business via a contract, and the ability to convert the former Soviet Union currency, the ruble, into another currency, this investment involves very high risks. Financial claims greatly enhance the savings and investment process. They facilitate indirect investment.

Financial Markets

Financial markets facilitate the savings and investment process by making it more efficient. Markets provide mechanisms to reduce the time and effort for CSUs to search for CDUs. They provide much needed information on prices and volume of transactions. In that respect, financial markets provide information about the income that can be expected on different financial claims and their current prices. There are many financial markets in developed economies. In Chapter 6, we will spend time discussing the taxonomy, or classification system, for different types of markets. That is, we will look at different ways to describe the structure of the many financial markets we enjoy in developed economies.

The importance of financial markets is also apparent when considering the development of a nonmarket economy. This economy has no mechanism for determining the value of goods and services. These values are determined by central government bureaucracies. The result of foregoing markets that provide information on the supply-and-demand interaction for goods and services is the mispricing of most goods and services. This leads to waste. Many goods are produced even though there is no market for them. Other goods are produced using very costly materials, when less expensive substitutes could be used. This also leads to the well-known shortages. The price is low, but goods are not available. Creating a market economy in goods and financial claims is a solution to many of these problems.

Global Markets in Financial Claims

The markets for financial claims truly became global in the 1980s. Consider the data in Table 1.2 on page 8. The table shows the total dollar volume of foreign investor transactions in U.S. equities and bonds in 1980 and 1990

Table 1.2

Transactions in Equities and Long-Term Bonds by Foreigners and U.S. Investors 1980 and 1990
(dollars in billions)

Type of Transaction	1980	1990	% Change 1990/1980
Purchase or sale of U.S. equity by foreigner	$ 75	$ 361	381%
Purchase or sale of U.S. long-term bonds by foreigner	123	3,852	3,032
Purchase or sale of foreign equity by U.S. investors	18	253	1,306
Purchase or sale of foreign long-term bonds by U.S. investors	35	650	1,752

Source: Peter A. Abken. "Globalization of Stock, Futures, and Options Markets." *Economic Review,* Federal Reserve Bank of Atlanta. (July/August 1991): pp. 1–22.

and the volume of U.S. investor transactions in foreign equities and bonds. The data show that the volume of transactions of these four types has increased from a low of 381 percent to a high of 3,032 percent between 1980 and 1990.

Financial managers today must be prepared to consider investment and financing alternatives throughout the world. The sharp growth in international trading of foreign securities is the result of two factors. First, international investors have turned to foreign markets to expand the investment opportunities to improve risk and return possibilities of their investment portfolios. Second, large trade surpluses, such as those experienced by Japan in the 1980s, have led to the growing supplies of capital that have been channeled into foreign denominated securities.

International competition among financial firms, especially commercial banks and investment banking firms, has resulted in many structural changes in the markets for financial claims. Today, trading rooms operating 24 hours a day are commonplace. In addition, to accommodate longer trading hours and to provide more efficient services, many markets are becoming automated.

Another indication of the global reach of financial markets is in the contracts for options and futures. These contracts are discussed fully in Chapter 5. The point to be made here is that the types of financial contracts upon which futures and options contracts are written has increased in number significantly while the types of contracts have a global reach. Table 1.3 shows the top ten financial futures and options contracts measured by contract volume for 1990. Notice that many of the contracts are written on financial claims of foreign countries. As recently as ten years ago, the futures and options markets were totally dominated by the United States. That's not true any longer.

Financial Institutions

Financial institutions provide an indirect way to bring CSUs and CDUs together. Many financial institutions put themselves between savers and borrowers by issuing their own financial claims to savers and lending the funds they raise to borrowers. In this process, financial institutions provide a variety of services that reduce costs of saving and borrowing for the participants in the economy and at the same time provide risk sharing, which reduces risks for savers.

Financial institutions are also providers of important services. One of the most important is providing a medium of exchange and payment services. Although our payments system is taken for granted, an efficient payments system facilitates economic growth and development. In countries without an efficient payments system and without confidence in the government's currency, barter becomes a necessary means of carrying out commerce. *Barter* is an exchange process in which producing economic units trade goods and services directly with other producers rather than using

Table 1.3

Ten Most Actively Traded Financial Futures and Options Contracts for 1990

Contract Type	1990 Contract Volume
T-bond (futures)	75,499,000
S&P 100 (option)	58,845,000
Eurodollar (futures)	34,694,000
Japanese government bond (futures)	16,307,000
Notionnel government bond (futures)	15,996,000
Euroyen (futures)	14,414,000
Nikkei 225 (futures)	13,589,000
S&P 500 (futures)	12,139,000
S&P 500 (option)	11,423,000

Source: Ibid. p. 7.

currency to do so. This is very inefficient and greatly slows economic development.

Our nation's largest financial institutions are *depository institutions*. These firms are chartered by the federal and state governments to provide a variety of deposit-issuing and lending services. They are the primary providers of payment services. The largest of the depositories are *commercial banks*. Commercial banks are followed in size by *thrift institutions:* the savings and loans, mutual savings banks, and credit unions.

The major *nondepository institutions* are *finance companies, insurance companies* (both life and property and casualty), *investment banking firms,* and *pension funds*. Finally, the United States has a wide variety of *investment intermediaries* that provide specialized asset management services. These include *mutual funds, real estate investment trusts,* and *limited partnerships*.

In addition, the federal government has chartered *government sponsored credit enterprises (GSEs)* to provide lending services to a variety of borrowers from farmers to college students. The largest of these GSEs provides funds for residential mortgages. Most of the GSEs are privately owned and compete directly against other financial intermediaries.

Agency Theory and Intermediaries

Most investments held by households are indirect investments represented by financial claims issued by the financial intermediaries just discussed. These assets represent claims on the income and real assets of other institutions. In most cases, the role of the investor is passive. The owner of 100 shares of stock in a company must rely on the management and board of directors to fulfill their preferences as owners. Owners of debt also rely on management of the companies in which they hold debt to fulfill the debt contracts. These relationships, referred to as *agency relationships,* are between the holders of financial claims, referred to as the *principals,* and those people who actually make investment decisions for firms and financial institutions, referred to as *agents*. *Agency theory* refers to the study of agent behavior. Agency theory has identified many circumstances in which the behavior of agents differs from the behavior that the owners and debtors of the firm would prefer.

Because agents can deviate from the behavior sought by the owners of the firm, the supplier of capital must devise various means to control and monitor the actions of their agents. This involves creating costly legal contracts, accounting systems, reporting systems, as well as systems of regulation. In the case of depository institutions, the federal government is an insurer of the liabilities of these firms and thus has its own need to recognize agency issues.

Agency relationships involve large costs called *agency costs*. These involve the costs related to the principal's need to control and monitor the agent's management of the firm's capital. Annual reports, regulatory reports and examinations, trustees used to monitor corporate behavior under debt agreements, independent auditors, and boards of directors are all agency costs that direct investors must incur. In fact, federal insurance of deposits is justified partly on the basis that it eliminates agency costs of depositors. The costs involved in agency relationships are significant. Consequently, it is incumbent on suppliers of capital to consider the incentives under which the users of their capital operate.

Government's Role in the Financial Process

A government's role in the financial system ranges over a large number of functions. In the United States, the federal government is very involved in the financial system. Indeed, many would say that the federal government has taken on too many functions that could be more effectively accomplished by privately functioning financial markets. The primary functions performed by governments in the developed countries are the following:

1. Providing for an efficient payments system
2. Creating a currency with the objective of stable prices
3. Providing a means for the central government to finance its activities
4. Altering the taxation of income earned on specific types of financial claims as a tool to allocate savings
5. Using direct and indirect lending by government chartered institutions, financial guarantees, and other means to allocate savings to investments deemed important by central government officials

In the Appendix to Chapter 8, we will discuss in some depth the U.S. payments system and the role of the Federal Reserve System in attempting to make it efficient. Central governments in every developed country have central banks or similar institutions that are involved in providing a payments system.

Most economists believe that another important responsibility of government is to provide a currency in which economic participants have confidence and to control the stock of the currency to avoid unexpected price volatility. The establishment of the Federal Reserve System in 1913 was designed, in part, to bring control over the stability of the money supply as well as to provide an efficient payment system.

Governments also tend to be involved in chartering financial institutions. The rationale for this involvement is multifaceted. First, governments believe that by controlling the charters of financial institutions they can safeguard the payment system and avoid breakdown and inequitable distribution of financial services. Second, using much the same rationale, many believe that governments have a responsibility to insure the stability of the financial institutions in order to carry out monetary policy in a stable and predictable way and to avoid economic depression or hyperinflation. Thirdly, governments are involved in the financial markets and in financial institution chartering so that they can facilitate their own fiscal activities. Central governments around the world are concerned with having institutions in which they can confidently invest government funds generated from taxes and borrow savings when there is inadequate revenue. In the early days of U.S. banking, the federal government only chartered national banks in the time of war, when it needed an institution that would facilitate borrowing funds. Fourth, central governments impact the allocation of savings. One approach is through the tax law. In the United States, the tax deductibility of home mortgages, federal tax-free status of state and municipal bonds, and tax-deferred nature of savings bonds all have an impact on the after-tax interest rates savers earn on these investments. This impact on after-tax interest rates has a profound impact on the allocation of savings. Altering taxation of the income earned on savings affects the amount of consumption a saver is able to defer into the future. This, in turn, affects the amount saved. Central governments also use savings directly for public purpose investments. Roads, schools, airports, and seaports are but a few capital investments that benefit from public policy. In the United States, however, the federal government also taps a large percentage of the savings pool to finance transfer payments to individuals. The objective is to reallocate income. Finally, central governments are involved in the indirect allocation of credit. In the United States, the federal government is broadly involved in the allocation of savings. It guides the allocation of savings by guaranteeing deposits of certain financial institutions and then regulating how these institutions lend these deposits. The federal government also has a large number of government-operated and government sponsored enterprises that guarantee and lend money for specific purposes. These programs are designed to encourage investment in residential housing and other purposes deemed important by government officials.

On the other hand, Congress recently passed laws that prohibit using insured depository institutions from making bond investments to companies with weak financial conditions. By doing so, the government is discouraging investment in these types of businesses. Some economists argue that, as a result of this type of government involvement in our financial markets, many commercial and industrial needs for savings go unfulfilled and productivity suffers.

The Flow of Funds

Now it is possible to put all the players discussed above together in a conceptual design. The importance of financial claims in facilitating the savings and investment process has been discussed. The process in which financial markets and institutions both improve the efficiency of the savings and investment process and reduce risks has been demonstrated. It has also been shown that governments are major players in the savings and investment process. They are involved in helping create a payments system as well as providing a stable supply of money. Central government officials also like to command resources. They do that directly through taxation and the tapping of savings for selected public investments and income transfers. They also do it indirectly by establishing institutions that allocate savings to purposes desired by government officials.

Exhibit 1.1 on page 14 shows the savings and investment process and the position of financial markets, institutions, and government. Savings can flow (1) directly from CSUs to CDUs by the sale of claims traded in financial markets; (2) indirectly through purchases of claims by CSUs that are issued by financial institutions and then lent by these institutions to CDUs; or (3) indirectly by sales of bonds or levying of taxes by governments that are used to invest in public capital goods or finance transfer payments.

What the diagram does not show is that the government also influences the investments made by financial institutions through two primary means. The government can alter the price charged on claims issued by CSUs by providing tax incentives, credit guarantees, and other risk-reducing schemes and by chartering financial institutions that are given favored treatment in return for lending to certain government-favored CDUs. As we will learn in Chapter 13, the federal government through its many government-operated and sponsored credit programs controls over 25 percent of nonfederal lending; that is, lending not done by the U.S. Treasury to finance budget deficits. It is now appropriate to consider the management issues related to operating these firms.

Managing Financial Institutions

Thus far, the savings and investment process has been made to appear relatively simple. In fact, the process is anything but simple. It involves the development of sophisticated information systems, analytical tools, and organizations. Today, we deal in international markets for goods and services that require no less of our financial markets. They too are global. This presents the participants in these markets with new risks as well as longer hours.

The managers of our financial institutions must learn a number of important aspects of their operations. This includes understanding the functions they perform, a topic that is covered in Chapter 7. It also includes an understanding of the role of government in determining the activities of many of our institutions through their chartering authority. This is covered in Chapters 13, 14, and 15. Finally, it includes an understanding of the issues that impact the financial decisions important to operating a success-

Exhibit 1.1

The Savings and Investment Process

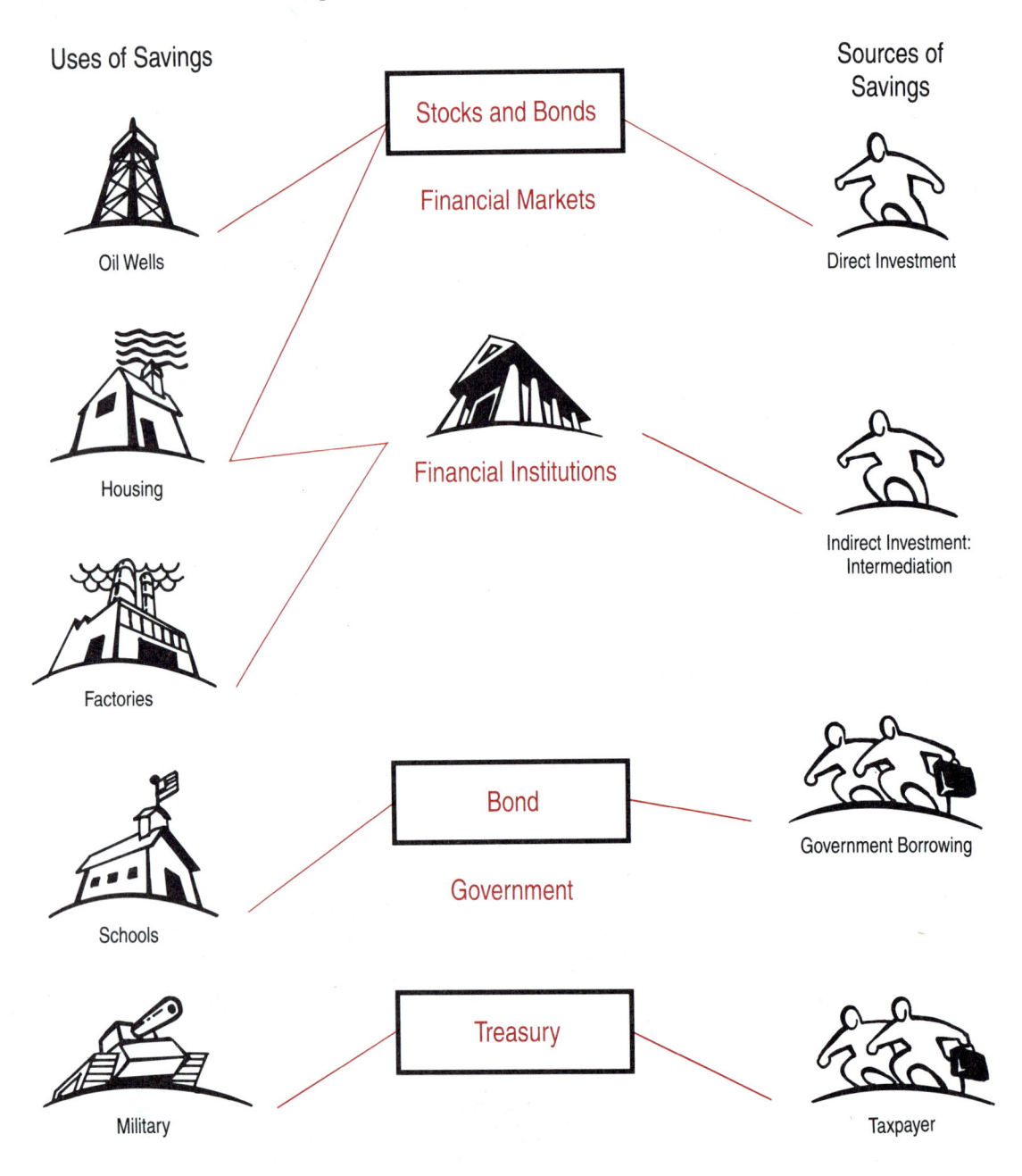

Uses of Savings
- Oil Wells
- Housing
- Factories
- Schools
- Military

Financial Markets: Stocks and Bonds

Financial Institutions

Government: Bond

Treasury

Sources of Savings
- Direct Investment
- Indirect Investment: Intermediation
- Government Borrowing
- Taxpayer

ful financial institution. These issues are the subject of the fourth section of this book, Chapters 16 through 24.

The primary issues that face the management of financial institutions are those faced by all businesses. The first relates to capital structure. *Capital structure* is the relationship between the amount of equity and debt used to finance the firm's assets. Financial institutions must determine their optimal levels of debt in their capital structure. They must also manage risk effectively. The primary risks they face are risks related to changing financial asset prices, which are risks resulting from interest rate and currency price changes, and risks related to the quality of the investments they make, referred to as credit risk. One has only to look at the carnage created by the failure of savings and loans, commercial banks, and insurance companies in recent years to understand the importance of risk management.

Financial institutions generally have many investment and financing options. As a result, maximizing the return on investments given acceptable risk and minimizing the cost of financing alternatives is a major function of management. Finally, financial institutions must be able to operate efficiently. Information is the primary resource of the intermediary. Information processing and communication technologies are critical to the success and everyday operations of intermediaries. Understanding why these two technologies are so important is another key to success.

Jobs in Financial Institutions

Financial institutions are major employers within the U.S. labor force. As of December 31, 1989, financial and real estate-related businesses provided jobs for over 6 million people. Table 1.4 on page 16 provides a breakdown of the employment within financial institutions by type of financial firm. Commercial banks are the largest employers in this group, followed by insurance companies and thrifts. Real estate employment is also shown, since a large percentage of real estate employment relates to financing real estate.

Employment growth in financial institutions weakened in the early 1990s as a result of the large number of financial institution failures and consolidations. This is likely to prevail for several more years. Ironically, the growth in jobs in the financial agencies, especially those dealing with failed institutions, has grown rapidly. As always, however, the prospective employee with good training and a solid understanding of the forces impacting financial institutions has a great advantage in the job market.

Table 1.4

**Employment in Financial Institutions
December 31, 1989**

Type of Financial Firm	Total Number of Employed People
Banking	1,665,000
Credit institutions other than banks (i.e., S&Ls, MSBs, and CUs)	866,000
Security, commodity brokers, and services	492,000
Insurance	1,432,000
Holding companies and other investment firms	210,000
Real estate	1,667,000
Total (without real estate)	**4,665,000**
Total (with real estate)	**6,332,000**

Source: *Statistical Abstract of the United States, 1991.* Department of Commerce, p. 495.

Summary

The financial systems of developed and developing free market economies represent major assets of these countries. They facilitate the savings and investment process and therefore have a major impact on economic growth and the formation of capital.

The development of an efficient financial system requires that the country's financial claims, markets, and institutions all be designed carefully. Generally, the federal government plays a major role in this process. As a result, the student of financial markets and institutions must also be a student of economics and political science as well.

Savers (CSUs) are economic units, individuals, businesses, governments, and foreign units that choose to forego current consumption in favor of future consumption.

Investors (CDUs) are economic units that have highly productive uses for savings. These uses create additional income and represent increases to the capital stock.

Financial claims are contracts that represent ownership of a future stream of income. It is important that governments provide for private ownership, legal contract rights, and a convertible currency to improve the savings and investment process through the establishment of less risky financial claims.

The nation's largest financial intermediaries are **depository institutions.** These include commercial banks, savings and loans, mutual savings banks, and credit unions. The nation also has many nonbank financial institutions and investment intermediaries.

Agency theory provides the basis for understanding the potential for conflict between the owners of capital and the agents who invest capital on their behalf. These agents include management and directors of commercial, industrial, and financial organizations. Since agents will not necessarily act in accordance with the owner's desires, there is a need to expend substantial resources on monitoring and controlling agents. These costs are known as **agency costs.** The federal government, as an insurer of deposits, must also spend significant resources for monitoring and control.

Financial markets and institutions make the savings and investment process more efficient and help to reduce risks.

Interest rates are the price mechanism in the private sector that allocate savings between CSUs and CDUs.

Governments are typically an active participant in the financial system. Governments can be helpful to private sector economic units by ensuring that an efficient payment system is developed and that the nation's currency does not fluctuate excessively in value relative to the value of goods and services. Stable prices and price expectations are desirable.

Governments are also active in the allocation of savings. Governments can impact the allocation of savings by (1) spending tax money and acting as a CDU in order to invest in public investments; (2) providing incentives for private sector financial institutions to allocate savings to specified borrowers; (3) chartering financial institutions and giving them financial incentives designed to allocate savings to specific borrowers; (4) using tax laws to influence the allocation of savings by altering after-tax interest rates; and (5) using government tax and borrowing authority to alter the allocation of income.

The primary duties of the management of financial intermediaries include (1) determining the optimal capital structure; (2) managing interest rate, currency, and credit risks; (3) pricing and selecting investments and liabilities; and (4) operating effectively using information processing and communication technologies.

Questions

Chapter 1

1. How do financial claims, markets, and institutions facilitate the savings and investment process?
2. If financial claims and markets did not exist, how do you suppose savings and investment would take place?
3. Why do individuals save? What is meant by the life cycle income pattern?
4. How does the level of interest rates and the expected returns on equity investments influence the level of savings?
5. What attributes make a financial claim so important?
6. Explain the importance of private property rights, legally binding contracts, and a convertible currency in facilitating the savings and investment process. What problems have the Eastern European countries and Republics of the former Soviet Union had in mobilizing savings for investment?
7. Explain the role of financial markets.
8. What is the role of financial institutions in our economy?
9. What role do governments normally play in the financial system? Which of these activities are the most important in creating a more efficient savings and investment process?
10. What is meant by an agency relationship? Give several examples. What problems do agents represent for the owners of financial assets?
11. How do governments influence which types of investments get funded?
12. What are the primary concerns of financial intermediary management?

Interest Rates and the Term Structure

chapter **2**

The purpose of this chapter is to study interest rates from several perspectives. The chapter begins with a discussion of the economic forces that cause interest rates to fluctuate with the business cycle. This builds off of the review of the savings and investment process introduced in Chapter 1. The factors that influence the supply and demand for loanable funds and the impact of inflation on interest rates are considered next. This is followed by a review of the relationship of interest rate levels to the maturity of a financial debt claim. This relationship is referred to as the *term structure of interest rates*. Lastly, the chapter identifies those factors that impact the level of interest rates that relate specifically to a given type of financial claim.

Fluctuations in Interest Rates

The reasons why interest rates fluctuate are covered in this section and the concept of the *real interest rate* is introduced. A discussion of the impact of each of the major sectors of our economy on interest rates over the course of the business cycle and the Federal Reserve System is included for perspective.

The Real Rate of Interest

One reason people are induced to save is so they can consume more tomorrow. Their ability to increase future consumption is based on the return they receive on their savings. Interest rates represent the return an individual saver (CSU) receives for foregoing consumption today. Conversely, interest rates are the prices that borrowing economic units (CDUs) pay for the privilege of consuming today. During any specified time period, the CSUs that supply and CDUs that demand savings create a market for loanable funds. For simplicity, assume that there is one market for loanable funds. In this market, all the CSUs and CDUs come together to make offers of and bids for the available loanable funds. Many of these CSUs and CDUs will determine how much they save and borrow based on the price that is eventually set in this market.

One of the major factors that influence the interest rate set in this market is the available investment opportunities of the CDUs. Consider a small undeveloped country that has just discovered it sits on top of a huge oil reserve. Such a country would have a large demand for savings to invest in oil exploration, drilling, and building a distribution system. Because of the large oil reserve, the country is able to offer to pay a high interest rate for loanable funds. Such a situation would induce the citizens of the country to save more, but it would also bring in foreign sources of savings as well.

It is the interaction of these investment opportunities and the propensity of consumers to consume now or defer consumption until later that defines the *real interest rate*. The real rate of interest is not the interest rate we observe in the financial markets, however. The interest rates we observe in the financial markets are *nominal interest rates*. These interest rates are affected by additional factors. These factors will be discussed later in the chapter.

The equilibrium real rate of interest is simply the intersection of the demand curve for loanable funds of CDUs and the supply curve of loanable funds of CSUs. Exhibit 2.1 shows the upward-sloping supply curve S and downward-sloping demand curve D. Equilibrium would include a supply and demand of loanable funds of $E1$ and real interest rate on the price of $i1$.

The exhibit also shows a demand curve $D1$. This additional demand curve shows what could happen in our small country after new oil reserves are found. Investment opportunities would increase, shifting the demand curve out to $D1$. The result would be to expand demand of loanable funds to $E2$, resulting in a higher real rate of $i2$.

The supply and demand of loanable funds within a particular country is impacted by the decisions made by households (individuals and families), businesses, central and state and local governments, and central banks. Countries also import and export their savings. The reasons why interest rates fluctuate over the course of the business cycle can be determined by exploring the supply-and-demand sides of the market for loanable funds.

Exhibit 2.1

The Real Rate of Interest Supply and Demand for Loanable Funds

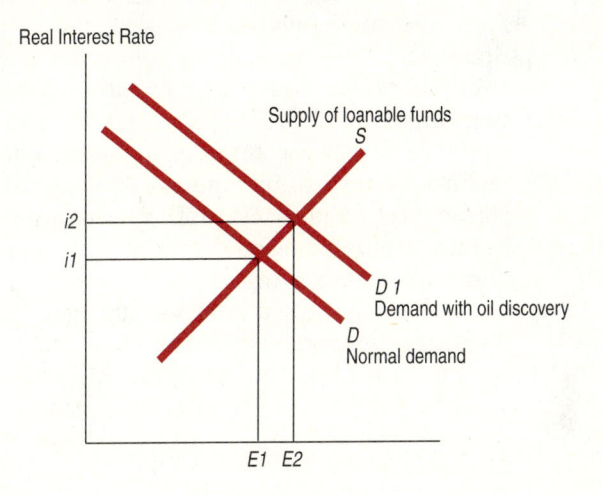

Real Interest Rate

Supply of loanable funds
S

i2
i1

D 1
Demand with oil discovery
D
Normal demand

E1 E2

Quantity of Loanable Funds

Supply and Demand for Loanable Funds by Sector

During short time periods, each sector of the economy is capable of being a CSU or CDU. Typically, the household sector is the primary capital surplus unit. This is because in the U.S., individuals hold the vast majority of the wealth. Although households as a sector are primarily CSUs, many younger householders are CDUs. These households are first-time homebuyers and purchasers of other durable goods, such as cars and appliances. Another example is students who go into debt to obtain a college education. Many more households are CSUs, however. Most of the financial savings of households is in the form of contractual savings. This includes reserves built up in pension funds and life insurance policies. The remainder is savings in depository accounts and investments in institutional forms of investment, such as mutual funds.

Governments, on the other hand, tend to be capital deficit units. This is partially because we do not produce balance sheets for our government units. We simply measure receipts and expenditures and ignore government capital spending by treating these expenditures as if they were for immediate consumption.

The international sector has, over time, moved from a capital deficit to a capital surplus unit. Here the driving factor is the U.S. balance of trade. When the United States experiences a balance-of-trade surplus, it sells more goods and services to foreign countries than it purchases. This condition results in the United States building up its holdings of foreign currencies, which are channeled into foreign investments. In the last decade, however, we have had balance-of-trade deficits. Japan and the other Pacific Basin countries have sold more goods and services to the United States than the United States has typically sold to foreign countries. As a result, foreign countries, particularly Japan, have been CSUs investing huge amounts of capital in the United States.

The business sector is also a capital deficit sector, although individual businesses may from time to time be CSUs. Businesses generate savings through retained earnings. However, as a group, businesses use all retained earnings plus additional borrowings for investments in plant-and-equipment and working capital, such as accounts receivable and inventory.

In summary, the business and government sectors have traditionally been net demanders of loanable funds, while the household and foreign sectors have been net suppliers.

Income and Interest Rate Impact on Supply and Demand for Funds

Changes in the net loanable funds position of these sectors of the economy —the difference between the sector's gross borrowing and gross lending— are dependent on two primary economic variables: total aggregate income, which can be approximated by a measure such as gross domestic product, and the level of interest rates. First consider the impact of income.

Periods of rapid income growth are associated with economic recoveries and mature economic expansions. These periods provide businesses with unusually good investment opportunities. Businesses also tend to increase accounts receivable financing and to hold higher inventories during expansions. As a result, business becomes more of a net demander of funds during periods of economic expansion than during periods of slow income growth, such as recessions.

The government sector, on the other hand, tends to develop spending plans well in advance of known tax receipts. In addition, when income growth is slowest, many government programs increase certain expenditures, such as unemployment insurance. As a result, during periods of rapid income growth, tax receipts rise more rapidly than expenditures. The opposite occurs when income growth slows—tax receipts fall and expenditures rise. This makes the government sector *countercyclical:* It borrows more during periods of slow income growth and less during rapid income expansions.

The household sector is not as easy to characterize with respect to its net demand and supply of funds in relation to income. Overall, the household sector's net contribution of savings is relatively stable. This is due in part to a large percentage of savings being contractual by nature.

Contractual savings includes reserves in pension funds and life insurance companies. Nevertheless, households tend to borrow for housing and durable goods during the early and middle stages of an economic recovery.

The international sector's net demand or supply of savings is affected by income changes. If income growth is rapid, U.S. consumers purchase more goods and services from foreign countries. This causes the balance of trade to worsen because imports rise faster than exports. As a result, foreigners build up holdings of U.S. dollars. Those that are not spent for U.S. goods and services are invested in real assets and financial claims, increasing the supply of loanable funds.

In sum, the business, government, and international sectors experience the most significant swings in their net demand and supply for funds in relation to changes in aggregate income. During periods of rapid income growth, the business sector's net demand rises, while the government and international sectors reduce demand (or increase supply). Overall, during economic booms the strong net demand for funds from households and businesses tends to more than offset the lesser net demands from governments and the international sector. The result is higher interest rates. These conditions are reversed during recessions, causing interest rates to fall.

Interest Rate Impact on Supply and Demand for Funds

As discussed earlier, the interest rate is the clearing price for establishing equilibrium in the demand and supply of loanable funds. It was shown that if all other factors are held constant, a higher interest rate will result in an increased supply of savings offered and a reduced amount demanded. This does not tell much about the degree to which changes in interest rates impact the amount supplied or demanded. The relationship of the supply offered and demand for loanable funds to changes in interest rates is called *interest rate elasticity*. If the quantities supplied and demanded change significantly due to small changes in the interest rate level, it is said that supply or demand is *interest rate elastic*. If the changes in quantities demanded and supplied change little for any given change in interest rate levels, it is said that demand or supply is *interest rate inelastic*. Consider the two supply and two demand schedules shown in Exhibit 2.2 on page 24. Both elastic and inelastic schedules are shown.

The elasticity of the demand and supply of loanable funds relative to interest rates is different for each sector of the economy. Borrowing businesses, younger net borrowing households, and foreign investors are all quite sensitive to changes in interest rates. Thus, the business sector's and younger household's demand schedules, and the foreign sector's supply schedules, would be interest rate elastic. Government demand and most other household savers' supply schedules tend to be relatively inelastic.

Exhibit 2.2

Interest Rate Elastic and Inelastic Supply and Demand Schedules

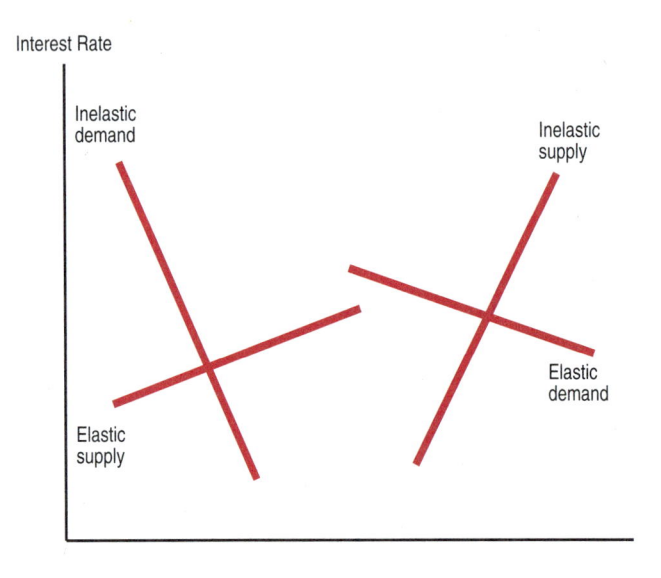

Demand and Supply of Loanable Funds and the Business Cycle

It is not a simple task to summarize the income and interest rate impacts in the supply and demand for loanable funds for four economic sectors simultaneously. In order to simplify this task, it is necessary to characterize each sector as a net supplier or net demander of loanable funds. A net supplier sector lends more than it borrows. A net demander sector borrows more than it lends. Table 2.1 shows the position of each of the sectors as it would normally be characterized during a period of weak economic income growth (recession) and a period of rapid economic expansion (boom).

The information in Table 2.1 is ambiguous with respect to the question of whether the aggregate quantity of loanable funds is higher or lower during recessions or booms. The answer to this ambiguity lies in the fact that the household sector is by far the largest net supplier of funds and the business sector the largest net user. This fact is important. As a generalization, the shifts in net supply and demand in the business and household sectors tend to swamp the changes in the government and international sectors. Consequently, as Table 2.1 shows, during recessions, household's supply is high and business demand weak, whereas during booms the reverse is the case. Exhibit 2.3 depicts these conditions. It shows the aggregate demand and supply schedules for loanable funds during an

Table 2.1

Change in Loanable Funds Position by Sector During Expansions and Recessions

Sector	Recession	Boom
Household	Net supply strong	Net supply weakens
Business	Net demand weak	Net demand strong
Government	Net demand high	Net demand weak
International	Net supply weak	Net supply strong

economic boom and recession. The boom shows a much higher demand schedule, *DB*, with only slightly stronger supply schedule, *SB*. During the recession, demand, *DR*, is relatively weak and supply, *SR*, only slightly less.

A main feature of Exhibit 2.3 is the change in interest rates from *rs* during recession to *rb* during boom. As the economy moves from a recessionary period of weak income growth to economic expansion, there is

Exhibit 2.3

Aggregate Supply and Demand for Loanable Funds During Economic Recessions and Booms

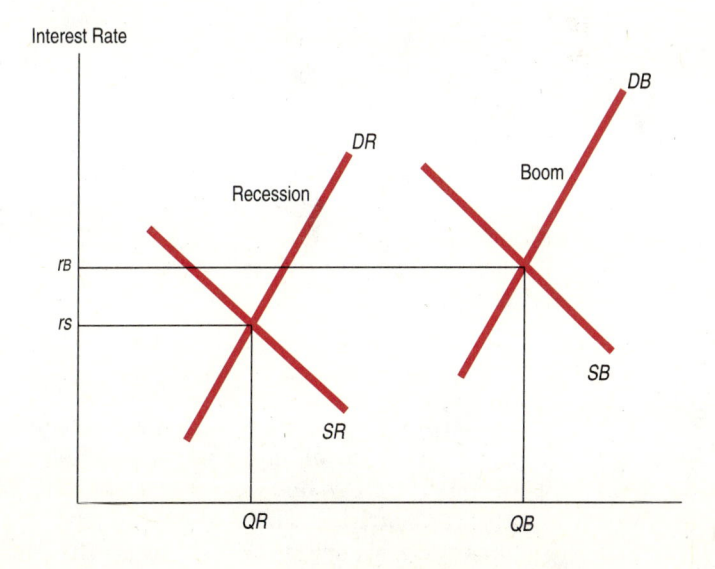

Exhibit 2.4

Interest Rate Fluctuations and the Business Cycle

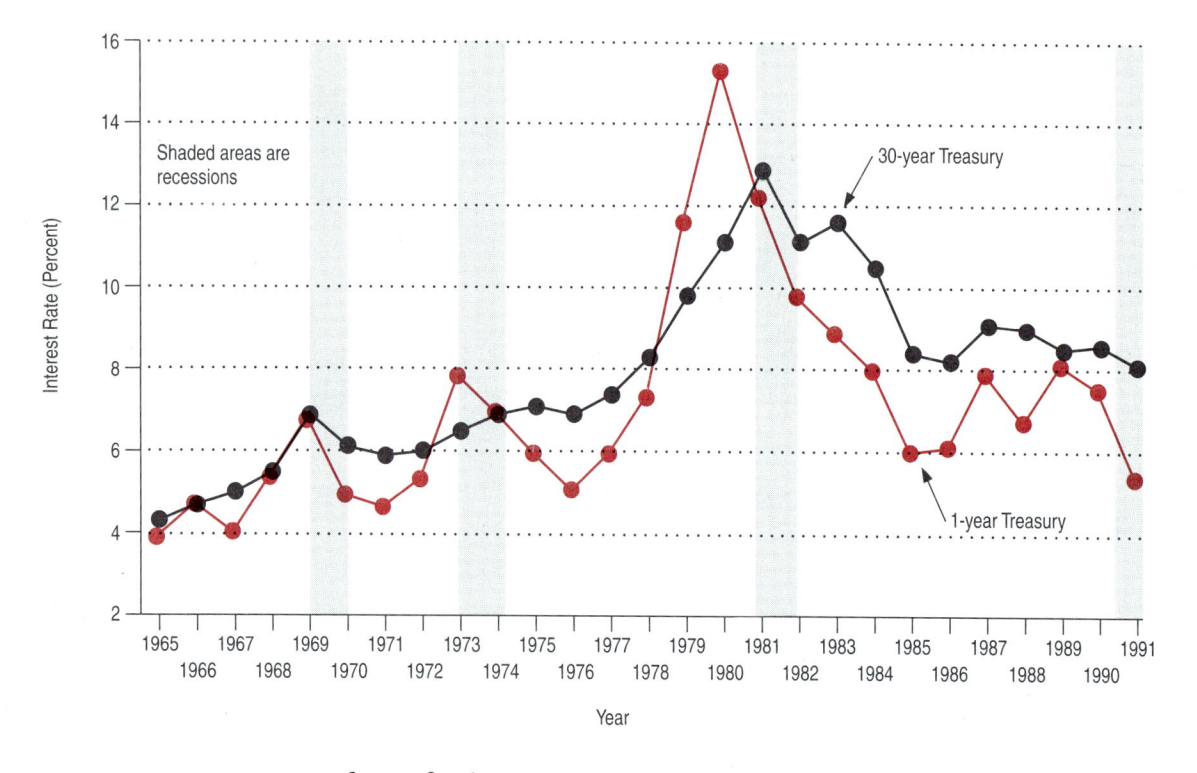

a tendency for interest rates to rise. This occurs regardless of Federal Reserve policy or inflation. Exhibit 2.4 shows the fluctuations in interest rates from 1965 to 1991. The shaded areas represent periods of recession. As the exhibit indicates, interest rates have tended to peak near the beginning of each recession. In every case, rates fell during recession periods.

Now, the Federal Reserve's impact on interest rates can be added to the list of factors.

Federal Reserve's Impact on Interest Rates

The Federal Reserve has considerable authority and powerful mechanisms to affect the level of interest rates. Their primary tool is open-market operations. Through open-market operations, the Federal Reserve purchases or sells securities. These are primarily Treasury securities. When they purchase the securities, they add to the supply of loanable funds. The sellers of the securities the Fed purchased can reinvest in other loans and investments. When the Fed sells securities, the opposite occurs.

Exhibit 2.5 shows how a *stimulative* Federal Reserve policy would be reflected in our aggregate supply and demand for loanable funds schedules. Here the Federal Reserve endeavors to increase the supply of loanable funds and to reduce interest rate levels, thus stimulating economic activity. The Fed also can reduce the level of the *discount rate* to stimulate credit growth. The discount rate is the interest rate it charges member institutions for short-term loans. Finally, the Fed can reduce the level of reserve requirements. *Reserve requirements* are deposits held in Federal Reserve banks and vault cash held by depository institutions as a percentage of certain types of deposits. Reducing reserve requirements increases the funds that depository institutions can lend.

Exhibit 2.5 shows the effect of the Fed purchasing securities, which adds to the supply of loanable funds. The supply schedule that had been *S1* shifts to *S2*. The result is an increase of loanable funds, from *Q1* to *Q2*, and a decrease in interest rates from *r1* to *r2*. A restraining Federal Reserve policy would, on the other hand, require the Federal Reserve to sell securities, increase the discount rate, and raise reserve requirements.

The actions of the Federal Reserve depend on many factors, the most important being the level of aggregate employment and inflation. The Fed tends to foster stimulative open-market policies when the economy has slack resources and high unemployment, and restrictive policies during periods of low unemployment and rising inflation.

Exhibit 2.5

Federal Reserve Open-Market Operations Used to Increase the Supply of Loanable Funds

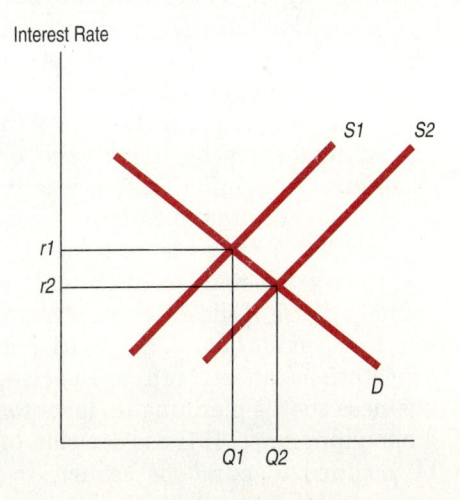

Exhibit 2.4 indicated that interest rates tend to rise during expansions and booms and to fall during recessions. This explanation does not tell the whole story, however. Note that from 1974 to 1981 interest rates rose significantly during this economic expansion. This is as expected. However, during the expansion from 1982 to 1990, rates generally fell. This is not consistent with the previous analysis. Consequently, it is necessary to look further to determine the other factors that impact interest rates.

Determinants of Market Interest Rates

So far, only the relationship of interest rates to broad supply-and-demand factors as they relate to the business cycle has been discussed. However, the discussion hasn't gotten very specific. For example, there has been no discussion of the way interest rate levels have been determined. The reasons why interest rates rose during the economic expansion of the 1970s and fell during the expansion of the 1980s have not been explored. This investigation begins by looking at the relationship of inflation and interest rates. Then the term structure of interest rates will be discussed, which will provide an indication of how interest rates vary in terms of *maturity*. Thus far, interest rates have been treated as if there were only one term for all financial debt claims. Finally, we will identify a number of factors that impact the level of interest rates that are financial-claim specific.

Inflation and Interest Rates: The "Fisher Effect"

The sharp rise in interest rates in the 1970s and their decline in the 1980s suggests other factors that impact the level of rates. Indeed, the main factor left out is expected *inflation*. The interest rates we observe in the money and capital markets are referred to as *nominal interest rates*. These rates are higher than the real interest rate we discussed at the beginning of this chapter. One factor that can account for the significant differences in the level of interest rates is the rate of inflation. In the 1970s, inflation rose to double-digit rates by late in the decade. The early 1980s continued to experience high inflation that finally began to decline by the middle of the decade. The decline in inflation occurred during an economic expansion.

In 1930, Irving Fisher wrote *The Theory of Interest,* which developed the theory for real and nominal interest rates. He concluded that the primary cause of the difference between nominal and real interest rates was *inflation expectations*. This relationship is called the *Fisher Effect*. Inflation expectations affect both prospective borrowers and lenders. Consider a business that is planning its inventory levels or a household contemplating a home purchase. If these decision makers expect prices will rise, they will be inclined to purchase sooner. In fact, if prices are expected to climb considerably, they may purchase excess inventory or a larger house than first contemplated. Therefore, rising inflation expectations can cause households and businesses to consume earlier and borrow more.

Conversely, a prospective saver anticipating higher inflation will be less willing to lend funds if the interest rate is near the expected rate of inflation. It would not pay to postpone consumption today in order to consume tomorrow if the principal and interest received on the investment purchases will be less than can be purchased with today's dollars.

This behavior results in a tendency for borrowers to willingly pay a higher interest rate if inflation is expected to increase, and savers to demand a higher interest rate when they anticipate a decline in the dollar's purchasing power. The relationship between the nominal interest rate r_n and the real interest rate r_i is approximated by Equation 2.1.

$$\text{Nominal interest rate } (r_n) \cong$$
$$\text{Real interest rate } (r_i) +$$
$$\text{Expected change in price } E \text{ (\% change in P)}$$

$$r_n = r_i + E \text{ (\% change in P)} \qquad [2.1]$$

The equilibrium nominal rate of interest will be approximately equal to the real rate of interest plus an incremental interest return that is approximated by the expected percentage change in the general price level.

Interest rates are related to the actual rate of inflation. However, that relationship is not perfect. Moreover, it is not possible to measure "expected" inflation. The actual rate of inflation may be unexpectedly higher or lower than that reflected by the level of nominal interest rates. Moreover, changes in nominal interest rates may be the result of changes in real interest rates stemming from the supply-and-demand factors discussed in the previous section. Most economists, however, believe that the real rate of interest is relatively stable, ranging from 2 to 4 percent, while the E (% change in P) is far more volatile.

So far, the discussion has focused only on fluctuations in interest rates that have similar maturities. Now another step in our interest rate investigation is added by considering how the maturity of a bond or other debt instrument might impact its interest rate.

The Term Structure of Interest Rates

The relationship between interest rates and debt securities that differ only in the length of their maturities is known as the *term structure of interest rates*. The term structure can be graphically represented by a *yield curve*. The yield curve is a graph of bond yields on a specified date and for a specified type of bond. The bonds differ only in respect to maturity.

Normally, the yield curve for Treasury bonds is used because of the large number of issues of varying maturities. A yield curve for Treasury bonds as of December 18, 1991, is shown in Exhibit 2.6.

Over time, the yield curve takes on a wide variety of shapes. Exhibit 2.4 indicates that the one-year rate is usually well below the thirty-year rate. This is referred to as an *upward-sloping* or *normal yield curve*. In 1969, the one-year and thirty-year rates were approximately equal. This is called a *flat yield curve*. Occasionally, as in 1979, the one-year rate is above the thirty-year rate. This is called a *downward-sloping* yield curve.

There are four useful theories for explaining the shape of the yield curve:

1. Expectations theory
2. Market segmentation theory
3. Preferred habitat theory
4. Liquidity preference theory

Each theory provides useful insights, and they should not be considered mutually exclusive.

Exhibit 2.6

Yield Curve for Treasury Securities (December 18, 1991)

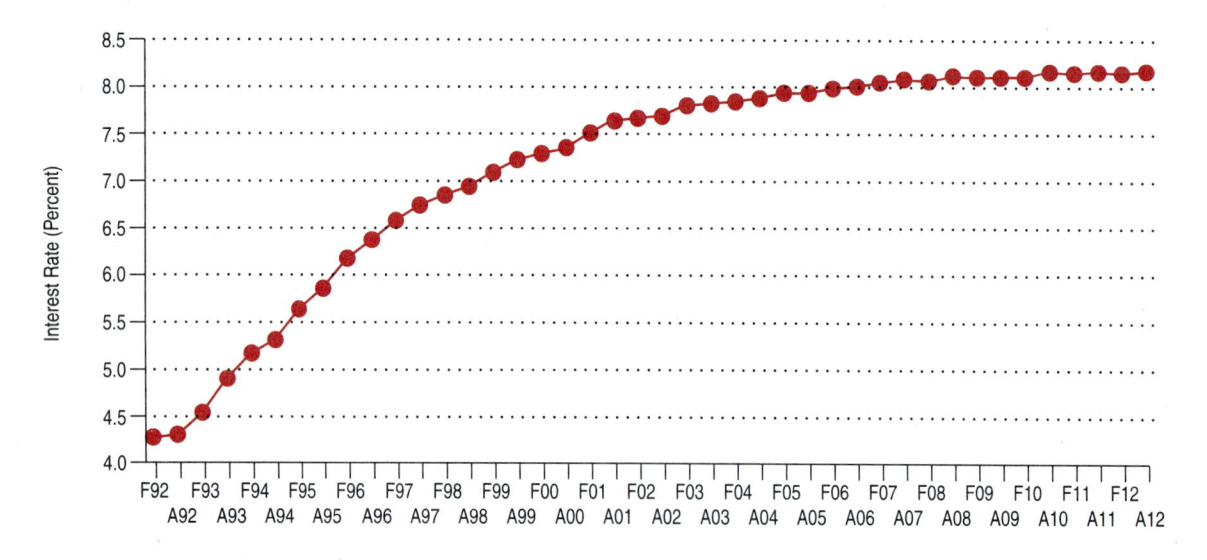

Source: "Treasury Stripped Bonds." *The Wall Street Journal*.

Expectations Theory

The basis for the *expectations theory* is the simple notion that borrowers and savers have choices to make with respect to the maturity of their loans and investments. A borrower needing funds for two years can borrow for two years, or alternatively borrow for one year and then borrow again for the next year. A saver with a five-year time horizon can buy a three-year bond and reinvest the proceeds in a two-year bond, or alternatively buy a five-year bond. How borrowers and savers make these choices according to the expectations theory is a function of their expectations about the future level of interest rates.

A simple example helps to illustrate this theory. Consider that you have just received $5,000. You are going to use it and any income you derive from investing it as a down payment on a car in two years. Your investment alternatives are (1) a one-year Treasury bond yielding 6 percent, the balance to be reinvested in another one-year Treasury bond at the prevailing rate one year from now; or (2) a two-year Treasury bond yielding 6.25 percent. In order to make this choice, you have to form an expectation of what you think one-year rates will be one year hence. Assuming reinvestment of interest payments, the two-year investment would be worth

$$(1 + .0625)^2 \times \$5,000 = \$5,644.53$$

The one-year investment, followed by the reinvestment, would only be worthwhile if the one-year rate one year hence was equal to or greater than *xx* in the following Equation 2.2:

$$(1 + .060)(1 + xx)\ \$5,000 = \$5,644.53$$
$$1 + xx = 1.065006$$
$$xx = .065006 = 6.5006\% \qquad [2.2]$$

The 6.5006 percent is called the expected *forward rate* on a one-year bond. If you believed the forward one-year rate would rise above 6.5006 percent, then it would pay to buy the one-year bond and reinvest. If not, then the two-year rate would make the best choice.

The expectations theory carries this type of trade-off to a market equilibrium. Savers and borrowers constantly consider these maturity trade-offs and regard the different maturities as close substitutes for one another. If there is a change in market expectations, so that more market participants feel that the one-year rate one year hence will be 7 percent instead of 6.5006 percent, then the market equilibrium rates will change. With 7 percent forward-rate expectations for the one-year rate one year hence, borrowers would be inclined to borrow for two years, and savers would be inclined to lend for one year and then reinvest. This would have the effect of lowering one-year rates (due to greater supply and lower demand) and raising two-year rates. This shift in rates would occur until the market's expected equality between the two-year investment return and the sequential one-year investments were equal once again.

The expectations theory can be boiled down into a simple premise: Long-term interest rates represent the market participants' expectations for future short-term rates. As our example indicated, knowing the one-year rate, the two-year rate represents the market's expectation for the forward one-year rate one year hence.

The expectations theory provides a plausible explanation of any yield curve. Consider Exhibit 2.7. It shows the three hypothetical term structures. The upward-sloping term structure would be present when the market participants expect short-term interest rates to rise. Such a condition would be expected at the bottom of a recession and early in an

Exhibit 2.7

Three Term Structures: Expectations Hypothesis

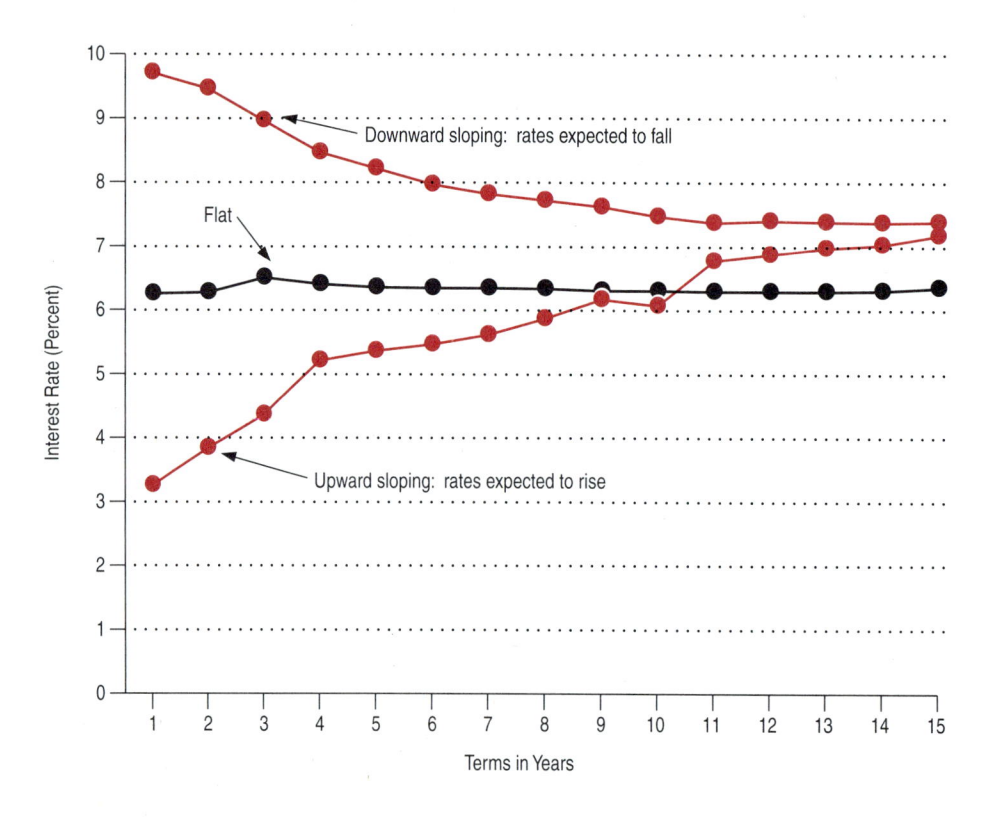

economic recovery when the demand for loanable funds and inflation are rising. The downward-sloping term structure would be expected when the economy is booming, credit demand is strong, and inflation is high. This condition would cause the Federal Reserve to adopt a restrictive monetary policy. During such a period, the market participants would be expecting that an economic downturn is ahead. Downward-sloping term structures are rare, but when they have occurred, economic slowdowns usually follow. The flat term structure occurs as a type of transition between the other two more pronounced curves.

Implied Forward Interest Rate

It is possible to calculate the forward expected interest rate for any forward period. This rate is referred to as the *implied forward rate*. Consider Equation 2.3.

$$(1 + {}_1r_{t-1})^1 (1 + {}_{t-1}r_0)^{t-1} = (1 + {}_tr_0)^t \qquad [2.3]$$

In this equation the r represents interest rates for selected periods. The subscript to the right of the r indicates the beginning point in time when the specific r applies. The left subscript denotes the number of the periods over which the rate applies. The rate ${}_1r_{t-1}$ is the implied one-year forward rate beginning in period ${}_{t-1}$.

Consider the following example. The current rate for a four-year bond, ${}_4r_0$, is 7 percent. The current rate on a three-year bond, ${}_3r_0$, is 6.8 percent. In this example $t=4$. Using Equation 2.3 we have

$$(1 + {}_1r_3)^1 (1 + {}_3r_0)^{t-1} = (1 + {}_tr_0)^t$$

$$(1 + {}_1r_3)^1 (1 + {}_3r_0)^3 = (1 + {}_4r_0)^4$$

$$(1 + {}_1r_3)^1 (1 + .068)^3 = (1 + .070)^4$$

$$(1 + {}_1r_3)(1.2182) = (1.3108)$$

$$_1r_3 = (1.3108/1.2182) = 1.0760 - 1.00$$

$$_1r_3 = .0760 = 7.60\%$$

Although the implied forward rate is easy to calculate, the market's forecast of implied future rates has not been found to be accurate. However, these implied rates do provide assistance in making investment decisions by comparing the investor's or borrower's forecast rates to that implied by the term structure. For example, in the previous example, if the forecast forward rate for one-year debt claims three years from now exceeds 7.60

> **DEMONSTRATION PROBLEM:** Computing Implied Forward Rate
>
> **Situation:** The interest rate on a three-year Treasury note is 10 percent, and on a one-year note 8 percent. Under the expectations theory, what would be the implied rate on a two-year Treasury note one year from now?
>
> **Result:** We must solve for the two-year rate $_2r_1$, one year from now. We assume that the returns from investing for three years will be comparable to investing for one year and then reinvesting the proceeds at the expected forward two-year rate.
>
> $$(1 + .08)(1 + {_2r_1})^2 = (1 + .10)^3$$
> $$(1 + .08)(1 + {_2r_1})^2 = 1.3310$$
> $$(1 + {_2r_1})^2 = 1.3310/1.08 = 1.1101$$
> $$_2r_1 = 1.110 - 1.00 = .1100 = 11.00\%$$

percent, it would pay to invest for three years at 6.80 percent, and then for one year at the expected higher forecast rate.

The expectations theory's validity depends critically on the notion of lenders' and savers' willingness to substitute investments and loans. The segmentation theory assumes that investors consider the substitution of maturities too risky.

Segmentation Theory

Consider that each maturity class of securities trades in its own distinct market. Under such a circumstance short, intermediate, and long-term bond rates would be determined by the unique supply-and-demand schedules for each of these markets. This notion of market separation is called the *segmentation theory*. A crucial assumption of the segmentation theory is that once the CSUs and CDUs have determined the best maturities for their loans and investments, they cannot be enticed into other maturities by higher levels of interest rates in markets for longer and shorter maturity assets.

The segmentation theory is capable of explaining each type of yield curve shape. An upward-sloping term structure is the result of strong demand and/or weak supply of short-term loanable funds with commensurately little demand and/or large supply of long-term loanable funds. The downward-sloping yield curve represents the opposite condition. Exhibit 2.8

Exhibit 2.8

Term Structure: Segmentation Hypothesis

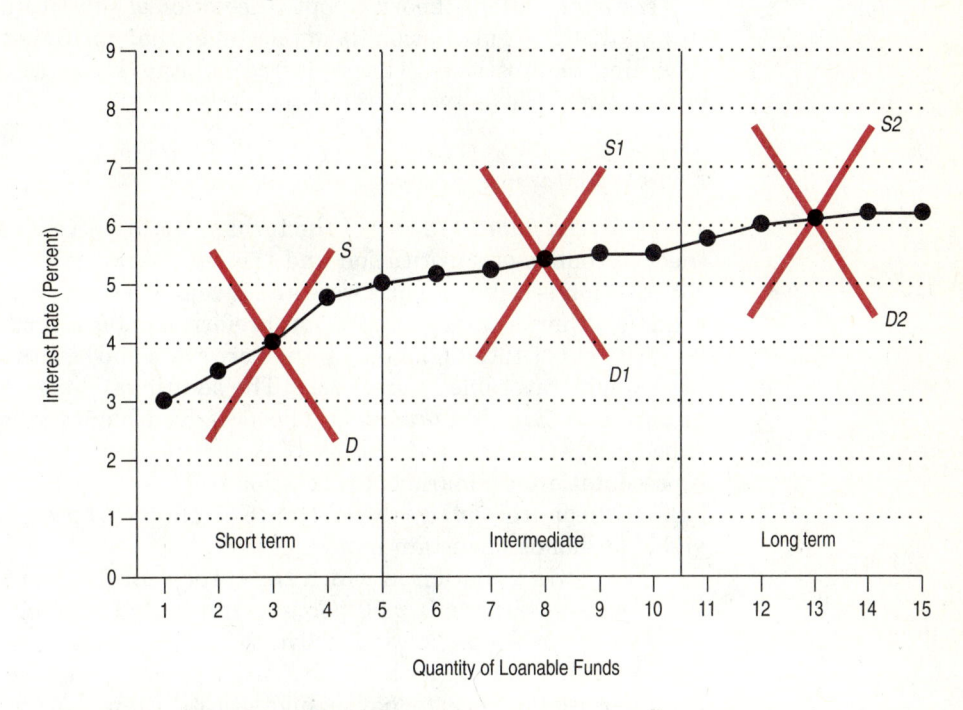

shows how you might depict the segmentation theory for short, intermediate, and long-term bonds. Each rate is determined by a unique set of supply-and-demand schedules.

One rationale behind the segmentation theory is that borrowers and savers want to match the maturities of their assets and liabilities. This matching process avoids the risk that interest rates will change in a significant way to upset the financial plans of the CSU or CDU. If a household wants to build a specified sum of funds to have during retirement, it can eliminate risk by buying long-term bonds that mature at the time the funds are needed for consumption. If the household buys short-term bonds and reinvests periodically, it faces the risk that interest rates will fall and the return on the investment will be less than expected. Consequently, the household will invest in long-term assets because they have long-term financial needs. Savers who invest for consumption a few years in the future, on the other hand, will invest in bonds of short maturities.

Efforts to prove the segmentation theory have been largely unsuccessful. As a result, the segmentation hypothesis is primarily used for explaining pricing differences in yields between markets. Such is the case in the markets for tax-exempt, taxable, and corporate bonds. Exhibit 2.8 explains how the unique supply-and-demand factors in these markets may cause pricing differences.

The expectations theory accepts the notion of substitutability of maturities, while the segmentation theory assumes that borrowers and lenders are unwilling to substitute. The preferred habitat theory attempts a compromise between these two extreme positions.

Preferred Habitat Theory

The *preferred habitat theory* of the term structure accepts the expectations theory premise of substitution and the segmentation theory premise that substitution is risky for borrowers and savers. However, this theory is not as rigid as either of them. Simply put, preferred habitat accepts the notion of maturity substitution, but only if the borrowers and savers are compensated with a more favorable interest rate. The additional return to the investor is known as a *liquidity premium*. The preferred habitat theory accepts the expectations theory, but claims that the yield curve is not an accurate representation of market expectations. This is because the preferred habitat theory recognizes the existence of a liquidity premium built into the yields for bonds of certain maturities.

Consider a situation in which the three-year interest rate is 9 percent and the five-year rate is 9.50 percent. If a large borrower wants to borrow more five-year funds, it would have to induce savers to substitute investments of other maturities to make more five-year funds available. This large borrower would have to pay a higher rate than 9.50 percent to induce investors to make more five-year funds available. This might raise the five-year rate to 9.60 percent. The additional .10 percent yield is the liquidity premium.

Preferred habitat says nothing about whether there is any systematic pattern to the liquidity premium as it regards bond rates of various maturities. This brings us to the liquidity preference theory.

Liquidity Preference Theory

The *liquidity preference theory* is derived from the premise that long-term bond prices are more volatile than short-term bond prices. Short-term investments reduce the risk that unanticipated interest rate movements will produce losses to investors. The additional price volatility of long-term bonds produces additional risk for investors. Since investors are risk adverse, they must be compensated for accepting it. Thus liquidity preference holds that the liquidity premium rises as the maturity of bonds increases. Savers must be compensated to lend long according to the amount of the liquidity premium.

Exhibit 2.9 shows how the expectations theory yield curve might look with a liquidity premium built into it. This upward-sloping yield curve has a steeper slope as a result of the rising liquidity premium.

The combination of the expectations theory and liquidity preference has the greatest support from the majority of economists today. Considerable empirical evidence supports the existence of a liquidity premium.

Specific Risk and Cost Factors Affecting Interest Rates

Look at the list of interest rates on the different types of debt securities for December 12, 1991, as shown in Table 2.2 on page 38. It includes a sample of debt instruments with maturities of about ten years. The table shows the U.S. government debt, the Pacific T&T and Reliance Electric corporate debts, and the Federal National Mortgage Association pass-through security, a bond collateralized by a pool of home mortgages. While it's not

Exhibit 2.9

Term Structure: Expectations Plus Liquidity Premium

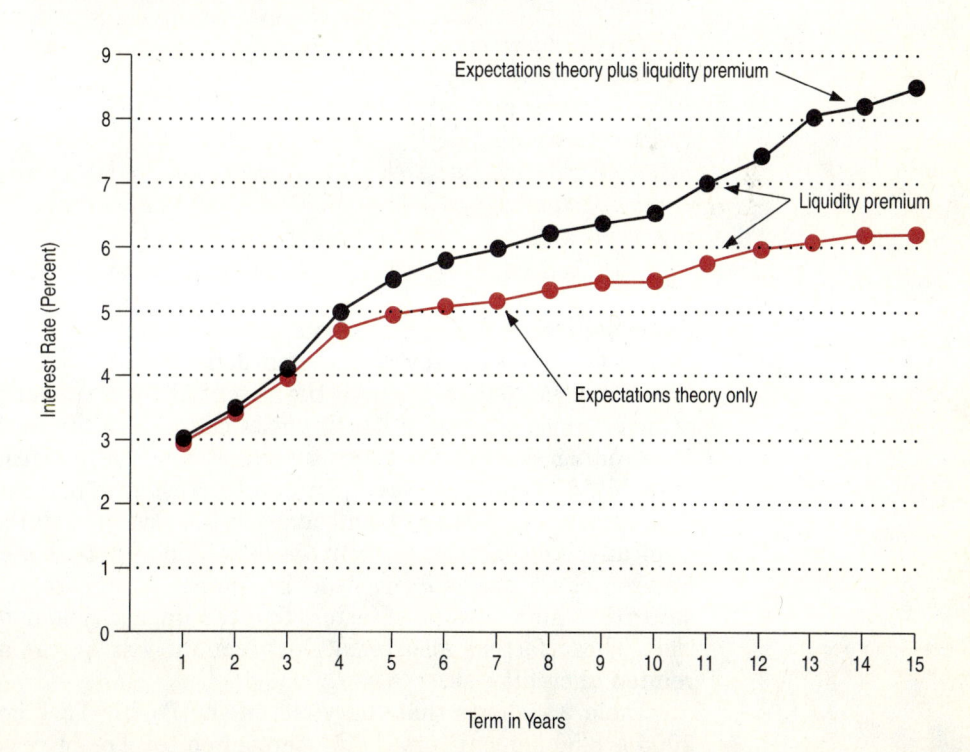

Table 2.2

**Interest Rates on Several Financial Claims
December 12, 1991**

Debt Instrument	Year	Yield
Treasury Bond 8.25%	2005	7.51%
Pacific Telephone and Telegraph 8.65%	2005	8.50
Federal National Mortgage Association pass-through 10% coupon mortgages		6.38
Reliance Electric 14%	2002	13.86

Source: *Wall Street Journal* (December 13, 1991).

important that you understand these debt instruments at this point, it is important that you are aware of the large differences in the market interest rates.

There are a number of factors influencing the differences in interest rates:

1. Credit or default risk
2. Marketability risk
3. Call or prepayment risk
4. Servicing costs
5. Exchange rate risk
6. Taxability

Credit or Default Risk

Financial claims involve the potential for loss to investors. The primary reason for loss on many claims is a default on the part of the borrower. *Credit or default risk* involves the potential that a saver will receive less principal and interest on the financial claim than the contract specifies.

Credit risk requires making estimates of the potential for loss. This probability is then converted into an interest rate premium, the *credit or default risk premium* (*crp*), and added to the saver's required nominal yield. Typically, the Treasury security is considered to be credit risk free. References to the *risk-free rate* in finance literature refer to Treasury securities. There are other factors that can impact yield in addition to credit risk. These factors also result in premium yields over and above those related to credit risk.

Table 2.2 shows that the yield on the Pacific T&T bond maturing in 2005 is 8.50 percent versus 7.51 percent on the Treasury bond maturing in the same year. A large percentage of this spread of .99 percent can be related to the higher credit risk of the Pacific T&T bond.

Marketability Risk

Marketability risk deals with the degree of difficulty in being able to convert a financial claim into cash at or near its most recent transaction price. This assumes, of course, that nothing has occurred to change the fundamental value of the financial claim. One of the best ways to understand marketability risk and to quantify it is to obtain the bid price and ask price for a particular financial claim. The *bid price* is the price that a willing buyer offers to purchase the claim. The *ask price* is the price a willing seller offers to sell. Most security dealers and organized exchanges quote bid and ask prices. For a Treasury security sold in $1 million trades, the difference between the bid and ask might be one thirty-second of 1 percent (.03125 percent). For the shares of an actively traded stock on the New York Stock Exchange, the difference might be an eighth to a quarter of a point. When a point in the price of a stock is $1, this amounts to 12.5 to 25 cents per share. For a $20 per-share stock, this bid–ask spread ranges from 0.6 to 1.25 percent of the stock price as compared to the .03125 percent in the case of the more marketable Treasury security. For a stock listed on the over-the-counter market, the difference between the bid and ask prices could be one half point or more. The over-the-counter market is operated by security dealers.

Savers who purchase investments with poor marketability expect to be compensated for the lack of marketability. This represents an additional interest spread, and is referred to as the *marketability risk premium (mrp)*. Exhibit 2.10 on page 40 shows some very revealing data reflecting the difference between the bid and ask prices of small market capitalization stocks as a percent of the price of the stocks. These are stocks with a small market value. Market value is computed by multiplying the number of shares by their market price. According to this analysis, the smaller the market capitalization, the less marketable the stocks. This is reflected in the exhibit by the very large ratio of the bid and ask spread to the market price. It is no surprise that smaller capitalized companies have fewer investors, less trading, and less investor interest than larger market capitalized companies.

Call or Prepayment Risk

Some financial claims offer the borrower the right to repay the principal debt prior to maturity. On financial claims like bonds, these provisions are referred to as *call provisions*. On financial claims such as home mortgages and installment auto loans they are called *prepayment provisions*. These

Exhibit 2.10

Bid/Ask Spread to Stock Price (Related to Market Capitalization)

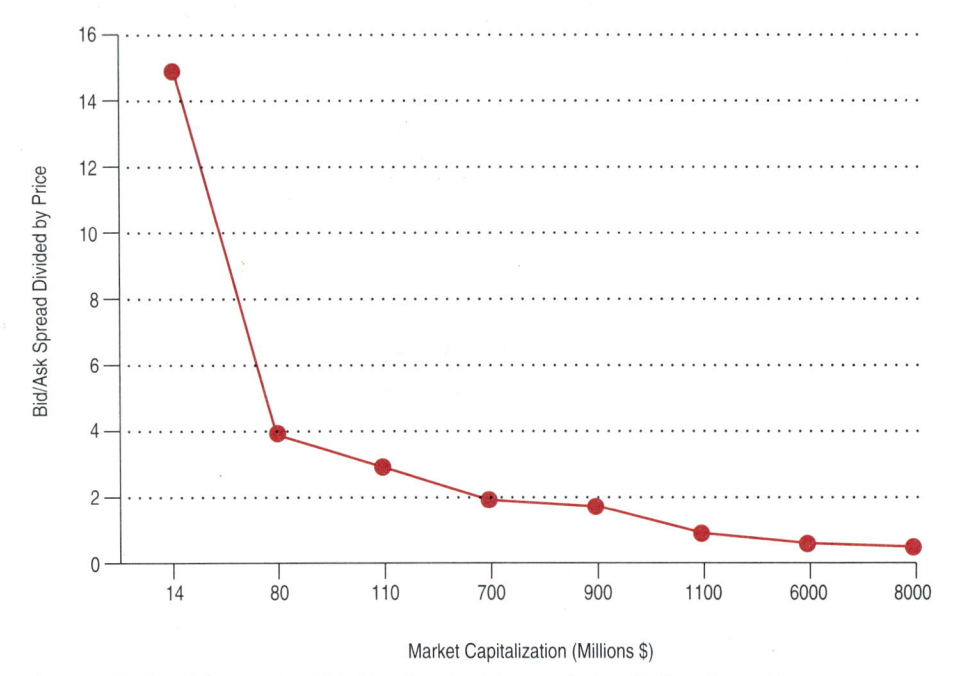

[Graph: Bid/Ask Spread Divided by Price (y-axis, 0 to 16) vs. Market Capitalization (Millions $) (x-axis): values approximately (14, 15), (80, 4), (110, 3), (700, 2), (900, 1.75), (1100, 1), (6000, 0.6), (8000, 0.5)]

Source: *Forbes,* August 19, 1991. Reprinted with permission Forbes, Inc. 1991.

provisions, which will be discussed in Chapter 5, are *options*. The borrower has the option to call or prepay the debt.

The investor in a financial claim that is callable or subject to prepayment accepts risk. The risk is that if interest rates fall, the borrower will call the bond or prepay the mortgage. The investor receiving the cash finds that he or she cannot reinvest it at an interest rate as high as the rate on the prepaid debt. This risk is called a *call or prepayment risk*. The compensation that investors demand to accept this risk is an additional interest spread referred to as the *call option premium (cop)*.

Servicing Cost

Some financial claims are difficult to service. This means that the process of collecting interest and principal payments, providing accurate records, or monitoring the ongoing credit position of the borrower involves considerable operating costs. Certainly it makes sense that the cost of servicing $10,000,000 of small auto loans is higher than the cost of servicing the same dollar amount of Treasury bonds. The auto loans would involve collecting payments and accounting for 800 to 1200 different loans. The Treasury bond involves two interest payments per year.

Lenders must be compensated for the servicing costs. This cost is included in the interest rate charged, and is referred to as the *servicing cost (sc)*.

Nominal Interest Rates on Taxable Debt

For the vast majority of taxable debt, it is necessary to make estimates of the order of magnitude of the factors just discussed to understand the level of nominal interest rates for specific domestic financial debt claims. This can be done by looking at Equation 2.4. It shows the risk-free rate of interest and the amount of additional yield each of the factors above is estimated to be worth for both borrowers and investors in order to create a market nominal interest rate for debt claims of type i for a term of t, r_i^t. In this equation, we use the risk-free rate for Treasury securities as the base rate. For many financial claims, the appropriate rate is the weighted cost of capital for the financial institution making the loan. This is discussed in full in Chapter 19.

$$r_i^t = r_{rf}^t + crp + mrp + cop + sc \qquad [2.4]$$

Nominal interest rate on claim i of term t = risk-free rate of term t

\+ credit risk premium + marketability risk premium

\+ call option premium + servicing costs

Exchange Rate Risk

As our financial markets have become more global, there has been a significant growth in the borrowing and investing in foreign denominated financial claims. A U.S. company establishing a manufacturing facility in Belgium might be inclined to issue bonds denominated in Belgium francs rather than U.S. dollars. Investors also have available to them many investments that are denominated in foreign currencies. These transactions involve *exchange rate risk*. This risk relates to the potential that the rate of exchange between the domestic currency and foreign denominated currency will change as a result of any number of factors. These factors will be discussed in Chapter 24. The primary risk for the borrower is that the value of the currency borrowed rises in relation to the domestic currency. This results in an unexpected cost on the international loan, since the loan would have to be repaid in the foreign currency that has risen in value relative to the domestic currency. This potential change in currency values

> **DEMONSTRATION PROBLEM:** Nominal Interest Rate on Specific Type of Debt
>
> **Situation:** Consider the yield on an auto loan. This loan has an interest rate of 10.25 percent in the marketplace. A comparable maturity Treasury rate is 8 percent. Auto loans include an expected credit loss premium of .75 percent per annum. They also cost 1.25 percent per annum to service. The loans carry a .2 percent marketability premium. Since these can be prepaid by the borrower before maturity, they also carry a call or prepayment option premium. What is this prepayment option premium?
>
> **Result:** Using Equation 2.4 we have
>
> $$10.25\% = 8.00\% + .50\% + .20\% + 1.25\% + X$$
>
> $$X = cop = .35\%$$
>
> This loan carries a premium yield of .35 percent to compensate for the fact that the borrower has an option to prepay the loan before maturity. This option is potentially costly to the lender, so lenders demand a higher yield.

must be reflected in computing the cost of borrowing. We consider this relationship in Equation 2.5.

$$r_{tc} = r_f + [(FX_d^{t+1}/_f - FX_d^t/_f)/FX_d^t/_f] \qquad [2.5]$$

Foreign total borrowing cost = foreign interest rate +
percent change in domestic currency price for one unit of foreign currency between period t and $t + 1$

r_{tc} = Total cost expressed as an interest rate of foreign borrowing

r_f = Interest rate on foreign financial debt claims

$FX_d^t/_f$ = One foreign exchange unit priced in terms of the domestic currency at time t ($.57 = 1 German mark)

Consider a situation in which the U.S. company plans to issue a one-year bond denominated in German marks, or DM. The domestic U.S.

annual interest rate, r_d, is 3.5 percent. The German annual interest rate r_f is 5 percent. The marks borrowed will be immediately converted to dollars and used in the United States. The price of one DM priced in terms of U.S. dollars is expected to go from .59 US\$/DM at point t to .57 US\$/DM at point $t + 1$. This represents a percent change of

$$[(.57\$/DM - .59\$/DM) / .59\$/DM] = -3.39\%$$

Since the U.S. dollar is expected to increase in value by 3.39 percent, the U.S. borrower will have to factor in the decreased currency cost of repaying at period $t + 1$ in German marks that are 3.39 percent less valuable in relation to U.S. dollars. This 3.39 percent reduced cost of borrowing German marks brings the true cost of borrowing to

German interest rate + increased (decreased) value of marks in

relation to the $

= total cost of German loan

$$5.00\% - 3.39\% = 1.61\%$$

Since this 1.61 percent is far below the U.S. borrowing rate of 3.50 percent, it would pay to borrow in the German market. Although it is not possible to accurately forecast future exchange rates, actual forward exchange rates in different countries do reflect differences in interest rates between countries. This will be discussed fully in Chapter 24. These forward exchange rates are not good forecasts of the future because they create exchange rate risk for borrowers and investors.

Taxability

The final factor influencing the changes in interest rates is *taxability*. Financial claim income is typically subject to taxation by both federal and state governments. Since the value of a financial claim is based on its anticipated cash flow, taxation acts to alter those cash flows.

Not all income generated by financial claims is taxed equally, however. A notable exception is income on U.S. government securities, which is not subject to state income tax. Most state and local municipal bonds are not subject to federal income tax. Other financial claims allow investors to defer taxation. Savings held in pension funds and as insurance policy reserves provide for income tax deferrals at the state and federal levels of government.

In Chapter 4 we will look closely at how these taxation differences affect the yields investors actually receive on different types of investments.

Reinvestment Risk

The *reinvestment risk* applies generally to all investments that generate cash flows for the investor prior to the maturity of the investment. When the *yield to maturity* is computed on investments, it is assumed in the calculation process that all cash flows are reinvested at the yield computed. The internal rate of return (IRR) calculation found in any textbook on business finance shows that one of the limitations of the internal rate of return calculation for investments is the assumption that all the cash flows received before the end of the investment period are reinvested at the IRR.

The reinvestment problem creates *reinvestment risk* for investors. This is the risk that the cash flows received before the maturity of the investment cannot be reinvested at the yield to maturity of the investment. To clearly see how the reinvestment risk works consider the following types of investments. Each of these investments has a yield to maturity of 6 percent, yet they have different cash flows.

1. Installment loan: Two equal payments received at end of each period.
2. Interest paying bond: Annual interest payments received at the end of each of next two years and principal due at end of the second year.
3. Discounted bond: All principal and interest due at maturity at the end of two years.

The cash flow for these three investments, each having a yield of 6 percent, is shown in Table 2.3.

Table 2.3

Cash Flows
6% Interest Rate
No Reinvestment of Cash Flows

Date	Installment Cash Flow (dollars)	Interest Bond Cash Flow	Discounted Bond Cash Flow
1-1-93	−1,000.00	−1,000.00	−1,000.00
1-1-94	545.44	60.00	—
1-1-95	545.44	1,060.00	1,123.60
Total	$90.88	$120.00	$123.60

Table 2.4

Cash Flows
6% Coupon Rate
Reinvestment of Cash Flows

Date	Cash Flow (dollars)	Reinvestment at 6%	Cash Flow plus Reinvestment Interest
Installment loan			
1-1-93	−1,000.00		−1,000.00
1-1-94	545.44	$(1+.06)1$	578.17
1-1-95	545.44		545.44
Total			**$123.61**
Interest-paying bond			
1-1-93	−1,000.00		−1,000.00
1-1-94	60.00	$(1+.06)1$	63.60
1-1-95	1,060.00		1,060.00
Total			**$123.60**
Discounted bond			
1-1-93	−1,000.00		−1,000.00
1-1-94	0.00	$(1+.06)1$	0.00
1-1-95	1,123.60		1,123.60
Total			**$123.60**

Note that each of the investments has a different net cash flow. This is because we have not yet reinvested the early cash flows. In Table 2.4, we will reinvest the early cash flows at the 6 percent yield of the investments.

Our reinvestment assumption results in the net cash flows becoming equal. This proves that as long as we can reinvest early cash flows at the investment's yield to maturity, each of these investments with 6 percent yields will produce the same net cash flow for the investor. Now consider what would happen if the reinvestment rate was not 6 percent, but rather 4 percent. The result of this reinvestment assumption on the net cash flows of our three investments is shown in Table 2.5 on page 46.

With this lower reinvestment rate, the three investments result in significantly different net cash flows. The differences that result from

Table 2.5

Cash Flows
6% Coupon Rate
Reinvestment of Cash Flows at 4%

Date	Cash Flow (dollars)	Reinvestment at 4%	Cash Flow plus Reinvestment Interest
Installment loan			
1-1-93	−1,000.00		−1,000.00
1-1-94	545.44	$(1+.04)^1$	567.26
1-1-95	545.44		545.44
Total			**$112.70**
Interest-paying bond			
1-1-93	−1,000.00		−1,000.00
1-1-94	60.00	$(1+.04)^1$	62.40
1-1-95	1,060.00		1,060.00
Total			**$122.40**
Discounted bond			
1-1-93	−1,000.00		−1,000.00
1-1-94	0.00	$(1+.04)^1$	0.00
1-1-95	1,123.60		1,123.60
Total			**$123.60**

changes in the reinvestment rate represent reinvestment risk. This risk can be eliminated by purchasing discounted securities, such as the discounted bond shown in the last table.

Summary

There are a large number of interest rates on different types of debt instruments, and these interest rates tend to move up and down together as they adjust to the changing supply and demand for loanable funds. Changes in the demand for funds from consumers, businesses, and governments, as well as Federal Reserve actions, cause the changes in the levels of rates. As a result, rates tend to be low during and immediately after the end of recessions when demand for funds is weak. They rise as the economy recovers and borrowers become more confident, and peak after a business expansion.

The **real interest rate** equates the next most desirable investment opportunity to the marginal interest return that is demanded. Increased investment opportunities tend to increase the real rate of interest—the rate of interest without consideration to inflation.

The **loanable funds theory** holds that interest rates are determined by the demand and supply of funds from the business, household, government, and foreign sectors of the economy and by actions of the Federal Reserve. Typically, during booming economic conditions the relative demand for funds rises in the business and household sectors and falls in the government and international sectors. During economic recessions, the reverse tends to occur.

Inflation expectations are known to be a major influence on the level of interest rates. Expectations of rising inflation cause businesses to build inventory and households to consume now, while causing investors to refrain from lending without being compensated for the expected loss in purchasing power. This is known as the **Fisher Effect.** This theory holds that

$$\text{Nominal Interest Rate} = \text{Real Interest Rate} + \text{Expected Inflation}$$

Interest rates on various types of debt instruments tend to rise and fall together, although some move farther and faster than others. **Short-term interest rates** fluctuate over a wider range than do **long-term rates.**

The **term structure of interest rates** or the **yield curve** shows the level of interest rates for different maturities. The factors that affect the shape of the yield curve are expectations of future interest rates, market segmentation, investor and saver preferred habitats, and investor liquidity preference.

The most powerful explanation of the term structure is the **expectations theory.** The expectations theory holds that long-term interest rates represent the market's expectation of what future short-term interest rates will be. Because of the typical behavior of interest rates over the business cycle, we usually find an upward-sloping yield curve during the early stages of a recovery and a downward-sloping yield curve when the economy appears headed for a recession.

The **market segmentation theory** holds that the relative demand for and supply of securities in different maturity ranges accounts for the changing shape of the term structure.

The **preferred habitat theory** is a compromise between the expectations theory and the market segmentation theory. This theory accepts the notion of the borrowers' and savers' willingness to substitute over maturities as long as the saver obtains a premium yield to shift from a desired maturity to a less desirable one. This premium is known as a **liquidity premium.**

The **liquidity preference theory** is based on the notion that investors are risk adverse and therefore prefer short-term investments with less interest rate risk than long-term investments. It builds off the preferred habitat theory by proposing that the liquidity premium rises as maturity increases. This theory holds that the term structure has a more pronounced upward slope than would be reflected if only the expectations theory yield curve was shown.

The **implied forward rate** is the market's expectation of future interest rates as reflected by the expectations theory and the prevailing term structure. It is possible to calculate the forward expected interest rate for any forward period. Consider the following equation:

$$(1 + {}_1r_{t-1})^1 (1 + {}_{t-1}r_0)^{t-1} = (1 + {}_tr_0)^t$$

In this equation the r represents interest rates for selected periods. The subscript to the right of the r indicates the beginning point in time when the specific r applies. The left subscript denotes the number of the periods over which the rate applies. The rate ${}_1r_{t-1}$ is the implied one-year forward rate beginning in period $_{t-1}$. The rates with the r_0 are known, which allows us to solve for the missing forward rate.

There are claim-specific factors that influence the structure of interest rates; that is, the spread between rates on different types of debt instruments at any given point in time. These factors include (1) **credit or default risk,** or the likelihood that the borrower will not pay in full and on time; (2) **marketability,** or the ease of selling the debt; (3) **call or prepayment risk,** the risk that the borrower will repay before maturity if interest rates fall; (4) **servicing costs,** the costs relating to collection and insuring that the debt performs according to its contractual terms; (5) **exchange rate risk,** the risk that attaches to debts repayable in a currency other than your own, which could depreciate in value; (6) **taxability,** the tax treatment of cash flows from the debt.

Reinvestment risk is the risk that early cash flows from an investment cannot be reinvested at the yield rate on the investment.

Questions

Chapter 2

1. Why do interest rates fluctuate?
2. What is the loanable funds theory of interest rates?
3. What is meant by the expression the "structure of interest rates"?

4. What does it mean to say the demand for loanable funds is interest rate elastic?
5. How does the Federal Reserve intervene to impact interest rates?
6. Why does the Federal Reserve intervene to impact interest rates and the supply of loanable funds? What tools does it use to accomplish its objectives?
7. What impact does inflation seem to have on the level of interest rates? What is meant by the Fisher Effect?
8. What is the relationship between the nominal interest rate and the rate of expected inflation?
9. How do interest rates tend to behave during periods of recession? During economic booms? During periods of abnormally high inflation? Explain your answers.
10. What is the term structure of interest rates?
11. Explain the expectations theory of the term structure. Explain the liquidity preference theory. Finally, explain the preferred habitat theory and the segmentation theory.
12. Explain what is meant by the following sentence. "It is impossible to test the empirical validity of the expectations theory because we can't measure expectations." Do you agree or disagree?
13. If you observe an upward-sloping term structure, what would the proponents of the expectations theory expect to be the course of future short-term interest rates? What about a downward-sloping term structure?
14. The interest rate on any specific debt is impacted by a number of factors. These include inflation and maturity. What other factors would be important in comparing the yield of a privately issued debt instrument to that of a Treasury security?
15. What is meant by *reinvestment risk?* Provide an example.

Problems

Problem 2-1   Implied Forward Rates

If the interest rate on a three-year Treasury is 9.50 percent and on the one-year Treasury 7.50 percent, what would the advocates of the expectations theory expect the yield on two-year Treasuries to be one year from now? Assume annual interest payments. Show your work.

Problem 2-2   Implied Forward Rates

The yields on Treasury securities over the next 24 months are

6-month	5.55%
12-month	6.00%
18-month	6.25%
24-month	7.40%

You have been asked to develop a forecast on the future 6-month Treasury rate using the expectations theory as your guide. Based on the above information, what do you calculate future 6-month Treasury bill rates to be 6, 12, and 18 months into the future?

Problem 2-3   Implied Forward Rates
You are going to invest funds for five years. An attractive three-year investment will provide an annual yield of 6 percent. A five-year investment is available at 7 percent. You believe that interest rates will be increasing. In three years, you expect that you can earn 8 percent on a two-year investment. Should you invest for five years at 7 percent or three years at 6 percent with a reinvestment for two years?

Problem 2-4   Specific Factors Affecting Risky Debt Rates
The yield on a ten-year Treasury is 8.50 percent. The yield on a conventional fixed rate mortgage is 9.55 percent. The credit risk premium on the mortgage is expected to be .15 percent and the marketability premium .20 percent. The mortgage also requires the investor to pay .10 percent to service the payments on the loan. What accounts for the remaining yield differential between the two debt instruments?

Problem 2-5   Foreign Borrowing Cost
Your firm is considering financing in the United Kingdom. The rate that would be required on a six-month bond would be 7 percent in pounds. The United States financing alternative would cost 9 percent. The U.K. pound (pd) is expected to change in value from $1.70/pd to $1.75/pd. Should the firm finance in the United Kingdom?

Problem 2-6   Foreign Borrowing Cost
The interest rate for a one-year loan in France is 6 percent. A comparable one-year loan in the United States would cost 8 percent. The exchange rate between U.S. dollars and French francs is $.18 per French franc (ff). What exchange rate would have to prevail in one year to make the borrower indifferent toward financing in the United States or in France?

Financial Claims

chapter 3

Financial claims are contracts between two parties. They identify the rights and obligations of the parties to each other. This chapter describes the basic requirements necessary for creating the major financial claims in our economy. Understanding the nature of these contracts is vital to understanding the value added by the creation of new claims and their associated risks and returns. The chapter begins by exploring the basic motivation behind the creation of financial claims, how they are created, and who creates them.

Why Financial Claims Are Created

Financial claims are used in a modern economy for many purposes, including (1) shifting the consumption of goods and services over time; (2) reducing risk through risk sharing or pooling; and (3) reducing the cost of financial transactions.

Consumers typically think of financial claims as a means to shift consumption and savings from one period to another. People save for retirement so that they can consume later in life. People borrow to purchase a home so that they can have a house before they have sufficient assets to purchase a house outright. Businesses borrow for investment in plant and equipment and inventory when the investment is too large to finance out of current income. Governments borrow to finance long-lived investments, such as roads and airports, so that their cost can be spread over the period of use. Shifting consumption from one period to another is known as an *intertemporal* transfer of resources.

Many financial claims are designed to reduce or alter the risk characteristics of other financial claims. Investment in a single mortgage could be very risky for a small investor: If the borrower defaulted, the investor might suffer a sizeable loss. However, if we place one thousand mortgages in a pool and sell a one-thousandth share to the small investor, the default risk is more predictable. A large pool of mortgages still has a risk of loss, but not all borrowers can be expected to default. If only a few do, the individual investor's loss is negligible. Diversification makes losses more predictable. This is an example of *risk pooling,* a common rationale for creating a financial claim.

Reducing transaction costs is an ongoing objective of many of our financial service intermediaries. Financial claims are often created as a means of reducing transaction costs. Consider mutual funds as an example. These financial intermediaries permit small investors to purchase diversified portfolios of securities. By aggregating the investments of many small investors, mutual funds permit a substantial reduction in transaction costs that result when you buy and sell securities in small amounts. Mutual funds obtain lower commission levels than are available to the large institutional investor. Also, analyzing the investment quality of a number of securities would be very costly for an individual, but by joining with other investors, it is possible to reduce the costs of investment analysis.

The Debt Financial Claim as a Contract

There are several basic characteristics of debt financial claims. Generally the debt contract includes the following:

1. A provision indicating the amount of interest the holder will receive or how that amount is to be determined
2. A provision stating the amount of principal to be paid at a date of maturity or a stipulated schedule for principal repayments
3. A provision that gives the borrower the option to repay the claim on or after a specified date, with or without a fee for prepayment
4. A series of provisions that require the borrower to fulfill certain conditions concerning its financial stability and/or the condition of collateral, if any, called *covenants*

Ordinarily the borrower or issuer of the claim will negotiate with the lender the provisions to be found in a financial claim. In the case of publicly issued securities, this is done by an investment banker acting as an underwriter on behalf of the investors. In practice, the underwriter discusses the provisions with the borrower and prospective investors as the contract is being drawn up to ensure that the securities will be sold.

Who Creates Financial Claims?

CSUs, which have surplus funds to invest, are generally found in the household sector, some state and local government units, and, in recent years, the foreign sector. CDUs, which borrow to consume or invest now, are generally businesses, some state and local governments, and the federal government. Each unit may from time to time switch from a CSU to a CDU or vice versa.

Households, businesses, governments, and foreigners are the principal creators of financial claims. At year-end 1990, these four sectors of the economy had over $10.6 trillion of financial claims outstanding. Table 3.1 shows the volume of outstanding financial claims by sector from year-end 1980 through year-end 1990. It also shows the growth rate for each of the sectors.

Table 3.1

**Year-end Financial Claims by Sector
1980–1990
(dollars in billions)**

Year	Total	U.S. Govt.	Private NonFin Total	Total	Home Mtge.	Local Consumer Credit	NonFin Business Total	Local and State Govt.
1980	3898	743	3155	1430	942	355	1438	286
1981	4280	830	3450	1549	1020	372	1597	304
1982	4668	991	3676	1626	1060	389	1719	331
1983	5209	1178	4031	1792	1156	438	1884	355
1984	5959	1377	4583	2019	1290	519	2181	383
1985	6805	1600	5204	2296	1441	602	2434	474
1986	7646	1815	5831	2596	1667	660	2725	510
1987	8344	1960	6384	2879	1888	693	2946	559
1988	9096	2118	6978	3192	2119	744	3182	605
1989	9805	2269	7536	3502	2353	791	3400	634
1990	10580	2569	8011	3832	2639	809	3531	649

Growth Rate

80–90%	10.5	13.2	9.8	10.4	10.9	8.6	9.4	8.5

Source: *Flow of Funds Accounts, Fourth Quarter 1990.* Board of Governors of the Federal Reserve System, Washington, DC (March 6, 1991).

Table 3.1 shows that the volume of financial claims issued by the nonfinancial sector of the economy grew by a compound rate of 10.5 percent in the decade ending in 1990. The fastest growth was registered in the obligations of the U.S. government, and the slowest in the obligations of state and local governments and in household consumer loans. Consumer debt for home mortgages grew rapidly during the decade.

Household Holdings of Financial Claims

The household sector is by far the largest holder of financial claims. Their holdings have changed over the years by becoming more institutionalized. Table 3.2 describes changes in the holdings of financial claims by the household sector, which includes trusts and nonprofit institutions, over the last forty years.

It is very clear that the composition of financial assets held by the household sector has changed significantly over this period. The table suggests the following conclusions:

1. After decades of increasing, household holdings of deposits are declining in share due to the availability of mutual funds that hold credit instruments and sell shares to households.

Table 3.2

**Select Financial Holdings of Households, Trusts, and Nonprofit Organizations
Select Years 1950–1990: Year-end Holdings
(dollars in billions)**

| | $ Amount and % of Total ||||||
Types of Financial Claims	1950	%	1970	%	1990	%
Deposits	$114	27.3	$543	28.7	$2429	23.8
Credit market instruments	92	22.0	247	13.1	2073	20.3
Corporate equities						
Mutual funds	3	0.1	45	2.3	497	4.9
Other	130	31.1	682	36.1	1858	18.2
Life insurance reserves	55	13.2	131	6.9	388	3.8
Pension reserves	24	5.7	241	12.8	2945	28.9
Total	$418		$1889		$10190	

Source: *Balance Sheets for the U.S. Economy 1945–90.* Board of Governors of the Federal Reserve System, Washington, DC (March 1991).

2. Pension funds, trusts established for employee retirement benefits, have become the fastest growing and largest of the financial intermediaries.
3. Household holdings of equities, common stocks of profit-making corporations have decreased in favor of mutual fund equity funds and pension funds that hold equities.
4. Households continue to disfavor holding savings in the form of reserves built up in policies with life insurance companies.

Another major conclusion from this table is that the professional asset management business has been growing very rapidly. Mutual funds and pension funds are capturing a larger share of assets to be managed, while households are less inclined to use traditional depositories and insurance companies.

The Taxonomy of Financial Claims

There are many different types of financial claims. The following classifications help to identify the types of issuers of financial claims and the structure of the claims. These classifications are not mutually exclusive with respect to specific financial claims.

Primary and Secondary Claims

Much of the discussion so far has been on financial claims that are issued by CDUs. These claims allow the borrower to use the funds for consumption or investment in goods or services. Financial claims issued by these economic units are known as *primary claims*. The individual who purchases an automobile using an auto loan obtained from a commercial bank is creating a primary claim, the auto loan. However, many financial claims are issued by institutions that use the proceeds to invest in other financial claims. Deposits, insurance policies with investment features, known as life insurance policy reserves, and pension fund reserves are liabilities of financial institutions issued for the purpose of investing the funds received in other financial claims through *intermediation*. These claims are known as *secondary claims*. Thus the commercial bank that issues a deposit to obtain the funds to make an auto loan is issuing a secondary claim, the deposit.

Derivative Claims

A wide variety of financial instruments derive their value from that of another financial claim. These are known as *derivative claims*. Financial options, futures options, swaps, and futures contracts are derivative claims. Options are financial contracts that permit the owner the opportunity, but not the obligation, to buy or sell a financial claim at a predetermined price. A financial futures contract is a financial contract that requires its owner to buy or sell a financial claim at an agreed-upon price. A swap is a financial contract in which two parties agree to pay each other income or currency based on a formula.

The value of an option, swap, or a futures contract is derived from the value of the financial claim upon which it is written. For example, the value of an option to purchase $100,000 of government bonds in six months is derived from the expected value of these bonds.

Asset-Backed Claims

Financial claims supported by assets have been an integral part of the financial markets for years. A *home mortgage* is a financial claim in which residential property serves as collateral. *Collateral* is the asset that is transferred to the investor if the borrower defaults under the obligation.

Another class of financial claims supported by other claims used as collateral are *asset-backed claims*. These claims pool other claims as collateral. A mortgage-backed security is a good example of an asset-backed financial claim. In this case, the collateral is a pool of mortgages on homes or apartments. This represents a new set of collateralized financial claims that pool other financial claims as collateral. Today, *mortgage-backed securities* represent the largest class of asset-backed claims. There are over $1 trillion of these securities outstanding. As we will see in Chapter 23, the asset-backed security can be used to finance a wide variety of different financial claims, such as auto loans and credit card receivables.

Hybrid Claims

Hybrid claims refer to a class of claims that are created by altering the cash flow and/or credit characteristics of an existing financial claim. The most popular hybrid claim is the Treasury zero coupon bond. Here the cash flows from a Treasury bond become the principal payments for a series of new zero coupon financial claims. A *zero coupon* is a financial claim that pays the investor one lump sum payment at some point in the future. Other hybrid claims involve altering the credit risk characteristics of an existing financial claim by creating multiple classes of claims using the original claim as collateral.

The existence of so many different types of financial claims has made the job of the financial market analyst extremely challenging. Many of the claims that exist today were not around ten years ago. Yet, each must be understood by investors and issuers so that it can be correctly valued.

Major Types and Issuers of Primary Financial Claims Outstanding

The questions of who issues financial claims, why they are issued, and the different types of claims have been discussed. Now, the volume of primary claims outstanding classified by type of issuer or CDU is considered.

Federal Government Claims

The federal government, through its large and persistent deficits in the last several decades, has become the nation's largest single creditor. The government finances its deficit position by issuing securities in a variety of different forms. At year-end 1991, U.S. Treasury issues reached $3,736 billion. The types of issues and their amounts are shown in Table 3.3.

As the table shows, U.S. government claims come in both marketable and nonmarketable forms. Almost two-thirds are *marketable securities*. These are known as *Treasury bills, Treasury notes,* and *Treasury bonds.* Treasury bills are sold at a discount price below their par, or redemption, value. The difference between the purchase price and the redemption value is considered interest. Bills are sold in three- and six-month maturities and

Table 3.3

**Types of U.S. Government Interest-Bearing Claims
December 31, 1991**
(dollars in billions)

Type of Claim	$ Amount
Marketable	$2,457
Bills	590
Notes	1,431
Bonds	436
Nonmarketable	$1,297
State and local government series	160
Foreign issues	42
Savings bonds and notes	136
Government account series	959

Source: Federal Reserve *Bulletin.* (May 1992) A28.

52-week maturities. Bills are very marketable. On a typical day U.S. government security dealers trade over $30 billion in Treasury bills.

Treasury notes and bonds are coupon securities. They pay interest on a semiannual basis. Treasury notes are issued with an initial maturity of two to ten years. Bonds are issued with maturities of ten years or more. Government security dealers trade about $90 billion in Treasury securities on an average day.

The Treasury's nonmarketable securities include a collection of securities issued to specific classes of investors. Series EE and HH savings bonds are the best known. They are issued in small denominations and sold to individuals. Nonmarketable securities also include issues specifically designed for government trust accounts, state and local governments, and foreign investors.

Primary Debt Claims Issued by Nonfinancial Businesses

The primary debt claims of nonfinancial businesses fall into two basic classifications. These are borrowings directly from suppliers, called *trade debt*. Other borrowings are accomplished through financial institutions and directly through the money and capital markets. Table 3.4 provides a breakdown of the types of claims issued by nonfinancial businesses.

The claims issued by nonfinancial business vary, as the table indicates. The business sector uses the money and capital markets to raise funds through industrial development bonds, corporate bonds, and commercial

Table 3.4

Primary Claims Issued by Nonfinancial Businesses
December 31, 1989
(dollars in billions)

Type of Claims	$ Amount
Tax-exempt bond (Industrial development bonds)	$114
Commercial paper	99
Mortgages	118
Corporate bonds	1,060
Bank loans	536
Trade debt	677
Other loans	236
Total	**$2,840**

Source: *Balance Sheets for the U.S. Economy 1960–1991*. Board of Governors of the Federal Reserve System, Washington, DC (March 1992) p. 5.

paper. Other claims such as mortgages and bank loans are issued to financial institutions. Businesses also issue claims to one another in the form of trade debt. The following are the primary classes of claims issued by nonfinancial businesses.

Corporate Bonds

Corporate bonds are financial claims representing an obligation of a corporation. Corporate bonds come in several different forms. The basic classifications include collateralized (secured) or uncollateralized (unsecured), senior or subordinated (junior), callable or noncallable, and convertible bonds.

Collateralized Bonds

Collateralized bonds are issued with assets that transfer to the bondholder in the event of default. They are considered secured bonds. Corporations use a variety of assets as collateral for a bond issue. Collateral may consist of fixed assets or intangible assets, such as stock of a subsidiary. If the stock of a subsidiary is used as collateral, the bond is known as a *collateral trust bond*. These bonds include provisions that protect the investor in case of default. These provisions might include transferring the voting rights of the subsidiary to the trustee for the bond-holder, and periodically establishing the value of the subsidiary stock to ensure that it exceeds principal value.

Mortgage bonds are issued by corporations with substantial investments in property, such as public utilities. Collateral in this case may be a power plant.

When a corporation uses equipment such as airplanes, railroad cars, or trucks as collateral, the bond is known as an *equipment trust certificate*. In the case of this type of certificate, a trustee for the bondholders retains title to the equipment and leases it to the corporation. The amount of equipment trust certificates issued is less than the value of the equipment. The remaining amount is paid by the corporation to the trustee to cover the cost of purchasing the equipment.

Debentures

Corporations issue bonds that carry no collateral, known as *debentures*. These are unsecured obligations of the issuer. If the company fails, the holder of a debenture is considered a general creditor of the company with no claim to the value of specific assets. As a result, in a bankruptcy, the unsecured creditor will ordinarily lose some or all of the money invested.

Subordinated Debentures

Corporations that are heavy borrowers will occasionally issue obligations that are of higher credit risk than even an unsecured debenture. These are called *subordinated debentures* because payment preference in bankruptcy is below that of secured lenders and general creditors.

Convertible Debentures

One way for corporations to increase the demand for their unsecured debt, and to provide for future growth of equity, is to issue bonds that can be converted into a specified number of shares of common stock in the company. Such bonds are known as *convertible debentures,* and the right to convert the bond into stock is called the *conversion privilege*.

Other Bond Provisions

Corporate bonds may carry a number of other provisions to improve their appeal to investors or to the issuing corporation. The *call provision* is designed to improve the flexibility of the issuer by providing the issuer the option to prepay, or call, the bond on or after a specified date and at a specified price.

A *sinking fund provision* improves a bond's investment appeal by requiring the issuer to periodically retire a specified percentage of the issue. This may be done by the issuer giving the bond trustee enough funds to redeem a percentage of the bonds chosen randomly or by delivering bonds purchased in the secondary market.

Serial bonds are designed so that a specified principal amount of the bond's par value comes due on predetermined dates during the life of the issue. These bonds are typically used when the collateral value is likely to decline over time, such as in the case of equipment trust certificates.

Investment Grade Ratings and Junk Bonds

Most publicly traded corporate bonds are rated as to their creditworthiness by one of the major rating services, such as Standard and Poor's, Moody's, and Fitch rating services. These private organizations perform an extensive credit analysis of a bond issuer and give the bond a credit rating. A rating of one of the top four highest ratings is generally considered investment grade. A rating below the top four grades is considered noninvestment grade. Noninvestment grade bonds became controversial in the 1980s due to their use in financing hostile takeovers and financial restructurings, as well as the fact that life insurance companies and savings and loans were investing in them. This controversy led to the adoption of the expression *junk bond*.

Prior to the 1980s, to obtain a below-investment-grade rating, the bond issuer had to experience deteriorating financial health. This would cause its bonds to be downgraded to the lower noninvestment grade. These bonds are called *fallen angels*. Thanks to the activities of Michael Milken, the investment banker most responsible for the huge growth in junk bonds in the 1980s, the primary new issue market was developed.

Primary Claims Issued by Households

The household sector issues financial claims for two primary purposes: home purchase and consumption of durable goods. The amounts outstanding of these two classifications are shown in Table 3.5.

The largest category of claims issued by households are mortgages on homes. These claims have become more complex in recent years due to the increase in the number of different types of mortgages issued. The following are several of the more important mortgages available:

Fixed-Rate Mortgages (FRMs)

FRMs are the most prevalent type of mortgage issued for financing a home. The typical FRM is a fully amortized, fixed-payment loan with a maturity of 15 or 30 years. An *amortizing loan* combines interest and principal payments in such a way that the principal is completely paid off at the end of the loan's term to maturity.

Borrowers can repay most FRMs at any time without a prepayment penalty. This prepayment option, also referred to as a *call option,* makes the fixed-rate mortgage very appealing to borrowers, but less attractive to lenders and investors. Mortgage borrowers commonly refinance a high-rate FRM during periods of cyclically low interest rates. Because the rates available to a holder of a prepaid mortgage are lower during such periods, the FRM is said to have high prepayment or reinvestment risk.

Table 3.5

Primary Financial Claims Issued by Households
December 31, 1991
(dollars in billions)

Primary Claim	$ Amount
Mortgages	$2,904
Consumer loans	
Auto	268
Revolving	235
Mobile home	19
Other	208
Total	**$3,634**

Source: Federal Reserve *Bulletin.* (May 1992) A36 and A37.

Adjustable Rate Mortgages (ARMs)

Adjustable rate home mortgages became popular in the 1980s. These mortgages come in a wide variety of different forms. One common feature is an interest rate that floats in relation to an index. The index may be for a specific security or an index of interest rates. For example, the index may reflect the one-year Treasury bill rate or the average cost of funds at savings and loan associations. A more detailed discussion of ARMs is found in Chapter 19.

Graduated Payment Mortgages (GPMs)

GPMs are fixed-rate mortgages with monthly payments that begin low and then increase during the early years of the mortgage. Often these payments are not large enough to cover the entire interest due, so the principal is increased periodically by the amount of unpaid interest. The low initial monthly payment helps homebuyers whose income is expected to increase to qualify for a larger loan than would be available using the more typical fixed-payment mortgage.

Primary Claims Issued by State and Local Governments

State and local governments are major issuers of primary financial claims. Two important reasons for issuing primary claims are to obtain funds for operating fund needs prior to tax collections and to provide funds for long-term capital expenditures. At year-end 1990, state and local governments had $649 billion in claims outstanding. The two basic types of state and local government bonds are general obligation bonds and revenue bonds.

General Obligation Bonds (GOs)

GOs are debt instruments issued by municipalities—states, counties, cities, towns, and districts—that are secured by the issuer's general taxing authority. Most of these bonds are used to finance long-lived, or capital, assets such as roads, jails, sewage treatment facilities, parks, and the like.

Municipalities also issue short-term GO securities to bridge the gap between the time when funds are needed and when they will actually be received. Government entities can receive funds through taxes, grants, such as federal government grants, fees charged for municipal services, and bond issuances. Short-term borrowings of one year or less that are issued in anticipation of receiving revenues are known as TANs (tax), RANs (revenue), GANs (grant), and BANs (bond) anticipation notes.

Revenue Bonds

Revenue bonds are issued by state and local governments to finance public projects and private enterprises that generate specific revenues, such as airports, college facilities, schools, industrial plants, hospitals, sports complexes, sewers and water facilities, and public-power plants. These revenues are pledged to repay the debt. The important feature of revenue bonds is that when revenues are insufficient to meet principal and interest payments, the municipality need not use other available funds or raise taxes to meet these payments. Thus revenue bonds are usually more risky than general obligation bonds.

Until now only claims issued by domestic individuals and organizations have been considered. As our markets have become more global, it has become necessary for financial market analysts to learn about claims issued by internationally based issuers.

International Issuers of Claims

Foreign governments and agencies, as well as foreign private corporations, issue claims that are purchased by investors in the United States. These claims are issued in foreign currency denominations and in U.S. dollars. The claims issued by foreign countries that are held by U.S. offices and foreign branches of U.S. banks are shown in Table 3.6.

Table 3.6

Claims of Foreign Countries Held by U.S. Offices and Branches of U.S. Banks
December 31, 1991
(dollars in billions)

Groups Issuing Foreign Claims	$ Amount
G-10 countries*	$137.5
Other developed countries	22.6
OPEC countries	14.6
Non-OPEC developing countries	64.3
Eastern Europe	2.4
Offshore banking centers	52.0
Other	47.7
Total	**$341.1**

*G-10 includes Belgium-Luxembourg, France, Germany, Italy, the Netherlands, Sweden, Switzerland, United Kingdom, Canada, and Japan.
Source: Federal Reserve *Bulletin*. (May 1992) A62.

Foreigners also issue a variety of private claims held by U.S. investors. These include bonds, trade credit, and other claims.

The claims we have just reviewed are all issued directly by individuals and organizations who need capital for consumption or investment. Many additional claims are issued by financial institutions which, in turn, invest the proceeds from the sale of these claims in other financial claims. This intermediation process accounts for the large number of secondary financial claims.

Secondary Claims Issued by the Financial Sector

Many of the financial claims issued in the United States are secondary claims. The principal issuers of secondary claims are the U.S. government's sponsored enterprises and agencies; depository institutions, such as commercial banks and thrifts; and nondepository intermediaries, such as insurance companies, finance companies, and pension funds. Table 3.7 provides a breakdown of the secondary financial claims issued by intermediaries.

The volume of secondary financial claims is very large. This is because the intermediaries are very well developed and our country is wealthy. As a result, most of the investment-allocation decisions relating to who obtains

International Focus

International Investments Boom

The sharp growth in world trade during the last decade has brought with it an awareness of foreign investment opportunities. U.S. investors have become more interested in foreign investments for several reasons. First, foreign companies are better known, since their products are widely purchased in the United States. Second, diversification into foreign securities is expected to improve overall investment performance by creating higher returns for any given level of risk.

During the 1980s, according to data published by the Federal Reserve Board, U.S. investor holdings of foreign corporate equities rose 17.9 percent per annum, rising from $44.6 billion at year-end 1980 to $231.2 billion at year-end 1990. Private corporate bond investments increased 11.5 percent per annum, rising from $43.5 billion to $129.1 billion.

Common approaches to investing in private foreign securities include mutual fund shares and *American Depository Receipts (ADRs)*. ADRs represent financial claims issued by U.S. banks that hold foreign securities in trust for investors.

Table 3.7

Secondary Financial Claims Issued by Major Private Domestic Intermediaries
December 31, 1991
(dollars in billions)

Type of Claim	$ Amount
Deposits and repos	
Checkable deposits	$ 585
Small time and savings	2,333
Money market fund shares	496
Large time deposits	267
Security repos	164
Credit market debt	1,073
Pension funds and insurance	2,286
Other	1,175
Total	**$8,379**

Source: Federal Reserve *Bulletin*. (May 1992) A43.

funds in the primary market are made by intermediaries, not by savers or investors directly.

The remainder of this section is devoted to a discussion of the types of claims issued by our major financial intermediaries.

Secondary Claims Issued by Depositories

U.S. depositories are the largest issuers of secondary financial claims. The most important of these claims are transaction accounts and time and savings deposits. The types of claims and volume of each outstanding is shown in Table 3.8 on page 66.

Transaction Accounts

These are funds on deposit that are withdrawable on demand by the use of checks or drafts. They can usually be withdrawn through automated teller machines, ATMs, and sometimes by debit cards and authorized telephone transfers.

Demand Deposits

Checking accounts used by corporations are called demand deposits and, by law, do not pay interest. Other types of organizations and individuals occasionally hold noninterest bearing demand deposits. Because they earn no interest, holders have a strong incentive to keep balances low.

Table 3.8

Secondary Deposit Claims of Depositories
December 31, 1991
Not Seasonally Adjusted
(dollars in billions)

Issuer and Type of Claim	$ Amount
Commercial Banks and Thrifts	
Transaction Accounts	
Demand deposits	$289
Other checkable deposits	333
Commercial Banks	
Time and Savings Deposits	
Savings deposits and money market deposit accounts	$582
Small time deposits	606
Large time deposits	374
Thrift Institutions	
Time and Savings Deposits	
Savings deposits and money market deposit accounts	$378
Small time deposits	465
Large time deposits	121

Source: Federal Reserve *Bulletin*. (May 1992) A14.

Other Transaction Accounts

These include negotiable order of withdrawal accounts (NOW), share drafts, and accounts authorized for automatic transfer to demand deposit accounts (ATs). These are checking accounts used by noncorporate customers and typically provide interest payments to the holder.

Savings Deposits

These accounts have no fixed maturity and the rate of interest paid can be changed at any time by the depository institution. Balances can be increased or decreased by the depositor at will. Savings deposits either require a low minimum balance or none at all and are typically held by small depositors. They are considered a stable and relatively low-cost source of funds by depositories.

Money Market Deposit Accounts

These accounts were developed to compete with money market mutual funds and security brokers' cash management accounts. Money market deposit accounts pay an interest rate that fluctuates in fairly close conformance with short-term money market rates. Minimum balance requirements are relatively high and withdrawals are limited. Fees are charged when balances fall below minimums or withdrawals are frequent. This is intended to discourage the use of money market deposit accounts as transaction accounts.

Certificates of Deposit

These are interest-bearing accounts that pay a fixed or indexed interest rate for a fixed term. The accounts may be redeemed by the holder before maturity, but usually after a penalty is assessed by the depository. Withdrawals cannot be made by check or through an ATM.

Negotiable Certificates of Deposit

Negotiable CDs are issued by depositories in large denominations, usually $1 million or more, and pay interest at maturity. Maturities generally range from several days to one year. These CDs are not redeemable prior to maturity, but because they are negotiable, they can be readily bought and sold.

Eurodollar Certificates of Deposit

These CDs are issued by foreign branches of U.S. banks, denominated in U.S. dollars, and sold to foreign investors. The use of the term *Eurodollar* is traditional and a matter of convenience; they may be issued in any part of the world and held by any foreign entity. Since they are issued through a foreign branch, they are not insured by government insurance funds.

Claims Issued by Government Agencies, Sponsored Enterprises, and International Institutions

Chapter 13 will provide a discussion of the major federal government lending programs. Consequently, in this chapter we will provide only a brief discussion of the volume of claims issued by these government-related entities. Table 3.9 on page 68 shows the debt outstanding at the major agencies and government-sponsored enterprises.

The claims issued by U.S. agencies and sponsored enterprises are all authorized through Congress. As a rule these claims are considered eligible collateral for Federal Reserve borrowings, and are considered legal investments by federally chartered depositories. Some of the debt is backed by the full faith and credit of the U.S. government, while others have their claims guaranteed by the Treasury or have a right to borrow from the Treasury. Some of these claims have interest payments that are exempt from state and local income taxes. These advantages place government agency and enterprise claims in a preferred position in the money and capital markets

Table 3.9

Debt Outstanding of Federal Agencies and Sponsored Credit Enterprises
December 31, 1991
(dollars in millions)

Agency or Enterprise	$ Amount
Agencies	
Defense Department	$ 7
Export-Import Bank	9,809
Federal Housing Administration	397
Tennessee Valley Authority	22,401
Total	**$32,614**
Federally Sponsored Enterprises	
Federal Home Loan Banks	$107,543
Federal Home Loan Mortgage Corporation	30,262
Federal National Mortgage Association	133,937
Farm Credit Banks	52,199
Student Loan Marketing Association	38,319
Financing Corporation	8,170
Farm Credit Financial Assistance Corporation	1,261
Resolution Trust Corporation	29,996
Total	**$401,737**
*Federal Financing Bank	$185,576

*The Federal Financing Bank is authorized to purchase or sell obligations issued, sold, or guaranteed by other federal agencies. Since the FFB incurs debt to lend to other agencies, its exclusion from the table is necessary to avoid double counting. The FFB may lend to agencies, but not to government sponsored enterprises.
Source: Federal Reserve *Bulletin*. (May 1992) A31.

by allowing them to borrow at lower interest rates than private sector institutions.

The agencies and sponsored enterprises borrow funds using securities similar in structure to those issued by the Treasury. Their short-term borrowing requirements are met by issuing discount notes similar to Treasury bills. Their intermediate and longer term needs are met by using bonds. However, the largest of these organizations issue a wide variety of obligations, such as collateralized mortgage obligations, and offer their claims to foreign markets. Some of the more important are shown in Exhibit 3.1.

Exhibit 3.1

Select Nontraditional Claims Issued by Agencies and Sponsored Enterprises

Federal Home Loan Mortgage Corporation (FHLMC)

Collateralized Mortgage Obligations (CMOs) These general obligations of the FHLMC are secured by a single pool of conventional mortgages. The CMOs are issued in different classes with varying maturities. Principal and interest is distributed semiannually. Principal on the pool of mortgages is first allocated to the short-term class until it is retired. Interest on each of the classes is paid on the principal outstanding. There is also an accrual class that receives any residual cash flows after the other classes are retired.

Real Estate Mortgage Investment Conduits (REMICs) A REMIC is a partnership that holds a pool of mortgages, which is collateral for multiple classes of securities. They are much like CMOs in structure. The advantage of the REMIC is that it permits issuance of multiple security classes without the issuer having to show the mortgages or the associated debt on its balance sheet.

Federal National Mortgage Association (FNMA)

Master Notes These are individual negotiated notes with variable principal amounts. These notes have floating interest rates tied to 91-day Treasury bills. The investor is allowed to increase or decrease the principal amount of notes held on a daily basis by a predetermined percentage above and below the initial amount.

Investment Agreements These are individually negotiated agreements similar to master notes that pay a fixed or variable interest rate and permit the principal amount to fluctuate.

Medium-Term Notes (MTNs) These claims are offered on a continuous basis with maturities ranging from one to thirty years. MTNs permit the issuer to set an interest rate for different maturities and allow investors to select from the offering on a daily basis. The issuer may or may not be successful in marketing these obligations on any particular day.

Banker's Acceptances

A *banker's acceptance (BA)* is a financial claim guaranteed by a commercial bank. The BA is used in foreign trade transactions in which the exporting organization wants to obtain payment immediately, but the importer needs to borrow to pay for the merchandise. If the importer expects to sell the merchandise within a short time after purchase, it can obtain a letter of credit from a bank for the amount of the import. This letter specifies the terms of the shipment and allows the exporter to obtain payment from the bank. At this point the exporter has been paid, but the importer's bank has a loan outstanding. To fund the loan, the bank may guarantee, or accept, the transaction. The BA can then be sold in the secondary market. At maturity, the importer must come forward with the funds to honor the acceptance or the bank is obligated to pay the holder. The use of BAs has fallen rather steadily. At year-end 1991, there were $43.8 billion dollars of BAs outstanding, down from $70 billion in 1987.

Fed Funds

All depository institutions whose deposits are federally insured must hold reserves at a specified percentage of demand deposits, and occasionally other transaction accounts. Cash that depositories hold in their vaults and on deposit at a Federal Reserve bank counts toward meeting the reserve requirement.

If a financial institution has excess reserves, it may sell them temporarily to institutions that have insufficient reserves. These are typically very short-term sales, usually overnight. Since the buyer is obligated to sell back the fed funds on the next working day at a previously determined price, the transaction is shown as a liability, or borrowing, on the buyer's balance sheet.

Repurchase Agreements

A repurchase agreement (repo) is a claim obtained as a result of one firm selling financial claims to another firm with the obligation to repurchase them at a specified point in time. A repurchase agreement is very much like a collateralized loan. The primary users of repurchase agreements are organizations such as investment banking firms that hold highly marketable securities as inventory in their trading activities. Because the repurchase agreement involves highly marketable collateral, these loans are relatively low-cost and low risk.

In order to raise funds, the holder of the claim enters into an agreement to sell them to another party, with the obligation to repurchase them later at a higher price agreed to in advance. The difference between the sale and repurchase price is income to the buyer. Repurchase agreements are shown as a liability on the books of the selling firm because of its repurchase obligation. The institution that buys the security shows an asset called a *reverse repurchase agreement (reverse repo)* on its balance sheet.

Repos are frequently used by security dealers who hold large inventories of securities in their trading portfolios. The repo provides an efficient way to finance those inventories for short periods of time.

Mortgage-Backed Securities

The largest and the fastest growing categories of secondary claims are mortgage-backed securities. Although many depository institutions issue mortgage-backed securities, the market is dominated by three government agencies and sponsored enterprises: GNMA, FNMA, and FHLMC. Table 3.10 shows the mortgage-backed securities outstanding for these three organizations.

Most mortgage-backed securities are *pass-through securities.* These are created by forming a pool of mortgages. The mortgages usually have the same or nearly equal stated interest rates and maturities. Borrower qualification criteria are uniform, and documents evidencing the mortgages are standardized. By having similar loans in the pool, the security is easier to value.

The holder of a pass-through security has the right to receive a specified share in the interest and principal payments made on all the mortgages in the pool. Prepayments of the principal on any mortgages are also passed through to the investors. In the case of agency and sponsored enterprise pools, a guarantee is provided to ensure that investors will receive timely payment of all principal and interest due even though mortgage payments may be in default and the property in foreclosure. The combination of a guarantee of timely payment and insurance against most credit losses means that investors are unlikely to suffer default losses.

Table 3.10

Mortgage-Backed Securities Issued by the GNMA, FHLMC, and FNMA December 31, 1991
(dollars in millions)

Issuing Organization and Type of Collateral	$ Amount
GNMA	
1 to 4 families	$416,425
Multifamily	13,347
FHLMC	
1 to 4 families	354,214
Multifamily	7,571
FNMA	
1 to 4 families	363,615
Multifamily	8,492
Total	**$1,272,155**

Source: Federal Reserve *Bulletin.* (May 1992) A36.

Pass-through mortgage securities have been issued by private financial institutions as well. These securities do not carry the guarantee of a federal government agency. The issuer must usually find some other means to protect against default risk. Several methods are used—insurance over and above that on the individual mortgages, a letter of credit from a highly rated bank, or a two-class offering of a senior and junior security, known as a *senior-subordinated pass-through*. The senior and junior securities are both collateralized by the same pool of mortgages. The difference is that the junior security must bear the loss of any interest and principal stemming from mortgage defaults before the senior security investor suffers any principal or interest loss. The senior security will not be affected until the principal amount of the junior security has been wiped out.

Summary

The primary economic function of **financial claims** is to facilitate the transfer of financial resources from capital surplus units, who wish to defer consumption, to capital deficit units, who desire to accelerate consumption or investment. Financial claims are also used to improve the efficiency of the financial system by altering the risk of claims, using risk sharing and pooling, and reducing financial transaction costs.

Financial claims are created by federal, state, and local government units, as well as businesses, households, and foreigners.

Financial claims are also used as legal contracts. Financial debt contracts include important optional provisions such as call provisions, collateral, and covenants.

At year-end 1990, financial claims of $10.58 trillion were outstanding. Of this total, the **U.S. government** issued $2.57 trillion, **households,** $3.83 trillion, **nonfinancial businesses,** $3.53 trillion, and **state and local governments** $649 billion.

Financial claims are classified as **primary and secondary claims.** Primary claims are issued by the borrower using the funds for consumption or direct investment in real resources. Secondary market financial claims are issued primarily by financial intermediaries who wish to invest in financial claims issued by others.

Financial claims whose cash flow or credit characteristics have been altered become known as **hybrid claims.** These claims have become significant in the last several decades. The major issuers of these securities are government agencies and government sponsored enterprises that use residential mortgages to issue **mortgage-backed securities** and create hybrid claims such as collateralized mortgage obligations from them. **Zero coupon bonds** use Treasury bonds to create a series of debt claims that have no interest payments.

Derivative claims include financial options, swaps, futures options, and futures contracts. The value of these contracts is related to existing financial claims that are issued and outstanding.

The major types of **primary financial claims** include the following:

1. **Treasury bills, notes, and bonds** issued by the U.S. government
2. **Corporate bonds, trade debt,** and **commercial mortgages** issued by nonfinancial businesses
3. **Residential mortgages and consumer loans** issued by households
4. **General obligations and revenue bonds** issued by state and local governments
5. **Government obligations, corporate bonds,** and **trade debt** issued by foreign governments and firms

The major types of secondary financial claims include the following:

1. **Deposits** issued by commercial banks and thrifts
2. **Policy reserves and pension reserves** of life insurance companies and pension funds
3. **Credit market debt** issued by financial institutions

The **federal government also sponsors large credit agencies** that are major issuers of financial claims. The credit agencies of the federal government are major suppliers of credit to the agricultural, residential housing, and business sectors of the economy.

Questions

Chapter 3

1. What are the motivations behind the creation of financial claims?
2. What is meant by the comment that "household savings are becoming increasingly institutionalized"?
3. What are the major provisions found in a financial credit claim?
4. Financial claims are referred to as primary and secondary financial claims. Determine whether each claim below is a primary or secondary claim.
    a. Credit purchase using bank credit card
    b. Savings account
    c. Initial public offering of common stock
    d. Demand deposit held at bank
5. Why has there been a reduction in the percentage of financial claims held as deposits by households?
6. Can the same household be a buyer and issuer of financial claims? Give an example.

7. Who are the largest issuers of foreign financial claims held by U.S. banks and branches?
8. Households have been holding a rising percentage of their financial assets in the form of pension fund reserves. They have also increased their relative holdings of mutual fund investments. Why do you think these changes have occurred? Do you think they will continue through the 1990s? Why or why not?
9. What is meant by the expressions *derivative claim, hybrid claim,* and *asset-backed claim?*
10. Claims are known as primary and secondary. Give three examples of each.
11. What is a junk bond? What do credit-rating organizations do for investors?

Valuation of Financial Claims

chapter 4

The valuation of financial claims is critical to the successful management of financial institutions. Throughout the study of finance, the question most asked is "What is it worth?" Financial institutions originate and purchase financial claims. They must be experts in valuation because determining value is critical to claim design and pricing. Valuation techniques are also used to determine whether an investment is worth more or less to the investor than its value as reflected by its market.

This chapter is divided into three sections. The first deals with the basics of present value theory. It reviews the basic formulations for present value, future value, yields, and compounding. The next section provides basic valuation and yield formulas for the most common types of financial debt instruments. The third section deals with fixed-rate mortgages and a number of the hybrid financial claims. This section also covers Treasury strips, interest-only and principal-only securities derived from mortgage securities, servicing strips, collateralized mortgage obligations, and senior-subordinated securities.

The Basics: Present and Future Values, Yields, and Compounding

Present value provides the basic theory for calculating values and yields for a series of cash flows. Students should have a financial calculator available to compute the basic calculations in this section and the next.

Present Value Theory

Present value theory is the foundation of the theory of valuation under certainty. This theory is used by corporations to make capital budgeting decisions. Present value techniques are also used to determine the value of commercial real estate. Finally, present value theory is used extensively in financial-claim analyses to determine the value of bonds and stocks.

Present value methodology is used to find today's value for a future stream of known cash flows to be received or paid. It is also used to determine the yield on a financial claim when the cash flows on the claim and today's value are known.

Present value calculations involve the use of the following four variables:

- the discount rate or base rate, r
- the cash flows, CF_t
- the present value, PV
- the number of annual periods over which the investment is outstanding, t

Equation 4.1 shows a financial claim with a simple future cash flow.

$$PV = CF_t/(1 + r)^t \qquad [4.1]$$

In this equation, present value, PV, is the monetary value measured in today's dollars of receiving a future cash flow, CF_t, at time period t. This future cash flow is referred to as *future value*. The variable used to represent future value is FV. The future cash flow is at a discount rate r for t periods. The interest is expressed as percent and hundredths of 1 percent, which are known as *basis points*. For example, consider a $2000 savings account on which a bank promises to pay a 9 percent annual return for two years. In two years it is worth

$$PV \times (1 + .09)^2 = CF_2 = FV$$
$$\$2{,}000 \times (1 + .09)^2 = \$2{,}376.20$$

In this case, the amount of money we expect to receive in two years is the future value $2,376.20.

The factors $1/(1 + r)^n$ and $(1 + r)^n$ are programmed into financial calculators and are available in the financial tables found in the back of this book. $1/(1 + r)^n$ is known as $PVIF_{r,n}$, and $(1 + r)^n$ is known as $FVIF_{r,n}$.

Many investments involve periodic cash flows. If these cash flows occur at equal intervals of time they are called *annuities*. An *ordinary annuity* is a series of periodic cash flows of equal dollar amount that occur at the end of a finite number of periods.

Equation 4.2 represents the present value of an ordinary annuity.

$$PV = CF\,[(1 - (1 + r)^{-n})\,/\,r] \qquad [4.2]$$

Consider a term loan. This type of loan requires a periodic constant payment. A term loan with a $314 annual payment, CF, due at the end of each of the next five years, n, would have a present value discounted at a rate of 9 percent, r, as shown using Equation 4.2.

$$PV = \$314\,[(1 - (1 + .09)^{-5})\,/\,.09]$$
$$PV = \$314\,[(1.0 - .6499314)\,/\,.09]$$
$$PV = \$314\,(3.8897) = \$1{,}221.37$$

The factor $[(1 - (1 + r)^{-n})/r]$, known as $PVIFA_{r,n}$, is also programmed into financial calculators and is available in financial tables found in the back of the book.

$$\text{Using tables: } PV = \$314 \times (PVIFA_{9.00,5})$$
$$PV = \$314 \times 3.890 = \$1{,}221.40$$

Compounding

Compounding occurs when interest is paid or accrued within a one-year period. This allows the investor to reinvest the interest to earn additional interest within the year. The number of interest payments or accruals, m, is the *number of compounding periods per year*.

We can easily incorporate a situation in which the bank *compounds* interest monthly by revising the equation to obtain Equation 4.3:

$$PV \times [1 + (r/m)]^{tm} = FV$$
$$\$2{,}000\,[1 + (.09/12)]^{2 \times 12} = \$2{,}392.83 \qquad [4.3]$$

In this equation, m is 12 for monthly compounding. The variable m would be 4 for quarterly payments and 2 for semiannual compounding. By compounding monthly instead of annually we have increased our future cash flow by $16.63 ($2,392.83 − 2,376.20).

Savings Certificate Compounding Wars

Before 1980, maximum interest rates on savings accounts paid by insured commercial banks and thrift institutions were regulated by the Federal Reserve Board and the former Federal Home Loan Bank Board. This rate-control regulation, known as Regulation Q, originated with the Great Depression of the 1930s for commercial banks, and was applied to savings and loans and savings banks in the 1960s. One impact of rate controls was that institutions had to find ways to appeal to savers' desires for higher rates without violating the controls. The result was to give customers free gifts, such as the ubiquitous free toaster.

Savings institutions also provided more frequent compounding of interest on accounts, thus providing the saver a higher interest return for any specific interest rate ceiling. The amount that is earning interest is determined by the initial deposit, PV, the number of compounding periods, m, the annual interest rate or base rate, r, and the number of years, t. In compounding, an interest rate called the *periodic rate* is applied. This is the determining time period between compounding, r/m. Here m is the number of compounding periods within a year, and mn is the number of periods. The future value is shown in Equation 4.4.

$$FV = PV\,(1 + r/m)^{mn} \qquad [4.4]$$

Table 4.1 provides an example of the future value of a $1,000 savings account after one year using five different compounding frequencies.

Table 4.1

Future Value of $1,000 Savings Account Using Different Compounding Frequencies (base interest rate 5.00%)

Compounding Frequency	Future Value of $1,000 Investment in One Year
Semiannually	$1,050.625
Quarterly	1,050.945
Daily 360 days	1,051.267
Daily 365 days	1,051.268
365/360 (360-day factor applied 365 days)	1,051.998

The future value calculation for the 365/360 is shown in the following equation:

$$FV = \$1{,}000 \times (1 + (.05/360))^{365}$$

This equation uses the interest factor for a 360-day year ($r/360$), and compounds for 365 periods. This is referred to as *compounding 360 over 365*.

It is also possible to use an infinite number of compounding periods. This is known as *continuous or infinite compounding*. This is shown in the following expression:

$$[1 + (r/m)]^{mt} \text{ approaches } e^{rt} \text{ as } m \to \infty$$

The variable e is the number 2.7183 . . . , r is the annual interest rate, and m is the number of yearly periods or fraction thereof. Many financial calculators have a function to calculate this expression. If we compound our 5 percent account for one year using an infinite number of periods we obtain

$$e^{rt} = e^{.05(1)} = 1.051711$$

Notice that the amount of 1.051711 is higher than our daily compounding, but below the 365/360.

Yield to Maturity

The yield to maturity on a financial claim is derived from the present value equation. The yield to maturity is the annualized interest rate, r, that equates the future cash flows to the present value, given a specified compounding approach. The interest rate on an investment is quoted in terms of a specified number of compounding periods. Bonds that pay interest twice a year have yields calculated using semiannual compounding. A mortgage in which the payments are made 12 times per year has its yield calculated using monthly compounding.

Now work out the yield to maturity on a corporate bond. A bond pays interest semiannually at the base rate of 9 percent per annum. For a bond, it is customary to refer to the base rate as the *coupon rate*. We use the coupon rate to calculate the actual interest cash flows (.09/2 × $25,000 = $1,125.00). The principal will be repaid on April 15, 1998. The par value of the bond is $25,000. A broker states on April 15, 1993, that the bond can be purchased at a price of 98.25. That means we can buy the bond for 98.25 percent of its *par value*. The bond is said to be selling at a *discount* from its par value. If the bond were selling at a price above 100, or above 100 percent of its par value, it would be selling at a *premium*.

To compute the yield on the bond, use the generalized present value Equation 4.5.

$$PV = \sum_{n=1}^{t} CF_n/[1 + (r/2)]^n + par\ value/[1 + (r/2)]^t \qquad [4.5]$$

Solving the problem using this equation results in

$$\$24{,}562.50 = \sum_{n=1}^{10} \$1{,}125/[1 + (r/2)]^n + \$25{,}000/[1 + (r/2)]^{10}$$

The yield to maturity, r, is 9.45 percent.

DEMONSTRATION PROBLEM: Yield to Maturity

Situation: Broader Bank offers a certificate of deposit that pays a 10 percent yield to maturity compounded quarterly. The managers of First Bank want to set a yield to maturity on their comparable maturity account that produces the same future value. However, First Bank compounds interest monthly. What yield to maturity should First Bank select?

Result: Yield to maturity at Broader Bank =

$$r = .10$$
$$(1 + r/4)^4 = 1.1038 = \text{future value}$$

Yield to maturity at First Bank =

$$(1 + r/12)^{12} = 1.1038$$
$$1 + r/12 = 1.0082638$$
$$r/12 = .0082638$$
$$r = .091659$$

The yield to maturity for First Bank's certificate should be set at $r = 9.91659$ percent.

Equivalent Annual Yield

Because the yield to maturity is expressed for different compounding periods, it is not appropriate to compare yield to maturity for investments involving different compounding approaches. To make comparisons possible, we use the *equivalent annual yield (EAY)*. The *EAY* is an annual interest rate that is computed without compounding. It shows what an investment would have to earn to produce the same future value as the same investment earns when compounding is used. The *EAY* allows us to compare interest rates on a variety of financial claims that have different compounding periods on a comparable basis. The *EAY* for an investment is shown in Equation 4.6 as

$$(1 + EAY)^1 = (1 + r/m)^m$$
$$EAY = (1 + r/m)^m - 1) \qquad [4.6]$$

DEMONSTRATION PROBLEM: Equivalent Annual Yield

Situation: Libor Bank pays 9 percent yield to maturity compounded quarterly on its certificates of deposit. The manager of Marion Bank wants to offer a certificate that provides the same *EAY* as Libor Bank. However, Marion's certificate will be compounded monthly. What yield to maturity must the bank offer?

Result: Find the *EAY* on Libor's certificate. It is computed in the equation

$$EAY = (1 + r/m)^m - 1.0$$
$$= (1 + .09/4)^4 - 1.0$$
$$= (1.0225)^4 - 1.0 = 9.31\%$$

Marion's certificate will have the same *EAY* of 9.31 percent. The yield to maturity that will produce that *SEY* with monthly compounding is

$$0.0931 = [1 + (r/12)]^{12} - 1.0$$
$$[1 + (r/12)] = (1.0931)^{(1/12)}$$
$$r/12 = .0074$$
$$r = .0893 = 8.93\%$$

The *EAY* for an investment with a yield to maturity of 9.45 compounded semiannually would be

$$(1 + EAY)^1 = (1 + .0945/2)^2$$

$$EAY = 9.67326\%$$

The *EAY* of 9.67326 percent will result in the same future value as a yield to maturity of 9.45 percent with semiannual compounding. The quantity called *effective yield* that is advertised by financial depositories for certificates of deposit is the *EAY*. The effective annual yield is sometimes referred to as the *simple interest equivalent yield*.

Cash Flows

The present-value equation is really quite simple. What isn't always so simple is knowing when and what the cash flows will be on any particular investment. The development of a *cash flow schedule* is the first and sometimes most difficult job in any valuation analysis. This schedule identifies the amount and timing for each cash inflow and outflow related to an investment. Present-value analysis must begin with the development of a schedule of the cash flows. If you are unable to determine cash flows, then you can go no further with the analysis. Sometimes an inability to determine cash flows with certainty is the sign that a financial claim has an option embedded within it. This is dealt with later in the chapter.

Let's take the case of a simple two-year bond. Consider a $10,000 investment in a bond with a par value of $10,000. The bond pays interest twice a year at the rate of 8 percent per annum, or $400 every six months. The investor also receives the original investment back at the time of maturity. The cash flows from this investment are shown in Table 4.2.

Table 4.2

Cash Flow Schedule

Date	Inflows	Outflows	Description
2-1-93		$10,000	Investment
8-1-93	$ 400		Interest
2-1-94	400		Interest
8-1-94	400		Interest
2-1-95	10,400		Interest and principal

This form of cash flow schedule can be used for any present value problem. It is often good to use a schedule like this if you get confused about how the cash flows on an investment behave.

Valuation and Yields for Common Debt Claims

In this section, we review the yield and valuation formula for the more common money market financial claims and bonds. The fixed-rate mortgage is left until the next section because the discussion of its valuation and yield requires introducing the concept of mortgage prepayment. We then build on that concept in the discussion of hybrid mortgage securities.

Discounted Treasury Securities

Treasury bills are the most actively traded debt security. These securities, known as T-bills, are issued by the U.S. Treasury in original maturities of 91 days (13 weeks), 182 days (26 weeks), and 364 days (52 weeks). They are also notable because they do not pay periodic interest. Rather, they are issued at a discount from par value and redeemed at par. The difference between the discount price and par is the gain or income.

The Treasury department has frequent auctions of Treasury bills. The Treasury used to use a group of forty large commercial banks and investment banking firms to conduct this auction. These dealers were known as *primary dealers*. As a result of irregularities, in 1991 the primary dealer auction was replaced by an auction system open to most institutional investors.

The Federal Reserve of New York reports the purchases and sales of U.S. government securities by the primary dealers. In 1990, the average daily volume of trading in outstanding T-bills was approximately $30 billion per day. Trading among this group in all types of Treasury securities was about $100 billion per day. In early 1990, the volume of T-bills outstanding was approximately $450 billion.

The dealers bid a percentage of the bill's par value. Thus a bid for a certain dollar amount of bills might be 97.787 on 182-day bills. This bid is a discount from the bill's par value of 100.

To compute the yield on this discounted security, we use the same present value methodology used in the example of the five-year bond. The equation for a $1 million par value bid on T-bills would be

$$\$977{,}870 = \$1{,}000{,}000 / (1 + (r/(364/182))^{(182/182)}$$

In this example, $r = 4.526$ percent. This is known as the effective annual yield on the 182-day bills. Since this yield is actually earned for only six months, when quoting an annual yield the assumption is made that the $1 million received at maturity can be reinvested for an additional six months at the same yield.

Bank Discount and Coupon Equivalent Yields on T-bills

Now that you have mastered the present value approach to calculating yields, we must throw you a curve. Back in the days before computers, government bond traders used a simple approach to calculating yields known as the *bank discount yield (BDY)*. This method of quoting yields on short-term securities is still around today.

The calculation involves Equation 4.7.

$$BDY = [(\text{par value}) - (\text{discounted price})]/(\text{par value}) \times (360)/(\text{days till maturity}) \qquad [4.7]$$

The bank discount yield on a T-bill of 91 days purchased at a price of 98.789 would be

$$BDY = [(100 - 98.789)/100] \times (360/91)$$
$$= .0479 = 4.79\%$$

The coupon equivalent yield, *CEY*, is also quoted for T-bills. This calculation is similar to the *BDY*, except that it recognizes that the T-bill is purchased at a discount. Consequently the discounted price, rather than the par value, is used in the denominator of the equation. The other difference is that it uses a 365- or 366-day year. The calculation is shown in Equation 4.8.

$$CEY = [(\text{par value} - \text{discounted price})/\text{discounted price}] \times (365/91) \qquad [4.8]$$

The coupon equivalent yield on the above T-bill using a 365-day year would be

$$[(100 - 98.789)/98.789] \times (365/91)$$
$$= 4.91685\%$$

The bank discount yield should not be used to compare the yield on T-bills to that of other investments, since it has a downward bias. The *BDY* underestimates the yield as compared to the effective yield. However, the *BDY* is quoted in the financial press when the results of the Treasury bill auctions are given, as shown in Exhibit 4.1. It is also used in secondary market transactions in T-bills.

Chapter 4 Valuation of Financial Claims   85

Exhibit 4.1

Report of Treasury Bill Auction, August 23, 1991

Report of Treasury Bill Auction

In early trading yesterday, the yield on three-month bills fell as low as 4.89%, but recovered before the bill auction. Here are details of yesterday's bill auction.

Rates are determined by the difference between the purchase price and face value. Thus, higher bidding narrows the investor's return while lower bidding widens it. The percentage rates are calculated on a 360-day year, while the coupon equivalent yield is based on a 366-day year.

	13-Week	26-Week
Applications	$29,124,050,000	$32,545,805,000
Accepted bids	$10,417,080,000	$10,400,915,000
Accepted at low price	83%	16%
Accepted noncompet'ly	$1,585,595,000	$1,248,235,000
Average price (Rate)	98.683 (5.17%)	97.356 (5.23%)
High price (Rate)	98.706 (5.12%)	97.361 (5.22%)
Low price (Rate)	98.691 (5.18%)	97.351 (5.24%)
Coupon equivalent	5.33%	5.46%
CUSIP number	93279WWW0	9327794YA6

Both issues are dated Aug. 22, 1991. The 13-week bills mature Nov. 21, 1991, and the 26-week bills mature Feb. 28, 1992.

Source: *The Wall Street Journal* Reprinted by permission of *The Wall Street Journal,* 1991 Dow Jones and Company, Inc. All Rights Reserved Worldwide.

Exhibit 4.1 shows the results of a T-bill auction. It indicates that there were applications to buy (bids offered) of $29,124,050,000 for 13-week bills. Of those, $10,417,080,000 were accepted. Eighty-three percent of the bids accepted were accepted at the low price of 98.691.

T-bills equaling $1,585,595,000 were sold on a noncompetitive basis. These are bids made to the Federal Reserve Banks by small investors who purchase less than $1 million and are willing to pay the average bid price of 98.693.

The *BDY* is calculated in this auction using a 360-day year as follows:

$$BDY = [(100 - 98.693)/100.00] \times (360/91) = 5.17\%$$

The *CEY* is calculated in this auction using a 366-day year as follows:

$$CEY = [(100 - 98.693) / 98.693] \times (366/91) = 5.33\%$$

Yield to Maturity on a Bond and Yield to a Call

Consider a bond trading at a price of 98.5 percent of par with eight years to maturity and a coupon rate of 8.75 percent. Our yield to maturity assuming semiannual compounding, r, is shown in Equation 4.9.

$$PV = \sum_{n=1}^{mt} CF_n/(1 + r/m)^n + Prin/(1 + r/m)^{mt}$$

where:

PV = value of bond

CF_n = interest payments

$Prin$ = principal/call payment

m = compounding periods = 2

n = period of cash flow

t = number of years until maturity

$$\$9{,}850 = \sum_{n=1}^{16} [\$437.50/(1 + (r/2))^n] + \$10{,}000/(1 + (r/2))^{16}$$

$$r = 9.017\%$$

Using tables: $\$9{,}850 = \$437.50\ (PVIFA_{4.50,16}) + \$10{,}000\ (PVIF_{4.50,16})$

$$r \cong 9.00\% \qquad [4.9]$$

Chapter 2 introduced the concept of a bond with a provision allowing the borrower to pay off the bond before its stated maturity. This bond has an embedded option referred to as a call option. The typical bond call option gives the borrower, the issuer of the bond, the right to pay off the bondholders after a specified date and at a specified price. A callable bond is illustrated in the following scenario: ACM Corporation issued a ten-year bond at a coupon rate of 8.75 percent. It has a call option that permits the company to redeem the bond at the end of five years at a price of 102.5 percent of par. It is purchased at $10,000 par value in the open market after it has been outstanding exactly two years. This means there are three years until the call. The yield to the call is

$$\$9{,}850 = \sum_{n=1}^{6} \$437.50/[(1 + (r/2))]^n + \$10{,}250/[(1 + (r/2))^6$$

$$r = 10.31\%$$

Using tables: $\$9{,}850 = \$437.50\ (PVIFA_{5.00,6}) + \$10{,}250\ (PVIF_{5.00,6})$

$$r \cong 10.00\%$$

The yield to the call is used to analyze the effect of the call provision on the investment results. The investor knows that the borrower is going to call the bond only if it is in the borrower's best interest to do so. That will occur when one of two events takes place: In the event of a sharp fall in interest rates, the issuer is likely to call the bond and then borrow in the open market at the lower prevailing rate. The other event might be that the borrower has experienced a substantial improvement in its credit rating, allowing it to borrow at a lower rate. The call effectively denies the investor the enjoyment of the full increase in the bond's value that would be expected if one or both of these two events had happened.

Repurchase Agreements and Reverse Repurchase Agreements

Government security dealers and financial institutions frequently have the need to borrow for short periods of time. They often carry large inventories of government, agency, and agency mortgage-backed securities. Since these assets have high marketability and virtually no credit risk, they are good collateral for a loan. A firm can use such collateral to borrow money using a repurchase agreement or repo.

Other financial institutions may find themselves in the opposite position. They have excess cash to invest for short periods of time. These firms are looking for safe short-term investments, frequently for as short as one day. The firm that purchases the securities in a repurchase agreement is involved in what is known as a reverse repurchase agreement, or reverse repo.

The repurchase agreement market has grown into a multibillion dollar marketplace. The borrowing institution agrees to sell its securities at a specified price and further agrees to repurchase the securities on a specified date and at a specified price. If the repurchase takes place in one day, it is known as an *overnight repo*. If the repurchase takes place over more than one day it is known as a *term repo*.

A typical transaction might involve a large investment-banking firm dealing in government securities selling $5 million par value of U.S. agency bonds to a medium-sized bank at a price of $4,998,990. The investment bank then agrees to repurchase the bonds at $5 million the next day.

The repo rate (RR) is based on a 360-day period, and in this case Equation 4.10 calculates it to be

$$RR = [(\text{repurchase price} - \text{sales price})/\text{repurchase price}] \times 360/(\text{days till maturity})$$

$$[(\$5{,}000{,}000 - \$4{,}998{,}990)/\$5{,}000{,}000] \times (360/1)$$

$$= .07272 = 7.272\% \qquad [4.10]$$

Perpetual Preferred and Consols

One type of security less common in the United States is the security that pays a fixed amount of periodic interest (CF) or dividend payments, but never returns the principal. Two such securities are the *perpetual preferred stock* sold in the United States and the *consol* sold in Britain.

To determine the value (*PV*) of the perpetuity, you must know the fixed-payment interest or dividend cash flows (*CF*) and the market base rate (*r*).

The valuation equation for the consul is shown below:

$$PV = \sum_{n=1}^{\infty} CF/(1+r)^n$$

This equation, fortunately, reduces algebraically to

$$PV = CF/r$$

It is important to note that the period between the cash flows must be the same as the period used for the rate *r*. If cash flows occur quarterly, then *r* must be a quarterly periodic rate. A perpetuity paying an interest payment of $50 per semiannual period at a periodic rate of 4 percent, or annual rate of 8 percent, would have a market value (*PV*) of

$$\$50/.04 = \$1,250$$

Zero Coupon Bonds

The *zero coupon bond* is just a longer maturity version of a discounted T-bill. This security usually has a maturity of several years to 30 years or more. It is designed for investors who do not want the reinvestment risk associated with interest-paying bonds.

To compute the yield to maturity on a zero coupon bond, assuming semiannual compounding, for a bond of $1,000,000 par value maturing in 9 years 6 months (19 periods), purchased at a price of 47 percent of par value, we use the following equation:

$$\$470,000 = \$1,000,000/(1 + (r/2))^{19}$$

$$r = 8.108\%$$

Valuation and Yields on Fixed-Rate Mortgages and Hybrid Financial Claims

Financial engineering is the name given to the creation of financial claims that are derived from other financial claims. This process involves altering the cash flows or credit risk exposure on new claims. The creation of hybrid financial claims has been a major innovation of the 1980s. A hybrid claim is created by altering the credit and/or cash flow characteristics of an existing claim or group of claims.

The process of creating these new claims owes its success to two important factors. First, hybrid securities are created from large volumes of more or less homogeneous securities. Our nation's large volume of Treasury bonds, agency, and government sponsored enterprise mortgage-backed claims easily fulfill that need. Low-cost computer power is the other requirement. The personal computer provides financial engineers with the ability to create a multitude of financial structures and to simulate how they would behave in various economic settings. These new claims rely on a significant analysis of varying cash flows, which only computers can accomplish.

Stripped Treasuries

One example of a hybrid security is the *stripped Treasury security*. In this case the cash flows of an outstanding Treasury security are channeled into two or more hybrid securities. One of these classes of the Treasury security is formed by using the interest cash flows. The other class uses the principal. Thus an outstanding Treasury security has its interest payments and principal payments stripped in the creation process.

In 1982, Salomon Brothers Inc. came forth with their Certificates of Accrual on Treasury Securities, known as CATS. At about the same time, Merrill Lynch Inc. created their Treasury Income Growth Receipts, known as TIGRs.

These new securities are principal-only zero coupon bonds. The process used to create these is known as *coupon stripping*. Table 4.3 is an example of a Treasury security whose cash flows are diverted by coupon stripping.

Table 4.3

Cash Flows from Treasury Securities
$1,000,000 Par Value
7.5% Coupon Rate
Five-Year Maturity

Date	Interest Cash Flows	Principal Cash Flows
6/30/90	$37,500	
12/31/90	"	
	"	
	"	
	"	
12/31/94	37,500	
12/31/94		$1,000,000

Eleven securities can now be created from these two sets of cash flows. The first ten of these represent zero coupon bonds with $37,500 semiannual interest payments representing the principal of the security. The other is the zero created by using the $1,000,000 principal payment as the principal for the zero coupon. In order to determine the market value of each of these securities we must discount each of the stripped security's cash flows by the relevant discount rates r_t. The variable t denotes the time period. The market value of each of these eleven securities is shown by the following equations. The market discount rate for each is r_t.

$$\text{Value of interest only}_1 = \frac{\$37{,}500}{(1 + (r_1))^1}$$

$$\text{Value of interest only}_2 = \frac{\$37{,}500}{(1 + (r_2))^2}$$

$$\vdots$$

$$\text{Value of interest only}_{10} = \frac{\$37{,}500}{(1 + (r_{10}))^{10}}$$

$$\text{Value of principal only}_{11} = \frac{\$1{,}000{,}000}{(1 + (r_{10}))^{10}}$$

Table 4.4

Market Values of Coupon and Principal Payments Discounted at Market Zero Coupon Rates

Date of Cash Flow	Cash Flow	Zero Market Rate	Period	Discounted Value
	(CF_n)	(r)	(n)	$(CF_n/(1 + r)^n)$
6/30/90	$37,500	4.75%	1	$36,630
12/31/90	37,500	5.00	2	35,693
6/30/91	37,500	5.25	3	34,695
12/31/91	37,500	5.50	4	33,644
6/30/92	37,500	5.75	5	32,545
12/31/92	37,500	6.00	6	31,406
6/30/93	37,500	6.75	7	29,725
12/31/93	37,500	7.00	8	28,478
6/30/94	37,500	7.25	9	27,218
12/31/94	37,500	7.50	10	25,951
12/31/94	1,000,000	7.50	10	692,020
Total				**$1,008,005**

In this example, it might be worthwhile to create the hybrid securities if they can be sold for a total value higher than the price of the Treasury notes. This can easily occur if the term structure of interest rates is upward sloping. If this is so, the shorter term strips of a stripped Treasury will be discounted by the market using a discount rate that is lower than the longer term strips. Referring to the equation, r_1 would be less than r_{10}. This would permit the issuer to obtain a higher price for the shorter term strips and a lower price for the longer strips. The result would be that the entire valuation of all the strips would be higher than the Treasury security trading as a whole. These prices would also have to be high enough to cover the costs of issuance, safekeeping, and distribution. Table 4.5 shows the yield on several hypothetical Treasury stripped securities.

Table 4.4 shows the market value of the cash flows for the five-year, 7.5 percent coupon Treasury if they are discounted at the prevailing zero coupon market interest rates, r_n.

In this table, the market value of each of the cash flows stripped from the Treasury security and discounted at the market yields for zeros is $1,008,005. This gives a good example of how the sum of the parts is worth more than the whole. If the Treasury security can be acquired for $1,000,000 and stripped so that it can be sold for $1,008,005, then there is a potential profit to be made for creating these hybrid securities and distributing them. In this respect, coupon stripping is like a leveraged buyout of a company—the various subsidiaries are sold at higher individual prices than they are worth bundled together.

Table 4.5

Reading the Financial Page

Yields on Stripped Treasuries
November 15, 1991
(typical listing)

Maturity	Type	Bid	Ask	Ask Change	Ask Yield
May 95	i	70–12	70–15	+2	10.28
Nov 96	p	65–14	65–17	+3	10.85

This table shows a typical listing of Treasury stripped coupon securities outstanding and their yields. The *i* stands for interest and *p* for principal. The investor can expect a higher volume of strips from the principal. This could also provide higher marketability. The prices are quoted as a percent of par in thirty-secondths of 100 percent. The change is shown in thirty-secondths. The yields are based on a semiannual compounding assumption. The May 95 security is assumed to mature on the fifteenth of the month. Its yield to maturity over seven semiannual periods would be

$$70.46875 = 100.00 \: [1/(1 + r/2)^7]$$

Ask Yield: $r = 10.28\%$

Thus far, the discussion has focused only on investments with cash flows that are easy to estimate. Now mortgages will be considered. These financial claims have cash flows that are difficult to estimate. As a result, it will be necessary to spend some time analyzing the nature of fixed-rate mortgages. There are two reasons why it is important to do so. Mortgages represent the largest type of financial claim. At year-end 1990, mortgage debt exceeded $3.8 trillion, well above the total Treasury debt. Also, mortgages have been used to create many of the hybrid securities that have become popular in recent years. It is impossible to understand the valuation of these hybrid claims until the valuation problems of fixed-rate mortgages are solved.

Fixed-Rate Mortgages and Mortgage-Backed Securities

The standard fixed-rate mortgage (FRM) is one of the most difficult of all securities to value. Why? It looks just like a normal annuity. The principal and interest are returned in a specified constant payment every month for the term of the loan. The one major difference is a provision in the mortgage contract that allows the borrower to prepay the mortgage at any time. One reason for doing this is to refinance the property. Refinancing could be profitable following a period of sharp declines in interest rates. The borrower could pay off the existing higher rate mortgage and refinance into a mortgage at a lower prevailing mortgage rate.

The standard mortgage contains a *prepayment option.* Many studies have been conducted in an attempt to understand the patterns of prepayment that can be expected on a single mortgage or portfolio of mortgages. Remember, present-value theory requires being able to specify the cash flows from any particular investment before calculating the yield. Herein lies the problem with the fixed-rate mortgage. It involves a prepayment option that can be exercised at any time. This makes it impossible to perfectly specify the cash flows. The following are some reasons for prepayment: (1) scheduled amortization of the principal on a mortgage (a known cash flow); (2) prepayment of all or part of the principal due to partial or total refinance; and (3) default. Reasons two and three are impossible to predict perfectly.

Inability to specify the cash flows with precision has forced mortgage market participants to use a number of assumed prepayment patterns for FRMs. It is critical to remember that these are nothing more than *assumptions* about how the cash flows on a mortgage or pool of mortgages will behave. These assumptions about the pattern of cash flows may have been based on a significant amount of theoretical and empirical analysis, but they remain assumptions.

Let's start our investigation of mortgages with a simple example. We will take a mortgage that does not prepay for any reason, including default. We use the standard present value equation in which we find the discount rate, or yield, r, assuming monthly compounding, $m = 12$, for a stream of equal monthly payments. Notice that the computation for determining the yield on an FRM is simply an ordinary annuity. The yield to maturity for a $100,000 mortgage with a monthly payment of $1,058 for 30 years is shown as

$$\$100{,}000 = \sum_{n=1}^{30(12)} \$1{,}058/[1 + (r/12)]^n$$
$$r = .1238 = 12.38\%$$

Using tables: $\$100{,}000 = \approx \$1{,}058\ (PVIFA_{1.00, 360})$

$$r \cong 12.00\%$$

Prepayment Assumptions and Mortgage Yields

The first attempt to simulate a more realistic cash flow for a mortgage was the adoption of the 10- and 12-year loan life assumption. This assumption held that a mortgage would repay according to its scheduled amortization until a specified date after 10 or 12 years, when it would prepay in full.

To see how this affects the yield on a mortgage, let's take three different mortgages. One is a 9.50 percent coupon rate mortgage that does not prepay, but rather, amortizes according to its normal amortization schedule. The others will have the same monthly payments and term, but will prepay at the end of 10 or 12 years. We will also assume that the mortgage can trade in a secondary market and be purchased at prices of 100 percent of par, 99 percent of par, or 101 percent of par. We can determine their yields using the previous equation, but we must modify the *PV* using 99 percent to 101 percent of par and use only 120 periods in the case of a 10-year loan life and 144 periods in the case of a 12-year loan life. The 120th and 144th cash flow will be the unpaid principal on the mortgage at that time. The impact of these prepayment assumptions is shown in Table 4.6 on page 94.

Table 4.6

Yield on a 30-Year, 9.50% Coupon FRM, Assuming 10- and 12-Year Prepayment Purchase Prices of 99%, 100%, and 101% of Par

Mortgage Prepayment Assumption	Purchase Price (% of par)		
	99%	100%	101%
No prepayment	9.62%	9.50%	9.39%
Prepay after 10 years	9.66	9.50	9.34
Prepay after 12 years	9.65	9.50	9.36

It is easy to see from the table that the cash flow assumption about prepayment has a very significant impact on yield. Whenever a mortgage is purchased at a price other than par, the prepayment of other-than-normal amortization of principal will affect the yield of the investment. Fast prepayment will increase (decrease) the yield on an FRM purchased at a discount (premium) from its par value. Slow prepayment will decrease (increase) the yield on an FRM purchased at a premium (discount) from par value. This is why so much effort has gone into trying to simulate the mortgage cash flows.

The next major breakthrough in the effort at estimating mortgage cash flow involved the use of information about how FHA mortgages actually prepaid. This new level of sophistication was driven by the rapid growth in mortgage pass-through securities issued by the Government National Mortgage Association (GNMA) and Federal Home Loan Mortgage Corporation (FHLMC). These securities contained pools of mortgages, which made the assumption of a prepayment on a specified date even more unrealistic. Also driving the change was the improvement in computer power.

The Federal Housing Administration (FHA) had been collecting data on the number of mortgages that prepay or default in each year following the year of origination. After 25 years they had filled out an entire prepayment schedule. The table is changed each year as another year's experience is added. The schedule allows computer-model builders to develop models incorporating the *FHA prepayment experience* on mortgage loan life, or mortality, as it has become known.

It is possible to assume faster or slower prepayment by taking a percentage of the FHA prepayment experience. Alternative prepayment rates were first used by mortgage analysts who realized that mortgages prepay faster in certain parts of the country than in others.

Different prepayment assumptions are also used to simulate faster or slower prepayment pools of mortgages that have coupon rates above or below the current market mortgage rate. A mortgage pool can be expected to prepay rapidly if it contains mortgages that have coupon rates above the current market rate. This induces homeowners to refinance. The opposite can be expected if market rates are above the coupon rate on the mortgage.

Two other approaches to estimating cash flows on FRM pools are the *Constant Prepayment Rate (CPR)* and the *Public Security Association Standard Prepayment Model (PSA)*. The CPR assumes that mortgages will prepay by some predetermined fixed percentage each month based on the existing principal outstanding, after the previous month's prepayment.

The PSA approach uses a more complicated assumption in which the prepayment percentage starts low in the early years of the mortgages and increases each month until it reaches 6 percent per year. Obviously, as with the FHA case, this approach can be sped up or slowed down by taking a percentage of the PSA prepayment assumption.

The embedded prepayment option in the standard FRM causes the relationship between the market value of the mortgage and open-market mortgage rates to be asymmetric. This means that if interest rates go down, a growing number of mortgages can be expected to prepay. This is due to higher home sales and refinance stimulated by the declining rates. As a

Exhibit 4.2

Market Value of 10 percent Coupon Mortgage Pool at Market Discount Rates of 7 percent to 12 percent

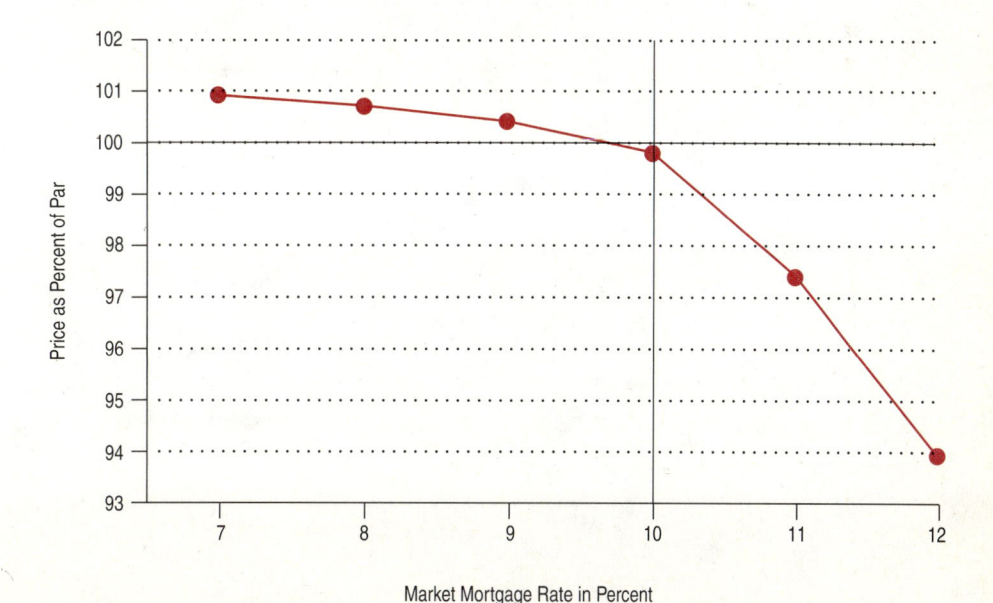

result, investors in mortgages and mortgage pools do not experience as much of a gain in market value as they do when the mortgages are not callable. Exhibit 4.2 on page 95 shows how we might expect the market value of a pool of 10 percent mortgages to change in value as open-market interest rates on new mortgages rise and fall.

Exhibit 4.3 shows the hypothetical cash flows for a pool of mortgages experiencing prepayment due to refinance and payoffs from normal home sales. The graph shows how the cash flows from a pool of mortgages would be expected to behave without a dramatic rise or fall in open-market interest rates.

In order to limit the impact of early prepayment, some mortgage lenders have incorporated a *prepayment penalty* in their mortgage contracts. This clause requires the borrower to pay an additional charge if the loan is repaid early. The prepayment penalty is the equivalent to a call premium on a corporate bond. Prepayment penalties are very common on mortgages made

Exhibit 4.3

Cash Flows for Hypothetical Mortgage Pool (Pool Principal: $1,000,000)

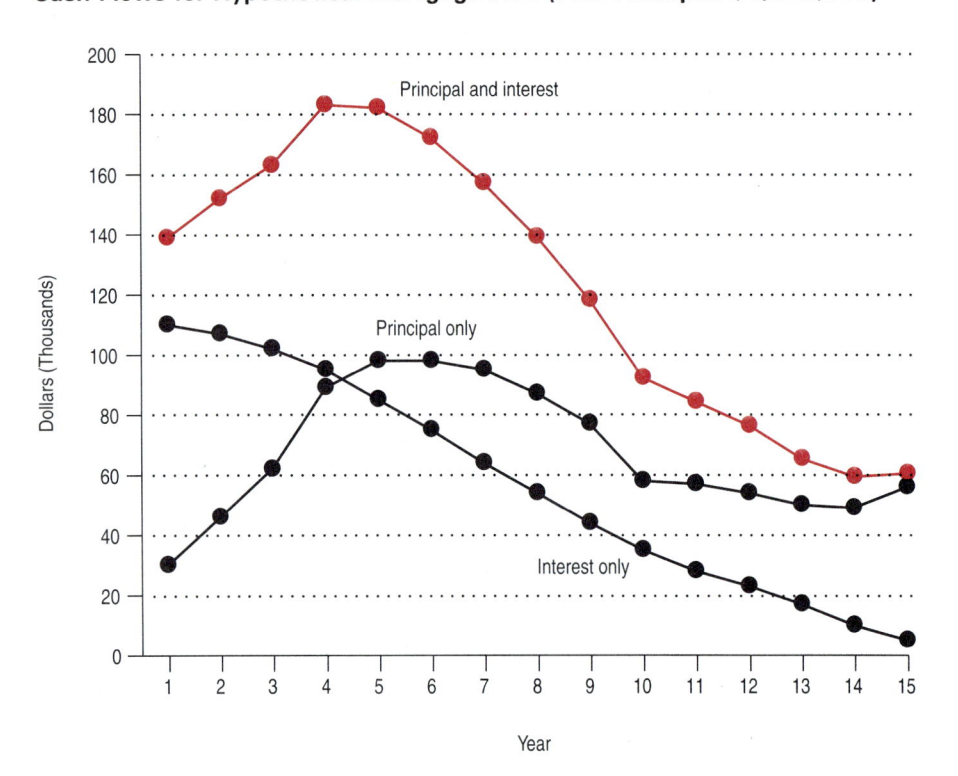

on office buildings and other commercial real estate, but are rare on home mortgages.

The asymmetric relationship between market value and changes in market interest rates makes the FRM a risky investment from a cash flow perspective. As a result, investors expect to be compensated for the additional risk relating to the embedded option in mortgage loans.

Even though pass-through securities of the GNMA have the full faith and credit guarantee of the U.S. government, the rates on GNMA securities typically range from 75 to 150 basis points over comparable maturity Treasury securities. The premium yield is the return for accepting the risk of early prepayment, as discussed in Chapter 2. If economic conditions stimulate prepayment, then the extra yield associated with the option premium is lost. It is lost because the prepayment assumption about cash flows was incorrect.

Table 4.7 shows how the financial press quotes yields on a hypothetical selection of mortgage-backed securities. The table shows one piece of information we have not yet discussed. This is the *weighted average life, WAL*. This figure is based on a specified prepayment assumption, any of those we have already discussed, or a proprietary estimate of a security dealer, which calculates the expected average length of time each dollar of principal is expected to be outstanding. Typically the high coupon securities are expected to have a very short weighted average life due to expected fast prepayment. Conversely, the low coupon securities have a longer expected weighted average life. This, of course, is because borrowers are more likely to prepay a mortgage that has a high coupon rate.

Table 4.7

Reading the Financial Page

Yields on a Hypothetical Selection of Mortgage Securities (typical listing)

Issuer	Coupon Rate	Remaining Life	Weighted Average Life	Price	Yield	Change in Yield
GNMA (30 Yr.)	8.5%	27.5	8.6	98–05	8.89%	+.12
FNMA (30 Yr.)	8.5	25.8	9.8	99–12	8.61	+.11
FHLMC (15 Yr.)	7.75	24.6	7.8	97–23	7.86	+.09

Table 4.7 gives typical information on several mortgage-backed pass-through securities. These are securities issued by the GNMA, FNMA, and the

FHLMC. The original maturity shown for the mortgages in the pool is either 30 or 15 years. The coupon rate on the security is shown. It is important to note that the coupon rate on the actual mortgages in the pool will be above that of the security. This is because the servicer of the mortgage will obtain about 25 basis points to service and the agency will obtain 15–25 basis points to guarantee the mortgages. The remaining life is the number of years from now until the last payment is received on the mortgages, if prepayment does not take place.

The remainder of the information is based on assumptions about prepayment. These assumptions usually vary between investment banking firms. The weighted average life is calculated based on the prepayment assumptions. These assumptions are also used to calculate yield. Prices are quoted in percent of par and thirty-secondths of 100 percent.

Interest-Only and Principal-Only Strips on Mortgage Securities

In much the same way we altered the cash flow on a Treasury bond to create a class of zero coupon bonds, it is possible to create interest-only (IO) and principal-only (PO) strips on mortgage securities. The IO is a security that receives all interest on all mortgages in the pool. The PO receives all of the principal.

Calculating yields or market values on interest-only and principal-only strips requires a cash flow assumption used by the FHA, CPR, PSA or other prepayment approaches. From this, the cash flows are simulated, and a present-value equation is formulated to solve for market value or yield.

These mortgage hybrid securities tend to alter the prepayment risk associated with investments in standard FRMs. Consider the IO security first. For the investor in the interest-only security, a decline in open-market interest rates that leads to the early repayment of principal will also reduce the amount of interest payments received over the life of the security. Thus the interest-only security is a better investment performer in a period of rising interest rates than it is in a period of declining rates. When interest rates rise, the amount of interest payments on the IO are higher. The principal-only security behaves just the opposite. If interest rates fall, investors will receive their cash flows much earlier than expected. Since the principal-only security is purchased at a deep discount, the earlier repayment of principal will provide a higher yield on the security.

Consider Table 4.8. It shows the direction of the change in the market value of an IO and PO from changes in open-market interest rates. The changes in market value are caused by two factors. The first relates to the change in discount rates resulting from changes in open-market rates. The second relates to changes in the cash flows of the two claims as a result of

Table 4.8

Market Value of IOs and POs Due to Changes in Open-Market Interest Rates

	Change in Value Due to Change in Market Interest Rate		Change in Value Due to Change in Prepayment Cash Flows	
	Type of Claim			
	IO	PO	IO	PO
Rising market interest rates	−	−	+	−
Declining market interest rates	+	+	−	+

changing prepayment experience. The table shows that the impact of a rise in open-market rates will decrease the value of a PO unambiguously. The higher discount rate decreases its value, as does the slowdown in cash flows. The change in the value of the IO, on the other hand, is ambiguous. The higher discount rate lowers value while the slowdown in prepayment causes the cash flows on the IO to increase. The IO could very well increase in overall value from a rise in interest rates. If so, it is the only debt security with this attribute. The opposite conditions prevail for a fall in open-market interest rates. The unusual property of the IO has made it popular with investors who want to earn interest on a financial claim that has limited interest rate risk exposure.

Servicing Income Contracts (Strips)

Now that the valuation of the interest-only strip is understood it is easy to understand a *servicing income contract* and its valuation. A servicing income contract is a contract granted to a loan servicing company for collecting payments, handling bookkeeping, and other responsibilities. The largest volume of servicing relates to servicing on home mortgages sold to the major government mortgage credit agencies.

The servicing organizations obtain a specified percentage fee on the outstanding balance of the loans serviced. Mortgage servicers attempt to earn at least 25 basis points (.25 percent) on standard FRMs, 37.5 basis points (.375 percent) on variable-rate mortgages, and 44 basis points (.44 percent) on FHA-insured or Veterans' Administration (VA) guaranteed mortgages pooled into GNMA securities.

The calculation of the value of the servicing contract is handled the same way as the calculation for the interest-only strip. After all, a servicing income stream is exactly equivalent to an interest-only strip. Servicing income is a fixed percentage of the outstanding principal of the loans serviced.

In determining the value of a servicing strip, all the costs and revenues associated with servicing must be incorporated into the analysis. In the case of a home mortgage, the servicer has to cover the direct costs of servicing the mortgage. In addition to a fee, the servicer may obtain benefits such as interest income on property insurance and tax impounds, if any. The servicer may receive profits from insurance sales and other products sold to the homebuyer, and interest on the funds received and invested during the interim period prior to remitting to the investor.

Once a cash flow statement is completed and a prepayment assumption incorporated into the analysis, the discounted cash flow algorithm can be used to determine the value of the servicing contract. Like the interest-only mortgage strip, the servicing mortgage income contract will decrease significantly in value if interest rates fall. In that case, the mortgages will repay early and the servicing income stream will end early. This occurred in a significant way in the summer of 1992 when open-market interest rates fell rapidly and by a large amount. The result was a nationwide refinancing of many high-rate FRMs. Consequently, the decline in interest rates wiped out the value of many financial institutions' servicing portfolios.

The same methodology can be used to establish value on all other types of servicing. Third-party servicing is done in large volume today on auto loans, credit card receivables, and commercial business loans. The valuation of servicing income contracts is very important since servicing is actively bought and sold. Mortgage banking companies are active as both buyers and sellers of mortgage servicing contracts. There is also active buying and selling among thrifts, commercial banks, and the Resolution Trust Corporation, which is charged with liquidating the assets of failed thrifts. Some of the assets being liquidated are servicing contracts.

Collateralized Mortgage Obligations and Real Estate Mortgage Investment Conduits

In 1983, a significant hybrid security was issued—the collateralized mortgage obligation (CMO). The CMO reduces some of the more disagreeable aspects of home mortgages, namely cash flow uncertainty. The concept is to repackage the cash flows from a pool of mortgages or mortgage pass-through securities into several newly created hybrid securities. These newly created securities have more appeal to investors because they have more predictable cash flows. They also have expected maturities that differ significantly from the mortgage itself. The Tax Reform Act of 1986 provided for the creation of a new tax entity called the *real estate mortgage investment conduit* or *REMIC*. This conduit allows CMO-type securities to be offered through a REMIC trust and allows the issuer to develop a multiclass CMO structure off the firm's balance sheet.

As discussed, a mortgage is like a series of monthly loans, each with a small amount of principal and interest due monthly. Viewed in this manner, it is easier to see how we can divide these cash flows to create a new class of securities. CMOs have three or more classes. A typical four-class CMO is discussed. The first is the short-term class called class 1, with an expected maturity of 2 to 4 years. The second is class 2, with an expected maturity of 4 to 8 years. Class 3 has an expected maturity of 8 to 12 years. The last class is the Z class. It is a residual class that receives cash flows only after all the other classes are paid off.

The CMO simply diverts all the cash flows on the mortgages so that the first three classes receive interest payments at a specified rate of interest and all principal repayments are used to pay off each class sequentially. Class Z then receives all remaining cash flows. This structure is easier to understand when you review Exhibit 4.4 on page 102. This graph shows the principal payments on each class. Note that classes, 2, 3, and Z receive no principal cash flows until the previous class is totally paid off.

The classes of the CMO, or *tranches,* as they are sometimes called, make the new mortgage securities more appealing investments. The creation of these classes reduces the liquidity premium embedded into the term structure of interest rates discussed in Chapter 2. Investors looking for shorter-term and intermediate-term investments can consider the first two tranches. These are typically priced near the prevailing market interest rates on two-year and five-year Treasury notes. If the term structure of interest rates is upward sloping, the shorter and intermediate-term tranches will have a yield that is below the coupon rates on the mortgages used as collateral to create the CMO. This lower rate on the short-term tranches sold creates much of the incentive for investment dealers and others to create CMOs in the first place. The return on the CMO to the issuer also includes float income. CMOs pay interest and principal semiannually, while the issuer receives a monthly cash flow that can be invested until paid out. The interest the issuer earns on that cash is called float income. The excess cash flows associated with a CMO are known as the CMO residual. These residuals can be bought and sold just like the other CMO classes.

It is possible to create a nearly infinite variety of CMO structures. For each one, however, it is necessary to make a prepayment assumption, such as an FHA, CPR, or PSA prepayment assumption. This will determine the relative size of each tranche. The investor must remember that while the CMO tranches have reduced cash flow uncertainty, it has not been totally removed. Thus, the true yield on a CMO can never be known in advance.

The financial press frequently quotes interest rates on CMOs as a spread over a specified maturity Treasury security. These CMOs have

Exhibit 4.4

Principal Cash Flows for Collateralized Mortgage Obligation (Four Class Series)

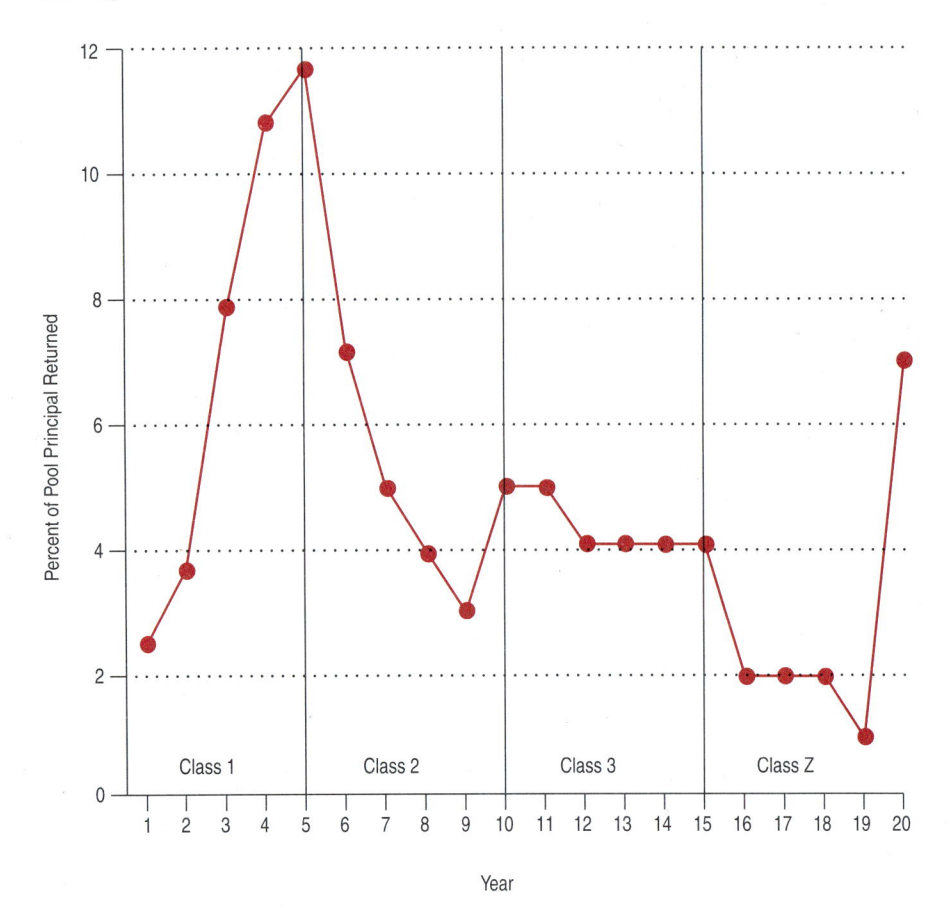

experienced yields approximately 110 to 120 basis points above the Treasury yield for a maturity closest to the weighted average life of the CMO.

Senior-Subordinated Securities

The creation of hybrid securities has not been limited to redistributing cash flows. Securities that redistribute the credit risk on the collateral underlying the security are also common today. An example of this is the senior-subordinated security structure.

A senior-subordinated class of securities is created by forming a pool of loans or securities. These securities or loans may be represented as mortgages or bonds. From this pool two or more new securities are issued using the loans or securities as collateral. A two-class senior-subordinated structure is comprised of senior and junior securities. The senior class is the lower-risk class. The junior, or subordinated, class has much higher risk, since this class will absorb the credit losses before the senior class is affected.

Consider an example starting with a pool of home mortgages totaling $50 million. Two securities are issued from this pool according to criteria provided by the credit rating services. The amount of the principal of the two securities depends on the credit quality of the collateral as evaluated by the rating services. Based on the quality of the collateral, we may assume that the rating organization will grant a AA rating to the senior class if at least 8 percent of the issue is made up of the subordinated class and no more than 92 percent is made up of the senior class.

In the case of the subordinated class, any loss of principal as a result of default and foreclosure on the mortgages in the pool will be charged against that class before the senior class is affected. In other words, the pool could experience foreclosure losses of principal of up to 8 percent of principal, or $4 million, before the senior class suffers any loss of principal.

The time for using the senior-subordinated structure is when the originator of the collateral believes that the credit quality of the assets is of higher quality than perceived by potential investors. This structure allows the issuer to sell a portion of the perceived risky assets at an investment-grade rating of AA or higher, for example, and realize a higher price that is attributed to a high credit quality rating. The issuer may choose to hold or sell the subordinated portion of the transaction. In any case, for there to be a profit on the transaction, the weighted cost of the senior and subordinated securities must be less than the coupon yield on the collateral. That spread must also cover the cost of issuance, servicing, and administration.

The following table is an example in which the issuer has home mortgages yielding 9.875 percent. The firm is able to issue a AA-rated security at a yield of 9.125 percent, which represents 92 percent of the pool. It must retain at least 25 basis points of the interest return on the mortgages to cover the cost of servicing the mortgages. It also learns of a potential buyer of the subordinated class that expects a yield of 10.50 percent on the remaining 8 percent of the pool. The cost of issuance and administration is seven basis points per annum. Table 4.9 on page 104 shows the weighted cost of this senior-subordinated structure to the issuer.

The weighted cost for each factor is derived from multiplying the weight percent (column 2) by the interest rate and costs expressed as interest rates (column 3).

In the table, the total interest cost of financing with this structure is 9.555 percent, or 32 basis points (.32 percent) below the 9.875 percent coupon yield on the mortgages. This will likely make this a very profitable transaction. Senior-subordinated securities have become very popular for intermediaries that want to decrease the volume of assets on their balance

Table 4.9

Example of Senior-Subordinated Structure for $50 Million in Home Mortgages (dollars in millions)

Security and Cost Factors	Amount (1)	Weight Percent (2)	Interest Rate and Costs Expressed as an Interest Rate (3)	Weighted Cost (%) (2 × 3)
Senior class	$46	92%	9.25%	8.395%
Subordinated class	4	8	10.50	.84
Servicing cost	50	100	.25	.25
Administration and issuance	50	100	.07	.07
Total weighted cost				9.555%

sheets. This financing structure allows the firm to sell a large percentage of the pool and remove it from the balance sheet.

As discussed earlier, the prepayment options embedded in a fixed-rate mortgage make its cash flows uncertain.

Municipal Securities and Tax Exemption

With the Tax Reform Act of 1986, the number of tax-preferred investments has been sharply reduced. A *tax-preferenced investment* is one whose income is taxed differently from ordinary income. This includes investment income that is tax exempt and tax deferred and subject to lower tax rates (such as the way capital gains income used to be taxed). State and local municipal bond tax preferences have largely survived tax reform. These securities are notable because they are exempt from federal income tax, and frequently state income tax also, for taxpayers living in the same state in which the bond is issued.

Because they are exempt from taxes, municipal bonds pay lower interest rates than taxable securities of comparable risk and term. The relationship between the yields on a tax-exempt bond and taxable bond is known as the *taxable equivalent yield (TEY)*. This yield allows comparison of yields between tax-exempt and taxable securities.

To use this yield you must know the taxpayer's marginal federal (*MFR*) and marginal state tax rates (*MSR*). The state tax rate only comes into play if the municipal bond is tax exempt in the state of issuance and the taxpayer is from that state. An example would be a municipal security with a tax exempt rate (TER) of 7.05 percent. The investor from the state issuing the bond would have a federal marginal tax rate of 34 percent and a state marginal tax rate of 6 percent. In this case the TEY is

$$TEY = \text{tax exempt rate} / [1 - (\text{marginal federal rate} + \text{marginal state rate}]$$
$$TEY = TER / [1 - (MFR + MSR)]$$
$$TEY = 7.05\% / [1 - (.34 + .06)]$$
$$= 11.75\%$$

Thus, a taxable security would have to yield 11.75 percent to provide an after-tax return equal to the return on a tax-exempt security yielding 7.05 percent for an investor in the 40 percent combined marginal federal and state income tax bracket. The Tax Reform Act of 1986 had a significant impact on the demand for municipal bonds by large federal taxpaying intermediaries such as commercial banks and insurance companies. The act mandated that by 1987 intermediaries would lose the ability to take the interest paid on debt sold to finance tax-exempt bond purchases as an expense for federal tax purposes. Consider the case of a commercial bank with a cost of funds (COF) of 4.00 percent that is considering purchasing a 7.05 percent yielding tax-exempt bond. To determine the taxable equivalent rate using the same federal and tax rates used above, we would use Equation 4.11:

$$TEY = [TER - (COF \times MFR)] / [1 - (MFR + SFR)]$$
$$TEY = [7.05\% - (4.00\% \times .34)] / [1 - (.34 + .06)]$$
$$TEY = 9.48\% \qquad [4.11]$$

It is easy to see why tax-exempt bonds have lost a lot of their appeal for many intermediaries that had been major investors.

Summary

The stock and trade of the financial intermediary is the financial claim. Consequently, people working in this industry must understand how financial claims are valued. This chapter briefly reviewed the basics of present value, future value, yield to maturity, and cash flow development. These are the basic tools needed to determine value and yield on all but the most complicated debt instruments.

The chapter presented the basic value and yield equations for the most common types of debt instruments, including discount Treasury securities, bonds with and without call provisions, and fixed-rate mortgages.

This chapter also introduced a wide variety of new types of hybrid financial instruments, such as Treasury stripped securities, interest- and principal-only strips, collateralized mortgage obligations, and senior-subordinated securities. Each of these claims is the result of recasting the cash flows or credit exposure on a pool of claims.

The following is a basic valuation equation for determining the **present value** on a cash flow or series of cash flows discounted at an interest rate of r:

$$PV = \sum_{n=1}^{t} CF_n / (1 + r)^n$$

This same equation is also used to determine the **future value** of a cash flow earning an interest rate of r.

$$FV = PV (1 + r)^n$$

Compounding is incorporated into this structure by calculating a periodic rate r/m where m is the number of compounding periods within a year. We then have the following PV equation:

$$FV = PV (1 + r/m)^{mn}$$

Discounted securities such as Treasury bills and zero coupon bonds are valued using the simple PV formula. **Zero coupon bonds** assume semiannual compounding so that their yield on a discounted security that pays no interest can be compared to bonds that pay interest.

A *perpetual* interest or dividend-paying financial claim, such as perpetual preferred stock or British consol, can be valued by using the following expression:

$$PV = CF / r$$

The value of a $1,000 par value bond is determined by using the present value equation with a semiannual compounding assumption. If the bond has a call provision then we modify the equation by replacing the par value of $1,000 with the call price and replacing the number of periods *tm* with the number of periods to the call.

$$PV = \sum_{n=1}^{tm} CF_n \, [1 + (r/m)]^n + \$1{,}000 \, [1 + (r/2)]^{tm}$$
$$m = 2$$

The equation shows that the bond is made up of two sets of cash flows. The first is a series of cash flows representing interest payments that form an ordinary annuity and a principal payment. The cash flows on any debt instrument can be stripped into as many securities as there are cash flows in the original security. A **coupon-stripped Treasury** security can be stripped into securities representing each of its interest payments and its principal payment. The valuation of the various stripped Treasury securities is determined by using the equation for a zero-interest bond and the relevant discount rate. The discount rate will likely be different for each portion of the stripped Treasury, since each strip has a different maturity.

Fixed-rate mortgages are some of the most difficult debt securities to value, because they have an embedded call option. Normally, an FRM would be valued as an ordinary annuity with equal monthly payments. Unfortunately, the assumption that a mortgage will remain outstanding for its full term is a poor assumption to make. As a result, it is necessary to make alternative assumptions about cash flows on mortgages resulting from early prepayment. Some of the alternative assumptions discussed include **FHA mortality experience, Public Security Association Standard Prepayment Model (PSA), and the Constant Prepayment Model (CPR).** Each of these approaches is designed to accurately simulate the cash flows on a pool of homogeneous mortgages.

Mortgage securities can also be stripped like Treasury securities. Interest only and principal-only securities have been developed by stripping the **interest payments (IO)** on a mortgage security from the **principal payments (PO)** and creating two new securities. Because of the prepayment option embedded in mortgages, the IOs and POs are very difficult to value. They require developing sophisticated cash flow models using the FHA, PSA, or CPR mortgage prepayment model structure or some alternative proprietary structure. The value of the PO will rise much more than an ordinary bond during a period of falling open-market rates because mortgages will prepay and the investor will obtain cash flows early. An IO will perform very poorly in a declining rate market and very well in a rising rate market. An IO is about the only debt instrument that may actually rise in value when open-market rates rise, because prepayments slow down and the security earns more interest.

The **servicing contract** value was shown to behave like an IO security.

Modifying the timing of cash flows is also the theory behind the **collateralized mortgage obligation (CMO)** and the **real estate mortgage investment conduit (REMIC).** Here the technique is to divert the cash flows into sequential classes or tranches of securities. The shorter-term tranches receive principal cash flows while the longer-term tranches receive only interest, until the short-term tranches are paid off.

Just as we can dissect a security's cash flows, we can also modify its credit risk. One method is the **senior-subordinated security.** A pool of homogenous loans or securities is used to create two or more new securities. The **senior securities** that have been created have lower credit risk because they do not suffer a loss unless the **junior** or **subordinated security** is wiped out due to credit losses.

The purpose for creating the senior-subordinated security is to be able to sell the senior portion at an interest rate less than the market yield on the underlying collateral. This permits the firm to get the assets off the balance sheet. It also earns an interest spread, which is computed to be the difference between the yield on the collateral and the yield on the securities sold, adjusted for the cost of issuance.

Tax-exempt securities are very popular investments for individuals with high marginal tax rates. They have also been popular investments for financial intermediaries. This changed, however, as a result of the **1986 Tax Reform Act.** The act eliminated intermediaries' ability to deduct the interest paid on deposits or debt used to finance the tax-exempt bond. The investor in a tax-exempt bond is interested in comparing the yield on a tax-exempt bond with a taxable bond. This requires using the before-tax equivalent yield (*TEY*). The equation for the *TEY* is

$$TEY = TER / [1 - (MFR + MSR)]$$

where *TER* is the tax-exempt yield, *MFR* is the marginal federal tax rate, and *MSR* is the marginal state tax rate.

An intermediary must adjust the equation to eliminate the tax deduction for interest paid on deposits or debt used to finance the purchase of a tax-exempt bond. We can do that by using

$$TEY = [TER - (COF \times MFR)] / [1 - (MFR + SFR)]$$

where *COF* is the cost of deposits or debt used to finance the tax-exempt bonds.

Questions

Chapter 4

1. Why is the development of a schedule of cash flows so important in using present value analysis?
2. What is meant by a discounted security? Give an example of one.
3. What is a zero coupon bond? What are the advantages from an investor's perspective of a zero coupon bond investment?
4. What is the motivation behind the creation of stripped Treasury securities?
5. What impact does a prepayment option embedded in a fixed-rate mortgage have on the value of the mortgage as rates rise and fall? Compare this to a noncallable long-term fixed-rate bond.
6. Why is it impossible to accurately forecast the principal prepayments on a pool of fixed-rate mortgages? What has been done to get around this problem?
7. Explain what is meant by an interest-only and principal-only mortgage pass-through security. Which of these is most similar to a mortgage servicing contract?
8. What is the objective of one who issues a collateralized mortgage obligation? What is a CMO?
9. A senior-subordinated security is designed to alter the credit-risk characteristics of a pool of risky assets. Explain how this works.
10. What are the advantages of tax-exempt bonds? Why are they less attractive to depositories that finance their purchases with deposits?

Problems

Problem 4-1   Compounding and Future Value

Which of the following would you rather have: (1) a savings account that pays 6.1 percent interest compounded semiannually or (2) a savings account that pays 6.0 percent compounded daily on a 365-day basis? Assume you invest $20,000 for one year.

Problem 4-2   Yield to Maturity

Broader Bank offers a certificate of deposit that pays a 10 percent yield to maturity compounded quarterly. The managers of First Bank want to set a yield to maturity on their comparable maturity account that produces the same future value. First Bank compounds interest monthly. What yield to maturity should First Bank select?

Problem 4-3   Bond Valuation

The Tyler Company has a bond outstanding that pays interest at the rate of 11 percent or $55 per semiannual period for each $1,000 of par value. The bond matures in exactly ten years. What is the market value of this bond if market interest rates for similar risky bonds are (1) 8 percent, (2) 11 percent, and (3) 12 percent?

Problem 4-4 Effective Annual Yield

Libor Bank pays 9 percent yield to maturity, compounded quarterly, on its certificates of deposit. The manager of Marion Bank wants to offer a certificate that provides the same effective annual rate as Libor Bank. However, Marion's certificate will be compounded monthly. What yield to maturity must the bank offer?

Problem 4-5 Yield to the Call

It has been exactly two years since Majestic Corporation issued a 30-year bond. The bond pays a semiannual coupon at a 12 percent annual interest rate. When it was issued, it had a five-year call provision that provided for a call at 110 percent of par any time after five years from the date of issue. Determine the present yield to maturity and yield to call, assuming the bond is selling at 112 percent of par.

Problem 4-6 Future Value and Taxation

You have $1,000 to invest. Your effective tax rate is 40 percent. Your savings options include

1. a savings account paying 8.5 percent compounded semiannually;
2. a savings account paying 8.35 percent compounded monthly; or
3. a tax exempt bond paying 5.1 percent paying interest quarterly.

What will your $1,000 be worth after one year for each alternative, with consideration to taxes?

Problem 4-7 Perpetual Preferred Yield

A perpetual preferred stock is paying 7.75 percent in dividends semiannually. What is the value of this stock if market yields on comparable preferreds are 8 percent?

Problem 4-8 Repo Rate

Mainland Investment has agreed to a repurchase agreement with a local commercial bank. Mainland will sell to the bank $10 million par value of Treasury bonds at a price of $9,995,980. Mainland has agreed to buy them back at par in two days. What is the repo rate based on a 360-day year for this transaction?

Chapter 4 Valuation of Financial Claims 111

Problem 4-9 Effective Annual Yield and Bank Discount Yield
A security dealer bids on a new issue Treasury bill at auction. The bid price was 98.7 percent for the 182-day bills. What was the bank discount yield and the effective annual yield (assume semiannual compounding) on this transaction? Use a 364-day year.

Problem 4-10 Repo Rate
An investment banker has agreed to sell to Pacific Bank $10 million par value of government securities at $9,995,899. The investment banker will repurchase the securities at par in three days. What is the repo rate (RR) and effective yield? Assume daily compounding.

Problem 4-11 Treasury Strip
A four-year Treasury bond is being considered as collateral for a coupon strip. It has a coupon of 9 percent with semiannual interest payments. The security is selling at par. The following table shows the market yield on comparable zero coupon Treasury securities.

Current Yields on Zero Coupon Treasuries

Maturity	Yield
.5 years	6.80%
1.0	7.20
1.5	7.30
2.0	7.80
2.5	7.90
3.0	8.00
3.5	8.20
4.0	8.50

The cost of creating the strip is $13,000 per million. Would you advise going ahead and creating the strip if you could sell it at the yields shown in the previous table?

Problem 4-12 Treasury Strip
Fitzgerald Investment Bank, Inc., would like to create and distribute to its customers a Treasury strip on a two-year remaining maturity bond. The date of the transaction will be the next interest payment date of July 1, 1993. The coupon rate on the bond is 8.50 percent. The following table shows the yields on the strips to be sold.

Market Yields on Zero Coupons to Be Sold

Maturity	Yield
January 1, 1994	6.25%
July 1, 1994	7.25
January 1, 1995	8.30
July 1, 1995	8.40

The cost of creating the strip is $20,000 per million of Treasury principal. What is the maximum price Fitzgerald can pay for the Treasury bonds to break even on the transaction?

Problem 4-13   Tax Equivalent Yield
   An investor is considering a federal tax exempt state bond that is also exempt from state taxation. The yield is 7.30 percent. The investor's federal and state marginal tax rates are 36 percent and 7 percent respectively. What is the taxable equivalent yield on this investment (*TEY*)?

Problem 4-14   Tax Equivalent Yield
   David wants to invest in a ten-year security. He has two choices: (1) a taxable bond yielding 8 percent or (2) a federal and state tax exempt municipal bond with the same credit risk yielding 4.90 percent. David's marginal tax rates are 35 percent federal and 6 percent state. Which security should he purchase and why?

Problem 4-15   Tax Equivalent Yield for Intermediary
   Bergen Bank is considering replacing some taxable securities with municipal bonds. As a financial analyst, would you recommend the security swap in either of the following situations? Answer yes or no and supply calculations to support your answers.
      1. The bank earns 7.3 percent on the securities held. They can be sold at no gain or loss. The municipal securities of equivalent risk would earn 5.5 percent. The bank's cost of funds is 4.5 percent. The bank's marginal federal and state tax rates are 36 percent and 5 percent respectively.
      2. The same conditions as above are true except the bank can earn 6 percent on the municipal bonds.

Problem 4-16 Tax Equivalent Yield for Intermediary
   Sanwan Bank has a cost of funds of 3.80 percent. It is contemplating investing in a tax-exempt bond. The marginal federal tax rate for the bank is 36 percent and the state marginal rate is 7 percent. Considering the impact of the 1986 Tax Reform Act, compute the taxable equivalent yield (TEY) on a municipal bond exempt from state taxes yielding 7.30 percent.

Problem 4-17 Senior-Subordinated Securities
   Lumbard Bank has a pool of $100 million in credit card receivables yielding an average of 17.5 percent. It forms a senior security class for 90 percent of the value of the pool and a subordinate class for the remaining 10 percent. Consider the following problems:
   1. The senior security can be sold to yield 15.75 percent and the subordinated class can be sold to yield 25 percent. If the total administrative costs for the issuance are 37.5 basis points per annum, what net yield spread will the bank realize from the securitization?
   2. How would you as the bank's portfolio manager justify such a securitization to your board of directors?

Problem 4-18 Senior-Subordinated Securities
   A pool of second mortgages yields 9 percent. For an administrative cost of 31.5 basis points per annum on the outstanding principal, a senior-subordinated structure can be formed with the senior class yielding 8.50 percent and the subordinated class yielding 10.35 percent. What is the maximum size the senior class can be as a percentage of the total pool without losing money on the securitization?

Futures and Options

chapter 5

Financial contracts whose value depends on the value of other financial claims are the subject of this chapter. These contracts are known as *derivative financial claims*. Financial futures contracts and options contracts are two of the most important.

The value of futures and options is derived from the financial claims on which they are written. These contracts are sometimes referred to as *contingent claims* because their value is contingent on that of another claim.

Functions of Futures and Options Contracts

Financial claims are created to provide for risk sharing and to reduce the cost of transactions. Futures and options are created for these same reasons. The primary role of these contracts is to provide an efficient method for sharing risks. Economic units face major risks and price risks are among those that can be reduced using futures and options contracts. The process of reducing price risks is known as *hedging*. Other economic units, known as *speculators,* are involved for the purpose of profiting from changes in prices. These contracts can be used to shift price risk from a hedger to a speculator or to another hedger. Futures and options contracts also provide a more efficient method for speculating on changes in prices of financial claims. These contracts allow an investor to benefit from a favorable change in the price of an underlying financial claim without having to put up all of the capital necessary to own it.

Using Futures and Options Contracts

The financial manager must be knowledgeable about futures and options in order to manage the price risk inherent in financial transactions. This is especially true for financial institutions that own and sell financial claims as their primary business. Although futures contracts were first created for agricultural commodities, today futures contracts in financial claims represent the greatest use of the organized futures markets. The primary use of the markets is to hedge the price risk associated with future purchases or sales of financial instruments.

Chapter 19 discusses in some depth how financial futures contracts can reduce the risk of changing interest rates. Some of the most common transactions include

- Hedging the cost of future financing
- Protecting the price of a financial asset to be sold in the future
- Reducing income volatility created by interest rate changes
- Hedging a commitment to lend money in the future

Financial options are also relatively new to the financial scene. Here, most of the action is related to the equity markets. Large institutional investors use options to hedge the price risk inherent in equity investments.

Financial Futures

The futures market in financial claims began relatively recently. In 1975, the Chicago Board of Trade (CBOT) developed a futures contract in Government National Mortgage Association pass-through securities. Several weeks later, the International Monetary Market (IMM) developed the Treasury bill contract, and two years later the Treasury bond contract was developed by the CBOT. Table 5.1 shows the most active contracts and the exchange where each is traded.

Table 5.1

Most Active Financial Futures Contracts and the Exchanges Where They Trade January 1992

Contract	Exchange
Treasury bill	IMM
Treasury note	CBOT
Treasury bond	CBOT
5-year Treasury notes	CBOT
LIBOR-1 month	IMM

What Is a Financial Futures Contract?

A *financial futures contract* is a legal agreement between the buyer or seller and an organized exchange or its clearing house. The exchange or clearing house will deliver (buyer) or accept for delivery (seller) an agreed-upon quantity and quality of the claim at a specified time and place. Since futures contracts are derivative claims, delivery of the underlying claim is not designed to take place, although it is possible. Rather, the buyer or seller of the contract is simply accepting the price risk inherent in the specific claim upon which the futures contract is written.

U.S. bond futures contracts are the most actively traded. Table 5.2 shows the trading information on the Treasury bond futures contract as it could be found in the financial press.

Table 5.2

Reading the Financial Page

Treasury Bond Futures Contract
(typical listing)

Treasury Bond $100,000; 32ndths of 100%
(Chicago Board of Trade)

Expiration	Open	High	Low	Settle	Chg	Yield	Open Interest
June	98-04	99-00	98-01	98-05	+ 7	8.12 − .07	175,000
Sept	97-18	97-30	97-16	97-19	+ 6	8.23 − .06	45,000
Dec	96-12	96-29	96-10	96-14	+ 7	8.30 − .06	32,000

Estimated volume: 300,000
Yesterday's volume: 250,000
Open interest: 320,000

The asset this futures contract is written on is a Treasury bond of $100,000 in principal value. The prices are quoted the same as the bond itself, in thirty-secondths of 100 percent. Thus the quote of 98-05 as the settle price for the June contract means that the contract price of the $100,000 in principal bonds is 98 5/32 or 98.15625 × $100,000 = $98,156.25. Each 1/32 is worth $31.25.

The columns include the month in which contract expires, prices for the open trade, high for the day, low for the day, and the closing trade or settle price. Also shown is the price change from the settle price of the previous trading day. The bond's yield to maturity are also shown computed from the settle price and the change in yield from the previous trading day. The open interest is the number of contracts outstanding for each month. The current trading volume is estimated and also given for the previous day. The open interest at the bottom represents all outstanding contracts in all expiration months. The Treasury bond contract requires an initial margin of $2,500 per contract and a maintenance margin of $2,000.

Valuation of Financial Futures Contracts

Financial futures contract prices are directly related to the prices of the cash market financial claim on which they are written. This relationship is so important that, if it were not so strong, there would be an opportunity to earn a profit from buying or selling in the cash market and offsetting the position in the futures market thereby earning a riskless profit. This process is called *arbitrage* and market forces work to eliminate this source of profit.

In the case of futures contracts, the relationship of the futures contract price and the spot cash price of the financial claim is shown in the following equation:

Futures contract price = Spot cash market price +

Cost of carry of the cash claim −

Return on holding cash claim

The relationship is easy to understand if you consider the following example of a Treasury bond. If this bond is yielding 10 percent and can be financed with a repurchase agreement at 6 percent, then this bond will be worth more in the cash market than the futures market. Consequently, the futures price will be less than the spot cash market price by the amount of the difference between the cost of carry and return on holding; in this case an annualized 4 percent (10 % − 6 %). If the difference between the futures price and spot price was less, it would be wise to buy the bond in the cash market, finance it with a repurchase agreement, and sell a futures contract to deliver the bond sometime in the future. This low-risk transaction would be replicated until the cash price of the bond was bid up and the futures price bid down, closing the gap once again at 4 percent annualized.

The difference between the spot, or cash, price and the futures price is known as *basis*. As a futures contract approaches expiration, the basis will converge to zero. The process that results in a zero basis is called *convergence*. Convergence occurs because the cost of carry and return on the financial claim approach zero at the expiration of a futures contract. Spot and futures prices converge at expiration, as shown in Exhibit 5.1. The graph shows an example of positive and negative basis and convergence.

Hedging

The theory behind the development of financial futures relates to hedging. Hedging is a process whereby the buyer or seller of a specified financial claim wishes to reduce the price risk inherent in holding a cash-market position. Agricultural commodity futures probably offer the best example. In futures terms the farmer is said to be *long* wheat. The grain mill purchases the wheat from the farmer after harvest and sells the flour to a baker. Since the grain mill has already contracted with the baker to supply a specified quantity of flour at a specified price and time, the grain mill is said to be *short*.

In this classic example, both the farmer and the mill are at great risk. The farmer is uncertain whether the price of wheat at harvest time will

Exhibit 5.1

Convergence of Spot and Futures Prices (Positive and Negative Basis)

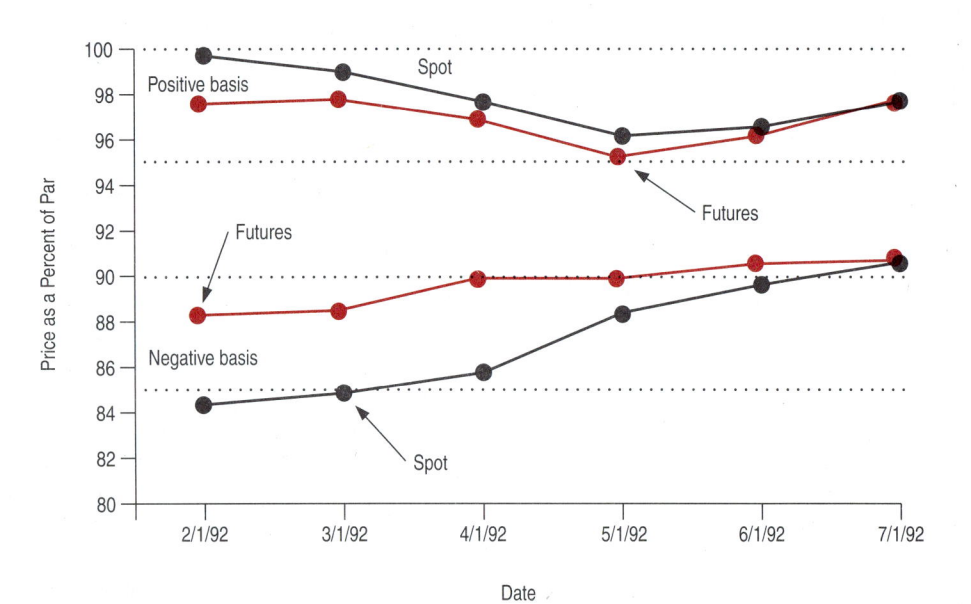

cover the cost of seed, fertilizer, fuel, and capital costs. The mill operator, on the other hand, is uncertain about the cost of buying wheat in the future in order to profitably honor the contract with the baker. Both the farmer and the mill have accepted price risk.

If the farmer knows the mill operator, they could reduce their price risk by contracting before harvest to have the farmer supply a certain quantity of wheat of a particular quality at an agreed-upon price. This transaction would be known as a *forward cash-market transaction*.

It is possible that the farmer doesn't know the mill operator, however. It is also possible that the farmer is unsure that, if prices go down, the mill operator will honor the contract, forcing a legal dispute. The farmer's next option might be to sell (go short) a futures contract in wheat for delivery around harvest time. Similarly, the mill operator would buy (go long) a futures contract to take delivery of wheat around harvest time. In the futures market, the clearing house of the exchange assumes the credit risk of both the buyer and seller. Both futures contracts would be bought back, or covered, at the time of the cash-market transaction. If wheat prices fall, the farmer would experience a loss on the wheat harvested, but a gain on the short futures contract. The mill operator would experience a favorable decline in the price of wheat, offsetting the loss on the futures contract. From this example, it is clear that a futures hedge can reduce the impact of price fluctuations. However, the hedger gives up a possible gain from a favorable change in prices in order to eliminate a possible loss from an unfavorable change.

Mechanics of the Futures Market

Some of the mechanics of using the futures market can be complicated. These aspects include margin and the existence of price circuit breakers.

Margin

Margin requirement relates to the amount of cash or Treasury securities that the hedging firm must hold with the member brokerage firm in relation to the equity value of the futures contracts outstanding. The opening of a contract requires the firm to put up an amount called *initial margin*.

After this, the amount of margin to be held with the futures brokerage dealer is determined by the value of the futures contract and the positive or negative equity. This is computed as the difference between the value of the price of the futures contract at the time it was executed and the current price of offsetting it in the market. The process of establishing this value is called *mark-to-market*. The holder of the futures contract must keep the margin sufficient to cover any loss related to the position currently outstanding (variation margin), plus an additional amount relating to the exchange's established margin requirements (maintenance margin).

For example, the initial margin on a Treasury bond contract is $2,500 and the maintenance margin is $2,000. This means that if the holder of the contract suffers a loss of more than $500, he or she must add additional margin to bring it back to the initial level of $2,500. A loss of less than $500 is acceptable.

Legal and Ethical Issues

Options and Futures Markets: Illegal Trading

In 1984 and again in 1989, the Chicago Board of Trade was shaken by allegations of illegal futures trading. The largest and most publicized allegations occurred in 1989 when over 40 members of the CBOT were indicted for illegal trading. These indictments were the culmination of approximately two years of investigations into trading practices by the FBI.

The alleged violations are very technical in nature. This is because the CBOT runs under a trading system called the *open outcry system*. Under this system, transactions are executed using hand and voice signals. As a result, there are poor records of transactions that take place and even a poorer audit trail for anyone seeking to substantiate specific trades.

Because of this system, the potential for abuse is high. The allegations included claims that traders executed orders off the exchange at prearranged prices with other traders. It was also alleged that traders were trading ahead of customer orders and profited from this knowledge in their personal trades. Some brokers were also accused of arranging to have other brokers take the other side of a customer's order to deny profits to other traders.

One result of the allegations was technological reform at the CBOT. At a cost of several million dollars, the CBOT installed a system to keep track of trade orders. However, the system does not automatically match orders, and thus does not eliminate the probability that many of the alleged violations will occur again. The CBOT experience called attention to the mechanics of how markets actually work. It also created more pressure to develop computerized trading systems with better audit procedures that lessen the chance of manipulation.

Price Circuit Breaker—The Daily Limit

One characteristic of the organized futures market is the existence of price volatility circuit breakers. Price volatility circuit breakers are used to limit the price movement of a financial claim on an organized exchange during a specified period. Futures contracts are subject to limits on price movements during a one-day period. These limits are known as *daily price limits*.

To the hedger, the existence of a circuit breaker can affect the efficiency of a hedge. If the hedging organization has a hedge outstanding, and the cash-market claim being hedged is sold or matures, a major price movement might result in a major change in the value of the outstanding futures contract, which triggers the daily limit circuit breaker. If this occurs before the hedge is taken off, the organization may be unable to offset the cash-market position by buying or selling the offsetting futures contract. At this point the hedge would come to a premature end. The cash claim would be eliminated, but the firm would have unhedged price risk in the futures position still outstanding. A loss is created on the futures contract without an offsetting gain in the cash market.

Periods of high price volatility frequently present severe problems to a hedging organization. Daily price limits may make it very difficult to coordinate the simultaneous unwinding of a cash position and its corresponding futures hedge.

Options

Options are frequently difficult to identify because they are embedded in a claim or are taken for granted in a transaction that otherwise seems straightforward. Also, options are difficult to value. This section looks at many types of options found in financial claims and transactions common to financial institutions. It will also review the basic Black-Scholes option-pricing model. This model includes all the primary factors that affect the value of options.

Options are the financial equivalent of a zero sum game. This is a game in which the gain of the winner is equal to the loss of the loser. There are two parties to every option transaction. The option writer must deliver or purchase the financial claim at a predetermined price. As a practical matter this only occurs when the market price of the optioned claim creates a profit for the party holding the option. The gain to the option holder is equal to the loss of the writer. So, why would anyone write an option? The answer is to earn an *option premium*. This is an amount of money that the option owner pays the writer to offer the option. The option writer receives the premium for risking economic loss.

Options are classified in a number of different ways. First, options are classified on the basis of whether the agreement is to buy or sell. A *put option* is a contract that gives the owner the right to sell a financial claim at a predetermined price on or before a predetermined date. Call options were covered in Chapter 3 and 4. A call option provides the owner with the right to buy a financial claim from the writer at a predetermined price on or before a predetermined date. *European options* stipulate that the purchase or sale must occur on the last date of the option period, or *exercise date*. An

American option, on the other hand, provides the owner with the right to buy or sell any time before the exercise date.

> ### International Focus
>
> ### U.S. Domination of Derivatives Threatened
>
> The United States has always been the undisputed leader in futures and options innovations and trading. Chicago, the heart of the agricultural midwest, took the leadership position with its Chicago Board of Trade and Chicago Mercantile Exchange. With the addition of financial derivatives in the 1970s, the markets boomed.
>
> The growth in derivatives for foreign securities, especially the German and Japanese, has resulted in significant growth in derivative trading outside the United States. Adding to U.S. problems is the growth in computerized trading and over-the-counter trading between dealers. The open outcry trading in the pits limits trading hours, whereas international financial markets know no time limits.
>
> The CBOT is fighting back with an electronic system of its own, called Globex. Most experts, however, feel that the United States will continue to fight a defensive battle for world domination on the derivative markets.
>
> Source: "Has Chicago Lost Its Edge?", *Business Week*. (March 9, 1992) pp. 76–78.

Common Options Found in Financial Intermediary Transactions and Claims

Options are common features in many financial transactions and claims. The following is a short discussion of some of the most common options found in the financial services industry.

Options on Common Stock

The most common options written today are puts and calls on common stock. The common stock option is the most frequently written option. Since the Chicago Board Option Exchange (CBOE) was founded in 1975, hundreds of option contracts have been offered. These include many traded stocks as well as stock indices, bonds, and futures contracts. Other forms of options on common stocks include warrants and bond convertibility features. A *warrant* is a call option on common stock that is sold in conjunction with a bond sale to enhance its desirability. A convertibility feature is a provision embedded in a bond contract that provides the owner with the option to convert the principal value of the bond into shares of common stock in the same company at a specified price on or before a specified date.

Commitments and Lines of Credit

Many financial institutions offer financial commitments to borrow money. This is the option equivalent of selling the borrower a put on a debt claim written against the borrower. These commitments can usually be written at a fixed or floating interest rate. The fact that a borrower has a commitment, however, does not mean that the borrower must borrow the money. The borrower has the option to deliver the debt claim to the lender. Most commitments are of the American variety.

A good example of a loan commitment is the commitment a mortgage lender gives a borrower on a home mortgage. Typically, the lender will give the borrower a commitment to borrow up to a specified amount of money at a specified interest rate. The option is usually written for 60 to 90 days. This option is a put option owned by the borrower providing the ability to sell a mortgage to the lender within the option period, an American option.

Lines of credit, even if written at a market or floating interest rate, involve a risk to the lender that funds may be very difficult for the lending institution to obtain when the customer decides to exercise the option and borrow the money. Consequently, lenders typically charge a commitment fee for the unused portion of a line of credit.

Prepayment Option in a Mortgage or Installment Loan and Call Provisions on Bonds

Most mortgages and installment loan contracts, particularly those written to consumers for durable goods and residential properties, have a provision in the contract allowing for prepayment of principal before the contractual maturity of the loan. This prepayment option is a call option, which allows the borrower to purchase the loan outstanding at its par value any time before maturity. It is an American option.

If market interest rates fall appreciably below the contract rate on the existing mortgage, then a prepayment can be expected to occur. This prepayment option is the equivalent of a call option on a bond issued by a corporation.

Many bonds also have call options. These provisions are just like the prepayment case, but they are not typically as advantageous to the borrower. Most call provisions require that, upon a call, the borrower must pay the investor a premium above the outstanding obligation. Also, the call provision is usually restricted to a single date in the future, as in a European option.

Interest Reinvestment on a Certificate of Deposit (CD Interest Reinvestment)

Most financial depository institutions allow the purchaser of a CD to either withdraw the interest credited to the account each quarter, or alternatively, keep the interest in the account to allow compounding of interest to occur at the CD contract interest rate.

This can be considered a call option held by the CD investor. In effect, the CD investor has a call option to purchase a CD for the amount of the interest paid at an interest rate that is prevailing on the initial CD. Consider what would happen if interest rates rise above the initial CD rate. In that case, the investor would withdraw the interest and invest in a newly issued CD at the higher market rate. If market interest rates fall, however, the CD investor would likely exercise the option to call, or reinvest in, the existing CD at the old CD rate for the amount of the interest paid.

Single Premium Annuity Withdrawals and Early Withdrawal of Funds from a Certificate of Deposit

Insurance companies that write single premium annuity contracts normally provide an option for the insured to withdraw the cash value of the policy through redemption each year. This option is a put option held by the insured. It is usually in the form of an American option. This redemption feature usually involves a penalty in the form of a discount from the policy's cash value.

Despite this discount, which acts as a call premium, the ability to put the policy back to the company is valuable to the insured should interest rates rise appreciably above the contract rate paid on the policy. The importance of this put option was very obvious to a number of insurance companies in the early 1990s. During this period, several large insurance companies that wrote large amounts of annuities experienced financial difficulties. In particular, Executive Life Insurance Company of California, First Capitol Life Insurance Company of California, and Mutual Benefit Life Insurance Company of New Jersey all experienced large redemptions of policies due to credit risk concerns of policyholders. This created severe liquidity problems for these companies that ultimately ended in their seizure by state insurance regulators.

A similar put provision is found in the certificates of deposit sold by commercial banks and thrifts. It is customary for these depositories to permit withdrawal of the funds in these accounts prior to maturity. Usually, the institution will charge what is known as an *early withdrawal penalty* in these cases. However, since these penalties differ from institution to institution, the penalty required by an institution may or may not be sufficient to make an early withdrawal advantageous to the investor holding the put option.

Policy Loan on a Life Insurance Policy

Many life insurance policies that build up cash value offer the insured an option to borrow an amount up to the cash value of the policy at an interest rate established at the time the policy is sold. This option can be viewed as a put option. It effectively allows the policyholder to sell or put a loan written against the insured to an insurance company at a predetermined interest rate.

During the late 1970s and early 1980s, life insurance companies experienced significant increases in policy loans. This was because the whole life policies they wrote in the period before the late 1970s had policy-loan options written with interest rates established at levels of 5 percent or less. When open-market rates hit post–World War II highs in the late 1970s and early 1980s, policyholders exercised their put options to borrow from the companies against the cash value of the policies and invest directly in either the money and capital markets or in deposits in depositories earning higher market interest rates. This created both earning problems and cash-flow problems for the insurance companies.

Understanding the Option Transaction

Obviously, an option only has value if there is some positive probability that the owner will be able to buy or sell a financial claim through exercising the option and earning a form of arbitrage profit. Profit is earned when the market value of the optioned claim is greater (less) than its option exercise price in the case of a call (put). For example, if you own a call option to buy a share of Sears, Roebuck and Company stock at $25 per share when the current price is $23 per share, then the option will have a value only if there is some positive probability that Sears stock will trade at a price higher than $25 per share during the period the option is outstanding. If such a positive probability is expected, then it is likely someone will be willing to pay a positive price for that option.

The owner of an option can be thought of as an investor, or speculator, in price volatility. Alternatively, the owner of the option may already be exposed to price volatility relating to a specific claim and may want to own an option to offset the price risk, in which case the option is used as a hedge. The greater the volatility in the underlying price of a particular financial claim, the more likely the investor exposed to this price risk will be interested in owning an option. Similarly, the greater the price risk of a claim, the greater will be the incentive for a speculator to be drawn into writing an option on that claim.

The owner of an option is also interested in financial leverage. The investor can receive the benefits (or losses) from the price volatility of a financial claim by purchasing an option, which will sell at a fraction of the price of the claim itself. This option transaction may be quicker and involve lower transaction costs than purchasing the financial claim directly and borrowing funds against the claim to produce the same financial leverage effect. For example, an investor can buy a call option on 100 shares of Sears, Roebuck stock or buy the stock itself on margin. If the option is purchased, the investor will forego any dividends paid on the stock, and will also be relieved from any interest on the margin loan. Most important, the holder of the option limits the potential loss, which could occur as a result of a sharp decline in the market price of the call-optioned claim. The ability to leverage and limit loss using options has a price, however. That price is the option premium paid to the writer of the option. A typical quote listing from a financial publication for options on the stock of Disney Corporation is shown in Table 5.3.

Table 5.3

Reading the Financial Page

Stock Option Quotation
Disney Corporation
(typical listing)

American Exchange
Disney

Closing Price*	Strike Price	Calls Jan	Calls Feb	Calls Mar	Puts Jan	Puts Feb	Puts Mar
135 3/8	100	35	nt	nt	no	1/8	1/4
	110	24 1/2	25 1/2	25 3/4	3/8	5/8	3/4
	140	1 1/8	1 7/8	5	8 1/4	10 1/2	11 7/8

nt: no trades
no: no option

*Closing price: New York Stock Exchange

The listing shows the last traded prices of three call and put options for Disney stock. The prices reflect the price of the option per share of stock. This listing shows three different strike prices. However, for a stock as volatile as Disney, strike prices are available in $5 increments. Not all strike prices are shown. A 100-share call option expiring in February at a strike price of 110 would cost $25.50 per share, or $2,550 for a 100 share block. There are additional contract months that are not shown in the Table. Most listings do not provide all the contracts. Typically the near-term contract months are shown.

Options are referred to as in-the-money, at-the-money, or out-of-the-money options. An *in-the-money option* has an immediate economic incentive. This is a put (call) option whose exercise price is above (below) the market price of the claim. All the call options on Disney that can be exercised at the strike prices of $100 and $110 would be in-the-money. An *at-the-money* option has a market price of the claim and the exercise price equal to the cash market price. An *out-of-the-money* put (call) option has an exercise price that is below (above) the market price. The Disney call options at the strike price of $140 are out-of-the-money.

Option Payoffs

One easy way to understand how an option works is to graphically present the payoff possibilities of holding an option. Consider the holder of a call option on one share of Sears, Roebuck and Company stock. The exercise price is $25 per share and the current market value is $23. The price of the call option is $3 per share. Exhibit 5.2 shows the profit or loss position of the option buyer for a wide range of possible prices for Sears stock. It is clear from the graph that the price of Sears stock must rise above the exercise

Exhibit 5.2

Payoff on Stock Call Option

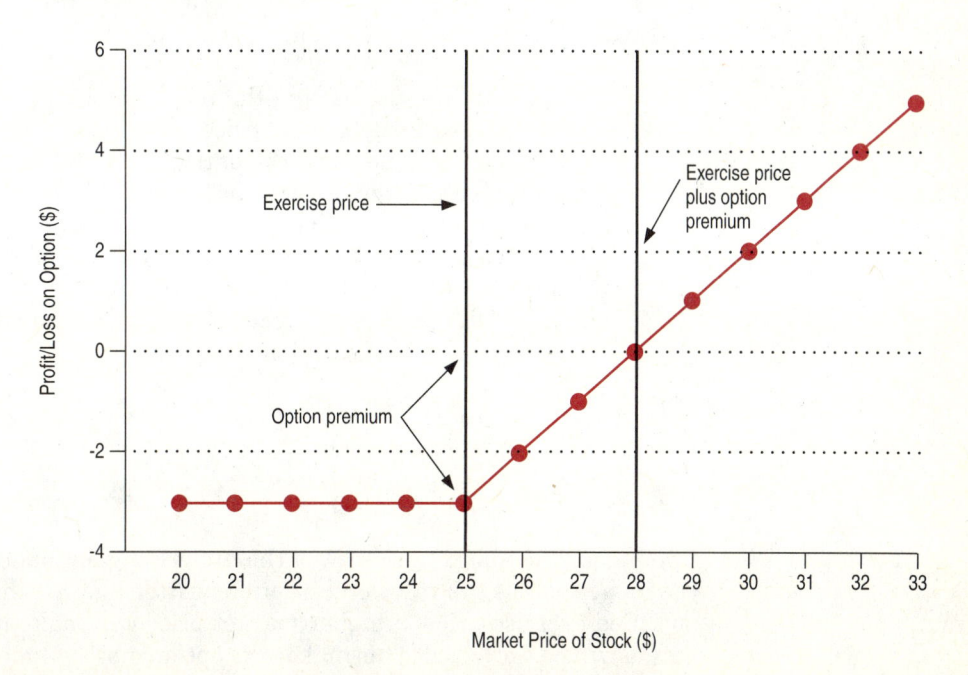

price by the amount of the option price or premium paid before a profit is possible. It is just as clear that the option holder has limited losses. The holder of the option cannot lose more than the price of the option no matter how low the price of the stock goes.

Intrinsic Value and Time Value

An in-the-money option is said to have *intrinsic value*. Intrinsic value is the difference between the option's exercise price and the spot price of the financial claim. For a call option to have intrinsic value, its current exercise price must be below the current spot price of the financial claim on which it is written. It must be in-the-money. If a call option on 100 shares of IBM stock has an exercise price of $99, and the current market or spot price is $102, then the intrinsic value of this option is $3 per share ($102 − 99). If the market price is $99 or below, it has no intrinsic value.

Typically, a marketable option will sell for more than its intrinsic value. Virtually all options that are written at exercise prices below the claim's spot price sell at some positive value. Also, most in-the-money marketable options sell for more than their intrinsic value. The difference between an options market price and its intrinsic value is known as *time value*. The time value of an option falls quickly as the option nears its exercise date.

Factors That Influence the Value of an Option

A number of factors are likely to affect the option premium or value of a particular option. These include the following:

1. The price of the underlying financial claim
2. The predetermined exercise price
3. The amount of time until the option expires, the expiration period
4. The interest rate on risk-free assets
5. The underlying volatility of the price on the optioned financial claim measured by the standard deviation of expected returns, sigma = σ
6. The dividend or interest received on the optioned financial claim during the period the option is outstanding

Let's see how each of these factors impact the value of a call option, C, by viewing each factor in isolation.

Price of the Underlying Claim

The higher the market price, P, of the underlying optioned financial claim, the higher will be the value of the option written against that claim. Given a specified exercise price, a higher market price will make it more likely the option will be exercised. This makes the option more valuable. Relationship: Higher P = Higher C

Exercise Price

The higher the exercise price, E, the lower will be the value of the option. The higher the exercise price, given a particular market price, the less chance the option will be in-the-money. This makes it less valuable. Relationship: Higher E = Lower C

Period Until Expiration

The length of time of the option period, t, will affect the value of an option. The longer the option period, the higher will be the option's value. The longer the option period the greater the chance that the option will come in-the-money. Relationship: Higher t = Higher C

Financial Claims Price Volatility

The higher the price volatility, σ, of the price of the underlying optioned claim, the higher will be the value of an option written against that claim. If the range of prices that the underlying claim may take during the option period is considered a probability distribution, then the claim with the highest standard deviation of return will have a greater value. This is because the greater the volatility of the stock's price, the greater the probability that the option will be exercised at a profit. Relationship: Higher σ = Higher C

The Risk-Free Interest Rate

The higher the interest rate, r, related to the cost of financing the underlying claim, the higher the option price. Using an option allows the investor to control an asset without tying up funds through owning it. Therefore, the higher the interest rates, such as the cost of a margin loan to finance the asset, the more valuable the option. Relationship: Higher r = Higher C

Income on the Optioned Claim

If the optioned claim produces income, I, such as stocks paying dividends or bonds interest, then the higher the income, the lower the option value. The fact that a financial claim pays income reduces the cost of holding the claim compared to holding the option. Relationship: Higher I = Lower C

Valuing Options: The Black-Scholes Option Pricing Model

In 1973, Fisher Black and Myron Scholes developed a model to value particular types of options. This model, commonly called the *Black-Scholes option pricing model,* and its many derivations have been used extensively in establishing the value of an option. Sophisticated models are used to determine the appropriate relationship between the price of an option trading on an organized exchange and the cash market price of the underlying financial claim.

The Black-Scholes model includes the first five factors in its specification:

1. The spot price
2. The exercise price
3. A measure of price volatility
4. The risk-free rate
5. The length of the option period.

This model cannot be used to incorporate income, I, received on the financial claim, however.

The model originally developed by Black-Scholes was designed for European call options. This discussion is concerned with one used to value a call option of the American variety. The model assumes no return on the underlying financial claim and that the options are marketable, that is, they can be bought and sold. This is a very important assumption, since many of the options discussed earlier in this section cannot be transferred. This means that the value of these options, absent transferability, will be less than would be calculated using the Black-Scholes methodology. The model also assumes that transaction costs are minimal and that all parties to the transaction have the same marginal tax rate.

Given these limitations, the model has been successfully used to value many types of options. The objective of the model is to estimate the market value of a call option, C. Consider a six-month call option to purchase 100 shares of IBM stock at $100 per share. This is the type of option that can be valued using a Black-Scholes type of model.

The model specification is given in Equation 5.1.

$$C = P\,N(d_1) - Ee^{-rt}\,N(d_2) \qquad [5.1]$$

C = the price of the call option, or the value of the option

P = the spot price of the underlying financial claim

E = the exercise price at the option's maturity

e = natural log e

r = continuous compound interest rate

t = remaining life of the option, expressed in years and percentages thereof

$N(d_1)$ = the cumulative probability distribution from a normal distribution for the value d_1

$N(d_2)$ = the cumulative probability distribution from a normal distribution for the value d_2

The values for d_1 and d_2 in the specification are

$$d_1 = \frac{[ln(P/E)] + rt}{\sigma\sqrt{t}} + .5\,(\sigma)\sqrt{t}$$

$$d_2 = d_1 - [\sigma\sqrt{t}]$$

σ = *the standard deviation of the continuously compounded rate of return on the underlying financial claim*

It is possible to work out an example of an option value using the Black-Scholes model. The model uses inputs that are generally available. However, it is structured for financial claims that do not pay interest or dividends. Thus, financial options on bonds generally do not fit. The values for σ must be estimated, since the distributions of returns in the future are not known. This requires using past data to estimate these parameters.

Example of Option Valuation

Consider an option to purchase a share of stock in Digital Equipment Corporation at $65 when the price of the stock is $62.50. The option will expire in four months or 120 days. The risk-free interest rate is 5 percent. The volatility of Digital Equipment stock as measured by the standard deviation of the return on the stock for the 120-day future period is estimated to be .40. Summarizing these data amounts to the following:

C = unknown option value, what we are solving for
P = $62.50
E = $65
r = .05
t = .33 years
σ = .40
d_1 = [[ln(62.5/65)] + .05(.33)/(.40)$\sqrt{(.33)}$]
      + .5(.4)$\sqrt{(.33)}$
d_1 = ((−.03922) + .0165/.229783) + .114891

$$d_1 = .016012$$

$$d_2 = .016012 - .229783 = -.213771$$

Using our estimates of d_1 and d_2 we are in a position to determine the values for the cumulative density of the normal probability distribution with a mean of zero. To do this we must use Table 5.4, which gives the cumulative probability under the unit normal probability distribution for d_1 and d_2 values of minus 3.00 to plus 2.95. Using this table it is necessary to interpolate the values of $N(d)$ for values of d between those given in the table. For example, d_1 is .016012 in Table 5.4. It falls between $N(d)$ values of .5000 and .5199. Since .016012 is between the table d_1 values .00 and .05 we interpolate

$$.016012/(.00 - .05) = 32.0240\%.$$

This percent of the range between .5000 and .5199 equates to

Table 5.4

Cumulative Normal Unit Probability Distribution: $N(d)$

d	$N(d)$	d	$N(d)$	d	$N(d)$	d	$N(d)$	d	$N(d)$	d	$N(d)$
-3.00	.0013	-2.00	.0228	-1.00	.1587	.00	.5000	1.00	.8413	2.00	.9773
-2.95	.0016	-1.95	.0256	-.95	.1711	.05	.5199	1.05	.8531	2.05	.9798
-2.90	.0019	-1.90	.0287	-.90	.1841	.10	.5398	1.10	.8643	2.10	.9821
-2.85	.0022	-1.85	.0322	-.85	.1977	.15	.5596	1.15	.8749	2.15	.9842
-2.80	.0026	-1.80	.0359	-.80	.2119	.20	.5793	1.20	.8849	2.20	.9861
-2.75	.0030	-1.75	.0401	-.75	.2266	.25	.5987	1.25	.8944	2.25	.9878
-2.70	.0035	-1.70	.0446	-.70	.2420	.30	.6179	1.30	.9032	2.30	.9893
-2.65	.0040	-1.65	.0495	-.65	.2578	.35	.6368	1.35	.9115	2.35	.9906
-2.60	.0047	-1.60	.0548	-.60	.2743	.40	.6554	1.40	.9192	2.40	.9918
-2.55	.0054	-1.55	.0606	-.55	.2912	.45	.6736	1.45	.9265	2.45	.9929
-2.50	.0062	-1.50	.0668	-.50	.3085	.50	.6915	1.50	.9332	2.50	.9938
-2.45	.0071	-1.45	.0735	-.45	.3264	.55	.7088	1.55	.9394	2.55	.9946
-2.40	.0082	-1.40	.0808	-.40	.3446	.60	.7257	1.60	.9452	2.60	.9953
-2.35	.0094	-1.35	.0885	-.35	.3632	.65	.7422	1.65	.9505	2.65	.9980
-2.30	.0107	-1.30	.0968	-.30	.3821	.70	.7580	1.70	.9554	2.70	.9965
-2.25	.0122	-1.25	.1057	-.25	.4013	.75	.7734	1.75	.9599	2.75	.9970
-2.20	.0139	-1.20	.1151	-.20	.4207	.80	.7881	1.80	.9641	2.80	.9974
-2.15	.0158	-1.15	.1251	-.15	.4404	.85	.8023	1.85	.9678	2.85	.9978
-2.10	.0179	-1.10	.1357	-.10	.4602	.90	.8159	1.90	.9713	2.90	.9981
-2.05	.0202	-1.05	.1469	-.05	.4801	.95	.8289	1.95	.9744	2.95	.9984

$[(.5199 - .5000) \times 32.024\% =] .006373$, which is the value added to .5000 we use for $N(d_1)$. These values and our estimate of the value of C are shown in Equation 5.2.

$$N(d_1) = .506373$$
$$N(d_2) = .415357$$
$$C = P\,N(d_1) - E\,e^{-rt}N(d_2)$$
$$C = 62.5\,(.506373) - 65\,(e^{-.05(.33)})\,(.415357)$$
$$C = \$5.0919 \qquad [5.2]$$

Our estimate of the value of the call option is $5.09 per share.

Sensitivity Analysis and Option Values

Table 5.5 shows the Black-Scholes determined option values for exercise price, X, risk-free rate, r, time to expiration, t, and σ. The table provides a sensitivity analysis of option values to changes in their parameters. In the analysis, σ takes the values of .4 and .6; X the values of $65, $67.5, and $70; r the values of 5 percent and 7 percent; and t the values of .33 and 1 in years.

Table 5.5

Sensitivity of Option Values to Changes in Parameters Using the Black-Scholes Option Pricing Model
(option values in dollars)

$t = .33$ years

X	\$65		\$67.5		\$70	
r	5%	7%	5%	7%	5%	7%
σ						
.4	5.09	5.27	4.15	4.31	3.35	3.49
.6	7.95	8.12	7.00	7.16	6.16	6.30

$t = 1$ year

X	\$65		\$67.5		\$70	
r	5%	7%	5%	7%	5%	7%
σ						
.4	10.19	10.73	9.21	9.73	8.31	8.78
.6	14.99	15.48	14.10	14.57	13.26	13.71

As the table shows, the values of the options given by the Black-Scholes model vary considerably. The impact of changes in σ and time to expiration have particularly large impacts on value. The risk-free rate and the exercise price have less impact for the ranges used in this analysis. A number of computer programs have been developed to permit analysts to calculate quickly the option values using this model and variations of it. This greatly simplifies the calculations for this relatively complicated formula.

Marketability and the Value of Options

The Black-Scholes model assumes that options are marketable. Marketability ensures that in-the-money options are exercised. This marketability assumption is very important to the valuations that arise from a Black-Scholes type of model. Many options are not marketable. The discussion of financial options disclosed a number that can only be exercised by one party, such as loan commitments and prepayment options. Frequently, in-the-money options, which would be expected to be exercised, are not. This is because the holder of the option may be unable to meet all the necessary conditions related to exercising the option. Or, it may not be rewarding enough to incur all the transactions costs. For example, many homeowners do not refinance a high-rate mortgage because they must pay large closing costs to exercise the prepayment option.

The Black-Scholes model will overvalue options that are not marketable. As a result, when making analyses of options that are exercisable by one entity, it is necessary to develop a probability distribution that provides an estimate of the probability that an in-the-money option will be exercised by those holding them. If only 50 percent of a particular type of in-the-money options are traditionally exercised, then the cost of writing that option would be 50 percent less than if the option were marketable.

Summary

Many financial futures and options contracts have been developed in recent years in order to facilitate risk sharing and reduce transactions costs. Financial futures contracts are used to reduce risks associated with price fluctuations of financial claims. Many financial futures contracts are traded in active markets with good marketability and an organized structure that provides limited credit risk.

Options are embedded in many financial claims and are involved in many transactions common to financial institutions. The Black-Scholes option pricing model was developed to value certain types of options. A number of factors impact on the value of options.

Financial futures contracts are legal agreements to buy (go long) or sell (go short) a specified quantity and quality of a financial claim on a specified date and place. A very small percentage of futures contracts involve delivery of the financial claim since it is customary to offset a futures position with an offsetting position before the contract expiration date.

The relationship between the spot price of a financial claim and its futures price is shown by the following equation.

$$\text{Futures contract price} = \text{Spot cash market price}$$
$$+ \text{Cost of carry of the cash claim}$$
$$- \text{Return on holding cash claim}$$

Users of the financial futures markets must be aware of the requirement to put up **margin** with a clearing house of the exchange. Margin is used to reduce the potential for a party reneging on a futures contract. Many futures contracts have **price circuit breakers** that can complicate the hedging process. The circuit breakers limit the size of a price movement over the course of a trading session.

Options are found in a wide variety of financial transactions claims. Sometimes they are hard to recognize. Options are classified as **puts** or **calls**. Puts (calls) give the option owner the right to deliver (receive) a financial claim at an agreed-upon price. The option may be an **American option** which is exercisable at any time before its exercise date or a **European option** exercisable only on its expiration date.

The **value of an option** is a function of six primary variables: (1) the optioned claim's **exercise price,** (2) the **spot price** of the claim, (3) the length of the period until **expiration,** (4) the level of **interest rates,** (5) the **underlying volatility** of the claim's investment return, and (6) any income earned on the optioned claim.

The **Black-Scholes option pricing model** and its many variations have been used for several decades to value options. The main difficulty with the model is its rigorous assumptions. These include:

1. There are no transaction costs.
2. The optioned claim pays no interest or dividend return.
3. The options are freely marketable.
4. The option is an American call option.
5. The basic parameters of the model, especially the probability distribution of returns, σ, are known.

Many options do not have **marketability.** Consequently, in valuing these types of options the analyst must estimate the probability that the option will not be exercised even though it may be in-the-money.

Questions

Chapter 5

1. What is meant by a derivative financial claim?
2. Describe the key provisions in a futures contract. What economic functions does a futures contract provide?
3. What is the role of margin in a futures contract?
4. The futures price and cash or spot price are said to converge. What is meant by convergence? Why do futures and spot prices converge?
5. What is meant by basis? Define positive and negative basis. Under what conditions of a futures contract valuation would you obtain a positive and negative basis?
6. What is an option?
7. What attributes of an option give it value?
8. Which of the following options will have greater value if all other factors are held constant:
   a. An option written on a claim with a highly volatile price or stable price?
   b. A long- or short-term option?
   c. The option whose exercise price is close to the spot price or the one whose exercise price is well above the spot price?
9. Why is the Black-Scholes option pricing model so important in finance?
10. Explain several options that are commonly found in financial claims and transactions.
11. Explain how the opportunity to allow interest to compound within a certificate of deposit or to withdraw it every quarter represents an option.
12. Explain a call and a put. Explain a European and American type of option.
13. Briefly draft a call option on one acre of land.
14. You hold an option to buy 100 shares of XYZ corporation at $23 per share. XYZ last traded at $21. Is it an in-the-money or out-of-the-money option?

Problems

Problem 5-1   Value of a Futures Contract

On January 14 Franklin Bank bought the March Treasury bond futures contract with a $100,000 par value at a closing price of 82 17/32, which also turned out to be the settlement price that day. The next day the opening price rose to 83, and later in the day the price fluctuated, reaching a high of 83 16/32 and eventually closing at a settlement price of 83 10/32. The account is marked-to-market.
   a. Show the contract value changes during the trading day (open, high, and close).
   b. How much is credited to the bank's margin account?

Problem 5-2   Futures Basis

A futures contract on Treasury bonds is available. The current yield on T-bonds is 9.8 percent. The repo rate that can be used to finance bonds is

5.9 percent. Based on this information will the basis between the futures contract price and spot or cash price for T-bonds be positive or negative? Give a reason for your answer.

Problem 5-3   Black-Scholes Option Valuation

A call option on Morgan Corporation common stock is available. The stock sells for $40 per share. It pays no dividend. The option has a nine-month exercise period. The call exercise price is $43 per share. Treasury yields are 4 percent. The option is available at a price of $4.90.

A security firm estimates the standard deviation of the return on Morgan's stock to be .35.

You have completed an analysis of the economic environment and the business activities of Morgan. Both suggest greater uncertainty in the earnings prospects for the company in the period ahead as compared to the past. As a result, you estimate the standard deviation of return to be .55.

Use the Black-Scholes model to estimate the value of the option at a standard deviation of .35 and .55. Do you think the current price of the option is too high or low? Use Table 5.4 as a guide.

Problem 5-4   Black-Scholes Option Valuation

Bob Smith has spent three years at Auto Supply Company. This large regional firm has stock listed over-the-counter. Bob was recently promoted. He received stock options for 1500 shares of Auto Supply common stock. The price of the stock is currently $6.00 per share, which is slightly below the exercise price of $6.50. The stock pays no dividend and the options can be exercised within three years.

Bob has obtained an investment banker's estimate of the standard deviation of the return on Auto Supply common stock of .20. The risk-free rate is approximately the Treasury note rate of 8 percent.

Estimate the value of Bob's options assuming they are transferrable. Does the lack of transferrability affect the value of these options? If so, why? Use Table 5.4 to estimate $N(d_1)$ and $N(d_2)$.

The Hot New Account

case 5.1

Southland Federal Savings Bank is an aggressive newly chartered federal savings bank located in the competitive Southern California market. Chartered in 1982, the bank had grown to $154 million in a single location. Its growth was fueled by fairly high rates paid in their single location, as well as the use of brokered deposits.

In 1993, Southland opened a new office in a very competitive and high-income section of their primary standard metropolitan statistical area. In order to promote the new office the president, Mr. Green, asked the marketing group to come up with some new ideas.

In March, several months before the office opened for business, Bob Stanley requested a meeting with Mr. Green. Bob was the head of marketing and branch operations. He indicated that he had a great idea for a new account.

The next week at the meeting, Bob briefed Mr. Green on the new account concept. He even provided a sample of the ad copy that would be used to promote the account. Bob was very excited with the concept. He indicated that none of the competition were offering anything like it. Moreover, focus group interviews indicated that savers considered the idea a great one. They received overwhelming support from the groups that looked at the new product.

Here is how the account was explained to Mr. Green. The account could be opened for as little as $2,500. The initial term would be nine months. The saver could add to the account any time in the first nine months up to a $50,000 total balance. The saver would still earn the rate that prevailed at the time the account was opened.

The account had another special feature. At the end of nine months, the account could be renewed at the same rate that prevailed at the time it was opened. If, however, interest rates

Southwest Savings FSB
7.75% Actual
8.13% Effective

Open a minimum $2,500 account with a nine-month initial maturity. Add at any time to a maximum of $50,000. At maturity, account can be renewed for another nine months at 7.75%, or higher if rates rise. If rates fall, continue to earn 7.75%. You can't lose with Southwest's "Competition Beater."

were to rise, the account would earn the higher rate at renewal time. Or the saver could close the account.

The first question Mr. Green asked was what the current Treasury bill rates were for comparable 9- and 18-month securities. He was given the information shown in Table C5.1. He was also told that Treasury securities with a 7.75 percent coupon maturing in nine months were selling at 100 28/32 and maturing in eighteen months at 101 4/32.

At this point in the meeting, Mr. Green called you in to answer several questions:

1. Does this account have any options embedded in it? Describe the option(s) as put or call. Describe the option(s) as clearly and carefully as possible.

2. If there are any options, are they American or European type?

3. Describe the option(s) as in-the-money or out-of-the-money.

4. Given the pricing recommendation for this account, does the institution seem to be pricing the account profitably? Why or why not?

5. Based solely on the information provided here, would you offer this program? Why or why not?

Table C5.1

Prevailing Treasury Bill Rates

Nine-month bill	6.54%
Eighteen-month bill	7.05%

Financial Markets

chapter 6

Several aspects of financial markets are discussed in this chapter. The discussion begins by identifying the different types of financial markets and then explaining how they operate. It answers the question of how markets allow participants to gather and analyze information to make informed purchases and sales of financial claims. This chapter also explains the process of arbitrage as it relates to tying together the value of claims in different geographic markets and between different periods of time. Finally, the efficiency of markets is discussed from both an operational and informational perspective.

Functions of Financial Markets

Financial markets, like markets for goods and services, provide participants with a number of benefits. The most important benefit is the reduction of transaction costs. These are the costs of gathering and communicating information about price and volume of trading. Most dealers and organized exchanges also provide safeguards for reducing the risk of settlement. Thus sellers can be assured of receiving the funds or securities they contract for on settlement day. Financial markets can also help reduce the costs of bringing buyers and sellers together. These costs are referred to as *search costs*. *Informational asymmetry* cost is reduced, as well. Informational asymmetry results when two parties to a transaction have unequal information about a financial claim involved in a transaction. Some organized markets attempt to reduce informational asymmetry by standardizing contracts and requiring security issuers to provide certain types of information. The major functions of financial markets, therefore, include

- Providing information on past and present prices and trading volume
- Reducing search costs by bringing buyers and sellers together
- Providing for standardization of contracts
- Reducing (transferring) credit risks for buyers and sellers
- Reducing informational asymmetry

By reducing transaction costs, financial markets allow for efficient transfer of capital to highly productive investments. Society benefits from these transfers, which increase economic productivity and create wealth.

The Taxonomy of Financial Markets

There are so many different types of markets for financial claims that it is necessary to describe the markets by categorizing them. This section will discuss the most common classifications of markets. It is important to note that these classifications are not mutually exclusive; that is, financial claims can fit several of the classifications discussed.

Types of Markets: Primary and Secondary

The first classification relates to the markets for newly created financial claims and the market for trading existing financial claims. The *primary market* is where financial claims are created. The primary market includes such transactions as the origination of new car loans or business loans. It also involves the underwriting of new common stocks or bonds sold to investors through investment banking firms. A home mortgage used to purchase a house is created in the primary market. When the Treasury sells newly issued bonds, they are sold in the primary market as well.

Once a claim has been created, any trading of the claim is said to occur in the *secondary market*. Secondary markets are this country's largest and most organized financial markets. The terms *stock market* and *bond market* are usually references to the secondary market. The largest secondary markets in our country are those for U.S. Treasury securities, common stocks, and mortgage-backed securities.

Types of Markets: Money Market and Capital Market

Financial markets are also categorized by the time period over which the funds are used. The *money market* refers to the market for short-term high-quality debt instruments. This class refers to the market for debt issued with a maturity of one year or less. The following is a list of primary securities found in the money market:

- Treasury bills
- Federal agency discount notes
- Commercial paper
- Negotiable certificates of deposit
- Repurchase agreements
- Banker's acceptances

The *capital market* is the market for long-term funds. They are used for more permanent financing purposes. This classification refers to financial claims issued with maturities over five years. The primary claims found in the capital markets include

- Treasury bonds
- Federal agency bonds
- Corporation long-term bonds
- State and local bonds
- Common stock
- Preferred stock
- Mortgages

Financial claims with maturities in the one- to five-year maturity class do not meet the customary definitions of either the money or capital market. They are referred to as the intermediate market. There is sometimes ambiguity as to which market they should be classified in.

Types of Markets: Dealers and Organized Exchanges

There are two different institutional structures for marketing financial claims: *dealer markets* and *organized exchanges*. The majority of transactions are handled in dealer markets. These markets are operated by one or more security dealers. Dealers may be investment banks, commercial banks, or any other intermediary that is able to hold an inventory in the financial claim and make markets in it.

Several of the largest dealer markets are for U.S. Treasury securities, the over-the-counter stock market, and the mortgage-backed security markets. The Treasury sells all its new issues of U.S. government securities to institutional investors, including commercial banks and security dealers, and in small denominations through the Federal Reserve Banks.

The *over-the-counter market (OTC)* in common stocks is well known as the market for thousands of corporate stocks that are not listed on organized exchanges. The firms that form the OTC each make a market in one or more stocks. Some of these dealers have created a national automated pricing network called the National Association of Securities Dealers Automatic Quotations (NASDAQ). This system provides automated bid and ask prices for the dealers who make markets in the OTC stocks. This automated system provides a single source for identifying prices, when as many as 10 to 15 different dealers may make a market in a particular stock.

Dealers in mortgage-backed securities such as GNMA, FNMA, and FHLMC mortgage-backed securities are among the largest traders in terms of dollar volume of transactions. In some periods, the trading volume of these securities has exceeded that of Treasury securities. The major dealers in mortgage-backed securities communicate with each other electronically, each sharing their bid and ask prices for various types of mortgage securities.

Organized exchanges provide more formal markets in a variety of financial claims. A relatively small volume of claims are actually traded in organized exchanges. The volume of trading is falling relative to the trading by dealers. This trend could change, however, with the growth in computerized trading markets.

Several organized exchanges, such as the New York Stock Exchange (NYSE) and CBOT, are institutions with worldwide reputations. These exchanges were formed at a time when communication technology was not well developed. As a result, a single physical location was an efficient way to bring buyers and sellers, or their representatives, together. Because of the growing average size of transactions generating from large institutional investors and improved communication technologies, organized markets are declining in relative importance. Dealers are now bringing large institutional buyers and sellers together outside of the exchange.

The matching of buy and sell orders is done by the specialists at the NYSE and by the members at the CBOT. The specialist acts as the intermediary at the NYSE, constantly changing the price of the security to match the orders to buy and sell. Specialists are also charged with the responsibility of maintaining an orderly market. This involves taking positions in the stock to avoid large price fluctuations. The specialists have the advantage of being the only party able to view the list of outstanding orders to buy and sell at limit prices. *Limit orders* are orders to execute a buy or sell of a stock at a predetermined price should the stock hit the limit price. Seeing the outstanding limit orders is a great advantage, since it permits the specialist to gauge the depth of the market and whether there are more buyers than sellers at or near the current price. This changed somewhat in 1992, as the order book for certain NYSE-traded securities became publicly available. This sharply reduced the advantage of the specialist by making the list of outstanding bid and ask orders available. This information provides a sense of the depth of the market.

Table 6.1 provides a listing of the major types of financial claims and the primary markets in which they are traded.

Table 6.1

Primary Claims and the Markets Where They Trade

Claims	Markets: Organized Exchanges and/or Dealers
U.S. Treasury and agencies	Investment banks
	Large commercial banks
Mortgage related securities	Investment banks
	Large commercial banks
State and local securities	Commercial banks
	Investment banks
Corporate bonds	Investment banks
	New York Bond Exchange
	American Bond Exchange
Common stock	Investment banks
	New York Stock Exchange
	American Stock Exchange
	Regional stock exchanges
Options	Chicago Board Options Exchange
	Investment bankers
	New York, Philadelphia, American, and Pacific exchanges
Financial futures	Chicago Board of Trade
	Chicago Mercantile Exchange
	New York Futures Exchange

Types of Markets: Spot and Forward

Markets for financial claims are further classified on the basis of whether the market represents purchases and sales of a claim for immediate delivery, known as a *spot market,* or for future delivery, known as a *forward cash market*. An example of a spot-market transaction would be the purchase or sale of shares of stock traded on the NYSE. Rules governing this transaction require that the seller deliver the stock and the buyer the funds within five business days from the date of the transaction, known as the *trade date*. The date the funds are due or the securities delivered is known as the *settlement date*.

A forward cash transaction usually involves a dealer who is willing to purchase or sell a financial claim for delivery at some future date. The delivery could take place 30, 60, or 180 days or more in the future. One of the largest forward cash markets is the home-mortgage secondary market. Originators of home mortgages frequently sell their mortgages to secondary market mortgage firms such as the FNMA and the FHLMC in a forward cash market operated by these firms. Firms also create mortgage-backed securities guaranteed by the GNMA, which are typically sold in the forward cash market before they are created. The forward cash market provides the seller with a guaranteed price for the security sold. It can also be used to hedge price risk.

Types of Markets: Human Interface Versus Computers

The computer is transforming financial markets worldwide. Financial markets in some countries are embracing computerized markets faster than the United States. This is partly due to the fact that the United States has established markets that rely on people, and changing to computer-operated markets would result in painful dislocations.

Computerized trading has taken on a variety of forms. At one level, automation is used simply to improve information flow on prices and transaction volume. These systems allow markets to be tied together worldwide. At another level, automation executes trades and extends trading hours, thus replacing people-based market systems. A number of computerized matching systems have been developed, and they compete with the major organized exchanges. Some of these systems permit off-hours trading after the organized market is closed. In May 1991, the NYSE responded to the inroads made by these systems by extending hours to allow trades to occur at the closing prices of each day.

Computers are making progress in the markets for derivatives, futures, and options as well. Several worldwide commodity exchanges are developing communication systems that will provide an interchange of contracts between them. The primary purpose of this effort is to extend the length of the trading day. Some international efforts also provide automated matching of orders.

With so many classifications for types of financial markets, it may seem as if there is no way to achieve rational pricing. Bringing about orderly pricing between markets and overtime is the role of arbitrage.

Arbitrage

As explained in Chapter 5, *arbitrage* ties prices of financial claims together in various markets. It is the act of buying a claim or group of claims in one or more markets and then selling the same claim or like claim in a different market or on a different delivery date. Arbitrage helps to establish that prices of claims are consistent across different markets and through time. It also provides consistency for claims that trade separately and those that are packaged into new forms, such as hybrid securities. The entity or person performing the arbitrage is known as the *arbitrageur*.

In a theoretically pure arbitrage transaction, the arbitrageur is able to create a portfolio of financial claims that cost nothing to hold and that produce a positive return with no chance of loss. In practice, there are many risks and significant transactions costs that make pure costless arbitrage impossible. However, less-than-perfect arbitrage transactions occur in our financial markets all the time, and they can sometimes produce substantial gains for the participants. Let's consider a few of these.

Arbitrage is a process that brings about a high degree of price consistency for financial claims that trade in two or more markets. Consider a share of stock that has an ask price of $52 per share and a bid price of $51.50 per share on the NYSE. An investor may notice that the stock has an ask price of $51 per share and a bid price of $50.75 on the Pacific Stock Exchange (PSE). At this point, the investor could become an arbitrageur. The arbitrageur would buy the claim at the low ask price in one market and immediately sell it in the other market, the NYSE, at $51.50. Assuming that the commissions and other transaction costs are less than $.50 per share, the arbitrageur makes a profit. This is an example of an arbitrage across different markets.

Arbitrage also takes place through time. Consider the earlier discussion of spot and forward markets. A financial claim's price should have a consistent relationship between buying it today in the spot market or in the future in the forward cash market. If the claim is an interest-paying security, then the relationship between the spot price and the forward price will depend on the cost of borrowing money to purchase the claim in the spot market, rather than waiting and purchasing it in the forward market. The forward market price must reflect the cost of holding the security in inventory until the forward delivery date. If the relationship between these two prices is not consistent with what theoretically sound valuation techniques would predict, then a profitable arbitrage can take place.

Consider the following situation. The investor is considering the following arbitrage transaction involving the spot and forward markets in a long-term Treasury security. A 20-year Treasury bond with a 10 percent coupon rate, $r_{20 \text{ T-bond}}$, is currently available to be bought in the 180-day forward market at a price of 100 16/32, F_{180}. The investor is able to borrow for six months at a six-month rate of 6 percent, $r_{6 \text{ month}}$. The spot price, S, of a comparable 20-year Treasury security is 101 4/32. If the investor borrows funds to buy the Treasury security in the spot market, and immediately sells it forward for delivery in 180 days, it would produce the following transactions and cash flows:

Transactions Undertaken

1. Borrow $1,000,000 at 6 percent per annum
2. Buy 20-year T-bonds in the spot market at 101 4/32 @ $1,000,000/ 101.125 = $988,875.15 par value Treasuries

3. Sell 20-year bonds in the forward market at 100 8/32 @ 9888.7515 × $100 8/32 = $993,819.53 to be received in 180 days

Summary of Cash Flows

1. Repay loan used to buy bonds − $1,000,000.00
2. Pay interest on $1,000,000 at 3 percent (6%/2) for 180 days − $30,000.00
3. Receive interest on $988,875.15 of T-bonds at 5 percent (10%/2) for 180 days ($988,875.15 × .05 =) + $49,443.76
4. Receive proceeds from forward sale of T-bonds + $993,819.53
5. Gain (or loss) + $13,263.29

This example of an arbitrage between the spot and forward cash markets in securities shows that a profitable arbitrage is possible. However, this group of transactions was accomplished in an artificial environment. This is probably why it produced a profit. First, there were no transaction costs. Second, the bid and ask prices of the securities were equal. Third, the arbitrageur was able to borrow 100 percent of the bond's value. These conditions would not be true in a real market situation.

There is a condition called *interest parity* that works to eliminate pure arbitrage possibilities between the spot and forward markets. Interest parity is an economic condition that relates the forward price of a security to its spot price. The relationship is between the level of the borrowing interest rate for the period covering the time between the spot and forward periods and the interest rate on the security to be delivered.

If interest parity had been in effect in the previous example, the forward price of the security would have been somewhat lower than 100 8/32. In fact, it would have been just low enough to wipe out the profit of $13,262.29. That would have occurred at a price approximately 1 5/32 below the price of 100 8/32. Interest parity is derived from the simple calculation shown in Equation 6.1:

$$F_{180} = S \times [(1 + r_{6\,month})/(1 + r_{20\,T\text{-}bond})]$$
$$= 101\ 4/32\ [(1.03)/(1.05)]$$
$$= 101\ 4/32\ [.9810]$$
$$= 99\ 3/32 \tag{6.1}$$

An easy way to understand the relationship of the forward and cash prices under interest parity is to consider Equation 6.2. This provides the interest parity identity.

$$F_t = S \times [\,(1 + r_{fc})\,/\,(1 + r_c)] \tag{6.2}$$

where:

F_t = Forward cash market price at period t

S = Spot price

r_{fc} = Cost of financing the claim

r_c = Interest return on the claim

Arbitrage transactions are also common in the markets for derivative and hybrid securities. Like financial futures contracts, options prices are related to the value of the underlying collateral or to the price of another financial claim. Chapter 4 discussed how it is possible to purchase Treasury securities at one price and strip the coupons to sell zero coupon securities at a higher price. This is a form of arbitrage. The arbitrageur is also an active player in corporate acquisitions. The arbitrageur attempts to buy stock in potential takeover companies that are subject to a tender offer or those that are expected to be the subject of an offer.

The Role of the Trader

Security dealers have *traders* who work to eliminate most arbitrage profit opportunities. Market efficiency is accomplished by the thousands of traders who work for financial intermediaries, many of whom are looking for potential arbitrage profits. When they find these opportunities, their actions to profit from them eliminate the profit potential. Consider an example. In the case of the forward and cash market example previously discussed, it was possible to profit from buying Treasuries in the cash market and selling them forward. This would prompt security dealers to bid up the price in the spot market and depress it in the forward market, thus eliminating the arbitrage profit.

Most trading occurs among security dealers. These organizations, primarily investment banks and large commercial banks, are set up to be market-makers and brokers for a select group of financial claims in which they choose to specialize. Traders are usually allowed to inventory securities for the account of the dealer. In fact, securities held in inventory are the primary assets of investment dealers heavily involved in trading. Trading for the dealer's own account is a risky activity, since the dealer must bear the price risk for any securities held in the portfolio.

Traders earn a profit by performing two basic functions. First they act as brokers, buying from one customer or dealer and selling to another customer or dealer. Second, they spend considerable effort looking for profitable investment and trading opportunities. Some of these opportunities are similar to the arbitrage transactions discussed in the previous section, representing investment securities thought to be undervalued or overvalued relative to other securities.

The trader is the focal point for all information on a particular claim. The dealer's sales force calls on customers and feeds the trader with information about the claims customers desire to buy and sell and the prices they are willing to execute orders at. In this respect, the trader is the keeper of the limit-order book that is available to the specialist in the NYSE. This information allows the trader to make informed decisions about whether the next change in price is likely to be up or down.

Traders also talk to other traders at competitor dealer's organizations, since they do much of their business with one another. Dealers also develop proprietary information systems to communicate among themselves information on current bid and ask prices and recent transactions. Many analytical students of finance are attracted to the trading function within dealer organizations, since it uses state-of-the-art financial models for valuing different types of financial claims. The other attraction is the isolated multimillion-dollar bonuses received by successful traders on Wall Street in New York. The growth in computerized order-matching effectively eliminates the trader's brokerage function. It also makes it much more difficult for the trader to take dealer positions in securities and to predict future prices because they no longer have access to the order book.

The ability to make trading profits depends on the efficiency of financial markets. Many economic and financial models assume that markets operate efficiently. By efficiently we mean that financial claims are correctly priced. Many traders believe otherwise. They search out situations in which the prices of certain financial claims are affected by institutional forces that provide arbitrage profit opportunities. Consider the fact that in late 1989, Congress passed a law requiring that all savings and loans stop buying junk bonds. It also required that bonds held by savings and loans be sold in five years. As a result, most of the large holders failed. Around the same time, the insurance regulators around the country put a limit on the amount of junk bonds that could be held by life insurance companies. All this publicity caused individuals to pull money out of junk bond mutual funds. Then, the government agency that took over the failed savings and loans began to sell the bonds aggressively in 1990. The result was a large supply and virtually no demand. Prices plummeted. The astute investor would have factored into their valuation model for these bonds the institutional factors at work. Once the government sold most of their bonds, the market stabilized and prices rose rapidly in 1991. Was the market pricing junk bonds efficiently? The economist would say yes and the trader no.

Globalization of Financial Markets

It is the investor's objective to seek the highest risk-adjusted rates of return on available investments. In the 1980s, investment opportunities expanded rapidly as international markets opened up to greater international capital flows. While most international capital flows take place through institutional investors, it is now possible for individuals to invest in the common stock of foreign companies and to purchase shares of mutual funds that hold foreign stock and bond portfolios. Consider the data in Table 6.2. They show the foreign purchases and sales of U.S. bonds with maturities in excess of one year in 1980 and 1990. The compound annual rate of growth in this trading was 41.13 percent per annum over the ten-year period. In 1990, the trading volume reached almost $4 trillion. Table 6.3 on page 152 shows the U.S. purchases and sales of foreign bonds with maturities over one year within the same time period. In this case the growth in the annual rate and equity trading has been almost as dramatic.

Investors' demands to diversify investments worldwide and seek higher risk-adjusted returns on investment possibilities outside of their own country are changing financial markets in very significant ways. The international demand for twenty-four-hour trading has resulted in the expansion of trading hours and new computerized trading systems. Investment dealers have had to expand internationally by opening offices in the major financial capitals around the world. Even individuals now have opportunities to invest in foreign securities directly and through investment funds.

Table 6.2

**Transaction Volume of U.S. Long-Term Bonds by Foreign Investors
1980 and 1990
(dollars in billions)**

Foreign Country	1980 Purchases and Sales of U.S. Securities	1990 Purchases and Sales of U.S. Securities	Compound Annual Growth Rate, 1980–1990
France	1.16	26.24	36.66%
Germany	7.75	85.18	27.09
United Kingdom	42.51	1,120.29	38.70
Total Europe	**60.65**	**1,578.17**	**38.53**
Japan	6.81	1,476.04	71.24
Canada	3.35	136.26	44.86
Total Worldwide	**122.86**	**3,851.99**	**41.13**

Source: Peter A. Abken. "Globalization of Stock, Futures, and Options Markets." *Economic Review,* Federal Reserve Bank of Atlanta (July/August 1991): p. 3.

Table 6.3

**Transaction Volume of Foreign Long-Term Bonds by U.S. Investors
1980 and 1990
(dollars in billions)**

Country Issuing Bonds	1980 Purchases and Sales	1990 Purchases and Sales	Compound Annual Growth Rate 1980–1990
France	1.28	30.17	37.22%
Germany	.88	34.14	44.24
United Kingdom	12.23	228.10	33.99
Total Europe	**18.68**	**375.25**	**34.99**
Japan	4.00	80.21	34.96
Canada	4.63	111.39	37.46
Total Worldwide	**34.98**	**649.50**	**33.93**

Source: Ibid.

Euromarkets

Euromarkets is a general term reserved for financial transactions carried out in currencies different from the domestic currency of the country in which the transaction takes place. The first major Euromarket transactions occurred in Europe as a result of a large build-up of U.S. dollars. This was caused by a balance-of-trade deficit between Europe and the United States. European exporters built up large U.S. dollar holdings that typically would be converted into their domestic currency. However, there was also demand for dollars by European borrowers. Consequently, some major European banks began to accept deposits in dollars and to lend in dollar-denominated loans. Foreign owners of U.S. dollars found it more advantageous to convert their dollar deposits drawn against U.S. banks into dollar deposits in banks in their own countries. Thus the *Eurodollar market* was born.

    The Eurodollar market got a real boost from the 1974 rise in oil prices. Middle East oil was priced in U.S. dollars. This resulted in oil export countries building up large holdings of U.S. dollars, many of which were invested in Eurodollar deposits in European banks and branches of U.S. banks in Europe. Active Euromarkets have developed in German marks, Japanese yen, and Swiss francs. The Switzerland activity is largely a result of the large foreign-owned deposits held in Swiss banks, which are available for investment in Swiss denominated loans and bonds.

Loans denominated in U.S. dollars that are made in the Euromarket are typically priced at a premium to the *London interbank offer rate (LIBOR)*. This is an interest rate at which European and British banks lend each other short-term funds. This rate was largely chosen because London is the most active international banking market outside the United States, specifically New York City.

Euromarkets have also developed in corporate bonds. Large corporations with recognizable worldwide names have the advantage of issuing U.S. dollar-denominated bonds in the Euromarkets. Foreign companies issue bonds purchased by U.S. investors as well.

Legal and Ethical Issues

Michael Milken: Junk Bonds and Rigged Market?

Few financial figures evoke the emotional responses Michael Milken creates. Mr. Milken joined the investment banking firm of Drexel Burnham Lambert in the mid-1960s and almost single-handedly created the new-issue junk bond market.

To many, Milken was a financial genius who worked to create a market that would provide funding for up-and-coming entrepreneurial companies and others who wanted to eliminate bureaucratic waste. Milken was a model of unostentatious living, despite annual incomes that once exceeded $500 million.

To others, Milken was a crafty and unethical charlatan who provided the financial resources for breaking up fine companies, resulting in losses of jobs and corporate bankruptcies. He was also accused of using unfair means to entice unknowing buyers to purchase high-risk investments.

In early 1990, Michael Milken was indicted on numerous counts of securities fraud. The charges included racketeering, insider trading, and stock manipulation. He eventually pleaded guilty to six violations of security law and agreed to pay $600 million in fines to cover potential losses. The judge in the case eventually estimated that investors lost about $300,000. Milken was sentenced to ten years in prison with the proviso that the sentence would be shortened if he contributed information concerning other legal violations in which he had knowledge.

Milken has also been subject to numerous civil lawsuits. The most controversial was a suit brought by the Resolution Trust Corporation alleging that he rigged the junk bond market and contributed to the failure of a number of savings and loans. This suit really goes to the heart of whether the junk bond market was an efficient market or a type of Ponzi scheme. The critics of the suit point to the fact that after the fall in the value of most junk bonds in the fall and winter of 1990, the market rebounded vigorously in 1991. They claimed that in true Ponzi schemes, the values of the assets involved don't recover. They argue that an embarrassed government regulatory bureaucracy is trying to take public attention off its own poor supervisory practices to focus attention on a scapegoat. Substantively, the RTC suit does raise questions about the nature of financial markets, the role of dealers, and the ability of one dealer to control prices. The suit was settled out of court.

The Efficiency of the Financial Claims Markets

Financial claims markets differ in the way they operate and in the way information impacts each market. The market for shares of IBM stock on the NYSE is generally considered an efficient market. Alternatively, the market for the paintings of a relatively obscure Austrian artist would be considered inefficient. Operationally, the NYSE provides efficient execution of a purchase or sale due to its central location and well-developed information system. IBM is also a highly traded claim with many buyers and sellers on the NYSE. The market for the Austrian's paintings, on the other hand, is not centralized, standardized, or of high volume. Information about the price of the artist's recently purchased paintings would be difficult to obtain. The IBM market is both operationally and informationally efficient, while the Austrian's painting market is not. Operational and informational efficiency of financial markets will be discussed in this section, and the question of why market efficiency is important will be answered.

Why Efficiency Matters

The efficiency of a market is extremely important to financial participants. According to Fama (1991), financial markets are said to be efficient if current prices reflect all available information. A weaker version of this definition was offered by Jensen (1978), who believes that prices reflect information to the extent that the marginal benefits from acting on the information reflect the marginal costs. Both economists agree that market efficiency is impacted by information costs and transaction costs. Since these costs are real, and sometimes significant, we can be reasonably certain that the stronger definition of market efficiency will not hold up. However, depending on the financial claim and the nature of the market in which it trades, it is possible to come close to that condition.

The cost of converting loans and securities into cash for liquidity needs is affected by efficiency conditions. It also affects the time needed to complete a transaction. Financial institutions involved in trading know that large transactions can be monitored by other dealers. These dealers will take advantage of known sellers or buyers by bidding up the price of the security in demand or short-selling the security a dealer is trying to unload. *Short-selling* describes a situation in which a financial claim is sold by borrowing it from an owner and later buying it in the market to replace the borrowed security. Short-sellers expect market prices to fall. They hope to sell high and buy low. Consider the government's liquidation of junk bonds in 1990. Dealers knew that when they received a phone call from the government or a savings and loan they were talking to a known seller. Institutions involved in hedging are also interested in market efficiency, since they must offset transactions in the futures and forward cash markets.

The risk in many of these transactions involves the ability of a market to absorb a transaction without a large price change. Another important factor is the transaction costs represented by the difference between the claim's bid and ask price. The greater the liquidity of a market, the more likely a transaction will not affect price, and the narrower the bid-ask spread. Sometimes the risk of a transaction is determined, in part, by the volume of trading in a specified financial contract. A futures market hedger may be forced to use a futures contract in a claim other than the one being hedged, because that futures contract has better liquidity.

Operational and Informational Efficiency

There are two ways to look at market efficiency. One way is from the perspective of the operational efficiency. This is a characteristic of how the market functions, with most of the emphasis on transaction costs. The other way is to look at it from the perspective of *informational efficiency*. Here the emphasis is on information costs. The concern in this case is whether market prices respond to available information. A favorable result would be market prices that closely approximate theoretical value of the financial claim.

Operational Efficiency

The operational efficiency of financial markets is very important to participants. Operationally efficient markets permit buyers and sellers to transact large volumes of financial claims with the confidence that the transaction itself will not affect the price of the claim. In an inefficient market, there is potential that the transaction costs will unduly affect price.

The attributes of operational market efficiency include

1. Availability of price information

2. Price continuity, or the potential that large transactions will impact price
3. Transaction costs

Availability of Price Information

The advances in information and communication technologies used in global financial markets have substantially improved the availability of information concerning the prices at which financial claims trade. Today, it is possible for even the individual investor to obtain on-line real-time information on common stock prices on the NYSE and many other markets. The rapid growth in the number of on-line price information services covering stocks, foreign currencies, and debt securities has significantly improved the efficiency of these markets.

Let's look at the example of the IBM stock and the Austrian paintings. The owner of IBM shares has information about the latest prices on the NYSE. Indeed, it will soon be possible to obtain quotations concerning the current number of shares bid (orders to purchase) and asked (orders to sell) outstanding at any time. Price and volume information are readily available. The market also is characterized by a minimal difference between the bid and ask prices.

It would be far more difficult for a potential buyer or seller to determine the prices at which the Austrian painter's art was sold. The seller might have to call several art dealers to determine if any recent transactions have taken place. Moreover, it would be difficult to determine from this information alone how similar in quality the paintings that were sold are to the one being offered.

Price Continuity

Another nice feature for the IBM market is that it is possible to buy or sell millions of dollars of stock without affecting the price significantly. This market is said to have *price continuity*. The market is said to be liquid. Few markets are able to sustain large trades without substantial changes in prices. However, many of the U.S. markets for financial claims are exceptions. Our markets for U.S. Treasury securities experience daily trading of approximately $100 billion. These markets are very efficient from a price-continuity perspective.

Table 6.4 shows the open interest for five futures contracts trading on the CBOT. It is clear from the open interest that the price continuity and the depth of these markets are likely to be much better in the Treasury bond contracts than the other financial futures contracts. This means that many participants in this market will find it necessary to use the contract with the best liquidity or price continuity, even though another contract may be more similar to the claim being hedged.

Table 6.4

Open Interest for Various Futures Contracts on the Chicago Board of Trade November 4, 1990

Contract	Open Interest
Treasury bond December	267,938
Treasury note December	63,816
5-year note December	73,114
2-year note December	6,996
Treasury bill December	36,546

Source: *Wall Street Journal* (November 5, 1990).

Transaction Costs

When someone buys or sells stock listed on the NYSE, the *transaction cost* is not substantial. Full-service and discount brokers will make the trade for a very small percentage of the total transaction. In addition, the market allows us to complete the transaction in just a few minutes. Usually, the stockbroker on a major exchange can execute an order and receive confirmation that it has been executed within a minute or two. The timeliness feature is another aspect of a liquid market.

Let's consider the case of the Austrian painting. In this case, it will probably be necessary to find an appraiser that has knowledge and appreciation of this artist's paintings. This will also involve shipping the desired painting to New York or Europe. The cost of the appraisal may be substantial and the quote only a rough estimate of value. Once this is completed, it will probably be necessary to retain an auction house to list the painting.

If it is sold successfully, the seller will pay at least 10 percent of the value to the auction house for providing a market. This transaction may take several months to complete. Moreover, if the seller has several paintings by the same Austrian artist, he or she will find that there are probably very few buyers. Consequently, this market can only absorb a few of these paintings at a time.

Circuit Breakers and Market Efficiency

Circuit breakers are rules incorporated into organized exchanges that protect market participants from operational market inefficiencies. The primary purpose of a circuit breaker is to reduce the possibility of excess price discontinuity. Such operational inefficiencies may be the result of other rules governing the market.

There are three types of circuit breakers. The first type prohibits trading when the balance of purchase to sale orders is significantly uneven. Under these conditions a circuit breaker is used so that market illiquidity does not lead to abnormal price fluctuations. This is called an *order imbalance circuit breaker*. A good example of this type of circuit breaker is used in the NYSE. It does not allow common stocks to open at the bell if an imbalance of purchase or sales orders exists. Order imbalances were a major issue in both the October 19, 1987 and October 16, 1989 stock collapses. During both of these days a significant number of Standard and Poor's (S&P) 500 companies trading on the NYSE did not open within the first half hour of the trading day. Following the 1987 crash, price limits were imposed on the S&P 500 futures contracts. An order imbalance circuit breaker triggers a trading secession if the index falls by a specific amount.

A second type of circuit breaker is designed to limit the amplitude of price increases or decreases. This is referred to as a *price-limit circuit breaker*. Many commodity futures contracts have daily limits on the maximum range of price. Once that daily maximum is reached, the trading stops until the next trading day, and a new limit is set from the previous day's close.

A third type of circuit breaker relates to an excessive volume of transactions. These are referred to as *volume circuit breakers*. In 1968, before the brokerage industry was properly automated, excessive trading volume taxed the ability of a number of these firms to handle the back-office bookkeeping and settlement duties. This resulted in the need to occasionally shorten trading hours and eliminate trading days until the problems were resolved. In the 1987 and 1989 stock market drops, the volume problems were related to the ability of the stock specialists to match sales orders with purchases in a timely manner.

One of the major issues raised by the existence of circuit breakers is that they can increase the credit risk of various participants in the financial markets. Circuit breakers both restrict liquidity and constrain price movements. As a result, a lender who takes securities as collateral for a loan, such as a margin loan, will experience an increase in risk exposure if a circuit breaker inhibits the ability of the lender to sell the stock to meet a margin call. Establishing the value of the collateral is also a problem when a circuit breaker is triggered.

Circuit breakers also increase the risk of loss in hedging transactions. Many hedges involve the purchase of a futures contract to offset price volatility of the cash market financial claim. Typically the hedge is lifted simultaneously with the execution of the cash market transaction. If the cash market transaction settlement occurs when the futures market is shut down due to a circuit breaker, the hedge may produce an unexpected loss.

Informational Efficiency

Thus far, the focus has been on the mechanical operations of markets. Equally important is how markets respond to information. If many potential investors believe that the price of a financial claim is undervalued, based on information made available to them, then their reaction will be to purchase the claim and drive up its price to the appropriate equilibrium level. Conversely, a claim that is thought to be overvalued will be sold by a number of owners driving the price down. It is profit motive that drives prices of claims up and down based on the valuations of buyers and sellers using information that is available.

An informationally efficient market is one that adjusts to new information quickly and in a way that is consistent with financial valuation theory. There has been considerable empirical testing of the efficiency of financial markets during the last several decades. These tests have endeavored to describe the informational efficiency of various markets as

1. Weak-form market efficient
2. Semistrong-form market efficient
3. Strong-form market efficient

Weak-form Market Efficiency

A market described as *weak-form market efficient* is a market in which past claim-price information provides no useful valuation information about future prices. Indeed, weak-form market efficiency strictly means that the expected value of the price of the next transaction is the current price. This hypothesis of market efficiency only relates to very short-term periods, when no new information enters the market that would influence the value of the good or claim.

This market efficiency standard does not preclude the possibility that the long-term value of a claim changes. New information will result in a reevaluation of the intrinsic value of the claim. The theory of market efficiency effectively discounts the theory of charting and technical analysis, which is based on analysis of past price and trading volume.

The theory that past prices of a financial claim are of no value in predicting future prices is also known as the *random walk hypothesis*. This theory simply states that the price in period $t + 1$ is independent of the price in period t. Illustrating an example of a simple random walk is much like tossing a coin for heads and tails. If a financial claim with the price of $10.00 has $.25 added for heads and $.25 subtracted for tails we will get a graph that looks like Exhibit 6.1 after 25 throws.

Most empirical work on stock and bond prices confirms the random walk hypothesis.

Semistrong-form Market Efficiency

The *semistrong-form theory* of market efficiency holds that the current value of a financial claim incorporates all generally or publicly available information about the claim. The market is semistrong-form efficient if the price of a claim responds almost immediately to new information. In the case of financial instruments, a bond's value will respond almost instantaneously to new information about Federal Reserve policy changes and inflation data, for example, while in the case of a common stock, the value adjusts equally fast to new unanticipated information on the firm's earnings prospects.

The semistrong-form theory of efficiency is much more difficult to test empirically than the weak-form hypothesis. Such a test typically requires

Exhibit 6.1

Price History of Random Walk (Heads = +$.25 and Tails = −$.25)

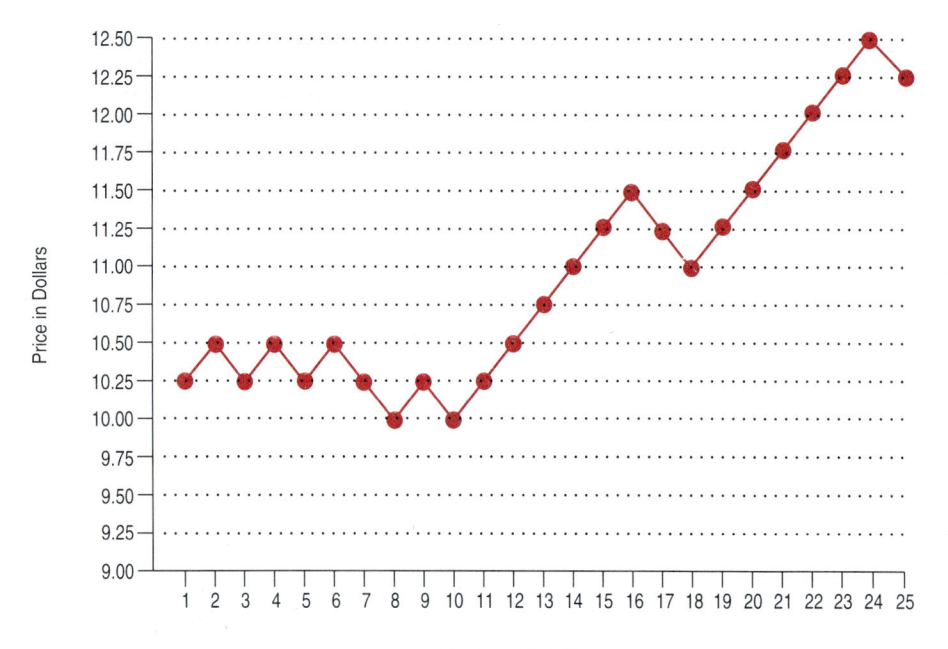

Number of Coin Tosses

identifying a valuation model that depends on a particular type of information. It is then necessary to carefully identify when announcements of this particular type of information take place. Frequently, this also requires knowing the difference between the market participant's expectations of what this information will be and what is actually announced. Finally, it is necessary to separate price changes resulting from the specific information being tested from all other information that may influence value. Overall, the empirical testing has confirmed the semistrong-form theory.

Strong-form Market Efficiency

Strong-form market efficiency goes one step further and states that current prices reflect all information available to specialists, security analysts, and corporate insiders. Specialists include economists and other market observers whose job it is to forecast the economy, Federal Reserve policies, inflation, and interest rates. On a superficial level, if specialists could systematically forecast price information, most specialists would be very wealthy, but we observe in the real world that these specialists are not gaining from this specialized information. On a more technical level, empirical testing of specialist's forecasts relative to market values has not produced investment performance significantly better than a random selection of stocks. Security analysts have also been tested with respect to their ability to systematically show better than market returns. Again, the results don't indicate that their information produces much more than normal returns.

The last group are corporate insiders, defined broadly to include anyone privy to nonpublic information. The empirical testing does indicate that insiders have meaningful access to information that can affect value. For this reason, insiders are prohibited from using their information for profit. Unfortunately, it is often difficult to determine who an insider is and what information is available at a particular time. To help categorize this information, publicly held companies are required to file monthly reports with the Security and Exchange Commission revealing every purchase and sale of the company's securities by officers and directors during the previous month.

Legal and Ethical Issues

Ivan Boesky: Insider Trading

Insider trading took on new meaning when Ivan Boesky, once a famous arbitrageur, was alleged to have profited from insider information obtained from an employee of Drexel Burnham Lambert. Ivan Boesky became the focal point in the high-stakes argument over whether hostile takeovers were good or bad for the U.S. economy. Even though Boesky was caught "red-handed," his actions created a national debate over the use of insider information and the role of junk bonds in hostile takeovers.

Boesky, a lawyer, eschewed the profession in the late 1960s to become involved in financial arbitrage. By 1986, he was reportedly worth several hundred million dollars as a result of taking large equity positions in companies that became takeover candidates. Boesky's downfall occurred when an employee of Drexel testified that Boesky paid him money for inside information on takeover transactions the investment banking firm was involved in.

Boesky eventually agreed to a settlement involving fines of $50 million and more if investors could prove loss. He also spent time in jail. His jail time, however, was considered minimal as a result of his willingness to provide prosecutors with information about others whom he claimed were involved in illegal activities.

Boesky's situation created a major debate among corporate chieftains concerning the role of arbitrageurs who contribute to the takeover of major corporations using borrowed money. It also highlighted the potential importance of insider information. Certainly, the question of how informationally efficient the stock market is will be impacted by the Boesky experience.

There have been a number of empirical tests to determine the potential use of inside information. Based on the number of convictions relating to the use of insider information, it does seem reasonable to believe that insider information is not always efficiently incorporated in current prices. Empirical testing also seems to confirm this result.

Empirical Tests of Market Efficiency: Valuation Anomalies

The theory of efficient capital markets holds that the prices of financial claims will equal the discounted value of the expected cash flows these claims generate for their owners. Although investors do not have perfect foresight, they are expected to act rationally by incorporating any new information about the prospects for cash flows into new valuations.

Over the last several decades, the increased availability of data, decreased cost of computers, and improvements in statistical methodologies have provided us with the opportunity to test many of the tenets of the efficient market hypothesis. Most of this research has been done using stock prices, and has been reviewed in a comprehensive manner by Fama (1991). The results have significant implications for any participant in the markets for financial claims because they suggest that market prices do sometimes deviate from the fundamental estimates of valuation.

If market prices can deviate from theoretical estimates of value, then these deviations provide opportunities for investors to make a profit. There has been considerable research in an attempt to identify the evidence of systematic differences in the performance of certain stocks or groups of stocks from the expectations of the efficient market hypothesis. These valuation discrepancies are known as *pricing anomalies*. The research studies the actual returns on common stocks of firms with different attributes, and then adjusts for risk to see if returns are systematically higher or lower. Several of the more significant ones are included in the following list:

- Winners and Losers: This research indicates that stocks that experienced price gains in the recent past tend to underperform the stocks that did very poorly in the previous period.
- Low Price-Earnings Ratio Stocks: This research indicates that stocks with low price-earnings ratios tend to outperform stocks with high P-E ratios.
- High Book-to-Market Value Stocks: This work indicates that stocks with high book-net-worth-to-market value achieve higher returns adjusted for risk.
- January Effect: This research indicates that stock returns tend to be higher in the month of January. One explanation is that stocks are sold for tax losses at year-end.
- Excess Volatility: The most important research in this area shows that stock and bond prices exhibit excess volatility compared to the prices they would exhibit if prices were efficiently determined by a theoretical valuation model. There are many other examples of research indicating that prices of certain financial claims exhibit excessive volatility compared to theoretical valuations.

Research that indicates that the prices of financial claims do not necessarily conform to the efficient market hypothesis is important. Prices impact on the allocation of resources. If prices are not good guides as to the productivity of those issuers of securities relative to other issuers, then resources can be misallocated.

For the investor, the notion that markets can exhibit mispricing based on some assessment of fundamental value raises the possibility that a wide variety of trading algorithms can be developed to profit from this mispricing. It explains why market participants talk in terms such as *market psychology, overreaction, overbought,* and *oversold.* These are all traders' terms, which suggest market-pricing anomalies of one type or another.

Summary

Understanding how financial markets operate is crucial to the success of the intermediary. The market for each type of financial claim differs from other claims in a variety of different respects. Participants must understand these differences to consummate transactions in these markets. Differences in market liquidity, transaction costs, information availability, and other factors can significantly impact on the success of a particular transaction.

Some market participants seek to gain advantages over other participants by creating exclusive information services. Others have the advantage of knowing the order book, such as NYSE specialists and traders at major dealers. This information provides a more accurate prediction of the price moves of a particular financial claim. Financial institutions must understand the operational and informational characteristics of the markets in which they transact their business.

Financial markets fulfill a number of important functions (1) providing information on past and present prices and trading volume; (2) bringing buyers and sellers together; (3) providing standardization of contracts; (4) reducing credit risks; and (5) reducing informational asymmetries. Collectively, these are known as **transaction costs.**

The taxonomy of markets consists of a number of classifications. **Primary markets** refer to the markets in which claims are created, and **secondary markets** are markets in which claims are traded after they are created. Money markets are those in which short-term high-quality debt is traded. **Capital markets** are markets for long-term financial claims such as long-term bonds and equities. Markets can be operated by one or more **dealers** or as **organized exchanges** such as the NYSE. Markets are also referred to as **spot** and **forward cash markets.** Spot markets refer to markets in which settlement is delivered within a few days and forward cash markets, in which settlement may be months in the future. Markets may also operate with human interface or computerized order matching.

Euromarkets refer to financial transactions that occur within a country in a currency other than the domestic currency. The **Eurodollar** market refers to a large market for deposits and loans in Europe denominated in United States dollars.

Arbitrage is the activity that brings prices of financial claims into relative consistency between markets, claims, and over time. Arbitrage takes many forms. Arbitrage transactions occur for claims trading in different geographic or dealer markets, between spot and forward markets, between closely related claims, between derivative markets and cash markets, and between cash markets and hybrid markets.

The relationship between prices in the spot and forward cash markets for debt securities is impacted by a condition known as **interest parity.** This condition holds that the forward price of a claim in period t, F_t, will equal its spot price, S, times the ratio of the financing cost of the claim, r_{fc}, over the claim's interest return, r_c. This is shown as

$$F_t = S\,(1 + r_{fc})\,/\,(1 + r_c)$$

Market efficiency can be evaluated with respect to the mechanics of a market known as **operational efficiency** or a claim's price response to new information known as **informational efficiency.**

An operationally efficient market possesses the following attributes: (1) It provides readily available prices. (2) It allows trading to occur with price continuity. (3) It involves low transaction costs.

The informational efficiency of financial markets is classified into three groups. Markets are considered (1) **weak-form market efficient,** if future prices are independent of past prices; (2) **semistrong-form market efficient,** if current prices incorporate all publicly available information; and (3) **strong-form market efficient,** if current prices include all information available to specialists, experts, and even insiders. Research indicates that while most markets in securities seem to be semistrong-market efficient, **pricing anomalies** exist, which sometimes refute the theory. Anomalies may provide profitable trading strategies.

Questions

Chapter 6

1. What is meant by the operational efficiency of a market? Name the attributes of an operationally efficient market.
2. What is meant by the informational efficiency of a market? Explain what is meant by weak-form market efficiency. Explain what is meant by semistrong-form market efficiency. Explain what is meant by strong-form market efficiency.
3. Explain what a circuit breaker is. Why have circuit breakers been used in organized markets?
4. List and explain the three types of circuit breakers.
5. How do circuit breakers impact market efficiency? How do circuit breakers impact credit risk?
6. Why are financial markets important to the economy? What roles do financial markets play?
7. Differentiate between a dealers market and an organized exchange. Give examples of each.
8. What is the over-the-counter market for common stocks? Differentiate this market from the NYSE.
9. Explain the difference between the forward and spot cash markets.
10. Explain the process of arbitrage. Give an example of an arbitrage transaction.
11. Arbitrage transactions can take place for like claims between markets and between different points in time. Explain how each type of arbitrage works.
12. Differentiate between the trade date and the settlement date.
13. Why is arbitrage an important financial concept? Why is a pure arbitrage opportunity unlikely to occur?

14. Market efficiency has been tested using a variety of empirical analyses. What types of results have these empirical tests produced with respect to how efficient our financial markets are? Explain some of the efficient market anamolies.

Problems

Problem 6-1 Forward Prices

An investor is considering an arbitrage transaction involving the spot and forward market in Treasury securities. The investor is able to borrow for six months at an annual interest rate of 4.5 percent. The long-term Treasury coupon rate is 8.5 percent. The long-term Treasury can be purchased in the spot market at a price of 99 16/32. The bond can be sold in the 180-day forward market at a price of 98. Should the investor borrow and purchase the Treasuries and then sell them forward? The transactions cost for a million-dollar transaction would be $4,000.

Problem 6-2 Forward Prices

The ten-year Treasury is selling for 97 percent of par in the spot market. It pays a coupon rate of 10 percent. It is possible to borrow for six months at a rate of 7 percent to finance the Treasury bond purchase. What would be the forward 180-day price, FX_{180}, of the bonds if interest rate parity holds?

Analyzing a Market

project 6.1

Pick a market for any tangible good for which you have some familiarity. If you are a collector of coins, art, baseball cards, or stamps you might pick one of those markets. If you are familiar with the market for used cars, bicycles, or other tangible goods you may pick one of those markets.

Project:

1. Describe the market you have chosen in terms of its operational efficiency. How do you obtain price information on recent transactions? Do prices show price continuity? Are transaction costs high or low?

2. What could be done to improve the operational efficiency of the market you selected?

3. How would you go about analyzing the informational efficiency of the market you selected?

Financial Intermediaries: Their Role in the Financial System

P art 2 provides an important theoretical overview of the functions of financial intermediaries. These functions include origination, servicing, brokerage, market-making, and portfolio management. The discussion follows a historical review of intermediation in the United States through the passage of the Federal Deposit Insurance Corporation Improvement Act of 1991.

Financial institutions are also presented. The first part of this section discusses commercial banks, both domestic and international. Thrift institutions are then covered, with special attention given to the savings and loan debacle. Life insurance companies and pension funds are finally covered, as well as other types of intermediaries, such as investment banks and property and casualty insurers.

Part Outline

Chapter 7:
The Theory of Intermediation and the Function of Intermediaries

Chapter 8:
U.S. Financial Intermediary History

Chapter 9:
Commercial Banks

Chapter 10:
Thrift Institutions

Chapter 11:
Life Insurance Companies and Pension Funds

Chapter 12:
Other Financial Institutions

The Theory of Intermediation and the Function of Intermediaries

chapter 7

The chapter begins by explaining the rationale behind the creation of intermediaries and the basic services they provide. Financial intermediaries have as their main role the processing of information, risk management, and the reduction of transaction costs.

These goals are achieved through their particular functions, which include origination, servicing, brokerage, market-making, and portfolio management. Intermediary management selects from the population of financial claims and the five functions to create a unique intermediary. This process is constrained by law and regulation.

This chapter also discusses the financial claim/function matrix, which is used to put an intermediary's selected functions into a comprehensive framework.

General Economic Rationale for Intermediaries

There has been considerable research aimed at better understanding the rationale behind the creation of intermediaries. A single dominant rationale has not been agreed upon. To explain the multitude of activities performed by intermediaries, the discussion in this chapter will focus on their four main functions:

1. The reduction in transaction cost rationale
2. The payment system rationale

3. The information processing and monitoring rationale
4. The asset and liability transformation rationale

These functions are not mutually exclusive by any means. As a group, however, they provide a fairly comprehensive understanding of the intermediary and the intermediation process.

Transaction Costs Reduction Rationale

Most researchers studying the rationale for the creation of intermediaries have focused on the lack of perfect markets. Perfect financial markets are defined as markets with negligible transaction costs, perfect and costless information for borrowers and lenders, and infinite divisibility in the denomination of financial claims. Relaxing these assumptions creates the opportunity to form intermediaries, which can perform various functions at a net cost lower than what governments, individuals, and firms could accomplish on their own.

One major efficiency concern is the transaction costs, or search costs, incurred when attempting to bring CSUs and CDUs together. This activity is referred to as *brokerage*. This search process takes considerable time and money to accomplish, and one way financial institutions can reduce search costs is through brokerage and the creation of their own financial liabilities.

Operator of the Payment System Rationale

Early research on financial intermediaries was mainly concerned with their role in creating liabilities. The focus was on the importance of intermediaries in the implementation of monetary policy and the creation of money demanded by central governments, households, and business units. Commercial banks were regarded as key to a smoothly functioning payment system and were regarded as very special economic units requiring special attention. Over time, near monies have broadened our concept of money and liquidity. These are not currency and demand deposits issued by commercial banks; they are liabilities of a variety of nonbank financial institutions that serve as a medium of exchange.

A money market mutual fund that offers a check-activated withdrawal feature is a near money, for example. Innovation, technology, and broadened liability powers for intermediaries have caused the payment system rationale to become less of a focus of attention.

Information Processing and Monitoring Rationale

Another major function of intermediaries relates to their role in collecting and analyzing information regarding potential borrowers. In this way intermediaries are producers of assets. Information processing and *moni-*

toring are important activities in creating loans and investments. Making good loans requires accumulating extensive data on the prospective borrower. Data must be monitored over time to ensure that a borrower is living up to the provisions in the financial claim.

Delegated monitoring is a term used to describe a basic function of intermediaries. Savers hire intermediaries to monitor the financial performance of borrowers over time. This is particularly useful when the firm's debt is held by many investors. Each investor would have to monitor the borrower separately, which would cost substantially more than having one agent perform this function.

Asset and Liability Transformation Rationale

Asset and liability transformation rationale is the process of intermediaries converting liabilities with one set of denomination, risk, and maturity characteristics into assets that may have entirely different characteristics. Related to this is the fact that intermediaries hold unmarketable assets and issue marketable liabilities. Marketability transformation is one of the primary economic rationales of intermediaries. Two types of asset and liability transformations undertaken by intermediaries are accepting various types of risk and managing portfolio activities.

One of the most important activities of financial institutions is transforming assets and liabilities. It is worthwhile to consider the nature of these transformations, since they are activities from which intermediaries earn profits and in which considerable innovation occurs.

Traditionally, transformations include denomination, maturity (or duration), and marketability. In addition to these, intermediaries transform the credit-risk characteristics, the monetary unit or currency, the extent to which the product serves as a medium of exchange, and the efficiency of a market. Consider each of these transformations separately.

Denomination Transformation

Denomination transformations involve selling liabilities in denominations that are different than the denominations of the assets they hold. The simplest case is the mutual fund that sells shares in denominations of several dollars, but invests in securities worth thousands of dollars.

Maturity or Duration Transformation

Some intermediaries issue liabilities that have different maturities than the assets in which they invest. For example, the liabilities of most thrift institutions remain very short-term in nature, while the primary asset of the thrift is a long-term mortgage. These maturities would undergo transformation through the activities of the intermediary.

Marketability Transformation

Marketability transformations refer to the activities of many financial institutions that hold unmarketable assets and issue marketable liabilities. Their ability to create marketable liabilities while holding unmarketable assets stems, in part, from the economies of scale in their own liquid asset management activities, as well as certain advantages they might have. One such advantage might be the ability to borrow from the Federal Reserve's discount window, the Federal Home Loan Banks, or the Credit Union Liquidity Fund. These emergency borrowing facilities allow depository institutions to hold smaller liquid asset holdings than they otherwise could.

Credit Risk Transformation

Credit risk transformations relate to the differences between the credit risk of an intermediary's assets and that of its liabilities. A large percentage of the assets of most financial depository institutions are below investment grade. Nevertheless, these intermediaries sell liabilities that have investment-grade ratings or the full faith and credit of the U.S. government, thanks to deposit insurance. This is a major transformation.

Less well known are the securitization activities of intermediaries. These are cases in which intermediaries use over-collateralization or subordination to transform the credit quality of a collateralized security.

Currency Transformation

With the growth in international transactions, the need for currency transformations has grown rapidly. Much of this involves foreign exchange. Somewhat less well known has been the growth in the currency swap market. Commercial banks have been leaders in arranging for foreign institutions to swap funds in two different currencies for repayment at a later date.

Providing a Medium of Exchange

There has been significant innovation in the creation of new mediums of exchange over the last several decades. The bank credit card is the preferred medium of exchange for many consumers. The nation's brokerage firms have also developed medium of exchange services through brokerage accounts, and balances available in money market mutual funds.

Enhancing Market Efficiency

Many financial institutions are engaged in brokerage and security trading activities, which have as their by-product the creation of more efficient markets. Financial firms specialize in buying, selling, and brokering specific types of securities. Market efficiency is improved through the reduction in the bid-ask spread for a specific security.

A Comprehensive Structure of the Functions of Intermediaries

The entire conceptual framework for the functions of all intermediaries includes the following:

1. Financial claim origination
2. Financial claim servicing
3. Financial claim brokerage
4. Market-making
5. Portfolio risk management

The first three of these functions involve information-processing as their primary feature. Portfolio management is a broad definition of a group of activities that includes the management of all asset and liability risks.

Market-making may be the most difficult concept to describe because it is really the nexus between the portfolio management activities of the firm and its other information-processing activities, especially brokerage. Market-making is really a by-product of the other functions of the intermediary. The activity produces no revenue for the firm, per se. Rather, the process of market-making can be considered a social benefit of the intermediary. Market-making is very dependent on the brokerage function, since market-making cannot take place without brokerage. Brokerage can and frequently does take place without market-making. It is in the portfolio management and market-making functions that so-called transformation services of intermediaries take place. Consider each of the functions separately.

Financial Claim Origination

From an intermediary's perspective, the creation of a financial claim may be an asset or a liability. *Origination* involves the primary activities associated with the creation of a new financial claim—underwriting, document preparation, creation of covenants, as well as the processing activities related to closing the transaction.

Origination also involves the selection of the most cost-effective channel of distribution for attracting loan, investment, or liability customers. For a retail bank, for example, deposit-gathering might include using branch banks, telemarketing, direct mail, and an agent. Similar choices would be available for the selection of a channel of distribution for a credit card. Originating a financial claim often includes the following activities:

- Credit underwriting (or credit scoring)
- Financial claim documentation
- Development of covenants

- Collateral review
- Loan disbursement
- Document control
- Selection of channel of distribution

Financial Claim Servicing

Servicing is a term that often means the collection and payment of principal and interest on assets and liabilities. It is also a loan-monitoring function that ensures borrowers are able to adhere to the loan covenants. Another important servicing function relates to collateral control and problem-loan activities.

An outsider looking at a financial institution may not think of its servicing responsibilities. If they do understand servicing, then it is likely they will underestimate its importance to the intermediary. In many institutions, most of their human resources are devoted to servicing assets and liabilities.

Financial claim servicing relies heavily on the use of information-processing technology. Computers process the collection of payments on consumer and business loans and update records on the many deposit accounts, mutual fund shares, and insurance policies.

Other servicing activities include loan restructuring, repossessions and foreclosures, collateral disposition, and implementing legal remedies. Loan-servicing units within a financial intermediary must keep good records on the performance of borrowers meeting their obligations under loan contracts. This information permits the firm to respond quickly to default situations. It also can determine how to obtain the best value for repossessed and foreclosed assets. Key servicing activities are

- Processing payment
- Collecting payment
- Controlling collateral
- Safekeeping collateral
- Monitoring covenants and borrowing
- Repossessing and foreclosing on collateral
- Restructuring debt
- Developing delinquency and credit risk reports
- Implementing legal remedies
- Disposing of collateral

Financial Claim Brokerage

Brokerage involves two very significant information-processing functions. It includes identifying potential buyers and sellers of various financial claims the intermediary is interested in, and gathering information related to establishing the market value of a particular claim.

Brokerage is also involved in reviewing various distribution channels to determine the best price for an asset or liability that might be created by the intermediary. For example, should the firm fund its needs with retail or wholesale funds? Should the firm originate home mortgages or purchase them in the secondary market? These questions may be answered through a process involving nothing more than surveying competitor prices for a given financial claim, such as a loan or deposit. Key activities of the brokerage function include

- Identifying borrower needs
- Identifying saver needs
- Monitoring prices of financial claims
- Monitoring other terms and conditions of the claims

Market-Making

Market-making enhances financial market efficiency. The interaction of intermediaries and other market participants creates liquidity in various markets. In market-making, the intermediary establishes clearing prices for financial claims it wishes to buy or sell. Market-making is considered the nexus of several intermediary functions because it involves the portfolio management function of the firm as well as origination and brokerage. To be a market-maker, the firm must put the asset or liability on the books for at least a brief period of time. It must be a principal in the transaction by putting capital at risk. The key activities of the market-making function includes bidding to purchase assets and bidding to sell liabilities.

Portfolio Risk Management Function

The *portfolio risk management* function refers to the selection of assets and liabilities the firm chooses to purchase or issue. All risk aspects of the portfolio are considered. The intermediary performs its asset and liability transformation services in the portfolio risk management function. By combining the information on customer needs gathered in the brokerage function with information on the status of the firm's portfolio, claims may be transformed by altering marketability, credit, maturity, currency, and denomination.

Portfolio risk management uses information from the brokerage function and the servicing function to help establish the firm's asset and liability strategies. Information on loan delinquency and other risk characteristics are available from the servicing function, while current market needs and prices are available from the brokerage function. Major activities of the portfolio risk management function are

- Setting prices for assets and liabilities
- Establishing credit risk parameters

Chapter 7 The Theory of Intermediation and the Function of Intermediaries

- Managing interest rate risk
- Managing credit risk
- Managing liquidity
- Managing mortality risk
- Performing arbitrage
- Providing financial guarantees

Portfolio risk management in many respects calls the shots for the other functions within the firm. It is responsible for pricing the assets and liabilities to ensure that the institution can operate profitably. It also has the primary responsibility for interest rate risk management. Analysts that provide quantitative measurements of the interest rate position of the firm submit their reports to the portfolio risk management function. Chapters 18 and 19 discuss the management of interest rate risk as a portfolio concept.

Although assisted by many other groups within the firm, the portfolio risk management group is responsible for understanding the credit risks inherent in the firm's asset portfolio. Again, credit risk is a portfolio concern since the risks of various types of assets differ, and many respond differently to changing general and local economic trends. Diversification reduces credit risks to manageable levels. Portfolio credit risks must also include any financial guarantees that the firm provides on securities or assets it sells or to securities it guarantees for others. For insurance companies and pension funds, the portfolio risk management group is responsible for managing the mortality risk of the firm or portfolio.

The Financial Claim/Function Matrix

The *financial claim/function matrix* puts each of the five functions into a comprehensive framework. This structure is used to describe the functions of intermediaries on both the asset and liability sides of the balance sheet. The matrix is shown in Table 7.1 on page 178. The financial intermediary is seen as an information-processing firm that processes and analyzes information in its origination, servicing, and brokerage functions, and manages a portfolio of assets and liabilities. The portfolio management activities are seen as the risk management activities of the firm. Interest rate and credit risks are present whenever the firm takes a financial claim onto its balance sheet. This may be for a very short time, as would be the case of a commercial bank or investment company with a security-trading activity.

The matrix is useful for any intermediary, since every financial claim is represented. The matrix also reflects where the claim came from, the primary or secondary market. As the table indicates, all claims originated by the firm are by definition primary market transactions. However, when it comes to brokerage and market-making, the firm may be involved in the primary or secondary markets or both. Table 7.2 on page 179 provides a

Table 7.1

Financial Claim/Function Matrix for Assets

Type of Claim	Origination	Servicing	Brokerage	Market-Making	Portfolio Management
	Pri		Pri-Sec	Pri-Sec	
Government					
United States					
Agency					
Municipal					
Business					
Corporate bonds					
Equities					
Mortgages					
Leases					
Loans					
Household					
Installment					
Credit card					
Mortgages					
Foreign					

Pri = Primary market
Sec = Secondary market

similar comprehensive schematic for the liability side of the intermediary's balance sheet.

One can take every intermediary and describe it by identifying which activity the firm has chosen and for which financial claim. The differences between firms will be determined by management preferences, law, and regulation. The financial claim/functional matrix is useful as a structure of any intermediary, from the most complex money center bank to the simplest mutual fund. It makes the focus of individual institutional differences less important, especially in light of the frequent changes in asset and liability powers of institutions.

The structure permits management of financial intermediaries to plan for all necessary functions before becoming involved in new financial claim markets.

Table 7.2

Financial Claim/Function Matrix for Liabilities

Type of Claim	Origination	Servicing	Brokerage	Market-Making	Portfolio Management
	Pri		Pri-Sec	Pri-Sec	
Demand deposits					
Certificates of deposit					
Retail Funding					
Insured deposits					
Life insurance					
Premiums					
Pension fund					
Contributions					
Mutual funds					
Capital Market Funding					
Collateralized debt					
FHLB advances					
Reverse repos					
Asset-based					
Unsecured Debt					
Negotiable CDs					
Bankers acceptances					
Commercial paper					

Pri = Primary Market
Sec = Secondary Market

An Example of the Small Commercial Bank

The financial claim/function matrix can be used to describe the functions of any intermediary. Consider the case of the 1st National Bank of Cedar Falls, Iowa. This bank of $40 million in assets is located in a small isolated town. It has few investment options. The balance sheet is shown in Table 7.3 on page 180.

Table 7.3

1st National Bank of Cedar Falls, Iowa
Balance Sheet for December 31, 1990

Assets		Liabilities	
Cash and government bonds	$12,000,000	Demand deposits	$14,000,000
Commercial loans	14,000,000	CDs	22,000,000
Mortgages	11,000,000		
Auto loans	2,000,000		
Building and equipment	1,000,000	Net worth	4,000,000
Total	$40,000,000	Total	$40,000,000

Table 7.4 shows the financial claim/financial function matrix for 1st National Bank. The matrix indicates that the bank originates and services commercial business loans, mortgages, and auto loans in the primary market. The bank also acts as a market-maker and portfolio manager for these assets. It purchases government securities in the secondary market, where it is a market-maker and portfolio manager.

On the liability side of the balance sheet, the bank originates demand deposits and certificates of deposit, both of which it services.

Mission Insurance Company Financial Claim/Function Matrix

Table 7.5 on page 182 is a financial claim/function matrix of a medium-sized life insurance company. Mission Insurance Company was founded in Indiana in 1925. It expanded into several other Midwest states and now does business in Illinois, Ohio, Michigan, Kentucky, and Iowa. The firm has grown to $125 million in assets. The firm writes primarily whole life policies and term insurance on individuals, relying on a small but successful in-house sales force. In recent years, due to competition in the industry, it expanded its product offering to include single premium annuities. The investment strategy of the company emphasizes very conservative investments including high-grade corporate bonds, U.S. government and agency securities, a small amount of preferred stock, and the balance in mortgage-backed securities. The firm obtains all its assets in the secondary markets. It has, however, recently created a small commercial real estate loan department that originates small-sized loans on office buildings and retail strip shopping centers in and around Indianapolis, where its main office is located.

Table 7.4

Financial Claim/Function Matrix for Assets and Liabilities
1st National Bank of Cedar Falls, Iowa

Type of Claim	Origination Pri	Servicing	Brokerage Pri-Sec	Market-Making Pri-Sec	Portfolio Management
Assets					
Government					
United States				X	X
Agency					
Municipal					
Business					
Corporate bonds					
Equities					
Mortgages					
Leases					
Loans	X	X		X	X
Household					
Installment	X	X		X	X
Credit card					
Mortgages	X	X		X	X
Foreign					
Liabilities					
Demand deposits	X	X		X	X
Certificates of deposit	X	X		X	X

Pri = Primary Market
Sec = Secondary Market

      The financial claim/function matrix for the Mission Insurance Company is shown in Table 7.5. Table 7.6 on page 183 shows the balance sheet for the company as of December 31, 1990.
      The financial claim/function matrix is a good reference for the activities of any intermediary.

Table 7.5

**Financial Claim/Function Matrix for Assets and Liabilities
Mission Insurance Company**

Type of Claim	Origination Pri	Servicing	Brokerage Pri-Sec	Market-Making Pri-Sec	Portfolio Management
Assets					
Government					
United States				X	X
Agency				X	X
Municipal					
Business					
Corporate bonds				X	X
Equities: preferred				X	X
Leases					
Commercial RE					
Loans	X	X		X	X
Household					
Installment					
Mortgages					
Foreign					
Liabilities					
Policy Reserves					
Term	X	X		X	X
Whole life and annuity	X	X		X	X

Pri = Primary Market
Sec = Secondary Market

Table 7.6

Balance Sheet
Mission Insurance Company
December 31, 1990

Assets		Liabilities	
Cash and U.S. money market instruments	$ 9	Policy Reserves	
		Term insurance	$15
Corporate bonds	56	Whole life	46
Preferred stock	14	Annuities	24
Mortgage securities	35	Single premium whole life	10
Commercial mortgages	11	Net worth	20
Total	**$125**	**Total**	**$125**

Summary

This chapter identified the primary conceptual functions of intermediaries. Rather than focus on specific intermediaries, it identified generalized functions that apply to all intermediaries.

The intermediary is an economic unit whose overall function is to reduce transaction costs. Intermediaries also provide a medium of exchange and contribute to the smooth functioning of the payments system. The chapter discussed the importance of information processing and delegated monitoring. These two functions are most important in allowing intermediaries to run efficiently.

The products and services of intermediaries were discussed in terms of financial transformations. Intermediaries typically sell liabilities that are different from their assets. This process is a financial transformation.

Reducing **transaction costs** is the primary function of financial intermediaries. The primary transaction costs include (1) providing a **medium of exchange and payment services;** (2) performing **loan servicing and monitoring;** and (3) acting as brokers by reducing **search costs.**

The products and services of intermediaries relate to the **transformation of assets and liabilities.** These transformations include (1) **denomination,** (2) **credit,** (3) **marketability,** (4) **currency,** (5) **maturity,** (6) **market efficiency,** and (7) **medium of exchange.**

The following are the primary functions of intermediaries: (1) **origination,** (2) **servicing,** (3) **brokerage,** (4) **market-making,** and (5) **portfolio management.**

Market-making refers to the activity of setting bid and ask prices for various types of financial claims. This does not produce revenue for intermediaries, but it does provide for greater market efficiency.

An intermediary's selection of financial claims and functions is a matter of law and regulation relating to the firm's charter and the choices of management. These decisions are summarized in a **financial claim/ function matrix.** This schematic describes the functions of a particular intermediary and the claims relating to each function.

Questions

Chapter 7

1. What types of transaction costs are financial institutions most likely to reduce for their users?
2. Financial institutions are said to be information processing companies. What types of information do they process?
3. What is meant by delegated monitoring? What is the economic justification for establishing commercial banks that relates to this concept?
4. Name at least four asset and liability transformations performed by financial institutions. Give examples of products offered by intermediaries that reflect these transformations.
5. How do financial intermediaries contribute to market efficiency?
6. List and explain the five primary functions of intermediaries.
7. Why is market-making considered a social benefit?
8. What are the primary management functions related to portfolio management?
9. What risks must be managed in the portfolio management function?
10. What determines the financial functions performed by any particular intermediary?
11. What are the primary activities associated with origination? What are the primary activities associated with servicing? What are the primary activities associated with brokerage? What are the primary activities associated with portfolio management?
12. What is the advantage of considering an intermediary in terms of the functions it performs?
13. If you were put in charge of a task force charged with establishing a unit within the commercial bank you work for to offer loans on recreational boats, what would you do to make sure the bank could handle this business effectively?

Chapter 7   The Theory of Intermediation and the Function of Intermediaries   185

Financial Functions: South Regional Bank

case 7.1

The South Regional Bank was founded in North Carolina in the 1800s. The regional amalgamation of banks in the Southeast was exactly what the management had hoped would happen to increase the growth opportunities for the bank. It now has over 125 offices in four states. Tables C7.1 and C7.2 show the bank's statement of sources and uses of funds and a balance sheet for 1993. This statement is used to develop a financial claims/function matrix.

The bank has several other activities that may not be apparent from the statements. The bank is a major originator and seller of loans on apartments to the FNMA and FHLMC. It currently services over $650,000,000 of such loans. In addition, the bank makes and sells immediately loans guaranteed under the federal student loan program. It does not service these loans. Finally, the bank will purchase U.S. Treasury securities for its customers. These securities are purchased in the name of the customer and the bank does not put them on its books.

Table C7.1

Sources and Uses of Funds Statement for 1993

Category	Source	Uses
Cash	$ 12,000,000	
U.S. Treasury securities		$ 5,000,000
U.S. agency securities		12,000,000
Mortgage pass-through securities		124,000,000
Consumer loans		
Auto loans		43,000,000
R/V and boat loans		12,000,000
Credit card receivables		13,000,000
Mortgage loans		
Home mortgages	74,000,000	145,000,000
Single family		
Apartment loans	34,000,000	34,000,000
Commercial mortgages		54,000,000
Business loans		
Commercial loans		143,000,000
Participations purchased (sold)		23,000,000
Municipal securities	44,000,000	15,000,000
Demand deposits	39,000,000	
Time deposits	125,000,000	
Subordinated debt	50,000,000	
Repurchase agreements		
Retained earnings	245,000,000	
Total	**$623,000,000**	**$623,000,000**

Table C7.2

South Regional Bank
Balance Sheet
December 31, 1993

Assets

Cash and due from banks	$ 324,000,000
U.S. Treasury securities	430,000,000
Agency securities	850,000,000
Municipal securities	332,000,000
Consumer loans	
Auto loans	724,000,000
R/V and boats	76,000,000
Credit card	
receivables	546,000,000
Mortgages	
Home mortgages	1,534,000,000
Apartment mortgages	123,000,000
Commercial mortgages	365,000,000
Business loans	
Commercial loans	2,700,000,000
Total	**$8,004,000,000**

Liabilities

Demand deposits	$2,345,000,000
Time deposits	4,900,000,000
Repurchase agreement	23,000,000
Subordinated debt	50,000,000
Capital	
Retained earnings	676,000,000
Stockholder's equity	10,000,000
Total	**$8,004,000,000**

Problems

1. Fill out a financial claim/function matrix for the bank. Use Tables C7.1 and C7.2. Indicate where the bank is involved in the secondary and primary markets.

2. For which financial claims is the firm involved in the secondary market?

3. How did you treat the Treasury securities the bank purchases for its customers?

U.S. Financial Intermediary History

chapter **8**

This chapter selectively reviews the history of U.S. intermediaries. The first part of the chapter covers from the prerevolutionary period to the beginning of the Federal Reserve System. The second part discusses the periods of most rapid financial change. This section begins with the 1930s depression. During this period Congress created a financial structure that worked well until the mid-1960s. During the period from the mid-1960s to the present, Congress passed significant legislation to deregulate financial institutions. This was a response to the financial innovations that were effectively dismantling the preestablished system. The chapter culminates with a discussion of the thrift crisis and the problems commercial banking and life insurance industries have endured in the 1990s and the legislation that responded to these problems. The chapter includes an appendix that discusses the U.S. payment system.

Early Financial Intermediary History

A study of early financial history provides several important lessons that help to put the development of our financial system in perspective.

A summary of major historical dates is provided in Exhibit 8.1 on page 190.

Exhibit 8.1

Time Line History of American Financial Institutions: 1781–1913

Commercial Banking	Year	Nonbank Intermediaries
Bank of North America	1781	
Bank of the United States	1791	
	1792	Insurance Company of North America
Bank of the United States disbanded	1811	
	1812	First life insurance company
Second Bank of the United States chartered	1816	First mutual savings bank
	1818	First trust company (commingled trust)
	1831	First savings and loan association
Jackson vetoes Second Bank of the United States	1832	
National Bank Act of 1863	1863	
National Bank Act of 1864	1864	
Financial panic	1873	
	1875	First pension fund (American Express)
Financial panic	1884	
	1890	First investment company (mutual fund)
Financial panic	1893	
Financial panic	1907	
	1909	First credit union
Creation of the Federal Reserve System	1913	

The Early History: 1620–1800

In early U.S. history, financial institutions were very primitive and financial needs were few. The United States had a perennial balance of trade deficit with England and a constant shortage of specie. *Specie* refers to the currency used as a medium of exchange. This problem was only partially corrected with a more favorable balance of trade with the Spanish colonies and the build-up of Spanish dollar specie (pieces of eight).

There were no major bank currencies available at that time, of course, and barter was the most common method of exchange. There were several attempts to create a domestic form of money that included wampum, which were beads of polished shells strung in strands and used by North American Indians. Tobacco was used as currency in the Southern colonies. This continued into the mid-1600s.

Banking activities such as deposit-taking and the discounting of merchant-held customer debt did take place. However, it was the merchants who handled these activities for their customers, not banks. Banks came into use in the early 1700s. These were primarily land banks, which used land as collateral on loans. The ratios of loan to value were conservative.

Revolution and the Bank of North America

Wars played a large part in shaping the history of the financial system. As the Revolutionary War began, Robert Morris pushed for the creation of a bank to assist in its financing. The first modern bank was a private bank, chartered in Philadelphia in 1782 as the Bank of North America. Its functions were to lend money to the government, hold government deposits, and act as a fiscal agent.

Agrarian Interests Versus the Merchants and the Wealthy

In time, the Bank of North America converted to a state charter, and its federal role diminished. During its short history as a federal bank, tension grew between the merchants and wealthy interests and the agrarian and small-business interests. Agrarian interests and small businesses favored locally based banks, ample lending volume, and few government controls. These attitudes were in direct conflict with the merchants and wealthy interests of the Northeast, who generally favored federalized banking, constrained lending, and stronger controls. This classic tension is the key to the eventual rise and fall of federally chartered banking during the 1800s.

Another effort to provide federal banking services was started in 1790. Alexander Hamilton pushed for the creation of the bank, which was to have the functions of increasing the quantity of capital available to the growing nation, assisting the government in borrowing, and facilitating the collection of taxes. The bank was a *fractional reserve bank,* meaning that it could create more bank notes than it had specie. The Bank of the United States was given a twenty-year charter.

State Banks Fill Void

The demise of the Bank of the United States in 1811 set off a period of fast growth in the chartering of state banks. However, throughout the 1800s, the state banks provided the nation with an unequal distribution of specie. In addition, the founders of these banks frequently attempted to conduct business in unprofitable locations. The banks were also weakly managed and frequently lacked sufficient capital. Despite these problems, and without a federally chartered bank alternative, the number of state banks grew rapidly. From 1811 to 1815 the number of state banks grew from 88 to 208.

The War of 1812 and the Second Bank of the United States

It took another war to stir the federal government's interest in banking. The War of 1812 provided the necessary motivation. In 1816, the Second Bank of the United States was chartered. Initially, however, the bank did not serve its interests well. During the years 1816 to 1823 the United States suffered from a serious financial crisis. During this crisis there was a significant reduction in the supply of money and many banks failed. Many other state banks, meanwhile, refused to redeem their notes for specie. In 1819, the United States was in a severe depression. In 1823, Nicholas Biddle took over the management of the Second Bank of the United States.

Suffolk System and New York Safety Fund

The failure of so many banks led to several individual efforts to shore up the banking system. In Boston, the Suffolk Bank brought stability to the Massachusetts banking system by establishing the *Suffolk System*. This system provided quick redemption for the notes of rural banks that joined as members. A rural bank that held reserves, a noninterest earning deposit of specie, in the Suffolk Bank could be assured that its note would be redeemed at par, that is, at face value. By 1825, most Massachusetts banks outside Boston had joined. The Suffolk approach provided strong evidence that reserves kept in a clearing or central bank can provide a safety net for the member institutions, helping them to meet liquidity needs.

New York tried another approach. In 1829 the legislature put into place the *New York Safety Fund*. The fund took premiums of one-half of 1 percent of the member bank's capital, up to a 3 percent maximum, and placed it in a fund to finance insurance against bank failures. It also limited the member banks from issuing notes equal to more than 2.5 times capital. The New York Safety Fund was fairly successful in demonstrating the value of insurance and capital requirements. Unfortunately, the fund's resources were not sufficient to withstand the financial panic of 1837. The New York Safety Fund was the first of many bank and deposit insurance programs to fail.

Second Bank Falls to Political Pressures

The Second Bank of the United States stabilized under the management of Nicholas Biddle. The election of Andrew Jackson in 1828 concerned the bank, however, since Jackson was against federal involvement in banking. The nomination of Henry Clay to run against Jackson in the election of 1832 put the bank in a precarious position. Clay supported the bank and his supporters urged the bank to seek early rechartering. The act passed both houses of Congress, but laid dormant until after the election. Apparently, too many bank officers vocally supported the losing candidate Clay. Jackson vetoed the rechartering and the Second Bank of the United States closed a few years after.

State Banks Blossom and Then Bust

The end of the Second Bank gave encouragement to the state bank movement. From 1829 until 1837, the number of state banks grew from 329 to 788. This period was one of industrialization and *laissez-faire* political economic thinking. In fact, wide-open banking grew so extensively that the federal government was left without a safe place to put its own deposits. In a number of Northern states, banking charters were obtained by anyone who could meet the minimum capital and bond deposit requirements with the state. This became known as free banking.

The panic of 1837 was caused in part by the reduction of British investment dollars. As many banks stopped redeeming notes for specie, the bank failure rate increased, sending the United States into an economic depression that lasted until 1843. The inelastic nature of the U.S. currency supply became evident once again. *Inelastic currency* means that the nation's supply of currency is affected by events largely outside the control of the government.

The era of free banking ended in failure. The United States needed a more *elastic currency,* one that was more responsive to the decisions of government. The unregulated banking system was unstable and subject to frequent failures, which resulted in regional economic disruptions.

Additional Efforts at State Banking Regulation

Free banking continued after 1837. Now, the state governments were taking a hand at regulation. During the period from 1844 to 1860, state governments passed many laws similar to the fractional reserve requirement in New York, in which banks could only issue notes up to a certain percentage of their capital.

This did not stop the proliferation of banks or bank notes, however. By 1860, there were 1,600 banks and over 7,000 different bank notes in circulation. Despite this difficult situation, it would take another war to get the federal government bank into the bank chartering business.

Civil War Brings National Banking

The Civil War quickly depleted the federal government's resources. As a result, the government resorted to borrowing funds from banks by issuing two installments of loans of $150 million each. This currency, called greenbacks, quickly depreciated after the second $150 million loan was obtained in 1862.

As a result, a national bank system was created to facilitate the government's financing effort. In 1863, the *National Bank Act* was passed. State banks were encouraged to convert to a national bank charter. The requirements were so tough, however, that very few converted. Another Act was passed that liberalized the requirements, and by 1864, there were 508 national banks. National banking had become a reality.

What really convinced the state banks to convert, however, was a federal tax that was placed on state bank notes outstanding. This tax increased to 10 percent in 1865 and by the end of that year, the country had 1,513 national banks.

The national bank charter and the new law had several very important provisions:

- It created the office of Comptroller of the Currency. This government office operated as the national bank regulator within the Department of the Treasury.
- It established capital requirements relative to the size of the community in which the bank served.
- It required the investment of bank assets in U.S. government bonds up to one-third of the bank's capital.
- It made national bank notes legal tender for most uses.
- It established reserve requirements of 25 percent.

Early History of Nonbank Intermediaries

While banking was developing in a more or less haphazard fashion, the commercial and individual needs of the country were also developing. With industrialization, a class of nonagrarian workers was beginning to concentrate in the cities. These changes created the demand for new types of financial services, such as deposit services, mortgage loans, life insurance, and consumer loans.

Insurance Companies

In 1792, the Insurance Company of North America was created to handle the insurance needs of the shipping industry. By 1800, there were about 32 insurers of property related to the shipping industry. The first life insurance company was founded in 1812. It provided a limited form of life insurance to the industrial workers and those that no longer looked to the farm as their family protection. Life insurance had a slow start, however, since the country was still largely agricultural.

The Thrift Institutions: The Banks' Missed Opportunities

Thrift institutions, as they have come to be called, included the mutual savings banks of New England, the building (later savings) and loan associations, and the credit unions. These were all imports from Europe. Each of these institutions can be traced to public services that the commercial banks of the day were unwilling to provide.

The organizers of the first mutual savings bank were initially denied a charter in New York because its business activities seemed too closely related to what commercial banks could already do. In 1816, the group went to Philadelphia and obtained a charter to start the first mutual savings bank. The bank was created as a safe and convenient place for the working class to keep their money.

In 1831, the first building and loan was chartered in Philadelphia. This institution provided loans for housing. The concept was to create a place for the community to aggregate savings so that a lucky member of the building and loan (usually by raffle) could obtain funds to build a house. Again, the commercial banks missed an opportunity by ignoring the market for home loans. Eventually these institutions became known as savings and loans.

The credit union came along much later. Again, the impetus was the lack of service by commercial banks. The emerging middle class had nowhere to borrow money for the purchases of consumer goods or for emergency purposes. At the time, a large group of wealthy Americans felt it was inappropriate for commercial banks to lend to the poor, since it might lead to default and harm the borrower's family. They felt that borrowing by the poor was socially and morally wrong. Credit unions were established in 1913 to provide the working class with credit that was not available from commercial banks.

All of these thrift institutions were created as mutual institutions. This means that they had no stockholders, but were owned indirectly by the savers and sometimes borrowers of the institutions who were their customers.

Pension Funds, Trusts, and Mutual Funds

In 1818, the first trust company was formed. This organization provided for a *commingled trust,* which allowed small investors to share the ownership of a pool of investments managed by a professional manager. This also gave investors an opportunity to diversify.

The American Express company started the first *pension fund* in 1875. Pension funds did not become popular until the large railroad companies began to provide pension fund benefits to their employees.

Investment companies came along in 1890. These firms were the precursor of the *mutual fund* and provided access to more sophisticated investments for middle-income households. The growth of investment companies coincided with the increased industrialization of the country.

Lessons from History

This short financial history has exposed several problems in the system. First, the country suffered from an inefficient payment system and state chartered banks subjected many smaller cities to erratic services. The large number of different bank notes and the lack of assurance that these notes would be honored at their par value contributed to the insecurity.

The nation continued to suffer from an inelastic supply of money. The money supply, such as it was, depended on conditions that were outside the control of government officials. In addition, the system of free banking resulted in frequent bank failures and losses of savings. Frequently, the poor were the biggest losers. It was evident that it would be necessary to devise a way to ensure the safety and soundness of banks. It was also clear that depositors were not equipped to analyze the quality of a bank's loan portfolio and its overall soundness.

Related to safety and soundness and the need to improve the efficiency of payment services was the need to provide emergency liquidity to commercial banks that were suffering temporary illiquidity. The concept of a lender of last resort satisfied this requirement. The *lender of last resort* is a central bank whose responsibility is to insure against a serious liquidity shortage. These shortages often resulted in bank runs, which caused severe economic dislocation to the communities in which they occurred. These conditions made the need for a central bank more and more evident.

The Federal Reserve System

The Federal Reserve Act was passed in 1913, creating the U.S. central bank, the Federal Reserve System. The rapidly industrializing nation was more willing to accept the concept of greater centralization and the need for a lender of last resort. The Federal Reserve Act was not passed without substantial compromise, however. There was a mixture of centralization (board of governors) and decentralization (twelve district banks) built in.

The act provided for the selection of seven members of the board of governors. The appointments are made by the president with Senate confirmation. The board's term is 14 years.

The board of governors was given the following primary responsibilities, most of which are still performed today:

- Determine the level of reserve requirements.
- Set the discount rate for the Federal Reserve Bank's lending to commercial banks and other members.
- Sit on the Federal Open Market Committee (FOMC), which is responsible for the implementation of monetary policy, using primarily open-market operations.
- Implement a wide variety of regulatory and supervisory requirements that impact commercial banks and most other financial institutions.
- Determine the role of the Federal Reserve in managing the nation's payment system.

Two encompassing objectives of the Federal Reserve are to achieve greater safety and soundness of our financial system and to provide an adequate supply of money to foster economic growth without inflation.

Safety and Soundness Responsibilities

The Federal Reserve largely carries out its safety and soundness responsibilities through the *discount window* at the nation's twelve Federal Reserve banks. The FOMC establishes the discount rate in consultation with the district banks. The objective is to avoid financial panics leading to bank runs and other disruptive conditions. The Federal Reserve uses its power to avoid a breakdown in the payments system, reduce the potential for disruptive local and regional economic breakdowns, and avoid bank failures as a result of unanticipated liquidity shortages.

The discount window maintains the banks' and other members' liquidity in times of stress and when seasonal withdrawals adversely impact the banks' liquidity.

Implementing Monetary Policy

The Federal Reserve implements monetary policy through the following policy variables:

1. The level of the discount rate
2. The level of reserve requirements
3. The purchase and sale of securities through open-market operations

By far the most important of these policy tools is open-market operations. The Federal Reserve intervenes directly in open-market operations by buying and selling government and agency securities. This policy alters the level of bank reserves and tightens or loosens the availability of loanable funds.

The FOMC is the decision-making body made up of the seven governors and five presidents from the twelve district Federal Reserve Banks. The chairman of the Federal Reserve Board serves as the chairman of the FOMC and the president of the Federal Reserve Bank of New York, by virtue of that bank's special responsibilities in international monetary settlements and its proximity to the U.S. financial center, is a permanent member among the five district banks.

The FOMC establishes guidelines regarding the level of interest rates, such as a target for the federal funds rate, or the growth of a monetary aggregate. The targets are based on the Federal Reserve's overall assessment of inflation, employment, economic growth, international foreign exchange rates, and other economic trends. Each month the FOMC receives briefing books from each of the twelve district banks discussing recent economic trends in their respective regions of the country.

Modern Financial Intermediary History: Creating a Segmented Financial Structure

The Great Depression of the 1930s, and the period leading up to it, provided the catalyst for the most sweeping financial legislation in U.S. history. During the period from 1927 to 1938, Congress passed the following legislation:

1. It determined the legality of banks branching across state lines.
2. It established several deposit insurance funds.
3. It created the Federal Home Loan bank system and the first federally chartered specialized home mortgage lending institutions, namely, the savings and loans associations, and federally chartered credit unions.
4. It denied commercial banks from engaging in security underwriting and distribution.
5. It created the first home mortgage guarantee program and the first secondary market government sponsored credit organization.
6. It established interest rate ceilings on time and demand deposits held in commercial banks.

These major legislative initiatives created a highly segmented and constrained financial system. Overall, the system operated without significant social costs and direct taxpayer assistance until the 1980s.

McFadden Act of 1927: No Interstate Branching

For the most part, commercial bankers did not open branch offices until the early 1900s. State chartered banks were the most aggressive in adopting branching. Prior to 1927, the branching issue was a state issue. In those states permitting branching for state chartered institutions, the national banks wanted parity. As a general rule, banks that had only one office, called *unit banks,* were against branching, considering it a competitive threat. Large money center banks were also against branching, since they felt they would lose their valuable correspondent bank business. They were uninterested in retail customers at the time.

Congress passed the *McFadden Act* in 1927 after considerable debate. It provided that nationally chartered banks could branch within cities in those states where state chartered banks were given that authority. Later in 1933, the Douglas Amendment of the Banking Act of 1933 liberalized this restriction on branching by permitting national banks to branch within a state to the same extent that state chartered banks were able to branch.

Deposit Insurance: The FDIC and FSLIC

Deposit insurance was a direct result of the widespread bank failures in the early 1920s and 1930s and the losses experienced by middle-class depositors. The Banking Act of 1933 created the Federal Deposit Insurance Corporation (FDIC) to provide insurance coverage up to $2,500 on deposits in commercial banks. In 1934, the Federal Savings and Loan Insurance Act (FSLIC) provided similar coverage for deposits held in savings and loan associations.

Much later, in 1970, deposit coverage was extended to credit unions through the National Credit Union Share Insurance Fund (NCUSIF). Over time, the coverage limits were extended until, in 1980, they reached $100,000 per deposit in any one institution.

In 1989, the FSLIC was abandoned and the Savings Association Insurance Fund (SAIF) was created as a separate entity under the FDIC, while the commercial banks' insurance fund was renamed the Bank Insurance Fund (BIF).

Federal Charters for Specialized Thrifts

In 1932, liquidity problems in the nation's mortgage-lending institutions led to the creation of the Federal Home Loan Banks (FHLBs). These institutions were designed to provide short and longer-term advances to mortgage-lending institutions. Shortly thereafter, the *Home Owners Loan Act* of 1933 created federal charters for savings and loans. Savings and loans became the first thrifts to receive a federal charter due to Congressional concern over the lack of mortgage money for home buyers and the lack of long-term fully amortized mortgage instruments.

In 1934, Congress passed the Federal Credit Union Act, which allowed credit unions to be chartered in all states. Thus, the credit union was the second thrift Congress recognized with a federal charter.

The last financial institution to attain federal status is the mutual savings bank. These institutions have broader powers than either savings and loans or credit unions. Mutual savings banks were given a federal charter in 1989.

Glass-Steagall: The Wall Between Investment and Commercial Banking

Prior to 1933, large commercial banks were heavily engaged in the underwriting and distribution of securities. Although these activities were not expressly authorized under the National Bank Act of 1863, commercial banks pursued these activities by establishing state-chartered securities affiliates. During the 1920s, the union of commercial and investment banking was very close. The stock market crash of 1929 led several political observers to question the relationship of commercial banks to investment banking. Congress considered several proposals to separate these two activities in 1932, but none were passed.

In 1933, the nation's banking system virtually collapsed and the economy fell into deeper recession. In the midst of this financial chaos, the Senate Banking and Currency Committee reopened the hearings it began in 1932 when they were exploring the relationships of commercial banks to their security affiliates. They found considerable evidence that (1) commercial banks made loans to attempt to artificially fix security prices, (2) security affiliates had sold difficult-to-sell securities to the bank's correspondents and trust accounts, and (3) commercial banks and their affiliates engaged in insider trading.

These investigations convinced the financially conservative members of Congress that commercial and investment banking should be separated. The Banking Act of 1933, known as the *Glass-Steagall Act,* was passed with three major provisions relating to commercial and investment banking. The first of these prohibited any Federal Reserve member bank from engaging in or being affiliated with any organization that is principally engaged in the issuance, underwriting, public sale, or distribution of securities. The second prohibited any organization involved in underwriting, selling, or distributing securities from engaging in taking deposits. The third provision prevented Federal Reserve member banks from sharing personnel with entities engaged in the issuance, underwriting, public sale, or distribution of securities.

Over the years, the Federal Reserve has liberalized the interpretation of Glass-Steagall in a number of important ways. Today, commercial banks or their holding companies may engage in a full range of investment banking activities outside the United States. They also may originate, underwrite, and distribute certain securities, such as general obligation municipal bonds and certain types of municipal revenue bonds. Commercial banks now offer discount brokerage services as well.

There are many controversial issues that remain as a result of the Glass-Steagall Act. Sometimes conflict arises when a commercial bank is put in the promotional role of the investment banker. There is also potential for a bank to use trusts under its control to sell securities it is unable to sell elsewhere. Another possibility is that a bank will encourage a company to sell securities and use the proceeds to pay off a weak bank loan. Or, the bank could make favorable loans to the bank's security affiliate, to issuers of securities distributed by the bank, or to support the price of a security.

Federal Guarantee and Government Sponsored Credit Agencies

During the Depression the government became very active in the residential mortgage finance business by taking three important steps: (1) the establishment of the Home Owner's Loan Corporation (HOLC) and its conversion of mortgage loans into fully amortized loans; (2) the creation of the Federal Housing Administration and its mortgage guarantee program; and (3) the creation of the National Mortgage Association of Washington, later to be renamed the Federal National Mortgage Association.

In 1933, the government passed the Home Owner's Loan Act. This legislation provided a means for defaulted loans on the books of financial depository institutions to be sold to the HOLC and refinanced. Between 1933 and 1936, over 1 million loans were purchased by the HOLC. It is also important to note that the HOLC converted these loans into fully amortizing loans. Prior to that time many of the loans were mortgages with balloon clauses. A balloon clause requires the loan to be fully repaid within a few years.

The National Housing Act of 1934 created the FHA, which widened the acceptance of fully amortized mortgages. In addition, the increased importance of government insurance led lenders to be more willing to extend the term of the debt. The actions of the HOLC and the FHA were important factors contributing to the almost exclusive adoption of the fully amortizing fixed-rate mortgage.

Another provision of the National Housing Act was designed to encourage the creation of national mortgage associations. These financing organizations were to buy, service, and sell mortgages originated by private lenders. No one stepped up to create one of these associations, however. As a result, President Roosevelt in 1938 persuaded a member of his administration to form the National Mortgage Association of Washington. This firm was designed to issue commitments to purchase FHA mortgages on single-family housing and also originate mortgages on multifamily housing. The firm was soon renamed the Federal National Mortgage Association, and it became the first secondary market mortgage entity.

Regulation Q: Interest Rate Price Controls

Another major legacy of the Depression were price controls on demand and time deposits, called Regulation Q. Many people blamed the massive bank failures on the tendency of commercial banks to aggressively compete with one another for deposits by paying higher interest rates. To eliminate all incentives to take risks by lending high-cost deposits to risky borrowers, the Glass-Steagall Act prohibited commercial banks from paying interest on demand deposits and subjected time and savings deposits to ceilings.

During the period following the Depression until the mid-1960s, these price controls were not particularly debilitating because inflation and interest rate cycles were modest. In the mid-1960s, however, open market interest rates rose significantly. Savings and loans were not subject to Federal Reserve controls under Regulation Q, and there was a concern that savings and loans would suffer under a rising rate environment. They were brought under Regulation Q in 1966 with the passage of the Interest Rate Control Act.

There were many changes to the Regulation Q format after 1966. The ceilings were adjusted and new innovations, such as the money market mutual funds, were created to keep the depositories competitive. As open market interest rates were moving to record high levels in the late 1970s, the battle to maintain the ceilings became competitively and politically impossible. Negotiable order of withdrawal (NOW) accounts, transaction accounts that paid interest, provided a competitive threat to the commercial banks' demand deposit monopoly, while the money market mutual fund was competing with commercial bank and thrift time deposits. Adding to the pressure were several senior citizen lobbying groups, who testified before Congress that the Regulation Q ceiling discriminated against them. They were the country's largest group of net savers and one of the most politically active. Regulation Q was eliminated in the 1980 Depository Institution, Deregulation and Monetary Control Act (DIDMCA).

Modern Financial Institution History: On the Road to Deregulation

Over the years, the financial structure of the United States has been the subject of much study and debate. Indeed, the inadequacies of the legal and regulatory structure were first pointed out in 1958 by the Commission on Money and Credit. A similar study, the Commission on Financial Structure and Regulation (Hunt Commission) followed in 1970. The Congressional response to these recommendations came years later. In 1975, the Senate passed the Financial Institutions Act, a financial restructuring bill, but it never passed the House of Representatives. In 1976, the House Committee on Banking, Currency and Housing developed and held hearings on a set of discussion principles entitled *Financial Institutions and the Nation's Economy (FINE)*. In 1981, some of the same issues were taken up by the president's *Commission on Housing*. This study led to strong recommendations to eliminate protectionism, controls, and separation of powers. The implementation of these recommendations came too late, however.

Political forces pushing for change received an unexpected ally in the late 1970s. Several lobbying organizations representing older Americans lobbied Congress for higher interest rates on their savings accounts. They contended that the interest rates they received on insured deposits were too low as a result of Regulation Q constraints. One of the leaders in pushing for change was the Gray Panthers, a senior citizen lobbying organization headquartered in California. Congress found the pressure for change too great and eventually passed significant financial reform legislation. The first response was the Depository Institution Deregulation and Monetary Control Act (DIDMCA). The following are the major provisions of the DIDMCA:

- Permits nationwide NOW accounts
- Eliminates deposit rate ceilings
- Applies reserve requirements to all depositories
- Provides federal override of state usury laws
- Provides access to discount window for thrifts
- Provides increased deposit insurance ceilings to $100,000

The DIDMCA took one very large step toward creating a more universal depository charter. Savings and loans, in particular, received transaction account powers and broader asset investment powers. Moreover, the act brought thrifts under many of the Federal Reserve provisions which, heretofore, concerned only commercial banks.

Shortly after the passage of the DIDMCA, Congress was again forced to address problems in the financial services industry. This time the impetus for the legislation was the increasingly weak state of the thrift industry. The prime rate hit 21.5 percent in 1981. This record high level of interest rates left the savings and loans with their huge holdings of fixed-rate mortgages and deregulated short-term savings accounts in a financial vise. By 1983, most of the net worth of the industry was all but wiped out. Congress responded to this dire situation with the Garn-St. Germain Depository Institutions Act (DIA). The following are the major provisions of the DIA:

- Authorizes a new account called the money market demand account to compete with money market mutual funds
- Provides broader power for federal savings and loans, including consumer loans, business loans, and expanded nonresidential real estate loans
- Provides authority for federally chartered institutions to offer adjustable-rate mortgages
- Permits thrifts to change charters
- Provides the FSLIC and FDIC with broad authority to assist weak and failing institutions

The DIA's most significant provisions broadened the powers of the FDIC and FSLIC to assist weak and failing institutions. These FDIC and FSLIC powers included the following:

1. Issuing financial guarantees
2. Assuming a weak institution's assets and liabilities
3. Making loans and contributions to troubled institutions
4. Arranging for mergers and other consolidations
5. Organizing mutual to stock conversions
6. Issuing net-worth certificates to banks and thrifts

The DIA also permitted out-of-state mergers and acquisitions of weak institutions. As early as 1982, for example, Citicorp of New York was given the authority to acquire a weak California thrift.

The DIDMCA and DIA did not undo the damage that the thrifts sustained during the high interest rate period in the late 1970s and the early 1980s. Although legislation provided the tools for regulators to overcome some of the problems, the basic weakness in the capital position of many thrifts and their limited earning potential continued to require Congressional and administration attention. In 1987, the main issue was the failing FSLIC, and Congress responded by legislating the Competitive Equality Act. The following are the major provisions of the act:

- Puts restrictions on commercial ownership of limited service banks (nonbank banks)
- Provides a mechanism for the FSLIC to receive $10.8 billion
- Requires that the Federal Home Loan Bank Board (the savings and loan regulator) provide forebearance to savings and loans with .5 percent capital
- Creates the Federal Asset Disposition Association to dispose of assets of failed thrifts
- Expands credit union powers

The Competitive Equality Act signaled Congress's first real recognition of the troubled state of the financial service industry. The act was only the first installment in a number of actions required to stem the tide of thrift and commercial bank losses.

A New Structure at Hand?

Of all the anticompetitive provisions discussed in the previous section, only Glass-Steagall remained a serious constraint. By 1990 the U.S. financial system looked quite different.

1. Interest rate ceilings on time and savings deposits were eliminated in 1980 with the passage of the DIDMCA.

2. The commercial banks' monopoly in offering demand deposits was eliminated through the Garn-St. Germain bill of 1982 and the Financial Institutions Reform, Recovery and Enforcement Act of 1989 (FIRREA). This legislation authorized commercial demand deposits for savings and loans.
3. Interstate branching had almost become a reality by 1990, as all but four states allowed out-of-state banks to compete in their state through holding company affiliates. The regulators of the federally chartered savings and loans have permitted nationwide branching by savings and loans.
4. Fixed commission rates on security brokerage were eliminated.
5. Fixed-rate mortgages were supplemented with adjustable rate mortgages.
6. The powers of thrifts were expanded.
7. Commercial bank holding companies could form investment banks.

Despite these evolutionary changes over the last 30 years, the U.S. financial system still shows signs of stress. Financial institutions have been failing at the highest levels since the Great Depression. Congress passed the FIRREA in 1989 as a means of dealing with the savings and loan crisis. Congress also set up a new agency, the Resolution Trust Corporation, to liquidate the failing thrifts. A deposit insurer, the Federal Savings and Loan Insurance Corporation, has failed and a new fund has replaced it, the Savings Association Insurance Fund (SAIF). The regulator of the savings and loans, the Federal Home Loan Bank Board, was eliminated and replaced by a department of the Treasury, the Office of Thrift Supervision. The Bank Insurance Fund created by the FIRREA has had to obtain additional capital sources. The following is a brief summary of the major provisions of the FIRREA:

- It replaced the independent Federal Home Loan Bank Board with the Office of Thrift Supervision.
- It replaced the Federal Savings and Loan Insurance Corporation with the Savings Association Insurance Fund.
- It replaced the Federal Deposit Insurance Fund with the Bank Insurance Fund.
- It reduced investment powers of savings and loans.
- It created the Resolution Trust Corporation to manage the liquidation of failed thrifts.
- It expanded supervisory powers.

A complete discussion of FIRREA is found in the Appendix to Chapter 14.
The weakness in the savings and loan and commercial banking business did not end with the passage of FIRREA, however. The structural overcapacity problems in commercial banking remained and a high number of failures continued. By 1991, Congress was informed that the newly

created BIF, like its failed sister the FSLIC, was about to run out of the resources to handle the large number of anticipated bank failures. So, in December 1991, Congress passed the Federal Deposit Insurance Corporation Improvement Act (FDICIA). The following is a brief summary of the bill's provisions:

- Increase borrowing authority of BIF
- Increase borrowing authority of FDIC
- Restrict use of brokerage insured deposits
- Increase powers of bank regulators over weakly capitalized banks
- Increase regulatory powers of Fed over foreign banks
- Curtail protection of uninsured depositors
- Require FDIC to implement risk-based deposit premium program

The main features of this bill are as follows:

1. To allow the BIF to borrow up to $70 billion to liquidate banks
2. To increase the borrowing power of the FDIC
3. To increase the powers of bank regulators to control banks whose capital falls below certain levels
4. To eliminate the flexibility to insure depositors with accounts over $100,000 and reduce the use of insured brokered deposits
5. To strengthen the supervisory authority of the Federal Reserve with respect to foreign banks operating in the United States
6. To authorize the FDIC to implement a risk-based deposit insurance premium program by 1994.

Overall, the bill did little more than toughen existing capital requirements and examination powers beyond those established in the FIRREA. The bill was passed after a year of effort by President Bush to eliminate constraints on interstate branching, liberalize ownership of banks by commercial and industrial firms, and liberalize Glass-Steagall restrictions. Congress instead ignored the liberalization provisions and strengthened the restrictive and examination provisions. Clearly, the political sting from the thrift debacle had not passed by 1991. A more complete discussion of the FDICIA is found in the Appendix to Chapter 14.

Looking ahead, it seems clear that the period of rapid and sometimes violent financial change is not yet over. Today, our financial institutions must respond not only to changes in the financial structure within the United States, but internationally as well. Foreign financial institutions have become major players in the United States, while the United States has lost its leading position in international banking. Competitive forces are impacting hard on the insurance industry as well.

Our financial system remains in the midst of a sea of change. Consequently, it is necessary to focus on the concepts and principles that not only help explain change, but also make it possible to predict the future.

Summary

The United States has one of the most complicated financial systems of any industrialized country. One reason is that the large geographical area of the United States worked against the early establishment of nationwide institutions due to communication and transportation limitations. Another reason is that most people were opposed to a major federal government role in the chartering of financial institutions. As a result, the United States created a complex structure of state and then federally chartered commercial banks and thrift institutions.

The system was impacted by the willingness of states to charter specialized financial institutions such as savings and loans, mutual savings banks, and credit unions. Each had its origin in a European institution.

Prior to the establishment of the Federal Reserve System, our financial system was characterized by financial panics and wide fluctuations in the supply of money and credit. The Federal Reserve was created to reduce the potential for these cycles and improve the payments system.

The Depression of the 1930s significantly altered the structure of our financial system. Deposit insurance, separation of commerce and banking, deposit rate regulation, separation of investment banking and commercial banking, and the federal chartering of thrift institutions established a protective and anticompetitive framework for many of our country's financial institutions for decades to come.

The 1960s inflation and rise in interest rate volatility provided the catalyst for financial innovations that were destined to threaten the 1930s system of separation and controlled competition. Money market mutual funds in the 1970s made interest rate controls ineffective. All this led to the deregulation of depository institutions in the late 1970s and early 1980s. Interest rate controls fell, assets and liability powers were expanded, interstate activities were authorized, and new financial innovations became frequent events.

The 1980s closed out on a sour note. Savings and loans, weakened by high interest rates in the late 1970s and early 1980s, were unable to successfully use their expanded powers to build capital. Many expanded into highly risky loans and investments. Adding to the crisis was inadequate regulation and supervision. The result was the failure and forced liquidation of a large portion of the industry in the late 1980s and 1990s. Commercial banks and life insurance companies were also affected by the new heightened level of competition and financial innovation. They too suffered high levels of failure and generally reduced performance.

As we enter the mid-1990s, public policy has moved toward two distinct objectives. First, there is a conscious effort to encourage the consolidation of depository institutions. Many experts feel that there is excess capacity. Second, the regulators of financial institutions want to avoid future taxpayer costs of liquidating failed institutions. This is manifesting itself in the form of higher capital requirements, stronger examination and supervision, and reduced risk-taking powers for these institutions.

In early U.S. history, wars were a primary motivation for the government to either establish commercial banks or legislate added powers for existing banks. **The Bank of North America** (Revolutionary War: 1782), **The Second Bank of the United States** (War of 1812: 1816), and **National Bank Act** (Civil War: 1863) are all a result of armed conflict.

Early efforts at bank regulation included the establishment in the early 1800s of the **Suffolk System** in Boston, Massachusetts, which provided for a type of **fractional reserve system** for smaller banks outside Boston and the establishment in 1829 of the **New York Safety Fund,** which was the first depository insurance program.

The **National Bank Act** of 1863 provided the framework for the federal chartering of financial intermediaries. It provided for the establishment of the first regulator, the office of the **Comptroller of the Currency,** established federal chartering standards, and set reserve requirements and established capital standards.

Thrift institutions were chartered to provide specific financial services that commercial banks would not provide. **Mutual savings banks** (1816) were designed to provide a safe place for low and moderate income savers to save; **savings and loans** (1831) provided mortgages for residential property purchase, and **credit unions** (1913) provided access to consumer loans for the middle class.

In the early 1900s, the U.S. **payment system** was deemed inefficient, the money supply was **inelastic** and subject to excessive fluctuations, and the **free banking** system resulted in excessive failures, financial losses, and regional economic dislocations.

The establishment of the Federal Reserve System in 1913 corrected a number of these deficiencies. First, it controlled the supply of money through **open-market operations** and changes in **reserve requirements** for commercial banks. Second, it provided a **lender of last resort** function and established the discount window. Finally, it put the Fed in charge of the **payments system.**

The Great Depression was the most active period in U.S. financial history. The following are the primary legislative changes in the system: (1) Congress insured the deposits of commercial banks (**Federal Deposit Insurance Corporation**) and savings and loans (**Federal Savings and Loan Insurance Corporation**). (2) It provided for federal chartering of saving and loans and credit unions and established the federal savings and loan regulator (**Federal Home Loan Bank Board**) and lending institutions (**Federal Home Loan Banks**). (3) It established interest rate controls for demand and time deposits at commercial banks (**Regulation Q**). (4) It set up federally sponsored programs for residential mortgage guarantees (**Federal Housing Administration**) and the establishment of a secondary market (**Federal National Mortgage Association**). (5) It prohibited interest banking (**McFadden Act,** 1927) and mixing investment and commercial banking (**Glass-Steagall,** 1933).

The inflation of the 1960s and 1970s was a great impetus for financial innovation. Money market mutual funds, interest-paying payment drafts (**NOW accounts**), money and capital market innovations, the creation of securities using loans as collateral, and other innovations put regulated depository institutions under growing competitive pressure. The following resulted from a series of deregulation laws: (1) **Interest rate regulations** of depositories were eliminated. (2) The powers of **thrift institutions** were expanded. (3) **Adjustable rate mortgages** were promoted. (4) The **thrift bailout effort** was started. Congress accomplished this by legislating the **Depository Institutions Deregulation and Monetary Control Act** of 1980, the **Garn-St. Germain Depository Institutions Act** of 1982, and the **Competitive Equality Act** of 1987.

Deregulation came too late to save the savings and loans. It also exacerbated the overcapacity in the financial services business. The 1980s closed and the 1990s opened with a thrift crisis, significant commercial bank failures, and the failure of several very large life insurance companies. The **Financial Institutions Reform, Recovery and Enforcement Act** of 1989 was designed to reduce the threat of future thrift failures and improve regulation. This act **reduced asset and liability powers** of thrifts, **changed the thrift regulator and insurance corporation,** and **strengthened capital requirements.** It also created the **Resolution Trust Corporation** to liquidate the failed thrifts. The FIRREA was followed up in 1991 by the FDICIA. This act bolstered the resources of the BIF and sharply increased the powers of commercial bank regulators, while curtailing the insurance of accounts of large depositors and authorizing a risk-based premium for insurance of accounts.

Questions

Chapter 8

1. What role did wars have in early bank history?
2. What was the Suffolk bank system? What modern day institution performs a similar function?
3. What was the New York Safety Fund? What modern day counterparts does it have?
4. The period of free banking from 1837 to 1843 taught us what lessons about the limitations of our financial system?
5. What is meant by fractional reserve banking?

6. Why were the National Bank Acts of 1863 and 1864 important?
7. What is meant by a thrift institution? Why did thrift institutions get a foothold in the United States?
8. What lessons did we learn in our financial experiences of the 1800s that finally created the impetus to establish the Federal Reserve?
9. What are the primary responsibilities of the Federal Reserve? What were the Federal Reserve's safety and soundness responsibilities and how were they carried out? What tools does the Federal Reserve use to implement monetary policy?
10. What precedents did the legislation of the 1930s establish for the structure of our financial system?
11. What is the McFadden Act and how did it impact the financial structure of the United States? What is the Glass-Steagall Act?
12. What legislation was passed during the late 1970s and 1980s? How did this legislation impact on the competitiveness of our financial structure? What factors were behind the passage of this legislation?

The Objectives of an Efficient Payment System

appendix

Society's objective for a cost-effective payment system is the provision of a quality medium of exchange characterized by low production and transaction costs. A quality medium of exchange is defined as one that provides adequate safety and reliability as well as accessibility for everyone. Providing this optimal mix of payment services is difficult given the vast number of organizations across the country that require transaction services. The optimal mix is further upset by the existence of float, which has a distorting impact on the selection of payment devices. *Float* is a positive financial balance created by a transaction that is available to the payer (the paying party) prior to the time the payment is credited to the payee (the receiving party).

Also affecting the mix of payment services is the presence of the Federal Reserve. The Federal Reserve has not always priced its services to cover the costs of providing them. As a result, financial institutions have favored the use of certain payment devices at the expense of others. The controversy over what role the Federal Reserve should play in the transactions of the private sector ended when Congress passed the Monetary Control Act.

This act stipulates that the Fed must charge prices for the services it provides, which fully cover the direct and indirect costs of providing them. This action was designed to assist the private sector, since the Fed's prices for specific payment services undercut the private sector. The act also required the Fed to provide equal access to its services.

Electronic Payment Devices

There are major ongoing efforts to introduce new and more efficient electronic devices. Still, paper-based checking services continue to dominate. According to

Humphrey and Berger (1989) the primary nonelectronic payment devices in order of number of transactions in 1987 were cash, checks, credit cards, travelers checks, and money orders.

The number of cash transactions was put at 278 billion, checks were 4 billion, and credit cards were 5.1 billion. The following is a list of the primary electronic payment devices in terms of dollar volume:

- Automated clearing house (ACH) transactions
- Wire transfers
- Point of sale (POS)
- Automated teller machines
- Preauthorized bill payment

Humphrey and Berger also estimated the dollar volume of these transactions. The estimated dollar volume for *wire transfers* in 1987 was $281 trillion. Checks accounted for $56 trillion. The next two were *automated clearing houses* at approximately $4 trillion and cash at $1.4 trillion.

Humphrey and Berger estimate that the direct and indirect cost of the U.S. payment system in 1987 was approximately $60 billion. This total is made up of production costs, such as the cost of producing paper and coin money, and processing costs, such as running the check and credit card clearing systems and float. The largest of these costs is float. Businesses are the largest beneficiary of float for two reasons. First, they have large cash management capabilities to reduce the float cost. Second, as the largest writer of checks, businesses try to maximize float benefits. A person who receives a check for payment and does not cash it immediately creates a float benefit for the party writing the check.

Much has been done over the last several decades to improve the efficiency of the payment system. There have been major improvements in the check-clearing system, which has reduced cost through productivity gains. Two major developments of the payment system are the direct deposit of social security and payroll payments. Still, with a cost of $60 billion there remain many opportunities to improve our payment system. There are several other improvements that have been the focus of recent attention:

1. Additional improvements in check-processing efficiency
2. Accelerating the switch from paper-based to electronic-based payment devices
3. Consolidating the banking system
4. Requiring the largest dollar transactions to be electronically transferred.

Check-Processing Improvements

The greatest source of float relates to the processing time embedded in the check-clearing system. Much of the effort of cash managers in businesses is aimed at reducing these processing delays. Lock-box services, used by corporations to reduce the time between when a payment is mailed and when it is deposited in the firm's account, is just one of a number of approaches used to reduce float. Over the years, the Federal Reserve has taken many steps to reduce check-processing delays. The Fed's regional check-processing centers and the privately run automated clearing houses are designed to reduce the processing delays in the check-clearing system.

Paper to Electronic Transfers

Electronic transfer is the most promising way to increase the efficiency of the payment system. One reason for this is simply because the direct costs of production and processing of most electronic transfers are less than the cost paper-based transfers, not to mention the substantial reduction in float. In the early 1970s, discussions about the impending "cashless society" were in vogue in financial institution circles. Now, over 20 years later, few anticipate such a development any time soon. Some are wondering when the growth of paper-based checks will stop. The volume of checks continues to grow each year despite efforts to encourage the development of electronic systems.

The largest electronic system is the ACH. These are used in major metropolitan areas to facilitate the clearing of direct deposit transactions. They also assist the direct bill-paying programs used for monthly reoccurring transactions. In dollar volume, the wire transfer is the largest electronic system because its transactions are usually high dollar denominations.

One relatively new technology that could speed electronic transfer use is known as the *electronic data interchange (EDI)*. The financial EDI is a system that allows businesses to hook up with one another to share data. An EDI business hooked up to a supplier could invoice, query a supply catalog, determine inventory position, order goods, delivery specifications and prices, and create purchase orders. One add-on to the system is the electronic payment. The emergence of EDI in more businesses may produce a major impetus for the use of electronic payments in the business sector.

Several decades of effort to reduce the proliferation of checks and increase electronic transfers have failed, however. The major reasons are that the check offers its user large float benefits, control over the particular transfer, and a receipt. Any move to displace checks will have to address each of these advantages.

Another major reason in support of electronic banking is that it could substantially reduce the amount of float in the payment system. Some have suggested that all transfers above $50,000 to $100,000 be put onto electronic systems.

Consolidating the Banking System

One reason that check clearing takes so long is simply because we have so many institutions that provide checking-type services. In Canada, for example, over 90 percent of all bank deposits reside in only six institutions. This substantially increases the probability that the paying bank will also be the receiving bank, thus reducing processing time. The 1990s is expected to be a period of accelerated consolidation of the bank system. As this consolidation takes place, the efficiency of the check-clearing system will increase.

Commercial Banks

chapter **9**

This chapter is an overview of domestic and international commercial banking. The chapter covers the asset and liability structure of commercial banks and shows how this structure differs depending on the size and location of the bank and the type of customers it serves. The asset and liability structures of community banks are decidedly different from the large money center and international banks. This chapter also reviews recent bank performance statistics to illustrate the factors that affect bank profitability. The number and size of banks is an important consideration when analyzing competition and profitability, which is why applicable laws that affect operational efficiency are discussed. The chapter concludes with a discussion of the international banking activities of the U.S. domiciled banks and foreign banking activities in the United States.

Asset and Liability Structure of Commercial Banks

Commercial banks are the most diversified of our nation's depository institutions. This is because they have the broadest asset and liability powers among the different types of depositories. Many small commercial banks, however, have simple asset and liability structures because they are not large enough to offer a broad range of services effectively. Many of these banks have asset and liability structures that are not significantly more varied than savings and loans or savings banks. Generally, the larger the bank, the more diversified is its asset and liability structure.

Commercial banks are often classified as community, regional, super-regional, and money center or international banks.

- *Community banks* are banks with assets below $500 million that service medium-sized cities or rural counties. They may also be located in neighborhoods of larger cities.
- *Regional banks* generally range from $500 million to over $10 billion in assets. They serve large metropolitan areas or whole states.
- *Super-regional banks* refer to bank holding companies (BHCs) that have expanded to include multiple states and metropolitan areas. The super-regional banks are usually over $10 billion in assets.
- Money center or international banks are the nation's largest banks, with assets of $25 billion or more. These banks usually provide virtually all types of bank products and services and have significant international activities.

Asset Structure of Commercial Banks

Commercial banks have considerable latitude in choosing the types of financial assets they will hold. Table 9.1 on page 216 shows the various types of loans and securities that commercial banks hold. The numbers indicate that commercial banks hold a wide variety of financial claims, including securities, commercial and industrial loans, real estate loans, and loans to individuals.

Securities

Commercial banks hold large security portfolios for two primary reasons. First, commercial banks are the largest issuers of transaction accounts. They need to hold highly liquid securities, such as Treasury and agency securities, to meet potential withdrawals. Second, commercial banks invest in state and local municipal obligations, since these investments provide attractive yields. This is due in part to their exemption from federal and some state income taxes. The Tax Reform Act of 1986 reduced the favorable tax treatment for commercial banks holding these securities and, as a result, municipal securities are declining in importance as a bank asset. Many municipalities and local government entities, however, rely on banks for their financing, since there is a limited market elsewhere for their securities. Therefore, banks are likely to continue to hold significant amounts of such securities.

Table 9.1

Loans and Securities Held by All Commercial Banks
December 1990
(dollars in billions)

Loans and Securities Held	$ Amount	% of Total
U. S. government securities	$ 454.2	16.7%
Other securities	175.6	6.5
Total loans and leases	2,093.8	76.9
Commercial and industrial	648.1	23.8
Bankers' acceptances held	7.5	.2
Other commercial and industrial	635.1	23.3
Real estate	836.5	30.7
Individual	378.9	13.9
Security	40.6	1.5
Nonbank financial institutions	34.7	1.3
Agriculture	33.0	1.2
State and political subdivisions	34.3	1.3
Foreign banks	8.2	.3
Foreign official institutions	3.2	.1
Lease financing receivables	32.7	1.2
All other loans	44.6	1.6
Total	**$2,723.6**	**100.0%**

Source: Federal Reserve *Bulletin*. (July 1991).

Commercial and Industrial Loans

Commercial banks are by far the largest lenders to commercial and industrial firms. Even though many larger companies use the corporate bond and commercial paper markets to finance their needs, commercial banks are still major lenders in this market, especially to medium-sized and smaller companies. Loans to commercial and industrial businesses are provided on a secured and unsecured basis. Secured loans include accounts receivable, inventory, and equipment financing.

Real Estate Loans

Real estate loans include construction loans for new projects, residential first and second mortgages, and multifamily and commercial mortgages. Over the last decade, commercial real estate lending has become far more important to commercial banks. It has also become a growing source of losses. In the future, the residential mortgage market is expected to become more important to banks as savings institutions shrink and commercial banks reduce their exposure in the commercial real estate market.

Individual Loans

Loans to individuals, also known as consumer loans, include auto, credit card, personal, boat, RV, and a host of other types of loans not secured by real estate. This has been a major growth area for banks in the last decade.

Agricultural Loans

Loans to farmers represent a significant volume of bank loans, but are shrinking as a percent of assets. Loans to farmers for machinery, seed and fertilizer, buildings, animals, and a number of other needs put commercial banks into direct competition with the federal farm credit agencies. These agencies have grown to represent a major percentage of the agricultural market at the expense of commercial banks.

Leases

The last major asset type is equipment leasing. Commercial banks are involved in consumer leasing of autos and equipment leases to businesses and not-for-profit organizations. Banks make leases rather than loans, even when the funds are used for the same purpose by the borrower, in part because of the tax advantages to leasing.

Liability Structure of the Banking System

Deposits of individuals, governmental units, and businesses represent the primary sources of funds for banks. In the last several decades, commercial banks have also developed wholesale funding sources to augment deposits. These include federal funds, repurchase agreements, and commercial paper. Table 9.2 on page 218 provides a breakdown of the major classes of commercial bank liabilities.

Deposits

Commercial banks are by far the largest supplier of transaction or checking accounts. Until 1980, commercial banks had a monopoly in the offering of checking accounts, but a series of regulatory changes allowed thrift institutions and credit unions to enter the market. Banks eagerly seek transaction accounts because they have low or no interest costs (although they are expensive to service), and because they constitute a primary account relationship from which other products can be sold.

Savings deposits represent a substantial but declining share of bank liabilities. These accounts, often called *passbook accounts,* offer interest rates that are usually higher than checking accounts but lower than time

Table 9.2

Major Liabilities of Commercial Banks
December 1990
(billions of dollars)

Liability Type	$ Amount	% of Total
Deposits		
Transaction deposits	$ 637.1	20.9%
Savings deposits	573.3	18.8
Time deposits	1152.9	37.9
Borrowings	548.7	18.0
Other liabilities	226.4	7.4
Total liabilities		
and capital	$3041.6	100.0%

Source: Federal Reserve *Bulletin*. (July 1991).

deposits. They are attractive to small savers because of the ease of adding and withdrawing funds.

Time deposits are the largest and fastest growing category of deposit accounts. Time deposits include certificates of deposit offered primarily to individuals, as well as large denomination negotiable certificates of deposit offered to businesses, nonprofit organizations, and governmental units.

Borrowings

Commercial banks have developed a range of nondeposit sources of funds, which are often referred to as *wholesale funding sources*. One of the most useful are federal funds. All banks are required to hold a percentage of certain types of deposits as reserves at Federal Reserve banks. These reserves can be transferred from one bank to another to adjust actual reserves to required levels. The bank in need of reserves is a buyer in the federal funds market. Generally, smaller institutions with less sophisticated cash management procedures are sellers of federal funds.

Commercial banks are also major borrowers in the repurchase agreement, or repo, market. Here the bank sells securities it owns to another institution with an agreement to repurchase them at an agreed upon price and time, usually overnight. Although bank activities in the fed funds and repo markets are in reality borrowing and lending transactions, technically they involve purchases and sales of assets. As a result, it is customary to refer to borrowing in these markets as selling and to lending as buying.

Banks also borrow on a longer-term basis using capital notes and debentures. These are unsecured bonds issued by the bank. Banks usually do not use capital notes as a major source of funds, but rather as a way to meet their capital requirements.

Banks also hold funds of the U.S. government in the form of Treasury tax-and-loan accounts. They also borrow occasionally from the Federal Reserve discount window.

Asset Structure Differences by Size of Bank

As mentioned earlier, banks of different size and focus are significantly different in terms of their asset and liability compositions. Smaller community banks typically have a more limited range of assets and liability choices. Large international banks have more diversified asset and liability structures and are more dependent on wholesale sources of funds.

Table 9.3 provides a comparison of the asset composition of commercial banks for three size groups and for all banks combined. This table shows interest-earning asset categories as a percentage of total assets.

Table 9.3

Asset Composition of All Commercial Banks by Size Year-end 1990

Interest-Earning Assets	All Banks	Under $300 Million	$300 Million to $5 Billion	Over $5 Billion
Total interest-earning assets	87.72%	91.17%	88.82%	86.96%
Loans	61.16	55.00	63.31	63.62
Commercial and Industrial	18.59	11.78	16.71	22.39
Real estate	23.51	28.00	26.85	21.25
Consumer	11.23	10.92	15.00	11.41
Foreign	.79	.01	.08	.50
Other	5.61	.89	3.91	6.88
Securities	17.25	28.29	18.78	14.38
U.S. and agency	11.85	21.22	12.98	10.28
State and municipal	2.65	4.58	3.18	2.08
Trading, reverse repo, and deposits	9.31	7.89	6.37	8.96

Source: Federal Reserve *Bulletin*. (July 1991) p. 518–26.

The primary differences in the asset structure of banks relates to the lower percentages of loans and the higher percentage of securities held by smaller banks. Smaller banks find it difficult to make a large volume of commercial and industrial loans because they are limited to smaller-sized loans to provide sufficient diversification. Also, small banks located in capital surplus areas are unable to support out-of-area loan offices and therefore are largely confined to the needs of the local borrower. Smaller banks are also more inclined to hold home mortgages because the mortgages generally are small, available locally, and low risk.

Larger banks have greater access to wholesale funding sources and therefore do not need to hold a large number of securities for liquidity purposes. As a result, they can hold a higher percentage of assets in loans.

Liability Structure Differences by Size of Bank

Just as there are significant differences in the asset composition of banks by size, their liability structures differ as well. Larger banks can attract wholesale funds more easily than small banks, and large banks have loan origination units that can usually supply more loans than retail deposits alone can support. Table 9.4 provides a look at the liability composition of commercial banks using the same size breakdown as in the previous table.

Table 9.4 shows that large banks are much heavier users of wholesale funding sources such as foreign deposits, large time deposits, federal funds, and repos than small banks. Small banks rely to a much greater extent on retail deposits, especially small time deposits and nonbusiness checking (other checkable) accounts. The table also indicates that smaller banks have significantly more equity than larger banks, while larger banks use more long-term debt (included in other liabilities) to meet capital requirements.

Regulation of Commercial Banks

The regulatory structure for commercial banks is complicated. This is due to the presence of both state and national chartered banks. The chartering of commercial banks by both state and federal authorities is known as the *dual banking structure*. The legislation that established national banks in 1864, the Federal Reserve in 1913, deposit insurance in 1934, and holding companies in 1960 led to further division of regulatory duties. Consequently, four entities share the various regulatory duties for commercial banks. These regulatory bodies include the state banking authorities, FDIC, Federal Reserve System, and Comptroller of the Currency. The duties shared by these organizations include the following:

- Chartering
- Approving interstate and intrastate branches and mergers
- Promulgating consumer protection legislation
- Enforcing consumer protection legislation

Table 9.4

**Liability Composition of Commercial Banks
Year-end 1990**

Liabilities	All Banks	Under $300 Million	$300 Million to $5 Billion	Over $5 Billion
Deposit liabilities	76.20%	87.75%	79.28%	71.35%
Foreign offices	6.55	N/A	1.78	7.29
Domestic	66.65	87.75	77.50	64.06
Demand deposits	12.98	12.49	14.42	13.71
Other checkable	6.22	10.52	7.45	5.08
Other core				
MMDA	10.81	10.67	12.66	11.91
Savings	5.75	7.90	7.08	4.54
Small time	19.71	34.99	23.97	15.78
Large time	11.18	11.11	11.92	13.02
Fed Funds and Repos	7.75	1.33	7.94	12.46
Other liabilities	4.85	.56	3.26	5.88
Equity	**6.26%**	**8.45%**	**6.85%**	**5.58%**

Source: Ibid.

- Providing deposit insurance
- Establishing reserve requirements
- Approving the formation or acquisition by a holding company

Table 9.5 on page 222 explains the overlapping nature of commercial bank regulation. The table shows the various types of commercial banks, including state and federally chartered banks, and Federal Reserve member and nonmember banks. State chartered uninsured banks are not shown. They are regulated by the same groups that regulate state insured nonmember banks, except that the FDIC has no role in their regulation. A bank is a nonmember bank if it does not belong to the Federal Reserve System.

Financial Claim/Function Matrix

As we have seen, the assets and liabilities and functional activities of commercial banks differ significantly from one bank to another. A financial claim/function matrix for a hypothetical community, regional, and international bank is shown in Table 9.6 on page 223.

Table 9.5

Commercial Bank Regulators

Regulatory Duty	National Bank	State Member Bank	State Nonmember Bank
Grant Charter	Comptroller	State	State
Interstate and intrastate branching and mergers	Comptroller	Fed and State	Fed and State
Promulgation of consumer regulations	Fed	Fed and State	Fed and State
Enforcement of consumer regulations	Comptroller	Fed and State	FDIC and State
Deposit insurance	FDIC	FDIC	FDIC
Reserve requirements	Fed	Fed	Fed
Holding company creation or acquisition by	Fed	Fed	Fed

Comptroller = Comptroller of the Currency
State = State Bank Regulatory Agency
Fed = Federal Reserve Board
FDIC = Federal Deposit Insurance Corporation

As the table shows, the larger the bank, the more varied the financial claims it chooses to hold as assets and issue as liabilities. In addition, the larger the bank, the more likely it will perform more functions, because only the larger banks are able to support the costs associated with developing the capability to originate and service different types of assets. The bank must be a reasonably large investor in many of these assets to reach an acceptable level of asset portfolio diversification.

Commercial Bank Financial Performance

The performance of the commercial banking industry has deteriorated by most financial measures throughout the 1980s. U.S. banks have been harmed by defaulted loans to developing countries, the severe depression in the southwestern states due to sharp declines in oil prices, and commercial real estate lending problems in a number of major metropolitan markets. Moreover, the poor performance of commercial banks has not been centered exclusively on large banks involved in international lending, oil belt credits, or commercial real estate finance. Many other banks have also experienced weak performance.

Table 9.6

Financial Claim/Financial Intermediary Production Matrix for Assets and Liabilities

Type of Claim	Origination Pri	Servicing	Brokerage Pri-Sec	Market-Making Pri-Sec	Portfolio Management
Assets					
Government					
United States	✲		❖✲	◆❖✲	◆❖✲
Agency	✲		❖✲	◆❖✲	◆❖✲
Municipal	❖✲		❖✲	◆❖✲	◆❖✲
Business					
Corporate bonds					
Equities					
Mortgages	◆❖✲	◆❖✲	◆❖✲	◆❖✲	◆❖✲
Leases	❖✲	❖✲		❖✲	❖✲
Loans	◆❖✲	◆❖✲	❖✲	◆❖✲	◆❖✲
Household					
Installment	◆❖✲	◆❖✲	✲	◆❖✲	◆❖✲
Credit card	◆❖✲	❖✲	✲	◆❖✲	❖✲
Mortgages	◆❖✲	◆❖✲	◆❖✲	◆❖✲	◆❖✲
Foreign					
Liabilities					
Demand deposits	◆❖✲	◆❖✲	◆❖✲	◆❖✲	◆❖✲
Certificates of deposits	◆❖✲	◆❖✲	◆❖✲	◆❖✲	◆❖✲

Pri = Primary market
Sec = Secondary market
◆ = Community bank
❖ = Regional bank
✲ = International bank

Table 9.6 continued on page 224.

Table 9.6 continued

Financial Claim/Financial Intermediary Production Matrix for Liabilities

Type of Claim	Origination Pri	Servicing	Brokerage Pri-Sec	Market-Making Pri-Sec	Portfolio Management
Capital Market Funding					
Collateralized debt					
FHLB advances	◆❖✻	◆❖✻		◆❖✻	◆❖✻
Reverse repos	❖✻	❖✻		❖✻	❖✻
Asset-based	❖✻	❖✻		❖✻	❖✻
Unsecured Debt					
Negotiable CDs	❖✻	❖✻	❖✻	❖✻	❖✻
Bankers acceptance	❖✻	❖✻	❖✻	❖✻	❖✻
Commercial paper	❖✻	❖✻	❖✻	❖✻	❖✻

Pri = Primary market
Sec = Secondary market
◆ = Community bank
❖ = Regional bank
✻ = International bank

Exhibit 9.1 shows the return on average assets (ROA) and on average equity (ROE) for all domestically insured banks from 1985 to 1989. The ROE is shown on the right-hand scale and the ROA on the left. Both series show high profit volatility and relatively low levels of profitability. Bankers customarily use a 1 percent ROA as a reasonable target. On average, bank performance has been well below these targets during the period shown. Weak earnings have made it difficult for U.S. banks to raise capital externally for expansion. Table 9.7 on page 227 indicates the percentage ROA and ROE for six different-sized commercial bank groups from 1985 to 1989. As the table indicates, the largest and smallest banks fared the worst.

The reasons for poor profit performance of commercial banks during the 1980s, despite relatively stable economic growth, reflect major changes in technology, regulation, macroeconomic policies, and competitive forces. Overall, commercial banks have been unable to earn a sufficient profit margin to provide a market rate of return on stockholders' equity to compensate for new risks associated with the business.

Exhibit 9.1

Return On Average Assets and Shareholder's Equity 1985–1990: All Insured Commercial banks

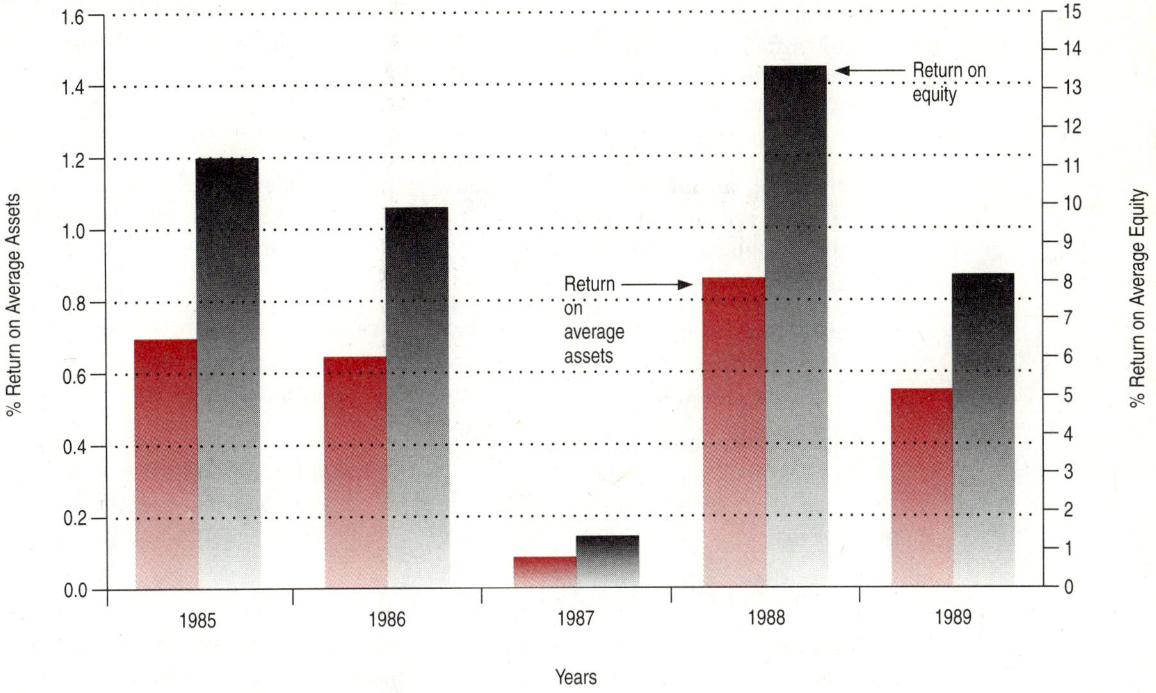

Source: *Statistical Abstract of the United States.* Washington, DC: U.S. Department of Commerce, 1991.

Management Highlights

Special Management Concerns for Commercial Banks

Community Banks

Achieving adequate economies of scale in operating efficiency: Smaller commercial banks have difficulty realizing processing efficiencies until they reach $50 million or more in size.

Achieving adequate asset portfolio diversification: Smaller banks cannot participate in many asset markets because they cannot assemble a portfolio of any given asset that is large enough to ensure diversification of risk.

Providing higher quality local customer service: Community banks are very dependent on a neighborhood or small city for deposits and loans. Since they cannot offer as many services as larger banks, they must provide better customer service.

Regional Banks

Achieving an adequate net interest margin: Moderate-sized banks confined to a region of the country may find that loan demands do not provide a high enough net interest margin without also accepting excessive credit or interest rate risks.

Achieving adequate diversification of regional economic business cycle risks: Regional banks typically must bear excessive credit risks due to their large concentration of loan assets within one region of the country.

Controlling operating costs: Regional banks typically must expand their loan origination activities to improve credit diversification and provide additional services to customers. This tends to increase expenses faster than revenues.

International Banks

Managing price risks on trading portfolios: International banks are generally active in trading securities for customers and their own account. This requires developing sophisticated risk-measuring and risk-management hedging systems.

Controlling foreign credit risks: International banks must manage foreign credit risks in addition to domestic credit risks.

Controlling foreign exchange risks: International banks typically trade foreign exchange in the cash and forward markets. Like securities, this trading involves substantial price risks that require developing sophisticated risk-measuring and management systems.

Management of off-balance sheet risks: International banks tend to have large portfolios of off-balance sheet exposures, such as interest rate and currency swaps, foreign exchange forward positions, letters of credit, and credit guarantees that involve considerable risks.

Bank Failures Climb

The sharp rise in bank failures represents one of the more important effects of the decline in commercial bank profitability during the last decade. Until

Table 9.7

**Percentage Return on Average Assets and Equity for Commercial Banks Grouped by Size
1985–1989
(insured commercial banks by consolidated assets)**

Percentage Return on Average Assets

Year	All Banks	0–$25 Million	$25–50 Million	$50–100 Million	$100–500 Million	$500 Million	$1 Billion +
1985	.70%	.36%	.69%	.75%	.87%	.72%	.67%
1986	.63	.09	.46	.62	.68	.61	.65
1987	.10	.26	.46	.66	.75	.51	−.15
1988	.84	.37	.62	.78	.81	.58	.89
1989	.52	.63	.77	.91	.94	.91	.37
Avg.	.56	.34	.60	.74	.81	.67	.49

Percentage Return on Average Equity

Year	All Banks	0–$25 Million	$25–50 Million	$50–100 Million	$100–500 Million	$500 Million	$1 Billion +
1985	11.31%	3.67%	8.00%	9.30%	11.96%	10.29%	12.53%
1986	10.10	.91	5.34	7.72	9.43	9.00	11.84
1987	1.63	2.75	5.39	8.02	10.08	7.51	−2.80
1988	13.56	3.88	7.03	9.24	10.66	8.70	16.47
1989	8.21	6.45	8.52	10.43	12.15	13.10	6.49
Avg.	8.96	3.53	6.86	8.94	10.86	9.72	8.91

Source: Robert E. Goudreau and B. Frank King. "Recovering Bank Profitability: Spoiled Again by Large Bank's Loan Problems." *Economic Review,* Federal Reserve Bank of Atlanta. (May/June 1990): adapted from tables on p. 37.

the 1980s, bank failures occurred infrequently in this country since the end of the Great Depression. Commercial banks, protected by price controls on deposits and legal impediments to competition from other depositories, were able to earn steadily growing profits. In the period from the 1950s through the 1970s, bank stocks were considered comparable to those of public utilities, meaning steady earnings and relatively high dividend payments. This favorable connotation ended for many banks in the 1980s as profits fell and bank failures rose to record high levels. Exhibit 9.2 on page 228 shows the number of insured commercial bank failures and the dollar

Exhibit 9.2

Bank Failures 1934–1989: Number and Dollars of Assets

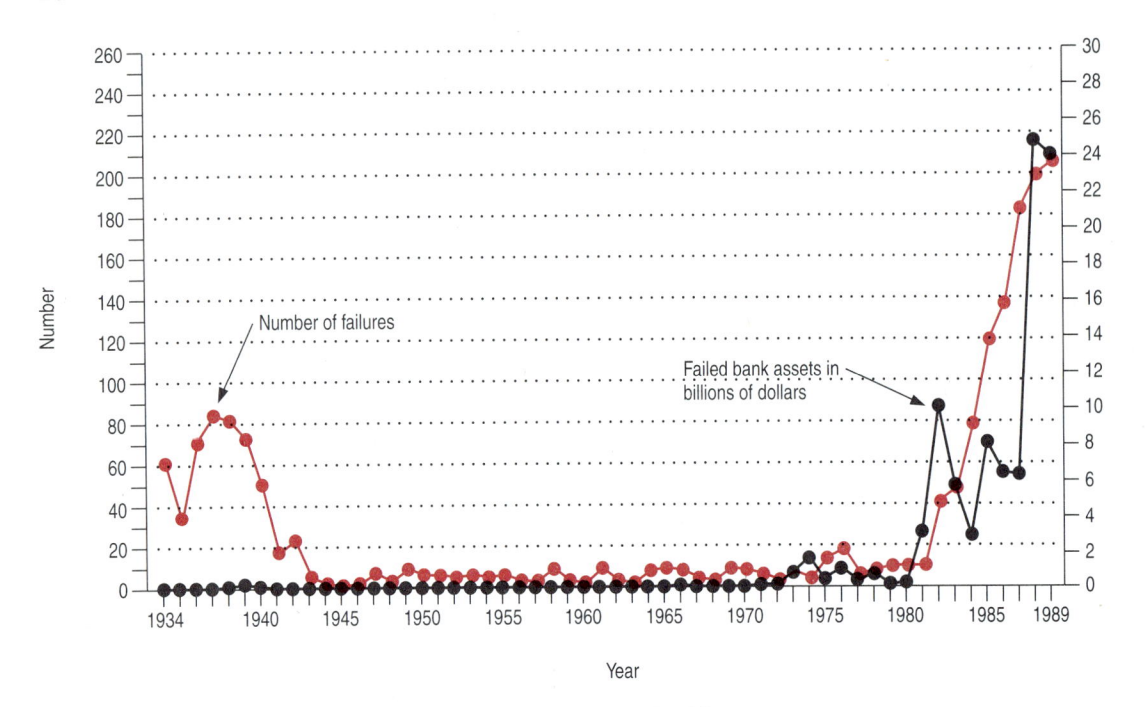

Source: *Statiscal Abstract of the United States.* Washington, DC: U.S. Department of Commerce, 1991.

amount of failed bank assets from 1934 to 1989. The large number of bank failures continued into the early 1990s.

Competition from Thrifts and Nonbanks

Probably the most significant changes to impact the competitive position and market power of commercial banks involve thrift institutions and nonbank financial intermediaries. These financial institutions have carved large holes in the markets traditionally served by commercial banks.

Since 1980, thrifts have received NOW account and demand deposit powers, eliminating the commercial banks' monopoly on this service. They have also received broad consumer lending authority and received limited commercial lending power. Nonbanks and conglomerates have developed competitive asset and liability services, including a variety of mutual funds, consumer finance products, corporate lending products, and corporate cash management services. As we will see in Chapter 13, commercial banks also face severe competition from government sponsored enterprises. All this new competition occurred at a time when rate ceilings on time and savings accounts were eliminated, forcing banks and other depositories to pay more competitive rates on deposit liabilities, narrowing their profit margins further.

All these changes have served to weaken the once-favored position of commercial banks and reduce their franchise value. Keeley (1990) analyzed the changes in the value of bank charters resulting from deregulation and new forms of competition. He concluded that one factor contributing to the decline in the market value of commercial bank equities relative to their book value was the decline in the value of a bank charter resulting from increased competition.

Bank Structure and Competition

A central fact of commercial banking in the United States is that there are probably more banks and related financial institutions operating domestically than the combined number of similar institutions operating throughout the rest of the world. Many banks operate as subsidiaries of holding companies owning more than one bank. Others have common or significant overlapping ownership. As a result, they may not operate as separate, independent entities. Nevertheless, the U.S. banking business is distinctive because of the number of competing institutions.

Banking *market structure* is the term used to cover the number, size, ownership, and geographic location of banking offices. Controversy over the best or optimum banking market structure continues to rage among researchers, regulators, legislatures, and the courts. The following section reviews several features of bank structure.

Size Structure

One feature of U.S. banking that has not changed dramatically in the last 50 years is that it is dominated by small banks. The vast majority of small banks are single-office organizations with limited product lines. They provide personal service to a local community, neighborhood, or rural area.

The other end of the spectrum includes the few large commercial banks. At year-end 1989, Citibank N.A. was the largest bank in the United States, with deposits of over $111 billion. Table 9.8 on page 230 shows the size distribution of commercial banks as of year-end 1989.

The overall concentration of banking as measured by the assets controlled by the largest banks has not changed materially in the last several decades. Despite the acceleration in the number of mergers and acquisi-

Table 9.8

Asset Size Distribution of U.S. Banks as of Year-end 1989

Size Range of Assets Held (in million $)	Total Number of Insured Commercial Banks in Size Group	Percent of All U.S. Insured Banks	Total Assets Held By Bank Size Groups (in billion $)	Percent Industry Assets
Less than $5	153	1.2%	$ .5	0%
$5 to $9.9	619	4.9	4.8	.1
$10 to $24.9	2,668	23.4	51.7	1.6
$25 to $49.9	3,238	25.5	117.2	3.6
$50 to $99.9	2,744	21.6	191.3	5.8
$100 to $499.9	2,370	18.6	463.3	14.0
$500 or more	614	4.8	2,470.4	74.9
All Domestic Insured U.S. Banks	12,706	100.0%	$3,299.2	100.0%

Source: *Statistical Abstract of the United States, 1991.* Department of Commerce, p. 499.

tions, the banking system has experienced a continued supply of newly chartered banks.

Even the continued rapid liberalization of branch banking has not resulted in a significant concentration of commercial bank assets. One reason for this is that many of the very large banks did not experience strong profitability in the late 1980s. As a result their ability to grow through acquisition has been hampered.

Branching and Interstate Banking

The ability of banks to operate branch offices has a major impact on the level of market competition and bank concentration. Branching by commercial banks is regulated by a complicated patchwork of state laws. The McFadden Act of 1927, for example, prohibited national banks from branching, except to the extent that state chartered banks may branch. This act effectively outlawed interstate branching.

State branching laws have been changing continually for the last half-century or more. Table 9.9 shows changes in branching laws in each state from 1910 to 1990. As a result, bank branching activity has increased in almost all states. Branching within a state can be classified into three categories: unit banking, limited branching, and statewide branching. In

Chapter 9 Commercial Banks 231

Table 9.9

State Branching Laws in Selected Years

State	1910	1929	1939	1961	1979	1990
Alabama	✧	●	◆	◆	◆	◆
Alaska	✪	✪	✪	✺	✺	✺
Arizona	✪	✺	✺	✺	✺	✺
Arkansas	◆	●	●	●	◆	◆
California	✺	✺	✺	✺	✺	✺
Colorado	●	●	●	●	●	●
Connecticut	●	●	✺	✺	✺	✺
Delaware	✺	✺	✺	✺	✺	✺
Florida	✺	●	●	●	◆	✺
Georgia	✺	◆	◆	◆	◆	◆
Hawaii	✪	✪	✪	✺	✺	✺
Idaho	✧	●	✺	✺	✺	✺
Illinois	●	●	●	●	◆	◆
Indiana	●	◆	◆	◆	◆	◆
Iowa	✧	●	●	●	◆	◆
Kansas	✧	●	◆	◆	●	✺
Kentucky	✧	✧	✧	◆	◆	◆
Louisiana	◆	◆	◆	◆	◆	◆
Maine	◆	◆	✺	✺	✺	✺
Maryland	✧	✺	✺	✺	✺	✺
Massachusetts	●	◆	◆	◆	◆	✺
Michigan	✧	✧	✺	◆	◆	✺
Minnesota	✧	●	●	●	●	◆
Mississippi	●	◆	◆	◆	◆	◆
Missouri	●	●	●	●	●	●
Montana	✧	●	●	◆	●	◆
Nebraska	✧	●	●	●	●	◆
Nevada	●	●	✺	✺	✺	✺
New Hampshire	✧	✧	✧	✧	◆	✺
New Jersey	✧	◆	◆	◆	✺	✺
New Mexico	✪	●	●	◆	◆	◆
New York	◆	◆	◆	◆	✺	✺

Table 9.9 continued on page 232.

Table 9.9 continued

State Branching Laws in Selected Years

State	1910	1929	1939	1961	1979	1990
North Carolina	✧	✹	✹	✹	✹	✹
North Dakota	✧	✧	●	●	●	✹
Ohio	✧	✦	✦	✦	✦	✹
Oklahoma	✧	✧	✧	●	●	✹
Oregon	✹	●	✹	✹	✹	✹
Pennsylvania	●	✦	✦	✦	✦	✹
Rhode Island	✹	✹	✹	✹	✹	✹
South Carolina	✧	✹	✹	✹	✹	✹
South Dakota	✧	✧	✹	✹	✹	✹
Tennessee	✹	✦	✦	✦	✦	✹
Texas	●	●	●	●	●	✹
Utah	✧	●	✹	✹	✹	✹
Vermont	✧	✹	✹	✹	✹	✹
Virginia	✹	✹	✦	✹	✹	✹
Washington	✹	●	✹	✹	✹	✹
West Virginia	✧	●	●	●	●	✹
Wisconsin	●	●	●	●	✦	✦
Wyoming	✧	✧	✧	✧	●	✹

● Unit banking
✦ Limited branching
✹ Statewide branching
✧ No branching law
✪ Not yet a state

Source: David L. Mengle. "The Case for Interstate Branch Banking." *Economic Review,* Federal Reserve Bank of Richmond (November–December 1990): p. 6

unit banking, only single-office banks are permitted in the state. Allowances may be made for limited service facilities and automated teller machines. *Limited branching* refers to geographic limitations, such as within a city, county, or portion of a state. *Statewide branching* allows branches to open anywhere within the state provided they obtain regulatory permission.

As the table shows, branch laws have been liberalized significantly, particularly over the last ten years. By 1990, only 14 states did not permit statewide branching while only three, Colorado, Missouri, and Montana, were still unit bank states. Even in states that have restrictive branching laws, *multibank holding companies* may control several banks within a specific market. For example, multibank holding companies control several banks in the unit bank state of Colorado, and chain banking, common investor ownership of several banks, is also common in the limited branching state of Illinois.

Interstate banking, effectively forbidden by the McFadden Act and the Douglas Amendment, is the new frontier in bank structure change. During the 1980s, a new form of interstate banking emerged with the development of reciprocal, regional pacts between states, which permit a BHC to own banks across state lines. As a result, large regional BHCs began operating in the Southeast, Midwest, West, and Northeast states in the early 1990s.

As of 1990, 46 states and the District of Columbia had passed legislation permitting banks in their state to be owned by an out-of-state holding company. Of these, 26 states permit nationwide reciprocity, while the remaining 20 states and the District of Columbia permit regional reciprocity. Reciprocity refers to the agreements between states that bank holding companies from one state be allowed to purchase banks in another state as long as the first state allows the same privilege to the second state's bank holding companies.

The following are a number of strong arguments given in favor of branching at both the interstate and intrastate levels:

- Branch banks are less likely to fail due to their ability to diversify their assets and liabilities geographically.
- Branch banks provide greater consumer convenience by having offices available in a variety of locations.
- Branch banking is significantly more efficient as an organizational form compared to multibank holding companies.
- The efficiency of the payment system is increased.
- Branching enhances competition.

Opponents of branch banking argue that unlimited branching would increase concentration of the business into a few, huge banking organizations largely free of local control. Many people believe this would result in less competition and an insensitivity to local needs.

Efficiency Through Size: Economies of Scale and Scope

Much of the discussion surrounding bank structure laws focuses on whether large banks are more efficient and, therefore, able to deliver more services at lower cost. These attributes are referred to as economies of scale and scope. *Economies of scale* concerns the relationship between the quantity of a bank service produced and the cost per unit of that service. In other

Exhibit 9.3

Economies of Scale

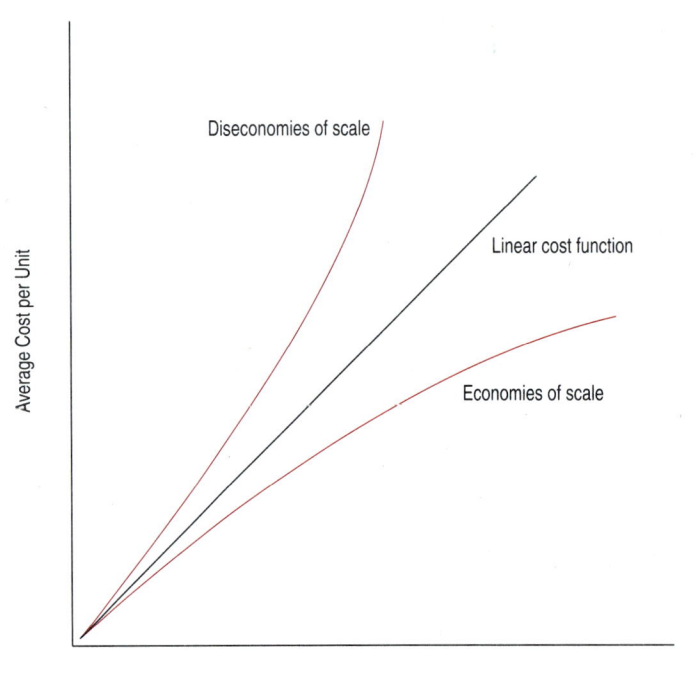

[Graph showing Average Cost per Unit on the y-axis versus Number of Units on the x-axis, with three curves labeled "Diseconomies of scale," "Linear cost function," and "Economies of scale."]

words, it asks the following question: "Can larger banks provide any given service more cheaply than smaller banks?" Exhibit 9.3 shows three hypothetical relationships of cost per unit is independent of the number of units produced. The linear cost unit line represents a situation in which cost per unit is independent of the number of units produced. The line labeled "economies of scale" indicates a product in which costs per unit decline as units produced increase, while the "diseconomies of scale" line shows rising cost per unit.

Economies of scope relates to the cost per unit of bank services that are produced jointly by sharing a common production system. For example, if a bank offers both first and second mortgages that are originated and serviced by the same unit within the bank, the cost per unit of the first and second mortgages originated and serviced would be less than if two groups provided the product. The issue in economies of scope is, "Can larger banks provide a wider range of services at lower per-unit cost because of shared joint production?"

Bank management and shareholders are interested in producing banking services at the least cost because, in a competitive market, the bank will survive and earn a reasonable profit. If technology, management structure, or joint service production results in lower costs as an activity grows in size, then there is a strong incentive for growing to maximize profits. From the government perspective, low-cost banking services are critically important to overall economic efficiency. Thus the question of whether the government should encourage or discourage the creation of large banks becomes a very important public polity issue.

Over the years, the great body of operating statistics on commercial banks has permitted extensive research on the subject of economies of scale and scope. Much of this work was done using the Federal Reserve Functional Cost Analysis data. The analysis provides cost and volume data for a large number of banks of various sizes and type of services provided, such as demand deposits, mortgage loans and others.

Research Analyses and Limitations

The first question addressed in the analysis relates to whether production functions of commercial banks display declining, level, or increasing average cost per unit as the output of a given service increases. Declining average costs indicate economies of scale. The second question relates to whether costs of two or more related services produced by the same bank have a joint production function that displays declining, level, or increasing average cost per unit of output. This analysis tests for economies of scope.

Unfortunately, the studies' results are not very convincing either way about economies of scale and scope in banking. According to Rose (1987), economies of scale showed up significantly only in relatively small banks with less than $100 million in assets. It should be recognized, however, that these empirical studies have many limitations. The data used in many of these analyses do not include large banks. Most banks supplying data for the Functional Cost Analysis were well below $1 billion in assets. Secondly, properly specifying the output of a bank is very difficult. Most of these studies have not used the framework discussed in Chapter 7, in which the functions of the bank are unbundled. It could be that some of these functions display economies of scale and others diseconomies of scale. When the functions are put together, however, the results are ambiguous.

The results, however, do suggest that public officials need not worry about larger banks monopolizing the market because they can achieve vast cost efficiencies. This may change as information processing and communication technologies change. Presently, the reduced cost of information and communication seems to favor the small banks as much as the large banks. Consider the greatly increased power and low cost of computers today compared to only a decade ago. As computer processing costs continue to decline, smaller institutions may well be able to stay competitive with larger banks.

Even if there are relatively few economies of scale and scope in banking, it is clear that larger banks see extensive opportunities to be gained through mergers and branching across state lines. Larger banks have been at the forefront of efforts to change the laws that inhibit geographic expansion. Their arguments are usually expressed in terms of operating efficiency and the benefits of lower costs to the public. Perhaps a more powerful argument is that geographic expansion will provide greater diversification of risk and fewer bank failures.

Entry and Exit

Another way that regulators impact the competitive structure of bank markets is by controlling the establishment of new banks and encouraging mergers and closings. During the last several decades, there has been a relatively constant rate of new bank charters. From 1980 through 1989, the number of new banks that were chartered rose from a low of 120 to a high of 266 per year. This rather free chartering of banks is due in part to the presence of the dual banking system. Banks in the United States may be chartered as a national bank by the Comptroller of the Currency, or as a state bank by a state regulator. This means that the only effective way for the federal government to control the number of new banks is to limit the granting of deposit insurance.

Bank disappearances usually meant mergers and acquisitions until recent years, when the number of bank failures increased significantly. Mergers, consolidations, and absorptions of banks increased rather significantly in the 1980s, as did bank failures.

Overall, research relating to the effects of entry and exit of commercial banks on competition is not very revealing. There is no significant evidence to show that new charters increase competition or hurt existing banks in the market. Results of analyses of the impact of bank chartering on the number of bank failures have been even more ambiguous.

Bank Holding Companies

A BHC is a corporate entity that owns the stock of one or more commercial banks. BHCs have been a feature of U.S. banking since the turn of the century. However, the real growth in BHCs did not take place until the mid-1960s. By 1990, over 90 percent of all the deposits in commercial banks were in banks owned by BHCs.

The reason for this phenomenal growth is that the BHC allows a bank-related entity to expand its product and geographic base in ways that are not permitted to banks alone. Recently, interstate reciprocity laws have provided the impetus for banks to purchase subsidiaries in new markets.

This allows potential cost savings, since a centralized holding company organization can perform various services for each of the BHC-owned banks. Since each of the banks must be a separate entity, however, it is not clear that significant economies of scale result from the multibank holding company structure. The BHC permits the bank to diversify its lending risks by permitting geographical diversification and its funding risks by allowing the firm to establish deposit-gathering units in different markets.

The BHC also permits the bank organization to operate businesses within the holding company structure that a bank is not permitted to undertake itself. These activities are carefully restricted by the Federal Reserve, which has the authority to determine permissible activities under the Bank Holding Company Act.

The activities or potential activities of BHCs fall into three groups:

1. Activities approved by the Federal Reserve for BHCs
2. Activities permitted by order of the Fed
3. Activities expressly denied by the Fed

Table 9.10 provides a list of the more important activities that pertain to each group.

BHCs have caused major changes in the structure of commercial banking. First, the types of businesses in which bank-related organizations may engage has greatly expanded. This has served to reduce the separation

Table 9.10

Status of Major BHC Activities per Fed Order

Approved	Permitted	Denied
Extension of credit	Operating a distressed savings and loan	Underwriting life insurance
Trust company and fiduciary activities	Buying and selling gold and silver for customers	Land investment/ development
Data processing services	Employee benefit	Management consulting
Consulting		
Investment or financial advising	Cash management services	Travel agency services
Securities brokerage	Corporate bond trading	Property management

Source: B. F. King, S. L. Tschinkel, and D. D. Whitehead. "Interstate Banking Developments in the 1980s." *Economic Review,* Federal Reserve Bank of Atlanta (May/June 1989): pp. 48–50.

of powers that characterized banking after the Depression. Second, the BHC has gone a long way toward reducing geography as a constraint to a bank organization's marketing and distribution strategy, except for deposit-taking activities through branches. Today, the BHC is the preferred structure for all large and many medium-sized banking organizations.

Bank structure has been a topic of academic and regulatory interest for several decades. While still a topic of interest, competition from other depositories and nonbanks has made the question of whether banking markets are competitive less important as a public policy issue. This is especially true given the additional competitive pressures represented by international banks operating in the United States.

International Banking 1960 to 1990

The modern history of international banking can conveniently be divided into three periods. The first, the 1950s to early 1970s, is the period in which U.S. banks took the lead in establishing worldwide banking operations. During this period, international banking was needed primarily to facilitate trade expansion. U.S. banks and companies dominated international markets.

The second period, from the mid-1970s to the early 1980s, was a period in which U.S. international banks took on the role of recycling the petrodollars of the Organization of Petroleum Exporting Countries (OPEC). These huge dollar surpluses were created when the OPEC oil cartel successfully increased the worldwide price of oil. The billions of dollars earned by oil exporting countries were invested in U.S. international bank offices and other foreign banks and reloaned to oil importing countries around the world. Many of these loans were made to developing countries that could not afford to pay higher oil prices from export earnings. Other loans were made to oil exporting countries, such as Mexico, seeking to speed up their internal development by borrowing money and using their future oil revenues as the source of repayment. Since U.S. banks were in many instances international leaders, they were heavily involved in the petrodollar recycling program.

The third period began in the mid-1980s. Banks in Japan and Western Europe caught up and surpassed the United States in international banking. There are three main reasons why this occurred:

1. Strong foreign economies: The economies in these countries performed very well during this period, and they greatly expanded international trade, creating an internal market for international banking services.

2. Large trade surpluses: Most of these countries, especially Japan and Germany, developed large foreign trade surpluses, which stimulat-

ed the development of foreign investment programs and facilitated the growth of their banks' international activities.

3. Weakened domestic bank earnings: U.S. bank earnings and capital positions began to weaken, and the shortage of capital inhibited international expansion. Many U.S. banks actually reduced their foreign presence during this period.

Functions Performed by U.S. Banks Internationally

U.S. banks participate in international markets in a number of ways. The following are the most important activities in this area:

- Commercial banking
- Investment and merchant banking
- Consumer finance
- Security brokerage
- Leasing
- Trust services
- Commercial finance
- Foreign exchange trading and hedging

As the list indicates, U.S. banks perform virtually all the functions internationally that they perform domestically. Foreign banking activities of U.S. banks are more diversified than their domestic activities, however. Some international activities, such as security brokerage, investment, and merchant banking, are currently prohibited or severely limited for domestic banks. These services are possible internationally because many foreign countries do not have the same limitations on banks that the United States has.

How U.S. Banks Are Organized for International Banking

There are four primary organizations used by U.S. banks for international banking activities:

1. Foreign branch offices
2. Domestic offices engaged in foreign banking
3. Foreign subsidiaries
4. Edge Act corporations

The most important of these are foreign branch offices and domestic offices. Table 9.11 on page 240 shows the volume of international assets held by each.

Table 9.11

International Assets of Insured U.S. Commercial Banks and BHCs by Type of Office
Year-end 1987
(dollars in billions)

Type of Office	$ Amount
Domestic office of U.S. banks	$136.5
International Bank Facilities (IBFs)	70.4
Other	66.1
Foreign branches	250.0e
Foreign subsidiaries	110.0e
Edge Act corporations	7.4

e = estimate
Source: James V. Houpt. "International Trends for U.S. Banks and Banking Markets." Working Paper, Board of Governors of the Federal Reserve System. no. 156 (May 1988): p. 3.

Foreign Offices

Foreign branch offices are the most common organizational form used by U.S. banks for international banking activities. These offices have the same powers and capabilities as the domestic bank and need not be duplicated in a foreign subsidiary. A foreign office can also pursue larger lending transactions by utilizing the entire capital base of the parent bank. Finally, deposits taken in the foreign office are exempt from reserve requirements.

Domestic Offices of U.S. Banks

The simplest way to conduct international banking activities is through the bank's offices in the United States. The difficulty, however, is providing service in the country in which the bank does business. International activities performed by domestic offices include buying foreign loan participations, trading foreign exchange, and issuing letters of credit.

Foreign Subsidiaries

Ownership of a foreign subsidiary by a U.S. bank holding company is a more complex approach to foreign banking. U.S. banks generally set up foreign subsidiaries to circumvent some prohibition imposed on the domestic bank by U.S. regulators. Foreign subsidiaries are used for the following reasons:

- Taking advantage of favorable tax or banking laws in another country that are available only to a locally chartered institution
- Opening offices in countries that prohibit foreign branches
- Circumventing prohibitions against investment banking and other activities that are legal in the foreign country, but not permitted by a U.S. bank

In addition, U.S. banks often purchase foreign bank subsidiaries to develop an immediate local banking franchise.

Edge Act Corporation

Although relatively insignificant today, U.S. banks at one time needed to provide deposit services to foreign customers outside of their state of domicile. This was not possible because of the McFadden Act prohibition against interstate branches. Congress passed the Edge Act to allow banks to operate branches in other states as long as they accepted only foreign deposits. The number of these corporations has declined in recent years partly because of the growth of interstate bank holding companies. There were 120 Edge Act offices in 1987 located primarily in cities such as New York, Los Angeles, Miami, and Houston, where large volumes of foreign trade are transacted.

International Banking Facilities (IBFs)

Foreign deposit-taking activities of U.S. banks were stimulated in 1981 by the Federal Reserve's authorization of IBFs. This designation allows a U.S. domiciled bank to establish a separate set of accounts for foreign deposits, thereby making them exempt from deposit insurance premiums, interest rate ceilings, and reserve requirements.

IBFs, however, are subject to significant restrictions. The most important is that they may conduct business only with foreign residents and other IBFs. Their number and assets have increased dramatically since being authorized in 1981. At year-end 1987, assets held by IBFs exceeded $70 billion. Table 9.12 on page 242 shows the growth of foreign branches of U.S. banks from 1960 to 1987. The table indicates the sharp rise in U.S. foreign banking activities during the 1960s and 1970s and the subsequent slowdown in the 1980s.

Foreign Banks Operating in the United States

The United States has been one of the most popular banking markets for foreign banks. As European and Pacific Basin countries developed large export markets in the United States, they also began to expand their banking overseas to provide services for their customers. Since the early 1970s, there has been a rapid increase in the number of foreign banks

Table 9.12

Foreign Branches and Branch Assets of Federal Reserve Member Banks Selected Years 1960–1987
(dollars in billions)

Year	Fed Member Banks with Branches	Number of Branches	Assets
1960	8	131	$ 3.5
1970	79	532	52.6
1980	159	787	343.4
1985	162	916	329.2
1987	153	902	350.0e

e = estimate
Source: Ibid. p. 7.

operating in the United States. The total U.S. assets of foreign banks hit $530 billion at year-end 1989. This is up from only $26.1 billion in 1972. Much of the growth in the 1980s came about because of foreign bank inroads into U.S. domestic banking markets. More liberal capital requirements and low home country interest rates allowed foreign banks to lend to U.S. businesses at lower rates of interest than U.S. banks could offer. Aggressive expansion by foreign banks resulted in a sharp increase in their share of U.S. banking markets. Recent international agreements to equalize bank capital rules among developed countries and lower U.S. interest rates have served to slow down the domestic market share erosion of U.S. banks.

Organizational Forms for Foreign Banks Operating in the United States

Foreign banks operate in the United States using the same organizational forms as U.S. banks use internationally. Foreign banks participate in U.S. markets through the following:

- Home country offices working through correspondent banks in the United States
- Branch offices located in the United States
- U.S. domiciled bank subsidiaries
- Edge Act corporations

Declining Relative Position of the United States in International Banking

In addition to the inroads foreign banks have made in U.S. markets, the relative position of U.S. banks in world banking markets has declined substantially since the 1970s. This is partly because of the growth in the European and Pacific Basin economies relative to the United States, and the decline in the value of the dollar. The extent of the dramatically falling international market share of U.S. banks is seen in Table 9.13 which shows the international assets held by foreign banks. The numbers indicate that, in only four years, from 1984 to 1988, the market share of U.S. banks dropped from 26.4 percent to 14.6 percent. Meanwhile, the share of Japanese banks rose in these same years from 23 percent to 38.2 percent.

In considering these data, keep in mind that using assets as the measure of bank activity may exaggerate the apparent decline in U.S. international banking because of the significant volume of activities not included on the balance sheet. U.S. banks, for example, are very active in the currency swap market and other international transactions that are not reflected in asset figures. In addition, the decline in the value of the dollar relative to the yen in this period accentuates the measured market decline. Nevertheless, U.S. banks have seen their domination of international markets in the 1950s and 1960s erode sharply in recent years as Japanese banks especially have expanded their international presence.

Table 9.13

International Assets by Nationality of Bank
(dollars in billions)

Parent Country	December 1984 $ Amount	% Share	December 1986 $ Amount	% Share	December 1988 $ Amount	% Share
France	$200.7	8.9%	$276.1	8.1%	$384.1	8.4%
Germany	143.2	6.4	270.0	7.9	358.8	7.7
Italy	90.6	4.0	145.1	4.3	201.2	4.4
Japan	517.9	23.0	1117.7	32.8	1756.4	38.2
Switzerland	82.9	3.7	152.0	4.5	238.6	5.2
United Kingdom	168.9	7.5	211.7	6.2	238.6	5.2
United States	594.5	26.4	598.3	17.6	675.3	14.6
Other	450.7	20.1	635.4	18.6	749.8	16.3

Source: Federal Reserve *Bulletin*. (February 1990).

The growing international role of Japanese banks is due to a number of factors. First, Japan has had a very large balance of payments surplus for many years. As a result, the country has built up large foreign exchange balances. Second, Japan has become a major world manufacturer and trading country. This has provided Japanese banks with a growing market for international banking services among their domestic exporting companies. Third, Japan has a very high personal savings rate, which has provided a large reservoir of savings for international investment. Finally, Japanese banks own stock in many nonbanking companies in Japan. A sharp rise in Japanese stock prices during the mid-1980s provided huge profits for banks. Since a large part of these gains could be counted as capital by Japanese banks, their growing capital resources provided a strong base for international expansion. This came at a time when U.S. international banks' capital positions were eroding, partly because of deteriorating loans to less developed countries.

International Focus

Japan Bank Capital and the Nikkei Average

Japanese commercial banks have a close relationship to many of their commercial customers. In fact, the banks own common stock in many Japanese firms. During the 1980s, this investment worked to the advantage of the Japanese banks. The primary index of Japanese stock prices, the Nikkei average, similar to our Dow Jones Industrial Average, climbed to approximately 37,000 yen. Japanese banks are also able to count 45 percent of the appreciated value of their stock holding as capital under the international capital agreements. The rise in Japanese stock prices provided a supply of low-cost capital, which provided the base for the worldwide expansion of Japanese banks.

The early 1990s has been a different story. By mid-1992, the Nikkei average was approximately 15,000 yen. This put Japanese banks in a potentially capital-short position. The international risk capital guidelines agreed to at Basle could force Japanese banks into several actions to raise their capital ratios, namely, selling assets and shrinking, issuing stock, and raising profit margins to enhance profitability. Shrinking or raising profit margins will certainly slow the pace of Japan's growing dominance in world banking.

The growth of Japanese banking is portrayed in Table 9.14. This table shows the explosive growth in Japanese banks throughout the world. The

Table 9.14

Location of Japanese Bank Offices
Year-end 1981−1989

Year	Offices in Japan	Total	Foreign Branches United Kingdom	United States
1981	791	233	134	74
1982	811	310	161	97
1983	908	350	178	108
1984	926	421	194	131
1985	1339	600	257	151
1986	1927	837	359	208
1987	2854	1090	426	252
1988	3044	1120	445	307

Source: Federal Reserve *Bulletin*. (February 1990).

Japanese foreign branches located in the United Kingdom and the United States are highlighted.

Reasons for the Changing Relative Position of International Banks

The experience of the post–World War II era illustrates the notion that the growth in international banking by banks in a particular country is largely a reflection of that country's success in international markets for goods and services. It is also heavily dependent on the relative health of the country's domestic banking industry. The U.S. banking industry has weakened during the 1980s and early 1990s. This has manifested itself in poor earnings and low capital growth. As a result, U.S. banks have had to retrench from their earlier aggressive stance in international banking markets.

A study of a number of the factors relating to the changing relative position of U.S. and other foreign banks in the international banking market by Zimmer and McCauley (1991) is revealing. They found that the single most important factor affecting the relative international competitiveness of one country's banks versus another's is the relative cost of equity capital. Higher equity costs make a country's banks less competitive.

The study cites four primary factors that have influenced the relative cost of equity capital in various countries. The first factor is the nation's pool of household savings. Japan, Switzerland, and Germany have all experienced much higher household savings rates than the United States. This accounts for a portion of the lower capital costs in these countries.

Economic stability and the accompanying stability in bank earnings also contributes to the difference in the cost of capital between countries. This is the second factor mentioned by the study. U.S. banks have experienced volatile earnings over the last decade and this has increased their cost of capital by depressing stock prices. Because Japan and Germany have managed to avoid large economic fluctuations in the 1980s, consequently their bank earnings have been more stable.

Cooperation between industrial and commercial firms and a nation's banks is also cited as a factor affecting the cost of capital. In Germany and Japan, the relationship between the industrial and commercial sectors and commercial banks is much closer than in the United States. This has resulted in lower default rates for industrial and commercial firms while, at the same time, providing banks with a more stable earnings and lower cost capital.

Finally, overall government policies influence bank capital costs. Countries that provide government assistance to firms in financial distress also tend to insulate banks from credit losses on loans. Antitrust laws, trade protectionism, and industrial subsidies all serve to reduce bank lending risk. This can translate into lower capital costs for banks in countries that provide greater assistance to domestic businesses. These protectionist policies are used less frequently in the United States than in Germany and Japan.

Table 9.15 shows Zimmer and McCauley's estimates of the cost of equity capital for banks located in four countries for the years 1984 to 1988. The

Table 9.15

Estimated Cost of Equity Capital for Banks of Several Countries 1984–1988

Country	% Cost of Equity Capital
Germany	6.9%
Japan	3.2
United States	12.0
United Kingdom	10.1

Source: Steven A. Zimmer, and Robert V. McCauley. "Bank Cost of Capital and International Competition." *Quarterly Review,* Federal Reserve Bank of New York (Winter 1991): adapted from table on p. 52.

cost of equity capital for U.S. banks was estimated to be 12 percent versus 3.2 percent for Japanese banks. The low cost of capital at Japanese and German banks allows them to fund loans at interest rates that are much lower than U.S. and U.K. banks. This competitive advantage is reflected in the market share numbers shown in Table 9.15. From 1984 to 1988, the market shares of U.S. and U.K. banks declined while the share of German banks grew modestly and Japanese banks' share increased sharply.

Summary

Commercial banks are our largest and most diversified intermediaries. Commercial banks hold a special place in our financial system because of the key roles they play in the U.S. payment system, their large business financing role, and their international activities. Even though other financial institutions perform all the activities of banks, they still dominate our system of depository intermediaries.

The financial performance of commercial banks in the United States over the last decade has been very poor. Commercial bank profits have been very low by post–World War II standards, while commercial bank failures have reached the highest levels since the Great Depression. As a result, the system is likely to consolidate in the years ahead. The role of U.S. commercial banks in international markets has also diminished significantly. This is partly a result of the growth in European and Pacific Basin economies, and partly due to weaknesses in the U.S. system.

Commercial banks have very diversified asset structures. Loans are the largest asset category, amounting to 60 percent of total assets and spread between business, real estate, and consumer loans. These banks also invest heavily in U.S. government, agency, and state and local government securities.

Commercial banks also have very diversified **liability structures.** Banks raise funds by issuing deposits in a variety of forms, such as checking accounts and time and savings accounts, which together represent three-quarters of bank liabilities. Some banks rely on wholesale financing sources such as negotiable CDs, repo borrowing, and fed funds.

The **size of a bank** has a significant impact on its asset and liability structure. Smaller banks are more heavily invested in securities and loans to consumers and residential real estate. They also use few wholesale financing sources. Large banks are heavier business and international lenders and rely more on wholesale financing sources.

The following agencies share **regulatory duties** for commercial banks: (1) **Comptroller of the Currency,** (2) **Federal Deposit Insurance Corporation,** (3) **Federal Reserve System,** and (4) **state bank regulatory authorities.**

Bank market structure is a term used to describe a variety of laws that impact a bank's size and choice of location and activities. The **McFadden Act** and the **Douglas Amendment** effectively prohibited the branching of national banks, except to the same extent states permitted state chartered banks to branch. These restraints have been largely eliminated due to **regional pacts** that permit interstate activities for BHCs.

Economies of scale refer to the relationship of a bank's operating costs to the quantity of products it produces. **Economies of scope** refer to two or more products produced with a single production system. Studies indicate that economies of scale and scope are only significant in the case of very small banks.

Commercial banks carry out their **international activities** using domestic offices, foreign offices, subsidiary companies located out of the country, and Edge Act corporations. Commercial banks perform the same services internationally that they do in the United States except in some countries they can also be involved in merchant and investment banking.

The relative position of **U.S. banks in the international markets** has declined significantly in the last decade. This is due primarily to the growth in foreign economies relative to the United States, but also to the weakened conditions of U.S. banks. In 1991, no U.S. bank made the list of the top 25 largest banks.

Foreign banks have increased their activities in the U.S. market significantly in the last decade. Japan in particular has substantially increased the number of offices and assets it has in the United States.

Questions

Chapter 9

1. The structure of the U.S. banking industry is said to be a reflection of federal and state laws. Do you agree or disagree? What is meant by this statement?
2. What is meant by the concept *bank structure* as it is used to describe certain features of our financial markets? Why is financial structure important?
3. What are some of the reasons that the U.S. bank structure is dominated by small commercial banks?
4. What has happened to branching laws in the last several decades? What has occurred to facilitate the interstate activities of commercial banks?
5. Do you think interstate branching is good for users of financial services? Explain your answer.
6. Explain the concepts of economies of scale and scope. What does recent research seem to indicate about the presence of economies of scale or scope?
7. What are the advantages of BHCs and why do larger banks form holding companies?

8. How would you differentiate between the asset and liability structures of large, medium, and small banks? Focus on the differences in the relative holdings of various assets and liabilities by these different-sized banks.
9. Smaller commercial banks tend to have larger holdings of short-term securities as a percentage of total assets compared to larger banks. Why is this the case?
10. Smaller commercial banks tend not to use wholesale liabilities to the same extent as larger banks. Why is this the case?
11. Commercial bank financial performance has deteriorated in the last decade. What are some of the reasons you can identify?
12. U.S. banks dominated international banking in the 1960s and 1970s. Why did the United States achieve this dominant position?
13. What are the principle activities performed by foreign offices of U.S. banks?
14. How are U.S. banks organized to do business in foreign countries? Why do most U.S. banks use their foreign branches to carry out foreign operations?
15. Why has the relative position of U.S. banks in the foreign banking market declined so much during the 1980s?
16. What impact has the cost of capital to commercial banks around the world had on the relative position of a country's banks in the foreign markets? Why is cost of capital important? Why would the cost of equity capital be higher at U.S. banks than at Japanese and German banks in the 1980s?

Thrift Institutions

chapter 10

Savings banks, savings and loan associations, and credit unions are referred to as thrift institutions. These institutions all began as mutual institutions designed to serve individuals by providing savings deposit services and, in the case of savings and loans and credit unions, mortgage and consumer loans, respectively. These specialized roles were codified in law and regulation in the 1930s.

Today, savings and loan associations (S&Ls) and savings banks (SBs) still concentrate their investments in the residential mortgage market, while credit unions devote most of their lending to consumer loans. These narrow financial roles persist despite the broader charters they received as a result of the financial deregulation of the 1980s.

This chapter provides a description of thrifts, their business structure, and their recent financial performance.

Overview of Thrift Institutions

S&Ls and SBs thrived in the post–World War II period until the late 1970s. Despite their highly constrained asset and liability powers, these institutions grew as a result of a number of advantages granted them by the federal government. These advantages were largely eliminated in the 1980s as the institutions were granted broader asset and liability powers.

Beginning in the late 1970s, S&Ls and SBs fell on hard times. Record high interest rates in the early 1980s largely depleted their capital base. This was followed by excessive risk-taking by some of the firms and regulatory miscues that culminated in the "thrift debacle."

Table 10.1 shows the total financial assets and average annual growth rate of the three major thrifts and commercial banks covering five periods ending in 1990. As the table indicates, except for the savings banks, the thrifts grew rapidly until 1983. At that point, the S&Ls experienced severe profitability and capital shortage problems. These problems became so severe that by late 1989 the industry began to shrink. The industry's shrinkage has continued well into the early 1990s. The savings banks also experienced operating problems in the 1980s, but less severely than the S&Ls. Consequently, their growth in the period between 1983 and 1990 actually exceeded that of the S&Ls.

Credit unions, on the other hand, have continued to prosper and grow at double digit annual rates. The rate of growth of commercial banks also increased from 1983 to 1989. This is partly due to depositors' concern over the safety of S&Ls, which caused some depositors to shift their funds to commercial banks. At the same time, commercial banks have been purchasers of savings and loan deposits from shrinking S&Ls and the Resolution Trust Corporation (RTC).

Table 10.1

Total Financial Assets of Major Depositories and Average Growth Rate 1953–1990 (dollars in billions)

Institution	1953	1976	1973	1983	1990	1953–1963	1963–1973	1973–1983	1983–1990
Commercial banks	$171	$280	$696	$1595	$3400	5.1%	9.5%	8.6%	11.4%
Savings and loans	27	105	267	829	1083	14.7	9.8	12.0	3.9
Mutual savings Banks	27	50	107	194	261	6.3	7.8	6.2	4.3
Credit unions	2	9	28	103	201	17.9	12.2	13.9	10.0

Sources: National Council of Community Bankers, Washington, DC, and Federal Reserve *Bulletin*.

Savings and Loan Associations

Savings and loans are the largest of the thrift institutions. Their most rapid growth occurred in the 30 years following the end of World War II. As the nation's largest single supplier of single family mortgage credit, the S&Ls grew along with and contributed to the suburbanization of our nation's cities.

The industry's prosperous years were largely the result of very favorable government policies. Until 1952, S&Ls and SBs were not subject to federal income taxes. Although this condition changed slowly, by the 1980s these institutions reached a level of federal taxation that is just slightly below other corporations. S&Ls also were not subject to the Regulation Q deposit rate ceilings until 1966. This allowed the business to pay rates above the ceiling levels imposed on commercial banks and helped them to attract a large percentage of the savings and time deposit markets. Luck was also a factor. The industry was allowed to carry enormous interest rate risk. These firms invested in long-term fixed-rate mortgages using short-term savings and time deposits. For most of the post World War II period, the term structure of interest rates was upward sloping. As a financial firm that borrowed short and lent long, this provided an especially high profit margin and contributed to the businesses' success until the late 1970s. The business also benefitted from the availability of favorable loans from the FHLBs.

The regulatory agency responsible for these businesses did not concern itself sufficiently with the businesses' high interest rate risk position until 1981. At that time, the FHLBB finally authorized adjustable rate mortgages. Unfortunately this action came far too late to help the S&Ls, since most of the institutions were already technically insolvent. This means that the market value of the business's long-term fixed-rate mortgages is significantly less than the deposit liabilities of the firm.

The businesses' fall from grace occurred in large part because virtually all of the federal government's advantages were eliminated while at the same time the record high interest rates of the early 1980s led to record operating losses and the depletion of the businesses' capital base. The S&L disaster is the topic of the Appendix at the end of this chapter.

Mutual and Stock Institutions

Two aspects of S&L structure have stood out over the years. These concern the size distribution of S&Ls and the division between stock and mutual institutions. Both of these structural aspects of the business have changed significantly in the last decade and can be expected to continue to change. The relationship between mutual and stock ownership is discussed first.

One of the limiting characteristics of the S&L business has been its domination of mutual institutions. Mutual S&Ls have no shareholders.

Rather, they are owned by the existing depositors. At the time an account is opened, the customer typically signs a proxy statement that directs a named individual to vote for directors at the company's annual meeting. This person usually has a close association to the members of the board of directors. The depositors' ownership really has little meaning unless the firm were to be liquidated or converted to a stock institution. Then the depositor would have certain ownership rights.

In 1980, 80 percent of all S&Ls were mutually organized firms holding 73 percent of the total assets of the industry. The profitability problems in the early 1980s forced many of these firms to convert to stock charters. The regulations governing these conversions were liberalized in the early 1980s by the FHLB. Since many thrifts required additional capital, conversions took place in large numbers. As a result, as shown in Table 10.2, the percentage of S&Ls that are mutual dropped significantly to 55 percent by June 30, 1989. In terms of assets, however, the change was more extreme. Only 26 percent of the assets were held by mutual institutions on June 30, 1989.

Regulation and Insurance of Accounts

Federally chartered S&Ls are regulated by the Office of Thrift Supervision (OTS). This regulator, like the Comptroller of the Currency, is an office within the Department of the Treasury. The OTS replaced the FHLBB in 1989. The deposits of S&Ls are insured by the Savings Association Insurance Fund (SAIF), which is administered by the FDIC. The FDIC examines all SAIF-insured institutions. S&Ls are chartered by both federal and state governments.

Table 10.2

Stock Versus Mutual Charters
December 31, 1980 and June 30, 1989

Institution Charter Type	1980	1989
Number of mutuals	80%	55%
Number of stocks	20	45
Percent of assets in mutuals	73%	26%
Percent of assets in stocks	27	74

Source: James R. Barth and Philip R. Wiest. "Consolidation and Restructuring of the U.S. Thrift Industry Under the Financial Institutions Reform, Recovery, and Enforcement Act." Research Paper #89-01, Office of Thrift Supervision (October 1989): p. 17.

Prior to 1989, federally chartered and insured S&Ls were regulated by the FHLBB, and their deposits insured by the FSLIC. Both these organizations were disbanded by Congress in 1989.

All SAIF-insured S&Ls are members of one of twelve FHLBs. These banks serve as liquidity facilities for their member institutions, and also provide long-term credit. Today, commercial banks may also become members of the FHLBs.

Many S&Ls have changed their names in recent years by adopting a Federal Savings Bank charter. This charter does not really alter the asset and liability powers of the institution from that of a federally chartered S&L, but it does allow these firms to use the term *bank* in their name. The Federal Savings Bank, known by the use of the acronym FSB, has deposits insured by the SAIF and should not be confused with a state-chartered savings bank that is insured by the BIF.

The significant decline in the number of mutual institutions and the even more extreme decline in the assets controlled by the mutual segment of the business suggest that the capital needs of S&Ls will continue to be a major problem. Mutual institutions have virtually no way to raise outside capital, except through a *mutual-stock conversion*. Converting to a stock institution by selling stock to depositors and the public will probably continue to be a course followed by many of the remaining mutual firms in order to raise capital.

Size Structure of S&Ls

Like commercial banks, S&Ls have traditionally been dominated by small firms. This has changed dramatically in the last decade. Table 10.3 shows the percentage of total business assets controlled by the top 10, 50, and 100 largest S&Ls on December 31, 1980, and on June 30, 1989. The table indicates that the business has become significantly more concentrated in recent years as a result of mergers and consolidations.

Table 10.3

**Concentration of S&Ls in
10, 50, and 100 Largest Institutions Measured by Assets
December 31, 1980 and June 30, 1989**

	Top 10	Top 50	Top 100
December 31, 1980	10%	25%	35%
June 30, 1989	18	39	52

Source: Ibid. p. 16.

Federal and State Charters

Another major change of the last decade has been the increase in the percentage of S&Ls that have federal charters. At year-end 1980, 50 percent of the institutions holding over 56 percent of the assets had federal charters. This has risen to 59 percent and 73 percent, respectively, by June 30, 1989. The reduction in the role of the state-chartered institutions was partly the result of the deregulation of federally chartered S&Ls in the early 1980s. In addition, a federal charter permits institutions to branch across state lines, whereas a state-chartered S&L cannot. This was first authorized by the FHLBB for out-of-state acquisitions of failed S&Ls. More recently, federally chartered S&Ls have become more popular because federal law has preempted many of the more liberal asset powers once enjoyed by state-chartered S&Ls.

Asset Structure of S&Ls

Residential mortgages dominate the asset portfolios of S&Ls. Despite significant opportunities to diversify in the 1980s, the business remains largely a specialized mortgage-lending institution. This has become more pronounced with the passage of FIRREA in 1989. This act reduced the asset powers of S&Ls, particularly in the areas of corporate lending and commercial real estate. The new risk-based capital requirements also serve to steer these institutions toward residential mortgages. Table 10.4 shows the asset composition of S&Ls as of December 31, 1990, and a discussion of the primary assets of S&Ls follows.

Table 10.4

Asset Composition of S&Ls
December 31, 1990
(dollars in billions)

Selected Assets	$ Amount	% of Total
Mortgages	$639	59.0%
Mortgage-backed securities	179	16.5
Commercial loans	24	2.2
Consumer loans	47	4.4
Cash and investment securities	60	5.5
Bonds, notes, other securities	63	5.9
Other	71	6.5
Total	**$1,083**	**100.0%**

Source: National Council of Community Bankers.

Mortgages and Mortgage-Related Securities

At year-end 1990, over 75 percent of all the assets of S&Ls were invested in mortgages and mortgage-related securities. The vast majority of these mortgages are secured by residential properties, although S&Ls became more active in the commercial real estate market in the 1980s. Most of the mortgage-related assets of S&Ls are invested in permanent home mortgages. Since 1981, a growing percentage of this mortgage portfolio has been invested in adjustable-rate mortgages, as distinct from fixed-rate mortgages, which dominated their portfolios prior to the 1980s.

As the government sponsored enterprises have come to dominate the residential mortgage market, S&Ls increasingly find themselves as investors in mortgage-backed securities. These securities may be an S&L's own mortgages, which have been swapped with the FNMA or FHLMC for a guaranteed mortgage-backed security. These securities are more liquid investments than mortgages, but they also have lower yields.

Investment Securities

S&Ls must meet liquidity requirements imposed on them by the Office of Thrift Supervision. Typically, they hold Treasury securities, agency securities, or high-grade corporate money market debt. The liquidity requirements imposed on all SAIF-insured institutions requires that these firms hold about 5 percent of their assets in liquid form. The OTS may change the required liquidity percentage from time to time.

Commercial Loans

In the Garn-St. Germain Act of 1982, federally chartered S&Ls received commercial lending powers of up to 10 percent of assets. This authority also allowed these firms to purchase corporate bonds, including noninvestment-grade corporate bonds, or junk bonds. At year-end 1990, only $24 billion in S&L assets were in any form of commercial loan or investment. An estimate of S&L holdings of junk bonds on June 30, 1989, revealed that as a group S&L bondholders held only $12.55 billion. Of this, over 96 percent were held by 50 institutions. FIRREA will substantially reduce S&L participation in the commercial lending market because it requires divestiture of junk bond investments within five years. The largest S&L holders of junk bonds all failed by 1990. This was partially attributable to the fall in junk bond prices, which occurred after the federal government outlawed new investments in the bonds and required divestiture.

Consumer Loans

Another market that S&Ls entered in the post–Garn-St. Germain period was consumer loans. This included auto loans, personal loans, and credit card receivables. Overall, the consumer loan market has not become a major asset on the books of S&Ls. Unlike commercial loans, however, FIRREA will not have a major impact on future consumer lending by S&Ls.

Liability Structure of S&Ls

S&Ls finance their activities primarily with short-term liabilities consisting of deposits and collateralized borrowings. Savings and time certificates of deposit provide the primary financing sources of S&Ls. Over the years, however, S&Ls have become major collateralized borrowers using FHLB advances, which are collateralized by mortgages. Other borrowings of S&Ls include reverse repurchase agreements, commercial paper, and bank loans. Table 10.5 provides the liability and net worth accounts of S&Ls as of December 31, 1990.

Deposits

The deposit liabilities of S&Ls consist of savings deposits, time certificates of deposit, demand accounts, NOW accounts, and money market demand accounts. Since deregulation, S&Ls have had broad freedom to create many types of deposit accounts. This means it is much more difficult to generalize about the nature of S&L deposit liabilities. The vast majority of S&L accounts are in time certificates of deposit and savings deposits. Transaction accounts still represent only 5.4 percent of their liabilities.

FHLB Borrowings

S&Ls have made significant use of their authority to borrow from FHLBs. These twelve banks are owned by the member S&Ls who own their stock in relation to their size and borrowing level. The FHLBs provide a wide range of lending programs from very short to as long as 20 years. These banks also

Table 10.5

Liability Composition of S&Ls
December 31, 1990
(dollars in billions)

Selected Liabilities	$ Amount	% of Total
Savings deposits	$153	14.2%
Time deposits	623	57.5
Transaction accounts	59	5.4
FHLB advances and other borrowed	149	13.7
Fed funds and repos	43	4.0
Other liabilities	25	2.3
Net worth	31	2.9
Total	**$1,083**	**100.0%**

Source: National Council of Community Bankers.

provide credit guarantees for debt sold by S&Ls. FIRREA provided the impetus to expand the FHLB lending programs to other financial institutions, such as commercial banks.

Other Borrowings

Larger S&Ls have developed wholesale sources of funds just like commercial banks. Some S&Ls use reverse repurchase agreements, federal funds, and commercial paper. For the most part, however, S&Ls have very poor credit ratings and must borrow on a collateralized basis. Some S&Ls have participated in the growth in collateralized borrowing by using mortgages, auto loans, credit card receivables, and other assets as collateral in asset-backed securities.

Management Highlights

Special Management Concerns for S&Ls and SBs

Achieving an adequate net interest margin: S&Ls and SBs have a large concentration of their assets in home mortgages. These assets have a modest spread over their cost of funds. This makes it difficult to sustain an adequate net interest margin.

Controlling the cost of deposits: S&Ls and SBs have traditionally paid more for deposits than commercial banks. They have, therefore, cultivated a customer base that expects a higher rate of interest. In today's environment, S&Ls and SBs are not able to earn higher interest rates on assets than banks, which makes their high deposit rate strategy less viable.

Controlling operating expenses: S&Ls and SBs will face low net interest margins for the foreseeable future. They will also face higher deposit insurance premiums and examination and supervision costs. As a result, they must control operating expenses.

Managing interest rate risk: Mortgages involve prepayment options that are difficult to hedge. This means that interest rate risk is an ever-present feature of these institutions. Even adjustable-rate mortgages are not without difficult-to-hedge provisions, such as interest rate caps, lagging rate indices, and other provisions that involve substantial risk.

Controlling exposure to local and regional real estate price risks: Most S&Ls and SBs have a high concentration of assets in local markets that are exposed to regional economic real estate value cycles. These firms must successfully manage this risk.

S&L Financial Performance

The S&L business was devastated by the record-high interest rates that prevailed in the late 1970s and early 1980s. As a result, these firms, which assumed a significant amount of interest rate risk due to their large holdings of fixed-rate mortgages financed with short-term liabilities, suffered large losses during this period. In fact, by 1982, the business had largely exhausted its tangible equity. *Tangible equity* equals common stock, plus paid-in-surplus and retained earnings, minus intangible assets, such as goodwill. *Goodwill* is the result of acquisitions of firms at prices above the book value net worth of the acquired firm. Goodwill is a nonearning asset. Firms with large amounts of goodwill may appear to have adequate amounts of capital. Actually, since the goodwill asset is nonearning, many observers consider the book net worth to be inflated. In 1989, the FIRREA required that S&L regulators not count goodwill in the capital calculation. This is also required for commercial banks.

Table 10.6 shows the number of S&Ls, their assets, and capital as measured by three different approaches from 1980 to 1982. *Regulatory capital* is capital that was acceptable to the former FHLBB. It included goodwill, higher than book value valuations for certain real estate holdings, and subordinated debt. GAAP capital is also shown. *GAAP capital* is capital that is measured under generally accepted accounting principles and includes goodwill. Tangible GAAP capital is GAAP capital with goodwill subtracted from it. The table shows the percentage of assets of each.

The table clearly shows that by 1982, the tangible capital of the industry was largely wiped out. From that point on, S&Ls had little chance

Table 10.6

Capital Measures for S&Ls from 1980–1982 (dollars in billions)

Year-end	Number of S&Ls	Total Assets	Regulatory Capital $ Amount	Regulatory Capital % of Assets	GAAP Capital $ Amount	GAAP Capital % of Assets	Tangible Capital $ Amount	Tangible Capital % of Assets
1980	3,993	$604	$32	5.29%	$32	5.29%	$32	5.29%
1981	3,743	640	28	4.37	27	4.22	25	3.91
1982	3,287	686	25	3.64	20	2.91	4	.58

Source: Philip Bartholemew. "Estimating the Cost of Regulatory Forbearance During the Thrift Crisis." U.S. Congressional Budget Office. Unpublished Working Paper (June 30–July 3, 1991): p. 3.

to succeed. The exceptions were those firms that had extraordinarily large capital bases relative to assets and those mutual firms that were able to build capital through the process of mutual-stock conversions. Many large mutual S&Ls became stock companies during the period from 1983 to 1987. This process did add considerable new capital to the business.

The poor financial performance of the S&Ls during the last decade and into the 1990s is reflected by Exhibit 10.1. Here the net after-tax profits of all FHLBB and OTS S&Ls are shown. The graph also shows the total tangible net worth of the industry.

Another reflection of the businesses' continuing problems is the reduction in the number of S&Ls and the shrinkage of total assets. Exhibit 10.2

Exhibit 10.1

Profits and Tangible Net Worth of S&Ls 1980–1990

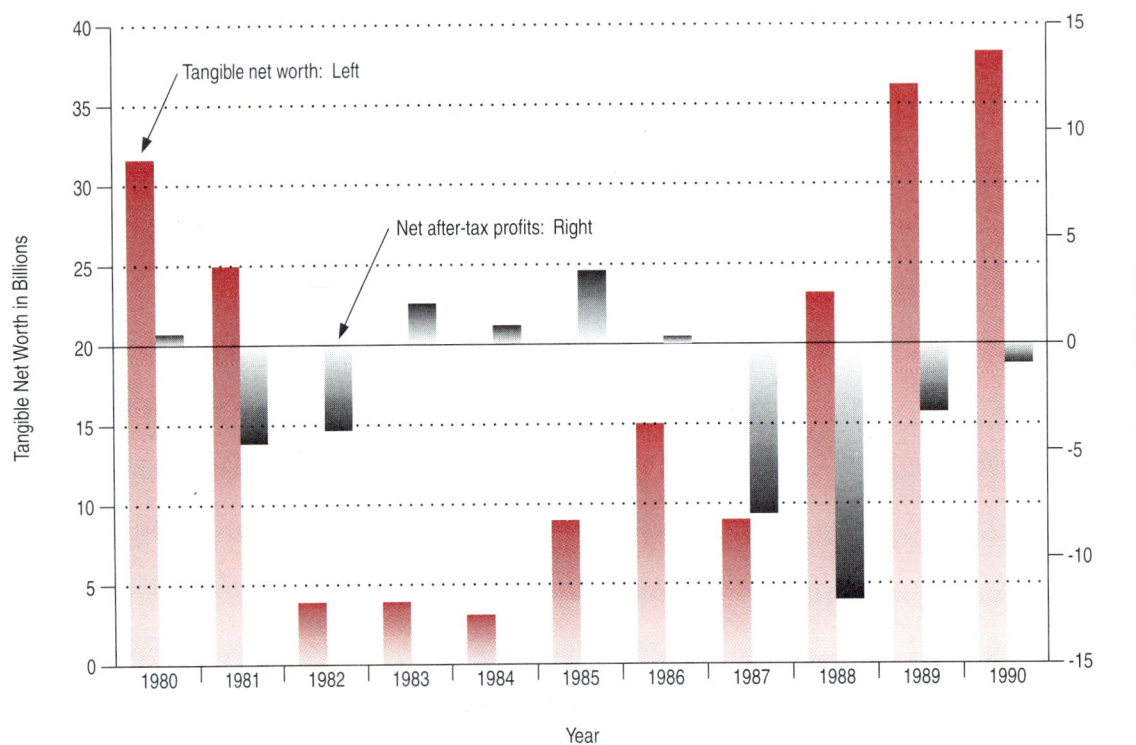

Source: Bartholomew, Philip. "Estimating the Cost of Regulatory Forbearance During the Thrift Crisis." Working paper. U.S. Budget Office, p. 3.

Exhibit 10.2

Number and Total Assets of S&Ls 1980–1990

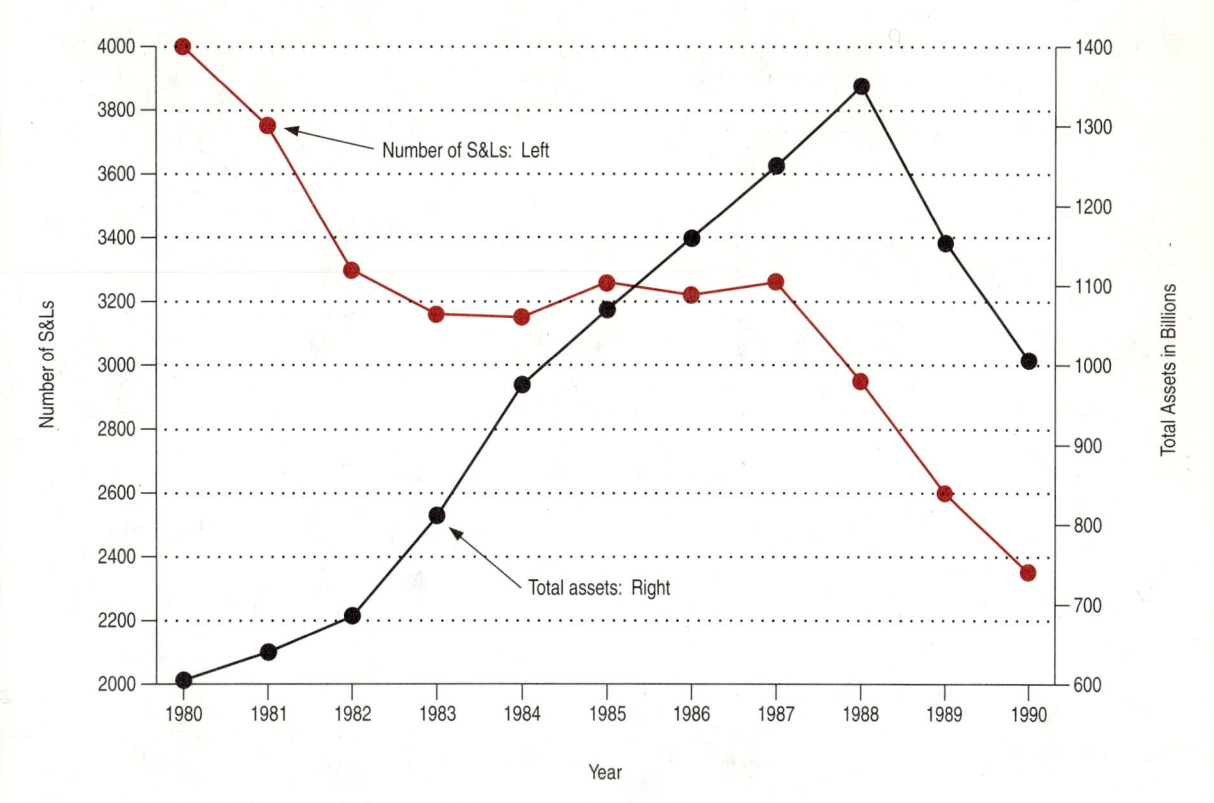

[Chart: Number of S&Ls (left axis, red line) declines from 4000 in 1980 to about 2350 in 1990. Total Assets in Billions (right axis, black line) rises from about 600 in 1980 to a peak of about 1350 in 1988, then falls to about 1000 in 1990.]

Source: *Statistical Abstract of the United States*. Washington, DC: U.S. Department of Commerce, 1991.

shows both these data series for the years 1980 to 1990. During this period, the number of S&Ls declined by 41 percent. This attrition will continue as more S&Ls fail and others are merged into stronger institutions. Many S&Ls and mutual savings banks are also being acquired by commercial banks. This is to be expected given the more flexible charter of commercial banks.

Taken as a whole, the performance of S&Ls since the early 1980s has been dismal. In the early 1990s, the RTC continued to take over insolvent firms and sell or liquidate assets. This process takes many years. Overall, SAIF-insured S&Ls suffered losses of over $8 billion in 1990. This bodes poorly for the future prospects of raising capital. Overall, it appears the industry will continue to shrink on both a relative and nominal basis.

The financial weakness of the S&Ls has resulted in a sharp increase in failures. From a trickle in the early 1980s, the number and dollar amount of assets represented by failed institutions taken over by the FSLIC and then the Resolution Trust Corporation (RTC) has increased to a flood. In 1980, 11 institutions with only $1.45 billion in total assets were taken over by government agencies. In 1990, the number reached 315 institutions with $110.25 billion in assets. The number and dollar amount of assets in S&Ls taken over by the FSLIC and the RTC is shown in Exhibit 10.3. It should be

Exhibit 10.3

Failed S&Ls Assumed by the FSLIC and RTC 1980–1990

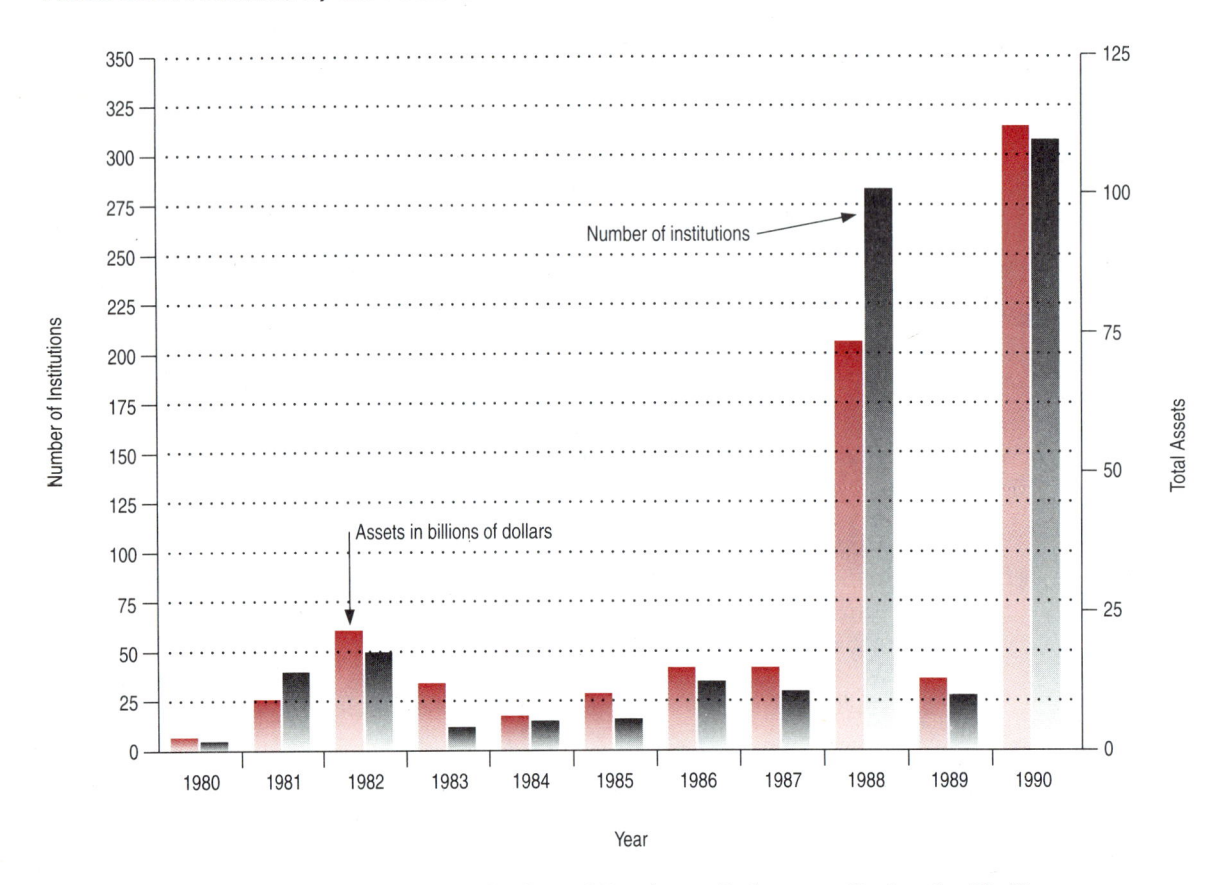

Source: Bartholomew, Philip. "Estimating the Cost of Regulatory Forbearance During the Thrift Crisis." Working paper. U.S. Budget Office, p. 3.

kept in mind that the timing of these takeovers is discretionary. Government regulators have wide latitude as to when to assume control over an insolvent institution. This accounts for the bunching of the failures during certain years in the 1980s and 1990s.

Another reason for the delayed regulatory response to the failed institutions has been the lack of available resources. The FSLIC had inadequate resources to assume failed S&Ls in 1989. To provide the necessary resources, the FIRREA established the RTC. The RTC arranged for the orderly liquidation and sale of failed savings and loans. The RTC did not receive unlimited appropriations from Congress, however. As a result, the assumption of failed institutions has depended on the available resources. Resources include the ability to borrow and funds received from selling assets of failed institutions. Each time the RTC has exhausted its resources, it has to go back to Congress for more. This process has created delays and may have even increased the cost of liquidation.

Legal and Ethical Issues

Lincoln Savings: Security Fraud, Influence Peddling, and the Dual System of Chartering Financial Institutions

No financial institution epitomizes the S&L tragedy more than Lincoln Savings and Loan does. Lincoln S&L was purchased in 1984 by American Continental Corporation, a large-scale real estate development company run by Charles Keating. Keating, like a number of other developers, considered the California state S&L charter to be an attractive way to fund real estate development. In fact, the state's new charter permitted unlimited direct investment in real estate.

The aggressive investment activities of Lincoln and several other institutions caught the eye of the federal savings and loan regulator, the former FHLBB. The board was responsible for insuring these institutions and promulgated a regulation that restricted the investment of insured institution assets in direct real estate to 10 percent. Keating allegedly responded by making political contributions to several highly placed U.S. senators (known as the Keating Five) in return for their help in pressuring the FHLBB to back off from their regulation, and later to impede the regulator's effort to gain control over Lincoln. The result was one of the most emotion-charged ethics hearings ever conducted by the Senate Ethics Committee as the Keating Five were asked to explain their activities concerning Lincoln.

Lincoln's officers and professional advisers also were the subject of numerous lawsuits by public and government units. The suit that gained the most publicity related to the sale of subordinated debt in Lincoln's parent ACC, which was sold in small denominations by using broker/dealers located in the branches of Lincoln Savings. These bondholders, many of them retirees, subsequently lost an estimated $200 million when Lincoln was taken over by the government. The suit alleged that ACC management, accountants, lawyers, and others committed negligent and fraudulent acts. This suit sent Keating to jail for ten years.

Aside from the press hype, the Lincoln situation raised several important issues. First, it provided clear evidence of the problem caused by having state-chartered institutions insured by federal insurance funds. This problem was partially resolved through federal legislation restricting the powers of state-chartered institutions. Second, Lincoln highlighted the potential for influence peddling, given a system in which regulators have very broad powers, and recourse and redress for overzealous regulators is difficult. The Ethics Committee didn't resolve that issue. Finally, the sales of subordinated debt raised additional issues about the responsibilities of management, directors, lawyers, and accountants in making representations concerning securities sold to the public.

Financial Claim/Function Matrix

Table 10.7 provides the financial claim/function matrix for a savings and loan association. In the origination function, S&Ls concentrate in mortgages and some consumer loans. Their liabilities consist primarily of transaction, time and savings deposits, and some wholesale funding sources.

Savings Banks

State-chartered savings banks (SBs) are the oldest of our thrift institutions. Although savings banks are in some respects indistinguishable from S&Ls, the state charters they possess provide greater flexibility than the S&L charter created under FIRREA. SBs are concentrated in New England, New York, New Jersey, Rhode Island, and Washington, and can obtain state charters in only 16 states. Savings banks received permission to charter nationally in 1978. These federally chartered savings banks are essentially federally chartered S&Ls with the name bank. The Garn-St. Germain Act of 1982 provided that savings banks with state or federal charters may obtain stock charters. Until then, all savings banks were mutual and were referred to as *mutual savings banks* (*MSBs*).

This section will focus on state-chartered savings banks, since federally chartered savings banks insured by the SAIF are included in the previous S&L discussion.

Table 10.7

Financial Claim/Function Matrix for Assets and Liabilities of Savings and Loans

Type of Claim	Origination Pri-Sec	Servicing	Brokerage Pri-Sec	Market-Making Pri-Sec	Portfolio Management
Assets					
Government					
United States	x			x	x
Agency	x			x	x
Municipal	x			x	x
Business					
Corporate bonds					
Equities					
Mortgages	x	x		x	x
Leases					
Loans					
Household					
Installment	x	x		x	x
Credit card	x	x		x	x
Mortgages	x	x	x	x	x
Liabilities					
Demand deposits and other transactions	x	x		x	x
Savings and CDs	x	x		x	x
Capital Market Funding					
Collateralized debt					
FHLB advances	x	x		x	x
Reverse repos	x	x		x	x
Asset-based	x	x		x	x
Unsecured Debt					
Negotiable CDs	x	x		x	x
Commercial paper	x	x		x	x

Pri = Primary Market
Sec = Secondary Market

Regulation and Insurance of Accounts

SBs are regulated by state regulatory commissions, as well as the FDIC. SBs' deposits were formerly insured by the FDIC also, as were the deposits of commercial banks. Today, they are insured by the BIF.

Asset Structure of Savings Banks

The asset structure of SBs is very similar to that of S&Ls. Table 10.8 shows the assets of BIF-insured savings banks. These data are for year-end 1990. The institutions shown include approximately 350 state BIF-insured savings banks, and represent approximately 27 percent as stock-owned and the balance mutual.

Like the S&Ls, the savings bank balance sheet is dominated by mortgages and mortgage securities. The major difference in the balance sheet from that of S&Ls is that savings banks have traditionally invested in the corporate bond and equity market. These investments amounted to less than 10 percent of assets in 1990.

Liability Structure of Savings Banks

The liability structure of savings banks is also similar to S&Ls except that savings banks generally have higher equity than S&Ls. Table 10.9 provides the liability structure of the savings banks.

Table 10.8

Asset Structure of Savings Banks Insured by BIF
December 31, 1990
(dollars in billions)

Asset Classification	$ Amount	% of Total
Cash and due from banks and U.S. Treasury and agencies	$ 15.2	6.1%
Mortgages	155.0	60.9
Mortgage securities	28.2	11.1
Corporate bonds, notes, and corporate stock	19.8	7.8
Commercial loans	10.1	4.0
Consumer loans	10.0	3.9
Other assets	15.7	6.2
Total	**$254.0**	**100.0%**

Source: National Council of Community Bankers.

Table 10.9

Liability Structure of Savings Banks
December 31, 1990
(dollars in billions)

Liability Classification	$ Amount	% of Total
Savings deposits	$ 64.3	25.3%
Time deposits	128.7	50.6
Transaction deposits	15.1	5.9
Borrowings	19.0	7.5
Federal funds purchased and repos	6.7	2.6
Other liabilities	3.5	1.4
Net worth	17.0	6.7
Total	**$254.3**	**100.0%**

Source: National Council of Community Bankers.

The savings banks also have a liability structure that relies more heavily on retail deposit sources than on S&Ls. In this respect, the savings banks more closely resemble community commercial banks.

Recent Savings Bank Financial Performance

Savings banks experienced net operating losses during the early 1980s. This was due to the sharp rise in open-market interest rates and the fact that most of their investments were in fixed-rate long-term assets. Unlike the S&Ls, however, the capital position of the savings banks was less impaired. This was because the savings banks entered the period with much stronger capital. At year-end 1990, savings banks had capital of 6.7 percent of total assets.

More recently, weaknesses in real estate values in the northeastern United States have contributed to operating losses at MSBs. In 1990, the BIF-insured MSBs lost $2.4 billion, up from previous years. So, even though the MSBs have a higher capital position than S&Ls, their lack of diversification makes them vulnerable to failure.

Credit Unions

Credit unions are the youngest and smallest group of thrift institutions. Organized successfully for the first time in 1909, credit unions grew slowly until the 1930s, when the credit unions' lobbying and service organization, the Credit Union National Association (CUNA), successfully obtained a federal charter permitting these organizations to be formed nationwide.

The success of credit unions is clear from Table 10.10. This table shows the number of credit unions, number of members, and total assets from 1970 to 1990.

As the table illustrates, credit unions have grown consistently in asset size and number of members for many decades. However, the number of credit unions has been declining for over a decade. This is because credit unions are tied to specific employers that may fail, merge, or move to a new location. In these circumstances, the credit union usually merges with another located close to it.

Regulation and Insurance of Accounts

Credit unions are regulated and supervised by the National Credit Union Administration (NCUA), if they have insured deposits. Some credit unions remain uninsured and are regulated by state commissions. The NCUA also administers the National Credit Union Share Insurance Fund (NCUSIF), which provides insurance of accounts. NCUA issues charters to federally chartered credit unions. Approximately 60 percent of all credit unions are federally chartered and the balance state chartered.

Common Bond

The *common bond* is a unique feature of the credit union. The common bond represents the affiliation of the credit union to a group, usually an employer. Historically, credit unions were formed by employers as a benefit.

Table 10.10

**Credit Union Growth Statistics
1970–1990
(dollars in millions)**

Years	Number of Credit Unions	Number of Credit Union Members	Assets
1990	14,906	61,700,000	$222,300
1989	15,144	60,490,312	205,444
1985	17,581	51,721,709	137,168
1980	21,467	44,047,759	68,996
1970	23,668	22,776,676	17,951

Source: *Statistical Abstract of the United States, 1991*. Department of Commerce: p. 504.

The formation of credit unions was designed to provide encouragement for savings and a place to obtain consumer loans. Over the years, the common bond concept has been broadened to include relatives. Some credit unions have incorporated geographic areas into their common bond definition. This has resulted in a major increase in the market potential of these firms and has accelerated their growth.

Credit Union Size and Ownership Structure

The most important features of the credit union business are that they are relatively small in asset size, and they are mutual institutions. Of the 14,906 credit unions in existence at year-end 1990, only 385 had assets in excess of $100 million and over 60 percent had assets of less than $5 million.

Asset Structure of Credit Unions

Credit unions' assets are concentrated in consumer loans and liquid investments. As Table 10.11 indicates, at year-end 1990, credit unions had over 65 percent of their financial assets in loans and almost 27 percent in U.S. government and agency investments.

The loans of credit unions consist primarily of consumer installment loans, with auto loans being the largest single category. Credit unions have also begun to add small amounts of mortgage loans to their portfolios. Because most credit unions are too small to adequately diversify, they tend to hold large portfolios of money market instruments. They are also large investors in commercial bank and S&L negotiable CDs, corporate commer-

Table 10.11

Financial Asset Composition of Credit Unions
December 31, 1990
(dollars in billions)

Asset	$ Amount	% of Total
Loans	$141.3	65.1%
U.S. government and agency investments	58.3	26.9
Cash	4.8	2.2
Other	12.6	5.8
Total	**$217.0**	**100.0%**

Source: *Flow of Funds Accounts, Financial Assets and Liabilities,* Federal Reserve System (January 31, 1992): p. 26.

cial paper, and Treasury and agency securities. Credit unions generally find it is easier to attract deposits than to invest their funds.

Liability Structure of Credit Unions

Table 10.12 provides the liability structure of credit unions as of December 31, 1990. The table shows that credit unions are well capitalized, with total capital of 7.9 percent of assets. They obtain essentially all their funds from deposits. Their deposit accounts consist of about 46 percent regular or passbook savings, 30 percent certificates and money market accounts, 14 percent individual retirement accounts, and 9 percent share drafts, a form of transaction account.

Table 10.12

**Liability and Capital Structure of Credit Unions
December 31, 1990
(dollars in billions)**

Liability and Capital	$ Amount	% of Total
Savings	$200.8	90.0%
Borrowings and other	3.9	1.7
Capital	18.5	8.3
Total	**$223.2**	**100.0%**

Source: Ibid. p. 26.

Management Highlights

Special Management Concerns for Credit Unions

Controlling credit risks: Credit unions make consumer loans to a sometimes small group of employees who may be subject to mass layoff or strike. The lack of employment diversification of the credit unions' customer base could present special credit problems.

Risks of employer changes: Credit unions frequently find themselves with significant operating problems due to sponsor failure, merger, or facility closure. These events can sometimes result in the need to merge the credit union or close it altogether.

Finding professional talent: Credit unions start small and then grow. Sometimes it is difficult to find and retain experienced management for a larger credit union.

Balancing funding sources with investments: Because of the lack of loans that small credit unions can safely invest in, they typically have an imbalance between their savings liabilities and a ready supply of quality loans. This can lead to large holdings of liquidity, which reduces interest income.

Recent Credit Union Financial Performance

Credit unions have been the most consistently profitable of our financial depository institutions. Since year-end 1980, the capital account of credit unions has grown at a compounded annual rate of 15.23 percent. The high level of profitability that credit unions have stems from some of their unique advantages. First, many credit unions receive nonmonetary assistance from their sponsor in the form of facilities and other expense-saving services. Many of the employees of some of the smaller credit unions are volunteers, as are the directors, who are elected from the membership. Second, credit unions market primarily to employed individuals. This lowers credit risks. Third, credit unions pay no federal income tax, which allows their capital account to grow rapidly.

Summary

Savings and loans, savings banks, and credit unions are known as thrift institutions, which emphasizes their role as depositories. S&Ls were formed to make mortgage loans for average-income citizens. Savings banks emphasized savings for low and moderate income families. Credit unions were developed around the concept of making consumer loans to employees of private companies and governmental units.

The 1980s and early 1990s have turned out to be difficult periods for S&Ls and savings banks. They have suffered huge operating losses and record numbers of failures. The humiliation of bad press, the loss of their independent regulator, and legislation have significantly reduced their operating freedom and increased their costs. The outlook for S&Ls and savings banks remains unfavorable. More failures will occur and more of these firms can be expected to be absorbed into commercial banks.

Credit unions are a happy exception. They have enjoyed strong growth and profitability during the same period. They make small consumer loans and have large holdings of government securities, and keep costs down. They also benefit from a lack of federal taxation. Their lack of risk-taking may also be the result of their mutuality.

S&Ls and **federally chartered savings banks** are the nation's largest thrift institutions. These firms emphasize **residential mortgage lending** and issue transaction, time, and savings deposits. S&Ls also rely on wholesale funding sources, especially advances from the FHLB. Approximately 55 percent of S&Ls are **mutual institutions,** but these hold only 26 percent of the industry's total assets. Both these percentages continue to drop.

State-chartered SBs are located primarily in the northeast states. They emphasize mortgage lending, but also have large portfolios of corporate bonds.

S&Ls, and to a lesser extent savings banks, have suffered huge operating losses and record failures. The result is that these financial firms are shrinking both in relative and absolute size and number. Consequently, they will play a decidedly reduced role in our financial system in the future.

Credit unions have performed better than any other depository in the last decade. They have prospered largely because of the lower risks they carry on their asset portfolios, low operating costs due to sponsor provided benefits, and their exemption from federal taxation.

Questions

Chapter 10

1. What advantages did thrift institutions have until the 1980s that helped promote their growth?
2. What differences are there between a savings and loan and a federally chartered savings bank?
3. Why have some savings and loans converted from a mutual to stock form of organization?
4. What changes have occurred in the savings and loan structure in the decade of the 1980s? Discuss concentration and form of organization.
5. How does the McFadden Act impact the interstate branching of federally chartered savings and loans?
6. How would you characterize the profitability and capital adequacy of S&Ls during the 1980s?
7. What do you expect to happen to S&Ls in the years ahead?
8. Why have credit unions continued to perform better than other thrifts?
9. What is meant by the *common bond?*
10. What advantages do credit unions have that have helped them remain profitable?
11. Why has the number of credit unions declined?

The Thrift Debacle

appendix

The primary contributors to the thrift debacle can be organized into several categories. The first group of causes can be called the "Pre-1980 Protectionist Era." This expression refers to government subsidizing the savings and loans with price ceilings on deposits, tax advantages, access to agency debt, and overall lower capital requirements than were imposed on commercial banks. This protective system also had its price in the form of constraints on legal investments and the use of adjustable-rate mortgages. The era ended in the late 1970s with an extremely tight monetary policy, which caused the price controls to lose their effectiveness.

The second group of causes can be called "Ineffective Regulation," since all the causes relate to the ineffectiveness of the regulatory agencies. After the industry was made virtually bankrupt in the early 1980s from the tight money policies, the industry and the regulators were both hoping that the industry's risky high growth and high risk asset investment strategy would pay off. It is apparent, however, that the regulatory gamble was a major failure.

The last group includes the regional recession in the oil belt and the growth in federal housing mortgage finance agencies. These causes are referred to as the "Government Macroeconomic Policies and Induced Competition." The growth of government sponsored enterprises is probably the most important, since the agencies have effectively eliminated the need for the mortgage-financing thrift. Indeed, given the state of the industry today, there remains serious questions concerning its viability.

Overview

The thrift debacle of the late 1980s will go down as one of the major financial events in U.S. history. It is easy to see why a series of events with such enormous costs could create highly emotional debate. Politicians, flamboyant and sometimes fraudulent individuals, ineffective regulators, and junk bonds are the subjects of front page headlines.

However, the causes of the thrift crisis cannot be left to newspapers and Congressional hearings. Academic research has provided valuable insights into the crisis and its causes, as well as recommendations aimed at preventing a replay. The primary conclusion from this research is that no crisis could have become this large without government policy error and misplaced economic incentives. While much of the crisis was the direct result of past government policy errors, it was the lack of regulatory will to step in early and control the government's exposure to loss through deposit insurance that ultimately broke the bank.

This finding, however, will not stop the regulators, Congress, and the industry from blaming each other. While it is true that government policies are at fault in the crisis, perhaps it is the political process of regulation that should also be the focus of our attention.

George Stigler (1971) correctly hypothesized a situation in which the regulated industry attempts to obtain benefits from a government regulatory system set up to oversee it. In the case of S&Ls, they benefitted from a form of price fixing (Regulation Q), subsidized deposit insurance rates (mispriced deposit insurance), and, ultimately, money (the bailout program). One cannot divorce the political process from an analysis of the thrift debacle.

Pre-1980 Protectionist Era

The protectionist policies of the period from the 1930s until the elimination of Regulation Q created a system of depositories that were unable to cope with interest rate volatility and growing competitive pressures. The main features of these policies include interest rate ceilings, constraints on the use of adjustable-rate mortgages, and other lending and liability constraints.

Excessive Adherence to Regulation Q and Fixed-Rate Mortgage

The Banking Act of 1933 prohibited banks from paying interest on demand deposits. It also required banks to control interest rates paid on time deposits. This system of price controls, known as Federal Reserve Regulation Q, became increasingly less effective with the innovation of money market mutual funds and other savings and time deposit substitutes. By the late 1970s, the political backing for these controls was weakened as lobbies for savers, mainly senior citizen lobbies, requested market rates on savings and time deposits. This political force, combined with the increased ineffectiveness of the ceilings, led to the passage of the Depository Institutions and Monetary Control Act of 1980, which removed the ceilings. This was happening at a time when the political constituency concerned with housing and mortgage finance was still strongly opposed to adjustable-rate mortgages.

The move toward market-rate savings also occurred when the portfolios of savings and loans were made up almost exclusively of fixed-rate mortgages made in the 1960s and 1970s at much lower rates than prevailed in the high-rate early 1980s. The result of deregulating the liability side of the savings and loan balance sheet without previously authorizing adjustable-rate mortgages resulted in massive operating losses at these firms. From 1980 to 1982 the tangible equity (net worth account less goodwill) at associations dropped from $32.2 billion to $3.8 billion. The industry was essentially bankrupt by the end of 1982. This left the unanswered question: Would the cost of liquidating the business have been higher or lower than its current cost if it had been done in the early 1980s? We have no answer. In the early 1980s, S&Ls held several hundred billion dollars of mortgages whose market value was substantially below their book value.

Mortgage Usury Laws and Due-on-Sale Prohibitions

Although less of an impact in the 1980s, the prevalence of mortgage usury laws in the 1960s and 1970s resulted in many institutions accumulating mortgage portfolios that had below-market interest rates. This also contributed to S&L losses in the 1980s. Usury laws are statutes that establish ceilings on the maximum interest rate that can be charged for a particular form of credit. In the 1960s and 1970s, a number of important states had usury laws that established a very low ceiling for home mortgages. Most of these statutes were subsequently removed or increased to very high levels, but many S&Ls ended up holding mortgages with low interest rates because of them.

In addition, the government and the courts acted in a variety of ways to strike down the use of due-on-sale clauses in existing mortgage contracts. This clause provided the lender with the ability to call the mortgage due if a sale of the property occurred. By denying the use of this provision, the lenders were forced to continue to hold low-rate mortgages.

Ineffective Regulation

By every account of the thrift crisis, regulatory failures were major contributing factors. Regulatory forbearance was also a major contributing factor. Moreover, examination and supervision was inadequate in addressing excessive risk-taking and fraudulent lending practices. Even the accounting data available to regulators was inadequate in identifying the severity of the problems.

Mispriced FSLIC Insurance: The Moral Hazard Problem

The regulators of savings and loans, primarily the FHLBB, were seemingly unable to manage the huge liability they carried as a result of the near bankrupt condition of the industry in the early 1980s. Rather than cut the losses and consolidate and liquidate the business at that time, the government policymakers effectively "doubled the bet." They lowered the cost of insurance of accounts in a number of very significant ways. This had the impact of increasing the exposure on the FSLIC. The moral hazard problem created the incentive for managers of essentially bankrupt institutions to take excessive risks.

The problem is related to the fact that with insurance of accounts, the depositors in weak institutions have no incentive to concern themselves about the financial position in which they entrust their funds. The other moral hazard is that owners of financial institutions have the incentive to increase risk taking, since the deposit insurance program helps to keep their cost of deposits low despite the relationship between debt and equity and despite the riskiness of their assets. This issue is discussed more fully in Chapter 16.

Looked at as an insurance program, the FSLIC can control its risks by altering a number of policy and pricing parameters. These include the following:

1. The explicit premium charged for the insurance
2. The capital they require the insured institution to have, which acts as a form of insurance deductible
3. The extent to which they allow the insured to take risks in the form of growth in deposits and/or acquisition of risky assets
4. The extent to which they allow owners and managers with conflicts of interest to control an institution
5. The extent to which they accept risk without spending on sufficient supervision and examination
6. The amount of exposure they are willing to assume as measured by the maximum dollar coverage of accounts (an amount that was raised to $100,000 per account in 1980)

In the case of the FSLIC, the cost of insurance was reduced in virtually every way possible in the late 1970s and early 1980s. The premium was not increased until the losses had already swamped the insurance fund. The amount of capital required of the insured savings and loans was allowed to go negative for many in the business, since the focus was on regulatory net worth, not tangible net worth. Many of the institutions were permitted to substantially increase the percentage of their assets in higher risk classes. This was especially true in the case of Texas and California state-chartered institutions, which had broad asset charters. Finally, inadequate funds were available for examination and few potential owners and managers were denied entry.

Inexperienced Management and Fraud

The abrupt expansion of asset powers for S&Ls that occurred in the 1980s combined with the reduced profits to entice S&Ls to expand into new asset markets in which profit margins looked more attractive. The lower profits were due to high open-market interest rates and increased competition from federal agencies. The combination resulted in the S&Ls sharply expanding their lending in markets where they had little experience. These markets included commercial real estate lending, consumer lending, corporate lending, high-yield securities, and real estate development. In many of these markets, S&L associations experienced operating losses.

Legal and Ethical Issues

Vernon Savings: Misuse of Corporate Resources and Political Influence Peddling

One of the most flagrant examples of the high-flying Texas thrift industry was Vernon Savings and Loan Association. This S&L was identified early in the growing S&L crisis as an example of the worst type of management abuse of an S&L charter. From 1981 to 1986, Vernon S&L grew tenfold in assets by offering brokered deposits and investing in high-risk real estate projects. Early profits in the mid-1980s became huge losses a few years later.

Members of Vernon's board and management were indicted on numerous counts of fraud and misapplication of association funds for personal use. The conviction of Vernon's president was based on a southern California beach house, personal junkets, and other questionable purchases at association expense. The Vernon case also involved allegations regarding the use of S&L funds to reimburse employees for political contributions. Vernon employees allegedly used political contributions to obtain support from elected officials to intervene with regulators.

The issues raised by the Vernon case include not only the obvious ones of corporate misapplications of funds and using political influence, but also the issue of what regulators should do to control who owns and manages governmentally insured institutions. Adding to the problem was the fact that managers, owners, and directors who entered the industry had little experience or were attracted by what appeared to be government endorsed wide open lending using government insured deposits. It appeared that the government regulators were so anxious to bring new capital into the institutions that they accepted just about anyone.

Accounting Conventions Masked Problems

A number of historical generally accepted accounting principles (GAAP) were found to be ineffective in assessing the deteriorating conditions. In the early 1980s, savings and loans were motivated to acquire other institutions using *purchase asset accounting*. This standard of accounting for the acquisition of another institution resulted in huge amounts of goodwill being created on the books of the surviving institutions. Moreover, once the assets were written down to market value, they could frequently be sold at a book profit if interest rates were low, as was the case in the mid-1980s. This led to an overstatement of the true profits of the business, since there continued to be a need to write down, or amortize, the goodwill for many years into the future.

Another accounting convention that created problems was determining whether the sale of assets was from a trading or investment portfolio. Many institutions sold assets from portfolios when they produced a book profit, but did not mark-to-market the balance of the portfolio. They took the gains into income and buried the losses. The accounting profession addressed this issue, but it was long after the business had artificially inflated profits and capital accounts.

Regulatory Accounting Weaknesses

Regulatory accounting policies also masked the extent of the thrift problem. The adoption of special regulatory accounting devices made the net worth of thrifts look better than it really was. In particular, the regulators came up with a regulatory net worth item called *appraised equity capital* that was defined as the appraised increase in value of the S&Ls' buildings and land used in the normal course of business. This only served to mask the true weakness of the institutions.

Unnecessary Restrictions on Bank Acquisitions of Savings and Loans

Federal regulators maintained strong restrictions on commercial banks acquiring S&Ls. Indeed, in the early 1980s the only acquisitions permitted were acquisitions of distressed institutions. The excess supply of financial service providers demanded policies that should have led to the consolidation of the business. However, political forces maintained highly restrictive acquisition policies.

Government Macroeconomic Policies and Induced Competition

The economic volatility that emerged in the 1960s and grew worse in the 1970s was especially debilitating to S&Ls. These firms were structured to perform in a stable economic environment with an upward-sloping term structure of interest rates. Unfortunately, macroeconomic policies did not produce that environment.

Monetary Policy, Inflation, and High Interest Rates

The extreme use of monetary policy was the primary macroeconomic stabilization tool used to control inflation after the Federal Reserve's shift to controlling the money supply in October 1979. This resulted in post–World War II record high open-market interest rates in the late 1970s and early 1980s. This stabilization policy contributed to the operating losses at S&Ls, since the asset portfolios of saving and loans were made up primarily of fixed-rate mortgages and their liabilities were short-term deposits. Savings and loans had enormous interest rate risk exposure, which impacted these institutions more than any other.

Competition from Federal Government Mortgage Credit Agencies

Adding measurably to the problems of the thrifts was the fact that the FNMA and the FHLMC were created with charter provisions allowing them to become the low-cost producers of mortgage credit. These agencies, which have private stockholders who demand maximum returns on invested capital, have several advantages over our system of insured depository institutions. These agencies are discussed in full in Chapter 13. Due to the profit squeeze between the deregulated deposit market and the agency-influenced mortgage market, many in the S&L business substantially increased investments in commercial mortgages, junk bonds, acquisition and development lending, consumer lending, and business lending in order to offset the decline in profit margins.

Oil Belt Recession/Depression

The sharp rise and then fall in oil prices during the 1970s and 1980s resulted in several areas of the country experiencing dramatic boom–bust conditions. Key among these states were Alaska, Texas, Colorado, Wyoming, Louisiana, Oklahoma, and Arkansas. Commercial development and mortgage lending on commercial properties were particularly hard hit. Even residential development and single and multifamily mortgages were victims of large defaults and massive devaluations. S&Ls were particularly hurt by this cycle.

Who Gained from the Crisis and Who Pays for the Bailout?

Without a doubt the most controversial aspect of the thrift crisis relates to its cost and the selection of the appropriate means of financing the bailout program. More than one government official was severely criticized for providing inaccurate information and estimates concerning the cost of the bailout program. As early as 1986, estimates were in the area of $5 billion. By 1992, the cost estimates, while still rising, were in the area of $200 billion, not including the cost of interest on the national debt that had to be raised to cover the paid-off depositors of failed institutions.

These estimates, needless to say, resulted in indignation on the part of government officials, the press, and the public. "How could these costs have gotten so high?" was the number one question on the minds of everyone. "Where did the money go?" "Who gained from these losses?" These questions were the source of hundreds of hours of testimony before both houses of Congress.

These straightforward questions rarely received a straight answer. Let's start with the question "Where did the money go?" As discussed, the primary cause was that insolvent or nearly insolvent institutions were allowed to continue to issue government-insured deposits and make loans and investments that were sometimes risky and ill-conceived. The losses relate to the simple fact that the value of the investments, plus the income received on the investments, was less than the amount of insured deposits issued, plus accruing interest on the deposits.

What bad investments were made by these failed institutions? According to the records of the RTC, the largest losses were on failed real estate investments in office buildings, apartments, shopping centers, land, and other development real estate. The beneficiaries of the thrift crisis must have been the developers, contractors, subcontractors, suppliers, laborers, and sellers of the land that went into these investments. Also, corporations that borrowed using the junk bond market must be considered beneficiaries of the thrift crisis. Finally, a number of homebuyers in the markets with the weakest thrifts such as Texas, Oklahoma, Colorado, and Arizona continued to receive financing from institutions that probably would have been closed otherwise. These were the primary beneficiaries. Of course, much has been made of the large salaries and bonuses, perks, and wasteful spending of a handful of thrift officers and directors. But that amounted to a drop in the bucket.

There was another group of major beneficiaries, however, that should not be overlooked. These were the savers in the institutions that pursued aggressive growth policies by paying high rates on their savings. The higher-than-market rates paid by these institutions on government-insured deposits resulted in these savers receiving billions of dollars of interest income.

The problem then turns to how to pay for the losses. The losses that the government began to recognize on the federal budget in 1986 and later years were losses that the government had already incurred off-budget. The best way to understand the situation is to think of the 1980s as a decade in which, for about seven years, the federal government ran a program to stimulate private investment. This program consisted of allowing a number of private financial institutions to issue government guaranteed debt, which was off-budget and called *insured deposits*.

The government allowed these investments to be in a wide variety of different loans and investments, from the safest home loan to the riskiest land loan. By the late 1980s, the government decided this program was not such a good idea and decided to shut it down. It then required the institutions to pay off the government-insured deposits that had ballooned during the early 1980s. These institutions found out, however, that a large percentage of the loans and investments they had made went sour. The institutions failed and the losses fell to the government to fund.

The government now had to go through the unpleasant task of shifting the losses from an off-budget insurance fund account to an on-budget account. Moreover, it would now require swapping insured government deposits for government debt. This made it look like the government was suddenly incurring large new deficit obligations, when in fact the spending had actually taken place in the early 1980s. The houses, businesses, office buildings, leveraged buy-outs, apartments, and shopping centers financed with the deposits were already a part of the capital stock of the country, even though the budget didn't recognize the expenditure until the late 1980s and early 1990s.

The source of payment for this newly recognized government debt appears to be falling on a wide variety of groups. First, the government turned to the insured institutions by raising insurance premiums on thrifts and commercial banks. Then the government expropriated funds from allied institutions such as the FHLB. Next, the government pursued a deficit-reduction program including new taxes, military expenditure cuts, and other measures.

Proposed Solutions

Now that the thrift debacle has been recognized and attention has turned to similar problems that commercial banks are having, there has been an outcry for solutions. These recommendations include actions that have already been taken or proposed. Some of the more important follow:

1. Increase the cost of insurance coverage. This has been done across the board or by instituting a risk-based premium program. The FDIC has been authorized to develop a risk-based program. Such a program has the most highly leveraged institutions and those with the most risky assets paying higher premiums.

2. Reduce coverage of deposit insurance. This set of recommendations involves such ideas as reducing coverage to a lower than $100,000 limit, limiting coverage to only $100,000 per individual regardless of how many institutions he or she does business with, or requiring a type of coinsurance whereby the government does not insure 100 percent of the deposits.

    The reduction of insurance coverage has occurred as a result of Congressional action to reduce the number of institutions that can use deposits sold through security brokerage firms, called brokered deposits.

3. Consolidate the financial services industry. Many experts believe that the long-term solution must involve considerably more consolidation within the financial services industry in the years ahead.

4. Increase capital and reduce risk-taking powers. FIRREA of 1989 and the FDICIA of 1991 were primarily designed to accomplish this objective. They substantially increased the capital requirements of thrifts while reducing their ability to invest in risky assets.

5. Increase powers of regulators. Both the FIRREA and FDICIA accomplished this. These recommendations relate to giving more powers to regulators to permit them to step in earlier to stop institutions that are involved in unsafe or unsound activities or allowing them to take over institutions that are just barely solvent.

6. Eliminate thrifts and merge them into banks. Many feel that the thrift is no longer necessary as a specialized financial institution. They feel that the institutions should merge or be converted to commercial bank charters. Many observers feel this is the long-term result of the passage of FIRREA of 1989.

7. Improve reporting and adopt mark-to-market accounting. A number of analysts believe that a form of mark-to-market regulatory accounting would have provided much more advance notice of the extent of the thrifts' financial problems. They want to see improved reporting. Mark-to-market accounting differs from accounting under GAAP. Under mark-to-market, the firm determines the market value of its assets and liabilities periodically. It no longer values its assets at historical book value. Such a system would have exposed the insolvent position of the S&Ls in the late 1970s and early 1980s. This accounting approach has been considered by the Financial Accounting Standard Board and has been recommended by the Securities and Exchange Commission.

Questions

Appendix

A1. What was the main cause of the thrift debacle?
A2. How did deregulation of the deposit rate contribute to the thrift debacle?
A3. What is meant by forbearance, and how did regulatory forbearance contribute to the thrift crisis?
A4. How did competition contribute to the thrift debacle?
A5. Who gained the most from the thrift debacle?
A6. Fraud and mismanagement have been blamed by some as the primary cause of the thrift debacle. Do you agree?
A7. What are some of the recommendations made to reduce the potential for additional thrift failure costs?

A8. How could savers in thrift institutions benefit from the thrift debacle?
A9. Should most of the thrifts have been liquidated in the early 1980s when they were technically insolvent?
A10. What is meant by moral hazard in relation to the thrift debacle?

Life Insurance Companies and Pension Funds

chapter 11

The purpose of this chapter is to describe the financial operations of life insurance companies and pension funds. These institutions share many of the same characteristics. One of their main similarities is that they both provide a source of retirement income. They are also alike in that they are funded with systematic contractual payments that are seldom withdrawn. As a result, both types of intermediaries enjoy steady growth and are able to invest in long-term assets.

Some families invest a portion of their retirement savings directly in the form of individual insurance policies with savings features. In many cases, retirement savings are accumulated in pooled pension plans, and the trustees of these plans invest the funds in group annuity policies. It is also possible to invest these funds in separate investment accounts with insurance companies. Life insurance companies compete with deposit institutions, mutual funds, and securities brokers for individual retirement savings. Pension fund assets are also managed by bank trust departments and investment advisory firms in addition to life insurance companies.

Because life insurance companies and pension funds have substantial overlaps in customer motivations and investment goals, it is logical that their discussion is included in the same chapter. Nevertheless, there are enough differences between these types of institutions that a full comparison is necessary.

Chapter 11 Life Insurance Companies and Pension Funds

Life Insurance Companies

Life companies are financial intermediaries that provide two primary services. First, they provide mortality risk management services. This is insurance against the loss of income due to death. Secondly, life companies offer savings and investment programs, mainly for retirement. Often these services are offered in a single policy with premiums split between them.

Life insurance companies, like other intermediaries, have undergone significant changes in the last several decades. Long known for conservative product development, investment policies, and marketing approaches, the industry found it necessary to respond to the many changes in the financial landscape in order to maintain market share.

Life companies have recently been very active in product development. New products have been developed to respond to the fact that investment returns on savings held by life insurance companies in the 1960s and 1970s were not competitive with other investments. This resulted in new products such as universal life and variable life policies and higher yielding, single premium annuities.

Life companies have also responded to the capture of a large percentage of household savings by pension funds. In order to compete for the management of these assets, life companies have developed fee-based, asset management services for pension funds. They have also improved their group annuity products to offer pension funds a product that can be used to guarantee lifetime income for retirees. Thirdly, life companies have developed investment products specifically designed for pension funds. The most popular of these is a life company contract that provides a fixed return and fixed maturity called a *guaranteed investment contract (GIC)*.

Partly because of these new products, life companies have become willing to invest in more risky assets. Many life companies have increased their investment in high-yield corporate bonds (junk bonds), commercial real estate and loans, and corporate stock. All of these have proven to have a higher volatility of returns as compared to the more conservative investments life companies have historically held.

Life companies have also responded to changes in the distribution channels for financial products. Some companies now actively sell annuities and life policies through securities brokers who have become licensed insurance agents. Savings and loans and commercial banks have also become active in marketing life insurance and annuity policies. Insurance is now being sold through direct mail and to employment and affinity groups. The traditional marketing approach of the life insurance salesperson sitting down at the kitchen table with the family to discuss insurance is becoming far less common. New marketing techniques, new products, and expanded investment choices have revolutionized the life insurance business, introducing more instability into the industry.

Mortality Risk

The two basic services purchased by life company policyholders are insurance against dying prematurely (life insurance) and insurance against living too long (annuities). Therefore, the probability that a policyholder will die at a certain age is highly important. This probability is called *mortality risk*. One of the functions of life companies is to pool mortality risk by insuring large numbers of individuals so that the life company's average mortality assessment approaches that which is expected from the whole or specified segment of the population.

In order to assess the probability of death, the insurance industry has developed extensive demographic data that it uses to estimate probability distributions for dying at various ages. These are known as *mortality tables*. Over the years, the average life expectancy of Americans has generally increased. This has worked to the advantage of life companies, since it defers the payment of death benefits. However, in the case of annuities, living longer means making annuity payments to policyholders for a longer period of time. As a result, insurance companies and their regulators use two sets of mortality tables, one for life insurance and another for annuities. The life insurance table, known as the Commissioners 1980 Standard Ordinary (1970–1975), assumes a population of individuals will all die by age 99. The annuity table, known as the 1983 Individual Annuity Table (1971–1976), assumes that the last death from a group will occur at age 115. These mortality assumptions, which are used to set insurance premiums, result in life companies accumulating more reserves on behalf of beneficiaries than if a more up-to-date set of statistics was used. A segment from these tables in shown in Table 11.1.

To understand how pure insurance, or *term insurance,* is priced consider an insurance company that sells a one-year $100,000 life insurance policy to 100,000 females who are all 25 years old. According to the table, the expected mortality at age 25 is 1.16 per thousand. Out of the 100,000 insured, 116 will be expected to die during the year. This would require a payout to their beneficiaries of benefits of $11,600,000 (116 × $100,000). Dividing this cost among the 100,000 insured women would result in a annual premium of $116 ($11,600,000/100,000). The costs of originating and servicing the policy and insurance company profits are added to this pure mortality premium. If the insurance company received all the premiums at the beginning of the year and the deaths occurred evenly throughout the year, it would then earn interest on approximately one-half of the premiums it receives. This investment income would serve to reduce the premium required.

When an insurance company offers a policy that has a premium above the pure insurance cost plus operating expenses and profit, it provides a policy with an investment annuity feature. Whole life, universal life, and variable life are several variations of policies that have investment features combined with the pure death coverage.

Table 11.1

Excerpt from Mortality Tables

| | Commissioners 1980 Ordinary |||| 1983 Individual Annuity Table ||||
| Age | Male || Female || Male || Female ||
	Deaths per 1,000	Expectation of Life (years)	Deaths per 1,000	Expectation of Life (years)	Deaths per 1,000	Expectation of Life (years)	Deaths per 1,000	Expectation of Life (years)
20	1.90	52.37	1.05	57.04	.51	59.50	.26	64.55
21	1.91	51.47	1.07	56.10	.53	58.53	.28	63.56
22	1.89	50.57	1.09	55.16	.55	57.56	.29	62.58
23	1.86	49.66	1.11	54.22	.57	56.59	.31	61.60
24	1.82	48.75	1.14	53.28	.60	55.63	.33	60.62
25	1.77	47.84	1.16	52.34	.62	54.66	.35	59.64
26	1.73	46.93	1.19	51.40	.65	53.69	.37	58.66
27	1.71	46.01	1.22	50.46	.68	52.73	.39	57.68
28	1.70	45.09	1.26	49.52	.70	51.76	.41	56.70
29	1.71	44.16	1.30	48.59	.73	50.80	.42	55.72

Source: *1990 Life Insurance Fact Book*. Washington, DC: American Council of Life Insurance, 1990. p. 122.

Basic Types of Life Insurance

Life insurance companies classify their insurance by type of customer. *Ordinary life* insurance consists of policies sold directly to individuals. *Group life* is sold to corporations and other organizations to cover their employees. Other group life policies are sold to members of affinity groups, mainly social organizations and professional associations. *Industrial life* insurance is a small and declining form of insurance more common from the 1930s to the 1950s. Customers pay premiums weekly in small amounts. This type of insurance appeals mostly to low-income wage earners. It has largely been replaced by group insurance. *Credit life* is sold in conjunction with a loan. It is designed to pay off the loan if the insured dies while the loan is outstanding.

Table 11.2 on page 288 shows the amounts of various types of insurance outstanding in selected years from 1960 to 1990.

Types of Ordinary Life Policies

There are three types of ordinary life policies: whole life, term, and other. The percentage of total ordinary insurance outstanding for each of the major types for various years from 1954 to 1989 is shown in Table 11.3.

Table 11.2

**Types of Life Insurance in Force in United States
1960–1990
(dollars in billions)**

Year	Ordinary	Group	Industrial	Credit	Total
1960	$ 341	$ 175	$31	$ 29	$ 586
1965	499	308	40	53	901
1970	735	551	39	77	1,402
1975	1,083	905	39	112	2,140
1980	1,760	1,579	36	165	3,541
1985	3,247	2,562	28	216	6,053
1989	4,940	3,469	24	260	8,694
1990	5,367	3,754	24	248	9,393

Source: *1991 Life Insurance Fact Book Update*. Washington, DC: American Council of Life Insurance. p. 10.

Whole life provides a combination of death benefit coverage and a savings feature that builds cash values that can be borrowed by the policyholder or withdrawn by terminating the policy.

Term life is death benefit coverage without a savings feature. Although insurance companies have developed term policies with a variety of premium payment plans, the basic structure of term insurance is that the premium pays only one year's death benefit coverage.

As shown in Table 11.3, whole life has declined sharply as a proportion of ordinary life policies sold, while term insurance has grown. This is largely because of the low returns paid on the savings or cash value portion of whole life policies.

Many ordinary life policies are also *participating policies* in that they pay a dividend. The dividend is paid to policyholders at the end of the premium year. For tax purposes, the dividend is considered a return of premium and therefore is not taxable. The insurance company pays dividends to the extent that mortality losses are lower and/or investment returns are better than anticipated. These dividends can also be used by the insured to purchase additional insurance or add to the policy's cash value.

Annuities

During the last decade, there has been a sharp growth in the sales of insurance annuities. *Annuities* differ from life insurance in that they promise to pay benefits over time to the person covered rather than death

Table 11.3

**Distribution of Ordinary Life Policies
1954–1989
(percent of total)**

Year	Whole Life	Other	Term	Total Permanent
1954	65.5%	18.3%	16.2%	100.0%
1966	65.9	7.3	26.8	100.0
1970	60.9	5.8	33.3	100.0
1981	58.0	3.5	38.5	100.0
1989	50.7	0.9	48.4	100.0

Source: *1990 Life Insurance Fact Book*. Washington, DC: American Council of Life Insurance. p. 27.

benefits to beneficiaries after the covered person dies. In this sense, annuities are truly "life" insurance since they cover you while you live. The growth of annuity sales has been prompted by two important developments. First, the 1986 Tax Reform Act left the single premium annuity, along with variable and universal life policies, among the few tax advantaged investments. Thus, the Tax Act gave life companies a major advantage in the marketing of these contracts. Second, pension funds have purchased annuities to provide for benefits owed to pensioners in active and restructured pension plans as permitted under the 1974 Employee Retirement Income Security Act (ERISA). The volume of annuity obligations under annuity contracts at year-end 1989 is shown in Table 11.4. In the table, "income now payable" means that these annuities are currently making payments to beneficiaries. "Income deferred but fully paid" means that the beneficiary is

Table 11.4

**Annuities Outstanding by
Status of Contract 1989
(dollars in billions)**

Status of Contract	Number	Annual Income
Income now payable	841,000	$ 3.8
Income deferred but fully paid	7,028,000	17.9
Income deferred but not fully paid	6,288,000	17.1

Source: Ibid. p. 39.

not yet receiving payments, but all premium payments required have been made. "Income deferred but not fully paid" means that the beneficiary is not yet receiving payments and all premiums have not been paid.

Annuities come in both fixed and variable form. The benefit payments in a fixed annuity are guaranteed by the insurance company. In a variable annuity, the payments are dependent upon investment earnings. Variable annuity funds are typically invested in common stocks. The appeal of a variable annuity is that retirement benefits will not be eroded by inflation since stock returns have typically outpaced inflation. The danger in buying a variable annuity is that the stock market is volatile and therefore annuity benefits can fall as well as increase.

New Policies Stress Investment Performance

The life insurance industry has had to develop new types of policies to compete with alternative retirement investment products. Sales of whole life policies, once the industry standard, declined sharply in the late 1970s and early 1980s. In addition, holders of whole life policies, seeing that investment returns on their cash values were below those offered elsewhere, borrowed the cash values in the form of *policy loans* or redeemed the policies and reinvested these funds in higher yielding investments.

A number of life company competitors persuaded insurance buyers to purchase term insurance only and place the difference between the term policy premium and the whole life premium in investments such as mutual funds. The success of this marketing tactic encouraged the life insurance industry to create new types of policies that provide higher investment returns. In most cases, life companies altered their investment portfolios by adding a greater proportion of higher return, higher risk assets. Some new policies are a type of wrap-around insurance. These include a form of term insurance with an investment feature that is directed by the beneficiary.

Variable Life Insurance

Variable life policies, like whole life policies, require level premium payments and combine a death benefit and a savings feature. Unlike the whole life policy, the savings or cash value in a variable life policy is held in a separate account and invested in assets designated by the policyholder. The cash value and death benefit on such a policy will increase or decrease depending on the amount of return on the assets in the account. The advantage of the variable life policy cash value account over a mutual fund is that investment earnings are tax deferred until withdrawn.

Universal Life Insurance

Universal life provides the policyholder with the flexibility to change the amount and timing of premium payments and thus the amount of insurance coverage and cash value. When premiums are received, they are applied first to the cost of providing the desired level of death benefit, and the remainder is invested in assets chosen by the insured. If the policyholder chooses not to make premium payments for a time, the cost of providing death benefits is deducted from accumulated cash value and the policy continues in force. In an ordinary life policy, failure to pay premiums could result in cancellation of the policy.

Flexible Premium Variable Life Insurance

The flexible premium variable life policy is a variation on the universal life policy in that premiums and insurance coverage can be changed and cash values invested in assets of the policyholder's choice. If the chosen assets earn a higher-than-anticipated investment income, the excess can be used to increase the death benefit.

The dollar amounts of variable, universal, and flexible premium life policies outstanding in several years from 1983 to 1990 are shown in Table 11.5.

Changing Pattern of Insurance Premiums

The inflation of the 1970s and early 1980s, with its resultant high interest rates, soured many on the use of traditional insurance policies as vehicles for savings. The low returns on these policies convinced many to use term insurance, with the difference between the term premium and whole life premium invested in common stock or other investments. As already noted, the life insurance industry responded to this situation by developing new policies that provide more rewarding investment opportunities.

Adding to the competitiveness of the industry in the 1980s were several relatively new companies that offered high-yield annuity policies using

Table 11.5

Variable, Universal, and Flexible Variable Life: Dollar Amount Outstanding (dollars in billions)
1983–1990

Year	Variable Life	Universal Life	Flexible Variable Life
1983	$14	$ 131	
1986	38	864	$ 26
1989	54	1,390	107
1990	52	1,619	114

Source: *1991 Life Insurance Fact Book Update*. Washington, DC: American Council of Life Insurance. p. 14.

distribution networks that bypassed traditional insurance company sales agents. Some of these companies also adopted more risky investment strategies that allowed them to pay higher interest rates on invested funds. In 1990 and 1991, several large companies and a number of smaller life companies failed because of losses sustained on investments in junk bonds and speculative real estate. This situation resulted in state regulators requiring insurance companies to follow more conservative investment policies.

The impact of the reduction in the traditional whole life policy and growth in the investment-oriented life policy from 1981 to 1990 was significant. Premium income on investment-oriented policies grew from less than 5 percent of all life company premium income to well over 70 percent. It will be interesting to see whether the failure of several companies specializing in investment-oriented policies in the 1990s will reverse this direction.

Asset Structure of Life Companies

The asset structure of life companies has changed in a number of important ways in response to the new types of services and the amounts being sold. The changes have come slowly, however, because of the long-term and largely predictable nature of traditional life company liabilities. As a result, life companies hold the majority of their assets in fixed-return, long-term investments, such as government securities, corporate bonds, and mortgages (see Table 11.6). At year-end 1989, these types of investments accounted for three-fourths of all life company assets.

Table 11.6

Life Company Assets by Amount and Percentage of Total Assets 1960–1990
(dollars in billions)

Year	Govt. Agency	Corp. Bonds	Corp. Stocks	Mortgages	Real Estate	Policy Loans	Other	Total
1960	9.9%	39.1%	4.2%	34.9%	3.1%	4.4%	4.4%	$ 119.6
1965	7.5	36.7	5.7	37.8	3.0	4.8	4.5	158.9
1970	5.3	35.3	7.4	35.9	3.0	7.8	5.3	207.3
1975	5.2	36.6	9.7	30.8	3.3	8.5	5.9	289.3
1980	6.9	37.5	9.9	27.4	3.1	8.6	6.6	479.2
1989	13.7	41.4	9.7	19.5	3.1	4.4	8.2	1,299.8
1990	15.0	41.4	9.1	19.2	3.1	4.4	7.8	1,408.2

Source: Ibid. p. 44.

Despite the historical emphasis on fixed-return investments, life companies have responded to the changing mix of insurance products by increasing investments in higher risk, higher return assets. This has resulted in increased holdings of common stock, less than investment-grade corporate bonds (junk bonds), and commercial mortgages and equity investments in commercial real estate. This has been offset somewhat by increased holdings of government and agency securities. Table 11.6 shows changes in the percentage holdings of life company assets by type over the last 30 years.

Size and Ownership Structure of the Life Insurance Industry

The life insurance industry is characterized by a slowly growing number of companies. Of the total of 2,343 life companies in existence at year-end 1988, 2,225 were stockholder-owned and 118 were mutual. However, mutual companies are among the largest in the industry. Metropolitan Life Insurance Company, New York Life Insurance Company, Prudential Insurance Company of America, Northwestern Mutual Life Insurance Company, John Hancock Mutual Life Insurance Company, and Equitable Life Assurance Society are mutual companies that are owned by policyholders rather than stockholders. They are among the top ten insurance companies in terms of total assets. Even though mutual life companies are few in number, they represent almost one-half of the total assets of the industry. There is a growing trend toward converting mutual life companies to stockholder ownership. In large part, this is intended to increase the capitalization of these companies and their ability to expand.

The number of life companies operating in the United States since 1950 is shown in Table 11.7.

Table 11.7

Number of Life Companies in the United States 1950–1990

Year	Number
1950	649
1960	1,441
1970	1,780
1980	1,958
1989	2,270
1990	2,200

Source: Ibid. p. 53.

Life Company State of Domicile

Life insurance companies are chartered by states rather than the federal government and as such, they are state regulated. Each state has its own capital requirements and other regulatory restrictions. However, in order to sell insurance outside of the company's state of domicile, it must obtain a license in those states and comply with their insurance regulations. Some states such as New York have very stringent requirements for companies operating in the state. In order to avoid these stricter requirements, some insurance companies operate subsidiaries in these states solely to write insurance on their residents. This allows the bulk of the company's business to be subject to less severe requirements of other states. The top ten states of charter for life companies is shown in Table 11.8.

Pension Funds

Pension funds are our economy's largest institutional source of long-term capital. Growth in private and state and local government pension funds over the last 20 years has exceeded that of most other intermediaries. Pension reserves of households represent their largest single class of financial assets. At year-end 1950, pension reserves represented only slightly more than 5 percent of total financial holdings of households. By year-end 1990, the percentage had climbed to 30 percent.

Table 11.8

**Ranking of States for Chartering Life Insurance Companies
Mid-Year 1990**

State of Domicile	Number of Charters
Arizona	699
Texas	237
Louisiana	104
New York	90
Illinois	81
Delaware	64
Pennsylvania	61
California	56
Indiana	54
Oklahoma	48

Source: Ibid. p. 52.

Pension funds are important institutions for several reasons. First, pension funds together control the largest stock of long-term financial capital in the country. This capital is available for long-term investment and it is growing rapidly. Secondly, the method by which corporations account for pension costs has made the earnings of private pension plans a major profit and loss item for a number of large corporations. For organizations with certain types of pension plans, investment performance of the funds accumulated to pay future benefits can have a significant year-to-year impact on the profit and loss statement.

This section looks at the major types of pension plans and the types of investments held by these plans. The principal factors that affect the cost of pension plans and the role life insurance companies play in the pension field are also analyzed.

Types of Pension Plans

There are two major types of pension plans that accumulate substantial investment funds. These are *private pension plans* and *state and local governmental pension plans*. Private pension plans are operated by private, profit, and not-for-profit organizations. State and local government pension plans are operated by governmental units for their employees, such as teachers, police and firefighters, and municipal employees.

Pension plans are also classified by the way benefits are determined. *Defined benefit* plans provide contractually determined benefits to recipients. A defined benefit plan might pay a retired employee a specified percentage (say 2 percent) of his or her annual pre-retirement income times the number of years employed. For example, if an employee worked for the employer for 25 years, he would receive 50 percent (2% × 25) of his pre-retirement salary.

In this type of program, the employing organization is obligated to pay earned benefits irrespective of the amount of funds set aside to provide for these benefits. By law, an employer having such a plan is obligated to fund these liabilities on a current basis. In addition, the employer risks having to make additional contributions if the investment returns on the funds set aside are poor.

The amount of contribution that must be made in order to adequately fund a defined benefit pension plan depends on a great number of factors. Actuaries help determine how much must be contributed to a defined benefit pension plan by making assumptions and estimates of these factors. The following are the most important of these variable factors:

1. Employee turnover (higher turnover reduces pension contributions)
2. Employee average age (older workers necessitate larger pension contributions

3. Expected income growth (higher growth in future income will increase pension contributions)
4. Expected income earned on pension investments (higher returns on pension assets will reduce pension contributions)
5. Vesting (earlier vesting increases pension contributions)

Defined contribution plans do not provide a fixed benefit. Rather, a contractual amount of contribution is established, which is typically a specified percentage (say 10 percent) of the employee's income. These contributions are invested and the employee benefits are dependent, in part, on investment performance. In some plans, the employee may have a choice of a number of possible investments. When this is the case, the employee's choice of investments will also affect the level of retirement benefits.

Pension plans can also be *insured* and *noninsured* programs. Insured pension programs are funded by annuities purchased from life insurance companies. The life company in these plans assumes the responsibility of paying promised benefits to beneficiaries.

Noninsured pension plans are administered by trustees selected by the employer, by the plan participants, or by both. These trustees have a fiduciary responsibility with respect to the funds set aside to provide benefits. This means they are obligated to oversee the investment of the funds, including specifying acceptable types of investments and obtaining investment management expertise. Trustees of noninsured pension plans often designate commercial bank trust departments, investment advisory firms, and insurance companies to perform day-to-day investment responsibilities. Nevertheless, the trustees are ultimately responsible for the prudent investment of funds accumulated to pay pension benefits.

Life Insurance Companies and Pension Programs

The life insurance industry and the pension fund industry overlap in a number of significant ways. Some pension plans simply purchase group annuities from life companies each year to provide earned benefits for employees. In this case, the pension plan retains no control over the assets accumulated to provide benefits. These assets become part of the general investments of the life company. The same thing occurs when an individual purchases an annuity to provide for his or her own retirement income.

Some pension plan trustees wish to retain control over how fund assets are invested. They can do so, and still employ the insurance company's investment expertise, by setting up a separate account. The insurance company manages the separate account for an individual pension fund or on a pooled basis for several funds having common investment goals.

Total life insurance company reserves attributable to pension fund annuities amounted to $641.7 billion at year-end 1989. Table 11.9 shows

Table 11.9

Private Pension Plans Held with Life Companies: Number of Persons Covered and Plan Reserves for Year-end 1989
(dollars in billions)

Type of Program	Number of Persons Covered (millions)	Dollar Reserves
Group annuities	42,280	$406
Keogh and IRA	5,585	52
Tax-sheltered annuities	5,120	63
Other	7,145	121

Source: *1990 Life Insurance Fact Book.* Washington, DC: American Council of Life Insurance. p. 57.

the number of persons covered and pension reserves represented under various annuity programs at year-end 1989. These numbers exclude funds managed by insurance companies under separate pension accounts. These dollars are included in pension fund assets.

Asset Structure of Pension Funds

Pension benefits are typically paid many years after the monies contributed to pay them are set aside. As a result, pension funds are long-term investors. This means that a large percentage of pension fund assets can be invested in corporate stocks, long-term bonds and mortgages, and real estate equities. Table 11.10 on page 298 shows the asset profile of private pension funds and state and local government pension funds. As the table shows, corporate stocks and bonds dominate the holdings of the two types of funds. Public pension funds tend to be more risk-averse in their investment strategy. This is reflected in a larger percentage of assets invested in U.S. Treasury and agency securities and a lesser percentage in corporate equities as compared to the private pension funds.

Growth of Pension Fund Assets

The rapid growth of pension funds in the last several decades can be attributed to a number of factors. With the addition of the "baby boom" age group, the number of employees covered has increased along with the level of benefits promised. People work longer now that age discrimination in

Table 11.10

Asset Structure of Private and State and Local Pension Funds
September 30, 1988
(dollars in billions)

Type of Asset	Private Pension Plans $ Amount	% of Total	State and Local Pension Plans $ Amount	% of Total
Demand deposits	$ 10.2	1.0%	$ 2.5	0.4
Time deposits	84.8	7.8	20.5	3.5
Corporate equities	539.6	49.6	205.7	35.0
Treasuries	78.4	7.2	121.0	20.6
Agencies	53.1	4.9	58.0	9.9
Corporate bonds	176.2	16.2	163.0	27.8
Mortgages	5.7	0.5	15.9	2.7
Open-market paper	85.0	7.8		
Other assets	52.6	4.8	0.7	0.1
Total	**$1,085.6**		**$587.3**	

Source: Ibid. p. 61.

employment has been outlawed. This increases potential benefits and delays their payment. As a result, the funds set aside to pay future benefits accumulate faster. In addition, the government has required employers to give employees greater vesting rights and to increase the amounts set aside in pension funds so that money will be available to pay benefits when employees retire.

Vesting refers to the right of an employee to receive employer-paid benefits under a pension plan even if the employee quits or is terminated before reaching retirement age. A few plans provide for immediate vesting, meaning employees can leave at any time without losing earned benefits. More frequently, employees are required to work for a minimum number of years, often three to five, before earned benefits are vested. If an employee leaves before the minimum service requirement is met, any benefits earned are canceled.

After the initial vesting period, an employee is usually vested in an increasing proportion of earned benefits as service time increases. For example, one-half of the benefits might be vested after five years' service, and 100 percent after ten years. Employers often delay full vesting of benefits as an inducement for employees to stay with the firm. However, Congress has established minimum vesting requirements for private pension plans by the passage in 1974 of the *Employee Retirement Income Security Act (ERISA)*. These requirements are designed to protect an employee from losing benefits if terminated after many years of service to an employer. Under the law, employee-paid pension contributions are fully vested.

Also under ERISA, employers with defined benefit plans must meet minimum funding requirements if pension fund costs are deducted for federal income tax purposes. In addition, pension benefits are insured by the federal Pension Benefit Guarantee Corporation if the sponsoring company goes bankrupt without providing sufficient funds to pay vested benefits.

Before the passage of ERISA, some companies promised employees pensions, but set aside insufficient funds to pay earned benefits. Employees were dependent upon the continued financial health of the company to receive benefits after retirement. If a company with an underfunded pension plan went bankrupt, its employees could be left without any prospect of retirement benefits even after many years of service to the company. After the passage of ERISA, companies with unfunded pension plan liabilities were required to increase contributions so that the plan could become fully funded over time.

The ERISA requirements for earlier vesting of pension benefits and the gradual funding of underfunded plans significantly increased employer contributions to private pension plans.

Putting Pension Obligations on the Balance Sheet

ERISA has not been the only factor driving change in pension plan financing. The Financial Accounting Standards Board, through accounting standards FAS-87 and FAS-106, has had a significant impact on how pension obligations are recorded on a company's books. FAS-87 requires employers to account for pension liabilities by using a uniform method of cost recognition. It also requires immediate recognition of liabilities. As a result, unfunded liabilities of pension funds must be recognized and reflected on the company's balance sheet. Employers with overfunded pension plans (pension plans whose assets exceed its liabilities) are required to recognize the excess funding as income over a period of time. FAS-106 requires employers to count as a current expense other types of retirement benefits, such as health benefits, paid after retirement.

Investment income on money set aside to pay future retirement benefits can greatly reduce the out-of-pocket cost of providing such benefits under defined benefit plans. If the money is invested wisely and produces superior investment returns, employers can reduce contributions and expenses. Also, investment income on pension fund excess is not taxable to the employer. As a result, there is a strong incentive to maximize investment performance in order to hold down pension costs. In contrast, poor investment performance will result in a need to make larger contributions. This can greatly increase expenses and lower earnings. To the extent that poor investment performance creates increases in unfunded liabilities, these will need to be reflected on the employer's balance sheet.

Overfunded pension plans have also played a role in a number of leveraged buyouts and other corporate restructuring. An overfunded plan can be terminated and employees' rights to benefits provided by the purchase of annuities. The balance of the funds not needed to purchase annuities can then be recaptured and used to retire debt, paid out as dividends, or for other corporate purposes.

Summary

Life insurance companies and pension funds have a number of common features. First, both types of intermediaries are funded largely by contractual savings. Second, life company and pension fund liabilities are long term. This results in both types of intermediaries investing a high percentage of assets in long-term bonds, mortgages, and corporate equities. Finally, life companies provide annuities, investment products, and asset management services to pension funds.

Life insurance companies provide **investment and mortality risk management** services. Life insurance companies are both **stock** and **mutual** in organization. The largest individual companies are mutual in form.

The basic insurance products of life companies have changed significantly in recent years. **Whole life insurance** has become less important, while policies with prospects of higher returns and risk have increased in importance. Policies that have become more popular are **annuities** and **variable life. Term insurance** has increased as policyholders have purchased pure insurance and invested savings in other forms of investment.

Life companies have altered their investment strategies to improve the investment appeal of their policies. The change involves accepting higher risk in investments in high-yielding corporate bonds, commercial mortgages and real estate, and corporate equities.

Life companies have created a number of products and services for pension funds. These include the following:

1. **Annuities** to cover lifetime incomes to pension fund beneficiaries
2. **Guaranteed investment contracts** as investments for pension funds
3. **Asset management services**

Pension funds are the fastest growing of the major intermediaries. They include both private and public pension funds.

Pension funds are structured as either defined benefit plans, with the benefit contractually set, or defined contribution plans, with the contribution contractually set, but the benefits dependent on investment performance of fund assets.

The **Employee Retirement Income Security Act** provides a number of protections for employees with pension plans. These include the following:

1. **Minimum vesting requirements**
2. **Funding requirements**
3. **Reporting requirements**

Pension plans have become more important to the nation's economy for two reasons. First, they represent the largest single source of investment capital. Second, the cost of pension programs has a significant impact on business profits.

Questions

Chapter 11

1. Explain what is meant by term insurance, whole life insurance, and annuities.
2. How has the types of insurance sold by life companies changed over the last several decades? Which are the more popular life insurance policies today versus 20 years ago?
3. Explain the structure of the life insurance industry in terms of mutual versus stock companies and state of charter. Why do life companies tend to be chartered in certain states more than others? What is different about New York as a place to sell life insurance?
4. Why are the largest life companies mutual companies?
5. Some life policies have cash values. Why do life companies sell life insurance that has cash values?
6. Some life companies sell life insurance policies that pay dividends. This is known as a participating life policy. What is a dividend? Is this form of income taxable to the policyholder?
7. Why did term insurance become more popular in the 1970s and 1980s?
8. The Tax Reform Act of 1986 eliminated many tax shelters for individuals. However, life companies can offer certain policies that provide for the deferral of tax. How did the Tax Reform Act of 1986 affect life companies?
9. What accounts for the strong growth in single premium annuities?
10. There has been a significant growth in the percentage of life company premiums that represent sales of investment-oriented life policies. Why has this happened and what impact does it have on the investment strategy of a life company?

11. Why do life companies and pension funds work so closely? What products and services do life companies provide to pension funds?
12. How would you characterize the asset structure of life insurance companies?
13. Mortality risk is almost unique to life companies. How do life companies assume this risk? What are mortality tables used for?
14. Why is there a difference between a mortality table for a term or whole life policy and another for an annuity?
15. Explain the difference between private and state and local government pension funds.
16. Explain the difference between a defined benefit plan and a defined contribution plan. Under which plan does the employer accept more risk? Under which plan does the employee accept more risk?
17. What is meant by an insured pension program?
18. Explain the structure of a pension fund's assets.
19. Explain what the terms *vesting, underfunded,* and *overfunded* mean with respect to pension funds.
20. What variables does an actuary take into account when determining the required reserves to be held in a pension fund?
21. How have accounting rules impacted the way employers treat pension obligations?
22. Explain which of the following factors would be expected to increase or decrease an employer's contribution to a defined benefit pension plan:
    a. Employee turnover decreases.
    b. Vesting is reduced from seven years to five years.
    c. The plan's investment return increases.
    d. Mortality increases.
    e. The average age of employees increases.
    f. Average wage and salary gains decrease in percentage.

Problems

Problem 11-1 Pricing Term Life Insurance

Quality Life Insurance Company has an opportunity to sell $50,000 term policies to a group of 20,000 individuals. You have been asked to help them price these policies. There are an equal number of men and women in this group. They are all 28 years old. The current mortality tables tell us the factors are 1.92 and 1.53 per thousand for men and women, respectively. Origination and servicing costs amount to $18.25 annually and a $6.75 profit is being factored. (There is no interest income being considered at this time.)

What are the premiums for the men's and women's policies?

Problem 11-2 Pricing Term Life Insurance

An insurance company would like to write a $50,000 term policy to market to 100,000 28-year-old females. Assume the cost of issuing the policies is $25.50 each. The company also expects to make a profit of $5.00 per policy.

How much would an insurance company have to charge for selling each one-year term policy? (Assume no investment income.)

The Commissioners 1980 Standard Ordinary mortality table indicates the deaths per 1,000 females of age 28 to be .126 percent.

Problem 11-3   Estimating Mortality Rate

William James has come up with a great idea for a promotion. He will offer a free $10,000 one-year term life policy for each sale of his product. He expects to sell 20,000 widgets. He doesn't know much about life insurance and wants to keep costs down. He can afford to lose $50 per customer due to deaths. He will self-insure the program, so he has no issuance costs.

What is the maximum mortality rate that this program can sustain without creating a loss?

Other Financial Institutions

chapter 12

A number of very specialized institutions are active in the United States today. These institutions include investment banks, property and casualty companies, finance companies, mortgage banks, and diversified financial service companies. Additionally, a number of intermediaries exist to provide a wide range of investments, including the following:

1. Open-end mutual funds
2. Limited partnerships
3. Real estate investment trusts

These investment-oriented intermediaries result from income tax provisions that allow them to avoid corporate income taxation if they meet certain conditions.

Although some of these institutions are not thought of as intermediaries, they all issue liabilities against themselves. The only exception are the trust companies. These firms act only as asset managers for assets belonging to others. Their large professional financial management activities deserve some discussion.

Investment Banks

One of the least understood of all the major financial intermediaries is the investment bank. This is because investment banking institutions perform a variety of functions for both institutions and consumers. Adding to the mystique of investment banking are the stories of multimillion dollar incomes, multibillion dollar mergers and acquisitions, highly sophisticated trading activities, and the temptations that surround money and power. Ivan Boesky, the noted arbitrageur who went to jail for insider trading, and Michael Milken, the famed head of Drexel Burnham Lambert's high-yield bond department who also went to jail, became household names in the 1990s. Their stories added to the mystique.

Investment banking companies perform a vast array of financial services. The following is a list of the most important:

1. Originating (underwriting) financial claims such as stocks and bonds
2. Selling and distributing financial claims through brokerage and acting as dealers in specific claims
3. Acting as market-makers by serving as dealers and traders in specified claims
4. Acting as investment advisors on such transactions as mergers, financial restructurings, investments, acquisitions, hostile takeovers, corporate valuations, and other major transactions
5. Acting as lenders to customers using securities as collateral

It is the underwriting and distributing of securities that used to make an investment bank somewhat unique. All the other activities performed by investment banks are also performed by other financial intermediaries. Actually, the underwriting of securities is no longer the sole domain of investment bankers since commercial banks can now underwrite municipal, and in a few cases, corporate securities. In 1990, the J. P. Morgan Company, a large New York commercial bank holding company, received underwriting authority from the Federal Reserve Board for corporate securities.

Types of Investment Bankers

Investment banks can be broken down into three groups. The first group emphasizes retail customers. These banks act principally as brokers of financial claims created by other investment bankers or traded in the secondary markets. Although these firms are not active in originating financial claims for large companies, they may serve small firms in regional markets. A subset of this retail group are the *discount brokers*. These firms provide brokerage services, primarily to household customers, at discounted prices. These firms tend to offer little investment advice and emphasize low price and service. A number of commercial banks have created discount brokers as subsidiaries within their holding companies.

The second group of investment banks serves primarily the corporate sector. This group actually originates financial claims, provides financial services, and acts as a broker and market-maker for institutional clients.

The third group are the larger firms that have both institutional and retail orientations. These firms provide virtually all the services discussed in this section for institutional clients and maintain a large number of retail offices for distribution of financial claims to the household market.

Underwriting Debt and Equity Securities

The underwriting process typically involves three primary steps. First, the underwriter and the issuer must identify the type of security to be offered. The available financing options will be compared to determine which option provides the least cost with the most issuer flexibility. This is the supply side of the underwriting equation. Second, the underwriters will use their customer base to determine the potential market for a new security. This is the demand side of the equation. The underwriter will then attempt to put a final design in place, incorporating the provisions that are important to investors and acceptable to the issuer. They also provide a preliminary price indication.

The issuing company's management and the underwriting firm subsequently provide additional information about the issuer to prospective investors by communicating directly with investors face-to-face. In a large issue, the senior management of the company visits with potential investors from all around the country. A *syndication group,* made up of several investment banker underwriters, is formed when it is felt that the sales effort will require broader coverage of potential investors. This group may be augmented still further by bringing in smaller regional investment bankers as part of a selling group.

The next job is to price and sell the security. This selling job is typically done on an *indicative bid* basis. That is, the underwriters and other distributors of the security determine the potential buyers and estimate a price near what they think these buyers will pay. This is usually done in the days just prior to the issue date. The indicated bid price is usually expressed as a spread over or under some benchmark security in the case of debt. Needless to say, neither the issuer nor the investors know what might happen in the market from one day to the next. A sudden drop in the stock or bond market will unravel the most carefully orchestrated transaction. If the demand is strong at the indicative bid, then the issuer may feel confident that it can price slightly higher. If demand is soft, the opposite occurs.

Underwriters distribute securities on a *best efforts, negotiated bid,* or *competitive bid* basis. On a best efforts basis the underwriter agrees only to sell what it is able to distribute, and is not obligated to sell the entire issue. A negotiated bid and competitive bid basis puts the underwriters and other

Legal and Ethical Issues

Japanese Investment Banking Companies: Financial Guarantees for Customers and Influence Peddling

For industrial, commercial, and service firms in the United States, Japan has been a tough market to crack. Accusations of unfair business practices and government protection have been ongoing. In 1988 and again in 1991, the world capital markets shook with revelations that political influence peddling occurred in the highest levels of the Japanese government and that major Japanese investment banking firms gave sweetheart financial arrangements to a number of Japanese customers.

In 1988, a Japanese firm named Recruit Co., a powerful publishing and real estate conglomerate, was accused of contributing to a large number of bureaucrats, businessmen, and senior members of one of Japan's major political parties. Recruit's officials purportedly allowed these influential people to obtain shares of stock in a firm that subsequently went public, creating a large profit for them. The trail of influence peddling eventually led to Japan's Prime Minister and an aide. The Prime Minister resigned and the aide committed suicide.

In 1991, Japanese financial markets were again shaken by revelations that some of the largest and most prestigious investment banking firms had provided financial guarantees on stocks held by customers against losses in order to obtain their business.

These revelations merely provided additional ammunition concerning the purported unfair symbiotic relationship between Japan's financial institutions, commercial and industrial firms, politicians, and the Japanese Ministry of Finance. Foreign financial service companies claim to be seriously disadvantaged in their ability to compete for financial business against the entrenched Japanese firms with their alleged illegal business practices and cozy political relationships.

---

distributors on the line, since they will buy the issue and will end up owning what is not initially sold.

Mergers and Acquisitions

Investment banking companies are major participants in the merger, acquisition, and financing business. Merger and acquisition activities are typically categorized into three classes.

1. Leveraged buyouts (LBOs)
2. Financial restructurings
3. Divestitures

LBOs have received the greatest publicity because they have involved some of the largest financial transactions in U.S. corporate history. The RJR Nabisco, Inc. leveraged buyout by the Kohlberg, Kravis, and Roberts buy-out fund in 1989 at over $25 billion surprised many experts who felt that a transaction that large was not possible. Adding to the interest in LBOs is the fact that the high-yield bond was instrumental in financing many of these transactions.

Financial restructurings were also a major activity in the 1980s. Again, using high-yield debt, many companies purchased their own equity in the open market and sharply increased their financial leverage. Divestitures were also more prevalent, as companies attempted to increase shareholder value by selling subsidiary activities that did not strategically fit with the rest of their organizations. These transactions all provided significant fee income to investment banks.

Market-Making and Trading

Many investment bankers are involved in security trading. This activity involves three closely related kinds of trading. The first is pure brokerage. A number of securities lack marketability, are difficult to value, and may be volatile in price. For these types of claims, investment bankers usually act as a broker. The price risk of holding an inventory of these claims is high. In these situations, the firm chooses not to commit to buy the securities without simultaneously finding a buyer.

Second, for most liquid securities, the trading firm will stand ready to take a security into inventory. For these securities, the firm accepts the price risk. It can hedge this price risk using a number of hedging techniques, but will often own the securities without price protection. The objective of this trading activity is to mark up the price and find a buyer as soon as possible.

Third, investment bankers also deal in proprietary trading, which involves taking a position in a security for the firm's own account. No customer need be involved. Many times proprietary trading involves various forms of arbitrage. This occurs when the firm tries to profit from price differentials between similar securities. These transactions involve different markets such as forward and cash markets or markets in different countries.

Trading is very much an international activity today. Much of this trading is backed up by quantitative analysis. Sophisticated mathematical valuation models determine which securities are overvalued or undervalued

Legal and Ethical Issues

Salomon Brothers: Treasury Auction Irregularities

In August 1991, Salomon Brothers Inc., one of Wall Street's leading security trading investment bankers, shocked the investment community with a press release admitting to "irregularities and rule violations in connection with its submission of bids in certain auctions of Treasury securities." This release was followed by resignations and removals of several of Salomon's highest ranking officials, lawsuits by shareholders and others, and investigations by a number of regulatory bodies. Allegations against Salomon included market manipulation, fraud, misrepresentations to federal authorities, books and records violations, and wire and mail fraud.

Salomon Brothers' violations of Treasury auction rules are related to limitations on the percentage of the total volume of a Treasury auction that could be bid by a single dealer. Salomon admitted to submitting false bids in the name of customers who had not authorized the bids in order to control more than the 35 percent limit. The trail led to Salomon Brothers partly because several competitors felt that they had been squeezed by Salomon's control of a larger percentage of the auction. In the Treasury market, there is an active forward cash market called the "when issued market." Trading occurs in Treasury securities for forward delivery. Several of Salomon's competitors had sold Treasuries to customers expecting to be able to successfully obtain them in the auction. But, they claimed, the bogus Salomon bids forced them to bid up the price of the securities in the secondary market after they were unsuccessful in obtaining them in the primary auction. Thus, they were squeezed out and forced to suffer a loss.

The result of the Salomon revelations led to allegations that many dealers routinely overbid in several of the markets for government-sponsored securities.

Salomon's admission put considerable pressure on the Treasury department to review the structure of its auction procedures and its adherence to a relatively small group of primary dealers. This led the Treasury department to open up the auction to all dealers in late 1991.

---

relative to one another. Proprietary trading is the primary activity for a number of major investment bankers, and the bulk of their profits are generated from this activity. A handful of traders earn multimillion dollar bonuses from successful trading.

Assets and Liabilities of Investment Banks

Although investment banks are not involved in intermediation activities such as holding assets or issuing liabilities to create portfolio income, their trading and dealer activities create large asset holdings. Table 12.1 on page 310 shows the year-end 1990 balance sheet for security brokers and dealers.

The large financial asset holdings of investment banks is primarily the result of their security trading, security distribution, and dealer activities. Investment banks act as intermediaries for many securities for short periods of time. They do this to assist customers who expect to be able to buy quickly from the inventory of an investment bank or sell immediately into their inventory. Investment banks also trade securities for their own account. These holdings represent the bulk of their assets. Investment banks also offer security credit in the form of secured loans to customers called *margin loans*. Investment banks loan customers funds using the

Table 12.1

Financial Assets and Liabilities of Security Broker Dealers*
December 31, 1990
(dollars in billions)

Assets Type	Amount	Liabilities Type	Amount
Checking and cash	$10.2	Security repurchase	$88.1
Corporate equities	9.6	Security credit	
		From: banks	44.4
		customers	59.0
Credit market instruments (U.S. govt, state and local, corporate, and open-market paper)	177.9	Trade debt	15.3
Security credit	38.8	Other	43.3
Other	25.6		
Total	**$262.1**	**Total**	**$250.1**

Board of Governors of the Federal Reserve System, *Flow of Funds Accounts*.
*Assets and liabilities do not equal due to the absence of real assets and net worth.

customers' securities as collateral. The Federal Reserve regulates the maximum percentage of the loan as a percentage of the margined account's market value.

On the liability side of the balance sheet, investment banks borrow heavily using their own securities as collateral for repurchase agreements. They also borrow from commercial banks using credit market instruments.

Property and Casualty Companies

Property and casualty insurance companies provide risk-pooling services for a wide range of hazards. P&Cs pool property risk covering hazards such as loss, damage, or destruction. P&Cs also pool casualty risks covering injury to individuals or impairment of income producing ability. P&Cs charge the policy-holders premiums, which are pooled, invested, and used to pay claims for losses sustained by the insured.

Like the life companies, P&Cs operate as both stock and mutual companies. There are approximately 3,500 companies that make up the P&C business. P&C companies are regulated by state government insurance agencies. P&C companies' operations can be conveniently divided into operating, or underwriting performance, and investment performance.

Operating or Underwriting Activities

To the extent that a P&C charges its policyholders premiums to cover the losses and administrative costs sustained during the period of coverage, the P&C can earn an underwriting profit. An underwriting profit is not as easy for P&C companies to earn as might be expected. During the last several decades P&C companies have faced high claims costs as a result of an increasing number of civil suits. Many of these actions have resulted in substantial jury awards to plaintiffs in cases involving individuals and businesses.

P&C companies have a difficult time predicting the potential size of their claims. Inflation is also difficult to forecast. In the late 1970s, unexpectedly high inflation resulted in substantially higher than expected claims for automobile damage. In the 1990s, medical costs continue to inflate at higher rates than anticipated. P&C companies also base their premiums on their expectations of investment income. These investment results are difficult to forecast.

The P&Cs measure their underwriting results using measures called the *loss ratio* and *expense ratio*. The loss ratio is the ratio of claims paid divided by premiums earned. The expense ratio is the ratio of operating expenses to premiums earned. The sum of the loss ratio and the expense ratio is the combined ratio. In the late 1980s and early 1990s, P&Cs as an industry experienced a combined ratio of approximately 110 percent. This means they have suffered losses on their basic risk-management business, which had to be made up by their investment activities.

The result of these factors is that P&C underwriting profit performance evidences sharp cycles. During the 1980s, P&C companies showed losses on their underwriting activities every year.

Investment Performance

P&C companies have the use of their policyholders' premiums until claims must be paid. Income generated from these investments allows P&C companies to be profitable despite large underwriting losses. Needless to say, P&C companies have an incentive to defer paying claims as long as they can. P&C companies are, therefore, always balancing the importance of good customer service (defined by fast and fair claims settlement) against the desire to keep claims unpaid and earn an investment return for as long as possible. P&C companies are large investors in state and municipal bonds, common and preferred stock equities, and other credit market instruments.

Recent P&C Company Financial Performance

The financial performance of P&Cs has traditionally been volatile. This is partially the result of the lag between the time that property and casualty claims increase and the time premium rates are increased. Part of this lag is also attributable to the fact that P&C companies usually have to receive approval to increase premiums from state insurance commissions. Exhibit 12.1 provides a graphic presentation of the two major sources of income for P&Cs over the last 60 years. The graph shows the net investment income (as a percent of net premiums earned) and the ratio of underwriting gains or losses (as a percent of total premiums earned). In the 1980s, there was a substantial increase in the ratio of investment income to premiums earned and a commensurate decrease in the ratio of underwriting losses to premium income.

There are a number of factors that would cause a sharp decrease in underwriting income. First, an increasing percentage of premium income is represented by casualty losses. These losses occur sometimes many years after premiums are taken in by the company. A second factor is greater price competition. Over the last decade more state commissions have deregulated insurance premiums. This has given rise to price competition and lower rates for the insured and commensurately larger underwriting losses.

Other factors have impacted this source of income. The rise in the stock market gave P&Cs a substantial income boost in the 1980s. Additionally,

Exhibit 12.1

Underwriting and Investment Income and a Percent of Net Premiums Earned at Property and Casualty Companies (1922–1988)

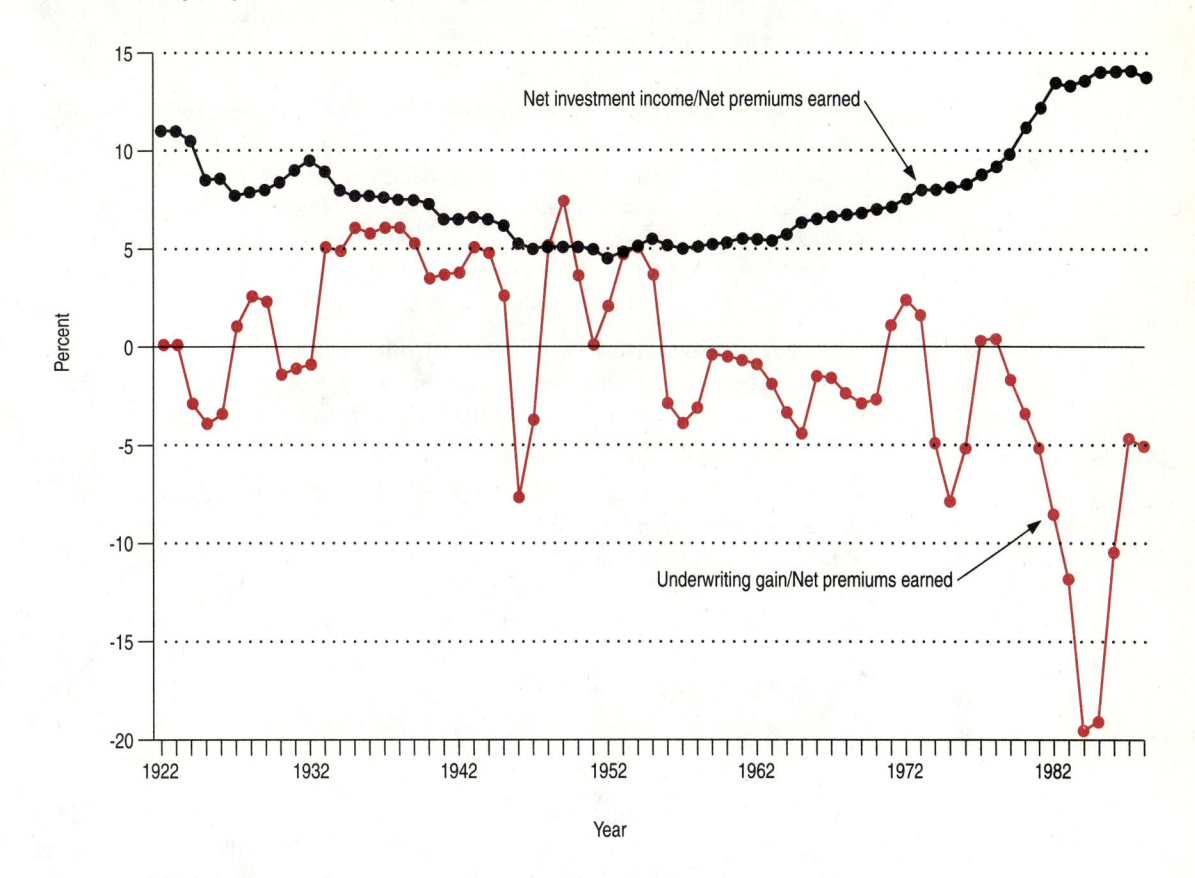

[Figure: Line chart showing two series from 1922 to 1988. Net investment income/Net premiums earned starts around 11% in 1922, declines to about 5% in the late 1940s–1950s, then rises to about 14% by 1988. Underwriting gain/Net premiums earned fluctuates around 0–5% through the 1950s, then declines, reaching lows near -19% in the mid-1980s.]

Source: Standard and Poor's Insurance Rating Services. *Industry Outlook on Property/Casualty Insurance.* Standard and Poor's Corporation, 1990. p. 3. (Reprinted with permission Standard and Poor's Insurance Rating Services.)

the Tax Reform Act of 1986 significantly increased the taxable income of P&C firms. The act taxed a greater portion of the loss reserves set up by these companies to cover future expected, but not yet realized, losses. These companies, therefore, had to increase the percentage of their assets in tax-advantaged state and municipal bonds as well as dividend-paying stocks, in which they benefit from the dividend exclusion. This lowered investment income.

Management Highlights

Special Management Concerns for Property and Casualty Companies

Predicting Future Costs and Hazards: Property and casualty companies must attempt to forecast future costs of claims as accurately as possible. Uncertainties concerning inflation rates, decisions arising from the judicial process, and new legal exposures all complicate this task. Increasingly, P&Cs are getting involved in the claims process by finding less costly providers of health and repair services for policy-holders with claims. Special efforts are also aimed at reducing fraud in the claims process.

Keeping Administration Costs Under Control: P&Cs operate on thin to negative underwriting margins. Therefore, the cost of operations must be carefully controlled. The cost of originating policies and servicing them is a major controllable expense for these companies.

Diversifying Hazard Risks: The hazards that P&C companies insure are impacted by state laws and judicial decisions. This means that P&Cs are subject to political risks that are not unlike international political risks. State agencies set insurance premium rates and mandate coverage. This means that P&Cs may be asked to write insurance that cannot be profitable. In recent years, a number of P&Cs have quit writing policies in states where they felt allowable premiums were inadequate.

Overall, the financial performance of P&Cs has been mixed. The greater price competition and risk of high casualty losses has had its toll on the industry. The number of insolvencies of P&Cs has increased significantly in the 1980s as compared to the 1970s.

Finance Companies

Finance companies are the largest and least regulated financial institutions in the United States. These firms got their start by providing financial lending services to two entirely different markets. The *commercial finance companies* developed largely as captives to large manufacturing firms. These business customers typically needed financing for equipment purchases. Firms that sold equipment developed their own companies to finance sales. Because many of these firms were subsidiaries of large highly capitalized manufacturing firms with strong credit ratings, they were able to obtain financing at highly favorable rates. A good credit rating is important to finance companies because they rely on open-market sales of debentures and short-term commercial paper.

Another group of finance companies began by financing low- and moderate-income consumers. The *consumer finance companies* had a business strategy far different from their commercial finance company sisters. Many of these firms lend money to individuals through retail offices. The consumer finance company succeeds by segmenting the market and concentrating on the lower income household that is unable to meet commercial bank underwriting credit standards.

Over the years, a portion of the market for unsecured personal loans, the specialty of the consumer finance company, has been served by the credit card. This caused many of the major consumer finance companies to alter their business strategies and find new ways to deliver their products. Some of these firms have become very large issuers of credit cards. Others have become large diversified holding companies that have entered the depository business through acquisitions.

Asset and Liability Structures of Finance Companies

Finance company assets are concentrated in consumer and business loans, while their liabilities are primarily open-market paper, such as commercial paper and other debt, as well as loans obtained from parent companies. Table 12.2 on page 316 shows the assets and liabilities of all U.S. finance companies as of December 31, 1990.

The assets show a large entry for reserves for unearned income. This contra-account is a special account set up for *add-on loans*. In these loans all the interest to be earned over the life of the contract is added to the balance of the loan when it is originated. This add-on interest accounts for the inflation in asset balances in the table and the need for the contra-account.

Although finance companies tend to be more highly capitalized than commercial banks, the increase in commercial bank capital requirements in recent years has eliminated some of the commercial bank's advantage in terms of financial leverage. Adding to the finance companies' advantage is the fact that a number of the largest and strongest finance companies are subsidiaries of the largest corporations in the United States, such as General Electric (General Electric Capital Corporation), General Motors (General Motors Acceptance Corporation), and the Ford Motor Company (Ford Motor Credit Corporation). Over the years, these finance companies have become major factors in the leasing business, secured business financing, auto financing, heavy equipment lending, and highly leveraged business lending.

Table 12.2

Assets and Liabilities of U.S. Finance Companies
December 31, 1990
(dollars in billions)

	$ Amount	% of Total
Assets		
Consumer loans	$136.0	25.9%
Business loans	290.8	55.4
Real estate	59.9	11.4
Total	**$486.7**	
Less		
Reserves for unearned income	$ 56.6	−10.7
Reserves for losses	8.9	−1.7
All other assets	103.6	19.7
Total Assets	**$524.8**	
Liabilities		
Bank loans	$ 18.6	3.5%
Commercial paper	152.7	29.0
Debt		
Due to parent	77.3	14.7
Net elsewhere		
Classified	157.4	29.9
All other liabilities	78.7	14.9
Net worth	40.2	7.7
Total Liabilities and Net Worth	**$524.8**	

Source: Federal Reserve *Bulletin*. (July 1991) A35.

Mortgage Banking Companies

Mortgage banking companies are true specialists in mortgage finance. Their primary role is to originate, service, and warehouse mortgages for short periods. The mortgages are subsequently sold in the secondary mortgage market, primarily to the GNMA, FNMA, and FHLMC. Although mortgage bankers are not thought of as investors in mortgages, the reality is that mortgage bankers assume both credit and interest rate risk. They must assume the interest rate risk that relates to the loan commitments made to a homebuyer. They also assume risk on the commitments made to the loan purchaser in the secondary market. The success of mortgage banking companies depends heavily on their skills in origination, servicing, and interest rate risk management.

Mortgage Loan Origination

Mortgage bankers originate both residential and nonresidential mortgages. They dominate the origination of residential mortgages guaranteed and insured, respectively, by the Veterans Administration and the Federal Housing Administration. The residential mortgages originated by mortgage bankers not sold to the government organizations are typically sold to commercial banks and S&Ls. The nonresidential mortgages are sold to insurance companies.

Mortgage bankers originate their residential business by calling on real estate agent offices and home builders. They compete for business on the basis of price and service. In the origination process, mortgage bankers typically charge a fee of approximately 1 percent of the mortgage balance to cover some of the costs of originating the mortgage. These costs include office rent, sales personnel, processing and administrative personnel, and administrative, documentation, and closing costs. Usually, the origination fee alone does not cover all the costs of origination. If that is the case, the mortgage bankers must rely on the value generated by the creation of a loan servicing contract to make a profit.

Servicing

Many mortgage bankers are in business to service mortgages for a small fee. This fee is based on the unpaid balance of the mortgage and is typically in the range of .25 percent to .44 percent for residential mortgages and less than .25 percent for nonresidential mortgages. It is easy to see that since the servicing fees are levied on the unpaid principal of the mortgage, the larger the average size of mortgages, the higher the servicing fees per mortgage.

The servicing portfolios of mortgage bankers are created in two ways. First, the mortgage banker can originate the loans for sale and subsequently service these loans. Alternatively, the mortgage banker may purchase servicing from other originating institutions. In the last ten years, the purchase and sale of servicing contracts has become a major activity for mortgage bankers as well as other mortgage-lending specialists. As the profit margins in the origination business have narrowed with increased competition, many institutions have been forced to sell the servicing contracts on some or all of the loans they originate to cover their costs.

Warehousing and Interest Rate Risk Management

Another key to a mortgage company's success is its ability to sell the loans it originates. This activity is called *secondary marketing* and is much more difficult to accomplish than it may seem at first glance. Mortgage bankers typically offer the homebuyer a guaranteed rate on the mortgage, which is excercisable until the mortgage transaction is completed. This guaranteed rate is really an option granted to the homebuyer, and it will likely only be exercised if it is to the borrower's advantage. The lender, having issued this option, must hedge this interest rate risk. Such a program is difficult and can frequently result in losses to the lending institution.

Secondary mortgage marketing can make or lose money in the following two ways: First, the mortgage banker will earn a warehouse interest-spread gain or loss until the mortgage is sold to the ultimate investor. The interest-spread gain or loss is determined by the difference between the interest rate earned on the mortgage held in the portfolio and the rate it pays to borrow the funds needed to finance the mortgages. Second, the mortgage banker will experience a gain or loss on the sale of the mortgage. Most mortgage bankers feel satisfied if they are able to merely break even on their secondary marketing activities.

Size Structure of Mortgage Banking Companies

Mortgage banking is a cyclical business with a changing market structure. Because a relatively small amount of capital is needed to enter the business, there tends to be a considerable number of new entrants during periods of high origination volume. Many of these firms exit during periods of low origination volume. During the 1980s, a number of large commercial banks and nonbank financial institutions became major mortgage banking institutions through the acquisition of independent mortgage banking companies.

A few very large mortgage banking firms dominate the industry from the standpoint of origination and servicing volume. There are a large number of smaller firms that specialize in small geographic areas and a few different types of mortgages. Some mortgage bankers act merely as brokers for large commercial banks, S&Ls, and other mortgage bankers.

Diversified Financial Service Companies

Large commercial and industrial firms have played an important role in our financial markets for many years. Retail firms also recognized the importance of providing credit to customers. For example, auto buyers have been able to finance their vehicles through the General Motors Acceptance Corporation. Department store shoppers can use credit programs offered by Sears, Roebuck or J.C. Penney. Most large retailing firms and gasoline companies have or had a captive credit card financing subsidiary at one time or another.

Several of the financial service subsidiaries of commercial and industrial firms have grown to be large diversified financial service companies. Life

Table 12.3

Major Financial Service Activities of Large Commercial and Industrial Firms 1990

Parent Company	Principal Business	Insurance	Real Estate	Securities	Regulated Deposits	Lending & Leasing
Aetna	Insurance	x	x			x
American Express	Credit	x	x	x	x	x
American General	Financial	x	x	x	x	x
Armco	Steel	x				x
Beneficial	Consumer Finance	x	x	x	x	x
Borg-Warner	Manufacturing	x		x		x
Chrysler Corp.	Auto	x	x			x
Equitable	Insurance	x	x	x		x
Ford Motor	Auto	x	x	x	x	x
General Electric	Manufacturing	x	x	x		x
General Motors	Auto	x	x			x
Household Finance	Consumer Finance	x	x		x	x
ITT	Conglomerate	x	x		x	x
Merrill Lynch	Securities	x	x	x	x	x
Parker Pen	Manufacturing	x			x	x
J.C. Penney	Retail	x	x		x	x
Prudential	Insurance	x	x	x	x	x
Sears, Roebuck	Retail	x	x	x	x	x
Transamerica	Insurance	x	x			x
USAA	Insurance	x	x	x	x	x
Westinghouse	Manufacturing		x		x	x
Xerox	Manufacturing	x			x	x

Source: Copyright 1991, *Los Angeles Times*. Reprinted with permission.

insurance companies and investment banking firms add to the number of diversified financial service providers. Table 12.3 shows a list of some of the largest diversified financial service providers. These firms are all very large providers of financial services without being in the commercial banking business. The table shows the parent company and whether or not it's financial service subsidiary is involved in insurance, real estate finance, securities, regulated deposits, or general leasing and lending.

The growth in the diversified financial services industry has added to the competitive pressures on depository institutions. Many financial service firms have used their consumer access and strong name recognition in the money and capital markets to build large financial service conglomerates.

Investment Intermediaries

Investment intermediaries comprise a group of institutions whose primary purpose is to provide portfolio management services to individual and institutional investors. The largest of these intermediaries are the open-end mutual funds. Less important are the limited partnerships and real estate investment trusts. All of these institutional forms, with the exception of the trust companies, have one thing in common. They are structured to avoid federal taxation at the intermediary level. These organizations pass their income directly to investors, where it is then taxed.

Investment intermediaries are among our country's fastest growing institutions. As individuals and institutional investors have become more experienced in managing their financial assets, they have searched out ways to diversify into more sophisticated investments. Investment intermediaries provide the vehicles to make these types of investments. Investment intermediaries pool the funds of many investors and make experienced investment expertise available.

Open-End Mutual Funds

The most successful financial intermediary measured by growth in assets for the last 20 years has been the *open-end mutual fund*. An open end mutual fund is an intermediary that issues shares representing a pro-rata ownership in a pool of assets. Mutual funds provide professional portfolio management skills and asset diversification for investors through the pooling of funds.

The rapid growth in the mutual fund industry started in the mid-1970s when the industry created the *money market mutual fund*. Money in this fund was invested in safe and marketable money market instruments and was designed to yield a higher interest rate than time and savings deposits. This was easily accomplished because the time and savings deposits of commercial banks and thrifts were still controlled under Regulation Q, and market interest rates reached post–World War II record high levels. This gave the money market mutual fund a good market in which to build market share.

Since then, the investing public has gained greater confidence in the mutual fund, and their number and variety have grown rapidly. Exhibit 12.2 shows the number of mutual funds and number of fund accounts from

Exhibit 12.2

Number of Accounts and Funds Invested in Mutual Funds 1975–1989

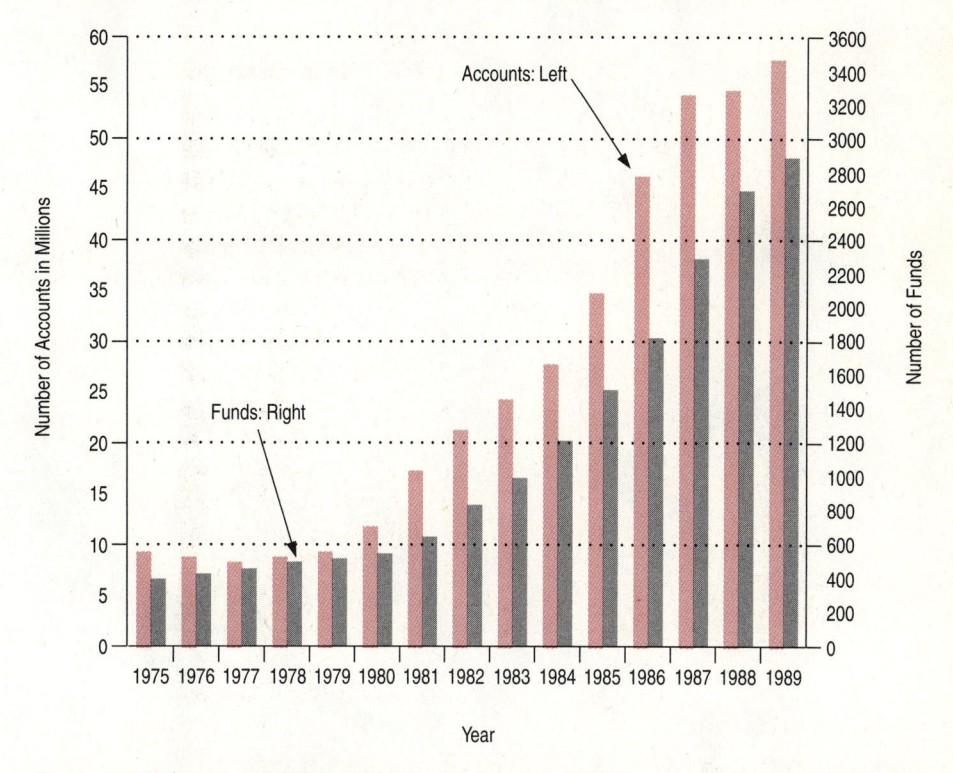

Source: *1991 Directory of Mutual Funds*. Washington, DC: Investment Company Institute, p. 4.

1975 through 1989. The number of funds is shown on the right axis of the graph and the dollar amount of assets on the left axis.

Exhibit 12.3 on page 322 provides a breakdown of the assets of mutual funds by the following four main categories:

1. Money market funds
2. Equity funds
3. Bond and income funds
4. Short-term municipal bond funds

The total for all four types of funds approached $1 trillion at year-end 1989.

Exhibit 12.3

Assets in Open-End Mutual Funds Classified by Major Type of Fund 1975–1989

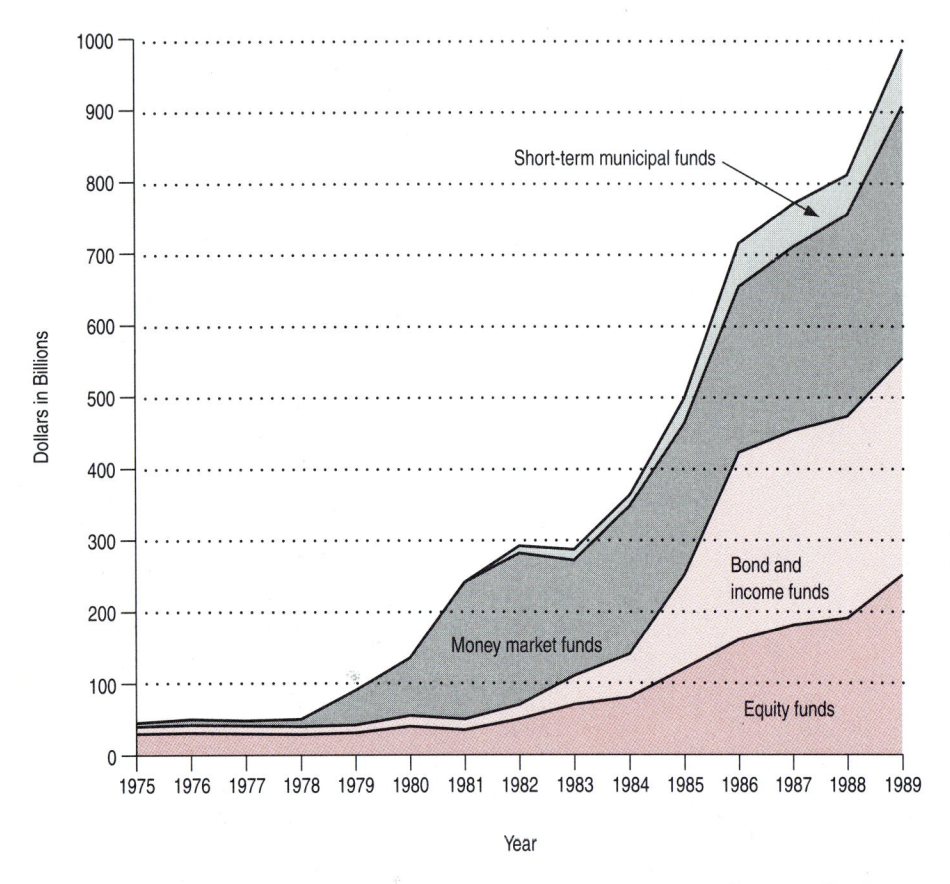

[Area chart showing Dollars in Billions (0–1000) from 1975 to 1989, with layers for Equity funds, Bond and income funds, Money market funds, and Short-term municipal funds]

Source: *Mutual Fund Fact Book, 1991.* Washington, DC: Investment Company Institute, 1991.

One of the main appeals of the mutual fund is access to professional management. Mutual funds are sold via a *prospectus,* which is a legal document describing the objectives of the fund, its management, and any fees charged for various services provided. It also describes in detail the fund's investment strategy. Exhibit 12.4 provides a list of the most popular mutual funds and some of the basic categories of investment objectives.

Exhibit 12.4

Types of Mutual Funds

Aggressive growth funds: Common stocks
Balance funds: Common stocks, preferred stocks and bonds
Corporate bond funds
Flexible portfolio funds: Common stocks, bonds, or money market debt (portfolio allocation)
Government National Mortgage Association funds: Also known as GNMA or Ginnie Mae securities
Global bond funds: U.S. and foreign bonds
Global equity funds: U.S. and foreign common stocks
Growth funds: Common stocks
Growth and income funds: Dividend-paying growth common stocks
High-yield bond funds: Corporate bonds below-investment grade
Income funds: Bonds
Income equity funds
Income mixed funds: Common stock and bonds
International funds: Foreign common stock
Long-term municipal bond funds
Money market mutual funds
Option/income funds: Common stocks and call options on stocks held
Precious metals/gold funds: Common stock of gold, silver, and precious metals producers
Short-term municipal bond funds
State municipal bond funds: Municipal bonds of a particular state
U.S. government income funds

Organization and Administration

Mutual funds are shareholder-owned corporations with a board of directors elected by the shareholders. Mutual funds are not taxed at the fund level, since they must distribute all current income and capital gains income to their shareholders. Typically, a mutual fund is created by a professional management company that is also involved in other aspects of the mutual fund business, such as servicing and portfolio management.

The management company earns profits from fees associated with each of these functions. Sometimes these functions are performed by more than one organization, with the origination, or sales and distribution, handled by one firm, a broker/dealer for example, and the portfolio management and servicing handled by a mutual fund management company. On December

31, 1990, the nation's largest mutual fund management company was Fidelity Investments, which managed assets of $118.8 billion.

Origination fees may include a commission paid out of the initial investment in the fund. Funds that pay this type of commission are called *load funds*. A typical load is 3 to 8 percent of the initial investment made in the fund. Funds without this charge are called *no-load funds*. There are also possible fees charged to the shareholders for ongoing promotion and distribution of funds called *12b-1 fees*. This name comes from the regulation number of the Securities and Exchange Commission, which regulates all mutual funds. Finally, some funds charge a fee at the time the shareholder redeems shares for cash. This is called a *redemption fee*. Each fund bears the cost of servicing itself. This includes portfolio management, administrative, legal, mail, telephone, and accounting costs, which are charged directly to the shareholders.

Limited Partnerships

Limited partnerships are one of the most versatile investment-oriented financial intermediaries. The limited partnership is composed of general partners that act as the operating entity for the partnership and accept unlimited liability for its actions, while the limited partners invest funds and accept liability only to the extent of the funds they have invested. Limited partnerships have the advantage of channeling income directly to the partners and thus avoiding a layer of corporate taxation. They also have one of the advantages of a corporate form of organization, the limited liability for the limited partners. Limited partnerships exist for many types of investments.

Typically, the limited partnership is best suited for specialized investments that do not lend themselves to large investment pools. Limited partnerships involve investments that have very long-term time horizons and volatile cash flows. One major drawback to the limited partnership is that it lacks marketability. Few investors in limited partnerships are able to find markets for the limited partnership shares they purchase. This tends to relegate limited partnership investments to a fairly small percentage of any investment portfolio.

Limited partnerships have been popular in the 1980s and 1990s with investments in real estate, leveraged buyouts, venture capital, and merchant banking. These are highly specialized investments that require expertise and uncertain cash flows. One of the major duties of the general partners is to attract investors. For partnerships with smaller investor groups, this usually requires marketing through an investment broker and paying a high distribution fee. For more specialized partnerships, the partners themselves will market the shares directly to institutional investors, such as life companies and pension funds. This is the way the large LBO partnerships are sold. Typically, the driving force behind a limited partnership is a group of general partners who have an established track record of successful investments in a specific area. Kohlberg, Kravis, and Roberts, the famous KKR leveraged buyout group, has used limited partnerships for years to attract equity capital to engage in their leveraged buyout activities.

The general partners in a limited partnership are compensated by the partnership for their investment expertise. They typically receive a salary and a portion of the investment income.

Prior to the 1986 Tax Reform Act, limited partnerships were used to channel tax losses on depreciable property to limited investors. Real estate, windmills, and solar collectors found their way into limited partnership investments largely because the investment tax credit and accelerated depreciation could be used to offset investors' income. The Tax Reform Act put a stop to that. This legislation limited the tax losses on partnerships to a maximum offset of the limited partner's passive income. This legislation resulted in billions of dollars of limited partnership investments becoming much less valuable to their investors.

Real Estate Investment Trusts

The *real estate investment trust (REIT)* is a very specialized investment intermediary that, like the limited partnership, is a creature of the U.S. tax law. A REIT is a corporation, trust, or association primarily organized to own or finance real estate. It may hold income-producing real estate, invest in mortgages, finance real estate development and construction, and acquire and lease property to developers. As a corporate entity, most REITs have a board of directors or trustees that are responsible to the REIT shareholders. Like the shares of most new companies, REIT shares are typically sold in a public offering. The major difference is that an initial public offering (IPO) of most companies is done after the company has established a track record. REITs, like limited partnerships, are initially sold based on representations made in a prospectus and before they have established an investment track record.

These investments have a marketing advantage over limited partnerships in that they are typically listed on a stock exchange. REITs are not limited to selling common stock. They may also sell preferred stock and issue warrants and debt.

The REIT has been granted a special position in the tax code. This special provision allows the REIT to be exempt from federal taxation if 95 percent of the income of the trust is distributed to its shareholders. This provision also makes the following requirements:

1. The REIT must be a corporation, trust, or association.
2. It must have a board of directors or trustees.
3. It must have at least 100 shareholders.
4. It must have no group of five or fewer shareholders controlling more than 50 percent of the shares.
5. It must derive at least 75 percent of its gross income from real estate activities.

The three major types of REITs are classified by their investment objectives. These types are mortgage, real estate equities, and hybrid.

Mortgage REITs invest at least 75 percent of their assets in mortgages. These include first mortgages, mortgage pools insured by government sponsored enterprises and private issuers, second or junior mortgages, and construction loans. Equity REITs invest 75 percent of their assets in the ownership of commercial, industrial, and residential properties. These REITs have an equity ownership in these properties either outright or in joint venture with other investors or developers. Hybrid REITs combine the investment objectives of the mortgage and equity REITs.

A new form of REIT has become popular in the late 1980s. This is the finite life REIT (FREIT). FREITs are organized with a stated expected life at their inception. Typically this ranges from 10 to 15 years. At that point, the FREIT is liquidated.

Trust Companies

Trust companies are financial service companies and not true intermediaries. Their primary functions are to invest funds for individuals and institutions and to service these accounts according to the requirements of the individual or agency, such as an employee benefit profit sharing or pension plan. At the end of 1988, it was estimated that the United States had approximately 3,600 trust companies. The majority of these trust companies, about 3,450, were independent trust companies and commercial banks providing trust services. The remainder were operating as savings banks, savings and loans, and nonfederally insured banks.

At year-end 1988, trust companies provided asset management services and serviced trust accounts with approximately $6,588 billion in assets. This represented over 7 million different accounts. Trust companies provide two basic services. First, they manage funds in *discretionary accounts* in which the trust company has the fiduciary responsibility for the investment of the assets. This represents about $1,157 billion of the total $6,588 billion in funds held in trust accounts. Nondiscretionary accounts are assets held by a trust company that does not have investment responsibility (see Table 12.4).

Table 12.4

Trust Assets by Type of Trust by Type of Investment
December 31, 1988
(dollars in billions)

Investment	Employee Benefit	Personal Trust	Estates	Employee Benefit	Other	Total
Noninterest bearing own institution	$ .517	$ .812	$ .071	$ .082	$ .436	$ 1.919
Noninterest bearing other institution	.210	.220	.003	1.003	.231	1.279
Interest bearing own institution	2.984	7.739	1.051	.471	2.681	14.925
Interest bearing other institution	34.390	7.577	.505	4.246	13.905	60.623
U.S. govt & agency	46.697	48.943	2.437	35.653	50.543	184.273
State, local, & municipal	.677	59.057	1.528	.343	28.297	89.901
Money mkt. fund	8.819	15.305	2.116	2.840	12.270	41.351
Other short-term debt	53.759	21.285	1.749	17.037	33.777	127.607
Other debt	38.327	20.768	.497	25.450	18.496	103.539
Equity	125.898	184.572	6.000	86.171	60.904	463.545
Mortgages	1.560	2.936	.301	.687	.852	6.336
Real Estate	4.617	20.537	2.946	2.098	3.281	33.478
Other	13.939	5.976	.754	2.715	4.622	28.005
Total discretionary assets	332.205	395.529	19.958	178.794	230.296	1,156.782
Total nondiscretionary assets	947.728	58.600	.902	368.571	4,055.320	5,431.121
Total assets	**1,279.934**	**454.129**	**20.860**	**547.365**	**4,285.615**	**6,587.903**
Number of accounts	2,602,808	1,536,344	77,567	2,499,930	561,101	7,277,750

Source: *Trust Assets of Financial Institutions, 1988.* Federal Financial Institutions Examination Council, Federal Deposit Insurance Corporation. Washington, DC, 1989.

Trust companies are also major servicers of investment funds for others. Their role is primarily one of safekeeping and account bookkeeping. A trust company's responsibilities may include the following:

1. Accepting employer and employee payments to an employee profit sharing or pension fund

2. Creating periodic statements to be distributed to the beneficiaries of the fund
3. Disbursing funds to retired employees or employees that leave the firm
4. Collecting income from investments directed by another party outside the trust company.

ERISA reporting requirements are a major problem for trust companies. Computer software packages have been designed to simplify the servicing of these accounts for trustees of individual and corporate trusts.

Table 12.4 shows the breakdown of the assets held by the following trusts at year-end 1988.

1. Employee benefit
2. Personal trusts
3. Estates
4. Other

Summary

This chapter provided a description of the nondepository intermediaries. Among these institutions, the most complex are investment bankers and diversified financial service companies. They perform a wide variety of financial functions. The more specialized institutions include property and casualty companies, finance companies, and mortgage bankers.

Investment intermediaries also were discussed. These firms provide individuals and institutions with the ability to pool resources for highly specialized investments and to benefit from specialized investment management expertise.

Investment banking firms provide a wide variety of financial services. In fact, as a group they provide just about every financial service except taking deposits. The following is a list of their primary activities:

1. Originating and distributing stocks and bonds
2. Acting as a securities broker for individuals and institutions trading in the secondary market
3. Trading securities for customers or for its own account
4. Acting as an investment adviser

Property and casualty companies provide a wide range of risk-pooling services. Their two primary businesses are **property insurance** covering hazards such as fire, property loss, or damage due to accident and theft. The other is **casualty insurance,** which covers loss of earning power, product failure, or accidents. P&Cs have experienced a sharp decline in their underwriting income in relation to premiums earned. This has been partially offset by growth in investment income.

Finance companies are the least regulated of our major intermediaries. They specialize in consumer lending to individuals and secured lending to businesses. The former are called consumer finance and the latter commercial finance companies. Both types finance their operations with money and capital market debt sold in the credit markets.

Mortgage banking companies are highly specialized firms that originate and service residential and, to a much lesser extent, commercial mortgages.

Diversified financial service companies are commercial, industrial, or nonbank financial firms that are involved in a broad spectrum of financial activities. In most of these activities, they compete with depository institutions.

Investment intermediaries represent a group of firms that specialize in pooling assets of investors and providing investment expertise. Investment intermediaries share a common feature in that the investments they hold are not taxed at the intermediary level. These intermediaries include **open end mutual funds, limited partnerships,** and **real estate investment trusts.**

Trust companies are not technically intermediaries, since they hold no financial assets. However, they are major providers of financial investment expertise and they act as servicers of pension and other employee benefit accounts.

Questions

Chapter 12

1. What makes investment bankers somewhat unique among our financial intermediaries?
2. Describe the differences among investment bankers referred to as retail, corporate investment bankers, and full-service institutional and retail. Give an example of each of these firms.
3. How do investment bankers make a profit by participating in securities issuances?
4. What functions do investment bankers play in the security issuance process?
5. If you were a company issuing a new security, would you have more risk under a best efforts, negotiated bid, or competitive bid agreement with the investment banker handling your distribution? Why?
6. Explain the types of merger and acquisition work performed by investment bankers.
7. Finance companies developed using basically two separate strategies.

Differentiate between these strategies and describe the differences in customer base.
8. How has the bank credit card impacted retail-oriented consumer finance companies? How did many of them respond?
9. Finance companies rely on debt sold in the money and capital markets. How have the changes in commercial bank deposit costs and insurance influenced finance companies?
10. What advantages do finance companies have as compared to insured depositories?
11. Describe the asset structure of finance companies.
12. Why are so many finance companies subsidiaries of large manufacturing companies?
13. Which government sponsored enterprises do mortgage banking companies rely on?
14. Which of the primary functions of financial institutions discussed in Chapter 7 are most important to mortgage bankers?
15. What are the major forms of interest rate risk that must be managed successfully for a mortgage company to prosper?
16. What are the risks of servicing mortgages relating to interest rate changes? Consider the discussion on servicing strips in Chapter 4.
17. What accounts for the presence of so many diversified companies in the financial services industry? How have they impacted commercial banks and thrift institutions?
18. Consider the types of investment-oriented intermediaries. How does taxation impact on these intermediaries?
19. What functions do investment-oriented intermediaries provide?
20. What accounts for the very rapid growth in open-end mutual funds since the mid-1970s?
21. What is meant by load and no-load mutual funds?
22. Why have many depositors left commercial banks and thrifts in favor of mutual funds?
23. What are the primary reasons for using the limited partnership? What impact does the tax law have on using the limited partnership?
24. What services do trust companies perform? How important are pension funds to most trust companies?
25. Do trust companies and life companies compete for some of the same business? Which customers would these companies focus on?

Part 3, on the role and impact of government in our financial system, discusses the concept of government as a regulator and as a participant in financing certain sectors of the economy.

Government's Role in the Financial Sector

Part Outline

Chapter 13
Federal Government Credit Activities

Chapter 14
Financial Institution Regulation, Insurers, and Regulators

Chapter 15
Structural Changes and the Performance of Financial Intermediaries

Chapter 13 reviews the many direct and indirect government credit programs. The most important of these programs are the government sponsored enterprises.

Chapter 14 presents the rationale for government's role as financial regulator and the many forms this regulation takes. The chapter also describes the process of regulation and its impact on managing financial firms and each of the major financial regulators and insurance organizations.

Chapter 15 offers an in-depth look at the many forces that have affected the performance of private financial institutions over the last decade or more. The role of the government is highlighted because of the large impact of government economic and regulatory policy on the performance of financial intermediaries.

Federal Government Credit Activities

chapter 13

The federal government is our nation's largest financial intermediary. Through its direct lending, guarantees, and sponsored enterprises, it is now about one-fourth the size of all private sector intermediaries.

This chapter details the growth in federal government credit activities. The significance of these programs relates to the following issues:

1. The rationale for the federal government's participation in the credit markets
2. The types of credit market programs used by the government
3. The impact that these programs have on the allocation of credit and on private sector financial institutions
4. The controversy surrounding the accelerated growth of these programs in the 1990s

Rationale for Federal Government Credit Activities

Federal credit programs have four principal rationales. First, these programs are seen as a way to reduce the impact of market imperfections. Many believe that without government involvement, certain groups of borrowers would be unable to obtain adequate credit, that worthy borrowers are not being adequately serviced either because of an inadequate number of lenders or because lenders inaccurately view these borrowers as having excessive credit risks. Farmers and small businesses have been selected for federal credit benefits because they cannot compete effectively for credit in the private sector. Credit agencies that have been established to assist these groups include the Farm Credit Banks and the Small Business Administration loan guarantee programs. Second, credit programs have been designed to achieve major national priorities. The federal government's desire to improve and increase the nation's housing stock as outlined in the 1968 Housing Act, for example, led to the creation of the GNMA and the FHLMC. Other national priorities provided the rationale for creating the Export-Import Bank, the Rural Electrification Administration, and the Agency for International Development. Third, credit programs are used in conjunction with direct subsidies to assist disadvantaged groups. For example, the student loan program of the federal government provides financing for college students and includes a large direct subsidy in the form of below-market interest rates, despite extremely high default rates. Finally, credit guarantees have been used for emergency loan purposes, such as the bailouts of Chrysler, Lockheed, and New York City. More recently, Congress has created agencies to raise money for the bailout of the federal insurance fund, which covers the deposits of failed thrift institutions.

Types of Federal Government Lending Programs

The credit programs of the federal government can be classified into the following three groups:

1. Direct loans
2. Loan guarantees
3. Government sponsored enterprises

There are about 350 different government direct and guaranteed lending programs that fall under these three classifications.

Direct Lending Programs

The federal government has a wide variety of programs that provide direct loans to individuals, businesses, and government units. These programs are financed through appropriated tax revenues and borrowing. Direct lending programs provide credit on more favorable terms than borrowers could obtain in the private market. This frequently means that loans can be made at interest rates that are below market rates and that credit can be extended for longer periods of time than would otherwise be available from the private sector.

Businesses and agriculture have been the primary beneficiaries of direct government lending programs. Business has benefitted from the activities of the Export-Import Bank, Small Business Administration,

Rural Electrification Administration, and the Agency for International Development. Agricultural interests have received loans from the Farmers Home Administration and the price support programs of the Commodity Credit Corporation.

Guarantee Programs

Federal government loan guarantee programs guarantee the payment of principal and interest, in whole or in part, in the event the borrower defaults on a loan. These loans are originated, serviced, and funded by private sector institutions. The loan guarantee effectively transfers the risk of default from the private sector institution to the federal government. By providing credit on more favorable terms than would otherwise be available, loan guarantees channel financial resources to favored groups. A borrower with a government guaranteed loan can, in effect, go to the top of the credit ladder.

The largest user of loan guarantees by far is the housing sector. Home mortgages insured by the *Federal Housing Administration* and guaranteed by the *Veterans Administration* represent over 70 percent of government guarantees in the 1980s.

Government Sponsored Enterprises (GSEs)

During the last decade, GSEs have become the largest federal credit program. The initial capital used to start these corporations was provided by government and private sources. In recent years, these organizations have largely converted to private ownership, but they still retain a special status in the credit markets because of their government sponsorship. The most recently created GSEs have been started as privately owned corporations with substantial government conferred advantages.

The advantages granted to GSEs include various combinations of the following:

1. The ability to issue stock and debt securities that can be held by federally regulated financial institutions, while similar securities issued by private companies are prohibited
2. An implied guarantee from the federal government, referred to as *agency status,* which allows these agencies to borrow at interest rates below even the best-rated private borrowers
3. Exemption from Securities and Exchange Commission registration requirements
4. National or regional monopolies in credit-granting activities
5. Regulatory net worth or capital requirements that are lower than those imposed on comparable private institutions

Table 13.1

**Government Credit Activities:
Direct, Guaranteed, and Sponsored Enterprises
1980–1987**
(dollars in billions)

Net credit advanced in nonfinancial credit markets	$4,782
Less federal borrowing from the public	−1,253
Net nonfederal borrowing	**$3,529**
Federal Credit Programs	
Direct loans	$116
Guaranteed loans	251
Government sponsored enterprises	442
Total Federal Credit Programs	**$809**

Sources: Table F-22, "Special Analysis F," *Special Analyses: Budget of the United States*, 1988 and Board of Governors of the Federal Reserve System, *Flow of Funds Accounts*, Fourth Quarter, 1987.

Through their overwhelming advantages over private sector competitors GSEs account for most of the rapid growth in government credit programs.

Table 13.1 illustrates the importance of federal government credit programs in our financial system. It shows the net amount of loans made directly by the government, guaranteed by the government, or made by GSEs over an eight-year period from 1980 to 1987.

This table reveals two important facts. First, the government's role in the credit markets is very significant. From 1980 to 1987, federal government credit programs covered $809 billion in funds borrowed (or 22.6 percent) of the net total of the $3,529 billion raised by nonfinancial borrowers. Second, the growth in federal credit programs is heavily concentrated in GSEs, which accounted for over 55 percent of total federal credit programs in recent years.

Table 13.2 on page 336 provides dramatic evidence of the growth of GSEs. This table shows the total assets plus the securities guaranteed by each of the privately owned GSEs, including the FHLBs, the FNMA, the FHLMC, the Student Loan Marketing Association (SLMA), and the Farm Credit Banks (FCBs).

These GSEs grew by $922 billion from 1979 to 1991, representing a compound growth rate of 20 percent per annum. This compares to a

Table 13.2

Total Assets Plus Guaranteed Securities of the Major Privately Owned Enterprises 1979–1991
(dollars in billions)

Enterprise	1991	1984	1979
FHLBs	$107	$ 65	$33
FNMA	476	120	49
FHLMC	384	81	18
SLMA	37	6	2
FCBs	52	72	33
Total	**$1,056**	**$344**	**$135**

Sources: Federal Reserve *Bulletin, Statistical Abstract of the United States,* and *Annual Economic Report of the President.* (Various Issues).

growth rate in total assets of all U.S. commercial banks for the same period of 8 percent per annum.

Private Financial Institution Involvement with Government Credit Programs

Private sector financial institutions have several reasons to be involved in the federal government lending programs. In fact, most of these programs rely on private sector institutions to make them work. Financial institutions can benefit from being involved with federal lending programs through origination of assets for sale to and/or guarantee by the government, servicing assets sold to an agency, and borrowing from or selling loans to an agency to increase liquidity. Each of these activities can generate increased profits for the private sector institution.

Origination Activities

Financial institutions are active in the origination of assets that carry government guarantees and loans sold to a GSE. Table 13.3 shows the major programs and institutions that are involved.

Private financial institutions profit from these programs by charging fees to originate loans, and, in some cases, selling loans to the agency at a price higher than the amount funded to the borrower.

Table 13.3

Private Sector Participation in Originating and Servicing Government Credit Programs

Federal Credit Program	Private Intermediaries Using the Origination and Servicing Programs
FHA mortgage insurance program VA mortgage insurance programs	Mortgage bankers, Thrifts, Commercial banks
GNMA, FHA, and VA mortgage guarantee programs; FNMA and FHLMC conventional single-family and multifamily mortgage purchase programs	Mortgage bankers, Thrifts, Commercial banks, Insurance companies
Small Business Administration loan insurance programs	Commercial banks
Student Loan insurance program	Commercial banks, Thrifts
Federal Agricultural Mortgage Corporation farm mortgage purchase program	Commercial banks

Servicing Activities

Private financial institutions service loans that are purchased by government agencies or guaranteed by government agencies and sold to others. These servicing activities can represent major profit centers for the servicing institution. This is especially true in the residential mortgage market in which the government purchases or guarantees a majority of the loans originated. Financial institutions service other types of loans for federal agencies as well. Some of these programs are shown in Table 13.3.

For a large number of private financial institutions, the servicing of government guaranteed loans sold to private firms and loans sold to GSEs are a major portion of their business activities. Their motivation to service these loans lies in the profit made from the servicing fees.

Liquidity Producing Activities

A number of federal lending programs are designed primarily to provide liquidity to financial institutions. There are two types of agencies that provide this service. The first type includes among its activities making loans directly to financial institutions. These include the Federal Home Loan Banks (FHLBs), the Central Liquidity Fund of the National Credit Union Administration, and the Federal Reserve Banks. The second type of liquidity-enhancing federal lending agency is one that purchases or guarantees loans, thereby increasing their marketability. Agencies designed primarily for this purpose include the GNMA, the FNMA, the FHLMC, the SLMA, and the Federal Agricultural Mortgage Corporation.

Of the three federal lending programs designed to provide liquidity to financial institutions, only the FHLBs are significant in terms of dollars lent. The Federal Reserve Banks' discount window and the Central Liquidity Fund are used infrequently, since most banks and credit unions hold a large percentage of assets in liquid forms. The FHLBs, by contrast, had total loans outstanding in excess of $120 billion at year-end 1990. The FHLBs provide short-term liquidity advances as well as long-term advances with maturities of up to ten years or more, primarily to S&Ls and commercial banks. The availability of longer-term advances has encouraged thrift institutions to borrow large amounts from FHLBs to fund long-term home loans. At year-end 1990, FHLB advances represented 10 percent of the total liabilities of S&Ls and federally chartered savings banks. The FIRREA of 1989 allowed commercial banks and credit unions to have access to FHLB loans when they are significantly involved in housing finance. This has encouraged growth in commercial bank and credit union borrowing from the FHLBs. In 1991, over 1,000 commercial banks borrowed from FHLBs.

The second government-supported source of liquidity for financial institutions comes through the use of government agencies and sponsored enterprises that purchase and/or guarantee loans. Such loans are readily marketable, and therefore can be easily converted to cash when necessary. The mortgage purchase and guarantee programs of GNMA, FNMA, and FHLMC have grown rapidly in the 1980s. They now account for more than one-third of all residential mortgage debt in the United States. Of this, FNMA and FHLMC accounted for almost 33 percent at year-end 1991, up from only 6.5 percent ten years earlier.

Primary Federal Lending Organizations and Programs

This section presents a short history of the major activities of the federal agencies that provide direct lending, guarantees, and government sponsored enterprise credit.

Farm Credit Banks

The FCBs are a farm credit system consisting of a number of cooperatively owned banks that provide credit to farmers. This system dates back to 1916 and was expanded during the Great Depression of the 1930s when farmers faced severe foreclosure problems. It represented the first government sponsored credit program.

The system includes the Federal Land Banks (FLBs), Federal Intermediate Credit Banks (FICBs), and Banks for Cooperatives (BCs). Today, the capitalization for these banks comes from the farmers and farm cooperatives that borrow from them. The banks provide credit to farmers who want to purchase farm land, equipment, livestock, seed and fertilizer, and inventory for farm cooperatives. At year-end 1991, the farm credit system had $52 billion in loans outstanding.

Government National Mortgage Association

GNMA or Ginnie Mae was created in 1968 to guarantee mortgage-backed securities that were backed by FHA and VA mortgages. Mortgage-backed securities were virtually unknown at the time. Today GNMA securities enjoy ready reception in the capital market because they carry the "full faith and credit" guarantee of the federal government, and their huge volume creates high marketability. As of year-end 1991, GNMA had guaranteed over $430 billion in securities. Over 1,100 lenders have participated in GNMA programs since its establishment.

GNMA does not issue securities itself; instead it guarantees securities of private issuers. The guarantee provides that the owner of a GNMA security will have prompt receipt of scheduled monthly principal and interest payments on the underlying mortgages, as well as prepayments of principal when the mortgage-borrower repays early or defaults.

Federal National Mortgage Association

FNMA or Fannie Mae is the largest of the mortgage finance GSEs. It was established in 1938 to purchase mortgages from lenders. It financed these purchases by issuing debt securities. In 1954 it became a mixed-ownership corporation. It was owned partly by shareholders, which were those organizations that sold it mortgages, and partly by the government. Then in 1968, Congress split the corporation into two entities, GNMA and FNMA, and FNMA became a privately owned entity. Today its stock is widely held and traded on the New York Stock Exchange.

FNMA operates by purchasing mortgages and issuing guaranteed mortgage-backed securities. In its purchase program, it buys FHA-insured, VA-guaranteed, and conventional mortgages on single and multifamily properties. The maximum dollar amount of each mortgage is set by law using an index. This is intended to limit the benefits of a government support program to moderate-income families. In 1992, the maximum exceeded $200,000. Loans qualifying for purchase are known as *conforming mortgages*. If a lender wishes to hold mortgages, but still have the benefits of an FNMA guarantee, it can swap the mortgages for a mortgage pass-through security backed by the same mortgages. The lender, in effect, holds the same mortgages as before, but now has the benefit of the greater marketability and safety of the FNMA security.

FNMA had assets of over $130 billion at year-end 1991, and in addition, had $372 billion of guaranteed mortgage pass-through securities outstanding. These securities are not shown as debt on the FNMA balance sheet, since they are not considered a direct obligation. They are not "owed" by the agency; like GNMA securities they are merely guaranteed by the agency.

Federal Home Loan Mortgage Corporation

FHLMC or Freddie Mac was established in 1970 to provide a secondary market for privately insured, or conventional, mortgages. At that time, GNMA and FNMA were limited to FHA-insured and VA-guaranteed mortgages. Funds to capitalize FHLMC were provided initially by the FHLB system. In 1990, it issued stock to the public and repaid the FHLBs. FHLMC stock is widely held and traded on the NYSE.

Because of the similarity of their programs, FHLMC and FNMA are strong competitors. Over the years, FHLMC has been a major innovator in the field of mortgage-backed securities, having created the first conventional pass-through security, guaranteed mortgage security, and collateralized mortgage obligation. At year-end 1991, FHLMC had total assets of over $24 billion. It also has guaranteed mortgage-backed securities over $361 billion.

Student Loan Marketing Association

SLMA or Sallie Mae is the nation's largest investor in and servicer of government-insured student loans. This GSE was established to provide a secondary market for student loans originated by commercial banks and others. SLMA stock is held by the public as well as a group of lending institutions that originate student loans. SLMA is also the nation's largest servicer of student loans. Many originators of student loans hold loans in portfolio until the student graduates and must begin to repay the loan. At that point, most financial institutions sell the loans to SLMA because of the complexity and high costs of servicing the default-ridden student loans. At year-end 1991, SLMA had debt outstanding of over $38 billion.

Federal Housing Administration

This mortgage insurance agency was established by the government in 1934 to provide insurance against risk of default on home mortgages. The objective was to encourage lenders to make longer-term mortgages than the customary 5- to 15-year maturities of that period. FHA is an agency within the Department of Housing and Urban Development. Today, FHA administers over 30 programs that provide insurance on single-family homes, multifamily projects, mobile homes, residential condominiums, cooperatives, and housing for the elderly.

Small Business Administration

The SBA was established in 1953. Today, the SBA provides financial and management assistance to small businesses and to victims of natural disasters. The SBA provides financial support through direct loans and guaranteed loans.

The SBA also provides guaranteed loans to small business investment companies (SBICs). These are privately owned and SBA-regulated organizations that supply venture capital and long-term financing to small businesses.

SBA-guaranteed loans, like GNMA securities, carry the full faith and credit guarantee of the federal government. As a result, they are considered free of default risk and can be easily bought and sold.

Allocational Efficiency of Government Credit Programs

The rapid growth of the federal lending programs has produced a growing controversy concerning the impact of these programs on the allocation of credit. *Allocational efficiency* refers in part to the issue of whether the full benefits of a government subsidy program reach the intended beneficiaries. Of particular concern has been the use of government-subsidized programs by borrowers who are able to obtain unsubsidized loans from the private sector. A borrower using an FHA mortgage that could have obtained financing using a conventional mortgage results in an inefficient use of government resources. The allocational impact of these programs is largest in those instances when the government provides a fairly large subsidy, as in some of the programs for farmers, students, and small businesses. Many of these subsidies represent pure windfall gains to borrowers eligible for unsubsidized credit. In these circumstances the programs produce no social welfare gain.

Other concerns over allocational efficiency deal with the *crowding out* impact of federal credit programs. Since the federal government and its agencies enjoy preferred borrowing status in financial markets, borrowers not covered by federal credit programs may be unable to borrow, or may have to pay a high cost when there is a shortage of loanable funds. This crowding out phenomenon is very hard to measure. Still, it is a very real concern.

Privately owned GSEs present a different allocational issue. Here the concern is that the GSEs will take advantage of their government status to reward stockholders. This can be done by capturing a large percentage of the benefits in the form of profits and letting only a portion of the government-derived benefits filter down to the ultimate borrowers. The high level of profits and return on equity at FNMA, FHLMC, the FHLBs, and SLMA in recent years suggests that this concern is valid.

Impact of GSEs on Private Intermediaries

Recent concern over the growth of GSEs comes at a time when both commercial banks and thrifts are finding it difficult to earn reasonable profits. Also, they are being accused of engaging in high-risk activities such as making loans to developing countries, participating in leveraged buy-outs, and investing in commercial real estate and junk bonds. In addition, banks and thrifts are feeling the sting of higher capital standards, more intense examination scrutiny, and higher deposit insurance premiums.

If these fast-growing agencies have used their preferred government granted borrowing advantages, lower capitalization requirements, and securities and tax exemptions to undercut the commercial banks and thrifts in markets they once dominated, then it could be argued that this has contributed to greater risk-taking by these institutions and increased failure rates. Agency inroads into traditional bank and thrift markets may be one of the major reasons that banks and thrifts began lending into riskier markets where yields have not been held down by government activity. Lower yields on traditional activities may also account for the poor profitability of depository institutions in recent years and their increased failure rate. If this is so, it makes the issue of GSE growth an important one for our public policymakers.

It also raises questions about the impact of new agencies that have been created in recent years. Congress has authorized the Federal Agricultural Mortgage Corporation (Farmer Mac), a secondary market for farm loans, and is also considering an agency to buy and package small business loans. The latter would cut into commercial banks' so-called "middle market" for business loans, which has been a major area of investment emphasis for banks in recent years, and raises the question of whether banks would have any unique lending role to play. This question has already been raised concerning thrift institutions in which government agencies dominate the residential mortgage market, historically the thrift's principal market.

Agency and Depository Pricing of Loans: The Agency Capital Advantage

Agencies can dominate a market by being low-cost producers when the privileges they have been granted by the federal government provide substantial cost advantages. The two principal advantages are low capital requirements and low cost of debt.

To evaluate the potential for market dominance, a model for pricing loans must be developed. This model is discussed more fully in Chapter 22. Using the model, it is possible to compare the break-even rate that must be charged for a given type of loan by an agency, such as FNMA, and a depository, such as a bank, to cover the costs of investing in the loan as well as costs associated with holding the loan, such as servicing, credit risk, and prepayment options risk. To do this, consider the recent data on the relative cost of liabilities for depositories and agencies. Also consider the impact of capital requirements imposed by regulators of insured depositories and the agencies to see how required capital levels impact the break-even loan rate for each lender.

The model used to get a first approximation of the break-even rate for depositories and agencies is a weighted average cost of capital model. The break-even risk adjusted asset yield (*BERAY*) is equal to the weighted average cost of equity and debt funds plus any unique cost or risk factors related to the particular loan being analyzed.

Capital requirements determine the weights assigned to equity and debt in our weighted cost of capital. The capital requirements used in the model are those prescribed in 1992 risk-based capital requirements by bank and thrift regulators for conforming residential first mortgages. The model is shown in Equation 13.1.

$$BERAY = (RCR \times RW \times CE) + [(1 - (RCR \times RW)) \times CD] + crp + cop + sc \qquad [13.1]$$

where:

$BERAY$ = Break-even risk-adjusted mortgage yield

RCR = Risk-based minimum capital requirement

RW = Risk weight

CD = Cost of debt

CE = Cost of equity

crp = Credit risk premium

cop = Option premium embedded in a fixed rate mortgage in percent

sc = Servicing cost in percent

Table 13.4 on page 344 shows the *BERAYs* for agencies, $BERAY_a$, and for depositories, $BERAY_d$, given regulatory capital requirements and risk weights adopted by the Federal Reserve, Federal Deposit Insurance Corporation, and the Office of Thrift Supervision. The values for *crp, cop,* and *sc* are assumed to be the same for depositories and agencies. Risk weights for depositories on mortgages are set at the proposed 50 percent of the total risk-based 1992 capital requirement of 8 percent. These risk weights are discussed fully in Chapter 22.

Capital requirements for the agencies are now set by law. The Department of Housing and Urban Development has imposed maximum leverage ratios on FNMA. The new capital ratios are considerably below depository ratios. The ratio of shareholders' equity to total assets plus guaranteed mortgage-backed securities for the years 1984 to 1989 are used, since they have been acceptable to those in government that oversee these institutions. The annual average of this ratio over the last five years is .652 percent for both FNMA and FHLMC.

Table 13.4 shows $BERAY_a$ and $BERAY_d$ for three hypothetical pretax cost levels for equity capital, CE, of 20 percent, 25 percent, and 30 percent. Other variables in the model are CD = 8 percent, crp = .12 percent, cop = .80 percent, and sc = .20 percent. These numbers are used merely for illustrative purposes.

Table 13.4 shows that FNMA's and FHLMC's substantially lower capital levels put them in a position to undercut the pricing of mortgages by depositories with much higher required capital levels. The range of this advantage is from .40 percent (9.60 percent–9.20 percent) to .74 percent (10 percent–9.26 percent).

Table 13.4

Break-even Mortgage Rate for Agencies and Depositories at Three Levels of Pretax Cost of Equity Capital

Assumed Pretax Cost of Equity Capital	Break-even Mortgage Rate
20%	$BERAY_d$ 9.60%
25	9.80
30	10.00
20%	$BERAY_a$ 9.20%
25	9.23
30	9.26

Agency and Depository Pricing of Loans: The Cost of Debt Advantage

The agency cost of equity capital advantage is significant, but it is probably less important in the long run than the advantage agencies enjoy in issuing liabilities. Government officials could mandate equal capital standards for regulated depositories and agencies. However, advantages in the cost of raising debt are more important and difficult to change. Government agencies are treated very well in the capital markets. Their cost of debt averages roughly 20 to 35 basis points over Treasury rates for comparable maturities. This is a low spread in comparison to private companies without the government affiliation.

To compare agency borrowing rates to the rates paid by commercial banks and thrifts for deposits, the average rates paid by commercial banks on the one-year retail CDs, one-year brokered CDs, and one-year negotiable CDs were calculated. Data on the average rates paid on these types of deposits were obtained from June 1989 through May 1990 from a survey completed by Banxquote Online as reported in the *Wall Street Journal* for the first Thursday of each month. These data show that commercial banks paid an average of 21 basis points or .21 percent above the one-year Treasury for retail CDs, a 67-basis point premium for brokered CDs, and 30 basis points more for negotiable CDs. Thrifts have historically paid even higher rates than commercial banks, typically 23 basis points or more. To these quoted rates must be added the cost of deposit insurance, which in 1992 was 23 basis points for the Savings Association Insurance Fund and 23 basis points for the Bank Insurance Fund. For some types of deposits, Federal Reserve noninterest earning reserves must be held, which effectively increases the cost of those funds. For retail funds, an approximated cost of servicing through branches at 30 basis points or more and other servicing costs must be added. To brokered CDs must be added commissions paid to the broker/dealer, which are usually 40 basis points.

Overall, the cost of deposits for banks and thrifts has ranged 30 to 80 basis points higher than for the agencies. This agency cost-of-debt advantage added to their cost-of-equity advantage makes the agencies the dominant low-cost producers of credit in the markets they serve. Thus, it is not surprising that in a recent study Hendershott and Shilling (1989) found that the impact of the mortgage GSEs was to lower agency eligible mortgage rates by 30 basis points relative to interest rates on similar mortgages not eligible for sale to or guarantee by GSEs.

This analysis strongly suggests that the financial problems of depositories in the 1980s can be attributed not only to deregulated deposit rates, as frequently argued, but also to agency induced downward pressure on loan yields in traditional lending markets. This situation is not likely to change in the 1990s.

Now that agencies no longer play a secondary role in the markets they serve, some analysts believe it is time to rethink the use of GSEs in our capital markets and to reduce the advantages they receive. During the last half of the 1980s, a variety of remedies have been proposed. The FIRREA of 1989 did include several provisions to increase oversight of FNMA and FSLIC by the Department of Housing and Urban Development. It also required them to demonstrate that they were adequately capitalized using a test of their own making. President Reagan's 1982 Commission on Housing went much further and recommended the complete privatization of the GSEs. The Office of Management and Budget has proposed a "user fee" to offset the agencies' advantage. This involves charging GSEs a premium on all debt issued or guaranteed by them. This would be similar to deposit insurance premiums charged to banks and thrifts. More recently, the U.S. Treasury has recommended that the agencies be required to obtain triple A ratings from the private rating services without relying on their special credit relationships to the Treasury. This would probably require higher equity capital ratios for GSEs and reduce their cost advantage. None of these proposals has received much support in Congress. This is partly due to the intense lobbying by the agencies and their customers who benefit from these advantages. In 1992, Congress passed legislation to establish capital requirements for the FNMA and FHLMC and required them to purchase more loans in low-income areas. Both GSEs had sufficient capital to meet the new requirements.

The growth in government guarantee programs and GSEs represents a huge government potential liability. In this respect, the liability is similar to the deposit insurance programs for commercial banks and thrifts. Despite this growing liability, there has been little action by Congress and the president to evaluate and monitor the actions of these organizations.

Summary

The federal government's role in the credit markets is not limited to borrowing to finance budget deficits. The government also plays an important part in supplying and directing credit to borrowers that Congress has decided deserve priority in the allocation of funds. At present, there are over 350 different government credit programs, including direct loans, loan guarantee programs, and government sponsored credit enterprises. Together these programs are about one-fourth the size of all private sector credit activity. Through federal credit programs, more generous credit is made available at lower cost to a wide range of borrowers, including homebuyers, farmers, small businesses, college students, rural electrical cooperatives, and exporters.

Of the three types of federal credit programs, government sponsored enterprises (GSEs) are the largest and fastest growing. To a large extent, GSEs compete with private sector intermediaries that provide the same or similar types of credit to the same borrowers. Normally it could be expected that private sector competitors of GSEs, such as banks and thrift institutions, would uniformly oppose the continuation or expansion of competing government agencies that have substantial built-in advantages. The advantages granted to GSEs by Congress include exemption from income taxes, lower capital requirements, and a host of other exemptions and privileges that allow GSEs to borrow at rates below even the highest quality private intermediaries. Since the GSEs rely primarily on private sector intermediaries to originate and service supported loans, and since these activities can be done profitably in most cases, leaders of private intermediaries are mixed in their views about further expansion of GSEs. However, many economists and financial executives object to federal credit programs on the basis that they (1) provide a form of subsidy to some borrowers who could easily borrow on an unsubsidized basis in the private sector and (2) crowd out of the credit markets some borrowers whose activities might be more economically productive.

A number of proposals have been advanced in recent years to reduce or remove some of the advantages of GSEs, and thereby slow down their growth. So far, the agencies' constituencies of favored borrowers and participating intermediaries have been successful in blocking change in the GSEs' preferred status. In fact, some GSEs have been able to expand the scope of their programs in recent years to cover more potential borrowers and participating private sector lenders. Thus, it is probable that government credit programs will continue to play a large role in the nation's credit markets.

The **federal government's credit programs** can be classified into three primary groups:

1. **Direct loans**
2. **Loan guarantees**
3. **Government sponsored enterprises**

The largest of these programs are the **GSEs.** Their substantial growth and profitability is the result of advantages granted them by the federal government. These include the following:

1. They issue debt that are allowable investments for many intermediaries.
2. They have the implied guarantee of the federal government.
3. They are exempt from Securities and Exchange Commission registration.
4. They have regional or national monopolies.
5. They are not subject to depository capital requirements.

Private sector intermediaries are heavily involved with the government's credit programs. They originate assets for these programs, service loans for these programs, and are able to borrow and sell assets to them to increase liquidity.

The growth in the GSE programs, in particular, has raised serious questions about the impact of these dominant programs on private sector institutions. Their ability to raise funds at lower costs than most depositories makes them the low-cost producer of credit for certain types of loans. They can undercut the private sector and create unfair competition and contribute to failures.

Questions

Chapter 13

1. Why is the federal government involved in the credit markets?
2. What national priorities have been identified for government credit assistance?
3. How have government credit programs been used for emergency purposes?
4. Name and describe the three basic types of government credit programs and give an example of each.
5. What government credit programs have grown the fastest? In which credit markets are the government credit programs most active?
6. What is a government sponsored enterprise? Give the names of several. What advantages have the GSEs been granted by Congress to carry out their various missions?
7. Which of these advantages seem to be the most important to GSEs in enhancing their competitive position?
8. What involvement do private sector institutions have with government credit programs?
9. Who are the major lending intermediaries that originate for government credit programs?
10. Which government credit programs provide liquidity to private financial institutions?
11. What do the FNMA and FHLMC have in common?
12. What is meant by allocational efficiency in the context of a government credit program? Should government credit programs be eliminated?
13. How might GSEs adversely impact private intermediaries? Which groups are helped and hurt by the GSEs?
14. Do GSEs have a lower cost of capital than many private intermediaries? If so, why?
15. What proposals have government departments made to control the growth of the GSEs?
16. Which private financial institutions are most likely to be adversely impacted by the GSEs in terms of their portfolio management activities?
17. What is meant by crowding out?
18. What would you do to reduce the growing dominance of the GSEs? Do you think the GSEs should dominate the markets in which they operate?
19. What do government guarantees do to help a distressed borrower like Chrysler and New York City?
20. Why do you think GSEs have been among the most profitable financial intermediaries in the late 1980s and early 1990s?

Financial Institution Regulation, Insurers, and Regulators

chapter **14**

Regulation is a fundamental feature of the U.S. financial system. Since the Depression of the 1930s, the regulation of financial institutions has grown considerably in both scope and breadth. Regulation is very important to managers of financial institutions because regulations and the regulatory implementation process can influence the performance of a financial institution as much as the quality of management.

During the 1980s, financial regulation underwent significant change. The primary impetus for this change was the thrift industry debacle and the rise in commercial bank and insurance company failures, which were exacerbated by weak regulation. The 1980s were also marred by scandal, fraud, and self-dealing in segments of the financial services business. These problems resulted in a substantial increase in legislation designed to increase penalties for such acts, while at the same time increasing the surveillance and monitoring of institutions by regulatory bodies. Today, most regulatory bodies have more authority, a greater assortment of potent tools to implement regulation, and more examination resources than ever before.

This chapter will look at the regulatory process from several perspectives. First, the question of why we have regulation is reviewed. This is followed by a discussion of how regulation is implemented. Finally, the major regulatory bodies and insurance organizations are identified and discussed. In the Appendix to this chapter, the most sweeping regulatory legislative change since the Depression, the Financial Institutions Reform, Recovery, and Enforcement Act of 1989 (FIRREA) and the Federal Deposit Insurance Corporation Improvement Act (FDICIA) of 1991, are discussed.

The Public Good Theory of Financial Regulation

The public good theory of regulation is the most useful model for understanding the rationale behind virtually all the regulation we find in the financial services business. The public good theory simply states that regulation may be justified to correct an alleged deficiency in the competitive market process.

Consider how the market may fail. According to the model of competitive markets, there must be many willing and able buyers and sellers and perfect information about the good or service involved in the transaction. This market structure does not always exist. As a result, society frequently imposes regulations designed to eliminate any undue advantage that one party to the transaction might have. Normally this advantage belongs to the seller. The perfect market model fails when the number of sellers is inadequate, such as in a monopolistic or oligopolistic situation. Finally, the model doesn't work if buyers are unable to understand the product due to its complexity.

The regulation of financial institutions in this country is aimed at accomplishing a wide variety of public policy goals. Because most financial institutions receive benefits from the federal government, such as deposit insurance, charters, or participation in federal government lending programs (FHA mortgages, for example), the Congress has required that these financial institutions pursue public policy goals. Laws and regulations are the method used to ensure that these public policy goals are accomplished.

The following is a list of nine public policy goals that have been used to justify the substantial amount of financial regulation. A discussion of each of these goals follows the list.

- Achieve competitive financial markets
- Reduce information imperfections or asymmetries
- Eliminate prejudice or bias of supply
- Achieve equal access
- Improve implementation of monetary policy goals
- Pursue socially desirable credit allocation
- Reduce potential of insider abuse and fraud
- Reduce potential for disruptive impact of financial institution failures
- Protect taxpayers from deposit insurance fund failures

Achieve Competitive Financial Markets

Concerns about the ultimate structure of a market for financial services has historically accounted for a considerable amount of regulation. Bank and thrift regulators formerly approved new branches by using as one of their criteria their judgment on whether a market was considered too highly concentrated. A highly concentrated market is a trade area with few institutions competing in it. Although market structure is still on the minds of regulators, it has not been a major issue for some time. This is because the market for financial services has been characterized by deregulation and overcapacity. Still, in 1991 when Bank of America and Security Pacific Banks of California were planning their merger, the banks sold branches in a number of markets in which the merger was likely to have produced high levels of financial concentration.

Likewise, the 1991 admission by Salomon Brothers, Inc., the large investment banker, that it had violated Treasury auction trading rules raised the issue of whether there was adequate competition in the primary Treasury security market. The result was a major modification of the auction process to allow more investors to participate.

Reduce Information Imperfections and Asymmetries

Claims of inadequate or misleading information accounts for a growing amount of consumer-based financial regulation. As financial contracts have become more complicated, there has been a growing demand from public policymakers and consumer groups for new regulations on disclosure and standardization of product and service descriptions. Regulations dealing with the standardization of insurance policies are designed to protect consumers who are unable to understand the complexity of many of these policies.

Truth-in-lending legislation, requiring that lenders quote interest rates on loans based on the effective interest rate basis, was passed because it was felt that consumers couldn't understand how to compare interest rates when some lenders included upfront fees, called points, while others did not.

Insurance companies are regulated to avoid putting an insurance customer at a serious informational disadvantage. Insurance policies are complicated financial contracts. As a result, the average consumer is at a significant disadvantage when attempting to negotiate with an insurance company. This informational asymmetry is a primary cause of insurance company regulation. Regulators are also concerned that companies provide prompt settlement of claims, and that the companies not be deceitful in the claims they make about the insurance products they market.

Reducing information asymmetries is also the object of the disclosure requirements mandated on publicly held corporations and other organizations that sell securities to the public. The different forms of market efficiency were discussed in the chapter on financial markets. The informational efficiency of markets depends on the availability of information to prospective investors.

Eliminate Prejudice or Bias of Supply

One of the most frequently cited goals of financial legislation relates to providing access to financial services on a fair and equal basis. During the decade of the 1960s and 1970s, when eliminating discrimination was a high social priority, many laws designed to prohibit discrimination in the financial markets were passed. Much of this legislation related to the discriminatory practices of institutions lending to specific classes of consumers.

The first major piece of legislation that dealt with fair and equal lending was the Consumer Credit Protection Act of 1968. The law required that lenders use a consistent methodology for quoting interest rates on loans, referred to as a truth-in-lending law. Since 1968, many laws have been passed to protect consumers from potentially unfair practices of lenders. Table 14.1 provides short descriptions of some of the most important of these acts.

Table 14.1

Major Consumer Lending Protection Laws

Law	Short Explanation
Consumer Credit Protection Act	Creditors must state the cost of borrowing in a common language to ensure easy comparisons of costs between lenders.
Real Estate Settlements and Procedures Act	Requires lender to estimate certain costs related to closing on a home purchase and obtaining a mortgage.
Equal Credit Opportunity Act	Requires all lenders to treat all credit applicants equally with respect to personal characteristics.
Community Reinvestment Act	Regulators will consider local lending experience of depository when considering approval of mergers and acquisitions.
Fair Credit Reporting Act	Establishes required procedures for correcting mistakes on a credit report.
Fair Credit Billing Act	Requires creditors to promptly correct billing mistakes.

Table 14.1 continued

Major Consumer Lending Protection Laws

Law	Short Explanation
Electronic Fund Transfer Act	Requires lenders and other institutions involved in electronic payments to meet certain conditions regarding transfers.
Home Mortgage Disclosure Act	Requires lenders to maintain records on mortgage lending by census tract.
Truth-in-Savings Act	Requires depositories to disclose the methodology used to access fees and pay interest on accounts.

All these laws were passed to help ensure that financial depository institutions do not discriminate in their lending practices on the basis of race, sex, or neighborhood, and that lenders provide adequate disclosure of their lending and deposit account practices. The regulations that were promulgated from these laws have a very real impact on the operations of the institutions affected. Much of this legislation requires costly reporting of certain types of information, while some provides for penalties such as the ability of regulators to deny mergers or other requests if the institution is found to be deficient in its lending practices. These laws also provide that consumers can sue the lender if a violation of these laws occurs. Suits may also be brought as class action suits on behalf of many individuals who may have suffered the same violation. The result of these laws has been to sharply increase the cost of doing business for all institutions, as they attempt to organize their lending practices to conform to these laws and regulations.

Achieve Equal Access

Equal access to a financial service is another justification for regulation. Just as years ago the highly regulated airline business had to fly to cities that were not profitable locations, a payment system operated partially by the Federal Reserve System helps to ensure that all parts of the country have access to the check-clearing system, despite the fact that providing service to some remote areas may be unprofitable. A fair amount of consumer-based legislation is concerned with equal access. The concept of *life-line banking* was promoted to ensure that lower income households could receive the services of a checking account at a low cost.

Insurance companies are regulated to ensure access for all who need coverage. Access is, of course, a price-related issue. Many regulations and a substantial amount of government involvement in the insurance industry relates to providing access to insurance for various groups. Flood insurance and earthquake insurance have been especially impacted by the federal government, to the point where this coverage has direct federal involvement. Another aspect of access relates to whether the premium charged a particular class of insured is discriminatory.

The goal of equal access is in direct conflict with the principle that a premium that is too low could lead to *adverse self selection*. Under adverse self selection, if poor risks are not differentiated by price, the loss experience of the insured pool will increase, bringing about the need for higher premiums. This will drive the lower risk groups out and the risk pool will get riskier, causing the need for another increase in premiums, and so on.

Improve Implementation of Monetary Policy Goals

A smoothly functioning financial system is considered essential to the successful implementation of monetary policy. Regarding monetary policy, the Fed is concerned that the banking system be responsive to a more stimulative monetary policy by increasing loans and investments. The central bank, attempting to achieve targets for the growth of several monetary aggregates or for specific interest rate levels, would find its effort frustrated by bank failures and financial stress in the financial system. A number of observers believe that the Depression was made more severe by the failure of commercial banks and the reduction in the monetary aggregates.

During the fall of 1990, the Federal Reserve expressed concern over the tightening of commercial bank lending policies brought on by the sharp growth in problem loans and investments and reduced real estate values. The regulator was also concerned that the increased regulatory sensitivity to commercial bank financial solvency was causing bank regulators to cause bankers to be too conservative in their lending policies. The Federal Reserve was concerned that tight lending policies would complicate their ability to pursue a more stimulative monetary policy and get the economy out of the 1990–1991 recession.

Pursue Socially Desirable Credit Allocation

The lending powers and regulations of financial institutions have occasionally been altered in an effort to help ensure a more socially desirable allocation of credit. *Socially desirable* is not an absolute standard, but is defined by Congress and government bureaucrats through legislation and regulation. The high percentage of assets that S&Ls must invest in home mortgages is an obvious attempt at increasing the supply of home mortgage credit. The creation of the GNMA and the expansion of the FNMA's authority in 1968 and the chartering of the FHLMC in 1970 were a direct result of the desire to improve the supply of home mortgage credit. A similar rationale was used to justify the establishment of the SLMA. Here the goal was to ensure an adequate supply of funds for student tuition at colleges, universities, and trade schools.

Reduce Potential for Insider Abuse and Fraud

Most of our security laws and regulations have as their primary purpose the protection of investors from insider abuse and fraud. Insider trading restrictions are designed to ensure that a company's officers and directors do not buy and sell a company's stock or bonds using insider information that they possess as a consequence of their position. Information that is released by companies and their officers is also subject to disclosure regulations to ensure that the information is factually correct and timely and to discourage insiders from providing misleading signals to unknowing purchasers of the company's securities.

Sometimes providing timely and adequate disclosure conflicts with the need for bank regulators to provide safety and soundness. One such situation relates to depository institutions and their examination reports. For example, federal regulators require that information in examination reports remain confidential to avoid the potential for a run on the financial firm should the report indicate that the firm is weak. On the other hand, there is the risk that without full disclosure, unknowing investors might purchase uninsured investments in the depository. These would not have been purchased if disclosure had been more revealing.

Reduce Potential for Disruptive Impact of Financial Institutions' Failures

Over the years, there have been a number of safety and soundness justifications for establishing, expanding, and defending the deposit insurance system. The primary safety and soundness justifications for regulation of commercial banks outlined in Benston and Kaufman (1988) include the following:

1. Concern about the costs resulting from financial panics and threatened interruptions to the payment system related to commercial bank failures
2. Concern over the possibility of local and regional economic disruptions caused by commercial bank failures that are concentrated in particular areas of the country
3. Concern over the loss of wealth of depositors

4. Concern that commercial banks will take excessive risk in their lending activities as a result of their ability to issue liquid deposits
5. Concern about the potential for excessive competition between banks and nonbanks, as well as the concern over conflict of interest between banking and securities issuance and commerce

The Great Depression of the 1930s left over 9,000 bank failures and resulted in a significant reduction in the nation's money supply which, many economists say, contributed to the Depression's length and severity. Partly as a result, important legislation was passed designed to promote the safety and soundness of our country's financial institutions and to protect low and moderate income households from sustaining losses on deposits held in failed depositories. During much of the period from the 1930s through the 1970s, the basic thrust of regulation was to protect financial institutions from excessive competition. Entry barriers were maintained, branching restrictions were widespread, controls on interest rates on demand deposits and savings accounts were maintained, and restrictions on the nonbank activities of bank holding companies were tight. These were all rationalized on the basis of safety and soundness. The provisions of the Glass-Steagall Act, which prohibits banks from underwriting corporate stocks and bonds, were rationalized, in part, under the banner of safety and soundness.

Safety and soundness is again a major theme of financial legislation. The failure of the FSLIC and the increased number of commercial bank failures in the 1980s were the primary impetus behind the passage of the FIRREA of 1989 and the FDICIA of 1991. These factors also account for the efforts of the commercial bank regulators to increase the capital requirements of commercial banks.

The goal of safety and soundness can be in direct conflict with the need for financial institutions to respond to increased competition from nonbanks, foreign banks, and federal government agencies. Safety and soundness concerns usually persuade regulators to restrict the ability of regulated firms to respond to competitive market forces.

Protect Taxpayers from Deposit Insurance Fund Failures

The problem with the safety and soundness goal is that it can be made to mean different things to different people. For example, should the regulatory body concerned with safety and soundness be concerned with protecting (1) the depositor's funds in the institution, (2) the deposit insurance corporation's reserves, and/or (3) the institution(s) in distress? The regulatory response to financial distress might be different for each case.

Since the 1930s, regulators have taken actions to protect each of these groups at one time or another. Depositors have been consistently protected even during the recent failure of the FSLIC. Moreover, very large financial institutions have occasionally been protected and their shareholders preserved despite the failure or impending failure of the institution. The failure of the Continental Bank of Illinois in 1984 was avoided due to assistance from the FDIC, which ended up owning stock in Continental, and from the Federal Reserve Bank of Chicago, which helped avoid a more severe liquidity problem at the bank.

While the rationale in favor of deposit insurance has been compelling, there remain real problems with operating governmentally based deposit insurance programs.

Costs of Regulation

The rationale behind regulation is well accepted today. However, there are extremely high costs associated with regulating the financial sector. The most obvious costs include the following:

1. The possible misallocation of resources caused by financial regulation
2. The administrative costs of regulation
3. The impact of regulation on the ability of regulated firms to respond to new market opportunities and competition

Much of the regulation we have discussed impacts the investment options available to financial institutions. Regulations that constrain the asset investment options of intermediaries can impact the cost of capital to various borrowers and industries. Capital requirements and charter restrictions can favor some borrowers over others in ways that can negatively impact real economic growth. They can also lead to excessive investment in less productive areas. Many economists have argued that the United States has many regulatory and chartering provisions that favor investment in residential real estate. These are said to reduce the capital available for plant and equipment investment.

Regulations also carry large administrative costs. The administrative cost burden of regulation is not easy to estimate. However, as any senior manager of a regulated depository will tell you, it is significant and growing. These costs include personnel time, reporting costs, and costs of examination and supervision, which are borne by the regulated institutions.

Finally, regulation inhibits the ability of regulated institutions to respond to new markets and competitive threats. The most obvious example of a regulation that contributed to many financial institution failures was the prohibition on savings and loans offering adjustable-rate mortgages. Largely as a result of this restriction, savings and loans went into the high-interest rate period of the late 1970s and 1980s with a portfolio of fixed-rate mortgages and sharply rising deposit costs. The result was insolvency for many. The regulatory price constraints on deposit interest rates that lasted until the early 1980s also contributed to the growth of money market mutual funds in the late 1970s. This competition is still potent today despite the absence of price ceilings.

Issues Related to Deposit Insurance Programs

The failure of the FSLIC in 1989 and the near insolvency of the *Bank Insurance Fund (BIF)* in 1991 have highlighted a number of issues that define public policy debate over how to operate a financially sound deposit insurance program.[1] These topics include the following:

1. The role of moral hazard in undermining deposit insurance programs
2. The too big to fail policy
3. The appropriate method for levying deposit insurance premiums on insured institutions
4. The effectiveness of competitive constraints and barriers to entry in reducing the probability for financial institution failure

Deposit Insurance and Moral Hazard

The rationale for deposit insurance is an outgrowth of the banking experience in the United States in the 1800s and the early 1930s. The periodic financial failures in the 1800s and the Great Depression provided substantial rationale to the advocates of a deposit insurance program. The protection of depositor funds is probably the strongest rationale behind depository regulation. The failure of the FSLIC and our other experience with depository failures has provided nearly conclusive evidence that the U.S. government will stand behind the safety of deposits in insured commercial banks and thrifts.

The stability that has resulted from these insurance programs has not been without costs, however. The single biggest problem concerns the relationship of deposit insurance to the willingness of insured institutions to take excessive risks. Insurance makes decision makers more willing to take risks. This is known as *moral hazard*. A moral hazard exists when depositors in institutions that take excessive risk are not affected by a high probability of failure of that institution.

In the U.S. system of deposit insurance there are three types of moral hazards present. First, there is the moral hazard relating to depositors who

---

[1] The history of the financial soundness of deposit insurance programs in the United States is generally not comforting. There was the failure of the New York Safety Fund in the 1840s and the numerous more recent failures of state-run deposit funds since 1985 in Ohio, Maryland, and Rhode Island. These failures dramatically focus attention on the difficulties of operating an actuarially sound government deposit insurance program.

are unconcerned about depositing funds in weak institutions as long as the funds receive deposit insurance. The second moral hazard relates to the management and shareholders of weak depository institutions. The presence of deposit insurance eliminates the market's natural response to a firm that has risky assets and low capital. Normally, as a firm increases business risk and financial leverage, we would expect its cost of capital to rise. With insured deposits, however, management and shareholders have the incentive to increase these risks as much as the regulators permit, since depositors will continue to supply funds anyway. Finally, even the regulators suffer from a moral hazard. If regulators are evaluated on the basis of whether depository failures occur when they are in office, then it stands to reason that regulators will attempt to delay taking over institutions as long as possible, preferably until a new government appointee is in office.

The general belief is that our deposit insurance system has all but eliminated the potential for financial panic and significant disruption to the payment system. The cost to society has been unnecessarily high, however. The taxpayer-financed bailout of the depositors of failed savings and loans and commercial banks in recent years points out the excessively high costs. The moral hazard problems point up the fact that the cost to society of maintaining the system is substantial and that new approaches need to be found to reduce these costs.

Too Big to Fail

One result of the post-1930s regulatory administration of depository failures is known as the *too big to fail (TBTF)* policy. This relates to the action on the part of depository regulators to support large financial institutions that are experiencing financial distress in ways that are not available to smaller institutions. Generally this support includes providing special liquidity sources and guaranteeing deposits over the $100,000 insurance limit. The too large to fail policy, which such rescues imply, has been defended by those concerned about the monetary policy and international banking implications of the failure of a very large bank. They contend that the failure of a very large bank could lead to a ripple effect on many other banks. Smaller banks, on the other hand, consider the too big to fail policy inequitable, because it helps large banks to raise funds.

The rationale behind this attitude toward large institutions is similar to the general concern over the cost of bank failures. Kaufman (1989) stated his opinion in this way:

TLTF [Too Large to Fail] is frequently used by bank regulators to avoid taking actions that could put them in conflict with powerful parties who would experience large dollar losses, such as uninsured depositors and other creditors, management, owners, and even large borrowers. In addition, the regulators frequently believe that such actions would be an admission of failure not only of the bank, but also of their own agency, which is charged with bank safety and evaluated by many on its ability to achieve this condition. In using TLTF, the regulators play on the widespread public fears of the contagiousness of bank failures, that is, on fears that individual bank failures may ignite a domino or chain reaction that would tumble other "healthy" banks nationwide, other financial institutions, and possibly even nonfinancial institutions and the aggregate macroeconomy.[2]

Over the last few years, the concern with TBTF has been used to deal with the Continental Illinois National Bank in 1984, the American Savings and Loan Association of Stockton, California, in 1984, and the Bank of New England in 1991. In each of these instances, large uninsured depositors were protected, and other benefits granted to creditors, owners, and management.

The primary concern has been that the failure of a large institution will create widespread panic withdrawals leading to bank runs. The failure of each of the institutions listed above was preceded by large disruptive withdrawals. However, there is no clear evidence that allowing these banks to fail with the attendant loss to uninsured depositors and creditors would be a serious economic problem, either locally or nationally.

Analysts looking at the TBTF history have concluded that uninsured creditors probably should bear some of the costs of failure. This would improve the monitoring of these institutions and reduce moral hazard risk. In addition, others feel that regulators should use early intervention as a tool to lessen the failure risk of large institutions.

In late 1991, the FDICIA was passed and the TBTF policy altered in a significant way. The bill prohibits paying off uninsured depositors in the event of bank failure unless the Federal Reserve, FDIC, and the Treasury deem it essential to protect against the disruption of the financial system. The policy goes into effect on January 1, 1995. The FDICIA also mandates early intervention by depository regulators for weakly capitalized institutions.

Protecting Deposit Insurance Fund Solvency

A major area of public debate in the 1990s has centered around how best to avoid another failure of a deposit insurance institution. The FIRREA legislation of 1989 attacked the problem directly by permitting higher insurance premiums for both the Savings Association Insurance Fund (SAIF) and the Bank Insurance Fund (BIF). Higher premiums were

---

[2] Kaufman, George G. "Are Some Banks Too Large to Fail? Myth and Reality." Working Paper Series, Research Department, Federal Reserve Bank of Chicago. (August 1989): 1.

implemented. Many consider this solution to be counterproductive, since the higher premiums will come out of already weakened profitability of depositories. Still, higher deposit premiums continue to be used to make the insurance programs more fiscally sound. The FDICIA also included a provision allowing the BIF to borrow from the Treasury with the proviso that the insured banks repay the loan out of higher deposit premium fees.

The potentially counterproductive impact of higher deposit premiums led to the complimentary emphasis on capital adequacy and stronger examination and supervision. These were also strengthened in the FIRREA legislation. In the area of capital adequacy, the emphasis has been put on a system of risk-based capital standards. The debate over insurance coverage has produced a large number of recommendations. Many of these concepts found their way into the FDICIA, which is discussed further in Appendix 14A. These proposals include the following:

- *Risk-based Insurance Premiums:* This system relates the amount of the insurance premium to the riskiness of the assets of the institution. The FDICIA permitted adoption of the risk-based insurance premium program by July 1993.
- *Co-insurance:* This plan would require that a portion of the deposit insurance coverage would come from a private insurance company. It is felt that private firms can provide the necessary depository surveillance more effectively and efficiently than the government. The FDICIA also permits the FDIC to implement a reinsurance coverage plan that, while not technically a co-insurance program, could make private resources available for deposit insurance.
- *Lower Deposit Coverage:* This proposal involves lowering the maximum deposit insurance coverage to below the current $100,000 per account, or putting a limit on coverage covering all accounts of a household regardless of how many institutions the funds are invested in.
- *Greater Disclosure:* This plan calls for greater disclosure of the financial position of the insured institution. The FDICIA mandated independent audits for more institutions and greater disclosure of the market values of assets and liabilities and contingent assets and liabilities.
- *Prohibiting Use of Brokered Deposits:* This proposal stems from the belief that financial depositories are able to grow excessively by distributing insured deposits through security brokers. Since many failed thrifts used brokered deposits, there are those who would prohibit their use. The FDICIA restricted the use of brokered insured deposits by denying this source of funding for all but the highest capitalized institutions.

- *Early Intervention:* The FDICIA also increased the role of capital and other measures of commercial bank financial soundness as criteria for regulatory intervention. The act directed the bank regulators to establish a program of five capital levels that, combined with other criteria such as bank earnings, would be used to determine the level of regulatory oversight and intervention. This gives regulators additional powerful leverage to effect change in weak financial institutions.

Constraints to Competition to Ensure Financial Soundness

Over the years, Congress and regulators of depositories have used a variety of means to protect the value of depository charters and thus reduce the chance of institutional failure. Some of the most notable examples of government efforts to limit the degree of competition among financial institutions since the 1930s include the following:

1. Glass-Steagall prohibitions on letting commercial banks underwrite securities
2. Prohibitions on allowing commercial banks to sell insurance
3. McFadden prohibitions on interstate banking
4. Use of price controls such as Regulation Q to ensure that depositories do not take excessive risks and pay excessive deposit rates
5. Maintaining a monopoly of transaction deposit services for commercial banks
6. Price controls on stock and bond brokerage rates

While most of these efforts to control the degree of competition have been rejected and modified since the mid-1960s, some still remain.

Many academicians have pointed out that entry barriers and other constraints to competition led to the development of near substitutes. The competition for savings accounts represented by money market mutual funds are pointed to as an example. Indeed, out-of-state loan production offices, nonbank financial institutions providing bank services, off-shore offices, and a host of technological systems that provide nationwide bank type services have effectively eliminated any institutional value of many of these competitive restrictions.

Despite the loss of most protective constraints to free and open competition among financial intermediaries, a few notable examples remain. Removing or liberalizing Glass-Steagall, McFadden, and prohibitions on insurance sales by banks were all actively debated and rejected in 1991 by Congress as it developed its FDICIA. The concern was that additional competition could weaken commercial bank and insurance companies just as deregulation was said to contribute to the S&L failures.

As the 1990s unfold, the debate will continue over whether higher capital requirements and stronger regulation or greater freedom to compete and earn a profit is ultimately the best financial protection of our deposit insurance system. This is the basic question: In an effort to ensure that no bank fails, will we develop a system in which banks cannot make a decent return for their shareholders?

How the Regulatory Process Works

In addition to the generalized theory of why regulation is needed, several theories about how the regulatory process actually works have been developed. George Stigler's special interest theory and Edward Kane's dialectical theory of regulation are two that draw the most interest.

Stigler Special Interest Theory

George Stigler's special interest theory of regulation grew out of the public good theory and his observation that, once the government acted to correct an alleged market deficiency, the regulatory body that was established to maintain ongoing supervision often became captured by the group it was set up to regulate. Stigler noted that the regulated group had more interest in the activities of the regulator than other groups. Therefore, this affected group would position itself to present its case more frequently and persuasively. He also noted that many times the staff of the regulatory agency went to work for firms within the regulated industry, or alternatively, individuals within the industry went to work for the regulator.

Some observers allege that the thrift crisis was exacerbated by the long-standing relationship between former FHLBB members and staff and the saving and loan industry and its trade associations. The regulated industry obtained undue influence over its own regulation. Many of the former presidentially appointed members of the FHLBB went to work for the industry after leaving the agency. For these reasons, among others, the agency was accused of being unable to be objective in protecting the public good.

Kane Dialectical Theory of Regulation

Edward Kane viewed the regulatory process as a *dialectical process* wherein society identifies a market failure and makes arguments to obtain regulation. The affected industry then responds by avoidance or innovating in such a way as to make the regulation ineffective, or presents counterarguments to weaken the impact of the regulation. This sets up a process of regulation and response followed by another regulation, and so forth.

Over the last few years, depository institutions have responded to higher capital requirements by developing off-balance sheet financing techniques designed to circumvent the new capital requirement. These innovations have resulted in another round of modifications to the regulatory capital requirements designed to strengthen them as a response to the regulated firms' actions.

Regulatory Procedures

Although the process of regulation is handled a bit differently by each regulatory agency, the primary activities are comparable. Regulation of financial firms involves *compliance examination* and *safety and soundness examination*.

Compliance examination relates to how well the regulated firm performs the many duties associated with its socially mandated responsibilities. Compliance examinations cover truth-in-lending disclosure, disclosure of real estate lending for the Home Mortgage Disclosure Act, and all the other compliance requirements imposed by law and regulation.

Safety and soundness examination considers the institution as an operating concern and attempts to determine the risk of failure. Safety and soundness examinations utilize various reports that are designed by the regulatory agencies and submitted on a monthly, quarterly, or annual basis. These reports include information that may not be reported by publicly held companies. In addition, examiners have access to all accounting information maintained by the firm and its independent accountants. For publicly held firms, the examiners can look at how the securities of the firm are trading. The market value of the firm relative to its book value and that of competing firms is a very good indicator of possible failure.

The examination process relies most heavily on an on-site review. It is during this review that the examination personnel have access to all information in the firm, including accounting, loan documentation, loan delinquency and loss experience, appraisals, and management committee and board of director minutes. The examination staff will meet with employees, management, and the board of directors if they deem it necessary. They are particularly interested in investment policies and procedures, the extent to which the board of directors monitors the actions of management, and the company's capital adequacy.

If the examination process uncovers conditions that are determined to be unsafe or unsound, examination personnel may use a number of means to interfere with the activities of the firm. They may issue cease and desist orders to stop an unsafe and unsound activity, remove management, limit growth, stop dividends, or request additional capital. The FIRREA and FDICIA dramatically increased the authority of the bank and savings and loan regulators and increased the penalties that can be assessed to management and directors of firms that do not operate within the scope of the laws and regulations.

Over the last decade, the regulatory process has increasingly focused on capital adequacy as the primary tool to ensure safety and soundness. Regulators have devoted considerable time and effort to improving their understanding of how capital should be measured, the impact of off-balance-sheet risks, the proper way to measure interest rate risk, and the problems relating to reliance on accounting data alone to measure capital.

Like financial depositories, life insurance companies have important fiduciary responsibilities. Consequently, a substantial amount of the regulatory requirements concerning life companies involve solvency. Financial requirements, asset restrictions, and capital regulations relate to the desire to avoid insurance company failure. This aspect of solvency also relates to ensuring that premiums are kept high enough so that the insurers are not threatened by insolvency. Regulation is designed to ensure that premiums are not charged at levels that are unreasonable. However, defining what is reasonable is at best difficult.

Regulators' Impact on Financial Performance and Operations

There are several very important reasons why the manager of a financial institution is concerned about regulation. The regulators of most financial institutions have broad and usually far-reaching authority that greatly influences decision making and financial performance of regulated firms. Indeed, the shareholders of a regulated firm sometimes find that the regulatory environment in which the firm is operating may have more to do with the firm's performance than the efforts of management.

Regulators impact the institution in the following ways:

1. By establishing and defining equity requirements and other financial performance requirements for the firm
2. By interpreting the firm's charter with respect to such important decisions as allowable investments, liabilities, and various other transactions
3. By determining the indirect and direct costs of examination and supervision
4. By interpreting how the firm should respond operationally to legislation, such as the Community Reinvestment Act, which in turn, will impact the firm's cost structure
5. By rejecting management, directors, and controlling shareholders
6. By authorizing acquisitions and mergers and, thereby, impacting the competitive market structure the firm faces
7. By restricting a host of business transactions

In Chapter 7 the financial claim/function matrix was introduced. It was shown that financial institutions must determine which claims and functions to perform based on laws, regulations, and institutional strategy. Federal and state chartering laws apply the most significant constraints on the asset and liability activities of financial firms. Regulators, however, are charged with implementing the laws that Congress and the state legislatures pass. These laws and regulations have resulted in dramatic changes in the types of financial claims and markets intermediaries participate in and the functions they perform.

Financial Institution Regulators and Insurers

There is no easy way to describe the regulatory structure for the financial institutions in this country. The U.S. regulatory system is complex and intrusive. Virtually all financial institutions have some regulation, even if they may be fortunate enough to have no specific regulator.

Mortgage banking companies, for example, do not have a specific regulator, but they do have to conform to regulatory requirements relating to mortgages they originate that are insured by the FHA or to requirements imposed on them by the GNMA, if they happen to service mortgages guaranteed by GNMA.

Structure of the Regulatory System

The structure of financial institution regulation is really the product of two historic political forces: (1) the desire to preserve the role of the states in the regulatory and chartering process; and (2) the desire to maintain separate identities for our system of specialized financial institutions, such as savings and loans and credit unions.

As a result, we have a regulatory and insurance system that includes three deposit insurance funds, an insurance fund for assets held in brokerage accounts, and a guarantor for pension benefits. The system also includes insurance, commercial bank, and thrift regulators in all fifty states, five federal commercial bank and thrift regulatory groups, a regulator for pension funds, one for futures trading, and another that regulates securities firms that has overlapping jurisdiction for all publicly held stock financial companies.

Primary Regulators and Insurers

Table 14.2 provides an overview of each of the regulatory and insurance agencies and some of the firms and organizations they regulate and insure.

A brief description of each of the major regulatory agencies will help to explain their roles, responsibilities, and jurisdiction.

Table 14.2

Major Regulatory and Insurance Agencies Both Federal and State

Regulated Organization	Regulators and Insurers
Commercial banks	Federal Reserve System
	Federal Deposit Insurance Corporation
	Bank Insurance Fund
	Comptroller of the Currency
	State Banking Commissions
Thrift institutions (savings and loans, mutual savings banks, and credit unions)	Federal Deposit Insurance Corporation
	Office of Thrift Supervision
	Savings Association Insurance Fund
	State thrift regulators
	National Credit Union Administration
	National Credit Union Share Insurance Fund
Life insurance companies	State Insurance Commissions
Private pension funds	Department of Labor
	Pension Benefit Guarantee Corporation
Security firms (investment bankers)	Security and Exchange Commission
	Security Investor Protection Corporation
Commodity futures brokerage	Commodity Futures Trading Commission
Mutual funds	Security and Exchange Commission
Mortgage bankers	Department of Housing and Urban Development
	Federal Housing Administration
	Government National Mortgage Administration
	Veterans Administration
Publicly held institutions	Security and Exchange Commission

Office of the Comptroller of the Currency

The Office of the Comptroller of the Currency (OCC) is the oldest bank regulator. It was formed in 1863 to charter and supervise federally chartered commercial banks. This office is responsible to the Treasury department. The comptroller's office is responsible for chartering, examining, and merger and branching approvals for national banks. National banks that are owned by holding companies are also subject to Federal Reserve regulation.

Federal Reserve System

The Federal Reserve System, created in 1913, has responsibility for commercial bank holding companies. It is responsible for establishing reserve requirements for all depositories, and for overseeing the nation's payment system. The Federal Reserve also is responsible for the promulgation of many regulations that impact all depositories, such as truth-in-lending, home mortgage disclosure, and other regulations designed to protect the public. In addition, the FDICIA of 1991 expanded the regulatory powers of the Fed over foreign banks operating in the United States.

Legal and Ethical Issues

Bank of Credit and Commerce International: Money Laundering and International Influence Peddling

Few financial scandals cross borders. Even fewer involve allegations of misdeeds and influence peddling in over 70 countries around the world. The exception was the scandal involving the Bank of Credit and Commerce International (BCCI). BCCI was a large bank holding company headquartered in Luxembourg with approximately $20 billion in assets and 400 branches worldwide. Formed in 1972, the bank expanded out of its original market in the Middle East into Eastern Asia, the Caribbean, Africa, and the subcontinent of Asia. It was accused in 1991 of illegally acquiring controlling interest in several U.S. financial institutions and of unrecorded deposits with the Bank of England.

Within a few weeks, allegations of money laundering and influence peddling worldwide began to circulate. Representatives of BCCI were accused of using political influence to obtain favorable concessions for banking activities in Zimbabwe, China, Hong Kong, and the United Arab Emirates, among others. In the United States, BCCI-controlled financial institutions were investigated for political influence peddling. An affiliate of BCCI was indicted for money laundering in Florida and pleaded guilty, leading to the closing of a number of BCCI offices in the United States. BCCI was also found to secretly control a U.S. bank run by two individuals with considerable political influence.

The BCCI experience raised major questions worldwide about the structure of examination and supervision needed to control financial institutions operating worldwide. The Federal Reserve obtained additional supervisory authority over foreign banks operating in the United States. This additional authority was granted by the FDICIA. The Federal Reserve has also called for the development of stronger international agreements for bank regulation and financial reporting.

Federal Deposit Insurance Corporation

The FIRREA substantially increased the authority of the FDIC. Until the passage of this act, the agency had responsibility for the examination of all banks and thrifts (primarily state-chartered mutual savings banks) that were insured by the FDIC insurance fund.

In 1989, Congress, alarmed by the thrift debacle and the role played by the primary thrift regulator, the Federal Home Loan Bank Board (FHLBB), extinguished the FHLBB and eliminated the separate insurance fund, the FSLIC. Congress gave expanded powers to the FDIC and established a new insurance fund, the Savings Association Insurance Fund, which is managed by the FDIC. A new insurance fund, the Bank Insurance Fund, was also created from the old FDIC insurance fund. This new fund is also supervised by the FDIC. The FDIC also was given the responsibility for managing the newly FIRREA-created Resolution Trust Corporation. The RTC will be discussed more fully in Appendix A.

State Banking and Thrift Regulators

Each state has an agency or group of agencies responsible for commercial bank and state-chartered thrift regulation. In most cases, however, the states share the examination and supervision responsibilities with federal agencies. State-chartered banks that are insured by the BIF are also subject to FDIC regulation and examination. State chartered banks that are owned by holding companies are also regulated by the Federal Reserve. The Federal Reserve also establishes reserve requirements for all state banks. Federal and state regulators also oversee state-chartered thrift institutions that are insured by the SAIF.

Office of Thrift Supervision

The *Office of Thrift Supervision (OTS),* the youngest of the federal regulatory institutions, charters all federal savings and loans and federally chartered savings banks and supervises SAIF-insured thrifts and thrift holding companies. It was created by the FIRREA in 1989 as a replacement for the FHLBB. The OTS is not an independent agency like its predecessor the FHLBB, but is a department within the Treasury department like the OCC.

There is a debate as to whether the OTS should remain a separate agency, given the expanded role and responsibilities of the FDIC. Some would like to have the OTS eliminated.

National Credit Union Administration

The National Credit Union Administration (NCUA) is the principal regulatory agency for federally chartered and National Credit Union Share Insurance Fund (NCUSIF) insured credit unions. Approximately 60 percent of all credit unions have federal charters and are regulated by the NCUA. In addition, approximately 60 percent of the remaining state-chartered credit unions are members of the NCUSIF insurance fund and thus become subject to NCUA regulation and supervision.

Department of Labor

Private uninsured pension funds were largely unregulated until 1974, when Congress passed the Employee Retirement Income Security Act (ERISA). This legislation established minimum vesting, funding, and fiduciary standards for private pension funds. ERISA also created the Pension Benefit Guarantee Corporation (PBGC), which guarantees the benefits of insured and uninsured pension funds.

The Department of Labor is responsible for implementing ERISA requirements. Its primary provisions include the following:

1. Fiduciary standards covering asset managers, trustees, and advisors
2. Vesting requirements, which relate to the schedule used to establish an employee's right to benefits
3. Reporting and disclosure requirements to ensure timely information to plan participants and financial information to the Department of Labor
4. Portability provisions to permit vested employees changing jobs to roll over the funds into a new plan or into a self-administered individual retirement account
5. Funding standards, which establish minimum levels to ensure adequate funding for current and past participants
6. Plan termination insurance through the PBGC

Commodity Futures Trading Commission

The Commodity Futures Trading Commission (CFTC) was established in 1974 to centralize the federal government's regulation and supervision of futures markets. The purpose of the CFTC is to monitor for any potential manipulative behavior in the trading of various futures contracts. The CFTC must also ensure that new contracts serve an economically justifiable purpose and enforce exchange rules, audit brokerage firms, and clearing associations. The commission also investigates violations of laws and regulations.

Securities and Exchange Commission

The SEC was established in 1934 and acts as an independent bipartisan administrative agency. The broad mandate of the commission is illustrated in the following list of SEC administrative requirements and provisions relating to the many laws passed since 1933:

- Requirements that public offerings of securities include an SEC approved registration statement setting forth certain required information
- Provisions against false and misleading disclosures by public institutions
- Maintenance of reporting requirements of firms listed on particular national exchanges
- Provisions governing the solicitation of proxies for holders of securities
- Provisions governing the disclosure of information when control of a company is sought through a cash tender offer and for other stock acquisitions
- Provisions that stockholders are provided information on insider trading activities
- Requirements for the registration of security exchanges, security associations, brokers and dealers, and municipal security dealers
- Provisions for regulation of options on any securities and security indices

State Insurance Commissions

Insurance companies are not regulated by the federal government because of the *McCarran-Ferguson Act of 1945*. As a result of this legislation, the federal government exempted insurance companies from federal antitrust laws as long as they were regulated by the states. Publicly held companies must adhere to SEC requirements, and life companies involved in the investment of pension fund assets are subject to Department of Labor ERISA requirements.

Although insurance companies are regulated by their state of domicile, there is considerable coordination between the various state insurance commissions. These commissions have established the *National Association of Insurance Commissioners (NAIC)* to coordinate their actions and share information. In 1991, this body adopted a standard that limited the holdings of junk bonds to 20 percent of a life company's assets. The NAIC has also developed a new minimum standard from policy reserves based on the risk profile of each company.

Most states also provide protection of policyholders through state-run insurance guarantee funds. These are funded by the life companies that are licensed to sell policies in the state. Most of these funds, however, have limited resources in relation to the size of the companies whose policyholders they guarantee.

State insurance regulations define what kinds of assets an insurance company may invest in, and also how each asset is to be treated in terms of valuation. They also establish the minimum level of reserves needed to meet the obligations of policyholders. The states also regulate the reporting and accounting methods used by insurance companies.

Securities Investor Protection Corporation

The *Securities Investor Protection Corporation (SIPC)* was established in 1970 by Congress. Although not a regulator, SIPC insures most accounts in brokerage firms up to $500,000, including up to $100,000 in cash. Accounts at each brokerage firm are insured separately, and it is possible to achieve higher coverage using separate joint accounts and trust accounts.

The resources of the SIPC come from a fund that approximated $400 million at year-end 1989. It was developed out of assessments paid by member brokerage firms registered with the SEC. The agency also has a line of credit of $500 million from a group of commercial banks and, as a last resort, a $1 billion line of credit with the U.S. Treasury.

If a brokerage firm fails, the SIPC freezes all accounts and goes to court to have a trustee appointed. The trustee then tries to get another brokerage firm to assume the accounts. If such a firm cannot be found, the trustee processes the claims individually.

Department of Housing and Urban Development

For those financial institutions involved in the secondary mortgage market, such as savings and loans, commercial banks, and mortgage banking companies, the Department of Housing and Urban Development (HUD) has certain authority over them. HUD implements the FHA-insured mortgage programs and is also the manager of the GNMA. HUD establishes minimum capital requirements for servicers of mortgages as well as certain standards for servicing FHA loans and loans guaranteed for GNMA. GNMA also has certain standards that must be met by institutions that create securities guaranteed by GNMA.

Pension Benefit Guarantee Corporation

The *Pension Benefit Guarantee Corporation (PBGC)* is an insurer of employee assets in private pension funds. It was created by the Employee Retirement Income Act of 1974.

PBGC is not a regulator; the regulation in this area is carried out by the Department of Labor. The PBGC is financed by premium payments levied against private pension plans. The premiums are used to establish a fund to ensure that a minimum level of retirement payments can be paid even if a pension plan sponsor were to go bankrupt.

Chapter 14 Financial Institution Regulation, Insurers, and Regulators   373

Summary

Regulation is a fundamental feature of our financial system. On the one hand, it serves as a public policy tool to achieve certain social goals and objectives. On the other, it serves as a constraint and intruder into the planning and day-to-day operations of regulated financial institutions. Regulation may help firms by restricting competition in their markets or hurt firms by restricting them from pursuing profitable investment alternatives and requiring higher levels of stockholder investment. It also results in a major cost burden for compliance.

The **primary public policy goals** of financial regulation include the following:

1. Achieving adequate competition in our financial markets
2. Reducing imperfect information
3. Eliminating prejudice or bias in supply
4. Achieving equal access
5. Improving implementation of monetary policy
6. Pursuing socially desirable credit allocation
7. Reducing potential for insider abuse and fraud
8. Reducing potentially disruptive impacts of financial institution failures
9. Protecting taxpayers from deposit insurance fund failures

The **deposit insurance system** creates three moral hazards. First, insured depositors are not concerned about depositing in weak institutions. Second, management and owners of insured firms are willing to maximize business and financial risks on the basis that the cost of capital will not be affected by rising agency and distress costs. Third, regulators attempt to delay closing failed institutions until their successor is appointed to avoid being held responsible for the failure.

Two theories of how the regulatory process actually works have been developed by **George Stigler** and **Edward Kane.** Stigler observes that after a time the regulator develops a symbiotic relationship with the organizations being regulated. This results in the regulated industry achieving undo influence on the regulator's decisions. Kane sees regulation in financial services as a dialectical process in which regulations bring industry avoidance efforts and innovation to reduce the impact of the regulation. This is followed by another regulation and so forth.

The regulatory process consists of **compliance examinations** and **safety and soundness examinations.**

Regulators have very significant **impacts on the management** of financial institutions. The most important include the following:

1. Establishing capital requirements
2. Implementing laws covering assets, liability, and service powers

3. Affecting operating costs through examination and supervision
4. Determining the burden of compliance legislation
5. Disapproving management, directors, and controlling shareholders
6. Approving mergers, acquisitions, and consolidations

The **primary depository financial institutions regulators** are the Comptroller of the Currency, Federal Reserve Board, FDIC, OTS, NCUA, and state bank and thrift regulators. **Nondepository regulators** are the state insurance commissioners, Department of Labor, SEC, HUD, and CFTC.

The federal government also sponsors **insurance corporations** that include SAIF and BIF, which are supervised by the FDIC, the NCUSIF, the SIPC, and PBGC. States also insure **life insurance companies** through state insurance guarantee funds.

Questions

Chapter 14

1. What is meant by the public good theory of regulation?
2. Explain several points of rationale for regulation.
3. Explain the Stigler special interest theory of regulation and the Kane dialectical theory of regulation.
4. How is imperfect information used as a justification for regulation? Give several examples.
5. What is meant by an imperfect market structure? Give several examples.
6. How does prejudice relate to regulation?
7. What concerns do the monetary authorities have with respect to financial regulation?
8. What are the primary public policy goals concerning financial regulation? Which do you consider to be the most important?
9. Why is safety and soundness such a concern for financial regulators?
10. How is regulation used to affect credit allocation?
11. What is meant by the phrase *too big to fail?* Do you feel that financial regulators should attempt to provide special assistance to the depositors, creditors, and shareholders of very large institutions?
12. What is deposit insurance? Explain several recommendations designed to reduce the potential for deposit insurer losses.
13. How have competitive constraints reduced the potential for deposit insurer loss?
14. As a consumer, what is the most important aspect of life insurance company regulation?
15. What are the two primary activities that regulators engage in with respect to carrying out regulatory functions?
16. What are the major impacts of regulation on financial institutions?

Chapter 14 Financial Institution Regulation, Insurers, and Regulators

17. What problems were made obvious in the failure of BCCI?
18. How do regulators impact the operations and day-to-day activities of regulated financial institutions? Give several examples of actions that regulators have taken in recent years.
19. What are some of the problems in regulating international financial firms?
20. There are now insurance programs for accounts held in security firms, the Security Investor Protection Corporation, and for pension obligations of individuals, the Pension Benefit Guarantee Corporation. What problems does this present? How do these problems compare to the problems experienced in our deposit insurance programs?

A

The Financial Institutions Reform, Recovery, and Enforcement Act of 1989: A Case Study in Regulatory Retribution

appendix

The Financial Institutions Reform, Recovery, and Enforcement Act of 1989 was passed in response to growing evidence in the mid-1980s that there would be insufficient resources in the FSLIC to handle the costs of failed savings and loans. The events that led to the passage of the FIRREA provide an excellent example of the potential for regulation to create valuable financial institution charters and, in the case of the savings and loans, eliminate much of that value.

The legislation was passed in a highly charged emotional atmosphere. The eventual size of the FSLIC failure had grown, based on regulatory estimates, from approximately $10 billion in 1985 to over $50 billion in early 1989. By 1992, the estimates of the government's RTC had grown to as high as $180 billion.

Failure Due in Large Part to Early Economic Policies

Most of the failures were related to the substantial operating losses and erosion of capital that occurred in the late 1970s and early 1980s. These losses were due to the combined impact of tight monetary policy and resultant high interest rates, combined with the deregulation of interest rates on savings accounts. By the early 1980s, the tangible capital base of the industry was largely depleted.

The thrift industry prior to the late 1970s had performed very well. For most of the 1950s through the 1970s the thrifts were the fastest growing financial institutions. Their prosperity was primarily the result of a beneficial regulatory climate. The thrifts were allowed to leverage their capital resources much more than commercial banks due to a policy of regulatory forbearance. They had favorable access to low-cost credit advances from the FHLBs. Finally, when high interest rates threatened them in the 1960s, they were brought under savings rate controls,

Regulation Q, to protect them from having to pay high interest rates on their deposits. Moreover, Regulation Q was administered so that thrifts could always pay higher interest rates than their competitors, the commercial banks.

Unfortunately, these price controls stopped being effective during the rapidly rising interest rates of the late 1970s, and the thrifts were caught in a deregulation atmosphere holding a large percentage of their assets in low-yielding fixed-rate mortgages. It was in this environment that the thrift debacle of the 1980s took place.

During the 1980s, many examples of inadequate regulatory supervision and lax behavior fueled the emotional nature of the Congressional debate concerning what to do to the thrifts. Everyone wanted to know who was responsible. Moreover, a few of the failures were related to fraud and incompetent behavior on the part of a number of flamboyant thrift executives, whose actions and life-styles were not considered appropriate in a tightly regulated industry that benefitted from government guaranteed deposits.

Adding insult to injury, a number of representatives and senators were accused of applying pressure on federal regulators so that a number of the weak thrifts could be allowed to continue operating. Before the legislative process ran its course, virtually everyone connected with the business was singled out as a contributor to the costly *bailout,* as it was termed.

Finding the Scapegoat(s)

Industry representatives were accused of fraudulent and incompetent behavior. Regulators were accused of lax regulation and implementing forebearance policies that exacerbated the problem. Elected officials were accused of applying political pressure that served to prolong the improper activities of a few in the business. The thrift trade associations were accused of minimizing the severity of the problem and promoting policies that eventually increased the cost of the solution. Finally, the Reagan administration was accused of ignoring the problem until after the 1988 election.

The widespread media coverage of the events made it difficult for the legislative process to resolve this problem unemotionally. It became clear early in the deliberations that the causes of the crisis were too complicated for the average American to understand. The causes related to a number of regulatory and economic stabilization policies that were implemented over a period of several decades. It became difficult for the media to focus on these causes when the blame could be placed so easily and more colorfully on a few industry members, regulators, and politicians.

Congress Reregulates and Weakens the Thrift Charter

The process of resolving these problems resulted in a major reregulation of the S&Ls without much attention being given to the eventual implications of what narrowing the charter powers and authorities would mean to the industry and its insurer. Public opinion, shaped in large part by the press, convinced most elected officials that a balanced response was not called for, given the large and growing costs of liquidating a large portion of the industry. Consequently, the impact of FIRREA will be felt for many years. It will also contribute to the failure and poor financial performance of many additional thrifts into the foreseeable future.

FIRREA will have the following impact on the formerly FSLIC-insured institutions. First, their asset powers will be greatly reduced, as they are forced to concentrate a greater percentage of their investment activities in residential real estate and mortgage investments.

Second, the cost of their operations will be increased as the cost of deposit insurance premiums increases, while the dividends on their holdings of FHLB stock are reduced. This will occur since a portion of the FHLB earnings will be used to fund low-income housing programs and help pay for the bailout. They will also face a substantial increase in their examination and supervision costs.

Major Provisions Impacting Thrifts

The major provisions of the FIRREA that impact on thrifts relate to insurance of accounts, powers of thrifts, and regulatory structure.

Insurance of Accounts

The act changed the insurance of accounts for both FSLIC-insured and FDIC-insured institutions by creating a new insurance fund for FSLIC-insured institutions. This new fund is called the Savings Association Insurance Fund. The SAIF is administered by the FDIC rather than the FHLBB, which was abolished by the act. The FDIC insurance fund is renamed the Bank Insurance Fund and continues to be administered by the FDIC.

Of great importance, however, is that the cost of the insurance has changed for both SAIF- and BIF-insured institutions. In 1991, the cost of deposit insurance premiums was 23 basis points (bp) per annum for both commercial banks and S&Ls. This was up from 12 bp for commercial banks and 20.8 bp for S&Ls in 1990.

Powers of Thrifts

The asset investment powers of thrifts were substantially reduced in a number of ways by the legislation. This was accomplished by eliminating or reducing certain powers, and by redefining the *qualified thrift lender test (QTLT)*. The QTLT defines the percentage of a thrift's assets that must be invested in specified types of qualifying assets.

The more restrictive the QTLT, the less flexibility the thrift has in its investment strategy. The following are some of the changes made to this asset test:

- Nonresidential real estate lending is to be limited to 400 percent of the institution's capital.

- High-yield bonds have been deleted from the 10 percent commercial business loan authority for federally chartered thrifts, and all existing bonds must be divested of within five years of enactment.
- Limits on loans to one borrower have been tightened to that which applies to national banks. Generally, this is 15 percent of unimpaired capital and surplus, and an additional 10 percent if it is secured by readily marketable collateral.
- The QTLT has been made more restrictive. Essentially, the new test includes the following as qualified assets:

1. Loans and securities collateralized by residential mortgages
2. Obligations of the FSLIC and FDIC
3. A limit of 15 percent in a basket that includes personal, family, and educational purpose loans, 50 percent of loans made and sold within 90 days, and 200 percent of loans on low-income housing, churches, and nursing homes

By July 1, 1991, a new QTLT will be in effect at 70 percent of assets in qualifying loans and investments. The impact of the new test will be to reduce the asset powers of thrifts.[1]

Regulatory Structure

This FIRREA completely alters the regulatory structure relating to thrifts, since the FHLBB is eliminated. The Board's historical activities were to insure the deposits of FSLIC-insured institutions, to promote the activities of thrifts, and to advance thrifts funds through the FHLBs.

These three functions will now be performed by three new agencies. First, the new Office of Thrift Supervision will supervise, regulate, and charter federally chartered institutions. Next, a new Finance Board has been created to monitor the activities of the FHLBs. The act permits nonmember institutions to join the banks and obtain advances. Finally, the FDIC will be responsible for administering the SAIF and BIF.

Major Act Provisions Impacting Industry Structure

The FIRREA has a number of significant provisions that relate to the future structure of our nation's depositories. These provisions relate to the conversion of thrifts into banks and the acquisition of thrifts by banks.

---

[1] The QTLT was made less restrictive in 1991 by the FDICIA. The QTLT percentage was lowered to 65 percent. See also Appendix B.

Conversion of Thrifts into Commercial Banks

The act does not permit conversions of institutions from the SAIF to the BIF before August 10, 1994, except under special circumstances. Conversions before this date can only occur if they involve a conversion of less than 35 percent of a member's assets, or if the conversion assists a member in default, or in danger of default, and the loss to the insurance fund would be less through the conversion than through the default. Exit fees to the SAIF and entry fees into the BIF will be required if conversion takes place prior to 1997.

Commercial Bank Acquisitions of Thrifts

At any time, a bank holding company can merge or consolidate a thrift subsidiary with a bank subsidiary, if it receives approval. Certain asset and capital requirements must be met. SAIF deposits in a bank subsidiary will be subject to SAIF premiums.

The acquisition provisions suggest that public policy will encourage the acquisition of thrifts by banks, while discouraging the acquisition of banks by thrifts. Later in the decade they also will permit the shifting of SAIF-insured thrifts into the BIF. Both of these provisions will work overtime to reduce the importance of the thrift industry as a factor in our financial system.

Resolution Trust Corporation

The *Resolution Trust Corporation (RTC)* was established by Congress in the fall of 1989. The purpose of this corporation is to manage and sell the assets of failed S&Ls insured by the former FSLIC. The RTC was also charged with managing the assets of the Federal Asset Disposition Association, which was established earlier to manage the sale of failed S&Ls. From its inception in August 1989 until April 1992, the RTC has assumed control of 690 institutions with assets at the time of takeover totaling $358.3 billion. By April 1992, the assets of the institutions still controlled by the RTC had shrunk to $114.5 billion as a result of resolutions and asset sales and payoffs. The RTC manages these institutions as conservatorships upon assuming control, and then as receiverships when sale or liquidation occurs. The assets of these institutions consist primarily of cash, securities, and mortgages that represent 76 percent of the total.

The RTC finances its operations primarily from public funds. Table A14.1 shows the sources and uses of funds from the RTC from its inception through April 1, 1992. The vast majority of these funds will be used to fund the losses sustained in the sale and liquidation of failed S&Ls.

The majority of the RTC's funds come from Treasury appropriations. The twelve FHLBs contributed $1.2 billion as a requirement under FIRREA. The RTC also borrows using the Federal Financing Bank (FFB) and has assumed the obligations of the REFCORP, which was a forerunner of the RTC.

The RTC is one of the largest managers of financial and real estate assets in the United States. It used over 181 independent contractors to manage approximately

Table A14.1

**Resolution Trust Corporation
Sources and Uses of Funds
Until April 1, 1992**
(dollars in billions)

Sources

Initial Treasury appropriations	$18.8
Additional appropriations	55.0
FHLB contributions	1.2
REFCORP borrowings	30.1
FFB borrowings	56.9
Total External Sources	**$162.0**
Recoveries from receiverships	51.8
Total Sources	**$213.8**

Uses

Resolutions and receivership funding	$180.1
Conservatorship advances	3.8
FFB interest	5.3
Other disbursements	−0.2
Total Uses	**$189.3**
Net Cash Available	**$24.6**

Source: *RTC Review*. Vol. II, No. 5 May 1992.

$35 billion of assets as of April 1992. The RTC has been a major seller of assets in all the markets that S&Ls lent. It completed disposition of 640 institutions through April 1992. Most of these were through the purchase and assumption of the failed institution's deposit liabilities and a certain amount of assets. The others were resolved by the RTC contracting with other institutions to pay off depositors or by paying off depositors directly. Commercial banks were the acquiring institutions in 70 percent of the cases.

Because of its sheer size, the RTC has been the subject of considerable criticism and public scrutiny. It is organized in an unusual manner. It has an *Oversight Board* made up of the Chairman of the Federal Reserve Board and Secretaries of the Treasury and HUD. The Chairman of the RTC is the Chairman of the FDIC. This cumbersome structure has resulted in frequent accusations that the RTC is excessively bureaucratic.

B

Major Provisions of the Federal Deposit Insurance Corporation Improvement Act of 1991

appendix

The Federal Deposit Insurance Corporation Improvement Act of 1991 (FDICIA) was passed in the wake of new revelations about potential large failures of commercial banks and inadequate BIF resources. Bank reform measures, such as allowing interstate banking, reducing Glass-Steagall restrictions, and permitting commercial banks to sell insurance, were all debated in 1991. The support for these reform proposals, however, gave way to growing concerns about the financial soundness of the BIF and the potential for another taxpayer bailout similar to the thrift debacle.

As a result, Congress passed a bill that rejected the reform proposals in favor of a narrow bill designed to increase financial resources for the FDIC and BIF and increase examination and supervisory authorities. The bill provides for the first Congressionally mandated supervisory responses to financial institutions with low capital levels. Congress also used the bill to increase consumer disclosures and other protections.

Safety and Soundness Reforms

The FDICIA provided additional resources for the BIF to handle commercial bank failures. The line-of-credit of the FDIC on the Treasury was increased from $5 billion to $30 billion. Any loans taken down would have to be repaid over a 15 year period using assessment charges against BIF-insured institutions.

The FDICIA provided for supervisory reforms that required all insured depository institutions, with a few exceptions, to receive on-site examinations at least once a year. The act also required all institutions over $150 million in assets to provide their regulator with audited financial statements prepared by an independent accounting firm. Finally, the act required accounting reforms including the preparation of all financial statements consistent with Generally Accepted Accounting Principles, a method for valuing contingent assets and liabilities, and a disclosure requiring a market value accounting for the values of assets and liabilities.

Regulatory Powers for Dealing with Undercapitalized Depositories

Probably the most significant provisions of the FDICIA as it relates to the powers of depository regulators concerns the statute's requirements for regulators to deal with weakly capitalized insured institutions. Depository regulators classify depositories under the following five categories:

1. *Well capitalized:* An institution that significantly exceeds the required capital level for each capital standard
2. *Adequately capitalized:* An institution that meets the required minimum level of capital for each capital standard
3. *Undercapitalized:* An institution that fails to meet the required capital standards
4. *Significantly undercapitalized:* An institution that is significantly below the required capital standards
5. *Critically undercapitalized:* An institution that fails to meet the regulator's critical capital standard, which must be no less than 2 percent tangible equity and 65 percent of the permitted leverage limit (total assets divided by equity)

For the last three capital classifications the FDICIA spells out requirements that the depositories must meet. These are briefly discussed in Table A14.2.

Table A14.2

Minimum Restrictions Imposed on Undercapitalized Depositories by the FDICIA

Capital Classification	Permitted or Required Regulatory Actions or Restrictions
Undercapitalized and significantly undercapitalized	Must submit a capital restoration plan. Controlling companies of the depository must guarantee compliance with the plan or accept financial liability up to 5 percent of the insured's assets. Is prohibited from acquisitions, opening or purchasing new branches, and engaging in new businesses.

Table A14.2 is continued on page 384.

Table A14.2 continued

Minimum Restrictions Imposed on Undercapitalized Depositories by the FDICIA

Capital Classification	Permitted or Required Regulatory Actions or Restrictions
Undercapitalized and failing to meet capital plan goals	May have to sell shares or obligations to raise capital.
	May be required to have their institution acquired or merged with another.
	May have transactions with affiliates restricted.
	May have growth or other activities restricted.
	May have directors and officers removed.
	May have deposits from correspondents restricted.
	May have distributions from holding companies restricted.
	May restrict level of deposit rates paid.
	May be required to divest or liquidate certain subsidiaries.
	May be restricted from paying bonuses or increasing salaries of executive officers.
Critically undercapitalized	Restrict interest payments on subordinated bonds.
	Appoint a conservator or receiver unless firm is meeting capital plan goals.
	Restrictions on other unusual transactions.
	Prohibitions of credit in highly leveraged transactions.
	Prohibitions on changes to charter, bylaws, and accounting methods.
	Prohibitions on paying excessive compensation and bonuses.
	Prohibitions of paying excessive deposit rates.

Other Major Regulatory and Institutional Powers Changes

The following are changes in major regulatory and institutional powers:

- *Too big to fail policy restrictions:* The FDICIA effectively eliminated the TBTF option that has been available to depository regulators and reduced the use of the Federal Reserve's discount window. As of January 1, 1995, the act prohibits the FDIC from protecting deposits above the maximum insurable amount and other creditors in which the deposit insurance fund would suffer a loss. The only exception would require agreement by the FDIC, the Federal Reserve, and the Treasury in consultation with the president.
- *Discount window restrictions:* The act also restricted the Federal Reserve from making discount window advances to undercapitalized institutions for more than 60 days in a 120-day period.
- *Brokered deposits restrictions:* Undercapitalized institutions are restricted from selling brokered deposits. Adequately capitalized institutions that do offer the deposits are prohibited from paying a rate that is higher than deposits of similar maturity in the institutions market area or a national rate for similar deposits.
- *Risk-based insurance assessments:* The FDICIA is authorized to establish a risk-based assessment system by July 1993.
- *State bank restrictions:* The act effectively restricts state-chartered banks from engaging in activities not permitted to nationally chartered banks. There are several exceptions.
- *Restrictions on real estate lending:* The act requires the regulatory agencies to adopt standards for real estate lending.
- *Periodic capital standards review:* The FDICIA sets up a schedule requiring periodic regulatory review of capital standards along with any modifications necessary to minimize loss to the insurance funds.

Savings and Loan Qualified Thrift Lender Test Expanded

The very restrictive QTLT standards that were implemented as a result of FIRREA were modified in the FDICIA. The percentage of qualifying assets was reduced from 70 percent to 65 percent, a greater percentage of consumer loans, stock in GSEs, and loans to churches, schools, hospitals, and nursing homes included as QTLT assets were allowed, and the percentage of assets invested in liquid assets, which are excludable from the asset base when calculating the QTLT, was increased. Overall, the modifications increased the portfolio diversification potential of S&Ls.

Depository Acquisitions of Institutions with Different Insurers

The FDICIA increases the ability of a BIF-insured institution to acquire a SAIF-insured institution and vice versa. The resulting institution, rather than transferring insurance coverage to one insurer, will have deposits insured on a pro-rata basis by both insurers who will share coverage.

Questions

Appendix A and B

A1. Explain the major provisions of FIRREA.
A2. Argue for or against the opinion that FIRREA was really a bill designed to lead to the ultimate elimination of S&Ls.
A3. What kind of impact will the FIRREA provision requiring S&Ls to invest a higher percentage of assets in residential mortgages have on this industry given the growing dominance of mortgage government sponsored credit enterprises?
A4. What was the purpose of the FDICIA? What were the reform objectives when the FDICIA was first advocated and what happened to them?
A5. How did the FDICIA respond to the recommendations for changing the deposit insurance programs?

Structural Changes and the Performance of Financial Intermediaries

chapter 15

The 1980s and early 1990s has been a volatile period for U.S. financial intermediaries. In particular, the country's system of specialized home lenders, the savings and loan associations, has been reduced to a mere fraction of its pre-1980 role. The term *debacle* has been used to describe the near disintegration of this system. Record commercial bank failures, substandard financial performance, and large staff reductions characterized the commercial banking system at the turn of the decade. Investment bankers, although used to more violent swings in business activity, suffered significantly in the late 1980s with forced staff reductions and large operating losses. Even life insurance companies have faced serious problems including several major failures.

All this can be contrasted with the continued strong performance of several other classes of intermediaries. This period witnessed continued growth and overall strong financial performance for mutual funds and finance companies as well as GSEs. Here, growth in assets has been strong at a time when thrift institutions and many commercial banks have had to retrench.

This chapter will review the major factors that have caused these declines in institutional performance. These changes emerged in the 1960s when rising inflation and volatile interest rates altered the once stable operating environment for our more traditional financial intermediaries. Thus, to grasp what has happened one must go back in time.

Overview

During the last 20 years, the U.S. financial system has undergone rapid change. This period saw major advances in information processing and communication technology. A very stable period of gradual changes in inflation and interest rate levels in the 1950s and 1960s increased in amplitude and volatility in the late 1970s and 1980s. Also, the competitive structure and the costs of doing business for depositories have been greatly altered by government deregulation policies.

In the 1960s, a depository market structure characterized by oligopoly was the policymaker's concern. In the 1980s and 1990s, the concern about overcapacity and excessive institutional failures are the policymaker's worry. Finally, new competitors have picked holes in what were once highly regulated depository markets.

Understanding these change factors is essential to managers of financial institutions who are involved in developing strategic plans or policy actions. Exhibit 15.1 provides an overview of the major factors that have impacted the U.S. financial system during the last several decades.

Exhibit 15.1

Major Changes Impacting U.S. Financial Institutions

Technologically induced changes

- Advances in information processing
- Communication advances

Economically induced changes

- Inflation during Vietnam War years
- October 1979 change in Fed policy
- Effect of oil price decline on developing countries and oil belt states

Governmentally induced changes

- Regulation Q and delayed deregulation
- Creation and expansion of privately owned governmentally sponsored credit agencies
- Inadequate regulation and supervision
- Excessive constraints on interstate acquisition and merger
- State deregulation of thrift powers
- Loss of payment system monopoly

Exhibit 15.1 continued

Major Changes Impacting U.S. Financial Institutions

- FIRREA fallout
- 1986 Tax Reform Act

Competitively induced changes

- Mutual funds, especially money market funds
- Discount brokers
- Entry of foreign banks, especially Japanese banks
- Money and capital market access for high credit rated corporations
- Capital market access for low credit rated corporations
- Nonbank financial competition

Technologically Induced Changes

Financial institutions are information-processing companies. As such, changes in technology that impact the cost structure for processing information and communication will have an important impact on them.

Information Processing

Financial intermediaries process information in their underwriting, servicing, brokerage, market-making, and portfolio management functions. The cost of this information-processing activity has changed significantly in recent years with the advent of less costly computer power. Today, the power of what were once state of the art mainframe computers are now found on the desks of millions of personal computer owners and users. This has created less expensive data processing capabilities and has facilitated the decentralization of information-processing activities.

Some intermediaries have been adversely affected by these trends because they acted to reduce the value of their geographic customer franchise. Competitors can now serve customers at greater distances from their offices. Indeed, the bank credit card market is dominated by firms that distribute and service their product worldwide.

The new information technologies have helped other intermediaries by allowing firms to design and manage highly specialized computer software systems to handle large volume activities. The innovator has benefitted, while the less efficient providers struggle to compete.

Communication Technology

Much of the same can be said of communication technology. Today, the pronouncements of a highly placed government spokesman will be read simultaneously worldwide on one of a number of communication systems. This has led to greater efficiency of our financial markets. Efficiency, as used here, can be defined as narrower bid-ask spreads and more instantaneous market adjustments. It also means greater difficulties for financial firms in the brokerage business seeking to profit from their brokerage function.

The impact of technology in both data processing and communication is not straightforward in terms of which firms benefit and which are hurt. Lower cost provides a niche opportunity for the very small firm that is able to take advantage of the low-cost data processing and communication capabilities without large administration and bureaucracy costs. On the other hand, to the extent that economies of scale or scope matter, firms that specialize in large-scale activities might be advantaged by the technology changes.

Improved technology and communication have also had a major impact on our brokerage firms. Once a source of information and analytical expertise for retail and wholesale investors, today information and communication technologies make it possible for investors to do their own analysis and information gathering. The need for the broker to offer expertise in the form of investment information has been lost on many an investor. This has made the inroads of the discount broker, following the deregulation of brokerage commissions, that much easier.

Economically Induced Changes

The financial institutions in the United States were largely structured to meet the needs of the 1930s. The structure was designed for relatively stable inflation and interest rates. Indeed, the nation's savings and loan associations were called upon to invest short-term time and savings deposits in long-term fixed-rate mortgages. This policy had to be abandoned in the 1970s as rising inflation brought about interest rate instability, which severely impacted that industry. Macroeconomic events have been a major contributor to the performance of U.S. financial institutions during the last several decades.

Inflation During Vietnam War Years

The Vietnam War created the impetus for the end of relative price stability in the post–World War II period. During the mid-to-late 1960s, new words such as *disintermediation* were coined. This word simply meant that if open-market interest rates on securities exceeded what commercial banks and thrifts were permitted to pay under Regulation Q, then customers would invest directly in these open-market investments. The first major experience with disintermediation occurred in 1965. In the Vietnam War years, macroeconomic policies brought high interest rates and volatility that intermediaries had not previously experienced. These policies eventually undermined the system of rate controls under Regulation Q.

October 1979 Federal Reserve Policy Change

On October 6, 1979, Federal Reserve Chairman Paul Volcker shocked the financial markets by reporting that the Federal Reserve open-market committee would be focusing more on the rate of growth of the monetary aggregates and less on the absolute level of interest rates. Experts immediately interpreted this statement to mean that interest rates could go to levels unsurpassed in previous cycles. They were correct. In the late 1970s and early 1980s interest rates did reach new highs. The prime commercial bank lending rate finally peaked at a record 21.5 percent in the early 1980s.

The decision to abandon the policy to control the level of interest rates and focus on monetary aggregate growth left the thrift institutions with their large portfolios of fixed-rate mortgages unable to cope. Regulation Q became an even less useful tool for providing stability, and actually became a destabilizing tool for controlling bank and S&L interest rates. The inflation of the 1970s combined with the Fed's new policy strategy to essentially bankrupt the S&Ls by the mid-1980s, and much earlier, if solvency had been measured by determining the liquidation value of the firms.

These economic policies also had a profound impact on life insurance companies. Life companies financed a large percentage of their assets with policy reserves of whole life insurance policies. Many of these policies had options permitting the policyholder to borrow the amount of the policy reserves at low interest rates. This occurred to a significant degree in the late 1970s and 1980s, making it necessary for life companies to sell high-yielding market rate assets and replace them with low-yielding policy loans. This situation also soured many potential purchasers of life insurance policies on the investment merits of whole life policies. Instead, many chose term policies. Life companies responded by developing and marketing policies such as annuities and selling liabilities such as guaranteed investment contracts with higher investment yields to build their liability bases. These liabilities, however, carried much higher interest rates that cut into insurance company profit margins.

Oil Price Cycle

The rise and fall of oil prices in the 1973 to 1985 period caused significant financial institution stress. Some developing countries, such as Mexico and Venezuela, and states such as Texas, Oklahoma, and Louisiana, were able to borrow against the large oil reserves they had safely in the ground. As the price of this collateral rose, the collateral supported even higher lending levels. However, once the value of the collateral fell with the decline in oil prices, so did the ability of the borrowers to repay their debt. The result was that commercial banks and thrifts took heavy losses on loans made in states and countries that based their development and growth on the oil and gas business.

Governmentally Induced Changes

This U.S. financial system was designed during the 1930s and was characterized by governmentally established barriers between the various financial firms. The Glass-Steagall Act, for example, forbade commercial banks from underwriting and distributing securities. Savings and loans were denied the authority to make business loans or offer demand accounts until the 1980s.

As competitive conditions increased and interest rates became more volatile, the government system of protection, price controls, and competitive compartmentalizing became unworkable and impossible to sustain. Unfortunately, deregulation came too slowly and was poorly executed.

Regulation Q and Delayed Deregulation

The history of S&Ls is the story of government regulation and protection. A product of the 1930s, the modern S&L was envisioned as a narrowly defined home-lending intermediary. In return for operating with very narrow asset and liability powers, S&Ls were granted a number of government benefits. These benefits included their own supportive regulatory system, insurance corporation, and lending agencies. They were also given tax advantages and eventually were brought under Regulation Q and permitted to pay a higher interest rate on deposits than commercial banks. Finally, they were permitted to operate with lower capital requirements than commercial banks. Unfortunately, the social costs of trying to maintain this system in the face of rapidly rising interest rates in the late 1970s and early 1980s became evident. These institutions could no longer be expected to borrow short and lend long. First, the saving public began to politically campaign for higher rates on deposits. Second, the disintermediation from depositories into direct investments and money market funds proved the ceilings were no longer effective.

Popular opinion was that the thrifts must be deregulated and given expanded powers like commercial banks as the *quid pro quo* for eliminating Regulation Q. This was accomplished in two stages. The first was the passage of the Depository Institutions Deregulation and Monetary Control Act in 1980. Next was the Garn-St. Germain Depository Institutions Act of

1982. Unfortunately, the timing was off the mark. Interest rates reached such high levels in the early 1980s that the operating losses of thrifts all but wiped out their equity. New lending markets that were opened up by the legislation could not be expected to help decrease interest rate risk or produce higher operating income for many years. The elimination of Regulation Q and the expansion of thrift powers came much too late to save the industry.

Loss of Commercial Banks' Monopoly in the Payment System

The deregulation of the early 1980s had a significant effect on commercial banks, as savings and loans, mutual savings banks, and credit unions were now permitted to offer consumer interest-bearing transaction accounts. Providing payment services was a major franchise value embedded in the commercial bank charter. In a very short period, this value was eroded through deregulation. Unfortunately, the increase in competition did little for the thrifts who had to aggressively price their new services to obtain market share. It also did nothing to reduce the cost of providing payment services at banks. Indeed, 1980 also brought the Monetary Control Act, which required the Federal Reserve to price its payment services to cover direct and indirect costs. It also brought the thrifts into the credit and debit card business, again reducing the profit potential for commercial banks.

Commercial banks now faced a doubling in institutional competitors and the prospect of paying interest on a percentage of their demand balances. Thrifts received the costly right to invest in new processing equipment and build new payment system management organizations, while using price to attract a respectable market share.

Exhibit 15.2 on page 394 shows the results of an analysis of the capital-to-asset ratios of the 25 largest commercial bank holding companies from 1951 to 1986. The capital-to-asset ratios are computed in two ways. The hatched line computes the ratio using the stated book value of equity of the holding company as a ratio of total assets. The bold line uses the market value of equity as the measure of capital. Market value of equity is computed by taking the market value of the firm's outstanding common stock times its price. When the stocks of these banks rise above the book value per share, the market value capital-to-asset ratio will be above the book value capital-to-asset ratio. This is considered by many to be a rough measure of the franchise value of these banks. The decline in the market capital-to-asset ratio, relative to the book value capital-to-asset ratio, is probably due to the competitive forces that have reduced the monopoly market power of commercial banks. This is due largely to the growth in interstate and intrastate branching, the loss of the demand deposit monopoly of banks, and competition from thrifts and nonbanks. All these factors have resulted in excess financial service capacity.

Exhibit 15.2

Market and Book Capital-to-Total-Asset Ratios for Large Bank Holding Companies 1952–1986

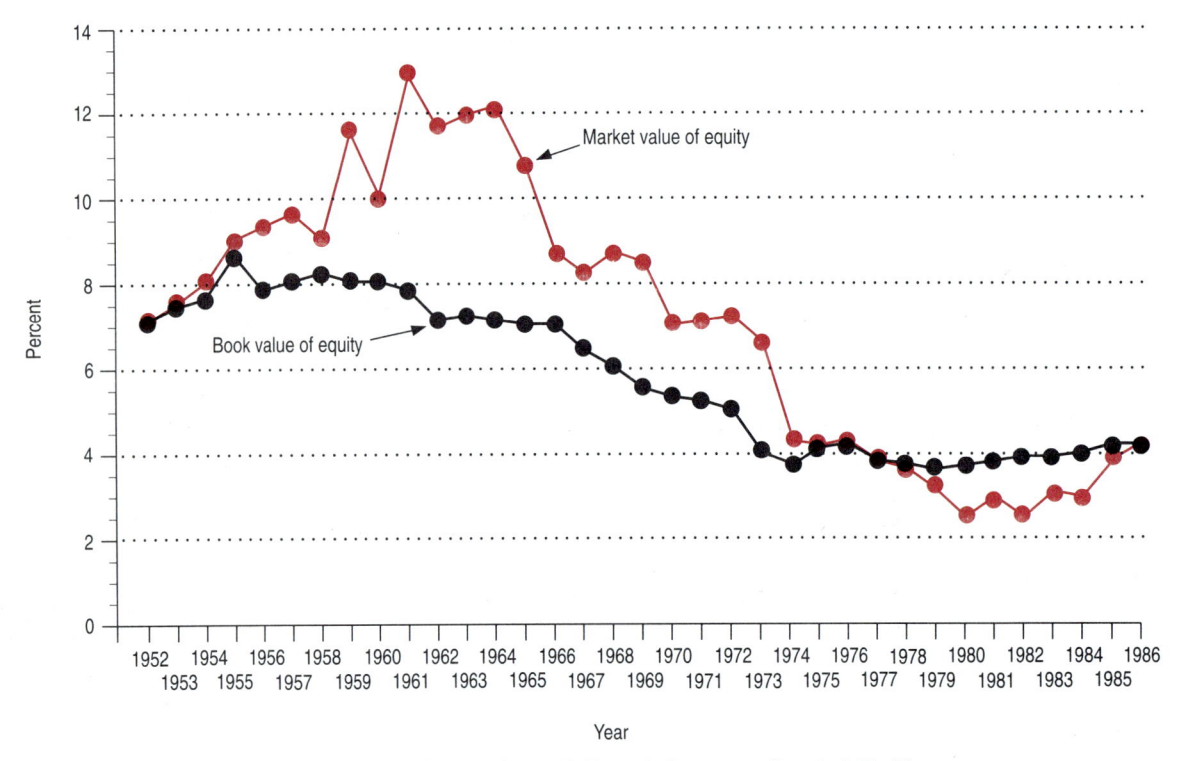

Source: Keeley, Michael C., and Frederick T. Furlong. "A Deposit Insurance Puzzle." *Weekly Letter,* Federal Reserve Bank of San Francisco. (July 3, 1987).

Government Sponsored Enterprises

The decade of the 1980s witnessed the maturation of government sponsored enterprises. The GSEs were set up harmlessly enough to ensure that certain well-defined borrowers would be able to obtain credit should the private sector not meet their needs for whatever reason. Ironically, one of the reasons the private sector did not meet the needs of certain borrowers was because of Regulation Q and disintermediation. This gave rise to the creation of the GNMA, FHLMC, and the privatization of the FNMA. It also resulted in the expansion of the FHLBs into long-term thrift lenders from lenders whose purpose was to provide short-term liquidity. The agricultural business was supported by the federal FCBs while the student loan market was supported by the SLMA.

As discussed in detail in Chapter 13, the GSEs have produced unintended side effects. Their status in the money and capital markets as agencies of the federal government permits them to borrow at preferred borrowing costs. An even more important advantage for them was the deregulation of deposit rates at commercial banks and thrifts in the 1980s and the rise in deposit insurance costs for banks and thrifts in the late 1980s and early 1990s.

With these significant advantages in raising funds, agencies have been able to dominate the pricing for certain types of credit. This has produced relatively lower interest rates on the loans the agencies are permitted to purchase. It has also caused a deterioration in the financial performances of commercial banks and S&Ls and has, at the same time, induced these institutions to search out markets in which agencies cannot lend. These markets have tended to be higher risk markets, such as loans to developing countries, commercial real estate and development, and highly leveraged corporate loans. Adding to the problem is the impact of the *fallacy of composition.* In this context, the fallacy of composition means that as more and more institutions feel the squeeze on profit margins in their traditional markets, they tend to search out the same higher risk markets. The fallacy of composition is that a more risky lending strategy implemented for a specific loan market might work for a few institutions, but cannot be supported if a large number of institutions simultaneously choose the same new strategy. There are only so many good creditworthy borrowers. This appears to have been the case with respect to both the junk bond market and commercial real estate development and mortgage markets in the 1980s.

Inadequate Regulation and Supervision

It is well documented that the large losses to the deposit insurance corporations in the 1980s and 1990s could be largely ascribed to inadequate regulation and supervision. Instead of increasing capital requirements in the early 1980s, they were lessened for S&Ls. Instead of carefully monitoring the experience of S&Ls with their new lending powers, S&Ls were frequently allowed to enter new markets with inexperienced personnel and control systems. Instead of carefully assessing the experience and capabilities of the many new owners and operating managers of these institutions, virtually no monitoring was done.

Overall, the financial institution regulators were ill-equipped for the financial turmoil of the 1980s. As discussed in Chapter 14, the moral hazard issues related to deposit insurance and regulation are difficult to solve. Indeed, it is likely that public policymakers will overreact on the side of conservatism. This would be manifested by demands for higher capital and reduced risk-taking authority. The FIRREA and FDICIA legislation are a good examples of this type of reaction. The impact of these policies will be to make it difficult for all but a substantially reduced segment of these businesses to achieve adequate profitability.

Expanded Deposit Insurance Coverage and Moral Hazard

In 1980, Congress increased deposit insurance coverage from $40,000 per account in any institution to $100,000. This action sharply increased the moral hazard problem for the depository regulators. Depositories could raise large volumes of deposits from depositors who could care less about the financial soundness of the institutions. The result was the creation of excess insured deposits.

These excess insured deposits tended to be invested in higher yielding, more risky assets as a result of the declining profit margins in traditional lending markets. It should come as no surprise that brokered insured deposits were used to fund many of the higher risk loans and investments. These deposits permitted institutions to grow very quickly, without taking the time to develop a consumer franchise.

The growth of the essentially insolvent S&Ls during the 1980s created serious problems. Table 15.1 shows the total assets and deposits of all

Table 15.1

Total Assets and Savings Deposits of Commercial Banks and FSLIC-Insured Institutions Year-end 1979–1988 (dollars in billions)

Institutions Assets and Deposits	Year-end 1979	Year-end 1984	Year-end 1988	Annual Growth Rate 1979–1984	Annual Growth Rate 1984–1988
Commercial banks					
Total assets	$1,143	$2,276	$3,047	14.76%	7.56%
Total deposits	1,030	1,604	2,146	9.26	7.54
FSLIC insured					
Total assets	579	902	1,350	9.27	10.61
Total deposits	470	724	971	9.02	7.60

Source: Federal Reserve *Bulletin*. Various issues.

commercial banks and FSLIC-insured institutions at year-end 1979, 1984 and 1988. The table also shows that FSLIC-insured institutions grew rapidly throughout this period. Ironically, and sadly, they actually grew faster than commercial banks between 1984 and 1988. During this four-year period, the deposits at FSLIC institutions grew at an annual rate of 7.60 percent per annum versus a lesser 7.54 percent at the commercial banks. Assets grew by 10.60 percent versus 7.56 percent at the commercial banks. This rapid growth in deposits and assets continued long after the thrift problem had been identified by industry experts. Regulation, however, seemed either unable or unwilling to arrest the rapid growth in insured deposits.

Constraints on Interstate Branching and Consolidation

Most observers of financial institutions would say that the United States has excess capacity in its financial system. It has more commercial banks and thrifts per capita than any industrialized country in the world. Compared to countries like Japan, Germany, France, and Great Britain, the number of depositories is five to ten times as many on a per capita basis. Despite this widely held view, the federal government did little to improve the climate for commercial bank mergers and consolidations and commercial bank acquisitions of thrifts until the early 1990s. Indeed, the FIRREA did little to induce commercial banks to acquire S&Ls. The reasons for this were mainly political. The thrifts have spent many political dollars over the years to maintain a separate system of home finance institutions despite years of evidence that the system was not working. Moreover, state banking regulators have been slow to offer up their regulatory turf to interstate banks. As a result, the pace of consolidation has been slow. Adding to the problem has been the tendency in the last few years for regulators of failed institutions to keep insolvent institutions alive and under government control. This has only exacerbated the overcapacity in the system.

State Deregulation and Chartering Impact

Following the federal government's deregulation efforts in 1980 and 1982, the state governments took up their own deregulation agenda. Concerned that many state-chartered institutions would convert to a federal charter, a number of states deregulated the investment powers of their state-chartered institutions far beyond what the federal government had already done. States such as Texas and California have been signaled out for their deregulation efforts. Many of the states also chartered many new institutions, which only added to industry overcapacity.

Having federal government agencies insure the deposits of state-chartered institutions has resulted in very significant problems. State governments, like depositors, have a moral hazard in that they feel free to permit broad risky lending powers for state-chartered institutions without facing the potential cost of failures. This certainly contributed to the cost of the savings and loan crisis and some bank failures.

FIRREA *Fallout*

The impact of the thrift crisis on financially sound intermediaries has largely passed. The weak firms are no longer creating excessive amounts of insured liabilities and underpricing risky asset acquisitions. According to the Federal Reserve Board, the total assets of SAIF-insured depositories dropped from $1.350 billion at year-end 1988 to $1 billion at year-end 1991. The rate of shrinkage is very likely to continue as the FDIC takes over more institutions and more S&Ls are bought by commercial banks.

However, the government's response to the thrift crisis is now being felt. This response, which is having a very negative impact on the depository institutions, includes raising the cost of deposit insurance and increasing the severity of examination-related loss reserves. These losses are due, in part, to more conservative asset valuations, which are sometimes based on mark-to-market revaluations at the fire sale liquidation values by the RTC.

The increase in deposit insurance premiums is the most apparent of the adverse impacts of recent government policies on the financial depository system. The cost of deposits to the SAIF-insured institutions is up to 23 bp and the BIF premium was raised from 12 bp to 23 bp. This represents an increase in the operating costs for all depositories and makes them that much less competitive with federal credit agencies and uninsured intermediaries. The insurance premium will go even higher under the 1992 proposed risk-based deposit insurance program.

The examination-induced loan loss reserving that has affected commercial banks and thrifts is more difficult to assess. First, it is difficult to determine how much of the estimated loss is due to a true reduction in market value, a change in market value valuation methodology, or a reduction in value based on the liquidation valuations impacted by RTC sales. There is also growing evidence that the RTC is having a significant adverse impact on the market valuation of a variety of assets held by depository institutions. Clearly, since the passage of FIRREA, a portion of the 1990 reduction in high-yield bond values can be attributed to the requirement that S&Ls liquidate their portfolios within five years. This led to an accounting requirement for mark-to-market of these portfolios, which caused several institutions to fall into insolvency. The portfolios then became the property of the RTC, which liquidated them as fast as possible. As any trader knows, a phone call from a party who is a known seller produces declining bid prices.

With government policies in place that increase the cost structure of depositories while reducing the value of their assets, it seems that depositories' problems will continue long into the 1990s.

1986 Tax Reform Act

Changes in tax legislation can have a significant impact on the financial performance of different sectors of the economy. Such was the case for the massive tax changes incorporated in the 1986 Tax Reform Act. This act reduced marginal tax rates for individuals and corporations and also eliminated a wide variety of deductions and tax preferences.

For financial institutions it had two very significant impacts in addition to changes in marginal tax rates. First, the bill reduced many of the tax preferences for investors in real estate. This included eliminating capital gains treatment for real estate and eliminating the ability to take depreciation losses against income for "passive investors." The result was that for many investors the after tax cash return on real estate fell. This, in turn, reduced the market value of many real estate projects. Some of this reduced market value affected the real estate lenders who foreclosed on many of these projects.

The act also affected the desirability of financial intermediaries to invest in state and municipal bonds. As discussed in Chapter 4, the act put an end to the deductibility of bank interest expense for tax-exempt securities purchased after 1986. This reduced the profitability of an asset that was an important component of the portfolio of commercial banks.

Competitively Induced Changes

Throughout the last several decades, the overall structure for U.S. financial institutions has become more competitive. New competition has come through innovations like the money market mutual fund. The money and capital markets have become more accessible to a growing number of U.S. companies. These firms found they could finance themselves outside of the commercial banking system. The globalization of the financial system has also resulted in increased competition while nonbank competitors have increased in number and importance.

Mutual Funds

The first real competitive threat to the well-protected depositories came in the 1970s with the emergence of the money market mutual fund. Regulation Q ceilings remained below the rates paid by mutual funds, and the result was substantial disintermediation. The increased sophistication of retail and institutional investors and the abundance of high-quality investments for money funds to invest in has made the deposit insurance guarantee of the banks and thrifts less valuable to investors. Added to this is the fact that many mutual funds offer transaction-activated accounts with only the convenience of a brick-and-mortar branch missing. The high cost of providing that brick and mortar is also working to the disadvantage of thrifts and banks, since most money market mutual funds offer their services with a relatively low expense load. This means they have been very rate competitive compared with the accounts of depositories.

By the end of 1989, the open-end mutual funds had accumulated assets in excess of $950 billion. They were providing retail customers access to municipal securities, junk bonds, mortgage-backed securities, and other investments that historically have been assets of depository institutions. Over the 1970s and 1980s, a large percentage of funds have been disintermediated from the depositories.

Money and Capital Market Access to High-Quality Borrowers

The entry of many of our nation's highest grade borrowers into our money and capital markets has been a major challenge for our nation's commercial banks. These borrowers had been a primary source of loans and deposits for banks. The growth of commercial paper and medium-term notes made the high-grade borrower a less frequent commercial bank customer. Moreover, the availability of the direct issuance of securities has reduced pricing of commercial bank credit. Today, only a few of the less creditworthy customers have to pay the prime rate for funds. Most other borrowers are able to price their bank loan off of rates in the money markets. This has acted to exacerbate the profit squeeze on banks. Less than 30 percent of all bank customers pay the prime rate or higher for their bank credit according to surveys of the Federal Reserve Board.

Capital Market Access for Lower Quality Credits

Just as the money and capital markets have provided viable alternatives to commercial banks for the high-grade borrower, the emergence of the high-yield security (junk bond) market has provided an alternative source of funding for the low-grade borrower. The junk bond market has become a viable funding alternative for many growing businesses. This has also taken a toll on the nation's commercial banks by allowing another important class of borrowers to avoid the commercial bank and use the investment banker to obtain funds. Fast-growing pension funds and life insurance companies have provided ample funds for the public and privately placed bond market.

Growth in Foreign Banking Activities

As discussed in Chapter 7, the last decade has witnessed a major increase in the activities of foreign banks operating in the United States and elsewhere. While the European banks have continued to increase their historically strong international activities, the rise of the Japanese banks has been the most notable. The Japanese banks, spurred by a strong market capitalization of their securities, large balance of trade surpluses, and a high national savings rate, have had to look beyond their borders for investment opportunities. All this has added to the competitive structure confronting U.S. banks.

Between 1981 and 1987 the ratio of assets of foreign banking offices in the United States to assets of U.S. domestic banks has increased over five percentage points to nearly 21 percent. Looking at international bank assets, we see the greatest increase in market share going to the Japanese banks between 1984 and 1988. The table showing these data is found in Chapter 9, Table 9.13. The biggest market share losses during the period were the U.S. banks. The Japanese market share increased 15.2 percent, while the U.S. market share decreased by 11.8 percent. Overall the major European banks held about steady despite the pickup in Japanese activity.

Competition from Investment Banks and Discount Brokers

Commercial bank holding companies offer brokerage services, and the large retail investment banking firms offer integrated accounts that provide transaction services, credit services, and a host of investment alternatives. The lines between the two types of institutions began to blur many years ago. The result has been a further increase in overall capacity to provide financial services without a commensurate increase in demand.

Nonbank Financial Competition

Competition has also come from nonbank competitors. Captive finance companies have taken a large and growing share of the secured auto loan and leasing markets. At the same time, Sears, American Express, and AT&T have been the most visible new major entrants into the consumer credit card market. Another major source of competition has been finance companies' affiliation with large manufacturing companies that have been able to secure strong credit ratings. These firms have become more successful partly because, since deregulation, banks and thrifts have lost their source of low-cost consumer deposits. Overall this new competition has acted to exacerbate the overcapacity in the financing industry.

Overcapacity: An Industry Curse

The factors so far discussed in this chapter point to one undeniable conclusion. The United States has more financial service production capacity than there is demand. Normally, market forces of merger, consolidation, and failure would correct such a market disequilibrium. That has not happened until recently in the United States for several reasons. First, the government allowed many depositories to remain in business and indeed expand their insured deposit liabilities when profit prospects were poor and capital for many inadequate. Second, the market cleansing process of allowing failed institutions to be liquidated and removed from the market was not followed by the government regulatory agencies for many failed thrifts and banks. Third, during the 1980s, the insurance corporations granted insurance to a large number of newly chartered banks and savings and loans. Many were chartered under liberal state chartering laws, but the insurance of accounts came from the federal government. This added more unneeded capacity. Fourth, the rising cost of deposit insurance has made it more difficult for U.S. banks to be international competitors, since the rising deposit insurance premiums and the need to hold reserves in zero earning accounts at the Fed further holds profit margins down. Fifth, the government has created and fostered major new competitors for commercial banks and thrifts in the form of GSEs. As more and more potential bank and thrift loans became government agency assets or government agency guaranteed securities, the potential market for good earning assets shrunk. The agencies also had the further disruptive impact of decreasing market yields on the assets created by the thrifts and banks on their balance sheets.

Impact Assessment 1970–2000

Each of the factors previously discussed has had a negative impact on depositories (see Table 15.2). Unfortunately, it would be very difficult, if not impossible, to quantify the financial impact of each. It is possible, however, to identify the period of time over which each factor has had its greatest adverse impact on the depository industry. This is necessarily an imprecise procedure, but it allows a determination of the potential for adverse conditions to prevail into the future. That is, it is possible to determine which of the factors will act as a drag on depository performance into the 1990s. These should be the factors public policymakers focus on.

Looking at the communication and technology factors first, it seems clear that these forces will be a continuing challenge for intermediaries. The cost of computer power continues to decline at a rapid rate. Consequently, information-processing companies, such as depositories, should expect to be affected significantly. However, as mentioned earlier, it is not clear how any particular institution will be impacted. Continued communication improvements are also expected. This will continue to increase overall competitive levels as local geographic markets are penetrated by institutions from great distances away. International banking competitive pressures are also expected to remain strong.

The economic problems of the 1970s and 1980s, on the other hand, should be of virtually no concern in the 1990s. Most depositories have developed much improved interest rate risk management measurement methodologies and techniques for minimizing the risk. The substantial growth in interest rate swaps is just one example of this improvement.

Chapter 15 Structural Changes and the Performance of Financial Intermediaries

Table 15.2

Impact of Factors on Depository Performance During the Last Two Decades and Expected Impact in the 1990s (subjective assessment)

Factor	1970–1980	1980–1990	1990–2000
Information processing	Neutral	Neutral	—
Communication	Negative	Negative	Negative
Vietnam	Major Negative	Neutral	—
October 1979	Major Negative	Major Negative	—
Oil price decline	Major Negative	Major Negative	—
Regulation Q and deregulation	Negative	Major Negative	—
GSEs	Negative	Major Negative	Major Negative
Regulation and supervision	Negative	Major Negative	Negative
Interstate branching	Negative	Major Negative	Major Negative
Payment system expansion	Negative	Major Negative	—
FIRREA fallout	—	Major Negative	—
Mutual funds	Major Negative	Major Negative	Major Negative
Discount brokers	Negative	Negative	—
Foreign banks	—	Major Negative	Negative
Capital market expansion: high-grade	Major Negative	Major Negative	Major Negative
Capital market expansion: low-grade	—	Major Negative	Negative
Nonbank financial competition	Negative	Major Negative	Major Negative

In the government area, significant problems remain. Although the impact of deposit interest rate deregulation through the elimination of Regulation Q has now largely worked its way through the system, as has the impact of the loss of the payment system monopoly of commercial banks, several other problems remain.

First, the GSEs seem to be untouchable. While numerous studies have resulted in various suggestions as to how their advantages might be reduced, little has been done. GSEs can be expected to continue to leverage their agency borrowing position in an effort to expand this advantage. More assets will carry the government agency guarantee, leaving still fewer profitable assets for depositories.

The regulatory implementation of FIRREA and FDICIA remains a significant problem. This has led to decreasing asset values. Deposit insurance costs have increased. The problem of keeping insolvent institutions open, sometimes simply to receive deposits, remains a problem.

As far as competitive pressures are concerned, each competitor remains a continuing challenge. The only one that seems to be less of a factor is foreign bank competition, at least temporarily. In 1990, both Japan and Germany implemented domestic macroeconomic policies that have substantially increased their cost of capital. The international risk-based capital standards are reducing some of the inequities as well.

Table 15.2 provides a summary of the factors discussed in this chapter and the likelihood that they will negatively impact on bank performance in the 1990s. The impact of these factors is also considered for the decade of the 1970s and 1980s. These decade periods are arbitrary. The table represents a subjective assessment of impact, without in any way attempting to quantify the factors. Overall, however, the assessment suggests that the relatively hostile environment of the last two decades will continue into the 1990s. It also suggests that many of the negative factors are within the control of government officials. Constructive government attention to the problems could reduce the severity of their impact.

Profits and Capital

The regulatory and Congressional actions of the late 1980s and 1990s have been partially counterproductive. FIRREA raised the operating costs of thrifts, decreased profit opportunities, increased capital requirements, and increased examination and enforcement costs. These actions do not solve the systemic problems confronting U.S. financial depositories. The problem is inadequate profitability under either a commercial bank or thrift charter given the current structure of our depository markets. FIRREA certainly did not increase the ability of thrifts to attract new capital or the Resolution Trust Corporation to obtain a good price for the thrift charters they control. FIRREA destroyed the potential for profits at many thrifts.

Regulators have also increased commercial banks' deposit insurance fees and capital requirements. To meet both higher deposit insurance fees and capital requirements, a firm must have a profitable charter value and positive future prospects. The basic problem is that banking and thrift institutions haven't had a good profit year in over a decade. Deregulation of liability pricing, expansion of competition in the payment system, and the explosive growth of GSEs are some of the primary reasons. The spread between asset yields and liability costs is low and shows only little promise of increasing as the number of competitors declines. Moreover, fee income, while increasing as fast as intermediaries are able, continues to be eaten up by increased operating costs, largely as a result of government regulatory system charges and, of course, problem loans.

Chapter 15 Structural Changes and the Performance of Financial Intermediaries

Table 15.3 shows the relationship between book value on December 31, 1989, and market value on November 19, 1990, for a representative group of large commercial bank holding companies. The table indicates that only six of the seventeen bank holding companies sold for greater than book value. Although book value is a poor measure of value, when newly issued stock cannot be sold for greater than book value, it usually acts as a deterrent to raising capital. By contrast, the FNMA stock shown in the table sells for approximately two and one-half times the book value. This is because FNMA and its sister agency the FHLMC have a charter that has comparative advantages over the insured depositories. Moreover, there are only two of them. All of this suggests that the franchise value of depositories has been reduced substantially in recent years.

Table 15.3

Relationship Between Book Value and Market Value for a Representative Group of Large Bank Holding Companies

Name of Bank Holding Company	Book Value per Common Share 12/31/89	Market Value 11/19/90
Bank of New York	$40.71	$18.75
BankAmerica	23.31	23.375
Bankers Trust	26.28	38.375
Chemical Banking	34.10	12.50
Citicorp	25.36	13.50
First Interstate	36.78	21.75
Manufacturers Hanover	41.49	19.625
J. P. Morgan & Company	21.78	40.875
Security Pacific	35.50	23.00
Mellon Bank	27.42	22.125
Signet Bank	28.15	10.00
Banc One	16.10	23.125
First Chicago	34.82	16.625
Norwest	13.13	18.50
Fleet/Norstar Financial Group	19.87	10.50
NCNB	26.79	25.00
First Wachovia	25.07	39.50
FNMA	12.52	32.625

Source: Moody Investor Service. (Summer 1990). *Wall Street Journal.*

Policy Options

Our financial structure could best be characterized as oligopolistic in many geographic markets from the Depression through the 1970s. Since then technology, deregulation, globalization of financial markets, credit agency competition, and the breakdown of institutional barriers have lessened the franchise value of insured depositories. Franchise value must be restored in order to reduce the chance of failure and improve the industry's prospects for attracting capital. This is likely to be a long-term effort. There is, of course, a risk that the process will swing too far toward concentration of market power. Shareholders in depositories should not be beneficiaries of governmentally induced efforts to concentrate markets. This outcome must be watched carefully by regulators. However, at this point, and probably for many years into the future, the problem of excessive concentration seems unlikely to come to fruition anytime soon. The following are some recommendations that have been made to improve the financial structure:

- *Increase capital requirements on GSEs and reduce the scope of their charter:* GSEs have indirectly contributed to our deposit insurance problems by adding enormous capacity to several major credit markets. Capital levels could be brought in line with depository institutions. They could be assessed a user fee at least equal to the insurance premium charged the depositories on their deposits. They could have their charters reviewed and narrowed with respect to their public policy objectives in light of their recent expansion tendencies and negative impact on depositories.
- *Interindustry acquisitions should be encouraged:* The FIRREA of 1989 made the acquisition of thrifts by commercial banks a costly undertaking. It also made thrift acquisitions of banks nearly impossible. Consolidation requires that mergers and acquisitions occur with ease. The FDICIA was a step in that direction.
- *Eliminate Fed reserve requirements:* The Regulation D requirement that depositories hold noninterest-bearing reserves against transaction and certain time deposits is a tax on these institutions. It makes them less competitive internationally and complicates their equity-building efforts at home. The Federal Reserve could pay interest on these reserves. Actions to reduce reserve requirements were taken in 1991 and 1992.
- *Failed institutions should be liquidated quickly after being seized by regulators:* If a suitable acquisition partner cannot be arranged within six months, a failed institution could be liquidated. A longer period exacerbates the excess capacity problem in the industry.
- *Authorize interstate branching for federally chartered depositories:* The process of consolidation would be substantially enhanced if

nationwide branching were authorized by Congress. The need to bring about greater consolidation while at the same time improving the ability of banks to diversify their asset portfolios should reduce the risk of bank failure and improve performance. A 1992 effort by the OTS to authorize interstate branching for federally chartered S&Ls was opposed by commercial banks.

- *Subject credit unions to federal taxation:* A remaining inequity that affects the competitive structure within the depository segment of the financial services industry is the lack of federal taxation of credit unions. Savings and loans went many years without federal taxation, but eventually pressure from commercial banks caused them to become fully federally taxed. Although the taxation of credit unions would do only a little to balance the competitive structure, it seems that such a change is justified.
- *Reduce deposit insurance coverage and let insured intermediaries shrink:* There are those who believe that the services provided by federally chartered and insured intermediaries are being competitively provided by other intermediaries. The finance companies, mutual funds, and nonbank financial firms are providing virtually any product that a commercial bank or thrift can provide. Thus, these analysts recommend reducing the scope of deposit insurance and letting insured depositories shrink their relative position in our financial system.

Summary

The plight of many U.S. financial institutions is a result of significant forces that have impacted the markets for financial services. These forces have served to reduce profit margins for many of our traditional and highly regulated financial intermediaries, while at the same time providing great opportunity for the less regulated mutual funds, finance companies, and discount brokers. Savings and loans, savings banks, commercial banks, and life companies have experienced the worst of these rising competitive forces. Adding to the problems has been poor government regulation and delayed government legislative responses to changing market forces. The resulting overcapacity in our financial services business will impact our financial intermediaries into the next decade.

The primary forces of change impacting the financial services industry in the last twenty years are **technologically induced changes, economically induced changes, governmentally induced changes,** and **competitively induced changes.**

Technological changes in data processing and communication have allowed financial institutions to expand markets and enter new markets, creating more competition. Technology has also permitted smaller firms to take advantage of the sophisticated financial tools and instantaneously communicated information that have made financial markets more efficient.

Economic policies of the last 20 years have resulted in greater amplitude and volatility of interest rates. This has created significant problems for financial firms that carried significant interest rate risk, such as savings and loans and life insurance companies. Sharp fluctuations in the value of certain resources such as oil have also led to significant credit problems.

Government legislative and regulatory responses to the changing competitive conditions in the financial services business have been largely detrimental. Deregulation of the nation's S&Ls came after many were insolvent. Regulatory forbearance policies exacerbated the size of the losses of the resulting failures. Until recently, governmental policies have discouraged consolidation and, therefore, contributed to overcapacity in the financial depository business.

Competition from less regulated financial institutions has resulted in a loss of market share and reduced profit margins at insured depositories. The globalization of financial markets and the economic resurgence of Western Europe and Japan has also increased competitive pressures on U.S. financial institutions.

Recommendations to reduce the potentially large cost of continued failures of insured depository institutions require government action. Some federally chartered financial institutions such as GSEs have special government-granted benefits that give them a competitive edge. This has complicated the overcapacity problems. Overall, the government must develop a consistent and effective set of policies to deal with the overcapacity in the depository markets.

Questions

Chapter 15

1. How do changes in information processing and communication technologies affect financial institutions?
2. Name several important impacts macroeconomic policies have had on depository institutions.
3. Discuss which government policies you feel have been most detrimental to depository institutions.
4. Explain how competition has impacted depositories in their ability to generate assets. Explain which competitive forces have impacted depositories on the liability side of the balance sheet.
5. Which of the forces impacting depositories are likely to be important in the 1990s?

Chapter 15 Structural Changes and the Performance of Financial Intermediaries   **409**

6. If depository services can be provided efficiently by others, why be concerned about their financial performance?
7. Is consolidation a viable means of reducing depository failures?
8. What impact do you think nationwide branching will have on the financial performance of depositories?
9. If the structure of our markets is such that competition is too severe, what can Congress and the regulators do to improve conditions? What changes are now taking place?
10. The mergers of BankAmerica/Security Pacific, Chase/Manufacturers Hanover, and NCNB/C&S/Sovran are important transactions. What do they seem to tell us about the future of commercial banking in the United States?

Part Outline

Chapter 16
Basic Financial Management for Intermediaries

Chapter 17
Distribution Channels for Financial Products

Chapter 18
Measuring Interest Rate Risk

Chapter 19
Managing Interest Rate Risk

Chapter 20
Managing Credit Risk

Chapter 21
Performance Analysis for Financial Institutions

Chapter 22
Asset Management and Pricing

Chapter 23
Liability Management and Pricing

Chapter 24
Foreign Exchange, Exchange Rates, and Managing Currency Risk

Managing Financial Intermediaries

Part 4 is concerned with the problems of managing financial intermediaries. The part begins with a discussion of basic financial management issues for a financial intermediary. Financial leverage, business risk, and the sources of intermediary profits are covered. The risks of operating intermediaries are discussed in the remaining chapters. These include interest rate risk, credit risk, asset management and pricing, liability management and pricing, and foreign exchange risk.

Basic Financial Management for Intermediaries

chapter 16

Financial intermediaries generate revenue from their portfolio management, servicing, origination, and brokerage activities. Each intermediary selects from the financial claim/function matrix the functions it wants to perform and endeavors to profit from these activities. This chapter reviews the basic principles of financial management for financial intermediaries.

Although certain portions of this chapter are relevant to a firm with insured deposits, most of the issues relate to all intermediaries. Thus, references are made to depositories, issuers of government-insured liabilities, and the all-inclusive intermediaries.

Financial innovation is discussed in the Appendix to this chapter. The last several decades have seen frequent innovations in our financial markets. From the types of financial claims being issued to the distribution systems being used, financial innovation has been a source of profit for many institutions and frustration for others.

Primary Financial Management Duties

The duties and responsibilities of managers of financial institutions now require greater sophistication than they once did. In years past, liquidity management duties were high on the list of important responsibilities. Today, a profit squeeze relating to the declining spread between the yield on assets and the cost of liabilities, rising interest rate risk related to a substantial increase in volatility of the price of financial instruments, and a profit squeeze related to deregulation and to the increase in competition have combined to complicate management duties.

The result of all these changes has been to necessitate an upgrading of the financial tools used in the field. Several of the more important financial duties and responsibilities include the following:

1. The valuation of financial claims
2. Interest rate risk measurement and management
3. Credit risk measurement and management
4. Pricing of loans and liabilities
5. Determining the optimal capital structure

Valuation of Financial Claims

Much of what financial firms do relates to valuing financial claims. The valuation of claims involves all the functional units of intermediaries—origination, servicing, brokerage, and portfolio management. Virtually all valuation models used in finance involve two basic methodologies, namely, present value theory and options pricing models. These were presented in Chapters 4 and 5, respectively. The job of the financial analyst is to determine the attributes of the financial claim in question in order to develop a cash flow statement for it, and then to determine the nature of any embedded options. Present value theory and options pricing are used to develop the tools needed for interest rate risk management, for the trading of loans and securities, and for designing and pricing new types of loans and liabilities.

Interest Rate Risk Management

The portfolio management unit usually assumes the responsibilities for managing interest rate risk. Interest rate risk is the impact of changes in market interest rates on a financial firm's asset and liability values and income stream. In many financial depository institutions, this job is assumed by a committee such as an Asset/Liability Committee (ALCO). This group prices assets and liabilities, develops the optimum asset and liability structures, manages interest rate risk of the firm, and oversees the management of liquidity. The roles of a typical ALCO committee are shown in Exhibit 16.1 on page 414.

The management of interest rate risk has become very sophisticated in the last decade as new risk management tools have become more common. Interest rate risk management necessarily involves using mathematical models to capture the complexity of today's financial claims.

Exhibit 16.1

Functions of Asset/Liability Committee

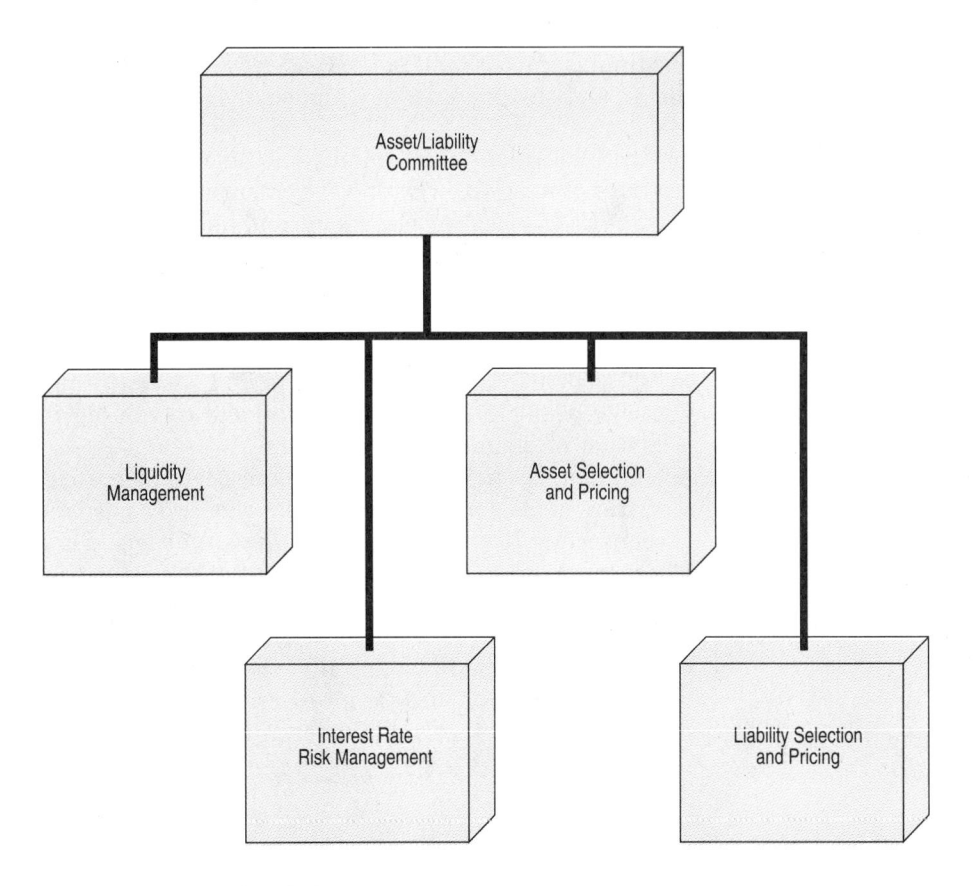

```
                    Asset/Liability
                      Committee
                          |
     ┌────────────────────┼────────────────────┐
     |                                         |
  Liquidity                                Asset Selection
  Management                                and Pricing
     |                                         |
 Interest Rate                            Liability Selection
 Risk Management                             and Pricing
```

The risk management models discussed in Chapter 18 include periodic *GAP*, duration, mark-to-market, and income simulation. Each of these tools is designed to measure the exposure of a financial intermediary to the impact on the firm's equity and income resulting from changes in open-market interest rates.

Altering the financial institution's interest rate risk position necessarily involves a risk/return tradeoff. Reducing the interest rate position of the firm will almost always lower the earnings of the firm in the short run. The trick is to develop an interest rate risk management strategy that provides acceptable earnings to the firm's shareholders without risking potential insolvency or creating unacceptable volatility in the income stream of the institution.

Credit Risk Management

It is the job of the firm's credit organization to manage the credit risk position of the firm. Credit risk is the probability of loss of interest and principal on a financial firm's debt assets. This function is usually performed by a group directed by a credit officer. This group is typically independent of the asset origination or servicing groups, and may report indirectly to the board of directors. This organization structure ensures an independent and impartial analysis of the credit situation. The credit function is performed by creating policies and procedures for underwriting loans in the origination units, analyzing the financial position of guarantors and issuers of securities held by the firm, creating policies and procedures for the servicers of assets, monitoring the credit experience of the institution's asset portfolios, and participating in the establishment of proper loan loss reserves. These are discussed fully in Chapter 20. The roles of a typical credit office are shown in Exhibit 16.2 on page 416.

To accomplish credit management duties and responsibilities, the firm must be knowledgeable about financial analysis, servicing, loan documentation, loan covenants, and environmental analysis. The firm must also maintain sound records on the credit performance of its portfolios of risky assets. Changes in underwriting, product design, servicing effectiveness, and laws and regulations can significantly impact the firm's loan loss experience.

Pricing Loans and Liabilities and Selecting Distribution Channels

The portfolio management group assumes the responsibility for determining the profitability of loans and investments. The objectives are to identify the lowest cost funding alternatives and, at the same time, identify potential asset acquisitions that provide expected returns equaling or exceeding the intermediary's cost of capital. These jobs are also frequently accomplished in the ALCO committee, which is the subject of Chapters 22 and 23. Whether a loan is destined for the portfolio or is to be sold in the secondary market, it is crucial that the firm knows how it should be priced. This involves obtaining knowledge of all the firm's costs, including debt, capital, servicing, origination, and credit.

Financial firms also have the responsibility of determining the least costly distribution channel for their products. Retail-based firms develop a franchise value related to their ability to market new products or cross-sell existing customers. Existing customers are normally less price-sensitive compared to the wholesale market or to potential new customers. This

Exhibit 16.2

Functions of Credit Office

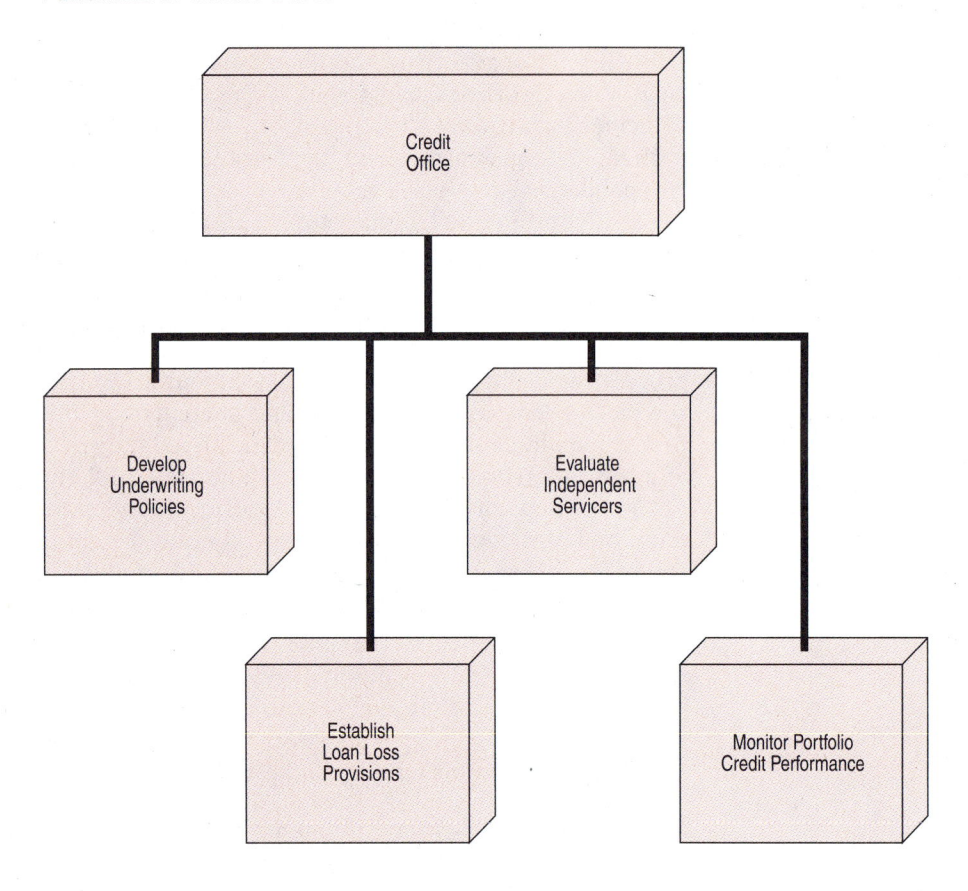

```
                    ┌──────────────┐
                    │    Credit    │
                    │    Office    │
                    └──────┬───────┘
         ┌─────────────┬───┴────┬──────────────┐
         │             │        │              │
   ┌─────────┐   ┌──────────┐  ┌──────────┐  ┌──────────┐
   │ Develop │   │ Evaluate │  │Establish │  │ Monitor  │
   │Underwr. │   │Independ. │  │Loan Loss │  │Portfolio │
   │Policies │   │Servicers │  │Provisions│  │Credit Pf.│
   └─────────┘   └──────────┘  └──────────┘  └──────────┘
```

requires developing new profit measurement tools designed to ensure that the firm maximizes the value of its retail franchise.

Pricing also requires the firm to evaluate the cost of selling its liabilities using a variety of different distribution channels. Is it more cost effective, for example, for a bank to raise funds with six-month maturities through its retail branches, negotiable certificates of deposits, or brokered deposits? The answer will change over time as competitive pressures in local markets change.

Capital Structure and Financial Leverage

A primary issue for any business is determining its optimal capital structure. This is no less important an issue for financial intermediaries. However, the job is made more complicated for intermediaries that are subject to minimum capital requirements.

One obvious difference between financial depositories and commercial and industrial businesses is the financial firm's high degree of *financial leverage*. Financial leverage describes the extent to which a firm uses debt in its capital structure. It is measured by the firm's debt, D, to total assets, A, ratio D/A. Financial depository intermediaries usually have debt that consists of 90 to 95 percent of its capital structure.

A depository's ability to issue government-insured deposits has significant implications for its use of financial leverage. These firms are able to utilize financial leverage to a much greater extent than other businesses. Indeed, as we will see, the depository has a tremendous temptation to leverage itself. Consequently, a government regulator's requirement to hold capital may be the only effective constraint on the leveraging of insured depository institutions.

A simple way to see how financial leverage works is to compute a financial firm's *equity multiplier (EM)*. The firm's *EM* is computed by dividing the firm's total assets by its net worth (*NW*). The *EM*, like the D/A, is a measure of financial leverage. A financial firm with $250,000,000 in assets and $15,000,000 in equity would have an equity multiplier of

$$EM = \$250{,}000{,}000/\$15{,}000{,}000 = 16.67$$

There is a mathematical relationship between the financial firm's return on assets (ROA), net income divided by total assets, and its return on equity, *ROE*, net income divided by total net worth. This relationship is expressed as

$$ROE = ROA \times EM$$

Return on Equity = Return on Assets × Equity Multiplier

It is difficult to achieve both a high *ROE* and low *EM*. This is because financial leverage tends to improve the return on equity. For financial firms, especially insured depositories, the cost of debt is significantly less than the cost of equity. Therefore, there is a great temptation to increase *ROE* by increasing *EM*. Of course, a higher *EM* also implies greater financial risk.

Financial Risk and Leverage

As a firm replaces debt for equity, its financial risk increases. As financial risk increases, the direct and indirect costs of debt go up. The tendency for lenders to impose greater costs on the firm that uses a higher percentage of debt in its financial structure is referred to as agency costs. Agency costs include monitoring and surveillance costs, the use of *restrictive covenants* in loan agreements, as well as the direct costs of higher interest rates on loans. A firm that has a high degree of financial leverage also has a higher probability of experiencing bankruptcy. *Distress costs* are estimated as the present value of the costs of bankruptcy times the probability of bankruptcy. Distress costs also increase, everything else constant, with the rise in financial leverage.

The impact of distress and agency costs on rising debt costs is short circuited when the firm can issue government-insured deposits. In this case, the buyer of the deposits is more concerned about the government's commitment to insure the obligations of the deposit funds than the viability of the individual firm that issues the deposits. As discussed in Chapter 12, the tendency for the depositor to be unconcerned about the strength of the institution in which they have their money is known as moral hazard. Because depository firms do not face significantly higher debt costs and other agency costs as financial leverage increases, they have a strong incentive to replace shareholder capital with government guaranteed debt.

The extent to which financial depositories leverage themselves also depends on whether they use uninsured or uncollateralized borrowings, such as commercial paper, large negotiable certificates of deposit, or Fed funds liabilities. The more uninsured debt in the capital structure, the more monitoring by private investors and the higher the agency costs. In other words, the uninsured investor does not present the same moral hazard problem as the insured depositor.

The other constraint on leverage is the government regulatory system. Government regulators can increase agency costs of the firm. They do this by putting limits on the holdings of risky assets by intermediaries and by limiting the extent of financial leverage through the establishment of minimum capital requirements. For a financial firm with inadequate capital, the government can impose a host of restrictions on growth, lending, asset composition, and mergers and acquisitions that have a direct bearing on the business' future financial performance. This represents significant financial agency costs.

In 1989 and 1991, the passage of FIRREA and the FDICIA gave OTS sharply expanded supervisory powers to deal with institutions deemed undercapitalized. These include the power to carry out the following actions.

1. Require shrinkage of assets
2. Prohibit lending
3. Implement conservatorship
4. Eliminate specific lending and investment activities
5. Force a merger
6. Change the composition of management or directors

Exhibit 16.3 describes the very difficult job of finding the optimal capital structure for a firm. It applies equally well for an insured depository as it does for a manufacturing firm. The graph has the market value of the firm's equity, *V*, on the vertical axis and the debt-to-asset ratio, *D/A*, on the horizontal axis. The line $V_e - V$, without regulatory agency costs, shows that if the management of a financial firm wants to maximize the equity value of the firm it will continue to replace equity with debt until it has virtually no

Exhibit 16.3

Optimal Capital Structure for an Intermediary

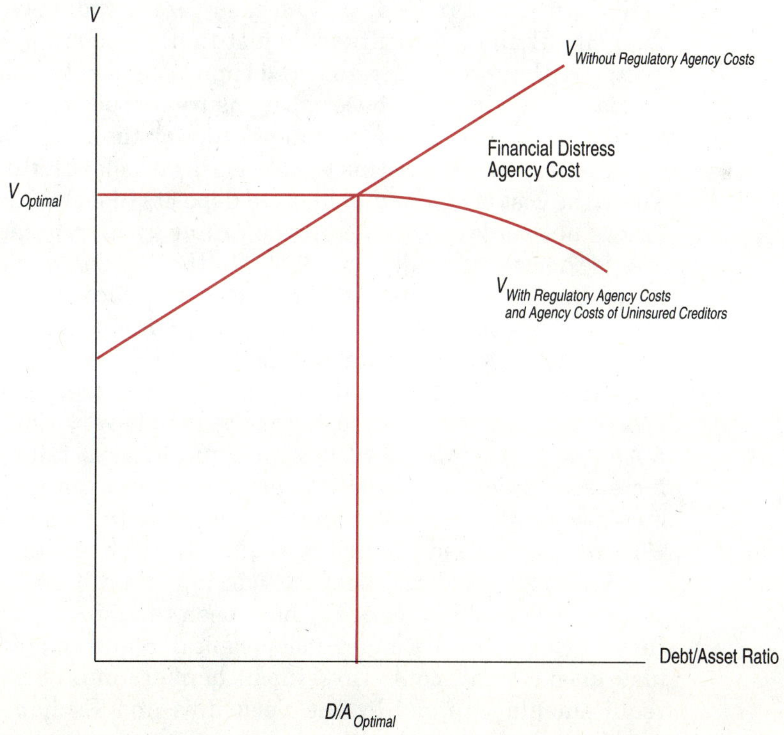
V
V Without Regulatory Agency Costs
Financial Distress
Agency Cost
V Optimal
V With Regulatory Agency Costs
and Agency Costs of Uninsured Creditors
Debt/Asset Ratio
D/A Optimal

equity in its capital structure. Two strong motivations for doing this are the tax deductibility of interest on debt and the low cost of deposits raised with the help of deposit insurance. In fact, the firm is motivated to continue to replace equity with debt until one of two events occurs. In the first event, the regulator will intervene and require more equity by establishing minimum capital requirements and threatening adverse regulatory sanctions, one form of agency costs. The second possible event would be for the firms using uninsured liabilities to experience private investors who demand higher interest rates and additional costly debt covenants, other forms of agency costs.

In addition, as financial leverage increases, the probability of bankruptcy increases. Distress costs also motivate management to limit the degree of financial leverage. Considering Exhibit 16.3, the firm will be motivated to increase its D/A ratio by moving along the upward sloping line until sufficient agency and distress costs cause it to bend down. The highest point, $V_{optimal}$, is where the optimal D/A for the firm is found and where the firm experiences its lowest weighted cost of capital.

In practice, both higher agency and distress costs occur as D/A increases. Were it not for these two costs, we would expect that insured financial intermediaries would leverage almost to the point of replacing all their capital with debt. Indeed, one can easily argue that between 1981 and 1988, the FHLBB allowed thrifts to do just that, since many had no tangible net worth. Without a strictly enforced capital constraint, the institutions kept increasing their asset base with insured deposits without facing either agency monitoring costs from depositors or their regulator.

It is easy to see why this is the case if we look at Exhibit 16.4. This graph shows the cost of equity and insured deposits (debt) to an insured depository that is not subject to a capital constraint by its regulator. On the vertical axis is the cost of equity and debt. On the horizontal axis is the firm's D/A ratio. Because the insured firm does not face meaningful agency and distress costs that increase the cost of raising deposits, the firm can lower its weighted cost of capital as its D/A ratio increases. This is true even though the higher financial risk of the firm increases its equity cost. The lack of significant agency costs results in only very slowly rising debt costs. As a result, the weighted cost of capital keeps falling as the D/A ratio increases. A lower weighted average cost of capital permits the firm to increase profits by increasing its size and taking on more investments whose yields exceed the firm's weighted cost of capital.

Although we have been discussing depository institutions in this section, we could just as easily have been referring to other intermediaries. Insurance companies must meet capital requirements imposed by state insurance commissions. Investment bankers must meet minimum capital requirements imposed by the Securities and Exchange Commission. Finance companies, on the other hand, finance their operations with privately issued debt. The investors in finance company debt impose very real agency

Exhibit 16.4

Cost of Equity, Debt, and Weighted Cost of Capital

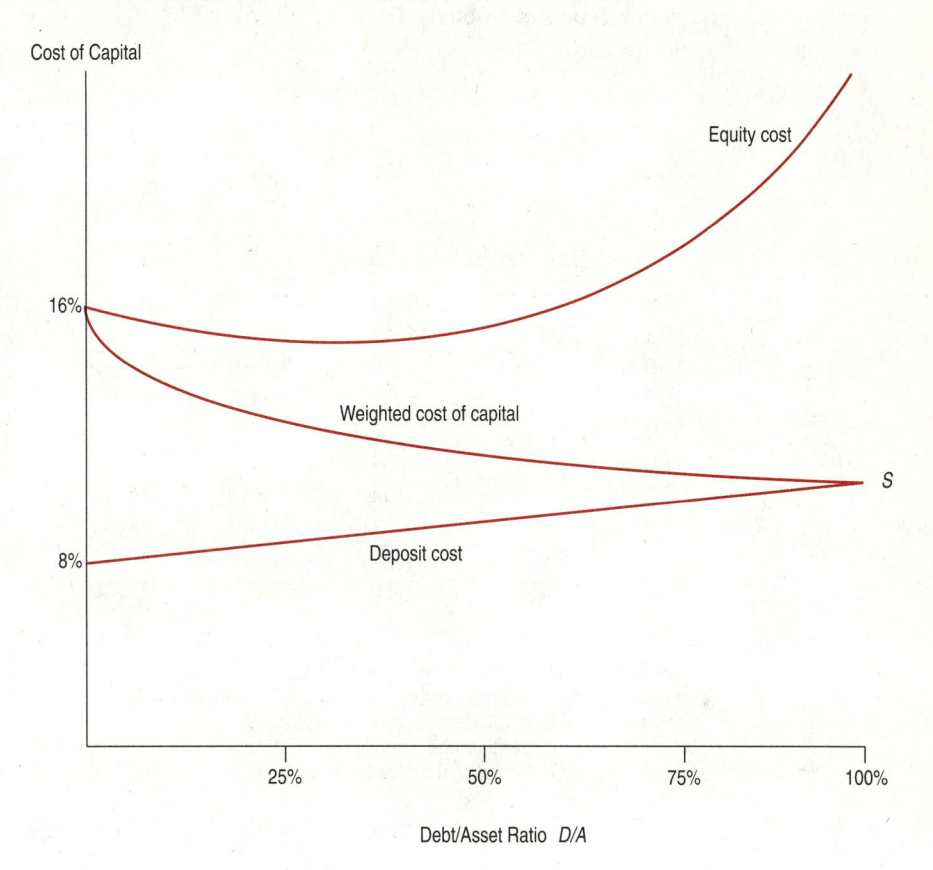

costs on these institutions, since they realize that there is no deposit insurance corporation to cover losses in the event of financial distress.

Relative Capital Positions of the Major Financial Institutions

Deposit insurance has a profound impact on the ability of these financial firms to leverage their capital base. As a result, the minimum capitalization of deposit firms must be determined by regulators. Consider the differences in the equity-to-total-assets ratios for commercial banks, security firms, insurance companies, property and casualty insurance companies and business and personal finance companies. Table 16.1 on page 422 provides

Table 16.1

Median Equity-to-Total Assets Ratios*
Major Types of Publicly Traded Intermediaries
(in percent)

Year	Large National Bank Holding Company	Securities Brokers and Dealers	Life Insurance	Property and Casualty Insurance	Business Finance Company	Personal Finance Company
1980	5.60	19.51	19.71	23.12	19.53	14.85
1981	5.67	24.49	21.06	24.20	20.42	14.71
1982	5.70	17.89	20.69	24.42	22.28	15.32
1983	5.72	28.92	19.92	23.08	20.42	14.22
1984	5.83	21.63	18.26	20.48	19.66	12.66
1985	5.94	19.94	15.44	16.85	19.16	12.34
1986	6.01	18.04	14.62	22.98	20.73	12.51
1987	6.03	23.41	13.40	21.91	17.04	14.26
1988	6.21	26.41	12.67	20.51	16.07	13.49
1989	6.27	19.69	12.37	22.29	13.76	13.30

*Data were taken from Standard and Poor's Compustat Service, Inc. Nonbank institutions with redeemable preferred stock have had the stock figures removed from their capital accounts so asset totals will be consistent.
Source: Department of the Treasury. *Modernizing the Financial System: Recommendations for Safer, More Competitive Banks*. February 1991. Section II, p. II-5.

data from 1980 to 1989 for publicly traded companies. These data show the commercial banks with the lowest equity-to-assets ratios and the property and casualty and securities firms with the highest. In all cases, the nondepositories have at least twice as much capital as the commercial banks. The data also show the trend toward lower capital ratios for life companies and, to a lesser degree, finance companies.

Business Risks

The optimal capital structure is also related to the riskiness, or volatility, of the firm's income stream. Financial firms with a high degree of interest rate risk will experience larger fluctuations in income than firms that have small interest rate risk exposure. Similarly, financial firms with large portfolios of risky assets or high concentrations of assets that are not well diversified will experience larger income fluctuations.

Private investors and government regulators are concerned with these portfolio characteristics when buying debt or insuring deposits. These risks are termed *business risks*. Intermediaries assume many types of business risks including the following:

1. Credit risks of the institution's asset portfolio and off-balance sheet obligations and guarantees
2. Interest rate risk including off-balance sheet exposures
3. Liquidity risks
4. Funding risks related to the mix of funding sources between more interest elastic wholesale versus less interest rate elastic retail funding sources
5. Operating cost risks relating to maintaining costly origination and servicing organizations

Because of business risks, deposit insurers and regulators must be concerned with each of these five sources of financial distress. If regulators simply established capital requirements in the form of maximum D/A ratios, financial firms would be motivated to take large business risks. This is because their insured deposit sources of funds are unaffected as to availability and cost by these risks. Consequently, regulators also look at these risks in their examination and supervision activities.

Regulators control these risks by establishing asset investment restrictions that limit undue concentrations in risky assets. More recently, they have established risk-based capital requirements so that there is a relationship between the amount of capital in the firm and the percentage of risky assets in the firm's portfolio. Congress has also worked to reduce the business risks of depositories by reducing access to the wholesale brokered deposit market and outlawing junk bonds for S&L portfolios. Insurance commissions have also limited junk bond holdings of life insurance companies.

Intermediary Profitability

Chapter 7 described the functional structure of intermediaries as origination, servicing, brokerage, market-making, and portfolio management. To the extent that these functions represent the primary activities of intermediaries, it would seem as though the income statement of these firms should be categorized using the same functional organization. Unfortunately, under generally accepted accounting principles, the income statements of intermediaries are not organized in this manner.

This doesn't mean, however, that a conceptual redesign of the income statement can't be developed for theoretical purposes using the functional breakdown from Chapter 7. This is done by unbundling the various functions of the intermediary and demonstrating how each of these functions generates its own revenues and costs. Equation 16.1 defines the intermediary's total profit.

$$\text{Total profit before tax } (TP) = NOI + NSI + NBI + NPI \quad [6.1]$$

where:

$$NOI = \text{net origination income}$$
$$NSI = \text{net servicing income}$$
$$NBI = \text{net brokerage income}$$
$$NPI = \text{net portfolio income}$$

Net Origination Income

The origination groups within any intermediary can be thought of as contracting with the portfolio manager to originate assets with specific risk and return parameters. The origination unit's revenue is derived from its contractual agreement with the portfolio management function. Origination units can also originate assets for other investors. If assets can be originated at a cost lower than the agreed upon contractual fee, the difference is profit.

The origination unit also sells its underwriting and investment expertise. One example of this revenue is from the firm selling whole loans, securities, or loan participations to third-party investors at higher prices than were originated.

The unit's origination income statement will look like Equation 16.2.

$$NOI = Ro - Co \quad [16.2]$$

where:

$$Ro = \sum_{i}^{n}(A_i\, F_i) = \text{Origination revenue for asset } i \text{ times fee } i \text{ for } n \text{ claims originated}$$
$$A_i = \text{Asset } i \text{ represented in dollars}$$
$$F_i = \text{Fee } i \text{ represented as a percent of } A_i$$
$$Co = \text{Costs of origination}$$

An example of *NOI* would be a mortgage originating unit that originates $42 million of loans in a year and receives a 1 percent origination fee. If the unit's cost of operations was $400,000 per year, the unit's profit would be ($42,000,000 × .01 − $400,000 =) $20,000.

Net Servicing Income

The servicing units also act as contract agents for the portfolio manager and any outside institutions that invest in assets serviced by it. All claims must be serviced. Consequently, the intermediary must determine who will service each claim it holds in portfolio. Servicing can be done by the firm itself or contractually by a third party. Chapter 2 discussed the fact that one factor making up the yield on a loan or investment is the cost of servicing. This servicing cost is the revenue stream to the servicing unit.

A commercial bank syndicating a commercial term loan would have to obtain a price from the servicing unit for the servicing activities it performs for outside investors. If the servicing unit is particularly efficient, it will be able to service at a price below the contract price. This creates profit for the servicing unit.

The income statement of the servicing unit is seen as Equation 16.3.

$$NSI = \sum_{i}^{n} (Rs_i - Cs_i) \qquad [16.3]$$

where:

i = Servicing for firm i

n = Number of firms serviced for

Rs_i = Revenue from servicing fees paid by the portfolio and outside investors, i

Cs_i = Servicing costs for servicing for i

An example would be a commercial bank that has sold loan participations on $80 million of loans. It services the loans for a fee of .25 percent per annum. If it costs the servicing unit $170,000 per year in operating costs, its profit from servicing would be ($80,000,000 × .0025 − $170,000 =) $30,000.

Net Brokerage Income

Brokerage income from third-party brokerage is easy to measure. This revenue is simply the difference between what the brokerage function is able to obtain as a commission, defined to be the difference between the price received by the seller, and the price paid by the buyer.

The broker's income statement would look like Equation 16.4.

$$NBI = Rb - Cb \qquad [16.4]$$

where:

$$Rb = \sum_{i}^{n} (Pb_i - Ps_i)$$

n = Number of brokerage transactions

Pb_i = Price of claim i bought from a third party

Ps_i = Price of claim i sold to a third party

Cb = Cost of operating the brokerage unit

An example would be a discount security brokerage that sells 10,000,000 shares of stock per year at an average commission rate of .30 per share. If this firm had a cost of $2,900,000 per annum, its profit would be (10,000,000 × $.30 − $2,900,000 =) $100,000.

Net Portfolio Income

Portfolio income is measured solely on the performance of the portfolio in terms of net interest margin and the gain or loss on loans and securities held in portfolio. The portfolio manager must manage interest rate risk, credit risk, mortality risk, and liquidity. The contribution of the portfolio manager is normally measured by the net interest margin. However, fees paid for origination, servicing, and brokerage are subtracted from the portfolio's income.

The portfolio management unit's income statement would be as shown in Equation 16.5.

$$NPI = Rp - Cp - La - Ro - Rs \qquad [16.5]$$

where:

Rp = Portfolio income from interest and gain and loss on sale of assets

Cp = Cost of portfolio management services

La = Loan losses

Ro = Fees charged by origination unit for their services

Rs = Fees charged by servicing unit for their services

An example would be a savings bank with interest income and gain on sale of securities of $120,000,000 in 1993. Its interest costs are $115,000,000 per annum. The firm pays the origination unit 1.5 percent of the loans it originates that are put in the firm's portfolio. In 1993, $30,000,000 were originated for the portfolio. The servicing unit services $90,000,000 of loans for the portfolio. It has negotiated a fee of .20 percent of the dollar amount of loans serviced. The portfolio unit's total operating costs are $1,000,000 per annum. This savings bank's income statement would look like Table 16.2.

A review of any intermediary's income statement would reveal that the interest margin from the portfolio and fees generated from origination, brokerage, and servicing are all major components. The revenues and costs shown here are accounted for differently under GAAP because in most intermediaries the functions are integrated for accounting purposes. Most firms do not have the system designed to measure the appropriate data. More firms are developing this ability, however. Consequently, this conceptual framework is important for developing management information and incentive systems.

Portfolio and Fee Income

As we have seen, intermediaries generate income from the origination, servicing, brokerage, and portfolio management activities they engage in. These are usually classified as *net interest income* and *fee income*. The interest and capital gains income generated by an intermediary's portfolio

Table 16.2

Savings Bank Income Statement

Interest income	$120,000,000
Interest expense	115,000,000
Net interest margin	5,000,000
Less cost of origination (.015 × $30,000,000)	−450,000
Cost of servicing (.002 × $90,000,000)	−180,000
Portfolio income (pre-tax)	4,370,000

after the liability costs have been subtracted is called *net interest income*. Depositories also generate fee income. In recent years, fee income has become a faster growing percentage of total income for many intermediaries. This income relates to the origination, servicing, and brokerage functions of intermediaries.

Because some of these firms are major participants in the nation's payment system, they generate fee income by providing demand deposit, credit card and debit card, telephone and wire transfer, and computer funds transfer services. These fee-based services are all related to the role of depositories as payment service providers. Mortgage loan servicing and student loan servicing are major sources of servicing income for loans sold to government sponsored credit enterprises in the secondary markets. Large depositories also syndicate large loans that are sold to other financial firms for which servicing income is earned.

Brokerage produces income through the brokerage of securities, foreign exchange, and other financial claims for individuals and institutional customers.

Intermediaries also generate fee income from their origination and portfolio management activities. Examples of these are loan modification fees, appraisal fees, letters of credit, and document preparation fees. Portfolio and fee income sources will be discussed more fully.

Net Interest Margin and Spread

The primary measure of the profitability of the portfolio management function of intermediaries is the *net interest margin*. The net interest margin measures the difference between the total interest income earned on the institution's earning assets and the interest expense on its interest-costing liabilities. The net interest margin for period t is shown in Equation 16.6.

$$\text{Net interest margin}_t = \text{interest income}_t - \text{interest expense}_t \quad [16.6]$$

The net interest margin is influenced by a number of factors. These factors are important to understand when comparing the net interest margin of several intermediaries, and when analyzing the trend in the net interest margin for a single institution over time. The primary factor affecting the net interest margin is the quantities of assets and liabilities of a firm. Size impacts the net interest margin in a significant way. As a result, the net interest margin is not very useful where comparing the portfolio management activities of different-sized institutions or in reviewing trends of a single institution that is growing or shrinking. To overcome this deficiency, the net interest margin is scaled by the total dollar amount of earning assets and interest costing liabilities. The result is the *net interest spread,* which is expressed as a percentage interest rate as shown in Equation 16.7.

Net Interest Spread$_t$ = [interest income$_t$/average earning assets$_t$] −

[interest expenses$_t$/average interest-paying liabilities$_t$] [16.7]

A problem with the net interest spread is that the dollar amount of earning assets and liabilities is rarely equal. Thus, firms with unequal dollar amounts of interest-earning assets and paying liabilities or a high level of nonperforming assets experience quite different net interest spreads. In order to eliminate the distortion caused by unequal dollar amounts of assets and liabilities, the net interest spread is frequently computed by taking the interest income and interest expense and dividing them by the average assets of the firm. This produces the *net interest spread to average assets* shown in Equation 16.8.

Net Interest Spread to Average Assets$_t$ = [interest income$_t$ −

interest expense$_t$]/average assets$_t$ [16.8]

The net interest margin, net interest spread, and net interest spread to average assets are shown in Table 16.3 on page 430 for the FNMA for the years 1988 to 1990.

Factors Influencing the Net Interest Spread and Net Interest Spread to Average Assets

The net interest spread and net interest spread to average assets are impacted by many factors which are influenced by management's selection of a portfolio strategy. Paramount in importance is the willingness of management to take interest rate and credit risk. Also of major importance is the selection of funding sources used by the firm. The relationship between the dollar amount of earning assets versus liabilities is a factor that impacts the net interest margin. It is worthwhile to review in greater depth how these factors influence net interest spread and net interest spread to average assets. The net interest spread to average assets for all commercial banks and other cost and revenue data are shown in Table 16.4 on page 431.

Credit Risk

The willingness of the institution to accept credit risk is a major factor influencing the net interest spread. Risky assets have a credit risk premium built into their yield. If properly underwritten, the loss experience will be

Table 16.3

Net Interest Margin, Net Interest Spread, and Net Interest Spread to Average Assets
Federal National Mortgage Association
1988–1990
(dollars in millions)

Item	1990	1989	1988
Average interest-earning assets (a)	$123,637	$112,446	$105,597
Interest income (b)	$ 12,069	$ 11,080	$ 10,226
Interest income to average earning assets % (c)	9.86%	9.96%	9.78%
Average interest-bearing liabilities (d)	$117,551	$107,802	$101,760
Interest cost (e)	$ 10,476	$ 9,889	$ 9,389
Interest cost to average interest-bearing liabilities (f)	8.91%	9.17%	9.23%
Net interest income (g) = (b − a)	$1,593	$1,191	$837
Net interest spread to average assets (h) = (g/a)	1.29%	1.06%	.79%
Net interest spread (i) = (c − f)	.95%	.79%	.55%

Source: Revised and adapted from Federal National Mortgage Association. *1990 Annual Report.* p. 8.

less than the risk premium and the firm will earn a higher profit. Whether this is the case or not, the net interest spread will tend to be higher for those intermediaries that invest in riskier assets.

Interest Rate Risk

The interest rate risk position of the intermediary will also influence the net interest spread. The acceptance of higher interest rate risk does not necessarily mean a higher net interest spread, however. An intermediary

Table 16.4

**Income and Expenses of Commercial Banks as a Percentage of Average Assets
1990**
(percent of average assets)

Interest income	9.57%
Interest expense	6.13
Net interest spread	3.44
Taxable equivalent	3.59
Noninterest income	1.63
Loss provision	.93
Noninterest expenses	3.45
Security gain (+) or loss (−)	.02
Before tax income	.70
Tax	.23
Extraordinary income	.02
Net Income	.50

Source: Federal Reserve *Bulletin*. (July 1991).

holding long-term fixed-rate assets funded with short-term floating rate liabilities experiences a higher net interest spread when the term structure of interest rates is upward sloping and a lower net interest spread when the term structure is flat or downward sloping.

For many decades, the thrift industry profited by taking large interest rate risks by investing in fixed-rate mortgages with short-term liabilities. During the 1950s and most of the 1960s, this turned out to be profitable, since the term structure was generally upward sloping. The reverse occurred in the early 1980s.

Funding Sources

The retail deposits of financial depositories usually cost less than the wholesale funding sources of these firms. Deposits attracted from retail customers may pay a lower interest rate, but there are hidden servicing costs, such as the cost of providing convenience through costly branches and other services. However, these operating costs do not influence the net interest spread. Consequently, depositories that rely more on retail funds will typically experience a higher net interest spread.

Another funding factor that impacts the net interest spread is the percentage of lower interest cost transaction accounts the depository has in its liability structure. A depository with a high percentage of demand deposits and other low interest-paying transaction accounts to total liabilities will, if everything else is unchanged, have a lower interest/expense ratio. Again, as in the case of the retail deposits, a high percentage of demand deposits may produce a higher net interest spread. However, because of the higher cost of servicing transaction accounts, the full cost of these liabilities will not be reflected in the net interest spread.

Tax Exempt Securities

Some depositories hold large investments in tax-exempt securities. These are held by institutions with high taxable income and high marginal tax rates. If a depository holds tax-exempt securities, it will appear to have a lower net interest spread due to the lower interest return on these assets. In order to compare these firms with others that do not hold tax-exempt securities, it is customary to use the taxable equivalent yield on the tax-exempt bonds in determining the net interest spread. The result is referred to as the *taxable equivalent net interest spread*. Table 16.4 shows the interest margin on an actual and taxable equivalent basis.

Nonperforming Assets

A financial firm that accepts high credit risk normally will have a high net interest spread. However, it will also tend to have a higher percentage of nonperforming assets. These are assets that no longer accrue interest income because of their delinquent status. Such firms may experience the apparent anomaly of a relative high net interest spread and a relatively low net interest margin.

Fee-Based Services of Financial Institutions

This section will focus on the fee-based income sources of financial intermediaries. Fee income is generated as a result of the three information processing functions of intermediaries: origination, servicing, and brokerage. The following are examples of fee income that relate to each of these functions.

Origination Sources of Fee Income

- *Loan Origination Fees:* Many types of loans involve the borrower paying an origination fee. This fee is normally assessed at the time the loan is funded. These fees are very common on real estate loans of all types including home mortgages, second mortgages, and equity lines of credit.
- *Appraisal Fees:* Virtually all real estate loans involve the assessment of the cost of a real estate appraisal. This might be

done by the lender's staff appraiser or an outside contract appraiser.
- *Loan Commitment Fees:* Financial intermediaries usually assess fees to borrowers who are interested in obtaining a commitment for future financing. A corporate acquisition, whether friendly or not, will normally require the purchaser to obtain a commitment from one or more lenders that financing for the transaction will likely be forthcoming. Investment banks and large commercial banks have made enormous fees for writing these commitment letters, which are sometimes called *comfort letters*.

  Real estate developers and builders also pay fees to arrange future mortgage financing or the permanent take-out financing on real estate developments. In both cases, the lender agrees to make a long-term mortgage to pay off the construction lender.

  Lines of credit and letters of credit are also major sources of fee income for financial institutions. Many borrowers want to arrange financing for future needs and will pay a fee to set up a line of credit, while other borrowers back up a loan or security with a letter of credit.
- *Underwriting Fees:* Investment banks and commercial banks earn underwriting fees for the creation of securities and syndicated loans. The fee represents compensation for origination activities relating to the claim, as well as the brokerage expertise that the institution brings to bear in order to ensure that the claim is distributed to investors.

Servicing Sources of Fee Income

- *Commercial Bank Correspondent Services:* Large commercial banks have provided a number of services for smaller commercial banks and thrifts over the years. The most important of these is check-processing services. In addition, larger banks with security trading departments provide security purchase and sale services, as well as the safekeeping of securities belonging to smaller banks and thrifts.
- *Trust Services:* Providing trust services is an important revenue source for a number of financial institutions. This activity involves managing a client's financial and real assets. The trust entity normally provides safekeeping, advisory, accounting, record keeping, and management services for the client. Trust fees are normally assessed on the amount of assets under management.
- *Portfolio Management Fees:* Mutual fund managers, managers of real estate investment trusts, the general partner in limited partnerships, and asset management companies derive most of their revenue from pure portfolio management services. These

organizations and individuals, like the trust company, manage assets for a fee.
- *Credit and Debit Card Annual Maintenance Fees:* Most providers of credit and debit cards charge an annual maintenance fee to offset the cost of account servicing.
- *Mortgage Servicing Fees:* A mortgage sold in the secondary market is serviced by the seller or another agent. This activity involves collection, statement production, payoff handling, delinquencies, and foreclosures. It is typical for the servicer to earn an annualized fee of 25 to 50 basis points on the outstanding loan balance.
- *Corporate Loan Syndications and Participations:* Large corporate loans are frequently sold, in part, to other lenders in the form of a syndication or participation. The originating institution, or lead lender, may sell off one or more participations in the loan to other lenders. The lead institution will earn a servicing fee by selling the loan to another lender at an interest rate that is somewhat below the loan contractual rate paid by the borrower. This creates servicing income for the selling institution.
- *Data Processing Services:* Financial institutions offer data processing services to other financial institutions. Most of these servicing activities are highly automated. Very expensive proprietary software has been developed by the leading firms. These firms will frequently sell or license the use of the software or process the work of other financial firms for a fee.

The most common data processing services include checking account, savings account, credit card, mortgage loan, general ledger, payroll, and commercial and industrial loan processing. American Express Company, for example, is the nation's largest supplier of data processing systems for credit cards.

Servicing Fees That Are Transaction Related

- *Credit and Debit Card Transaction Income:* Credit and debit card issuers earn transaction income related to the use of the card. Financial institutions earn a fee from the merchant that accepts the card. This fee is split two ways. A portion goes to the card-issuing institution and a portion goes to the institution that converts the card receipts to cash for the merchant (merchant fee).
- *Checking Account Fees:* Financial institutions earn a number of different types of fees on checking accounts. They include monthly maintenance fees, per-check use fees, nonsufficient fund (NSF) fees, and other fees for assisting the customer in using and maintaining the account.

- *Lock-Box Services:* The lock-box is a service involving mail-receiving boxes. Financial institutions that provide this service have local payment-processing centers that ensure the timely receipt of checks and timely depositing into the receiving firm's account. This cash management service assists the firm in minimizing its float.
- *Automated Transaction Machines:* Many financial institutions offer automated transaction services through automated transaction machines (ATMs).
- *Computerized Banking and Brokerage:* Although relatively new, computerized banking and brokerage are now being offered. These services allow the customer to review account balances, shift funds between accounts, implement security purchases and sales, and access an array of informational services.

Brokerage Sources of Fee Income

- *Security Brokerage:* Investment banking firms and other institutions provide security brokerage services to commercial customers and consumers. The primary revenue from this activity is the brokerage commission associated with each transaction.
- *Foreign Exchange and Advisory Services:* Financial intermediaries provide foreign exchange services to their clients. This involves selling foreign currencies that earn brokerage income.
- *Insurance Brokerage:* Financial institutions, other than insurance companies, sell insurance. This includes property and casualty and life. The income on this activity is in the form of insurance commissions.

Objectives of Mutual Institutions

Many savings and loans, insurance companies, savings banks, and all credit unions are mutual institutions. They are owned by their members, which may include depositors, borrowers, and policyowners. Over the years researchers have explored the question of whether mutual institutions behave similar to stock-owned institutions or whether they seem to be responsive to objectives other than profit maximization. These differences are important when comparing the financial performance of stock and mutual institutions and when trying to understand their decision-making framework. Some researchers have concluded that a number of objectives may be more important to mutual institutions than to stock-owned institutions.

Growth

Some researchers maintain that profit is not the primary objective of a mutual, insisting instead that maximizing the satisfaction of as many customers as possible is their objective. The assumption is that a potential customer will not become a client if they are not satisfied. The objective of a mutual institution would then be to maximize satisfaction by maximizing growth in assets or in number of customers. Put simply, maximizing growth will maximize satisfaction.

Management Income

There is another reason to consider growth in assets to be a major objective of mutual institutions. This relates to the often-observed fact that the managers of mutual institutions tend to be compensated based on the size of the institution they manage. This would certainly provide a major motivation for mutuals to become larger.

Management's Nonpecuniary Rewards

The mutual savings and loan business was jokingly characterized in the 1960s and 1970s as the 3, 6, 3 business. This means that the savings and loan would borrow at 3 percent, lend at 6 percent, and the senior management would be on the golf course at 3 P.M. *Nonpecuniary* means nonmonetary. Less job stress and more leisure time would be the objective of management here. The point is that the mutual institution has less incentive to be a profit maximizing firm when a lower level of performance is acceptable. Some have held that the expenses of mutual institutions also tend to be higher since mutual managers have less reason to produce profits for shareholders. These firms may have a tendency to provide higher management and employee perks than profit-maximizing firms.

Risk Minimization

Others feel that risk minimization is a strong objective of mutual institutions, as compared to stock-owned companies. Since the management and board of directors or trustees of mutual institutions are not rewarded based on profits and return on equity, they have less incentive to take potentially profitable business risks. Risk of failure is of greater concern because failure means loss of employment. Taking risks that result in higher returns does not benefit the mutual management group as much as those operating stock institutions. This one-sided aspect of the risk-return tradeoff for mutual managers could make them more risk averse.

Meeting the Competition

Some believe that market competition will influence how mutual institutions behave. Mutual institutions do not operate in a vacuum, rather, they are influenced by competitors who are frequently stock-owned institutions. Consequently, when competition is strong mutuals are forced by competitive market forces to behave more like stock institutions. Since stock institutions impact pricing, marketing, and the cost of inputs like employees, mutual institutions have to emulate stock companies to survive.

Control

Many believe that one advantage of mutual firms is that the board of directors and senior management maintain control of the organization. When depositors open accounts in mutual saving and loans, they typically sign proxies that name a person close to the existing board and management to vote at the firm's annual meeting. Many state-chartered savings banks have self-perpetuating boards of trustees that name their own successors. Mutual life companies also have essentially self-perpetuating boards. These practices create effective control by the group currently in authority. With control comes the ability to set salaries and other benefits for the management and board. Such effective control also stifles criticism from the outside.

There are important differences in the motivation and behavior of the management and directors of mutuals as compared to stock institutions. Unfortunately, motivation is not easy to quantify and measure. Nor is the number of hours management spend on the golf course easy to measure given available data. Nevertheless, it is important to consider alternative objectives of mutual institutions when evaluating them.

Summary

This chapter explained how financial intermediaries make a profit—by performing origination, servicing, brokerage, and portfolio management activities. The most clearly understood of these is the portfolio management function.

Intermediaries must make important capital structure decisions. These decisions depend not only on the regulatory environment in which they operate, but also on the degree of financial leverage and business risks that influence the firm's cost of capital. For intermediaries that issue insured deposits, the role of the regulator is critically important to the capital structure decision. This is because investors in insured deposits do not impose high agency costs on the firm. Consequently, regulators must impose these costs.

The chapter described the sources of intermediary income and the ways of measuring it. The chapter closed with a discussion of the possible objectives of mutual institutions.

The **primary duties of financial managers** are valuation of financial claims, interest rate risk management, credit risk management, pricing of loans and liabilities, and determining the optimal capital structure.

The **optimal capital structure** for an intermediary depends on the impact of agency and distress costs on the cost of debt and equity at intermediaries. **Intermediaries** with insured deposits face regulations that establish minimum capital levels. **Regulators** also influence the extent to which insured depositories can accept business risks.

Financial risk is a term that describes the increased probability of financial distress as a firm increases its debt-to-assets ratio. Financial leverage relates to the return on stockholders' equity in the following relationship:

$$\text{Return on Equity} = \text{return on assets} \times \text{equity multiplier}$$
$$ROE = ROA \times EM$$

Business risk relates to the extent to which a financial firm accepts risks that are unrelated to capital structure. For financial firms these business risks include the following:

1. Credit risks related to asset quality
2. Interest rate risk
3. Liquidity risk relating to available funding sources
4. Funding risks related to the mix of retail and wholesale liabilities
5. Degree of operating leverage relating to the cost of origination and servicing units

The primary measures of portfolio management income are the **net interest margin, net interest spread, and net interest spread to average assets.**

$$\text{Net Interest Margin}_t = \text{interest income}_t - \text{interest expense}_t$$
$$\text{Net Interest Spread}_t = [\text{interest income}_t/\text{average earning assets}_t]$$
$$- [\text{interest expenses}_t/\text{average interest-paying liabilities}_t]$$
$$\text{Net Interest Spread to Average Assets}_t = [\text{interest income}_t - \text{interest expense}_t]/\text{average assets}_t$$

The following are the primary factors influencing the net interest spread and net interest spread to average assets:

1. Credit risks
2. Interest rate risk

3. Funding sources used
4. Tax-exempt securities held
5. Nonperforming assets

Mutual financial institutions are motivated by objectives different from those of shareholder-owned institutions. Objectives that are thought to motivate mutual financial institutions include the following:

1. Growth
2. Management income
3. Management's nonpecuniary rewards
4. Risk minimization
5. Meeting the competition
6. Maintaining management and director control

Questions

Chapter 16

1. What activities do intermediaries perform to make a profit?
2. What are the primary financial duties performed in the management of intermediaries?
3. What is involved in interest rate risk management?
4. What is involved in credit risk management?
5. Do you think commercial banks are unique as financial firms? Why or why not?
6. How do insured depositors differ from other financial firms with respect to agency and distress costs?
7. How has the FIRREA of 1989 increased financial distress cost at insured intermediaries?
8. Explain which depositors are worried about the financial leverage of insured depositories and why.
9. Why did many S&Ls essentially replace all their equity with debt in the 1980s?
10. What are the business risks of an intermediary?
11. What factors impact on an intermediary's net interest margin?
12. Financial firms that hold tax-exempt securities as investments cannot directly compare the yield on their assets to firms that hold no tax-exempt securities. What should be done to allow such comparisons?
13. Discuss several fee-based services in the areas of origination, servicing, and brokerage.
14. Explain several objectives that might be adopted by mutual institutions.

Financial Innovation: Theory and Practice

appendix

The last three decades have witnessed an extraordinary explosion in financial innovation. Countless new financial claims, distribution systems, information processing capabilities, and risk management techniques have been created. Financial innovation is a necessary feature of financial management for three primary reasons. First, it is important to determine which forces give rise to financial innovation or alternatively, whether the innovation is simply a product of spontaneous random behavior. It is logical to assume that the events that provide the impetus for innovative behavior can also determine the conditions under which profitable innovation opportunities may be found.

Secondly, some theorists believe that financial innovations can alter established macroeconomic relationships. Financial innovation may make it more difficult to predict how the relationship between monetary and real economic variables change. This is important in the implementation of monetary policy.

Technological innovations are also responsible for improving the efficiency of the money and capital markets. Today, information systems tie together financial institutions throughout the world. These systems act to make our money and capital markets more efficient. They have also made it more difficult for financial institutions to profit from trying to monopolize information.

Finally, innovation involves change, and change can alter the fortunes of established institutions and create new opportunities for others.

Theories of Financial Innovation

There have been a number of excellent studies on the subject of financial innovation over the years. The basic premise of this research is that innovation tends to take place most frequently during periods of rapid change in technology, regulation, taxation, and price volatility. This Appendix looks at many of the theories developed in the last several decades.

Silber's Constraint Theory of Innovation

William Silber (1975) attributes financial innovation to attempts by profit-maximizing firms to reduce the impact of various types of constraints that have the impact of reducing profitability. Silber's theory is one of the most general of the theories and is, therefore, consistent with each of the others that follow. Silber postulates that financial institutions, as profit-maximizing organizations, will attempt to innovate to increase business opportunities or reduce costs. This may involve innovation in order to circumvent constraints that restrict the operations or market opportunities of the firm. Under this theory, the old law prohibiting the thrifts from offering transaction accounts provided the incentive for them to innovate. The result was the development of negotiable order of withdrawal accounts in 1978.

Kane's Market, Technology, and Political Theory of Innovation

Edward Kane (1984) sees financial innovation as an institutional response to financial costs created by changes in technology, market needs, and the political sphere, particularly laws and regulations. Kane refers to the interactive process of regulation that follows institutional avoidance and innovation as a *dialectical process*. Regulations create institutional responses that are designed to avoid the impact of regulation which, in turn, provides the seeds of a new round of regulation. Kane's contribution included technology and market needs.

Communication and information-processing technologies as well as market needs that relate to new products or concepts, such as leveraged buyouts, have provided the impetus for many financial innovations.

Miller's Regulation and Taxation Theory of Innovation

Merton Miller (1986) states that major innovations in the last 20 years have been almost exclusively the result of changes in tax laws and regulatory changes. He attributes the development of many new financial claims to attempts to alter the amount and timing of taxable income. He also notes that many innovations were the result of regulatory barriers and the desire of financial firms to avoid the impact of regulatory constraints.

Certainly every change in the tax law is a major event for tax lawyers, accountants, and investment bankers, who try to profit from finding profitable ways to reduce the tax burden.

Merton's Market Efficiency Theory of Innovation

Robert Merton (1990) also provides a valuable rationale for financial innovation. His theory is based on the notion that financial innovation is motivated by forces designed to increase market efficiency and improve social welfare. Financial innovation as it is used in this context must provide true economic benefits.

Merton gives three motivations for producing innovation: (1) the creation of financial claims that allow for risk sharing, risk pooling, and hedging, as well as new financial structures that allow for transferring resources over time; (2) the improvement of economic efficiency and liquidity; and (3) the reduction of agency costs. The latter is a result of unequal information between two parties to a transaction and imperfect information about a firm's performance and prospects. Like Silber's, Merton's theory of market efficiency is very general.

Legal and Ethical Issues

Centrust Savings Bank: Patents on Financial Products

Innovation in the financial services business has been routine during the last 20 years. New hybrid and derivative financial products have been created that have sometimes created great profits for the innovating firm. However, as many innovators have found out, their innovation lasts about as long as it takes for the ink to dry on the newly issued prospectus. A successful new product is quickly replicated by a multitude of competitors. Until the case of College Savings Bank (plaintiff) versus Centrust Savings Bank (defendant), the notion that the innovator of a financial product could protect itself with a patent by applying the concept of "intellectual property" was unheard of.

In 1988, College Savings Bank applied for several patents on a CollegeSure Certificate of Deposit. The CollegeSure CD is an adjustable rate CD that pays interest tied to an index of college costs. College claimed that Centrust infringed on the idea.

The suit was settled with the agreement that Centrust would pay license fees for using certain features of the CollegeSure CD. A number of years earlier, Merrill Lynch & Company won a settlement concerning its innovative CMA account, an account that consolidated security transactions and holdings with a transaction account and credit card. Merrill's legal action against several competing firms offering similar products eventually led to Merrill receiving license fees.

The issue of whether a financial product can be patented is still unresolved. Some believe that, like computer software itself, if a financial product relies on specialized computer hardware or software, it can be protected.

Technology and Financial Innovation

Technological advances in information processing have created many obvious innovations in the financial services business. Since financial institutions are information-processing companies, they have been impacted more than many other types of businesses by technological progress in data processing and telecommunication. The following are some of the more important innovations prompted by technology.

Automated Tellers and Home Banking/Brokerage

The advent of inexpensive computers has made it possible to deliver financial transaction and information services to many new locations, including the home. ATMs are found in airports, shopping centers, colleges and universities, and grocery stores. Today, many of these systems are tied together into regional and national network systems. These ATM networks will permit essentially nationwide 24-hour-a-day access to information and transaction capability.

The home personal computer coupled to a modem permits access to both depository and brokerage account information. These systems also are used to provide access to a wide variety of financial information services that permit security analysis.

Consolidated Statements

The ability to merge information from a number of data files and the increased speed and reduced costs of mainframe computers have led to the development of consolidated statement accounts. These accounts bring together financial information on credit, security, and transaction accounts into one statement. The Merrill Lynch "Cash Management Account" was one of the first and most popular of the consolidated statements.

Improved data processing and communication technology have impacted all financial institutions. Some institutions, particularly depositories, have found that the technologically driven lower costs of performing transactions have made it possible for their competitors to provide transaction services that are very competitive with the demand deposit and other transaction services they offer.

Technology has also greatly expanded the geographic boundaries serviced by financial institutions. Customers no longer have to be near the financial institution they do business with.

Regulation and Financial Innovation

Probably the single most important stimulant to financial innovation in the last several decades has been financial regulation. The structure of our financial system remained relatively unchanged from the Depression until the mid-1960s. That system was a product of extensive legislation passed in the 1930s. As the economy began to experience the inflation of the 1960s, increased interest rate volatility combined with technology to trigger major financial innovation. This volatility provided the impetus for financial institutions to find ways to reduce the adverse impact of the many controls and restrictions built into our 1930s financial structure.

The recent move to higher capital requirements for depositories has been the impetus for significant innovation in changing the credit risk characteristics of financial claims. One example of this type of financial engineering involves recent developments in the creation of new asset-backed securities.

New Collateralized Securities

One new claim created initially to avoid the imposition of capital requirements was the senior-subordinated security. The rationale behind these securities was to permit a financial institution to use the assets on its books as collateral for a multirisk class of securities. During the 1980s, this structure was used to create billions of dollars of mortgage securities on both home mortgages and apartment mortgages sold to institutional investors. Subsequently, the regulators tightened up on capital requirements for these subordinated securities.

The creation of these credit risk partitioned securities and the regulatory response to them is a excellent example of Kane's dialectical theory of financial innovation. First a new regulation is issued, the higher capital requirement. This caused the innovative response of the senior-subordinated security. The regulator then realizes that the new capital regulation has been circumvented and is forced to modify the regulation to bring about its desired goal.

Money Market Mutual Funds

Although taken for granted today, the money market mutual fund was not a significant competitor to depositories until the mid-1970s, when market interest rates rose to levels far above the interest rates that federal regulators permitted banks and thrifts to pay on deposits. The Regulation Q interest rate ceilings imposed on depositories at that time provided the impetus for this innovation.

Negotiable Orders of Withdrawal

The negotiable order of withdrawal (NOW) account was the innovation of a state-chartered savings bank in New England. Like the money market mutual fund, the NOW account innovation was stimulated by the fact that commercial banks could not pay interest on demand deposits and thrifts could not offer demand deposit services.

Foreign Currency Futures

The growth in foreign trade and the increased volatility in exchange rates created the climate for a formal market in foreign exchange futures. Prior to the establishment of this new market only large money center banks handled foreign exchange transactions.

Interest Rate Swaps

Interest rate volatility also played an important role in stimulating the development of the interest rate swap market. Here, financial institutions and other firms alter their exposure to changing interest rates by agreeing to pay the other institution's interest rate obligation on a specified amount of debt.

Interest rate swaps were given a major boost by the regulators of thrift institutions. In the early 1980s, these regulators wanted thrifts to reduce their interest rate risk. One quick way to do that was by using an interest rate swap.

Collateralized Mortgage Obligations

Collateralized mortgage obligations (CMOs) are securities collateralized by mortgages or mortgage pass-through securities. These securities partition the cash flows from the underlying mortgages. Because fixed-rate mortgages have long maturities and prepayment uncertainty, many investors are not interested in these securities. CMOs create a series of securities that appeal to particular investors, such as S&Ls, that require shorter-term assets to meet regulatory requirements.

In addition to regulation, CMO development requires significant computer simulation. These simulations required advancements in computer technologies that occurred at a rapid rate in the 1980s.

Taxes and Financial Innovation

Changes in the tax law have always been a major stimulant of financial innovation. Financial products such as those created by real estate investment trusts, limited partnerships, real estate mortgage investment conduits, and mutual funds are the result of specific sections of the tax code. The mortgage pass-through security is also a creature of the tax code that created a tax entity called a *grantor trust,* and more recently, the *real estate mortgage investment conduit*. The growth of the single premium life insurance policy in recent years is the result of the favorable tax treatment it obtains under the tax code.

Zero Coupon Bonds

One of the early stimulants to the growth of zero coupon bonds was the tax law in Japan. In the early 1980s, many American companies and federal agencies created zero coupon bonds to be sold in Japan, since the Japanese at the time gave zero coupon bonds favorable tax treatment.

Tax-Exempt Revenue Bonds

Ambiguity in the federal tax law regarding what is an appropriate use of funds from a tax-exempt state or municipal bond became the stimulant for considerable innovation in state and municipal finance in the 1970s and 1980s. Many government units created tax-exempt bonds, collateralized by mortgages on factories, shopping centers, and homes, for borrowers who never had the benefit of being financed at tax-free interest rates. The tax law was subsequently changed in the early 1980s to restrict the use of tax-exempt financing for the benefit of private sector households and businesses. This was another example of a dialectical process.

Lease Financing

Leases represent a form of financing that is a product of the tax law. A lease provides the depreciation tax benefit to the owner of the equipment. This allows a tax-paying unit to shelter income. At the same time, it allows a unit that does not pay taxes, a government unit or a firm that has tax losses, to obtain some of the benefit of the tax shelter.

New Products and Innovation

Probably the simplest innovations to consider relate to new products. Each new product, be it a computer, recreational vehicle, or newest imported auto, must establish its collateral value for a loan market to develop. Many times the manufacturer or distributor becomes the first organization to extend credit, when the collateral has no established secondary market and resale value cannot be readily established. Innovative lenders, however, will consider these new products, and for a sufficient reward, will extend credit on them.

Innovation and Monetary Policy

A large body of economic literature written in the 1960s and 1970s held that the growth rate of the narrowly defined money stock, known as currency and demand deposits, M1, was the most important monetary quantity for the Federal Reserve to measure and control through monetary policy. According to these theories, the growth of the narrowly defined money supply was the primary influence on prices, and indirectly, on economic stability. By the 1970s, however, it was becoming apparent that inflation, new financial instruments like money market mutual funds, and technology used to improve money management techniques had altered the historical relationship between the narrowly defined money supply and other macroeconomic stabilization variables.

While economists will not all agree, the question of what influence innovation has on various monetary policy variables has created a lively debate. Indeed, over the years the definition of M1 has been modified and additional measures have been devised and used for short periods of time.

To date, there is no agreement on which is the best measure of money. Many economists, however, believe that the narrowly defined money supply does not have the same relationship to real economic measures it once had. That raises the question of which monetary variables to monitor and control most carefully. It raises the related issue of how to predict the changing relationships between the selected monetary measure and the real economy. These questions are not likely to be resolved any time soon. They do, however, provide a useful illustration of how financial innovation can impact economic policymakers.

Questions

Appendix

A1. What is Silber's theory of financial innovation? Give an example of a financial innovation that supports this theory.

A2. What is Kane's theory of financial innovation? Give an example of a financial innovation that supports this theory.

A3. What is Miller's theory of financial innovation? Give an example of a financial innovation that supports this theory.

A4. What is Merton's theory of financial innovation? Give an example of a financial innovation that supports this theory.

A5. How might a change in the federal tax law motivate financial innovation? Give an example.

A6. How does technology influence financial innovation? Give an example.

A7. How does a change in financial regulation impact financial innovation? Give an example.

Distribution Channels for Financial Products

chapter 17

Many changes have occurred in the types of distribution channels used by financial service companies. Twenty years ago, financial services were distributed primarily through large sales forces operating out of company facilities. Cost considerations and improvements in telemarketing and direct mail technologies have caused a relative decline in the use of the traditional brick-and-mortar and direct sales channels of distribution.

Contributing to the changes has been the use of electronic systems for handling financial transactions. Electronic funds transfer systems have become a well-established means of servicing customers, and have helped spur the development of new types of financial products. This has left depository institutions, brokerage firms, and insurance companies with significant investments in branch offices and established sales forces. As pressures for consolidation within these businesses continue, better methods for assessing the effectiveness of traditional channels of distribution will be needed.

Alternative Channels of Distribution

Every business must determine the most cost-effective channels of distribution for its products and services. By *channel of distribution,* we mean the method chosen to market the product to the desired potential customer base. During the last 20 years, the financial service business has experienced major changes in the types of distribution channels used. Mutual funds proved that direct mail and telemarketing could be an effective way to distribute the money market mutual fund against strong competition from commercial banks and thrifts. Direct mail has been the most effective distribution channel for credit card issuers. Telemarketing and direct mail have also been the distribution channel of choice for discount brokerage firms.

There has also been an increase in the use of agents. Insurance companies selling single premium annuities and variable life policies have used retail brokerage firms and subsidiaries of commercial banks and thrifts to sell their products. Also during the 1980s, brokerage firms have become major distributors of certificates of deposit for banks and thrifts. These are known as insured brokered deposits.

For the management of financial institutions, the choice of distribution channels has become very important. Because of the high cost of brick-and-mortar facilities and direct sales forces, commercial banks, life companies, and thrifts have been threatened by competitors in the mutual fund and brokerage businesses as telemarketing and direct mail have grown in use. Indeed, the banks and thrifts have increased their own use of direct mail and telemarketing as the effectiveness of these channels of distribution has become more evident.

The old line brokerage and insurance companies have also been threatened by the use of new distribution channels. These firms have traditionally relied on direct sales forces to distribute their products and services. Some insurance companies have competed against these companies by using direct mail and sales through agents of brokerage and depository institutions. Telemarketing and direct mail have been used effectively in the discount brokerage business. Electronic methods of servicing and distributing financial products have also become more popular as well. The following are the primary channels of distribution.

- *Direct Sales:* Direct sales is still the primary channel of distribution chosen by most sellers of financial products and services. Most depositories rely on a direct sales force for distributing most saving and loan products. This is normally done within the offices of the institution. Direct sales forces solicit financial product sales from larger businesses and other institutional customers. Brokerage firms and most life companies still rely on direct sales forces to distribute their products as well. Usually, the more sophisticated the financial product or service, the more likely direct sales will be used.
- *Telemarketing:* Telemarketing has been one of the fastest growing marketing distribution channels in the last decade. Telemarketing is mostly used for products that are relatively simple to understand and frequently used. The security brokerage business uses telemarketing to develop prospect lists

for sales of securities. Depositories also use telemarketing to sell certificates of deposit and a host of other products.

- *Direct Mail:* Direct mail has also become an important distribution channel during the last decade. Many of the most common savings, investment, and loan products are offered through direct mail. Direct mail dominates in the distribution of credit cards. A number of lower cost insurance products such as credit life, mortgage life, and term life insurance are also marketed through direct mail.
- *Dealer:* A number of financial institutions have developed relationships with dealers who market products that are financed with debt. Automobile, boat, recreational vehicle, mobile home, and heavy-equipment dealers frequently have lending relationships with one or more lending institutions. Consumer and commercial finance companies are major users of this distribution channel.

  Financial institutions cultivate relationships with dealers because financial products can be marketed at the point of sale. This is also good for the dealer, since it eliminates one potential obstacle that could cause a sale to be lost. The point-of-sale advantage in marketing auto loans through a dealership is a prime example of this type of relationship.
- *Agents:* The high cost of direct sales and brick-and-mortar facilities has caused a number of financial service companies to use agents to distribute their product. The use of agents is common in the credit card business, in which many small banks and thrifts offer credit cards that are serviced by another institution.

Credit cards are sometimes offered to members of affinity groups. An affinity group is an association, club, or other organization having a large membership that is targeted by a financial institution to solicit financial products. The affinity group receives financial compensation for lending its name and membership list to the distribution effort. Similar arrangements are common in the life insurance business. Many organizations make their membership lists available to sponsor sales of low-cost term insurance.

It is also common for retail direct sales forces of brokerage firms to distribute the products of other financial firms including stocks, bonds, and other traditional products. For example, many retail brokerage firms sell investment life insurance products, like annuities and variable life policies, as well as certificates of deposit issued by banks and thrifts. Brokerage firms also distribute mutual funds and limited partnerships.

Table 17.1 shows the major financial service distribution channels and the extent to which they are used by financial service providers for a variety of financial claims. Managers of financial service intermediaries must continually reassess their distribution channels. Changes in life-style,

Table 17.1

Major Distribution Channels Used by Intermediaries by Type of Loan or Investment

Financial Claim	Direct Sales	Tele-marketing	Direct Mail	Dealer	Agent
Consumer loans					
Auto	X			X	
Boat	X			X	
Credit card	X	X	X	X	X
R/V	X			X	
Mobile home	X			X	
Mortgages					
Single family	X	X	X		X
Apartment	X				
Commercial	X				
Commercial Loans					
Business	X				
Equipment	X			X	X
Insurance Policies					
Property and Casualty	X	X	X	X	X
Life	X	X	X	X	X
Investments					
Mutual funds	X	X	X	X	X
Retail security brokerage services	X	X	X		
Savings accounts and CDs	X	X	X	X	X
REITs	X				
Limited partnerships	X	X	X		

product design and complexity, distribution costs, and pricing all influence which channel is selected. Generally, the larger and more complicated the transaction, the more likely that direct sales will be used. As products become well-established in the market, distribution channels that do not require interpersonal sales attention become more cost effective.

Electronic Banking

Electronic banking refers to a number of computer and telecommunication systems that are designed to permit financial transactions with little or no human interface. These developments are generically referred to as *electronic funds transfer systems (EFTS)*. Electronic banking was actively discussed in the 1970s and early 1980s when a number of analysts made bold predictions about how electronic systems would replace checks, currency, and tellers in depositories. These systems would pay bills, deposit paychecks, and dispense information and cash.

To be fair, many electronic systems have been developed and implemented. However, as discussed in the Appendix to Chapter 8 on the payment system, checks and currency have not gone away. They continue to grow in use, with electronic transactions still representing a fairly small percentage of total transactions.

Where electronics have had an impact, however, there have been clear advantages to businesses, employees, and consumers. The benefits have been a reduction in float, a reduction in transaction costs (such as postage), and greater convenience. Where these benefits have been significant, electronic systems have replaced paper and human-based systems. The more successful electronic systems firmly established in the marketplace include the following:

1. Direct deposit of paychecks, social security checks, and other recurring payments through the automated clearing house
2. Automated tellers and cash-dispensing machines found in financial depositories and offsite locations
3. Point-of-sale systems
4. Home banking systems

Direct Deposit Systems

Direct deposit systems were the first major electronically based systems to become popular. Direct deposit systems allow for individuals and businesses to preauthorize payments to be made directly into and out of a transaction account in a commercial bank or thrift. These transactions usually occur on a specified date.

Direct deposit transactions are accomplished through automated clearing houses (ACHs). ACHs are jointly owned associations made up of larger financial institutions in regional areas. They are responsible for clearing checks and making electronic transactions between financial depositories. ACHs are electronically tied together by the Federal Reserve's *Fedwire system*, which makes electronic transactions between ACHs in roughly 38 regions.

These systems permit employees to have their paychecks directly deposited into their checking accounts, thereby reducing float costs. ACHs also allow retirees to electronically deposit their social security and other government payments directly in their checking accounts. This provides security against lost or stolen checks. These direct deposit systems are also designed to make recurring payments, such as mortgage payments, utility bills, and insurance bills, that the individual preauthorizes. This helps to reduce the cost of checks and postage.

Automated Tellers (ATMs) and Cash Dispensers

Automated tellers and cash dispensers have become a major service in the last 15 years. ATMs eliminate the need for routine manual transactions and improve service by reducing lines and extending hours.

ATMs, and the less versatile cash dispensers, have become very popular. They have become so popular that financial depositories have joined together to create *shared ATM networks,* which permit individuals to obtain cash or perform an account inquiry at a machine at any institution that is a part of the network. Some of these networks cover large regions, and others the entire country. ATMs are also used by nonbank financial institutions such as American Express to provide 24-hour service to account holders.

The appeal of ATMs to depositories is straightforward. If the service is priced properly, the ATM will allow for fewer employees at teller stations, possibly shorten hours, and produce fee income. The fees are charged by some institutions as a service charge on the account activating the ATM. Some fees are for transactional usage, and others are charges for the use of machines owned by others that are part of the network.

Point-of-Sale (POS) Systems

Point-of-sale systems are designed to allow consumers to transfer funds directly from an individual's account to a merchant's account. These systems have been more a subject of discussion in financial circles than a reality. From the consumer's perspective, most of these systems have a serious disadvantage. They eliminate the float advantage a consumer receives by charging the purchase on a credit card. There is simply no good economic incentive for consumers to use POS systems as the service is now typically offered.

An offshoot of POS systems are systems designed to reduce credit card fraud. These electronic systems are used by merchants to obtain credit card authorization for purchases above a certain amount. The POS system is likely to expand when merchants decide on the type of incentive that would overcome consumer resistance. In the meantime, the electronic capital investment to run such systems is being put in place.

Home Banking

In the late 1970s and early 1980s home banking by telephone became a subject of heated competition among depositories. The primary services offered under home banking included telephone bill paying, account transfers, and inquiries. Interest in home banking was higher when Regulation Q was still in effect, and depositories looked for any type of competitive advantage to differentiate their services from the next institution. The home banking service was implemented by several hundred depositories as a value-added service.

Home banking systems have also been adapted to the home personal computer during the last few years. To date, however, both telephone and personal computer systems are not widely used services. Consumers have not been willing to pay the fees attached to these services.

Depository institutions are not the only institutions using telephone- and personal computer-based systems. Stock brokerage firms offer account inquiry and security services from both telephone- and personal computer-based systems. Mutual fund management companies also offer telephone-based services.

Overall, the economics of electronic financial transactions will continue to improve. Paper-based transactions continue to require physical movement and handling. Good cash management procedures require searching for new ways to reduce float. As postage costs continue to rise, electronics will find its way into the design of more payment systems. One interesting new variant of EFTS is the electronic filing of income tax returns with the IRS. Several banks have piggybacked onto this system with a loan program that lends the taxpayer the refund due on the return. In summary, EFTS is here, it simply hasn't lived up to its proponents' early dreams.

A Framework for Selecting Distribution Channels

The selection of the most cost-effective distribution channels for a given financial product is a complex process. This is because there is usually no objective measure for determining which distribution channel will maximize profitability. Multiple distribution channels are frequently used. These can be especially effective when firms are expanding into new markets and want to avoid high-cost permanent offices or sales forces.

Some of the factors that bear on the selection of a distribution channel include the following:

- The financial product's complexity
- The salability of the product without sales input
- The distribution channel's fixed versus variable costs
- The impact of new distribution channels on existing channels

A brief discussion of each of these factors follows.

- *Financial Product Complexity:* More complex financial products typically require more direct sales effort. Such products as commercial loans, mortgages, and most investment life insurance policies normally require significant sales effort. Consequently, direct sales forces are used.
- *Sales Effort Needed:* A number of financial products typically require more sales effort than others. Full-service full-commission security brokers use their sales forces to sell products rather than stand ready to receive orders. These brokers sell investment ideas. Discount brokers, on the other hand,

appeal to investors who make their own investment decisions and want lower transaction costs.
- *Channel Cost Structure:* Full-time sales forces and physical offices have high fixed costs compared to direct mail, telemarketing, and agents. The channels with high fixed costs may be less cost effective for expansion into markets with established competitors. These channels are also less cost effective for products with strong cyclical demand volatility.
- *Interaction Between Channels:* The financial firm with a well-established sales force or branch system will find it difficult to sell its products in the same market using competing distribution channels. The established sales force and branch personnel can become alienated.

The branch office is still the primary distribution channel for depository institutions and retail security brokers. As a result, special consideration should be given to how to evaluate the cost effectiveness of this distribution channel. The FDIC reports that at year-end 1989, commercial banks had over 48,000 branch offices.

A Model of Retail Depository Branch Profitability[1]

This section develops a theoretically sound and practical way for depository institutions to measure the profitability of deposit gathering branch offices.

Why a Branch Profitability Model Is Needed

The need to accurately measure the profit contribution of a branch is greater today than ever before. Consider the following six reasons. First, the deregulation of the deposit-rate ceilings has made the cost of retail deposit gathering from commercial branches more expensive.

Second, the deregulation of deposit rates has forced a change in the competitive service mix. In the days of Regulation Q, depositories competed with convenience in the form of many offices, free services, and a physiological feeling of safety that manifested itself in the form of large costly permanent facilities. Competing on the basis of interest rate or price was prohibited. These institutions need to evaluate the profitability of their branch networks.

Third, the Financial Institution Reform Recovery and Enforcement Act of 1989 has resulted in thousands of branch offices being offered for sale by the Resolution Trust Corporation. The RTC has been aggressively trying to sell many of the offices of institutions that have gone into receivership. Institutions wanting to bid on them will need to value these branches.

---

[1]This section describing the branch profitability model is taken with permission from the article: Thygerson, Kenneth J., "Modeling Branch Profitability," Journal of Retail Banking, Fall 1991, p 19–24.

Fourth, measuring branch profitability is necessary because of the growth and availability of other types of insured deposit distribution channels. Fifth, there is an established trend among insured depositories to buy, sell, and trade existing facilities. The feeling is that in many markets consolidation is necessary to restore and enhance profitability.

Lastly, a branch profitability measurement model assists in developing a branch personnel compensation incentive system that encourages behavior that is consistent with the profit measurement objectives of the model.

Model of Branch Functions and Activities

The retail branch should be looked at fundamentally as a distribution system for financial products and services. In this respect, it is no different than a retail store. It should be considered one of many alternative distribution channels available to the depository.

The major functions of the branch are the origination and servicing of various asset and liability products of the firm (as discussed in Chapter 7). Because of the substantially different operating strategies used by financial depositories around the country, each institution must perform this analysis for itself. Branch personnel may also be involved in a complete or partial underwriting or credit-scoring activity. Some depositories delegate branches to complete the underwriting as well as to see to the funding of certain loans. Others use the branch simply as a distribution channel, with the branch personnel acting as a direct sales force, but not a loan-processing or underwriting unit.

The servicing activities of the branch involve payment processing, deposit processing, and transaction processing to the extent that these activities occur within the branch. The branches of some institutions might also serve to distribute products and services not produced by the firm. In this case, the measure of profitability is based on the commission or service fee cash flows derived through the sale of safety deposit boxes, mutual funds, insurance, and agent-based credit card programs.

Measurement Model of Branch Profitability

The model for a branch's income statement is total branch profits, (TBP) equals branch servicing income (BSI) plus branch origination income (BOI) plus branch fee and commission income (BFC) minus branch total costs (BTC). This is shown in Equation 17.1.

$$TBP = BSI + BOI + BFC - BTC \qquad [17.1]$$

The variables used in this model are defined as follows.

Branch servicing fee income (*BSI*) includes an allocation provided to the branch from any servicing groups within the firm that receive services performed by branch personnel, such as loan posting, payment processing, and collection. A branch that collects and posts loan payments for mortgages may receive a revenue allocation of $.25 per payment, for example.

Branch origination income (*BOI*) is the largest and most important source of income for most branches. Origination income cash flows come in two forms. The first relates to financial products and services that the branch successfully markets to the public on behalf of the firm's asset managers. Asset managers can be thought of as product managers who market specific loans or other financial service products. Asset managers look at the branch as one of several alternative distribution channels available to them.

Here the branch should be allocated revenue based on what the asset or loan manager feels it can pay to obtain additional sales of the product. The revenue will be in the form of commissions, say, $12 per credit card issued, .25 percent of the funded dollar amount of any first or second mortgage originated through the branch, and so forth. Each loan or service sales unit that wants to use the branch to distribute a product must determine what type of commission and processing fee it can afford to pay the branch to market their product.

The second form of *BOI* relates to the origination of deposit products. This is typically the largest portion of *BOI*. The branch-generated retail deposit is but one of a number of alternative funding sources for the firm. Asset and liability managers of the firm monitor prices for all alternative funding sources. These prices, along with monitoring the competition, form the basis of the pricing used by the retail branch system.

This analysis also forms the basis for developing the cash flows for the branch relating to deposit origination. These cash flows are based on the assumption that the goal of the branch is to maximize the present value of the difference between the marginal cost of raising funds through the branch and the next least cost alternative for raising funds through other distribution channels. These alternative sources of funds might be negotiable CDs, brokered insured deposits, federal funds, or reverse repos.

The branch management can maximize profit by successfully marketing a large volume of deposits at a price that is below the cost of raising funds through alternative distribution channels. Because the cost savings may occur in the future, it is necessary to take the present value of these interest savings. The present value of these cash flows is computed on all deposits new to the depository and on all deposits repriced during the period under analysis. The appropriate discount rate would be the firm's weighted cost of capital (*coc*). This analysis assumes that deposits such as demand deposits, money market demand accounts, and savings accounts are repriced each day. While having chosen to reprice transaction and passbook accounts daily, alternative assumptions should be based on the institution's experience. Many commercial banks, for example, have analyzed their transaction and passbook accounts and have concluded that an average effective maturity of one to three years is a good approximation.

This analysis will produce the present value of the interest savings cash flows (*PVIS*). To compute it, we take the difference between the interest rate on the alternative deposit source ($AR_{i,t}$) for account type i for period t and subtract the interest cost of the branch deposit interest rate ($DR_{i,t}$). The resulting interest spread is then multiplied by the amount of deposits of each type i originated or repriced by the branch during the current measurement period. The present value ($PV_{coc,t}$) of this series is then taken for cash flows over the number of periods the deposit is outstanding, t. The firm's weighted cost of capital is used as the discount rate. The weighted cost of capital is assumed to be 9 percent. The firm with a pretax cost of equity of 25 percent and an average cost of liabilities of 8 percent, with a 6 percent equity-to-asset ratio, would have a *coc* of approximately [(25% × 6%) + (8% × 94%)] = 9.02%. This is shown in Equation 17.2.

$$PVIS = [PV_{coc,t}(D_i \times (AR_{i,t} - DR_{i,t}))] \qquad [17.2]$$

where:

PVIS = Present value of interest savings for period t discounted at the cost of capital *coc*

$PV_{coc,t}$ = Present value with discount rate of *coc* for t periods

D_i = Deposits dollar amount of account type i sold or repriced at rate $AR_{i,t}$

$DR_{i,t}$ = Deposit rate for account type i for t periods

$AR_{i,t}$ = Deposit rate for alternative funding source i for t periods.

Table 17.2 shows how data might be organized to create the model input. The deposit cost data *DR* and *AR* must include the cost of deposit insurance,

Table 17.2

Example of Deposit Cost Comparisons for All Deposits Sold by a Branch in One Month

Branch-Generated Deposit	Rate DR_i	Alternative Funding Source	Rate AR_i	$AR_i - DR_i$
Demand deposits	0.00%	Federal funds	5.75%	5.75%
Savings accounts	4.25	Federal funds	5.75	1.50
3–12 month CDs	7.85	Negotiable 3–12 month CDs	8.58	.73
12–24 month CDs	8.24	Brokered CDs 12–24 month	8.90	.66

Regulation D reserves (reserves held in vault or Federal Reserve deposits that earn no interest), and brokerage commissions, if applicable. The term structure of alternative funding sources must be properly identified. The cost of alternative funding sources represents the next lowest cost of funding sources for the institution performing the analysis. These costs will vary from firm to firm. Exhibit 17.1 shows the difference between rates paid on retail, negotiable, and brokered insured deposits by banks from May 1989 through April 1990 as reported by the *Wall Street Journal*. The graph shows high volatility in the spreads, which translates directly into branch

Exhibit 17.1

Retail Cost of Deposits Less Negotiable CD Cost of Deposits and Retail Cost of Deposits Less Brokered Insured Cost of Deposits May 1989–April 1990
(differences in average monthly rates)

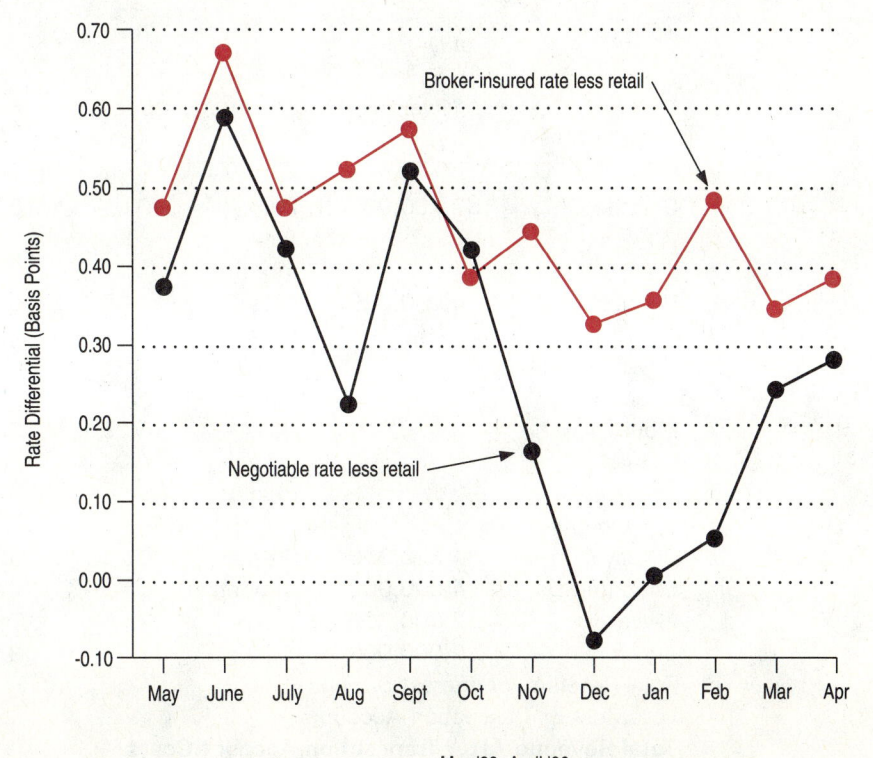

Source: Banquote Online. Reported in *The Wall Street Journal*. Various issues.

profit volatility. The alternative funding source cost is compared to the interest cost of the new deposits and repriced deposits sold during the reference period, t.

Table 17.3 provides all the information necessary to calculate the present value of the interest savings on funds renewed and those brought in as new funds into a hypothetical branch for a one-month period. An example will help to illustrate how the calculations are made. Take the case of the one-year deposits. These funds will stay on account for one year and save the firm .25 percent as compared to the next lowest cost of one-year money. This .25 percent translates into a quarterly positive cash flow of $[(.25\%/4) \times \$2,000,000 =] \$1,250$ received at the end of each of the next

Table 17.3

Present Value of Interest Savings Calculated at the Firm's Weighted Cost of Capital (9.00%) for all Deposits Rolled Over and New Deposits Received for the Month of July 1991

Deposit Type	Amount of Deposits Rolled Over or New	Term	Interest Rate	Next Lowest Rate	Present Value of Savings @ 9.00%
Checking	$2,100,000	Daily for a month	0.0%	5.75%	$10,063
Negotiable order of withdrawal accounts	4,000,000	Daily for a month	4.5	5.75	4,167
Money market demand accounts	3,500,000	Daily for a month	5.25	5.75	1,458
90-day CDs	4,800,000	90-day	6.25	6.75	6,000
6-month CDs	14,000,000	6-month	6.50	7.00	34,615
1-year	2,000,000	1-year	7.00	7.25	4,837
4-year	2,000,000	4-year	7.25	8.50	51,046
Total Revenue for Interest Savings					$102,186
Less Cost of Transaction Accounts					13,300
Total Revenue After Transaction Account Costs					**$88,886**

four quarters. Discounting this quarterly savings at a weighted cost of capital of 9 percent gives a total of $4,837.

The value of the checking account deposits is determined by taking the interest savings of 5.75 percent for a month and multiplying it times the average weekly balance to get [(.0575/12) × $2,100,000 =] $10,063. The NOW account balances are handled in the same manner. It is necessary to identify the extraordinary marginal costs associated with transaction accounts such as checking, NOW, and MMDA. In this example, the depository has determined that the monthly cost of servicing these accounts is $3.50 for activities performed outside the branch. The depository in the example has the following number and associated costs for these accounts:

Type of Account	Number	Cost per Month @ $3.50
Checking	1,800 accounts	$6,300
NOW	1,200	4,200
MMDA	800	2,800
Total Cost per Month		**$13,300**

Table 17.4 provides an example of the detailed schedules for branch fee and commission income (BFC).

Table 17.4

Schedule of Fee and Commission Income for a One-Month Period (BFC)

Product Type	Number Sold	Compensation per Unit	Total Income
Credit card sold	23	$ 12	$ 276
Second mortgages	5	80	400
First mortgages	12	120	1440
Safety deposit income	20	12	240
Checking fees received	120	6	720
Auto loans	12	25	300
Other loans	8	30	240
Annuities sold	10	80	800
Total BFC			**$4,416**

Table 17.5

Monthly Direct and Indirect Costs of Operating a Retail Branch (BTC)

Heat, light and rent	$15,200
Maintenance	1,290
Advertising and promotion	1,000
Staff costs plus benefits	8,765
Training and human resource allocation	765
Data processing allocation	32,453
All other allocations	12,776
Total BTC	**$72,249**

Branch total costs (BTC) include the direct costs of running the branch system (see Table 17.5 above). This includes personnel, heat, light, space, telephone, mail, maintenance, and upkeep as well as all supervisory branch personnel, branch advertising, and branch back office costs. Many of these costs will be allocated on a per account or per employee basis. Branch space costs can best be uniformly estimated by charging the branch the rental cost at the current cost per square foot for commercial space in the locale of the branch. Otherwise, branch space costs could be unduly influenced by whether the firm owns the branch, or if rented, by when the lease may have been signed. These represent sunk costs or benefits.

Added to this must be the allocation of all indirect costs related to running the branch system. Allocations for data processing, human resources and training, communication, accounting, space management, and

Table 17.6

Income Statement for Hypothetical Branch (TBP)

Income	
Deposit origination	$88,886
Fee income	4,416
Total income	93,302
Costs	
Direct and indirect	72,249
Income or (loss)	**$21,053**

executive time must be included. Typically, these allocated costs can be estimated quite accurately by making allocations on a per account basis, or per branch employee basis.

Table 17.6 provides a summary of each of the revenue and cost estimates assembled for the hypothetical branch. This branch was profitable during the month shown in the example.

Using the Model to Analyze Branch Purchases, Sales, Closures, and Swaps

This model has been used very successfully for analyzing the profitability of branches available for purchase and for valuing existing branches for possible closure, sale, or swap. To use it, it is necessary to forecast expected average spreads between the rates paid on deposits attracted through the target branch and alternative funding sources. The target branch expenses can usually be fairly estimated by using actual historical data. Then, a forecast of future deposit growth is made along with estimates of commission and fee income. By discounting these pro-forma cash flows over a five- to ten-year period, the analyst is able to determine the maximum deposit premium that might be offered to buy, sell, or swap a target branch.

Using this model, it becomes very easy to determine which branches might be candidates for purchase or sale. It also makes very clear the special advantages of branch purchases, in which the purchased branch can be merged into an existing branch office. This situation provides a large increase in deposits without a commensurate increase in costs. Branch swaps with other institutions that provide the same result for both parties is also very rewarding.

Summary

This chapter identified and reviewed the various distribution channels used by financial institutions. These channels of distribution have undergone great changes in recent years as the cost of physical facilities and direct sales forces have increased. The chapter also reviewed recent technological changes that have permitted the growth in EFTS-based financial systems.

Finally, a model for measuring branch performance for depository institutions was developed. This model uses the difference between the cost of branch deposits and the cost of alternative sources of funds as the major variable impacting performance. The model also makes it possible to evaluate the future success of branches and to value branches that might be purchased, closed, sold, or swapped.

The traditional distribution channels of depository institutions, insurance companies, and retail brokerage firms consisting of branch offices and direct sales forces are being relied on less today than in the past. **Dealer's,**

agents, telemarketing, and **direct mail** are now actively used by financial institutions.

Electronic funds transfer systems have grown to be an important means for financial institutions to service and distribute their products. **Direct deposit systems** are well established, as are **automated tellers** and **cash dispensers.** These systems provide economically proven ways to reduce float and provide added convenience. **Point-of-sale systems** and **home banking** have been less popular. This is because the benefits are less obvious and the costs of providing them higher.

The primary reasons for the acceptance of these systems are **reduction of float, reduced transaction costs,** and **greater convenience.**

Branches and the personnel that operate them represent major costs for depository institutions. One way to determine the **profit contribution of a branch** is to develop a model to compute the cash flows related to operating the branch. The model given in this chapter relies on estimates of fee and commission income and cash savings represented as the difference between the cost of funds generated by the branch and that available from other sources. This model is also used to evaluate branch sales, purchases, closures, and swaps.

The primary data inputs in the model include **cash flows** derived from **origination** and **servicing less the total cost of operations.** For depository institutions, the primary source of cash flow is the **present value of the interest savings** on branch originated deposits as compared to the next least-cost alternative.

Questions

Chapter 17

1. Explain why some financial intermediaries have reduced their reliance on physical branches as their primary distribution network and have developed other channels of distribution.
2. What new channels of distribution have become popular in the insurance industry in the last decade?
3. What did the success of mutual funds tell us about the potential for using new channels of distribution?
4. What is the primary function of a branch office for a financial depository?
5. The primary contribution to profit for a financial depository typically comes from what activity or product?
6. What types of activities do depository branch offices perform for which they should be compensated or credited?
7. Explain why branch sales and purchases have become important activities for financial institutions.

Chapter 17   Distribution Channels for Financial Products   **465**

8. Do you expect the number of depository offices to increase or decrease in the years ahead? Why?
9. Many discount stockbrokers have adopted new distribution methods for brokerage services. How have the channels of distribution for this business changed?

Case Study in Branch Profitability: To Keep or to Sell

case 17.1

Midpacific Bank is in the process of reviewing its retail branch network. It opened a number of branches during the early 1980s in a major expansion. Many of these branches performed very well. Several, however, did not live up to expectations. Their growth seemed to stall out as competitors with stronger locations and market shares were able to outperform the Midpacific locations.

The president of Midpacific has asked the financial officer and the head of the branch system to analyze the Crossroads branch. The bank has received an offer to buy the branch for a deposit premium of 1.5 percent from a competitor. This premium will be paid in cash and will represent 1.5 percent of the deposits in the branch at the time of the sale closing. This is a very small premium, but Midpacific has little confidence that this branch will perform well in the years ahead.

The financial officer and the head of branch operations put together the following data that they consider relevant to making the decision. Table C17.1 shows the marginal out-of-pocket costs of operating the branch. The table also shows the expected increase in costs over the next four years. Table C17.2 shows the deposit base for the branch and the expected growth over the next four years. It also shows the average expected spread between the

Table C17.1

Estimated Annual Cost of Operating Crossroads Branch

Costs	1991	Expected Annual Change
Personnel	$73,000	4%
Heat, light, and rent	48,000	3
Other operating costs	37,000	4

Table C17.2

Deposit Base, Growth Forecast, and Spread Between Deposit Costs and Wholesale Funding Source

Type of Account	Amount 1991	Annual Growth Rate	Spread to Wholesale Alternative
Transaction accounts	$3.5 million	2%	4%
Number of accounts	1,500		
CDs and savings	$20.5 million	2	0.25
Fees and loan profits	$13,000	0	
Total	$24.0 million		

The cost of processing transaction accounts is $24 per year per account.

cost of retail deposits from this branch and the alternative of raising wholesale money through negotiable CDs or other borrowings. The table also shows the profit contribution of the branch from sales of loan products and the fees earned on other services provided.

The two executives decided to do 1991–1995 pro-forma income statements for the branch to determine whether the branch would show improving or worsening profit performance. The branch profits to date have been very unsatisfactory. The cost of selling the branch will involve paying severance pay, notifying the customers of the sale, and performing the computer conversion to the seller's computer. This will cost $40,000. In addition, the bank will have to buy its way out of the remaining lease on the branch. This will involve a payment of $25,000. The bank estimates its pretax weighted average cost of capital at 9 percent.

Questions

Case 1

1. Using the data provided, develop a five-year pro-forma including 1991 as the base and 1995 as the last year. Show all costs and revenues developed by the branch. Ignore taxes in this analysis.
2. If the trends in costs and revenues continue beyond 1995, would you sell the branch at this low deposit premium? Why or why not?

Determining the Appropriate Branch Premium to Pay for Acquisition

case 17.2

The Resolution Trust Corporation has taken over several savings and loans in your market. They have put a number of branches of these institutions out for bid. First Bank is considering bidding for one of these branches located across the street from one of its existing offices. By purchasing the branch from the RTC, they can close it and shift the deposits to their existing branch without much increase in operating costs.

The branch for sale has deposits of $22 million. It has been declining in size since the RTC took over management. If First Bank purchases the branch and assumes the deposits without assuming assets, it can repay some of its wholesale deposits and lower its cost of funds. However, it expects to lose deposits because of customer confusion about the closing of the branch and the firing of personnel.

The president of First Bank has asked the head of retail banking and the financial officer to come up with a bid that will provide a solid profit. It will be necessary to determine the net present value of the investment in the branch assuming a pretax weighted cost of capital to the bank of 10 percent. The two executives have come up with the following data for analysis. Table C17.3 shows the expected deposit balances for the next three years through 1996 and their best guess beyond 1996. It also shows the expected average spread between the cost of funds for the deposits purchased in the RTC branch transaction and the cost of wholesale funds that can be expected.

The revenue from additional fees and product sales from the new customers is assumed to be zero. The additional one-time and ongoing costs of the addition to their customer base of the $22,000,000 in deposits is also shown in the table.

Table C17.3

Estimated Deposit Balances and Average Spread Compared to Wholesale Funding Source for 1993–96 and Beyond
(dollars in millions)

Year	Average Balance	Spread versus Wholesale	Number of Accounts
January			
1992	$22	.45%	5200
1993	17	.40	4500
1994	14	.45	3500
1995	12	.50	3300
1996–2001*	10	.50	2200

*No value ascribed to accounts after ten years

The additional costs of servicing the additional accounts are shown in Table C17.4. Converting the account files to First Bank's computer system and notifying all the new customers also involve some major costs. These are shown in the table as well.

Table C17.4

Account Servicing and Conversion Costs

Costs of Conversion

Computer costs	$12,000
Moving files	5,000
Closing out safe deposit boxes	5,000
Personnel for transition	5,000
Promotion and advertising	3,000
Total	**$30,000**

Costs of Servicing Accounts

Cost per account	$12 per account per year

Questions

Case 2

Construct a cash flow statement using the costs and revenues discussed in the case study. The statement should show the cash outflow representing the conversion and one-time customer costs of assimilating the new deposits. Then calculate the present value of the deposit cost savings less the servicing costs. The discount rate should be that of the firm's weighted cost of capital. Ignore any possible value of the deposits after ten years. All cash flows should be assumed to occur at the end of each year. Determine the maximum discount First Bank can pay for the deposit base. Ignore taxes.

(Hint: The initial cash outflow plus the maximum premium paid on the deposit base should equal the net present value of the interest savings.)

Measuring Interest Rate Risk

chapter **18**

Interest rate risk relates to the impact that changes in interest rates have on the market value of an institution's assets, liabilities, and its income stream. Although changing interest rates have always presented a major risk for financial institutions, the extent of this risk did not become clear until the record high interest rates in the late 1970s and early 1980s made virtually all savings and loans insolvent if their assets had been sold at market value and their liabilities paid off. Most experienced substantial operating losses during this period. Had it not been for regulatory forbearance, now considered most unfortunate, most savings and loans would have been taken over by the government by 1983.

This experience resulted in major efforts to improve interest rate risk management measurement tools and develop new risk management strategies and tools. In addition, financial regulators began requiring savings and loans to provide interest rate risk reports.

Three primary interest rate risk management tools are discussed in this chapter: periodic *GAP,* duration, and mark-to-market. Each provides a somewhat different view of a firm's interest rate risk position. Income simulation tools, which help the firm measure the impact of changes in interest rates on accounting income statements and balance sheets, are also discussed.

An Example of Interest Rate Risk

The concept of interest rate risk is presented in Table 18.1, which shows the balance sheet for a hypothetical financial intermediary, High-Risk Federal. This intermediary invests in long-term U.S. Treasury bonds and finances these bonds with short-term one-year liabilities and equity. It maintains a ratio of 5 percent equity to total assets.

At the time this balance sheet was developed, the yield on the bonds when they were purchased and the current market yield on the bonds were both at 10 percent. Thus, the market value of the bonds was equal to the book value of the bonds. Consequently, the firm could liquidate its bond holdings at its book value and experience no gain or loss on the transaction, except transaction costs.

The liabilities also carry a current market yield that is equal to the market yield when the liabilities were issued. As a result, the firm could, in theory, repurchase its liabilities in the secondary market at its book value. This would effectively pay off these liabilities. Again, there would be no gain or loss from this transaction, save that associated with transaction costs.

To see how interest rate risk manifests itself, consider the following. The day after this balance sheet was developed the management of High-Risk Federal woke up to find that interest rates had risen 4 percent over the entire term structure of interest rates. The term structure rose 4

Table 18.1

Balance Sheet for High-Risk Federal
(dollars in millions)

Assets					Liabilities				
Asset	Market Yield When Purchased	Current Market Yield	Book Value	Market Value	Liability	Market Yield When Issued	Current Market Yield	Book Value	Market Value
10-year T-bonds	10.00%	10.00%	$100	$100	1-year marketable paper	7.00%	7.00%	$95	$95
					Equity			5	5
Total			$100	$100	Total			$100	$100

percent in a parallel move. The yield for one-year liabilities rose to 11 percent from 7 percent, while the yield on Treasury bonds rose to 14 percent from 10 percent.

Table 18.2 shows the balance sheet of High-Risk Federal with the market rates and market values of its assets and liabilities updated to reflect the higher market interest rates.

Here, the current market values for the firm's ten-year Treasury bond assets and its one-year liabilities are compared to their old market values. The result is shocking. The value of the assets deteriorated by over 21 percent to the new market value of $78.81 million. This sharp decline in market value was due to the fact that these assets were long term and fixed rate. The liabilities, on the other hand, were short term in maturity. They declined in value by only a little over 3.5 percent. The 7 percent coupon one-year liabilities actually had a market value of 97.64 percent (92.76/95.00) of their original par value. Because High-Risk Federal took a considerable risk by purchasing long-term fixed-rate assets with short-term liabilities, the intermediary would be bankrupt if it were liquidated. Its assets would be sold for $78.81 and its liabilities would be paid off at $92.76. High-Risk Federal's shareholder's equity would be $-13.95.

It is important to keep in mind that High-Risk Federal does not have to liquidate its assets and liabilities or show an operating loss, even though it

Table 18.2

Balance Sheet for High-Risk Federal Adjusted for Rise in Open-Market Interest Rates (dollars in millions)

Asset	Market Yield When Purchased	Current Market Yield	Book Value	Market Value	Liability	Market Yield When Issued	Current Market Yield	Book Value	Market Value
10-year T-bonds	10.00%	14.00%	$100	$78.81	1-year marketable paper	7.00%	11.00%	$95	$92.76
					Equity			5	13.95
Total			$100	$78.81	Total			$100	$78.81

is effectively insolvent. This is because under GAAP, as long as High-Risk Federal intends to hold these assets until maturity, it is not obligated to value them at their new lower market value. Moreover, there will be no impact of this rise in open-market interest rates on High-Risk Federal's income statement until its one-year liabilities come due. This is because for accounting purposes, High-Risk Federal will still be earning interest on its assets at 10 percent and paying 7 percent for its liabilities. However, after a year, if interest rate levels remain at the new higher level, High-Risk Federal will have to replace the 7 percent liabilities with 11 percent liabilities and experience a larger negative spread between its asset and liability yields.

This example dramatically shows the impact of interest rate risk on the viability of a financial intermediary. In the late 1970s and early 1980s, savings and loans had long-term assets and short-term liabilities that created losses as significant as those for High-Risk Federal.

Interest Rate Risk Is a Portfolio Concept

In managing interest rate risk, it is necessary to recognize that interest rate risk involves analysis of the firm's entire portfolio of assets and liabilities. It is virtually impossible, except in a few circumstances, for a financial firm to manage interest rate risk by acquiring assets that have the same cash flow characteristics as their liabilities. The exceptions are mutual funds, real estate investment trusts, and limited partnerships. Most intermediaries also have many assets, mortgages are one example, that have embedded options that cannot be offset with liabilities with comparable characteristics. This is why all the tools used for interest rate risk management involve analysis of the entire portfolio. The interest rate risk position of the firm requires measurements based on the entire profile of assets and liabilities in order to understand their interaction.

It is also important to consider how off-balance sheet assets and liabilities impact the interest rate risk of the firm. A commercial bank with a large mortgage-servicing portfolio reflected off the balance sheet must include those servicing contracts in its interest rate risk measurement analysis. This is also important for firms that have large outstanding financial commitments to buy or sell loans or securities.

Periodic GAP

The *periodic GAP* is the simplest and most easily understood of all the interest rate risk management measurement tools available to financial institutions. The periodic *GAP* is defined as the dollar volume of assets that mature or reprice during period t, less the dollar volume of liabilities maturing or repricing during period t. This tool is widely used because of its simplicity.

The concept of periodic *GAP* is straightforward. It measures the potential that a change in interest rates will have a proportionately larger or smaller impact on the market value of the assets and interest revenue of the firm than it will on the firm's market value of liabilities and interest costs. A firm has a positive (negative) periodic *GAP* if it has a greater (smaller) dollar amount of assets maturing or repricing than it has liabilities maturing or repricing within period t. If interest rates rise, a firm with a positive (negative) periodic *GAP* can be expected to experience a rising (declining) net interest margin. The opposite will occur if interest rates decline.

The periodic *GAP*, GAP_t, of period t is shown in Equation 18.1. Here, RPA_t is the quantity of the firm's assets that will mature or reprice during the period from the present until period t, and RPL_t is the quantity of liabilities that will reprice or mature during the same period.

$$\text{Periodic } GAP_t = RPA_t - RPL_t \qquad [18.1]$$

The periodic *GAP* can be calculated for any period t. This is why it is referred to as the periodic *GAP*. *GAP*s can be calculated as a one-year *GAP*, a three-month *GAP*, or any other period one chooses. They are also calculated for interim periods, such as between 90 and 180 days. Periodic *GAP*s help determine both short-term and long-term exposures to interest rate risks. The length of the chosen period is determined by selecting those periods over which a high percentage of the firm's assets and liabilities will mature or reprice. A ten-year *GAP* report, for example, is of little value for a firm that has 95 percent of its assets and liabilities maturing in two years. Management uses its knowledge about bunching maturities or repricing assets and liabilities to select the most useful periods for constructing *GAP* reports.

An Example of a Periodic GAP Report

Table 18.3 on page 476 shows the balance sheet for a small commercial bank. Assets and liabilities are shown with information about when they mature or reprice.

Given this balance sheet, those assets and liabilities that will mature or reprice within the period chosen for the *GAP* report must be identified. Consider a one-year *GAP*, GAP_1. To create this report those assets that will mature or reprice within one year must be identified. For assets such as mortgages, it is necessary to estimate the percentage that will prepay during the year. For liabilities, such as NOW accounts and passbook accounts, it is necessary to determine whether the bank will treat them like a fixed-rate account or a repriced account. This will depend on the experience of the bank. Many banks do not frequently change interest rates

Table 18.3

Balance Sheet
First National Bank of Bard
(dollars in millions)

Assets		Liabilities	
Cash and due from banks + short-term liquid assets (less than 6 months)	$1	Demand deposits	$3
Governments and agencies (more than 1 year)	12	Money market demand deposits	12
Reverse repo agreements (less than 1 month)	1	Passbook account	12
Auto loans (initial maturity 48 months)	54	CDs	
		less than 3 months	34
		3–6 months	38
		6–12 months	40
		over 12 months	20
Fixed-rate mortgage (initial maturity 30 years)	50	Collateral mortgage bond (maturity 5 years)	70
Adjustable-rate mortgages (index 1-year Treasury)	87	Capital note (maturity 7 years)	10
Loans tied to prime	51	Capital accounts	32
Credit card receivables	15		
Total	**$271**		**$271**

paid on most transaction accounts, despite changes in open-market rates. They may, therefore, use an estimated maturity of two or three years for some of these accounts. If these accounts are treated as fixed rate, then it is necessary to determine the percentage that would be lost if open-market rates increased significantly.

Table 18.4 shows the schedule for repriced assets RPA_1. The assets have been divided into two groups. One group consists of those assets in which the analyst can make an accurate forecast of the percentage that will reprice or mature during the one-year period. The second group are those

Table 18.4

**Maturing or Repriced Assets
Within One Year, RPA_1
First National Bank of Bard
(dollars in millions)**

**No Estimation of Repricing or Maturity
Is Necessary:**

Cash and due plus short-term liquidity	$ 1.0
Loans tied to prime	51.0
Reverse repurchase agreements	1.0
Credit card receivable	15.0
Adjustable-rate mortgages	87.0

**Assets in Which Estimation of Repricing or Maturity
Is Necessary:**

Auto loans (assume 20% maturity in first year)	10.8
Fixed-rate mortgages (assume 12% prepay in first year)	6.0
Total RPA_1	**$171.8**

assets that require a forecast or estimate concerning their expected maturities. Table 18.5 on page 478 shows a comparable schedule for repriced and maturing liabilities, RPL_1.

In the case of Table 18.4, it was necessary to estimate the percentage of auto loans and fixed-rate mortgages that would prepay in one year. The analyst used an estimate of 20 percent of the principal balances for the auto loans and 12 percent for the mortgages based on past experience of the bank. Table 18.5 made estimates for the potential loss of passbook and demand deposits during the one-year period. The estimates assume that these accounts would not be repriced and that a certain percentage would be lost to competitors over the period. The estimate of deposit loss was 15 percent for the one year.

The resulting one year GAP is shown in Table 18.6 on page 478.

Table 18.6 indicates that the firm has a positive GAP_1 of $45.55 million. This simply means that during the next twelve months the firm can expect that $45.55 million more in assets will reprice or mature than liabilities. If everything else is held constant, except market interest rates, this firm can be expected to improve its net interest margin if open-market rates rise and to reduce its net interest margin if open-market rates fall over the next

Table 18.5

Maturing or Repricing Liabilities Within One Year, RPL_1
First National Bank of Bard
(dollars in millions)

Liabilities in Which No Estimation Is Necessary:

CDs less than 1 year	$112.00
Money market demand deposits	12.00

Liabilities in Which Estimation Is Necessary:

Passbook accounts plus demand deposits (assume 15% loss)	2.25

Total RPL_1	**$126.25**

twelve-month period. A positive *GAP* will improve the firm's net interest margin during a period of rising interest rates because more lower rate assets will be replaced by current higher rate assets than will lower rate liabilities be replaced by current higher rate liabilities.

Another way to express the GAP_t is as a percentage of the firm's total assets at $t=0$. This quantity, called the GAP_t *percentage,* scales the measure to standardize for asset size and permits the GAP_t of one firm to be compared over time with itself and with other peer group competitors. This expression is shown in Equation 18.2.

$$GAP_t \text{ percentage} = GAP_t / \text{total financial assets}_t \quad [18.2]$$
$$= \$45.55/\$271.00 = 16.81\%$$

Table 18.6

One-Year Periodic GAP_1
First National Bank of Bard
(dollars in millions)

Total repriced assets (RPA_1)	$171.80
Total repriced liabilities (RPL_1)	$126.25
1-year periodic $GAP = (RPA_1 - RPL_1) =$	$45.55

Another similar measure is to take the ratio of RPA_t to RPL_t, as shown in Equation 18.3. This is called the *GAP ratio*.

$$\text{GAP ratio} = RPA_t / RPL_t \qquad [18.3]$$
$$= \$171.8/\$126.25 = 1.36$$

The *GAP* ratio is another measure that permits the firm to make comparisons with itself over time and with other firms.

GAP Buckets

Periodic *GAP* statistics are also computed for interim periods. Consider the *GAP* report shown in Table 18.7. This report was developed for assets and liabilities that mature between several periods up to 365 days. These interim periods are sometimes referred to as *buckets*.

A *GAP* report divided into buckets can be used by the analyst to identify specific periods in which changes in the firm's asset and liability structure may be needed.

Limitations of GAP Reports

Periodic *GAP* reports have some important limitations. These limitations stem from the fact that *GAP* reports are computed at a point in time and they cannot properly account for uncertain cash flows and for the repricing limitations of certain assets and liabilities. The following are some of the limitations of GAP_t reports.

Repricing or Maturity Bunching

The *GAP* report only shows the relationship of repricing assets and liabilities during the period t. It does not show the interest rate position of

Table 18.7

GAP Bucket Report

	\multicolumn{4}{c}{Period of Maturity or Repricing}
	0–90 Days	91–180 Days	181–365 Days	365 Days+
Assets maturing or repricing (RPA_t)	121	72	62	255
Liabilities maturing or repricing (RPL_t)	132	93	52	232
GAP_t	−11	−21	+10	+23

the firm after period t or between two periods. This creates a problem when a firm has a large volume of assets or liabilities repricing or maturing during a period between two *GAP* periods. The periodic *GAP* report will not disclose the bunching of asset or liability repricing. Although the analyst producing the *GAP* report is probably aware of these bunching problems, this is still a limitation of the methodology.

Estimates of Cash Flows

The *GAP* report is only as good as the analyst's estimates of asset and liability cash flows. It is very likely that some of the assets and liabilities that reprice have prepayment options embedded in them. This is true with mortgages, for example. This means that the *GAP* report must rely on estimates of the percentage of mortgage principal that will repay during period t.

Another problem concerns assets whose repricing is discretionary. Some assets that may be repriced under the terms of the claim contract are rarely repriced, even during periods of interest rate volatility. Credit card receivables, for example, can be repriced within a short period of time, but they are rarely repriced in practice, even if market rates change significantly. Other examples are passbook accounts at commercial banks and thrifts and interest-paying negotiable order of withdrawal accounts. The rates on these accounts are rarely changed. This means the analyst is left with the task of making assumptions about whether assets are in practice more like adjustable-rate or fixed-rate assets. The analyst must then calculate the *GAP* statement by incorporating these assumptions.

Rate-Indexed Assets and Liabilities

Another limitation of the *GAP* report relates to the fact that when rate-indexed assets and liabilities reprice, there may be caps or other limitations on the magnitude of the adjustment. This usually occurs when the asset includes an interest rate cap. An *interest rate cap* is a contractual limit on the maximum level of the interest rate on an adjustable interest rate financial claim. These caps are found in many adjustable-rate mortgages, for example. Consequently, a firm with many capped adjustable-rate mortgages will appear from the *GAP* report to have a low interest rate risk exposure even though the assets facing upward adjustments are constrained by the cap.

Income Statement

Another limitation of the *GAP* report is that there is no stable mathematical relationship between the firm's *GAP* and its profitability. While it is possible to say that a firm with a positive *GAP* should perform better in a rising interest rate environment than in a declining rate environment, it is difficult to determine the extent of the income variation.

Off-Balance Sheet Risks

GAP reports usually do not disclose the interest rate risks related to off-balance sheet claims and commitments. Firms with large off-balance sheet investments in loan servicing contracts, for example, do not reflect the risks of prepayment of these assets. The interest rate risks related to options granted by an institution in the form of loan commitments and forward loan sales are also not reflected. These risks must, therefore, be incorporated in the overall risk assessment of the institution in other ways.

What Is the Right GAP?

The computation of the *GAP* is relatively easy. Determining the right *GAP* for a financial institution is far more difficult. If assets and liabilities did not have complications, such as embedded options, then the simple answer would be to have a zero *GAP*. This would be the right strategy for the interest rate risk averse institution. Such a firm might subscribe to the theory that predicting interest rates is impossible. After all, there is little evidence that forecasters are able to systematically forecast interest rates. For these firms, minimizing interest rate risk might be a sound strategy.

Unfortunately, for a firm desiring to minimize interest rate risk, a zero *GAP* is too simplistic an approach. Special risks, such as assets with prepayment options, interest caps, and off-balance sheet assets and liabilities that create interest rate risk must be considered. Additional analyses may dictate a move to a positive or negative *GAP*.

Other firms rely on interest rate forecasts to adjust their interest rate risk position. These firms seek a positive *GAP* when interest rates are expected to rise and a negative *GAP* when rates appear headed lower. Still others believe that the term structure is more likely to be upward sloping or normal most of the time due to the liquidity preferences embedded in the term structure. These firms will desire to have a slight negative *GAP* most of the time.

GAP *and Forecasting Business Cycles*

The financial institutions that are willing to expose themselves to additional levels of interest rate risk generally use interest rate forecasts based on the business cycle. These firms feel they can predict interest rates according to major turns in the business cycle. They believe that short-term interest rates are likely to rise in the middle to late stages of a cyclical recovery and fall during the middle to late stages of a recession. If they feel strongly about their forecast, then they would position the firm to have a positive *GAP* in the middle stages of a recovery and a negative *GAP* at the middle stage of recession. Table 18.8 on page 482 shows how the firm that is willing to take interest rate risk over the business cycle might choose to position itself.

Table 18.8

GAP Position During Business Cycle

Stage of Business Cycle	Expected Change in Rates	GAP Position
Middle stage of recession	Fall	Negative
Late stage of recession	?	Close to zero
Middle stage of recovery	Rise	Positive
Late stage of recovery with accelerating inflation	?	Close to zero

Duration

Unlike *GAP, duration* is a financial concept that has been around a long time. The concept was developed by Frederick Macaulay in a volume published by the National Bureau of Economic Research in 1938. Still, it did not find a wide audience in the financial literature and among practitioners until quite recently. One reason is that powerful computers are required to compute duration statistics. The emergence of powerful personal computers in the last decade has resolved this problem.

Duration is defined as *the weighted average period of time over which the cash flows of an investment are expected to be realized.* The weights used in duration are determined by the period in which the cash flows occur. Early cash flows have small weights and late cash flows large weights. Duration is used as an alternative measure of the maturity of an investment. It has some superior attributes, since it takes into consideration the timing and amount of cash flows received before the full payment of principal, as in the case of a bond. In the case of high coupon bonds, mortgages, installment loans, and annuities where the cash flows in early periods are usually substantial, the financial claim's duration is shorter than the claim's stated maturity.

Duration can be used to compare the cash flow profiles of a financial firm's assets and liabilities. The closer the weighted average duration of the firm's assets is compared to its liabilities, the lower the interest rate risk of the firm.

Calculating Duration

The formula for duration, *DUR,* is shown in Equation 18.4. It is the product of two summations. In the numerator, the sum of the discounted cash flows is calculated from any particular investment weighted by the period in which they are received. The discount rate in duration is the market interest rate, r. The first periodic cash flow, C_t, is weighted by the period it arrives, namely, $t=1$. The last cash flow, C_n, is weighted by the period it arrives, $t=n$. From this, it is easy to see that for two equal cash flows stemming from an investment, the one that arrives latest will have the more significant impact on the numerator of the duration equation. Late cash flows tend to increase the duration statistic. For this reason, a 10 percent, ten-year interest-paying bond will have a much longer duration than a 10 percent fully amortizing loan. This is because the principal cash flows on the bond arrive later.

The denominator of the duration formula is simply the present value of the investment's cash flows discounted at the market interest rate, r. The numerator is the time weighted present value of the cash flows discounted at the same market rate.

$$DUR = [\sum_{t=1}^{n} C_t(t)/(1+r)^t] / [\sum_{t=1}^{n} C_t/(1+r)^t] \quad [18.4]$$

where:

C_t = asset cash flow in period t

r = periodic open-market interest rate (discount rate)

n = number of periods the claim is outstanding

The duration of a three-year $1,000 principal bond with a coupon rate of 8 percent, calculated at an open-market interest rate of 8 percent, paying semiannual interest is shown as Equation 18.5. Notice that because the bond pays interest semiannually, six periods, $n=6$, are used.

$$DUR = \Big[[\$40 \times (1)/(1+.04)^1 + $$
$$\$40 \times (2)/(1+.04)^2 + \$40 \times (3)/(1+.04)^3 + \$40 \times (4)/(1+.04)^4 +$$
$$\$40 \times (5)/(1+.04)^5 + \$40 \times (6)/(1+0.4)^6 + \$1000 \times (6)/(1+0.4)^6 \Big]$$

divided by

$$\Big[\$40/(1+.04)^1 + \$40/(1+.04)^2 + \$40/(1+.04)^3 +$$
$$\$40/(1+.04)^4 + \$40/(1+.04)^5 + \$40/(1+.04)^6 +$$
$$\$1000/(1+.04)^6 \Big] \Big]$$

$$= 5.452 \text{ semiannual periods}$$
$$= 5.452/2 = 2.723 \text{ years}$$

[18.5]

Table 18.9 calculates each of the terms of Equation 18.4 for a bond with a ten-year maturity, a coupon rate of 5 percent, and a $1000 principal balance. The market rate used is 8 percent. The table shows a duration of 7.697 years versus a stated maturity of ten years. Table 18.9 was developed using one of several common software spreadsheets available on the market.

Table 18.9

Duration Calculation
Ten-Year, 5.00% Semiannual Coupon, $1000 Principal Bond
Market Rate = 8.00%

Period t	Cash Flow C_t	Present Value of Cash Flow Discounted at $r=8\%$ $PVIFA_{4.00,t}$	Present Value of Cash Flow Times Period $t \times PVIFA_{4.00,t}$
1	25	24.038	24.038
2	25	23.113	46.227
3	25	22.225	66.675
4	25	21.370	85.480
5	25	20.548	102.740
6	25	19.758	118.547
7	25	18.998	132.986
8	25	18.267	146.138
9	25	17.565	158.082
10	25	16.889	168.891
11	25	16.239	178.634
12	25	15.615	187.379
13	25	15.014	195.187
14	25	14.437	202.116
15	25	13.882	208.224
16	25	13.348	213.563
17	25	12.834	218.184
18	25	12.341	222.132
19	25	11.866	225.455
20	1025	467.797	9355.932
		Total 796.145	**Total 12,256.614**

Duration in Half Years = 12,256.614/796.145 = 15.39495
Duration in Years = 15.39495/2 = 7.6974751

Properties of the Duration Measure

The duration measure has certain interesting properties that make it a very useful tool for the financial manager. These properties of duration relate to maturity, coupon rate, and market rate.

Duration and Maturity: As a general rule, the relationship between a bond's duration and its stated maturity, assuming the bond has no sinking fund and is not a zero interest bond, is positive. An increase in maturity, if everything else is held constant, will increase the duration of a bond. Nevertheless, the duration will still be less than its stated maturity. The only exception is the case of a zero coupon security, which has a duration equal to its maturity.

Duration and Market Interest Rates: The duration of a bond will decrease as market interest rates rise.

Duration and Coupon Rate: The duration of a bond will decrease as the coupon rate on the bond increases. This is because the bond will generate larger cash flows in the early periods. As the coupon rate approaches zero, as in the case of a zero coupon bond, the duration approaches its stated maturity.

Duration and Interest Rate Elasticity

One measure of a financial asset's price behavior is the extent to which an asset's price will be affected by a rise or fall in open-market interest rates. This change in price, P, of a financial debt claim in relation to a specified 1 percent change in the open-market interest rate, r, is referred to as *interest rate elasticity*. The duration measure provides a reasonable approximation for establishing the interest rate elasticity of a bond.

Equation 18.6 provides the relationship between the change in the price of a debt claim and a given change in the interest rate.

$$\% \triangle P = - DUR \times [1\% \triangle r] \times [r/(1 + r)] \qquad [18.6]$$

where:

$$r = \text{market interest rate}$$
$$P = \text{price of the claim}$$

In this expression, $\triangle r$ refers to the number of basis points change in the open-market interest rate that equates to a 1 percent change in the base rate r. A 1 percent change in the open-market rate from a base rate of 8 percent would be 8 bp (.01 × 8.00%). Note that the relationship of %△P for a financial debt claim is negative, since −DUR (a negative term) is multiplied by the term 1%△r, which is positive. This is a normal relationship between a bond's value and a rise in market rates. This equation can be converted into a measure of interest rate elasticity by dividing both sides by 1%△r. This gives us Equation 18.7, which is our measure of elasticity, E.

$$E = (\%\triangle P)/(1\%\triangle r) \quad [18.7]$$
$$= -DUR \times [r/(1+r)]$$

The elasticity of the bond shown in Table 18.9 would be shown as Equation 18.8. Notice that the duration is measured in the same time units as the interest rate. In the example, both are annual. The open-market rate is 8 percent. A 1 percent change would be 8 basis points or .08 percent.

$$E = -7.697\% \times [.08/1.08] \quad [18.8]$$
$$= -0.57\%$$

Elasticity is interpreted as the percent change in the price of the bond for a given 1 percent change in open-market interest rates. In this case, the initial open-market discount rate equals 8.00 percent. A 1 percent change in this rate would be 8 basis points. Given an elasticity of −.57 percent, this 8 bp increase in open-market rates would result in a .57 percent decrease in the value of the bond. If an investor held $1 million of market value of these bonds, the 8 percent change in open-market rates would decrease the value of the bonds by (−.0057 × $1,000,000 =) − $5,700.

The relationship between the price change on a financial claim and changes in open-market interest rates is not linear, as suggested by this equation. Thus, Equation 18.7 only gives an accurate estimate of the elasticity for very small changes in r. For these small changes in interest rates, it works quite well. For large changes in r, the estimate is less satisfactory.

Portfolio Durations

Managers of financial firms interested in measuring interest rate risks are not particularly interested in the duration of a particular asset or liability, but rather in the duration of a portfolio of assets (DUR_A) and liabilities (DUR_L). Fortunately, the duration measure has a very convenient additive property. It is possible to calculate the duration of each asset or liability separately and then calculate the duration of a portfolio of assets or liabilities by computing the weighted average of the durations of each asset or liability. The weights are the percentage of the firm's total financial assets or liabilities represented by each asset or liability.

The firm's net worth is excluded from a duration analysis. Although net worth, either as retained earnings or newly issued equity, is a financing alternative for all financial firms, its duration is essentially infinite. For purposes of a duration analysis, however, it doesn't make sense to use infinity as the duration of net worth. In portfolio duration analysis, net worth is ignored and treated as a *residual*. It is the change in net worth that needs to be analyzed after changes in open-market interest rates affect the value of the firm's assets and liabilities.

For example, Table 18.10 on page 488 shows the weighted average portfolio durations for a small life insurance company. The table shows the duration for each of its financial assets and liabilities. Then, a weighted average duration is calculated using a weight representing the percentage that each financial asset and liability represents of the total financial assets and liabilities. The result of taking this weighted average portfolio duration is 5.67 years for assets and 8.14 years for liabilities.

Using Duration GAP for Interest Rate Risk Management

Having reviewed the properties of duration, it is now appropriate to calculate it for specific financial claims as well as portfolios of assets and liabilities. This portfolio duration is used for analyzing a financial firm's interest rate risk position. With the estimates of portfolio durations for assets and liabilities, it is possible to calculate the duration *GAP*. This is a measure of the difference between the duration of the firm's financial assets less liabilities and the percentage of financial assets financed by financial liabilities. The duration *GAP*, DUR_{GAP}, is defined as shown in Equation 18.9.

$$DUR_{GAP} = DUR_A - [(w_L) \times DUR_L] \quad [18.9]$$

In the equation, w_L is defined as the percentage of financial assets financed with financial liabilities. This is shown in Table 18.10 to be $200 million of financial liabilities divided by $266.67 million of financial assets of ($200/$266.67) = .75. The w_L weight is used to adjust for the fact that the volume of assets and liabilities affected by a change in market rates is rarely equal. In our example of Security Life w_L is .75.

The estimate of the duration *GAP* for Security Life is shown in Equation 18.10.

$$DUR_{GAP} = 5.67 - [.75 \times 8.14] = -.435 \quad [18.10]$$

Table 18.10

**Weighted Average Portfolio Duration
Security Life Company of Cleveland**

Assets $266.67 Million	Percent of Total Assets (1)	Duration Years (2)	Weighted Duration (1) × (2)
Cash and government < 1-year bonds	5%	.30	.015
1–2 years	4	1.20	.048
2–3	10	1.90	.190
3–5	12	3.00	.360
5–7	16	5.25	.840
7–10	15	6.30	.945
10–15	8	8.10	.648
15+	5	8.90	.445
Mortgages fixed rate (remaining maturity 20 years)	25	8.70	2.18
Weighted Duration (DUR_A)	**100%**		**5.67**

Liabilities $200 million	Percent of Total Liabilities (1)	Duration Years (2)	Weighted Duration (1) × (2)
Insurance reserves: Term life	22%	.40	.09
Insurance reserves: Whole life and annuity	63	10.70	6.74
Guaranteed investment contracts	15	8.70	1.31
Weighted Duration (DUR_L)	**100%**		**8.14**

Net Worth: $66.67 million

A duration *GAP* of −.44 years is quite low. The firm, therefore, would experience little change in its market valuation as a result of a change in interest rates in the open market. The negative duration *GAP* means that a rise in market rates would lead to a larger decline in the market value of the firm's liabilities than in the value of its assets. This condition would increase the value of the firm.

Duration *GAP* can be used just like periodic *GAP* to measure the relative exposure of the firm to interest rate risk. In the case of DUR_{GAP}, however, a positive and negative DUR_{GAP} have the exact opposite interpretation compared to periodic *GAP*. Unlike periodic *GAP*, a positive DUR_{GAP} implies that the firm will be hurt by rising interest rates.

Duration and the Market Value of Equity

Earlier in the chapter, an elasticity measure using the duration statistic was developed. Since the portfolio duration *GAP* is a cumulative weighted average measure of the asset and liability portfolio durations, then it follows that the elasticity of the duration *GAP* provides a measure of the sensitivity of the firm's equity to changes in interest rates. Changes in the equity account are the result of changes in the market value of assets less the market value of liabilities. This change is what the duration *GAP* measures when it is converted into an elasticity. This statistic provides another powerful tool for measuring a firm's interest rate risk exposure.

The equity or net worth account is the residual account on the balance sheet that is impacted by changes in the value of assets less liabilities. The statistic that estimates the change in market value of equity for a specified change in open-market interest rate is called the *interest rate elasticity of the market value of equity, MVE*.

This approach to interest rate risk management assumes the following:

1. All the assets and liabilities are readily marketable
2. Any changes in their respective values are accounted for immediately
3. There is no corporate taxation

Since none of these assumptions hold in the real world, the elasticity calculated from the duration *GAP* is used simply as an estimation procedure to provide a rough estimate of the impact of changes in interest rates on the residual market value of the firm. This analysis cannot, however, be used to simulate what occurs in the income statement or balance sheet under GAAP.

Another assumption related to the use of the duration *GAP* elasticity statistic is that when it is used, it is assumed that any change in interest rates is the same amount for interest rates of all maturities. This is known as a parallel shift in the term structure. From our study of the term structure, we know that a parallel shift in the term structure of interest rates is quite unlikely. However, the calculation of a portfolio duration incorporates the implicit assumption that interest rates over the entire term structure will rise uniformly by 1 percent from their base level.

Despite these limitations, the elasticity measure used to determine the percent change in the market value of equity is still a very useful interest rate risk measurement tool. Equation 18.11 shows the elasticity using the duration *GAP*, $E_{DUR\,GAP}$, calculated at an interest rate of 9 percent.

$$E_{DUR\ GAP} = DUR_{GAP} \times [r/(1 + r)] = -.44 \times [r/(1 + r)] \quad [18.11]$$
$$= -.44 \times [.09/(1 + .09)] = -.44 \times [.08257] = -.0363$$

Using this statistic, it is possible to calculate the percentage change in the market value of equity. A base interest rate of 9 percent is assumed. Then a rise in open-market rates to 9.40 percent is simulated. The equation for the market value of equity is shown as *MVE* in Equation 18.12.

$$MVE = E_{DUR\ GAP} \times [\Delta (r) / (r)] \quad [18.12]$$
$$= -.0363 \times [(9.40 - 9.00) / 9.00] = -.0363 \times .0444$$
$$= -.001612$$

If Security Insurance Company had financial assets of $266,670,000, a forty basis point instantaneous parallel increase in open-market interest rates would decrease the market value of equity by (−.001612 × $266,670,000 =) −$429,872. In the Security Insurance Company example, equity was $66,670,000. Consequently, this change in rates of 40 basis points would reduce equity by only .645 percent.

Problems and Limitations in Calculating Duration

The duration calculation is not an easy one to handle without fairly powerful computers. Even with computers, however, the analyst must first precisely specify the cash flows of each asset or liability. That can be very difficult. Mortgages and installment loans have prepayment options, and many liabilities such as certificates of deposit and annuity life insurance reserves have early withdrawal options embedded in them. These make the cash flow estimation process very difficult.

Consequently, duration, like periodic *GAP*, must necessarily rely on approximations of cash flows that may turn out to be inaccurate. Duration also suffers from the limitation of not being able to capture the impact of many off-balance sheet transactions that impact interest rate risk. In this regard, it mirrors the limitations of periodic *GAP*.

Mark-to-Market

Many firms have interest rate risk management needs that require very precise techniques for measuring this risk. The most precise technique available is mark-to-market. Mark-to-market, sometimes referred to as *market value accounting,* is used to establish the value of assets used in trading portfolios. Unfortunately, as a tool for measuring interest rate risk, such precision is difficult to attain. Mark-to-market is a process whereby the financial assets and liabilities of the firm, or a sub-group thereof, are valued at their current market value calculated at a point in time.

The need for some firms to use mark-to-market relates to (1) the need to establish the value of the assets of the firm for operating purposes, as in the case of a mutual fund, that must mark-to-market in order to be prepared to redeem old and sell new shares; (2) the requirement to mark-to-market in order to meet security or loan sale and trading accounting requirements under GAAP; and (3) the need for additional interest rate risk management measurement information.

In the first two situations, mutual fund operators and security traders and dealers act as market-makers for various securities. They must mark-to-market under GAAP accounting rules. The mutual fund operator must be prepared to sell and redeem shares at market value. The management of security trading firms must know the value of their portfolios throughout the trading day to ensure against loss due to volatile interest rate conditions. Likewise, a mortgage banker or other originator of mortgages having outstanding mortgage commitments to sell in the secondary market must monitor the value of these mortgages against the price at which they have been committed to be sold. Under GAAP, these firms must account for their transactions and asset holdings using the mark-to-market methodology.

In the third situation, still other firms use mark-to-market not because they have to, but because it provides yet another interpretation of the interest rate risk position of the firm. These firms are interested in using mark-to-market as a tool to analyze the impact of changes in interest rates on the value of all their firm's assets and liabilities.

In recent years, the use of mark-to-market has been recommended by a number of government regulatory institutions. Representatives of the OTS and the former FHLBB have been the most prominent proponents of mark-to-market. Representatives of the Securities and Exchange Commission have also advocated it as a way to improve the financial reporting of financial firms. In early 1992, the Financial Accounting Standards Board (FASB) took up the issue of how the security portfolios held by commercial, industrial, and financial firms should be marked-to-market. The FASB establishes the generally accepted accounting principles used by the accounting profession. This new FASB ruling will make mark-to-market an integral part of depository accounting practice.

The primary reason that mark-to-market is not used more frequently relates to the difficulty in developing mathematical functional relationships between open-market interest rates and the value of specific loans and investments.

Mark-to-Market Equity Valuations

The last section developed the concept of the duration market value of equity. This statistic was used to monitor the impact of changing interest rates on the residual value of the firm, its equity value. This is computed by subtracting the market value of assets from the market value of liabilities. Mark-to-market valuation is also used to estimate the residual mark-to-market valuation of equity for financial firms.

Mark-to-market has an advantage over duration market value of equity because the marketplace impacts the market value of financial assets in ways that cannot be measured by duration alone. Duration only considers the impact of changes in interest rates on value. In the money and capital markets, however, the market value of financial claims is affected by factors in addition to interest rate changes. These factors are sometimes equally important in the valuation process. These factors include the following:

1. Changes in the relative default risk premium
2. Changes in the marketability or liquidity premium
3. Changes in the value of embedded options in the claim
4. Changes in the supply and demand conditions for a particular asset

In other words, mark-to-market aims to capture the impact of as many of the factors that impact on the value of a particular financial claim as possible. Looking at the duration percentage change in the market value of equity, for example, means looking solely at the impact of interest rates on the price of the financial claim.

Most mark-to-market accounting systems base their valuations on actual estimates of the market values of assets and liabilities. These values are typically based on secondary market price quotations. Where price quotations are unavailable, it is necessary to establish valuation models that relate in some functional way the value of specific assets and liabilities on the books of the institution to financial claims that do trade in an established secondary market. Sometimes this is a very imprecise process.

Mark-to-Market Valuation of Equity Sensitivity Analysis

Mark-to-market equity valuations are also used for managing interest rate risk. This process involves the use of *sensitivity analysis,* that is, estimating the value of assets and liabilities under different interest rate scenarios. The analysis to be carried out here will involve a mark-to-market valuation of equity sensitivity on the assets and liabilities of a medium-sized credit union named the Pine Valley Community Credit Union. The management and directors of this small firm want to learn how the firm's assets and liabilities will change in market value as a result of a change in open-market interest rates. This will be accomplished by creating a mark-to-market equity sensitivity analysis of the firm.

The objective of this sensitivity analysis is to determine how the existing portfolio of assets and liabilities will change in value assuming interest rates rise or fall by a specified amount, say, by one and two hundred basis points from their current levels. To make these estimates, the cash flows of each asset and liability must be modeled. In the case of mortgages and installment loans with embedded prepayment options, it is important to properly estimate how these assets will prepay in different interest rate environments, since the market value of these assets will be influenced by these cash flow changes. Notice that the liabilities of the firm are also marked-to-market. The concept here is to treat the liabilities as if they are all traded in a secondary market and can be purchased by the firm at their secondary market prices.

In this analysis, an instantaneous change in interest rates is assumed. It is as if one day the entire term structure of interest rates had risen or fallen by one or two hundred basis points. This is not a realistic assumption, of course, but it provides a basis for measuring the sensitivity of the firm's assets and liabilities to interest rate shocks. It also greatly simplifies the computational procedures. Of course, any schedule of interest rates can be used to mark-to-market.

Tables 18.11 and 18.12 on page 494, and Table 18.13 on page 495 show the balance sheet, expected percentage of the firm's assets that will amortize or pay off under several assumptions about changes in open-market rates, and the initial market discount rates used to discount assets and liabilities under the assumed prevailing term structure. The tables also include off-balance sheet assets and liabilities, which, in this case, include a portfolio of mortgage servicing contracts that had a market value of $650,000 on December 31, 1990. Exhibit 18.1 on page 496 shows the five term structures used in the analysis.

From these data, a statement showing the impact of a change in the market value of the firm's assets and liabilities resulting from a parallel change in open-market rates of (+/−) 200 bp and (+/−) 100 bp is developed. The cash flow payoff and prepayment assumptions represented by Table 18.12 and the cash flows for each of the other assets and liabilities are discounted at interest rates that are 100 bp and 200 bp higher and lower than those shown in Table 18.13. The result of this discounting process is shown in Table 18.14 on page 497.

The mark-to-market equity sensitivity analysis reveals that the Pine Valley Community Credit Union has considerable interest rate risk. If interest rates rise unexpectedly by a large amount, the credit union will experience a dramatic decline in the market value of its assets less liabilities. The results of this type of analysis can be depicted in a graph. In Exhibit 18.2 on page 498 the actual mark-to-market value of equity is shown with a hypothetical line called the hypothetical low-risk mark-to-market. This line represents the profile that a risk-adverse firm would prefer, if attainable.

Table 18.11

December 31, 1990 Balance Sheet
Pine Valley Community Credit Union
(dollars in millions)

Assets		Liabilities	
Cash and short-term and agency securities	$ 8.0	Savings accounts	$35.0
Auto loans	23.0	NUCIF advance (3-year)	1.0
Mortgage loans	9.0	Term certificates (2-year)	8.0
Mortgage securities	6.0	Reserves	3.0
Reverse repurchase agreements	1.0		
Total	**$47.0**		**$47.0**

Off-Balance Sheet

Mortgage servicing portfolio of $45 million @ 37.5 basis points per annum	Valued at a 11% discount rate = $650,000

The decline in the mark-to-market value of equity is primarily because Pine Valley holds long-term fixed-rate mortgages in whole loans and mortgage securities. These are not offset by long-term fixed-rate liabilities. The institution could reduce its interest rate risk position by selling some of

Table 18.12

Payoff and Prepayment Assumptions
Annualized Payoff and Amortization Rate*
(five interest rate levels assumed)

Asset	−200 bp	−100 bp	Current Rates	+100 bp	+200 bp
Impacted auto loans	25%	15%	12%	11%	10%
Mortgages	18	13	8	7	5
Mortgage securities	15	12	7	6	5
Mortgage servicing	14	10	8	7	5

*Based on initial principal balances.

Table 18.13

Initial Market Discount Rates for Assets and Liabilities
December 31, 1990

Asset and Liability Class	Current Market Discount Rate
Cash and agency securities	6.50%
Auto loans	11.25
Mortgages	9.65
Mortgage securities	9.30
Reverse repurchase agreements	6.25
Savings accounts	5.25
NUCIF advance	7.50
Term certificate	7.10

Off-Balance Sheet

Mortgage servicing portfolio	11.00%

its fixed-rate mortgage whole loans and mortgage securities and replacing them with adjustable-rate mortgages or additional auto loans that have shorter duration.

Limitations of Mark-to-Market

Mark-to-market is a simple process for some financial firms that hold widely traded securities on organized exchanges. Most mutual funds, for example, hold a portfolio of very liquid stocks and bonds, whose values are normally readily ascertainable in the organized markets. This is not the case in many other circumstances, however. As a result, mark-to-market valuation techniques have a number of limitations that make them difficult to use.

Establishing the Value of Infrequently Traded Assets

Mark-to-market is a very difficult process for firms that hold securities, loans, and other investments that are infrequently traded. These might include assets such as high-yield corporate bonds, commercial loans, and consumer loans. Some of these assets have no organized exchange or group of dealers that are able to quote market prices precisely. As a result, to use mark-to-market means relying on estimation techniques that are imprecise and complicated to administer.

Exhibit 18.1

**Term Structures Used for Sensitivity Analysis
(Base and Change from Base +/− 100 and 200 Basis Points)**

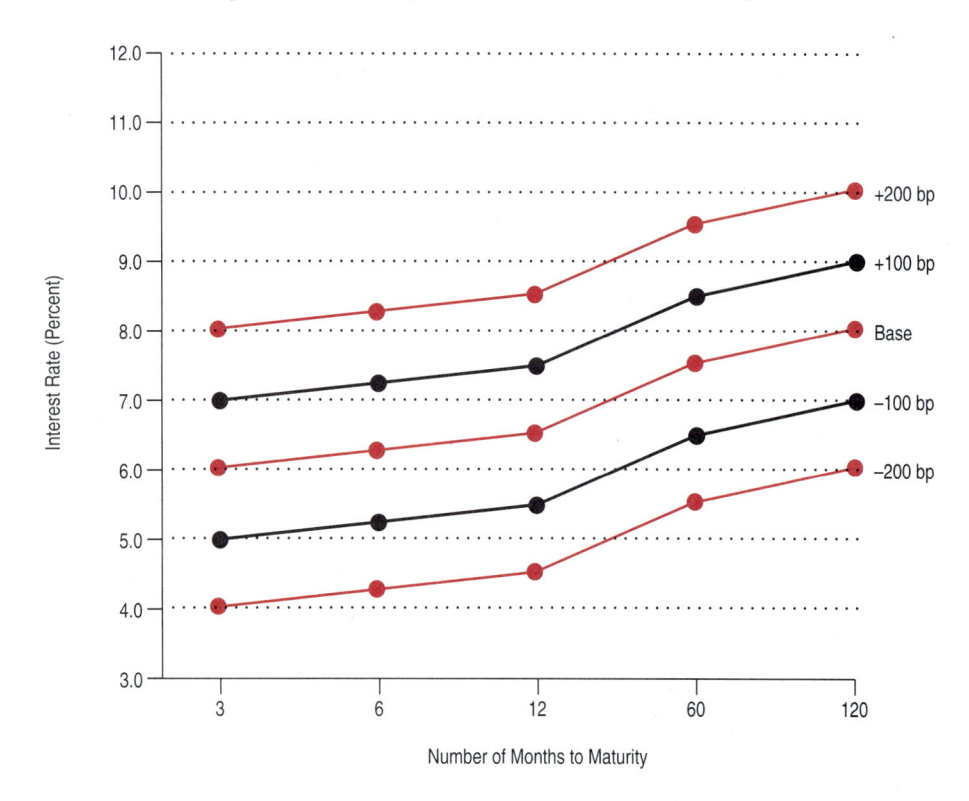

The firm using mark-to-market valuation techniques may attempt to establish valuation benchmarks based on information from dealer groups and others who have a working knowledge of the value of a particular security or loan. Other firms rely on analytical models that provide statistical relationships between the value of a liquid security and the less liquid security held by the firm. In this case, the value of an illiquid security is based on a historical mathematical relationship to another highly marketable security.

Mark-to-Market Difficulties for the Financial Firm's Liabilities

It is also difficult to mark the liabilities to market. Many liabilities do not trade at all, such as insurance reserves held for policyholders. Establishing

Table 18.14

Mark-to-Market Equity Valuation Sensitivity Analysis for Parallel (+/−) 100 and 200 bp Changes in Open-Market Interest Rates
(dollars in millions)

Assets	−200 bp	−100 bp	0 bp	+100 bp	+200 bp
Cash and agencies	$ 8.00	$ 8.00	$ 8.00	$ 8.00	$ 8.00
Auto loans	25.00	24.00	23.00	22.00	20.00
Mortgages	9.50	9.30	9.00	8.50	8.10
Reverse repurchase agreements	1.00	1.00	1.00	1.00	1.00
Mortgage securities	6.30	6.20	6.00	5.80	5.60
Mortgage servicing	.45	.52	.65	.71	.76
Total	$50.25	$49.02	$47.65	$46.01	$43.46
Liabilities					
Savings accounts	$35.00	$35.00	$35.00	$35.00	$35.00
NCUIF advance	1.05	1.02	1.00	.98	.96
Term certificates	8.90	8.60	8.00	7.60	7.20
Total	$44.95	$44.62	$44.00	$43.58	$43.16
Mark-to-Market Value of Equity					
Market value of assets less liabilities	5.30	4.40	3.65	2.43	.30

the market value of a certificate of deposit in a changing interest rate environment is much easier, but still requires the analyst to make a number of simplifying assumptions.

The Assumption of Parallel Term Structure Shifts

In most cases, the analyst using mark-to-market to perform a sensitivity analysis for changes in the firm's asset and liability values will do so by

Exhibit 18.2

Market Value of Equity Sensitivity Analysis

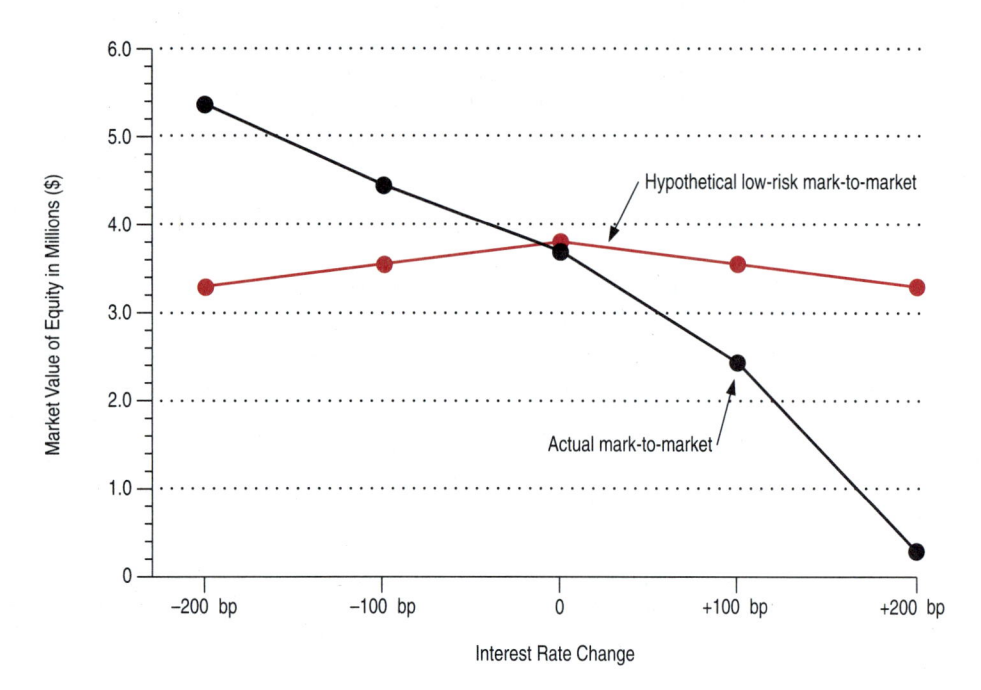

[Chart: Market Value of Equity in Millions ($) vs. Interest Rate Change, showing two curves — "Hypothetical low-risk mark-to-market" (relatively flat near $3.3–3.8M across −200 bp to +200 bp) and "Actual mark-to-market" (declining from ~$5.4M at −200 bp to ~$0.3M at +200 bp).]

estimating equal nominal percent changes in interest rates along the entire term structure, referred to as *parallel changes in the term structure*. In reality, changes in the economy normally result in other than parallel shifts. This causes the mark-to-market estimates to be less than realistic. Analysts can, of course, make any assumptions they want about how interest rates will change in the next period.

Picking Bid or Ask Prices

Another knotty problem is that there are sometimes large spreads between the bid and ask prices on various assets to be marked-to-market. This gives the analyst using mark-to-market a range of prices upon which to establish value. The firm using mark-to-market has to decide how to handle this seemingly innocuous dilemma.

Take the case of a firm that just purchased a portfolio of commercial mortgage loans in the secondary market at the ask price. Such a transaction might have a one-half to three-quarters of a point difference between the bid and ask price for the asset. If interest rates did not change and the firm marked-to-market this portfolio the next day using the bid price, the firm would have lost the one-half to three-quarters of a point according to their mark-to-market report. For a financial firm with only 5 to 6 percent equity, this is a major reduction in value. This situation dramatizes one of the limitations of mark-to-market. In the valuation of illiquid assets, the bid-ask spread can be very wide. This distorts the valuation process. It may lead to too high a valuation of assets if the ask price is used, and the opposite if the bid price is used.

For purposes of simulating changes in equity value, it is probably wise to use the average between the bid and ask price when it is available. In any case, it is important to recognize the computational problem created by the bid-ask spread and to apply the methodology consistently over time.

Income Simulation

Each of the interest rate risk measurement techniques assists in measuring how changes in interest rates affect the repricing of assets and liabilities in relation to one another and the market valuation of the firm. However, as useful as these measurement tools are, none of these approaches is useful in determining the impact of open-market rate changes on the accounting income of financial institutions. This is because, except for trading portfolios, accounting under GAAP does not require marking-to-market the assets and liabilities of the firm. Consequently, market gains or losses due to interest rate changes are generally not recognized in the income statements of depositories, finance companies, and insurance companies, except over time.

In order to determine the impact of interest rate changes on the reported accounting income of a financial intermediary, it is generally necessary to use an *income simulation* model. This permits the firm's management to simulate accounting statement income resulting from changes in interest rates and from changes in interest rate risk strategies.

Simulation models have been used for decades to help guide management in selecting various assets and liabilities strategies. Today, it is possible to develop relatively robust simulation models using personal computers with spreadsheet software. The problems in developing these models are the same faced in the periodic *GAP,* duration, and mark-to-market techniques discussed previously, namely, determining reasonable assumptions for cash flows of assets and liabilities that have embedded options.

It is also difficult to model changes in the relationship between the prices and yields of various assets and liabilities. That is, the market price or yield on a particular asset or liability may experience a change in its relationship to the price or yield of the firm's other assets and liabilities. These changes may be totally unrelated to changes in the term structure of interest rates. A particular deposit, for example, may become relatively more costly to the firm as a result of local competitive conditions that require paying more to retain that deposit. Consequently, the price and yield of this liability will change relative to the firm's other assets and liabilities. Such changes are generally unpredictable. However, simulation models can be used to perform sensitivity analyses of these changes.

Management will generally use a simulation model in conjunction with the interest rate risk management measurement tools presented in this chapter to obtain a more comprehensive understanding of how the firm is impacted by interest rate risk changes.

Example of an Income Simulation

Security Federal Savings Bank is a traditional savings institution with a large portfolio of fixed-rate mortgages. Despite a major effort by the firm in recent years, it has been unable to originate adjustable-rate mortgages. During the mid-1980s, this situation produced profitable results, since interest rates in the open market fell from 1985 through most of 1986. The directors of Security have become very concerned about its large holding of fixed-rate mortgages that are financed with short-term liabilities. At year-end 1986, the financial officer prepared a periodic *GAP* report. This report is shown in Table 18.15.

The *GAP* report in Table 18.15 indicates that the institution has a very severe interest rate mismatch. This means an increase in open-market interest rates could have a severe impact on the solvency of the company. With this information at hand, the directors have requested a simulation using a rising open-market interest rate scenario. The forecast interest rates to be used in the simulation are shown in Table 18.16.

The board of directors has decided to reinvest all of the firm's cash flow into new adjustable-rate mortgages. They are interested in what will happen to reported income. The simulation result of this strategy is shown in Table 18.17 on page 502.

As the directors anticipated, the simulated rise in open-market rates would be extremely harmful to Security Federal. The income simulation allowed the management and directors to see just what type of impact a rise in rates would actually have on the pro-forma income statement. The simulation confirmed the information supplied in the periodic *GAP* report indicating a substantial interest rate risk problem. While this simulation is an extremely simple model, it serves to show how a simulation can be used to create pro-forma income statements under a variety of economic scenarios and investment strategies.

Table 18.15

One-Year Periodic GAP_1 Analysis Report
Security Federal Savings Bank
December 31, 1986

Assets

Cash and short-term liquid assets (less than 1 year)	$10,000,000
Fixed-rate mortgages and mortgage securities (Prepay 12% of $95,000,000)	$11,400,000
Total assets maturing or repricing in 1 year (RPA_1)	$21,400,000

Liabilities

Money market accounts	$10,000,000
3-month CDs	$85,000,000
Total liabilities maturing or repricing in 1 Year (RPL_1)	$95,000,000

$RPA_1 - RPL_1 = $ −$73,600,000
Periodic GAP percentage (GAP/financial assets) =
 −$73,600,000/$105,000,000 = −70.1%
Periodic GAP ratio (RPA_1/RPL_1) = $21,400,000/$95,000,000 = 22.5%

Table 18.16

Interest Rate Forecast for Simulation

Claim	Quarter 1	Quarter 2	Quarter 3	Quarter 4
Money market accounts and CD rates	6.00%	6.5%	7.00%	8.5 %
Mortgage rates	7.00	7.5	7.75	8.00
Liquid asset earning rates	6.00	6.5	7.00	8.5

Table 18.17

Income Simulation
Security Federal Savings Bank

	Quarter 1	Quarter 2	Quarter 3	Quarter 4
Interest Income:				
Old mortgages	$1,662,500	$1,612,625	$1,562,750	$1,512,875
New mortgages		$53,438	$110,438	$171,000
Liquidity	$75,000	$81,250	$87,500	$106,250
Interest Expense:				
Savings	$1,425,000	$1,543,750	$1,662,500	$2,018,750
Net Interest Income	$312,500	$203,563	$98,188	−$228,625
Other income	$125,000	$125,000	$125,000	$125,000
Operating expenses	$375,000	$375,000	$375,000	$375,000
Net Profit Before Tax	**$62,500**	**−$46,437**	**−$151,812**	**−$478,625**

Summary

Interest rate risk, along with credit risk, is one of the two major financial risks borne by most intermediaries. For intermediaries that do not issue liabilities that are cash flow equivalents of their firm's assets, interest rate risk is inevitable. Interest rate risk became recognized as a severe intermediary concern when S&Ls experienced financial problems in the late 1970s.

This chapter focused on the measurement of the interest rate risk position of financial intermediaries. A number of measurement techniques have been developed over the years that establish the interest rate risk position of the firm and also measure the sensitivity of the firm's market value and income to changes in open-market interest rates.

Some of these measures are rather simple to calculate and understand conceptually, such as **periodic GAP.** Others, such as **duration GAP** and **mark-to-market,** require significant modeling of asset and liability cash flows and complex computations. All these measures, however, have limitations that make them less than perfect. As a result, many firms use several methodologies to obtain an overview as well as different perspectives of their firm's interest rate risk position.

Interest rate risk is defined as the impact that changes in open-market interest rates have on the value of a financial firm's assets and liabilities and its income stream.

Interest rate risk is measured by considering all the firm's assets and liabilities as well as off-balance sheet commitments. Because interest rates affect values of specific asset and liabilities differently, interest rate risk measurement should be implemented as a portfolio concept.

Periodic GAP, (GAP_t), is defined as the difference between the dollar amount of assets, (RPA_t), and liabilities, (RPL_t), that mature or reprice within a specified period of time.

$$\text{Periodic } GAP \text{ is defined as } GAP_t = RPA_t - RPL_t$$

Periodic *GAP* measures may be computed for any period t that management concludes would be useful based on their knowledge of the firm's asset and liability structure. While periodic *GAP* is an easy concept to compute and understand, its value as a measurement tool is limited due to (1) the somewhat arbitrary nature in which periods are selected, (2) the difficulty in estimating cash flows for certain assets and liabilities, and (3) the inability of *GAP* to measure the impact of interest rate caps on various assets.

Duration is an alternative measure of a financial claim's maturity that more accurately weighs the cash flows of a financial claim as they occur over time. Duration is defined as:

$$DUR = [\sum_{t=1}^{n} C_t(t)/(1+r)^t] / [\sum_{t=1}^{n} C_t/(1+r)^t]$$

where:

$$C_t = \text{asset cash flow in period } t$$
$$r = \text{periodic open-market interest rate (discount rate)}$$
$$t = \text{number of periods the claim in outstanding}$$

The duration of a financial claim has the following functional relationships: (1) It is positively related to the financial claim's maturity. (2) It is negatively related to the level of open-market interest rates. (3) It is negatively related to a financial claim's coupon interest rate.

Portfolio durations can be simply computed by calculating the weighted average durations for the firm's assets and liabilities. From these asset and liability portfolio durations, DUR_A and DUR_L, a duration GAP, DUR_{GAP}, measure can be calculated by using the following formula:

$$DUR_{GAP} = DUR_A - [(w_L) \times DUR_L]$$

w_L is defined as the percentage of financial assets financed with financial liabilities.

Duration measures have the valuable property that they can be used to calculate the change in value of a financial claim resulting from small changes in the level of interest rates. This is known as **interest rate elasticity,** E. It is defined as

$$E = -DUR \times [r/1 + r]$$

Using portfolio duration GAP statistics, it is possible to calculate the change in value of a financial firm's portfolio of assets and liabilities due to a small change in interest rates. This is known as the **interest rate elasticity of the market value of equity, MVE.** This is defined as

$$MVE = -DUR_{GAP} \times [(\triangle r)/(1 + r)]$$

This is a very important measure of the impact of changes in open-market interest rates on the shareholder's equity in the firm.

Mark-to-market is a interest rate risk tool and accounting methodology that serves as a required approach to the valuation of a firm's assets and liabilities for certain firms, such as mutual funds and firms that trade financial claims, and also as a powerful sensitivity analysis tool for measuring the impact of changes in open-market interest rates on the equity of the firm.

Conceptually, mark-to-market is a straightforward methodology for performing sensitivity analysis whereby the firm values its assets and liabilities at different levels of open-market interest rates. With several of these valuations calculated at different interest rate levels, a **mark-to-market valuation of equity sensitivity analysis** is developed that provides estimates for how the firm's equity value, viewed as the residual of the market value of assets less the market value of liabilities, changes as the level of interest rates changes.

Because each of the previously mentioned interest rate risk measurement methodologies does not provide good estimates of how changes in interest rates will impact the reported financial income of the firm, **income simulation techniques** are used. Income simulations forecast how changes in interest rates, given specified financial asset and liability strategies, will impact the reported accounting income of the firm.

Questions

Chapter 18

1. Explain what is meant by interest rate risk.
2. Describe several methodologies for measuring interest rate risk.
3. What is meant by the proposition that interest rate risk is a portfolio concept?
4. Define periodic *GAP*. What is the appropriate *GAP* period(s) *t*?
5. Why are cash flow estimations so important in *GAP* reports? What types of assets and liabilities are the most difficult to make cash flow estimates for?
6. Which is more risky from an interest rate risk perspective, a positive one-year *GAP* percentage of 23 percent or a negative one-year *GAP* percentage of -23 percent? Why?
7. Explain some of the major limitations of *GAP* reports.
8. Do you think it is wise corporate strategy for a financial firm to manage its *GAP* based on an interest rate forecast? Why?
9. Explain the properties of the duration calculation. How does the duration of a bond relate to the bond's maturity? How does duration relate to market interest rates? How does duration relate to a bond's coupon rate?
10. One nice property of duration is its use in calculating a bond's interest rate elasticity. How would you use this measure?
11. Durations of various assets held by a firm are additive when weighted. What does this mean and how important is it?
12. If a firm has assets, 90 percent financed by liabilities with a portfolio duration of 2.3 years, and liabilities with a portfolio duration of 4.3 years, what would you expect to happen to the firm's profit margin if interest rates dropped? What if rates rose?
13. Explain the concept of the duration market value of equity. If a firm with $300 million in assets has a duration percent change market value of equity of -24 percent calculated at a 1 percent rise in open-market interest rates, what impact would a 1 percent change in rates have on the firm's equity?
14. Mark-to-market is used by a number of firms as their standard approach to the valuation of assets and liabilities. What types of intermediaries use mark-to-market?
15. Explain some of the limitations of using mark-to-market.
16. What are the advantages of mark-to-market as a interest rate risk management measurement tool?
17. Mark-to-market simulations are used to determine the sensitivity of the firm's equity to changes in interest rates. How is this accomplished?
18. What is meant by a parallel shift in the term structure of interest rates as it relates to duration market value of equity analysis and mark-to-market valuation of equity sensitivity analysis?
19. It is said that measures of interest rate risk exposure obtained from periodic *GAP,* duration, and mark-to-market analysis do not translate into useful

forecasts of earnings. Why? What methodology might you use to obtain useful earnings forecasts?

Problems

Problem 18-1   Periodic GAP

A thrift institution has total assets of $520 million and total liabilities of $476 million. Within the next year, $212 million in assets and $330 million in liabilities are subject to maturity or repricing if interest rates change.
1. What is the firm's one-year periodic *GAP*?
2. What is the *GAP* percentage and *GAP* ratio?
3. Would the firm expect to see its net interest margin rise or fall if market interest rates rise during the next year? Why?

Problem 18-2   Periodic GAP

A commercial bank has total assets of $1.35 billion and total liabilities of $1.08 billion. Within the next year, $464 million in assets and $420 million in liabilities are subject to maturity or repricing.
1. What is the firm's one-year periodic *GAP*?
2. What is the *GAP* percentage and *GAP* ratio?
3. Would the firm expect to see its net interest margin rise or fall if market interest rates rise during the next year? Why?

Problem 18-3   Duration and Elasticity

You own a $1,000 bond with a term of maturity of four years. The coupon rate is 9 percent, paid semiannually. The current market yield on similar bonds is 8.25 percent.
1. What is the duration of the bond?
2. What is the market value of the bond?
3. What is the interest rate elasticity of the bond at the current market interest rate?
4. What would you expect the market value of the bond to be if market interest rates should fall to 8 percent?

Problem 18-4   Duration Elasticity/Portfolio Duration

As portfolio manager for a large bank you have a choice of three equally risky assets to invest in with the following durations:

Asset A DUR = 3.5 years
Asset B DUR = 6.0 years
Asset C DUR = 15.5 years

1. Assume the current term structure is relatively flat and that market yields for each of these instruments is currently at 9 percent. Compute the interest rate elasticity for each asset.

2. Compute the duration and interest rate elasticity of a portfolio consisting of 20 percent of Asset A, 35 percent of Asset B, and 45 percent of Asset C. Assume market rates are 9 percent.
3. If you commit half your portfolio to Asset A, what portions of Assets B and C would you need to purchase to have a portfolio duration of 7.5 years? What would be the interest rate elasticity of that portfolio if market rates are 9 percent?

Problem 18-5 Portfolio Duration/Duration GAP

Midwest National Bank has the following balance sheet:

Midwest National Bank
Balance Sheet
December 31, 1990

Assets	$ Millions	Avg. *DUR*
Cash	$ 3	—
Short-term Treasuries	20	0.4
Long-term Treasuries	18	7.5
Commercial loans	30	3.2
Real estate loans	25	9.1
Property, plant, equipment	4	—
Total Assets	$100	
Total Financial Assets	**$96**	

Liabilities		
Demand deposits	12	—
1-year certificates	35	0.7
5-year certificates	35	4.3
Other liabilities	7	3.8
Total Liabilities	$94	
Net Worth	6	
Total Financial Liabilities	**$94**	

1. Compute the weighted average duration of the bank's assets. Compute the weighted average duration of the bank's liabilities.
2. Compute the duration *GAP* and the interest rate elasticity of the market value of equity for the bank. Market rates are averaging 7 percent.
3. From your answers in number 2, by how much would you expect the market value of the bank's equity to change if market interest rates moved to 8 percent?

Problem 18-6 Portfolio Duration/Duration GAP

Providence Savings and Loan has the following balance sheet:

Providence Savings and Loan
Balance Sheet
December 31, 1990

Assets	$ Millions	Avg. *DUR*
Cash	$ 22	—
First mortgage loans	180	14.5
Second mortgage loans	53	6.6
Auto loans	75	3.0
Other assets	12	7.2
Property, plant, equipment	8	—
Total Assets	$350	
Total Financial Assets	**$342**	

Liabilities		
NOW accounts	40	—
Passbook accounts	36	—
1-year time deposits	84	0.8
2-year time deposits	78	1.5
3-year time deposits	42	2.7
Other liabilities	50	5.4
Total Liabilities	$330	
Net Worth	20	
Total Financial Liabilities	**$330**	

1. Compute the weighted average duration of the firm's assets. Compute the weighted average duration of the firm's liabilities.
2. Compute the duration *GAP* and the interest rate elasticity of the market value of equity for the firm. Market rates are averaging 6.5 percent.
3. From your answer in number 2, by how much would you expect the market value of the firm's equity to change if market interest rates moved to 6.25 percent?

GAP Measurement of Interest Rate Risk for North Savings Bank

Introduction

case 18.1

North Savings Bank is a shareholder owned institution located in the upper Midwest. The company was chartered in 1952 as a mutual institution and was managed by Robert Rine from its formation until Mr. Rine retired in 1983. The company experienced significant difficulties in the late 1970s and early 1980s due to the high market interest rates, its large holdings of fixed-rate mortgages, and the deregulation of savings deposit rates in 1980.

North SB is now managed by Martin Went. Mr. Went was hired from outside of the organization by the board to accomplish several objectives. He was first to accomplish a mutual conversion of the institution into a stock-held company. This was completed in the spring of 1985. He was also asked to implement a portfolio diversification program that would substantially reduce the company's holdings of fixed-rate mortgages by increasing the company's investment in adjustable-rate mortgages, consumer loans, and business loans tied to the prime rate. The board has made it very clear that they want to reduce the firm's interest rate risk.

North SB is a very dominant institution in a three-county area. Unfortunately, the demand for loans is relatively weak. This means that finding a suitable supply of loans that reprice or mature in a short period has proved difficult. Reducing the firm's interest rate risk has been a very slow process, and not altogether successful.

The Problem

Mr. Went has asked you to review his firm's overall operating position. In particular, he is interested in the firm's interest rate risk position. He would like you to identify where the firm stands with respect to interest rate risk. He would also like your ideas concerning what can be done to reduce it.

Some of the firm's primary operating statements for the year 1992 are shown in Tables C18.1 and C18.2.

Gathering Data

In discussing the consulting assignment with Mr. Went, it was determined that a periodic *GAP* report should be prepared for North SB. This report would include the one- and three-year *GAP* for the bank. Mr. Went would like you to explain the overall *GAP* position of the firm.

To prepare the *GAP* report, you met with Mr. Bender, the chief financial officer, to determine various assumptions for the maturity, cash flows, and repricing of the various liabilities.

In discussing the mortgage portfolio, Mr. Bender indicated that the large portfolio of fixed-rate mortgages was expected to

Table C18.1

North Savings Bank
1992 Income Statement

Interest on mortgages	$145,119,000
Interest on investments	7,315,000
Interest on other loans	26,070,000
Total Interest Income	**$178,504,000**
Cost of deposits	$107,340,000
Cost of borrowings	17,675,000
Cost of other liabilities	9,200,000
Total Interest Cost	**$134,215,000**
Net interest margin	$44,289,000
plus	
Fee and other income	6,500,000
less	
Loan loss provision	7,990,000
less	
Operating expenses	34,000,000
Net before tax income	8,799,000
Fed and state taxes	3,518,000
After Tax Income	**$5,281,000**

Table C18.2

North Savings Bank
Balance Sheet
December 31, 1992

Assets	$ Amount	Rate in %
Cash and short term investments	$110,000,000	6.65
Auto loans (60 months)	75,000,000	10.75
Credit card receivables	35,000,000	19.75
Second mortgages fixed (15 year)	32,000,000	11.50
Second mortgages variable (15 year)	12,000,000	10.50
First mortgages fixed (30 year)	658,000,000	8.25
Variable (30 year) tied to cost of funds	234,000,000	7.50
Variable (30 year) tied to 1-year Treasury	276,000,000	7.75
Variable (30 year) tied to 5-year Treasury	321,000,000	7.40
Business loans tied to prime rate	98,000,000	11.50
Building and fixtures	87,000,000	0.00
Foreclosed and repossessed assets	34,000,000	0.00
Total	**$1,972,000,000**	

Liabilities	$ Amount	Rate in %
Demand deposits	$78,000,000	0.00
Money market demand accounts	233,000,000	6.75
Savings passbook deposits	254,000,000	5.00
Retail certificates of deposit	930,000,000	7.80
Certificates over $100,000 (less than 6 months)	85,000,000	7.50
Federal Home Loan Bank borrowing	202,000,000	8.75
Collateralized mortgage bond	100,000,000	9.20
Retained earnings and paid in surplus	90,000,000	
Total	**$1,972,000,000**	

prepay at a rate of approximately 12 percent per annum over the next five years. The adjustable-rate portfolio was expected to prepay at the rate of 8 percent per annum. The second mortgage portfolio, both fixed and adjustable, was expected to prepay at the rate of 15 percent per annum. The adjustable second mortgages are tied to the one-year Treasury.

The five-year adjustable-rate mortgages are tied to the five-year Treasury. Mr. Bender feels that it is safe to assume that they will reprice by equal amounts each yearly period. The cost of funds adjustable mortgages reprice monthly.

The other loans are all essentially adjustable at any time, except for the auto loans, which Mr. Bender indicated are likely to mature equally over the next five years. On the liability side, Mr. Bender has prepared Table C18.3 showing the remaining terms of the certificates of deposit and the borrowing.

Reviewing Other Operating Statistics

Once the *GAP* report is complete, Mr. Went would like you to review some of the other conditions of the firm. In particular, he is concerned that the net interest margin is quite weak. The industry average for 1992 was 2.75 percent. He would like you to measure North SB's net interest margin and see how it stacks up to the industry. He would also like you to provide ideas for improving the interest rate position of the firm, if you feel it needs improvement.

Table C18.3

Maturity Structure of Certificates of Deposit and Borrowings

Retail Certificates	
Less than 90 days	$130,000,000
90 days to 6 months	250,000,000
6 months to 1 year	350,000,000
1 year to 3 years	200,000,000
FHLB Borrowings	
Less than 1 year	120,000,000
1 year to 3 years	50,000,000
Over 3 years	32,000,000
Mortgage Collateralized Bond	
Over 5 years	100,000,000

Questions

Case

1. Prepare a one- and three-year *GAP* report for the bank. Compute the GAP_1 percentage and ratio.

2. Analyze the report concerning the interest rate risk position of the bank. Discuss what would likely happen to the net income of the institution if interest rates rose or fell by a significant amount.

3. Compute the weighted yield on earning financial assets and liabilities. (This is similar to the net interest spread discussed in Chapter 16, except you can use the actual current yields and balances rather than average balances.) How does the net interest spread compare to the industry? What can management do to improve it?

Managing Interest Rate Risk

chapter 19

Now that the techniques for measuring the interest rate risk position of the firm have been mastered, it is necessary to gain an understanding of how to alter a firm's interest rate risk profile. During the last decade there has been a significant increase in the number and sophistication of interest rate risk management techniques. This increase coincided with the increase in interest rate volatility in the late 1970s.

A number of major risk management techniques will be covered in this chapter. These include the following:

1. The financial futures and forward cash markets
2. The futures options market
3. The interest rate swap market
4. The use of adjustable rate lending

The selection of one of these approaches over the others relates to the objective to be accomplished, the length of time over which the transaction will extend, and the profit impact of producing a given change in the company's interest rate risk profile.

The Income and Interest Rate Risk Tradeoff

Students of finance should by now believe in the often-cited adage, "There is no such thing as a free lunch." This applies equally well to the reduction of interest rate risk.

Interest rate risk management techniques involve difficult tradeoffs. The primary tradeoff is usually lower current income for the probability of higher future income under certain possible future economic scenarios. Reducing interest rate risk, however, almost always has a negative expected value with respect to future income in an environment of unchanged interest rates. This is why it is so important to consider the costs as well as the benefits of reducing interest rate risk.

Consider the case of a firm with a high negative *GAP*. This firm's objective is to reduce its interest rate risk by reducing its negative one-year *GAP* on $50 million of assets and liabilities. To do so, management has identified the following strategic policy options covering $50 million of assets and/or liabilities:

Option 1: Stop originating the next $50,000,000 of 8.5 percent fixed-rate mortgages and begin origination of 7.25 percent adjustable-rate mortgages to hold in portfolio.

Option 2: Replace $50,000,000 of maturing three- and six-month liabilities costing 5.25 percent with longer term maturity liabilities over one year costing 6.75 percent.

Option 3: Complete an interest rate swap of $50,000,000 of short-term liabilities to receive a floating rate tied to the 30-day Treasury bill rate currently at 5.4 percent for a fixed-cost five-year liability obligation costing 6.70 percent.

Each of these strategies will reduce the firm's interest rate mismatch. They will also reduce the firm's income in the short run under scenarios of unchanged interest rates or lower interest rates. These transactions will only help the firm in the case of rising interest rates.

In order to analyze this tradeoff, it is necessary to complete an analysis to determine the impact these strategy options have under alternative economic scenarios. The customary approach is to use an income simulation model. Consider Table 19.1 on page 516. It shows the impact on the pro-forma pretax income of Second National Bank for the next 12 months under several interest rate scenarios after simulating the implementation of the three strategies. The process of developing this schedule involves simulating income under five different interest rate strategies (0, +/− 100, and +/− 200 basis points changes in interest rates) for each of the three new strategies and a 0 change in rates for the present strategy. The simulation of the current strategy with interest rates unchanged will be used as the baseline income level that each of the other strategies will be compared to.

It is obvious from the table that implementing interest rate risk-reducing strategies can be costly. This is why so much analysis is required to evaluate different strategies for improving the interest rate risk position

Table 19.1

One-Year Income Impact Compared to Baseline Income of Implementing Three *GAP*-Reducing Strategies for Five Interest Rate Scenarios

		Change in Interest Rate Forecast		
+200 bp	+100 bp	0 bp	−100 bp	−200 bp
		Option 1		
+$375,000	+$187,500	−$62,500	−$450,000	−$775,000
		Option 2		
+$525,000	+$270,000	−$467,000	−$678,000	−$1,050,000
		Option 3		
+$467,000	+$205,000	−$178,000	−$425,000	−$725,000

of the firm. In order to select the least costly strategy, a probability can be applied to each of the five scenarios and the expected value of each strategy can be calculated. For the firm that applies a simple probability of 20 percent to each interest rate scenario, the expected values of the three scenarios are −$145,000, −$280,000, and −$131,200, respectively. This can be interpreted as the cost of reducing the firm's interest rate risk on $50 million of assets and liabilities. In this case, management would choose option 3 if they wanted to reduce their interest rate risk.

Financial Futures and Forward Cash Markets

Financial futures and forward cash markets were discussed in some depth in Chapters 5 and 6. Because of the greater operational difficulties in using the futures market, it will be emphasized in this chapter. However, it should be kept in mind that many hedging transactions that can be accomplished in the financial futures market can also be accomplished in the forward cash markets operated by security dealers, GSEs, and foreign exchange dealers.

Futures and Forward Cash Market Hedges

The function of futures and forward cash market hedges is to offset price fluctuations of a cash market claim held by an institution or a claim committed to be bought or sold with another contract whose price changes are perfectly negatively correlated with the cash market position. These offsetting positions can be either in the forward cash markets or futures market.

Active forward cash markets are maintained by dealers in Treasury securities, mortgage-backed securities, and foreign exchange. The major GSEs in mortgages, the FNMA and FHLMC, maintain active forward markets in residential mortgages. These forward markets make it possible to sell, and sometimes buy, financial claims for forward delivery. This can eliminate price risk for an institution that holds or contemplates investing in these claims and does not want to accept the risk of price fluctuations between the current period and the future period, when purchase or sale is contemplated.

One of the first duties of the analyst is to determine whether the forward cash market or futures market is best for reducing interest rate risk. This decision is not always easy. It usually depends on the unique circumstances of the institution and its relationship to dealers. Some of the important differences between the forward cash and futures markets include the following:

1. Futures contracts have established margin requirements that reduce credit risk between the parties to the transaction.
2. The forward market may provide a lower cost due to lower margin requirements.
3. Forward contracts are more flexible in terms of timing and type of claim.
4. Futures contracts are generally easier to offset than forward cash contracts.
5. Futures contracts may be more marketable.

A main point to remember is that futures prices and forward prices move closely together in active markets. As a result, the efficiency of the hedge is not seriously compromised by the selection of one of these markets over the other.

The greater complexity of the financial futures market, however, necessitates a closer look at the mechanics of determining the hedge ratio for a financial futures hedge. This is an important problem because frequently the claim to be hedged does not have a futures contract equivalent.

Hedge Ratio

A major problem in using the futures market is determining the number of futures contracts needed to hedge the cash market position. The objective is to find the best type and number of futures contracts that provide the highest correlation between the price changes of the cash market position and the futures market position. The hedger wants to create a situation in which, as nearly as possible, the change in price of the contract used to hedge, such as a futures contract, will offset the change in price of the cash market position. The target *hedge ratio* is the quantity of futures contracts needed to provide the most effective hedge for a given cash market position. It is given by Equation 19.1.

$$\text{Hedge ratio} = [PV_{cc}/PV_{fc}] \times b_{cc/fc} \qquad [19.1]$$

The hedge ratio is made up of two parts. The first, PV_{cc}/PV_{fc}, is the relationship of a price sensitivity for the cash market claim divided by the price sensitivity of the futures contract. The second part is the correlation between the actual yield change of the cash market claim and the futures market claim.

The first part of the hedge ratio requires establishing the relationship between changes in the price of the cash market claim and the futures market contract in relation to a specified change in open-market yields. This is defined by the ratio in Equation 19.2.

$$\frac{\text{Price value of one basis point change in cash claim}}{\text{Price value of one basis point change in futures contract}} =$$
$$PV_{cc}/PV_{fc} \qquad [19.2]$$

The quantity in Equation 19.2 is simply the elasticity of the price of the cash market claim, PV_{cc}, in the numerator divided by the elasticity of the price of the futures contract claim, PV_{fc}, in the denominator. These elasticities will depend on the market interest rate, maturity of the cash and futures market claims, and the coupon rate on each. These elasticities must therefore be calculated carefully for the cash and futures claim. Moreover, as market conditions change during the life of the hedge, market yields and maturities change. Consequently the hedge ratio that is needed to provide the most efficient hedge will change. This makes it necessary to change the number of futures contracts in the hedge during the hedge period.

Consider the change in the price of a high-grade ten-year corporate bond with a coupon rate of 10 percent and a yield to maturity of 9 percent. A one basis point change in rates to 9.01 percent will result in a decline in price of $-.0639$ percent of par. If a ten-year Treasury futures contract is used with an 8 percent coupon and 8 percent yield to maturity, then a one basis point change in yield to maturity to 8.01 percent will decrease price by $-.0680$ percent of par. The factor in Equation 19.2 would be $-.0639/-.0680 = .9397$. In this example, the price of the futures contract will change more than the price of the cash market claim for a given change in interest rates. Therefore, fewer futures market contracts are needed as compared to the dollar amount of cash market claims being hedged. In the previous chapter, duration was used to determine the price elasticity of a financial debt claim. The duration price elasticity measure can also be used to determine the hedge ratio.

The second part of the hedge ratio concerns the relationship between the yield movement of the cash market claim and the futures market contract. This is shown as Equation 19.3.

$$\frac{\text{Change in the yield of the cash market claim}}{\text{Change in the yield of the futures market contract}} = b_{cc/fc} \quad [19.3]$$

The relationship in Equation 19.3 is nothing more than the beta, b, in a simple correlation [(Y: change in yield of cash market claim) = $a + b$ (X: change in yield of the futures contract) + error]. In these correlations, the length of time over which changes in yields are collected should correspond to the length of the hedge period. For short hedges of several days, then, the beta should be calculated using daily changes in yield to maturity for the futures and cash market claims. For hedges of several months, changes in yield to maturity measured over weekly or monthly periods will be appropriate. An example of a daily yield correlation is shown in Exhibit 19.1 on page 520.

A high correlation between the yield on the cash and futures claims would be reflected by a high coefficient of determination, or R^2. R^2 values range from a low of 0 to a perfect correlation of 1.00. A high correlation between the yield change of the cash and futures market claim does not ensure a riskless hedge, however.

In our example, the beta for the correlation between the change in yields between a ten-year high-grade corporate and ten-year Treasury is .92. This means changes in the yield of ten-year corporate securities change only 92 percent as much as the ten-year Treasury. Thus, fewer futures contracts are needed to hedge the change in the corporate securities than if the beta were 1.0 or higher. The hedge ratio is computed by taking the product of Equation 19.2 and Equation 19.3.

$$\text{Hedge ratio} = .9397 \times .92 = .8645$$

The hedge ratio of .8645 indicates that less than one dollar of the Treasury futures contract is needed for each dollar of cash claim to be hedged. In this example $.8645 of Treasury bond contracts is required for each dollar of corporate bonds to be hedged.

The hedge ratio shows the price relationship between one dollar of the cash market claim to be hedged and one dollar of the futures contract. Unfortunately, futures contracts do not come in one-dollar denominations. Therefore, it is necessary to compute the number of futures contracts for each hedge transaction. This is easily done by multiplying the hedge ratio by the ratio of the dollar amount of the cash market claims being hedged divided by the dollar amount of the futures contracts.

Exhibit 19.1

Correlation Between Yield Changes for Cash and Futures Claim

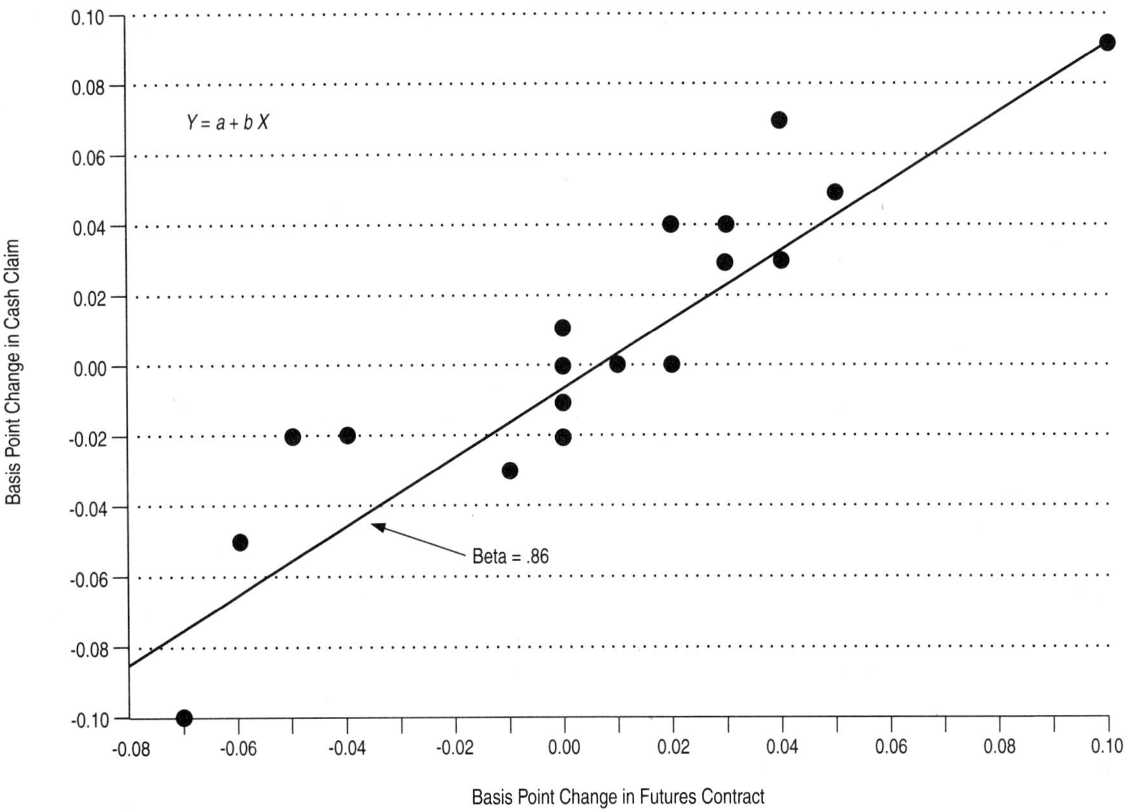
Y = a + b X
Beta = .86
Basis Point Change in Cash Claim
Basis Point Change in Futures Contract
0.10
0.08
0.06
0.04
0.02
0.00
-0.02
-0.04
-0.06
-0.08
-0.10
-0.08
-0.06
-0.04
-0.02
0.00
0.02
0.04
0.06
0.08
0.10

In the previous example, the hedger is interested in hedging \$3,000,000 in corporate bonds. The Treasury bond contract is offered in \$100,000 units. Therefore, to hedge \$3,000,000 in corporate bonds requires multiplying the hedge ratio by the ratio of the dollar of cash claims to the dollar amount on the futures contract chosen.

$$\text{Number of futures contracts} = \text{Hedge ratio} \times \$3{,}000{,}000/\$100{,}000$$
$$= .8645 \times 30 = 25.94, \text{ or } 26 \text{ contracts}$$

DEMONSTRATION PROBLEM: Futures Hedge

Situation: A pension fund manager expects a $20 million corporate contribution into the plan in 60 days. The funds will be invested in agency mortgage-backed securities at that time. The pension fund manager is concerned that interest rates will fall. Consequently, she considers hedging the price risk by going long on Treasury bond futures.

On the day of the transaction the pension manager has assembled the following information needed to design the correct hedge:

Data Input:
(December 5, 1992)

Spot price of 8 percent coupon Treasury bonds	100–03
Spot price of 8 percent mortgage security, 8 percent FNMA	99–22
March price of 8 percent coupon futures contract for Treasury bonds, March 1993 delivery	99–07
Beta (Treasury bond versus mortgage security)	.84
PV_{fc} per 8 percent Treasury bonds	−.08415
PV_{cc} per 8 percent mortgage security, 8 percent FNMA	−.08723

Establishing Hedge Transaction:
Step 1: Determine hedge ratio

$$\text{Hedge ratio} = PV_{cc}/PV_{fc} \times b_{cc/fc}$$
$$= -.08723/-.08415 \times .84$$
$$= .8707$$

Step 2: Determine number of futures contracts

$$\text{Number of contracts} = \$20{,}000{,}000/\$100{,}000 \times .8707 = 174.1$$
$$= 174 \text{ contracts}$$

Step 3: Buy 174 long contracts on Treasury bonds

Data Input:
(Feb. 15, 1993)

Treasury bond futures price, March 1993 contract	101-08
Mortgage security, 8 percent FNMA	101-12

> **Results:**
> Cost Without Futures Hedge
>   Purchase 8 percent FNMA, $20 million par value
>   March 15, 1993 cost = $20,000,000 × 101–12   = $20,275,000
> Cost With Futures Hedge
>   Purchase 8 percent FNMA, $20 million par value
>   March 15, 1993 = $20,000,000 × 101–12   = $20,275,000
>   Futures gain [(101–08)–(99–07)]% × 174
>   × $100,000   – 358,875
> **Cost**   **$19,916,125**
>
> Futures hedge reduced cost of mortgage securities resulting from the fall in interest rates.

Types of Risk-Reducing Hedging Transactions

There are two types of futures positions. The first is a long futures position. A *long futures* position is analogous to buying the financial claim with an obligation to sell it on or before a specified date at the market price prevailing at the time of sale. This position is used for hedging when the firm has sold or is committed to sell a financial claim in the forward cash market that it does not own. In this case, the hedger is concerned about a rise in price. The firm has an outstanding contract to deliver a claim at a predetermined price, but does not yet own the claim. A *short cash* position involves selling the claim in the forward cash market. The short cash position is used to hedge the price risk on a financial claim that is owned or if there exists a firm commitment to buy. The firm, however, has no contract to sell at a predetermined price. In this case, the hedger is concerned about a possible drop in price on the claim in the future when the sale takes place.

    The trading activities of commercial banks and investment banking firms routinely involve selling financial claims to customers with the expectation that they will cover their short position at some future time. This situation frequently involves the need to hedge. Another example is an insurance company that sells a guaranteed investment contract to a pension fund at a fixed yield, when the sale will not fund for a specified period. The insurance company has committed to a fixed-cost liability without locking in the yield on the assets to ensure a positive interest margin. Such a firm could be thought of as being short, fixed-rate assets. In the futures market, the firm could go long on a futures contract in a long-term bond in order to lock in the value of assets to be acquired in the cash market at some future point.

    The other basic futures transaction is a *short futures* position. This position is analogous to selling a financial claim in the forward cash market with an obligation to buy it back on or before a specified date at the prevailing price. There are many circumstances in which a financial firm will find itself needing to hedge a *long cash* position. Financial firms routinely commit to make loans at an agreed upon rate to be funded at some future date. This transaction creates a long cash position. A firm that has not yet funded this commitment or sold the loan in the secondary market, as in the case of a mortgage commitment, would be exposed to interest rate risk.

A common example of such a situation would be a mortgage banking firm that has made commitments to homebuyers to fund mortgages at a specified rate. Such commitments usually take 60 days or more to fund. With this long cash position, the firm might consider using the futures market to create a short sale of a futures contract to cover their long position. Another example would include a firm that has very short-term liabilities and longer term assets, a large negative *GAP*. Such a firm could be thought of as being long on long-term assets. To hedge such a position, the firm could go short in the futures market for long-term bonds.

Exhibit 19.2 on page 524 shows a number of common unhedged positions in which financial institutions might find themselves. These positions could create the need for an offsetting futures market hedged position. The exhibit also shows a hypothetical futures position that might be used to hedge the risk of the cash position.

Hazards of Futures Market Transactions

Although the concepts involved in futures market transactions appear straightforward, the actual mechanics of using the futures market are complex and represent potential risks. Several of the more common problems in using the futures market for hedging the types of transactions shown in Exhibit 19.1 include the following:

1. Managing basis risk
2. Hedging options risk with futures contracts
3. Accounting for futures transactions

Basis Risk

A primary underlying assumption in using the futures market for hedging price risk is that the price of the futures contract will closely track the movements of the price of the claim in the cash market. *Basis risk* is defined as the probability that the price of two financial claims do not closely correlate to one another over time. That is, the functional price relationship between two financial claims shows low correlation, as in the calculation of

Exhibit 19.2

Common Unhedged Financial Positions of Financial Institutions and the Futures Position to Hedge Them

Cash Market Position	Futures Market Position	Futures Market Transaction
Hedging Commitment Lender makes a fixed-rate loan commitment to borrower to be funded in 60 days: long cash position in fixed-rate assets	Lender requires a short futures contract	Short a Treasury note or bond contract due 60+ days
Reducing Negative GAP Intermediary has a large negative periodic GAP between assets and liabilities: long cash position in fixed-rate assets	Intermediary requires a short futures contract	Short a Treasury note or bond contract due long term
Reducing a Positive GAP Intermediary has a large positive periodic GAP: short cash position in fixed-rate assets	Intermediary requires a long futures contract	Buy a Treasury note or bond contract due long term
Locking in Borrowing Rate Intermediary has a collateralized borrowing coming due in three months and would like to lock-in today's interest rate on the refunding: long cash position in a fixed-rate asset	Intermediary requires a short futures position	Sell a Treasury note or bond contract due after refunding date
Locking in Asset Yield Intermediary has sold a fixed-rate liability due to be funded in 90 days and wants to lock in an asset yield: short cash position in fixed-rate assets	Intermediary requires a long futures position	Buy a Treasury note or bond contract due after funding date

the hedge ratio. This statistic was defined for the hedge ratio as R^2. This coefficient is the correlation between the change in yield of the cash market claim and the change in yield for the futures contract.

Clearly, basis risk is very important in futures market hedging transactions. This is because the primary purpose of a hedge is to go long or short on a futures contract whose price will be perfectly negatively correlated with the cash market claim's price. Such perfect negative correlation will provide an effective portfolio hedge.

The following example will vividly show how basis risk can adversely impact the success of a futures market hedge. Consider an institutional investor that is interested in using a portfolio of high-yield securities (junk bonds) as collateral in a collateralized bond obligation. Such an issue is to be priced at a yield premium over the five-year Treasury note. The securities chosen as collateral are five- to ten-year high-yield bonds with a weighted average yield-to-the-call of 14 percent. The bond issuer is concerned that interest rates will rise, which will reduce the spread between the weighted return on the high-yield bonds and the collateralized financing.

In order to hedge this position, the finance department concludes that the firm should sell a five-year Treasury note futures contract. If interest rates rise, then the firm will be able to cover (buy back) the futures contract at a lower price, creating a gain to offset the expected loss in the price of the high-yield bonds. The department believes that if the general level of interest rates falls, it will impact the high-yield market as much as the Treasury market. In other words, it computes the $b_{cc/fc}$ to be 1.0. However, the R^2 is only .3, a very poor correlation. To the extent the correlation is poor, it represents basis risk to the firm.

The firm's hedge works as follows. The firm sells $5 million of five-year Treasury securities in the futures contract. At the end of 60 days the firm completes preparations to issue the collateralized bond obligation. A major event takes place, however, to complicate the situation for the firm. Ten days before the bond issue, the nation's largest high-yield bond dealer files for bankruptcy, sending the high-yield bond market into a tailspin. The price of the portfolio of high-yield bonds falls by 4 percent. In the meantime, the Treasury market rallies and the five-year Treasury note increases in price by 2 3/32. The result of the hedge program is shown in Table 19.2 on page 526.

Clearly, in the example, the finance department did not fully understand the potential impact of basis risk represented by the low R^2. The relationship between the value of the high-yield bonds and the Treasury securities was very unstable. In this particular case, the relationship was actually negative for a short period of time during which the price of the futures contract and Treasury securities rose, while the price of the high-yield bonds fell. The hedge actually exacerbated the loss to the firm. This is an extreme example, but it does serve to show the potential impact of basis risk on the effectiveness of a hedge.

Table 19.2

Result of Hedge Program

	Position	Amount	Change in Price	Change in Value of Position
High-yield bonds	Long	$5 million	−4%	−$200,000
Treasury futures	Short	$5 million	+2 3/32	−$104,678
Gain or loss on hedge				−$304,678

Mixing Futures and Options

Exhibit 19.2 showed a number of situations in which a firm might want to hedge a financial position. A careful look at the exhibit will indicate that a financial firm has actually issued an option in one of the hedge positions. It is very risky to hedge option price risk with a futures contract.

In this case, the firm has an outstanding fixed-rate loan commitment. This type of commitment is an option owned by the borrower. Such a situation could result in a dangerous use of a futures market hedge. Consider a mortgage banking company that makes fixed-rate mortgages. Its customary practice is to make a mortgage commitment to a potential homebuyer at the prevailing fixed-rate mortgage rate. The commitment will be honored if the loan is funded within 60 days. This is tantamount to the lender writing an option to a homebuyer to deliver (put) a mortgage at a specified price and interest rate on or before a specified date.

What might happen if the mortgage banker uses the futures market to provide price protection between the time the commitment is made and the loan is sold in the secondary market? The mortgage lender decides to use the ten-year Treasury to hedge the risk of price volatility in the value of the mortgage to be delivered to the secondary market agency within 90 days. As conditions unfold over the course of the 60-day commitment period, the trend of interest rates is down. The commitment made to the homebuyer at a rate of 10.25 percent for a 30-year mortgage can now be obtained at a competing lender at a rate of 9.5 percent. The homebuyer discovers this and decides to obtain a loan commitment at another lender. Table 19.3 illustrates this transaction.

In this example, the firm used a futures contract to hedge an option. The futures contract requires that the firm fulfill the obligation to deliver. The option does not. Consequently, the firm lost money on the futures position with no offsetting gain in the mortgage cash market. The firm attempted to hedge option risk with a futures contract.

Table 19.3

Result of Hedge Program

	Position	Amount	Change in Price	Change in Value of Position
$200,000 ten-year Treasury futures	Short	$200,000	+3.25%	−$6,500
$200,000 mortgage	Long	0	N/A	N/A
Gain or loss on hedge				−$6,500

Despite the obvious risk in using futures contracts to hedge the risks of options, it is frequently done in practice. In the case of the mortgage banker, it is typical to determine an average percentage of loans that close as a percentage of the total dollar amount of commitments written. The *closed loan ratio* is used to determine the number of futures contracts to use. This ratio is adjusted higher during periods of rising open-market interest rates when a high percentage of the outstanding commitments move to an in-the-money condition and are, therefore, expected to be exercised. The ratio is decreased in a falling interest rate environment when a high percentage of outstanding commitments are out-of-the-money and are, therefore, expected not to be exercised. The closed loan ratio is raised when open-market rates are rising and lowered when rates fall. However, the possibility still remains that if interest rates fall, the firm will have a large loss on the futures position and no offsetting gain in the cash market.

Accounting Issues

Making matters somewhat more complicated in the world of futures are the GAAP requirements affecting futures transaction accounting. Although accounting for a futures position does not affect the economic consequences of the transaction, it could affect the timing of when gains or losses are reported. Accounting for a futures position requires that the futures position be marked-to-market if the firm is unable to specify the cash market financial claim being hedged that has potential price volatility.

If the firm can identify a specific financial claim cash market position or outstanding commitment that represents a financial risk due to price fluctuation, then the firm would account for it by offsetting the gain or loss of the futures contract against the gain or loss in the cash market at the time the positions are closed out. If there is no current cash gain or loss, then the gain or loss on the futures contract is used to adjust the cost basis of the hedged cash market instrument. This results in the amortization of the gain or loss over the life of the hedged asset or liability.

The problem with using the accounting rules relates to circumstances in which a specific cash market claim cannot be easily identified, as in the case of an entire asset portfolio being hedged to reduce a large positive or negative *GAP*. This is also the case when the relationship between the change in the futures market price and the hedged cash market claim price is not highly correlated, with a low R^2, due to high basis risk. In these circumstances, accounting for the transaction would require that the futures contract be marked-to-market and the cash position accounted for at the lower of cost or market. The firm could be experiencing a successful hedge, but would be required to report the futures gain or loss without reporting the offsetting cash market gain or loss.

This accounting practice effectively reduces the desire to implement the generic type of portfolio hedge listed in Exhibit 19.2, even though such a hedge could be effectively used to improve the firm's overall periodic or duration *GAP* position. To avoid having to mark-to-market a futures position, a firm would have to pick a specific group of assets or liabilities to hedge. It would also have to demonstrate that the hedge contract's price is highly correlated with the cash claim's price.

Futures Options

Fortunately, there is an alternative market for hedging the price risk associated with being the writer of options. This is the options on futures market. *Futures options* contracts are options to buy or sell a specified futures contract prior to its expiration at an agreed-upon price.

In October 1982, the Chicago Board Options Exchange (CBOE) of the CBOT began trading options contracts on Treasury bond futures contracts. These contracts, known as futures options, are offered on Treasury bonds, notes and bills, a municipal bond index, interest rate swaps, Eurodollar bonds, LIBOR bonds, British gilts, and mortgage-backed securities. Despite all these contracts, the largest volume of outstanding contracts is concentrated in Treasury bonds and Eurodollar bonds.

The logic of having options written against futures contracts may not seem readily apparent. However, the standardization of futures contracts, the organized trading of futures contracts that creates marketability, and the future's market exchange margin system all make the futures contract a good alternative for writing option contracts. This is especially true since it has been shown that futures prices closely track forward cash market prices. For these reasons, the futures contract provides an excellent vehicle to establish an option for hedging price risk. These advantages do not mean that investment dealers do not write and broker negotiated price options directly. They do. However, the futures options market has several advantages over the dealer market, the two most important being marketability and standardization.

Futures Options: A Description

Recall from Chapter 5 that options are written as either call (a right to buy) or put (a right to sell) options. A call (put) option written on a futures contract provides the owner with the right to buy a long (short) futures contract. That is, the call (put) option on a futures contract is a right to go long (short) on a futures contract. The advantage of the option is that the price of the futures contract is set at the time the option is written. And, like all options, a futures option is exercised at the discretion of the holder.

Futures options are written to coincide exactly with traded futures contracts. Indeed, they are written against existing traded futures contracts. Thus, the exercise dates of the options are the expiration dates for the futures contracts. Table 19.4 shows typical quotes as they might appear in the financial press for several futures options on Treasury bonds. Notice that there are three call and put contracts at six different strike prices.

Table 19.4

Reading the Financial Page

**Futures Options
(typical listing)**

Treasury Bonds $100,000 bonds; 64ths of 100%
Chicago Board of Trade

Strike Price	Calls Jan	Calls Mar	Calls June	Puts Jan	Puts Mar	Puts June
98	2–14	3–41	3–56	0–08	0–25	1–14
100	0–12	1–31	1–42	0–10	1–01	2–01
102	0–02	0–42	1–45	1–05	2–06	3–20
104	0–01	0–25	0–52	3–20	4–11	5–21
106	–	0–02	0–06	–	6–02	7–01
108	–	–	–	–	8–00	8–42

Estimated Volume 75,000
Previous Volume   52,000:   23,000 calls;   29,000 puts
Open Interest   340,000 calls; 185,000 puts

This table shows a typical listing for futures options contracts on Treasury bonds. The options are written against futures contracts listed on the CBOT. The prices are expressed as points and 64ths of 100 percent. Thus, a price of 1–31 for the $100,000 March contract at a strike of 100 would cost (1 31/64% × $100,000 =) $1,484.375.

Consider the March call at 100. The contract amount is for $100,000 par value of bonds. This option provides the owner with the right to purchase a long futures contract at a price of 100 31/64 percent of par on or before March. The call premium, or price, of this option is 1 31/64. Each 1/64 is worth (1/64% × $100,000 =) $15.625. Thus, the price of one call at a strike price of 100 would be (95/64 × $15.625 per 1/64 =) $1,484.38.

At the time this option could be purchased, the March T-bond futures contract was selling at 99 7/32. Consequently, the option in question would be considered to be out-of-the-money. This means that there is no profit from exercising the option at the current price of the futures contract. If the futures contract was selling for 100 5/32, however, the option would be considered to be in-the-money, since the option could be exercised immediately at 100 and the futures contract sold at 100 5/32.

Intrinsic Value and Time Value

When an option is in-the-money it is said to have *intrinsic value*. When an option is out-of-the-money or at-the-money (option price equals exercise price) it has no intrinsic value. In the case of the option, which can be exercised at 100 when the futures contract is selling at 100 5/32 percent of par value, the intrinsic value is the difference between the futures selling price and the exercise price for a call option. This option's intrinsic value is (100 5/32 − 100 =) 5/32% per option or, (5/32% of par value × $100,000 =) $156.25.

Options sell for more than their intrinsic value. This is because an option also has additional value related to the fact that the option holder has the prerogative of holding the option, selling the option, or exercising it. The remaining life of an option gives it additional value. This additional value is known as *time value*. The time value is the difference between the option premium price and the intrinsic value of the option. In our example, the time value would be (1 31/64 − 10/64 =) 1 21/64. The shorter the expiration date for an option, the lower is its time value. Thus, the time value of an option quickly declines as an option approaches its expiration date. The fact that options have time value is the reason why marketable American-type options should not be exercised before their expiration date. If they are, the holder wipes out the option's remaining time value, which could be realized if the option were sold instead of exercised.

Using Traded Futures Options

In practice, futures options are used for two primary purposes. First, they are used to hedge the price risk of writing options. On many occasions, financial institutions write options to customers. A loan commitment with a rate set in advance is a good example of a put option sold to a potential borrower. In this situation, the lender has written a put option to accept a debt claim of a borrower at a specified interest rate on or before a specified date. If interest rates rise, the borrower can be expected to exercise the option and deliver the debt claim. If rates fall, however, the borrower will likely borrow at a lower rate elsewhere.

One way to hedge the risk inherent in writing this put is for the lender to buy an offsetting put futures option that expires around the time of the loan commitment. If interest rates rise, the lender will lose on the loan commitment and gain on the put futures option. Thus, a futures put (call) option can be used to hedge a cash market put (call) option written in the cash market.

Secondly, futures options can be used to purchase price insurance. The owner of an option stands to lose only the option premium paid, but stands to gain an unlimited amount if the price of a futures contract rises in the case of a call option or falls in the case of a put. Consequently, a futures option may be purchased to provide protection from an adverse price change in a cash market position without giving up a potential gain from a favorable price change.

Exhibit 19.3 provides several examples of how futures options can be used to manage interest rate risk.

Exhibit 19.3

Selected Futures Options Transactions for Managing Interest Rate Risk

Cash Market Transaction	Cash Market Risk Position	Option Used to Hedge Interest Rate Risk
Fixed-rate commitment outstanding	Sold put option on loan	Buy futures option put on debt similar to loan
Hold large bond portfolio. Concerned over possible change in Fed policy raising rates	Long cash position on Treasury bonds	Buy futures option put on Treasury bonds
Sold certificates of deposit with clause permittting additional deposits at existing interest rate	Sold call option on additional CDs	Buy futures option call on debt claim similar to CD

The primary advantages of futures options relate to the fact that, unlike futures contracts, an option provides a safer hedge for options written by the institution than do futures contracts. In theory, options price risk should be hedged with offsetting options. Another advantage of options is that there is no margin required.

The disadvantages of futures options include the presence of price circuit breakers on the financial futures contracts on which the options are written. This can serve to complicate a hedge program. Secondly, options do not provide offsetting price protection until the futures price exceeds the strike price by the amount of the option premium. Options are not cost-effective for small adverse price moves.

DEMONSTRATION PROBLEM: Futures Option Hedge

Situation: A mortgage lender has made a $1,000,000 commitment to a borrower on March 2, 1994. The loan has a rate of 9.25 percent and a 20-year maturity. It must be closed within 60 days.

The lender is concerned that if interest rates fall, the loan will not close. This is a problem since the loan has been presold to a life insurance company to yield the life company 9 percent. Consequently, if the loan does not close, the lender will have to purchase another loan in the secondary market to yield the rate promised to the life company. If rates fall, buying a loan to cover the committed sale to the life company will result in a loss.

The solution is purchasing a call option on a long-term futures contract to offset the put option offered the borrower.

Data Input: Note: Futures and cash quoted in 32ndths and options in 64ths of 100 percent.

(March 2, 1994)

Spot price of 8 percent coupon Treasury bonds	96–03
Spot price of 9 percent mortgage	100–22
March price of 8 percent coupon futures contract for Treasury bonds, June 1995 delivery	95–07
Beta (Treasury bond versus mortgage)	.82
PV_{fc} per 8 percent Treasury bonds	−.8415
PV_{cc} per 9 percent mortgage	−.8945
June Treasury bond call option price, strike price 97	1–50

Establishing Hedge Transaction:

Step 1: Determine hedge ratio

$$\text{Hedge ratio} = PV_{cc}/PV_{fc} \times b_{cc/fc} = -.8945/-.8415 \times .82$$
$$= .8716$$

> Step 2: Determine number of futures options contracts
> Number of contracts = $1,000,000/$100,000 × .8716
> = 8.716 = 9 contracts
> Step 3: Buy nine call options @1–50 per option = 9 × $1,781.25
> = $16,031.25
>
> **Data Input:** Rates fall, loan does not close, lender must purchase mortgage in secondary market to deliver to life company.
> (May 4, 1994)
>
> | | |
> |---|---:|
> | Treasury bond futures price, June 1994 contract | 100–08 |
> | Mortgage, 9 percent | 102–30 |
> | June Treasury bond call option price, June 1994 | 6–50 |
>
> **Results:**
> Without Futures Options Hedge
> Purchase 9 percent mortgage = $1,000,000 × 102–30 = −$1,029,375
> Deliver 9 percent mortgage = $1,000,000   +1,000,000
> **Loss**   **−$29,375**
>
> With Futures Options Hedge
> Purchase 9 percent mortgage = $1,000,000 × 102–30 = −$1,029,375
> Cost of options   −16,031
> Deliver 9 percent mortgage = $1,000,000   +1,000,000
> Futures options gain [6−50−(1−50)]% × $100,000
>   × 9 = $5,000 × 9 =   45,000
> **Loss**   **−$406**
>
> Futures options hedge reduced the loss. The loan commitment was not excercised and the lender had to buy a mortgage in the secondary market to meet its obligation to the life company.

Interest Rate Swaps

One of the fastest growing interest rate risk management tools is the *interest rate swap*. This is a contractual agreement between two parties who agree to make periodic payments to one another. Such an agreement typically has one party receiving payments on a fixed nominal amount of principal based on a specified long or intermediate term interest rate. The other party receives payments based on a short-term interest rate, which floats over the term of the agreement.

The interest rate swap was first accomplished in England in 1981. The United States accomplished its first swap when the Student Loan Marketing Association completed a swap in 1982. The market has grown swiftly. It is estimated by Marshall and Kapner (1990) that over $550 billion in swaps were accomplished in 1988 alone.

The concept of the interest rate swap is to assist both parties. Some consider the transaction to be motivated by a condition in which both parties have a comparative advantage in raising funds—one party with a comparative advantage in the short-term market and the other in the longer-term market. This comparative advantage condition provides the motivation for each party to enter into an interest rate swap.

The primary purpose of the swap is to assist the financial firm in altering its interest rate risk profile. A financial firm with a high interest rate risk position stemming from an excess of maturing or repricing liabilities compared to assets, a negative *GAP*, could reduce this *GAP* by converting short-term liabilities into longer term liabilities.

The Typical Swap

The typical interest rate swap has two primary players and frequently a third party player. The two primary players are the institutions that want to alter the cash flow on a specified amount of nominal principal. *Nominal principal* is the amount specified in the contract on which interest will be paid to each party. In an interest rate swap, actual principal does not change hands. Exhibit 19.4 shows an interest rate swap in which party A agrees to pay a floating rate of 2.5 percent over the 90-day Treasury bill rate on $15 million of nominal principal for five years. Party B, on the other hand, agrees to pay a fixed rate of 9.5 percent on $15 million of nominal principal for five years. The payments are made semiannually in this case. The two parties are often brought together by a broker. More typically, however, the swaps are arranged by a third party that acts as an intermediary. This third party is frequently a commercial bank or investment banker.

Exhibit 19.5 shows the swap arrangement with the commercial bank as the intermediary. The commercial bank is typically compensated by increasing the rate to parties A and B and keeping this interest rate spread as a profit. As a result, in Exhibit 19.5, party A pays 2.625 percent over the 26-week Treasury bill rate and party B, 9.625 percent. This allows the bank

Exhibit 19.4

Interest Rate Swap
Payments Made Semiannually Between Two Parties

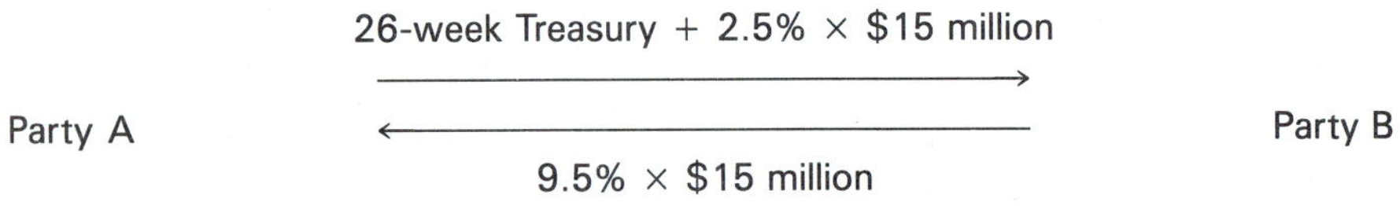

Party A ⟶ 26-week Treasury + 2.5% × $15 million ⟶ Party B
Party A ⟵ 9.5% × $15 million ⟵ Party B

Exhibit 19.5

Payments Made Semiannually Among Three Parties Swap with Bank Intermediary

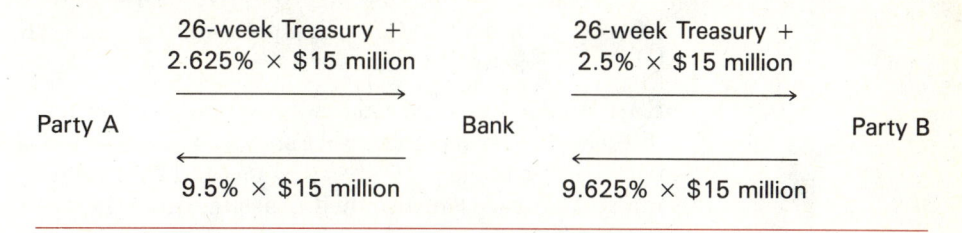

```
              26-week Treasury +              26-week Treasury +
              2.625% × $15 million            2.5% × $15 million
              ─────────────▶                  ─────────────▶
  Party A                          Bank                          Party B
              ◀─────────────                  ◀─────────────
              9.5% × $15 million              9.625% × $15 million
```

to obtain a profit of .25 percent for the five-year life of the contract. The bank is compensated this .25 percent spread for providing three services. First, it is compensated as a broker bringing both parties together. Secondly, it is compensated for its activities as an originator of the transaction. This involves legal documentation and underwriting costs. Finally, it is compensated for acting as an intermediary. This involves accepting the credit risk that one or the other party will default on the swap.

In Exhibit 19.5, the commercial bank is an intermediary between the two parties. This does not have to be the case. The bank could write a swap agreement with just one of the two parties. In that case, the bank could assume interest rate risk. If it wrote only the swap to party B, for example, and a rise in short-term interest rates caused its cost of funds to rise, it could face an interest rate squeeze, since it would be receiving a fixed return from party B. Many commercial banks act as primary dealers in swaps where they take credit and interest rate risks.

DEMONSTRATION PROBLEM: Interest Rate Swap

Situation: Southern Savings Bank has a large negative one-year periodic GAP_1. This situation can be improved by completing an interest rate swap. The bank will accept a fixed-rate obligation for five years at a fixed rate of 7 percent. In return, it will receive income at the three-month Treasury bill rate plus .50 percent. The term of the swap will be five years.

Data Input: The bank's quarterly income statement, ignoring operating expenses and loan losses, is shown below. The bank's GAP_1 is negative $3,000,000. The bank is contemplating a $3,000,000 nominal principal swap.

> Quarterly Net Interest Margin
>
> Interest income $8,500,000
> Interest expense   6,250,000
> Net interest margin $2,250,000
> Interest swap $3,000,000 principal five years fixed @ 7.00%
> Interest swap $3,000,000 principal, floating quarterly, @ 3-month bill + .50%, current bill rate 4.5%
>
> **Result:** The result of this swap will depend on future changes in interest rate levels. Table 19.4 shows the change in the net interest margin for changes of (+/−) 0%, 1%, and 2% changes in the level of interest rates. (For simplicity, assume all assets and liabilities, except the swap, reprice or mature after the period shown in the sensitivity analysis.)

Table 19.5

**Sensitivity Analysis of Net Interest Margin
Changes in Interest Rates of (+/−) 0%, 1%, and 2%
(dollars in thousands)**

Change in Interest Rates

	−2.00%	−1.00%	0	+1.00%	+2.00%
Without Swap					
Interest income	$8.50	$8.50	$8.50	$8.50	$8.50
Interest expense	5.95	6.10	6.25	6.40	6.55
Net Interest Margin	**$2.55**	**$2.40**	**$2.25**	**$2.10**	**$1.95**
With Swap					
Interest income	$8.50	$8.50	$8.50	$8.50	$8.50
Interest expense	6.70	6.55	6.40	6.40	6.40
Net Interest Margin	**$1.80**	**$1.95**	**$2.10**	**$2.10**	**$2.10**

Southern Savings Bank's swap has the impact of insulating its net interest margin from increases in open-market interest rates. There is a cost to doing this, however. The firm will experience a decline in its net interest margin initially (under the 0 change in rate scenario), since the cost of the five-year swap payments is 2 percent higher than the current receipts under the short-term swap. This is because the term structure is upward sloping at the time of the swap. Another cost of the swap is the spread that the counterparty takes out of the transaction. This is a net loss shared by the two swapping organizations.

Commercial Bank Profit from the Swap

In the case of Exhibit 19.5, the commercial bank has written two swap agreements that provide a .125 percent margin each between the interest payments it receives and the interest payments it makes. This amounts to .25% on $15 million of total principal. The profit from this transaction can be considered the present value of these interest rate margin cash flows. The swap is outstanding five years or ten periods ($n = 10$). When discounted at a weighted cost of capital of say 12 percent, the present value of an n period swap to the bank, ignoring administrative costs and credit risk, would be shown by the equation below:

$$\text{Present Value of Swap} = \sum_{n-1}^{10} [(.0025 / 2) \times \$15{,}000{,}000] / [(1 + .12 / 2)^n]$$

$$= \$146{,}282$$

In January 1989 the Federal Reserve Board issued regulations establishing the capital requirements required of commercial banks holding a swap portfolio. Until that time, the swap portfolios of commercial banks required no capital. This was due, in part, to the fact that swap transactions are off-balance sheet transactions, since the nominal principal of swap transactions is not shown on the balance sheet.

In order to recognize the credit and interest rate risks inherent in swaps written by commercial banks, the Federal Reserve developed a methodology that determines the minimum capital requirement to be held against swaps. The amount of this reserve is based primarily on a mark-to-market calculation using the notational principal, swap coupon rate, and prevailing market interest rate.

Consider a commercial bank that has written a swap with four remaining years to maturity, calling for a 10.5 percent fixed-coupon payment. If after a one-year period, the current prevailing swap rate for the remaining three-year term on this swap is 7.5 percent, then it is clear that the bank could lose 3 percent per annum to replace the swap if the counterparty that was making the 10.5 percent payment to the bank defaulted. The risk-based capital requirement is based on the recognition of this potential loss to the bank.

Risks in Managing Swap Portfolios

An institution managing a large swap portfolio must understand the risks involved. These risks include credit, interest rate, and basis risks.

Credit risk: Swap credit risk is the risk that a counterparty will default on a swap agreement at a time when the replacement of the swap would represent a loss to the intermediary.

Interest rate risk: Swap interest rate risk is the risk that a swap that is written by the intermediary is unhedged by offsetting swaps or other assets and liabilities. This would represent an unhedged swap position. This situation would occur if an intermediary was making floating payments to a counterparty under a swap agreement when the firm had a large negative periodic *GAP*. Such a swap would exacerbate the interest rate mismatch of the organization.

Basis risk: The intermediary accepts basis risk to the extent that one floating rate swap payment is tied to one index and an offsetting swap tied to another. If these two indices are not perfectly correlated, then the firm will face basis risk. If an intermediary contracted to pay 6-month LIBOR + 2.25% to a counterparty and accepts a payment of 26-week Treasury + 2.50% and the relationship between the two rates changes, then the intermediary will be exposed to basis risk.

Interest Rate Swaps and Interest Rate Risk Management

The usefulness of interest rate swaps in interest rate risk management should be obvious at this point. The interest rate swap can be used to convert liabilities whose cost is predominantly short-term into fixed-rate liabilities and vice versa. The swap can be used very much like the interest rate futures contract to hedge against the price risk of debt securities. The advantage of the swap is that the term of a swap can frequently far exceed that of a futures contract. Some swaps are written for up to 20 years. In addition, swaps provide more flexibility due to the negotiated nature of the transaction.

A financial institution with high interest rate risk due to a large positive or negative periodic *GAP* would use the swap as shown in Exhibit 19.6.

Exhibit 19.6

Use of Swap for Interest Rate Risk Management

Interest Rate Risk Position	Indicated Swap
Large negative periodic *GAP*	Assume fixed-rate interest payment for short-term interest receipt
Large positive periodic *GAP*	Assume short-term interest payment for fixed-rate interest receipt

Adjustable-Rate Lending

Many financial contracts have adjustable-rate interest provisions. Loans tied to the prime rate, Treasury bill yields, or LIBOR are common examples. The reason so many financial intermediaries lend using adjustable-rate contracts is to reduce interest rate risk. Most depositories, for example, have limited access to long-term liabilities. However, they have ample short-term liabilities, since this is the depositors' preference. As a result, these lenders prefer loans whose interest rate closely tracks the changes in short-term liability costs.

The problems in the thrift industry in the late 1970s and early 1980s were the impetus for the development and widespread adoption of adjustable-rate mortgage (ARM) programs for residential housing. It also led to the adoption of adjustable-rate indexed claims in other contracts as well. Until the early 1980s, only a handful of state-chartered institutions had the clear legal ability to write these mortgages. Even in those states that permitted ARM lending, however, the majority of state-chartered institutions made fixed-rate mortgages (FRMs). In the early 1980s, however, that changed as the thrift and commercial bank regulators adopted regulations permitting ARMs. Until that time, ARMs were criticized by groups of homebuilders and real estate sales groups who felt that the "inferior" ARM would drive "superior" FRMs out of the market. These groups contended this would hurt the sales of new and existing houses. With the deregulation of deposit rates, however, the pressure for regulators to authorize ARMs was overwhelming.

Regulators in the early 1980s demanded that the nation's savings and loans reduce their interest rate risk positions. They strongly encouraged institutions to originate these loans for portfolio investment. By the mid-1980s, close to 50 percent of all newly originated mortgages were ARMs. By 1990, still only about 30 percent of the nation's single family mortgage stock were ARMs. These percentages compare to virtually no ARMs in the mid-1970s.

The Basic ARM Features

The ARM has been the source of significant innovation over the last decade. Several features of ARMs, however, have to be established at the time they are originated. Because there are so many features, it is easy to see why ARMs have been the source of so much innovation and consumer confusion. The main features include the following:

1. The interest rate index
2. The margin over the index
3. The adjustment period
4. The option of using interest rate caps and floors

5. The option of a lower than coupon initial rate (sometimes known as teasers)
6. The option of payment limits
7. The option of negative amortization

The first three of these provisions are necessary in any adjustable rate contract, and the others are optional.

Interest Rate Index

The interest rate index specifies the base upon which the mortgage's interest rate is established. Exhibit 19.7 shows a number of the more commonly used indices.

Interest Rate Margin

The interest rate margin determines the percentage amount of spread the borrower's rate is established over the index. The index is determined at a specified time and the margin is added to it. For example, the 11th District cost of funds index for the Federal Home Loan Bank of San Francisco is determined to be 8.02 percent in March 1994. The margin on a particular mortgage is 2.25 percent. The rate on the mortgage would be 10.27 percent (8.02% + 2.25% = 10.27%).

Adjustment Period

The adjustment period determines the amount of time between adjustments to the mortgage rate. Within the adjustment period, the changes in the index do not influence the rate on the mortgage. However, at the adjustment period, the index value will affect the mortgage rate. Adjust-

Exhibit 19.7

Common ARM Indices
One-year Treasury
Three-year Treasury
Various LIBOR rates
Cost of funds index, various Federal Home Loan Banks
Cost of funds index, national

ment periods are typically monthly (on cost of funds ARMs), semiannually, annually, or every three years (on certain Treasury and LIBOR ARMs).

Interest Rate Caps and Floors

An ARM can be written to incorporate a maximum rate life-of-loan *cap,* which establishes the highest rate the index plus margin can rise to, regardless of the rise in the index. The mortgage may also incorporate a *floor,* which is the minimum rate the index and margin can fall to.

Initial Rate Discount or Teaser

It is common to have ARMs quoted in the market with an initial rate that is below the index plus margin. This lower rate has come to be known as a *teaser*. The teaser has been used to encourage the use of the ARM at the expense of the FRM. Occasionally, the lender allows the borrower to qualify for the mortgage at the lower monthly payment computed at the teaser. This allows some borrowers to qualify for a larger mortgage.

Payment Change Limits—The Annual Cap

Some ARMs have a maximum payment increase feature built into them. This is known as an annual cap. These ARMs will constrain the rise in the index to say, 1 or 2 percent within any 12-month period. In the case of a cost of funds ARM, the limit has frequently been set so that the maximum adjustment in rate will be limited to no more than what will produce a maximum, say, 7.5 percent payment increase in any annual period. This feature is designed to limit the payment "shock" to the borrower and lessen the probability of default.

Negative Amortization

Most mortgages provide for a portion of each monthly payment to reduce the principal balance on the mortgage. This is called amortization. Some ARMs have a negative amortization feature. The principal goes up instead of down. This occurs when the index plus margin increases, but the payment is held constant or is not permitted to rise enough to pay all the interest, thus creating a negative amortization situation. A mortgage with a 7.5 percent payment increase limit, as in the previous example, might include a negative amortization feature.

These ARM features can be put together in an infinite variety of combinations and have clearly been a major tool in reducing interest rate risk at the nation's depository institutions.

Many depositories will originate ARMs for portfolio investment and fixed-rate mortgages for sale in the secondary market. This permits the institution to create two valuable income streams that act as an interest rate hedge against rising interest rates. In the firm's portfolio, it will have an adjustable-rate asset whose rate increases as open-market interest rates rise. In addition, the firm will also produce a servicing contract that also acts as a hedge against rising interest rates. A servicing contract will tend to rise in value as open-market interest rates rise, due to the slower prepayment experience anticipated during a period of rising interest rates.

Other Adjustable Loans

The success of the ARM has led intermediaries to develop a wide array of adjustable-rate consumer loan contracts. Today, the adjustable-rate feature is used on second mortgages, credit card receivables, lines of credit, and security loans. On other than first mortgages, the more popular indices include the prime rate, Treasury bill rate, and cost of funds.

Summary

The objective of interest rate risk management is to alter the interest rate risk profile of a financial institution in such a way as to control the impact of changes in market interest rates on the value of the firm. Few financial intermediaries are able to issue liabilities that have cash flows that mirror the cash flows of its assets. The exceptions are mutual funds, limited partnerships, and real estate investment trusts.

For depositories, finance companies, and insurance companies, interest rate risk management is a major concern. As was discussed in the chapter on measuring interest rate risk, interest rate risks involve the firm's overall asset and liability profiles. Yet, when it comes to managing interest rate risks, accounting and institutional barriers frequently require that specific assets or commitments be identified before a risk reducing transaction can take place.

The primary tools used to reduce interest rate risk are financial forward and futures contracts, interest rate swaps, and adjustable-rate loans.

The **financial futures market** is less than 20 years old. Financial futures contracts can be used to hedge the price risk of claims held by financial institutions or commitments outstanding by these firms.

Financial futures contracts are legal contracts that commit the buyer (**long position**) to take delivery of the financial claim for which the contract is written or to repurchase the contract (cover the position) before its expiration date at the prevailing market price. A seller (**short position**) of a futures contract is committed to deliver the financial claim at the contract expiration date or repurchase the contract at its prevailing market price anytime before expiration.

Hedging in financial futures involves identifying the cash market financial claim that presents price risk to the firm and offsetting that cash market position with an opposite position in the futures market.

The mechanics of using the futures market can be very complicated. Futures transactions require holding **margin** in the form of cash or certain marketable securities to cover any potential loss that may occur should the firm immediately reverse its futures market position. Futures market hedging also involves determining the correct relationship between the price changes in the cash market claim and the contract used in the futures market. This involves calculating a **hedge ratio,** which is defined as follows.

$$\frac{\text{Price value of one basis point change in cash claim}}{\text{Price value of one basis point change in futures contract}} =$$

$$PV_{cc}/PV_{fc}$$

$$\frac{\text{Change in the yield of the cash market claim}}{\text{Change in the yield of the futures market contract}} = b_{cc/fc}$$

$$\text{Hedge ratio} = [PV_{cc}/PV_{fc}] \times b_{cc/fc}$$

The relationship between the yield of the cash market claim and the futures market claim is rarely a perfect correlation. This presents the hedger with **basis risk.** Basis risk is the risk that the interest rate change of the cash market claim is not perfectly correlated to the futures market claim. Basis risk can produce unexpected losses and gains to the hedger.

Futures options provide the most theoretically sound approach for hedging the price risk associated with writing options. Futures options are options written on outstanding traded futures contracts. These options allow the owner to purchase (call) or sell (put) a long or short futures contract at an agreed-upon price prior to the expiration date of the futures contract.

Interest rate swaps are the fastest growing financial technique for altering the interest rate risk position of a firm. Swaps involve two parties that wish to alter the interest rate they pay on a fixed amount of **nominal dollar principal.** One party that is currently obligated to make a fixed-rate payment wants to convert to a floating rate, and the other party the opposite. Typically a third party, such as a commercial bank or investment banker, will act as a principal in a swap transaction between the two other parties. This is performed to earn a profit for providing origination, portfolio management, and brokerage services. The compensation is earned through acquiring an interest margin.

Adjustable-rate financial claims are widely used by financial firms to modify their interest rate risk position. A major increase in adjustable-rate lending has occurred in the residential mortgage market.

Adjustable-rate financial claims require that certain provisions be specified. The necessary provisions include **interest rate index, adjustment period,** and **interest rate margin.** Other provisions found in adjustable-rate claims are optional.

Questions

Chapter 19

1. Explain a number of important approaches for managing interest rate risk.
2. Explain what a futures contract is.
3. Financial futures contracts are used to hedge the price fluctuations related to changes in interest rates. Give several examples of situations that might suggest the use of a futures market hedge.
4. What is meant by a long and short futures position?
5. What is basis risk and why is it important in hedging using the futures market?
6. Why is it risky to hedge the risk of writing an option with a futures market hedge?
7. Explain some of the accounting issues that relate to using the futures market.
8. In the futures market, what is meant by margin? Who must put up margin?
9. What is the hedge ratio as it relates to using the futures market? How do you calculate the hedge ratio? Why is a correct hedge ratio so important?
10. What type of circuit breaker do you frequently find used in the futures market? Why is the existence of such a device important to implementing a hedge transaction?
11. Explain an interest rate swap.
12. Why are commercial banks involved in the swap market?
13. How does a commercial bank or other intermediary writer of swaps make a profit on swap transactions?
14. What types of risk are inherent in swap transactions?
15. How would you use an interest rate swap to help manage interest rate risk?
16. Why has there been an increase in the use of adjustable-rate financial contracts?
17. What are the basic features of most adjustable-rate financial claims?
18. What are some of the problems in the valuation of financial claims with caps, floors, payment change limits, teasers, and other features found in many adjustable-rate financial claim contracts?
19. What are the most common indices used in adjustable-rate financial claim contracts?
20. Increasing the use of adjustable-rate loans in the portfolio will decrease interest rate risk for most depositories, but this action could also decrease the firm's interest rate margin. Explain this statement.

Problems

Problem 19-1   Hedging

You are a mortgage banker and have just agreed to make a $3 million apartment loan. It will take 60 days to process the loan, at which time you will sell it in the secondary mortgage market at the then-prevailing interest rate.

1. You decide to hedge your position with the five-year Treasury note futures contract. You sell $3 million worth of contracts at a price of 100 8/32. After 60 days, interest rates have risen and the futures contract price has fallen to 98 12/32. The mortgage can only be sold for 97.5 percent of par. What is the net gain or loss from the hedge?
2. Was this a perfect hedge? Why or why not?

Problem 19-2   Hedging

As portfolio manager for a commercial bank, you are examining the refunding of $55 million in brokered CDs, which are maturing in six months. You would like to construct a hedge that will protect you from rising interest rates that would increase your refunding costs.

1. You choose the five-year Treasury note futures contract as your hedge instrument. What will rising interest rates do to the price of the contract? Should you sell the contract (short futures position) or buy the contract (long futures position)? Why?
2. What will be the effect of the hedge if interest rates fall? What would be the effect of falling interest rates if you don't use a hedge?

Problem 19-3   Interest Rate Swaps

Progressive Federal Bank has created a new type of IRA account that pays depositors 7.25 percent annually for seven years. The bank has issued $80 million of these IRA accounts. Because its seven-year funding requirements are only $45 million, the bank decides to seek an interest rate swap into a short-term obligation to cover its obligations on the remaining $35 million.

1. The six-month LIBOR rate is 7.95 percent. If the bank swaps payments at the six-month LIBOR rate on $35 million for seven years in return for a series of fixed receipts at the current six-month LIBOR rate plus ten basis points over the same seven years, what gross yield spread will the bank lock in on the $35 million?
2. If annual servicing costs for the IRAs are 55 basis points and the annual transaction costs for the swap are 20 basis points, does the swap still make sense?
3. The bank wants to use the $35 million to fund assets that have minimal interest rate risk. What kind of assets should it seek and how should those assets be priced?

Problem 19-4   Interest Rate Swaps

A bank and a savings and loan association both find themselves in an awkward interest rate risk position. As an investment banker, you are interested in the possibility of constructing a double interest rate swap for the two institutions.

1. The bank has commercial loan assets that are returning the one-year T-bill rate plus 3.5 percent, net of all servicing costs. The savings and loan association has variable rate savings accounts that cost 1 percent below the one-year T-bill rate, including servicing costs. If you split the available spread equally between the two institutions after taking a 50 basis point annual spread, what will be the prices of the first swap? Assume a Treasury bill rate of 7 percent.

2. The savings and loan association has fixed-rate mortgages yielding 9.5 percent annually, net of all servicing costs. The bank has fixed-rate long-term certificates of deposit on which it pays 7 percent annually, including servicing costs. If you split the available spread equally between the two institutions after taking 50 basis points annual spread, what will be the prices of the second swap?

Managing Credit Risk

chapter **20**

Credit risk has not been the focus of as much academic analysis as interest rate risk analysis. The techniques for managing interest rate risk were largely mastered in the 1980s as a result of the thrifts' problems. However, there are fewer methodologies for managing credit risk. Yet, credit risk is a more important topic to master and understand today because of the dynamic competitive forces shaping the financial services industry.

This chapter identifies the primary areas of focus in the credit risk management function and provides an overview of credit analysis. First, the primary types of credit risks are identified. This is followed by an extensive discussion of portfolio diversification techniques used to control credit risk. Then specific techniques for managing credit risk of individual loans are discussed. Finally, the topic of off-balance sheet transactions is introduced.

Overview of Credit Risk Trends

During the last decade, the United States has experienced an international debt crisis, the credit problems of the thrift debacle, large and growing credit problems in the nation's real estate markets, and losses from the highly leveraged loan and junk bond era. These are all related to credit risks.

Chapter 15 presented the reasons why credit risk is likely to continue to be a major issue for financial intermediaries. Intermediaries have lost their largest and most creditworthy customers. The highly credit-rated corporations have gone directly to the capital markets. The less creditworthy customers have found the high-yield bond market. Corporate money managers have stopped giving banks idle balances as they and their consumer counterparts have found the retail and wholesale money market mutual funds. The thrifts have watched the federal credit agencies dominate the residential mortgage market. In sum, financial markets have become more competitive and efficient. Profit margins have been reduced to the point where a large segment of our financial service providers have excess capacity.

The most significant impact of these competitive forces is the pressure put on financial institutions to find higher yielding assets. Since many of the traditional assets of banks and thrifts no longer have adequate profit margins, the managements of these institutions have looked to other markets or have created new markets to find higher yields. The following are some of the results of their efforts:

- Growth in international lending to third world countries in the late 1970s and early 1980s
- Growth in acquisition, development, and construction lending by thrifts and commercial banks in the 1980s
- Growth in investment in high-yield bonds by thrifts and insurance companies in the 1980s
- Increased commercial bank lending to leveraged buy-outs and corporate acquisition financing by commercial banks
- Increased lending and liberalization of terms on consumer loans, such as five-year automobile financing by commercial banks and finance companies
- Increased use of limited documentation on residential real estate loans in which various underwriting requirements are eliminated or reduced
- Use of off-balance sheet credit exposures including interest rate and currency swaps, loan commitments, recourse sales, and securitization of assets

The tendency of financial institutions to pursue these types of transactions and investments puts a premium on credit risk management. The roles of credit officers, loan underwriters, institutional credit analysts, loan servicers, and loan monitoring groups have taken on considerably more importance. The loan workout departments in financial institutions and those working for the government have increased their activities substantially in the 1990s.

Major Types of Credit Risks

Credit risk is the probability of financial loss on a loan or investment. Principal losses on loans, however, represent only one portion of total losses on defaulted loans. The total loss includes the following:

1. Accrued, but uncollected, interest
2. Management and outside legal expenses dealing with such activities as loan documentation and analysis, restructuring, repossession of collateral, and sale of collateral
3. Costs to pursue legal remedies
4. Opportunity costs relating to the lag between when the loan stops accruing interest and any recovery of principal takes place

The major types of credit risk exposures faced by a lender according to Donaldson (1989) include pure credit risk, underwriting risk, settlement risk, documentation risk, operating risk, political risk, and event risk.

Pure Credit Risk

Pure credit risk is what most people think of when they consider credit risk. In the case of pure credit risk, the borrower does not live up to the terms and conditions of the loan agreement. This results in a financial loss to the lender. A borrower in distress is likely to require a loan restructuring. The amount of pure credit risk in any lending transaction will depend critically on how the loan or investment was structured. Collateral, guarantees, sound documentation, covenants, and other lender safeguards are used to limit pure credit risk.

Underwriting Risk

Underwriting risk relates to the probability of loss assumed by the loan originator between the time of origination and sale of a financial claim in the secondary market. Frequently, investment bankers hold securities for their own account prior to distribution. Commercial banks lend money with the expectation that a loan participation will be sold to other banks. Mortgage lenders originate mortgages with the objective of selling into the secondary market. In each instance, there is an element of credit risk accepted by the originator that is related to the probability that the originated financial claim does not meet the credit standards of the buyer.

Settlement Risk

Settlement risk relates to the risk that a counterparty to a transaction is unwilling or unable to complete the transaction. The greatest settlement risks are borne by investment banking firms and commercial banks that handle large trading portfolios of securities, foreign exchange, or other secondary market instruments.

Settlement risks are related to the price volatility of the underlying claim. The greater the price volatility, the greater the likelihood that a price will cause a loss for the counterparty, which creates the motivation to renege on the purchase or sale commitment. If settlement does not take place, the broker/dealer is exposed to a loss.

Documentation Risk

Documentation risk relates to a loan that creates a loss due to poorly drawn legal documents or a poorly structured loan agreement. These documents involve many provisions, covenants, and descriptions that monitor and resolve disputes if a loan or investment goes into default. Unfortunately, the legal profession tends to write these contracts for other lawyers and judges. Many of the financial intermediary's personnel responsible for monitoring, servicing, and complying with these complicated provisions may be unable to understand or properly comply.

To deal with this problem, there have been many efforts to standardize legal documents. The secondary market mortgage GSEs have spent millions of dollars developing standardized mortgage contracts, servicing contracts, and other documents to facilitate the sale and servicing of mortgages. Despite these efforts, documentation risk is inherent in the lending and security origination processes.

Operating Risk

Operating risk relates to a loan originator's operating difficulties that are caused by inadequate training or capacity. Occasionally, the demand for loans is so strong that it puts significant pressure on the originator's ability to complete the necessary tasks for properly originating the loans. In 1986 and again in 1992, for example, sharp declines in mortgage rates created a record demand to refinance home mortgages. Many lenders were unable to process these loans within the time frames that the borrowers expected or had been promised. This led to lawsuits and major public relations problems for many firms.

Operating risk problems have increased due to credit legislation and regulation. The truth-in-lending, equal credit opportunity, and home mortgage disclosure acts have all increased the operating risks of the loan origination process by increasing its complexity.

Political Risk

There are several types of political risks. One type of political risk relates to whether a country will honor its debt commitments and those of private companies in its jurisdiction. Another type of political risk relates to how countries regulate and supervise their financial institutions. The latter problem was evident in the case of the Bank of Commerce and Credit International (BCCI) scandal. In this case, an international bank carried out alleged illegal activities by taking advantage of differences in supervisory diligence among the countries in which it operated.

Recent agreements reached in Basel, Switzerland, led to the establishment of internationally accepted capital standards for commercial banks around the world. This represented an effort to provide more uniform regulation of the world's banking institutions. The Bank for International Settlements also works to provide for greater uniformity of bank regulation.

All financial institutions must be concerned about international credit risk exposures and the foreign institutions with whom they deal. International banks must also be concerned about the impact that regulations promulgated by other countries and international organizations have on their institutions.

Event Risk

Event risk relates to unanticipated changes in the ownership, control, capital structure, or business activities of a firm that impact materially on its creditworthiness. For example, a leveraged buy-out frequently leaves the senior holders of high-grade debt in a less secure position. A major equity repurchase program also adversely affects existing debt holders. An acquisition in an industry that is highly risky, compared to the historical activities of the acquiring firm, can lead to debt rating downgrades and losses for debt holders.

Techniques for Managing Credit Risks

Managing credit risks does not lend itself to the use of the powerful analytical techniques and methodologies associated with the measurement and management of interest rate risk. As we have seen, credit risks come in a wide variety of forms. Credit risks are impacted by macroeconomic, industrial, international, legal, and ethical considerations. Models for predicting the impact of this wide array of forces are difficult to develop. In fact, the job of measuring and managing credit risk is considerably more difficult than measuring and managing interest rate risk.

This chapter discusses some of the more important techniques that have been deployed to manage and control credit risk. Diversification is the primary theoretical technique for controlling losses due to credit exposure at the loan and the portfolio level. Likewise, credit analysis is the primary technique for controlling credit risks at the loan level. Loan covenants are most often used to alter credit risks associated with individual loans and debt securities.

Diversification of Credit Risk

In modern finance, asset diversification is the theoretically correct technique for reducing the return volatility for any given level of expected risk within a portfolio of investments. The rationale for diversification of risk is of more than theoretical concern, however. The failure of many financial institutions in the 1980s and early 1990s demonstrated the hazards of undiversified asset portfolios. The rationale behind diversification has led one group of analysts to advocate substantially increasing the size of financial institutions to ensure that proper diversification takes place. Diversification by type of credit, by type of borrower, and by geographic area are advocated by this group. Another group of analysts, however, point toward the diversification efforts of thrift institutions in the 1980s as proof that, while diversification may be a good theoretical concept, it does not work. These analysts maintain that specialization is needed to understand the unique risks and to provide for the sound underwriting of the loans.

These arguments really serve to highlight two dimensions of credit risk diversification. The first is referred to as credit risk diversification relating to the *law of large numbers* for investments in one type of credit. The second type of credit risk diversification relates to the reduction in risk that comes about through investing in more than one type of asset. Here the variance of return is reduced through portfolio diversification. Both types of diversification are important in understanding the risks faced by financial intermediaries. Indeed, managers of intermediaries must be ever mindful of the possibility that the advantages of one type of risk-reducing diversification are not offset by failing to consider the other. That is, the benefits of portfolio diversification can be more than offset by inadequate attention to how each type of asset is acquired.

Law of Large Numbers Diversification

The first type of diversification to understand relates to investments made in a particular type of risky asset. This is referred to as the law of large numbers diversification. It is defined as the probability that a specific lender's credit loss experience on a portfolio of a particular type of loan will deviate from the actual loss experience for the population of loans from which they are drawn.

Consider a financial institution developing a loan program for auto lending. After an analysis of this market, management determines that it will underwrite loans that provide credit to potential buyers who are unable to meet the higher credit standards used by the captive auto finance companies. After determining the underwriting requirements, the institution completes a study to determine the likely credit loss experience on such a program. This analysis reveals that, properly implemented, the program would result in an expected average 3 percent repossession rate. The losses, after sale of the repossessed cars and holding costs were considered, are expected to be 60 percent of the loan balance at time of repossession. Given the pricing the bank can obtain in the market for this type of loan, management determined such a loss experience to be acceptable.

The problem is to determine how big a program would be required to ensure that the portfolio assembled by the institution is large enough to produce the expected loss rate of the population with a high degree of confidence. The bank has only $40 million in assets, and has decided to devote $2 million to the new program. Given this limit, the bank officials are concerned that it might not be able to create a program that provides an adequate number of loans to come close to the 3 percent repossession rate.

The analyst considering this problem concluded that it was essentially a statistical sampling problem. The distribution of the mean loss percentage for the sample of loans the bank originates from the population of auto loans is a binomial distribution. Each loan made could be considered a draw from a distribution of loans that had three bad loans out of every hundred loans from a population of loans underwritten according to the selected standard. The standard error of sample means from a binomial distribution taken from a population with a known loss parameter, b, is shown in Equation 20.1.

$$\text{Standard Error, SE: } (b = .03) = \sqrt{b\,g/n} \qquad [20.1]$$

In this equation, n is the number of loans, b is the percentage of bad or repossessed loans in the population, and g is the percentage of good loans in the population. Clearly, $b = (1 - g)$. Table 20.1 shows how the standard error of the mean of a sample repossession rate changes as n increases.

In this example, the lender set 4 percent as the maximum loss rate acceptable to commence with the program. They also want to be 99 percent confident that their loss percentage will be less than or equal to 4 percent.

Table 20.1

Standard Error of Sample with Repossession Rate of Population of 3% as *n* Increases from 25 to Infinity ($g = .97$, $b = .03$)

Standard Error of the Sample Mean

n	$\sqrt{b\,g/n}$
25	.0341
50	.0241
100	.0171
300	.0098
400	.0085
500	.0076
750	.0062
1000	.0054
Infinity	.0000

Table 20.1 shows it would take a sample of over 300 loans to get a standard error of the sample loans originated from the population to be 3 percent (+/−) one standard error of .98 percent. This occurs with 84 percent degree of confidence. The degree of confidence is based on the fact that the mean of samples taken from a binomial distribution will approximate a normal distribution if n is large. The standard error of the sample will fall within one standard error of the population mean with 84 percent degree of confidence, 97.7 percent within two standard errors, and 99.9 percent within three standard deviations. However, we are concerned only with the probability that the loss percentage is above the mean. Consequently, we need only consider the area under the standard normal distribution above the mean. This is known in probability theory as a single-tailed test. For one standard error, the area under the single tail is [1.00 − ((1.00 − .841)/2) =] 92 percent, for two standard errors the area under the single tail is [1.00 − ((1.00 − .977)/2) =] 98.85 percent, and for three standard errors [1.00 − ((1.00 − .999)/2) =] 99.99 percent. Using the one-tail test, we could achieve 98.85 percent degree of confidence at (2(SEs)/2 ≅ .01). This occurs with approximately 300 loans.

Comparing this analysis with the institution's goal of no more than $2 million in auto loans indicates a problem. The average auto loan in the market is determined to be $12,000. This means the bank would have to make (300 × $12,000 =) $3,600,000 in auto loans before it could be satisfied that its sample would have a repossession rate of 4 percent or less with 98.85 percent degree of confidence. This suggests that the bank should reject this program. This example shows how difficult the law of large numbers diversification is to achieve for small lending programs.

In recent years, financial institutions of all types have suffered very large losses on loans on commercial real estate. The average size of these loans is fairly large. Consider a situation in which it is determined that to provide adequate diversification the institution should hold a portfolio located in at least five distinct metropolitan areas in at least three geographical regions of the country. If the loss experience is 1.5 percent on commercial loans, then the number of loans needed to diversify in each market in order to reduce the standard error to 1 percent or less with 98.85 percent confidence (2 SE for a one-tail test) would be Equation 20.2.

$$\sqrt{b\ g/n} = .015 \times .985/300 = .0098 \qquad [20.2]$$

$$n = 300$$

In this example, it would take a portfolio of 300 loans to achieve the confidence level required. This would require a portfolio of $150,000,000 in each market, if the average loan size was only $500,000. Such diversification would be very hard to achieve for all but the very largest institutions.

This example again serves to highlight one reason so many financial intermediaries experienced large losses on commercial loan portfolios. They had portfolios that were not large enough to provide law of large numbers diversification, not to mention being inadequately diversified geographically. This is true even for institutions that underwrote these loans in a very professional manner.

The law of large numbers diversification also indicates why many institutions would not be well served to diversify their portfolios into many different types of assets. Most institutions are simply too small to accumulate a portfolio that is representative of the population from which it is drawn. Since most financial institutions are very small, they are forced to specialize in a few lending programs in which they can achieve an adequate number of loans. This, by necessity, ignores portfolio diversification. Another alternative for these small firms is to hold a high percentage of their portfolio in very riskless assets, such as U.S. government and agency securities. This is the case for many of our nation's smaller intermediaries.

Portfolio Diversification

Although modern portfolio theory has progressed significantly since Harry Markowitz wrote his monograph entitled *Portfolio Selection—Efficient Diversification of Investments* in 1959, his theory remains as the basis for the diversification of portfolio assets. Portfolio diversification concerns the variance in the return on the firm's entire asset portfolio when it consists of different combinations of assets.

The basis of the Markowitz theory is that investments should be evaluated on the basis of two dimensions, expected return on the ith asset, $E(r_i)$, and the expected volatility of return, measured by the standard deviation of return, $E(SD_i)$. The breakthrough in the Markowitz theory is that he showed that two or more investments whose returns are not perfectly correlated can be combined to produce a portfolio whose risk, as measured by expected standard deviation of the expected return on the portfolio, $E(SD_p)$, is lower for a given expected portfolio return, $E(r_p)$. In other words, diversification can produce a more optimal result for the risk-adverse investor—a higher return for any specific degree of risk. The key to this result relates to the covariation of returns of the various assets comprising the portfolio. The objective is to define what Markowitz referred to as the *efficient frontier*. This frontier consists of that unique set of portfolios that have the highest expected return, $E(r_p)$, for any given level of risk, $E(SD_p)$.

Consider the case of the institution that is investing in home mortgages (Table 20.2 on page 556). Its management considers a portfolio consisting of three-year adjustable mortgages tied to the three-year Treasury with a spread of 2.25 percent. The other asset is a GSE guaranteed mortgage pass-through security collateralized by 15-year fixed-rate mortgages. The

Table 20.2

Computation of Returns, $E(r_p)$, Standard Deviations, $E(SD_p)$, and Covariance of Returns, Cov_{ij}, for a Three-Year Adjustable Rate Mortgage and 15-Year Fixed-Rate Pass-Through: 1991

Month/Year	ARM return r_a %	Pass-through return r_p %	$r_a - E(r_a)$ %	$r_p - E(r_p)$ %	Covariance $(r_a - E(r_a)) \times (r_p - E(r_p))$
1/91	6.5	9.5	−1.4375	.875	−1.2578
2/91	7.8	6.5	−.1375	−2.125	.2922
3/91	9.3	7.5	1.3625	−1.125	−1.5328
4/91	7.0	10.9	−.9375	2.275	−2.1328
5/91	7.0	10.5	−.9375	1.875	−1.7578
6/91	7.25	9.5	−.6875	.875	−.6016
7/91	7.02	9.5	−.9175	.875	−.8028
8/91	8.1	6.5	.1625	−2.125	−.3453
9/91	8.6	7.5	.6625	−1.125	−.7453
10/91	7.2	6.6	−.7375	−2.025	1.4934
11/91	8.4	9.5	.4625	.875	.4047
12/91	8.9	9.5	.9625	.875	.8422
Average	**7.9375**	**8.625**		Sum =	**16.6797**

monthly returns on these two assets computed on a mark-to-market basis, which includes accrued interest plus or minus the change in market value between periods, is shown in Table 20.2. The table also shows the values for the difference between the monthly return and the mean, or in this case the $E(r_a)$ and $E(r_p)$, and the standard deviations and covariance between the two assets. For simplicity, it is assumed that the returns for the last year are a good estimate of future expected returns and standard deviation.

The key to portfolio diversification is the covariance between the two assets and the impact this has on the portfolio standard deviation. Equation 20.3 is the formula for the portfolio standard deviation derived by Markowitz.

$$\text{Portfolio standard deviation} = SD_p = \sqrt{\sum_{i=1}^{n} W_i^2 SD_i^2 + \sum_{i=1}^{n} \sum_{\substack{j=1 \\ i \neq j}}^{n} W_i W_j Cov_{ij}} \quad [20.3]$$

where:

W_i = the weight in percent of asset i in the portfolio

SD_i = standard deviation of asset i return

SD_p = standard deviation of portfolio return

Cov_{ij} = covariance between returns on assets i and j

n = number of assets

Table 20.3 provides a summary of the results of calculating the expected portfolio return and portfolio standard deviation for different weightings (W_i) of the two assets. In our two-asset example, $W_j = 1.00 - W_i$.

Table 20.3 provides the weighted average returns and portfolio standard deviations for several combinations of fixed and three-year Treasury-based adjustable-rate mortgages. A combination of three-year ARMs combined with fixed-rate mortgages provides a higher return and lower standard deviation than a portfolio of three-year ARMs alone. This occurs, as shown in Table 20.3, when a portfolio is made up of 80 percent, 3-year ARMs and 20 percent, 15-year pass-through securities. With this combination, the expected portfolio return exceeds the 100 percent ARM portfolio with a lower standard deviation of expected return.

Exhibit 20.1 on page 558 provides a graphic representation of the portfolios shown in Table 20.3. Table 20.3 shows a situation in which the combination of the three-year ARM and fixed-rate mortgages with a weighting of 80 percent ARM and 20 percent fixed actually provides a higher return and lower standard deviation than the three-year ARM portfolio would by itself.

In recent years, some of the largest U.S. commercial banks have begun to develop asset portfolio diversification strategies based on the risk/return framework previously discussed. The primary limitation of these approach-

Table 20.3

Portfolio Expected Returns, $E(r_p)$, and Standard Deviation, $E(SD_p)$, for Different Portfolio Weighting of Assets: Three-Year ARM = i and Fixed-Rate = j

Portfolio	W_i Weighting	W_j Weighting	$E(r_p)$% Return	$E(SD_p)$% Standard Deviation
ARM 1.0	1.00	0.0	7.755	.764
ARM .8	.80	.20	7.930	.656
ARM .6	.60	.40	8.104	.920
ARM .4	.40	.60	8.277	1.354
ARM .2	.20	.80	8.451	1.841
ARM 0	0.0	1.00	8.625	2.349

Exhibit 20.1

**Risk–Return Frontier
(Fixed and Adjustable Rate Mortgage Portfolio)**

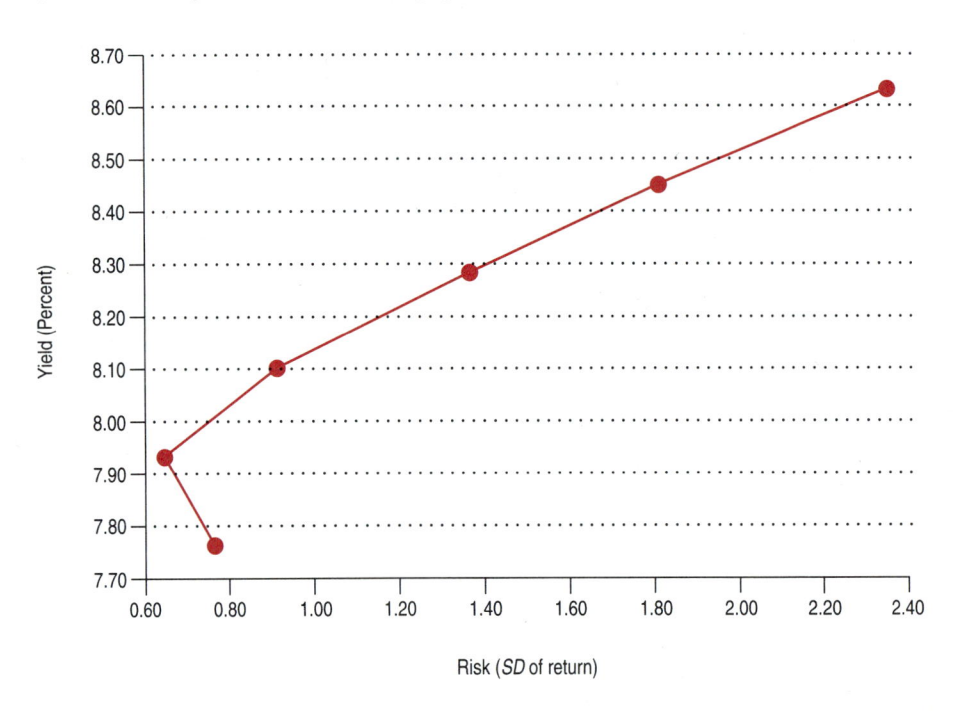

es is that the data used to determine expected risk and return are typically based on historical experience.

The Law of Large Numbers/Portfolio Diversification Tradeoff

The reality is that few financial institutions are large enough to enjoy the benefits of both the law of large numbers and portfolio diversification. This means that management must usually make a tradeoff between the two. Most smaller institutions determine a few markets in which they can achieve a large enough activity to enjoy the benefits of a large number of loans. The rest of the portfolio is then usually invested in relatively risk free assets, such as U.S. government and agency securities (as in the case of a small commercial bank), high-grade bonds (as in the case of a small insurance company), or GSE guaranteed assets, such as mortgage securities (as in the case of thrifts).

Given the U.S. financial structure, which is comprised primarily of smaller institutions, it is clear that most institutions are unable to diversify their assets in an effective way. This is shown in Exhibit 20.2, which shows a hypothetical efficient frontier for a large diversified intermediary, such as a large bank, a large less diversified intermediary, such as a large S&L, and a small intermediary, such as a credit union. The larger institutions are able to diversify to a greater extent than the smaller ones. Some intermediaries, such as commercial banks also have charters granting greater investment opportunities, which improves diversification potential.

The ability to diversify is also impacted by the availability of underwriting and servicing talent for the markets being considered. It is prudent to diversify a loan portfolio by geographic location. However, the ability to diversify geographically is also limited by the availability of mortgage loan underwriters and origination experts with local experience.

Exhibit 20.2

Efficient Frontier for Commercial Banks and Thrifts

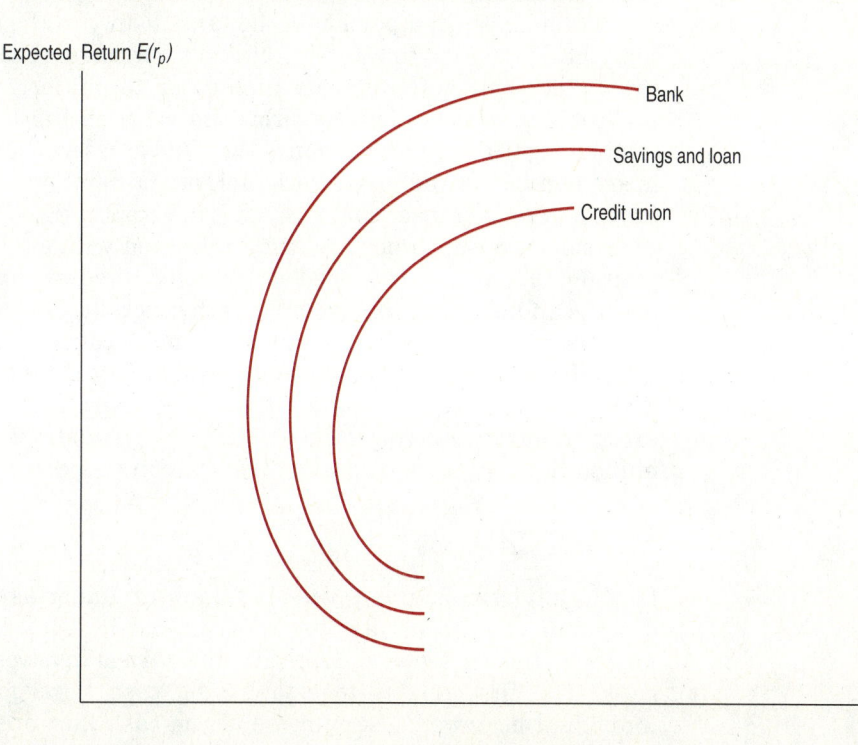

Expected Return $E(r_p)$

Bank
Savings and loan
Credit union

Expected Risk $E(SD_p)$

The Large Loan Exposure: Risk-Sharing Through Participations and Reinsurance

The methods discussed so far have relied on statistical techniques for diversification that assume each of the loans or investments are of nearly equal size. In reality, the sizes of loans and investments vary significantly. This presents the credit-risk manager with a special problem. The failure of several large loans in the firm's portfolio would substantially increase the potential for the institution's failure.

Financial institution regulators have long recognized this problem. As a result, commercial banks and S&Ls have to conform to regulations that restrict the size of loans made to one borrower. In the case of nationally chartered banks and S&Ls, the limit is 15 percent of unimpaired capital and surplus and an additional 10 percent, if the loan is secured by readily marketable collateral. Many S&L failures in the 1980s and 1990s were exacerbated by the fact that there were no limits on loans to one borrower if the loan was collateralized by real estate.

Large loans present special risk problems for intermediaries. A lending institution can deal with excess loss exposure by selling *participations*. For years commercial banks have cultivated relationships with *loan correspondents* who invest in a portion of the large loans. In the case of a participation, the originating institution retains a portion of the loan in its portfolio, say 15 percent, and sells the remainder to one or more correspondent institutions. The originating firm also services the loan. In return, the originating firm earns a portion of the yield as a servicing fee to augment its income and cover the costs of origination and servicing. The profit analysis for this type of transaction is covered in Chapter 22.

Insurance companies are also confronted with similar large scale risk positions. They have developed a technique called *reinsurance*. Reinsurance permits an insurance company to sell the excess coverage that is beyond the risk tolerance of the company to one or more companies that can properly diversify the risk. Some insurance firms, called *reinsurers,* specialize in assuming a portion of the risk from large exposures. Such a firm would assist in insuring a very large oil refinery against fire or providing a $10 million life insurance policy on a key person in a corporation, for example.

Credit Analysis

Credit analysis is the process of inquiry undertaken by a lender to determine the probability that a borrower will fulfill the obligations of a loan or other evidence of debt. Credit analysis involves three basic objectives. The first relates to establishing cash flows for the company or individual borrower. The purpose of the cash flow analysis is to analyze historical financial statements so that the sources and uses of cash are identified and then forecast into future cash flows.

The second objective of credit analysis involves reviewing the company's activities in the context of historical performance, industry performance, competition, changes in technology, and market structure.

The third aspect of the process deals with verifying the accuracy of the information supplied by the potential borrower. This process is referred to as *due diligence*. This includes verification of such information as deposit balances, collateral values, and financial statements, for example. Since fraud is a common problem in the lending markets, due diligence is a vital aspect of the lending process to reduce the probability of its occurrence.

In previous times, lenders usually relied on collateral as the primary basis for granting a loan. In this context, credit analysis was much less important, since it was primarily the market value of the collateral that determined the likelihood of repayment. Today, however, many loans rely only on the ability of the borrower to generate sufficient cash flow out of operations. In addition, credit analysis is more important than in previous periods because more loans are of longer term. These longer maturing loans are called *term loans,* and are far more common today. Term loans expose the lender to a much higher degree of risk than shorter term loans.

Another change that has occurred in credit analysis is the increased emphasis on the value of the firm as a going concern. Lenders now know that a loan is most likely to be repaid out of the earnings of a company as a going concern as opposed to the liquidation of the firm's assets. This is a change from 50 years ago, when lenders stressed working capital and the liquidation of the firm's assets as the most important variables relating to credit quality. The major exception to this relates to the recent growth in highly leveraged acquisition and buy-out financings. Some of these loans and bond financings are made with full recognition that the ongoing firm does not have adequate cash flows from operations to repay the debt, and that only through the sale of assets (subsidiaries, real estate, or operating divisions, for example) can the debt be repaid. Despite these changes, analysis of cash flow remains the primary credit review process. To many lenders, pro-forma estimates of *earnings before interest and taxes (EBIT)* are synonymous with credit analysis.

Cash Flow Analysis

Since cash flow statements are the major financial statement for the credit analyst, cash flow analysis should be considered in the broadest possible context. It is the job of the credit analyst to identify and forecast the operating cash flows of the firm. It is also necessary to analyze the risks of the firm and to incorporate those risks in cash flow scenarios.

The major cash flow risks include the following:

- *Production:* It is necessary to analyze the impact on production that can occur as a result of access to raw materials, suppliers,

technology, fuel, and anything else that can upset the firm's production of goods or services.
- *Marketing:* The analyst reviews the market for the product and asks the following questions: Who are the competitors? How price elastic is the product or service? What substitutes are available? Do a few major customers control a high percentage of the sales?
- *Personnel:* The analyst is concerned about labor availability, cost, and harmony.
- *Finance:* Here the analyst determines how vulnerable the firm is to sharp rises in the cost of credit. The analyst determines the exposure of the firm to credit problems the customers of the firm might have. Analysis of accounts receivable and delinquency rates on the firm's liabilities are the focus of attention.
- *Domestic and International Competition:* The analyst focuses on the potential for increased domestic and international competition. This analysis involves assessing the potential for changes in trade restrictions and other trade policy changes that could increase competition.
- *Government Actions:* Everything from environmental restrictions to antitrust is the focus of this area of analysis.

Altman's Z Score

In 1968, Edward Altman did an extensive empirical analysis of financial ratios to determine which provided the best predictive information about financial distress leading to bankruptcy. He used an empirical methodology called *discriminate analysis*.

The result was a *Z score,* which is used to help determine the probability of distress for a firm. The analysis identified the following five variables:

1. Working capital divided by total assets
2. Retained earnings divided by total assets
3. Earnings before interest and taxes divided by total assets
4. Market value of equity divided by book value of total debt
5. Sales divided by total assets

Later, Altman and others extended the study and added several other variables to the analysis including stability of earnings, equity divided by total assets, and total assets of the firm. The discriminate analysis work of Altman has been used extensively in underwriting loans and other credit analysis work.

Altman's Z score is used by commercial banks in their commercial business lending departments. Unfortunately, the analysis has not been done for many smaller companies that use bank credit facilities. Consequently, there is no guarantee that the factors related to financial distress and bankruptcy in the Altman analysis will be related to failures of smaller businesses.

Argenti's Analysis

In 1976, John Argenti also spent considerable time studying failed companies. His more subjective approach attributed failures to several causes, including the following:

1. Management weakness
2. Inadequate management information
3. Failure to respond to change
4. Excessive growth or overtrading
5. Launching a big project
6. Financial leverage

The findings on management skills require elaboration. Argenti concluded that poor or weak management was frequently evidenced by one man rule, nonparticipation by the board of directors, unbalanced top management, a lack of management depth, a weak finance function, and a combined chairman-chief executive.

There was also ample evidence of the use of creative accounting in weak companies. By creative accounting, Argenti referred to the use of accounting conventions that increase the firm's revenue and decrease the firm's costs. Many times assumptions must be used to arrive at a firm's audited financial statements. If the firm's management systematically distorts these assumptions through creative approaches that inflate revenue and reduce costs, it is frequently a sign of a firm approaching a financial distress point.

Credit Analysis and Consumer Loans

Consumer loans are also the subject of intense credit analysis. Consumer loans include collateralized loans such as installment loans as well as uncollateralized credit card and line of credit loans. A large number of statistical studies have been carried out over the years to identify those factors that would differentiate between performing and defaulted loans. Some of the factors that have been identified include borrower age, marital status, income, status as home owner or renter, job stability, credit record, occupation, and number of dependents.

Many large consumer lenders have developed computer models to screen potential borrowers using information available from credit agencies and elsewhere. This analysis is called *credit scoring*. Financial institutions that are major solicitors of credit cards through direct mail use computerized credit scoring techniques to develop mailing lists and set preapproved credit lines.

Covenants in Financial Claims

Originators of financial claims have an arsenal of techniques designed to alter the risk characteristics of specific financial claims. These are known as *loan covenants*. They are used to reduce the probability of credit losses. Loan covenants spell out borrower obligations under the debt contract regarding financial performance, establish standards of business conduct, and constrain actions of management and directors.

This section will show how lenders and investors protect their interests in the creation of financial claims through the use of covenants in financial contracts. These covenants are generally developed by the staff involved in loan origination and drafted by a financial firm's legal counsel.

Covenants are also used to protect the position of the firm in those cases in which collateral is present. In such a case, the firm attempts to ensure that it can get its hands on the collateral quickly. It also wants to ensure that the collateral's value is not eroded as a result of use by the borrower or by negligence in the event of default before repossession or foreclosure can take place.

Although loan covenants are written by the legal staff, they are a crucial part of the risk and return parameters of the lending decision. Because covenants are designed to reduce the probability of principal loss, it is important that the financial organization's loan origination, servicing, and portfolio management groups understand and participate in the drafting of the covenants.

The origination unit must be involved because they are responsible for negotiating the contract and documenting the transaction. The servicing unit must be involved since they will be responsible for monitoring the transaction to determine whether any events take place that could trigger a violation of a covenant provision. The portfolio manager is interested in the covenants because they will affect the forecast of the probability of loss and will, therefore, affect the pricing of the loan.

Typical Covenants Found in Car, Boat, or Recreational Vehicle Loans

The following are common covenants on consumer durable loans:

- *Collateral:* The collateral covered shall include all accessories and parts now and any replacements in the future. The borrower must be the owner of the collateral and the collateral must be free of any lien, security interest, and/or encumbrance.
- *Sale or Transfer:* The borrower will not sell, contract to sell, or dispose of the collateral, or any interest therein, without prior consent of the lender.
- *Location:* The borrower will not remove the collateral from the state for more than three days without the express written consent of the lender.
- *Protection of Collateral:* The borrower will keep the collateral in

good condition and will not use the collateral illegally or improperly.
- *Insurance:* The borrower will insure the collateral with companies acceptable to the lender against such casualties and such amounts as the lender shall require with a standard clause in favor of the lender.
- *Premiums, Taxes, and License Fees:* The borrower will pay promptly all insurance premiums, taxes, license fees, and other charges affecting the collateral.
- *Decrease in Value of the Collateral:* If the collateral has materially decreased in value, the borrower will provide enough additional collateral to satisfy the lender. Otherwise the loan amount will be reduced.
- *Lender May Declare Security and Take Possession of Property:* Upon the occurrence of default, the lender may declare all obligations secured immediately due and payable or seize collaterals and sell them.

Typical Covenants in a Municipal Revenue Bond on an Electric-Generating Facility

The following are several covenants on a municipal revenue bond:

- *Electric Rates:* The bonds are payable solely out of the net operating revenue of the electric system of the city. Net operating revenue is defined as gross operating revenue less operating and maintenance expense. The City is obligated to establish rates and collect charges in an amount sufficient to service the bonds, after meeting its expense of operation and maintenance.
- *Reserve Account:* The City will maintain a reserve account in an amount equal to the maximum amount of annual debt service (principal plus interest) on the bonds.
- *Insurance and Other Issues:* The City will maintain adequate insurance on the electric system, will maintain and enforce valid regulations for the payment of bills, will not invest the proceeds of the bonds in a manner that would result in the bonds constituting a taxable bond, and will pay and discharge all lawful claims.

Typical Covenants in Noninvestment-Grade Corporate Bonds

The following are common covenants on a noninvestment-grade corporate bond:

- *Minimum Net Worth:* The company must meet the minimum net worth to ensure that the company's affairs are managed responsibly and that the bondholder's interests are protected.

- *Limitation of Restricted Payments:* Restricted payments that include stock dividends, stock repurchases, and advances by the company are prohibited when the company's net worth falls below $XXX or if a condition of default exists with respect to the note.
- *Limitation on Additional Indebtedness:* The company is prohibited from incurring additional debt unless its fixed charge coverage ratio has been at least 1.3 to 1.0 for the four quarters preceding the desired date of indebtedness.
- *Restrictions on Dividends:* As long as any notes are outstanding, the company is not allowed to pay a dividend or make any other distribution on its capital stock.
- *Restrictions on Affiliate Transactions:* The unusual transaction payment, including sale, purchase, lease, or loan by affiliates or subsidiaries, is restricted unless such a transaction is demonstrated to be in the best interests of the company.
- *Limitation on Redemption of Junior Debt:* The company is prohibited from purchasing or redeeming any junior debt unless it concurrently redeems at least twice as much of the senior notes or its capital base is at least $XXX.
- *Limitation on Conduct of Business:* The company is prohibited from engaging in any business other than the XXX business.
- *Limitation on Ranking of Future Indebtedness:* The company is prohibited from incurring any debt that would cause the current notes to be ranked lower than they are now.
- *Restriction on Merger, Consolidation, or Sale of Assets:* The company may merge with or consolidate into another company if no event of default is created and the net worth of the company is not reduced.
- *Effects of Certain Takeover:* The holders of the notes shall have the option to require the company to redeem the notes if there is a takeover attempt.
- *Right of Holder to Require Purchase Upon Change of Control:* The note holders shall have the right to require the repurchase of their notes upon a change of control.
- *Limitation on Amendment to Indenture:* Amendment to indenture is limited in a number of ways to a majority of bondholders and in other cases to the consent by all bondholders.

These lists present representative samples of covenants that are found in a variety of the most common forms of debt contracts. The long list of covenants associated with below investment-grade debt is a reflection of the large losses associated with these loans. Many investors in high-yield bonds learned firsthand the impact of event risk. The existence of event risk accounts for the many covenants dealing with business activities, sales of assets, and changes in ownership and control. As a result, noninvestment-grade bonds and highly leveraged loans today include many more covenants than in the past.

These lists make it clear that a knowledgeable lender can negotiate loans and security terms that can significantly affect credit risk. Despite these protections, however, the borrower can quickly take actions that can all but neutralize the protective value of many of these covenants. Moreover, loan covenants are merely legal provisions that must ultimately, if a dispute arises, be adjudicated in a court of law or by a judge in bankruptcy. This process is costly and time consuming. As a result, the job of assessing credit risk, controlling it, and monitoring outstanding loans and investments remain the primary duties for financial institution management.

Fraud and Credit Losses

Unfortunately, fraud is an ever present feature of the lending and investment process. *Fraud* is defined as a deliberate deception perpetrated to obtain an advantage. In order to receive favorable treatment on a loan application, potential borrowers have been known to falsify information on income, employment, tax returns, credit reports, deposits held in institutions, appraisals, financing outstanding, and a host of other relevant underwriting data that significantly impact the lending decision.

Collateral lenders have been victims of fraud committed by borrowers who advance payments on loans they use as collateral even though the loan is in default. Some loan sellers have been known to double sell loan contracts they service. This means selling the same loans to two buyers. Sometimes borrowers attempt to pledge assets as collateral to more than one lender. Borrowers also provide business pro-formas that do not include relevant information or are knowingly too optimistic. All these are examples of fraud that are common in financing. Lenders can rarely detect fraud. They do develop audit and due diligence procedures to improve detection and reduce the severity of it.

Bankruptcy

Borrowers who have little prospect of paying their debts may choose to use our nation's bankruptcy laws. Chapter 7 of the Bankruptcy Reform Act provides for the complete dissolvement of debts by individuals except for federal tax obligations, child support, and debt resulting from fraud or obtained in contemplation of bankruptcy. Chapter 13 provides for the partial repayment of debt under a court administered plan for individuals with less than $1 million in assets. Chapter 11 is used by businesses to provide protection against creditors seeking restitution by allowing the company to continue to operate.

The nation's bankruptcy law was revised significantly in 1978. The result was to increase the asset exemptions that apply to bankruptcy. This liberalization, combined with the growth in consumer credit, has led to a sharp increase in the number of bankruptcies per capita. Exhibit 20.3 shows the number of personal bankruptcies per 100,000 population from 1960–1990. The number is fast approaching 300 per 100,000 population after ranging around 100 from 1960–1980. The 1990 number represents over 700,000 bankruptcy filings.

This increase in bankruptcy is also associated with a sharp increase in the percentage of debt to disposable personal income. Exhibit 20.4 shows the ratios of total, home mortgage, and consumer debt to total personal income from 1980–1990.

Lenders to both consumers and businesses must be aware of the impact that bankruptcy has on their ability to be repaid. They must also seek timely possession of collateral that frequently gets tied up in a bankruptcy proceeding.

Exhibit 20.3

Personal Bankruptcies 1960–1990

Source: "Payment of Household Debts." Federal Reserve *Bulletin*. (April 1991): p. 223.

Exhibit 20.4

Household Debt as a Percent of Personal Income 1980–1990

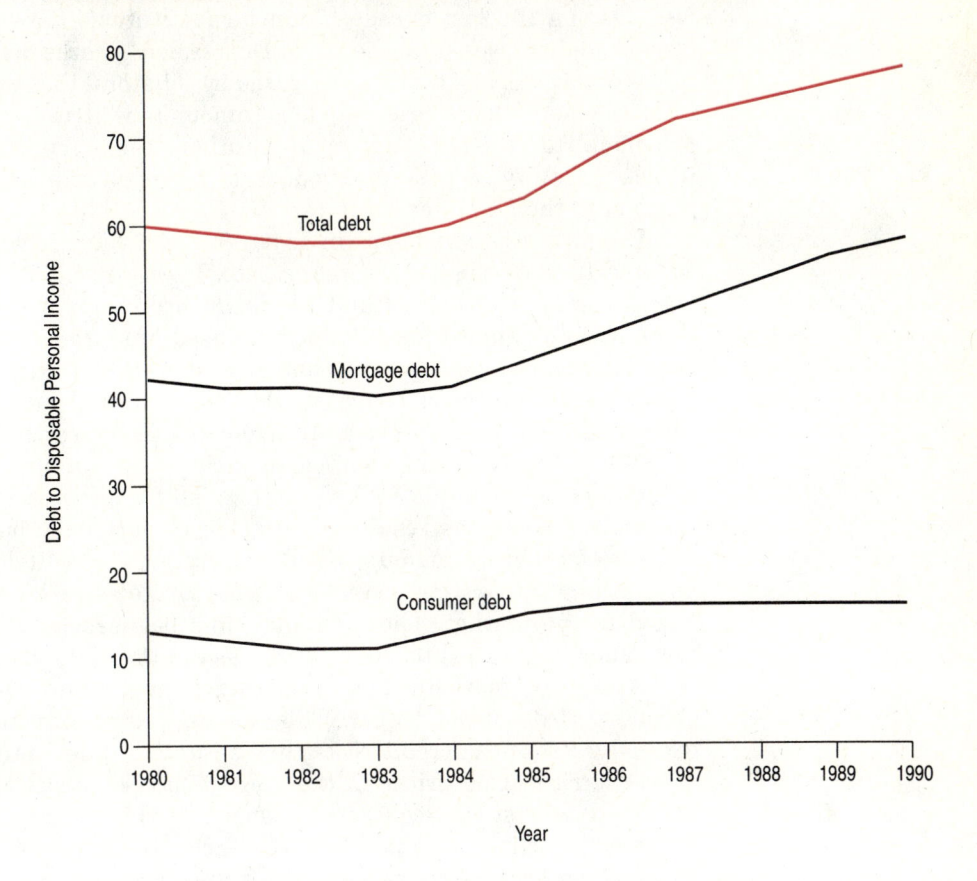

[Line chart showing Debt to Disposable Personal Income (0–80%) on the y-axis versus Year (1980–1990) on the x-axis. Three lines are plotted: Total debt (rising from ~60% to ~78%), Mortgage debt (rising from ~42% to ~59%), and Consumer debt (relatively flat around 11–17%).]

Source: "Payment of Household Debts." Federal Reserve *Bulletin*. (April 1991): p. 219.

Creditors of businesses that file bankruptcy must decide whether to accept a Chapter 11 filing, which seeks to preserve value by allowing the company to operate, or force a Chapter 7 filing, which involves liquidation. Creditors have the right to request that a company be put into liquidation. This depends on the number of creditors and their view of the prospects for recovery. In either case, large fees will go to the court-appointed trustee for services involving the liquidation of assets and to lawyers who represent all the parties involved. Their fees are given preference over other creditors in any liquidation. As a result, it is in the creditor's interest to make decisions quickly.

Collateral and Credit Risk

For loans relying on collateral to reduce credit risk, it is important to recognize the limitations of collateral as the ultimate protection against loss. During the last decade, financial institutions have experienced the largest credit losses since the Great Depression. A large percentage of these losses involved loans that were secured by collateral that was valued, at the time the loans were originated, at amounts well in excess of the loan principal. How then did so many institutions lose so much? The answer lies in the volatility of collateral values and the structures of the loans in relation to their collateral values.

The largest credit losses in the 1980s and early 1990s were on loans collateralized by commercial real estate. These losses were experienced by S&Ls, commercial banks, and life insurance companies. All these loans were based on appraisals of value that used pro-forma estimates of future rent levels and space absorption. The appraised values were generally mathematically correct based on the assumptions, but the assumptions turned out to be terribly incorrect. From an office vacancy rate of 5 percent in 1980, the national rate of office vacancies shot up to nearly 20 percent by 1990. Rent levels, adjusted for inflation, fell from the early 1980s through the early 1990s. The result was that developers built buildings using a variety of different lenders based on forecasts of rent levels and space absorption that became increasingly inaccurate as each new building was added to the market. The long lead time between building concept and occupancy only added to the problem, as did the 1990–91 recession.

The cycle of market values in commercial real estate is measured in half decade periods, if not longer. This makes it very difficult for lenders to correctly assess the credit risks they assume. Similar problems occurred after the rise in oil prices in the mid-1970s. Countries with oil reserves borrowed against that collateral to speed up their economic development. The sharp decline in oil prices in the early 1980s reduced their ability to repay those loans. Commercial banks were the holders of many of these oil-based loans, both internationally and domestically. Because collateral values may experience very long and unpredictable cycles, there is little that a lender can do to avoid credit losses. At best, the lender can diversify risks through portfolio diversification.

The other important feature of asset-based lending relates to the structure of a loan in relation to the collateral's value. An automobile provides good collateral for many auto lenders. However, this collateral depreciates. Consequently, lenders must decide how to structure loans and leases in relation to the expected depreciation in the value of autos. In the mid-1980s, the five-year installment auto loan and lease became very popular. This only served to exacerbate a credit problem that auto lenders already knew existed. Namely, the market resale value of used cars fell faster than the principal balance on the loans used to finance them. The lower the down payment required and the longer the amortization period, the greater the credit risk faced by the lender. The large defaults and repossessions experienced on many of these loans caused a number of lenders to revise their loan structures to provide for higher down payments and shorter terms.

Off-Balance Sheet Transactions

During the last several decades there has been a substantial growth in the number of financial transactions that are not required to be shown on a financial institution's balance sheet. An *off-balance sheet transaction (OBST)* involves risks to financial institutions. These risks include liquidity risk, credit risk, foreign exchange risk, and interest rate risk. One reason that so many of these OBSTs are structured so that they do not show up on the balance sheet is that managers of financial institutions want to avoid capital requirements. This rationale has become less appealing in recent years, since the depository institution regulators have developed risk-based capital requirements that cover OBSTs. Another reason for the increase in OBSTs relates to efforts of institutions to maximize their origination and servicing capabilities, while at the same time avoiding a heavy concentration of undiversified risk.

The types of OBSTs that involve risk fall into several categories. These include the following:

1. Loan commitments involving liquidity and credit risks
2. Foreign exchange trading activities in the forward markets involving foreign exchange and credit risks
3. Interest rate and currency swaps involving credit risk and interest rate risks
4. Subordinated securities created from senior-subordinated security structures involving credit risks
5. Sales of higher quality assets, leaving portfolios of higher credit risk
6. Sales of assets with recourse involving credit risk

Table 20.4 on page 572 provides a recent breakdown of the primary OBSTs of commercial banks from 1984 to 1990.

The growth in these OBSTs has been significant. The following is a discussion of the risks involved in this type of transaction.

Loan Commitments Including Commercial Lines of Credit, Banker's Acceptances, and Financial Guarantees

Most financial institutions that originate financial claims issue loan commitments. These commitments potentially involve interest rate risk, credit risk, and liquidity risk. A financial institution that creates a line of

Table 20.4

Bank Off-Balance Sheet Activity (dollars in billions)

Year	Standby Letters of Credit (1)	Letters of Credit (2)	FX Commitments (3)	Commitments (4)	Futures (5)	Options (6)	Swaps (7)
1984	$145.5	$30.0	$584.0	$495.6	$68.3	$4.5	NA
1985	175.0	28.4	735.2	542.4	97.7	15.7	$186.2
1986	169.7	28.4	890.8	570.5	179.3	39.6	366.6
1987	169.8	30.5	1504.1	611.6	260.3	65.3	714.9
1988	170.4	30.2	1683.2	655.0	408.8	96.8	928.6
1989	179.3	30.3	2261.0	685.9	518.6	193.4	1347.0
1990	184.6	30.6	2586.9	1034.6	895.0	386.8	1714.7

1. Standby letters of credit net of conveyances
2. Commercial and similar letters of credit
3. Commitments to purchase foreign currencies and U.S. dollars
4. Commitments to make or purchase loans or to extend credit in the form of leasing financing arrangements
5. Futures and forward contracts, excluding foreign exchange
6. Standby contracts and other option arrangements
7. Notional value of interest rate swaps

Source: Gary Gorton and Richard Rosen. "Overcapacity and Exit from Banking." Unpublished working paper. (November 1991) Table 1. Reprinted with permission.

credit for a customer accepts the liquidity risk that the customer may draw down the line at an inopportune time. The loan commitment may also involve interest rate risk if the loan involves a fixed rate and the rate is set before the loan is closed. Loan commitments also involve credit risk. A line of credit may be established at a time when the credit standing of the borrower is high. However, unforeseeable events may make the commitment far more risky if the business experiences distress. This leads to what is known as adverse self-selection in the loan commitment process. The least creditworthy customers are most likely to draw down outstanding loan commitments.

Commercial banks are major issuers of standby letters of credit (SLCs). These agreements obligate the commercial bank to honor a claim brought against a commercial bank's customer in the event the customer defaults. SLCs involve considerable credit risk for the issuing institutions. SLCs are used to guarantee commercial paper, bonds, and notes issued by commercial customers and to guarantee performance under such transactions as construction. Businesses pay banks for SLCs in order to obtain credit at a lower cost, since the investor will look to the creditworthiness of the bank as the ultimate credit behind the transaction.

Foreign Exchange Transactions

Large commercial banks and investment bankers are active in the foreign exchange markets. They act as brokers and traders. This involves taking a position in the forward markets for foreign currencies and accepting considerable foreign exchange risk that is not reflected on the balance sheet.

Interest Rate and Currency Swaps

Interest rate and currency swaps are arranged by a number of commercial banks and other financial institutions. These transactions typically put the intermediary between two other parties. The intermediary may issue a fixed rate for variable-rate swap to one party and, sometime later, issue an offsetting, or partially offsetting, swap to another firm. The result is that the intermediary must accept credit risk and interest rate risk if the offsetting swaps are not completed simultaneously.

Senior-Subordinated Securities

As securitization has become more popular, the financial restructuring of credit risk has resulted in the creation of the senior-subordinated security. This innovation was discussed in Chapter 3. It involves creating at least two classes of securities collateralized by the pool of assets. The senior class is of higher quality, since it suffers no credit losses until the subordinated class's principal has been eliminated through credit losses. The risk of these securities is highest for the subordinated holder. In some cases, the issuer of the security finds it difficult to sell the subordinated class and leaves it on the balance sheet. This gives the appearance of a higher capital ratio, even though the risk of the entire issue is concentrated in the subordinated security.

Loan Sales and Asset-Backed Financing

Many financial institutions are involved in loan sales and asset-backed financings designed to increase origination and servicing activity. Frequently, however, financial institutions find it easiest to sell or securitize those assets of least credit risk. This serves to increase the overall credit risk exposure of the firm. One reason selling risky assets is so difficult is that the underwriting of these assets is costly and time consuming. In addition, with an asset-backed security, the rating agencies will require loans of a uniform high quality in order for the security to meet a specified rating.

Loans Sold with Recourse

Occasionally financial institutions sell loans with *recourse*. This means that the seller agrees to repurchase the loan if it goes into default. The result is that the selling institution bears all the credit risk on these assets even though they are off-balance sheet.

The increased number of financial institution failures in recent years has heightened the attention paid by regulators and analysts to the nature of the risks accepted by institutions that are not reflected on their balance sheets. Today, the disclosure of these transactions is mandatory. However, disclosure is usually in a footnote to the financial statements. An example of such a disclosure is shown in Table 20.5, made by Security Pacific Bank of California. It shows the outstanding OBSTs that involve some element of risk to the institution.

Table 20.5

Off-Balance Sheet Transactions Outstanding
Year-End 1989 and 1990
Security Pacific Corporation
(dollars in billions)

Financial Instruments Whose Contract Amount Represents the Amount of Credit Risk	1990	1989
Commitments to extend credit	$35.0	$33.2
Standby letters of credit and foreign office guarantees	7.4	7.2
Other letters of credit	0.9	1.0

Financial Instruments Whose Contract Amount Exceeds the Amount of Credit Risk	1990	1989
Forward and futures contracts		
Foreign exchange	$177.8	$126.0
Other commitments to purchase or sell	30.0	35.9
Interest rate contracts		
Swaps	122.3	113.3
Caps, floors, and other	23.8	10.7

Source: Security Pacific Corp. Annual Report 1990, p. 61.

Summary

Despite the tools of credit analysis and management, financial intermediaries still experience large credit losses. This is due in part to business cycles, the presence of fraud, and the unpredictable nature of collateral values. Making matters more difficult is the fact that the value of collateral that supports so many loans has long price cycles that are difficult, if not impossible, to predict. As a result, credit risk remains the number one cause of failure for financial intermediaries.

There are many different types of credit risks. This chapter discussed: **pure credit risk, underwriting risk, settlement risk, documentation risk, operating risk, political risk,** and **event risk.**

The **law of large numbers** and **portfolio diversification** are the two primary methods intermediaries use to reduce credit risk exposure. The law of large numbers diversification refers to the probability that a lender's credit experience will approach that of the population from which the loans are drawn. Portfolio diversification deals with combining assets with different expected returns and standard deviations of return to obtain the highest expected return for any given level of expected risk.

The law of large numbers diversification can be reduced by establishing a loan portfolio with a sufficient number of loans so that the expected credit losses fall within an acceptable level around the population's loss percentage. The **binomial distribution** was shown to be one method for determining the minimum size of the portfolio needed to achieve such confidence. The equation for the standard deviation of the mean of a sample taken from the binomial distribution is

$$\text{Standard Error of Sample Mean} = \sqrt{b\,g/n}$$

Portfolio diversification was shown to be effective if the firm develops a diversification of assets strategy. This strategy is accomplished by selecting assets having sufficient covariance with one another so that the portfolio expected return is maximized for any level of expected portfolio return variance.

Large loans are a special area of credit concern. Credit exposures from large loans or large insurance coverage on a single risk exposure can be effectively reduced through **loan participation sales** and **reinsurance.** Regulators are also concerned about loans to one borrower and frequently establish limits on such loans.

Credit analysis is the primary method of reducing the credit risk on a single loan request. Credit analysis relies most heavily on cash flow analysis for business credit. **Credit scoring,** using a variety of different individual factors, is used in analyzing consumer loans.

Altman's Z score and **Argenti's analysis** of factors that are related to failed companies were found to be helpful in identifying financial ratios and other factors that influence the probability of bankruptcy.

Loan covenants are an important technique used by lenders to reduce the credit risk on a wide variety of loans.

Despite major efforts to reduce credit losses, **fraud** and the cyclical and often unpredictable nature of **collateral prices** have continued to produce significant credit losses at financial institutions.

Bankruptcy provides a legal means for individuals and corporations to protect themselves against creditors seeking restitution of unpaid debt. Individuals and businesses used bankruptcy in record numbers in the late 1980s, partially as a result of the liberalization of bankruptcy laws.

Financial institutions carry considerable credit risks off their balance sheets. The primary **off-balance sheet transactions** involving sometimes significant credit risks include loan commitments, foreign exchange trading, interest rate and currency swaps, subordinated securities, sales on high quality assets, and assets sales with recourse. OBSTs have grown significantly in recent years.

Questions

Chapter 20

1. Explain some of the forces that have led financial institutions to increase their credit risk exposure in the 1970s and 1980s.
2. Provide a short explanation of pure credit risk, underwriting risk, settlement risk, and documentation risk.
3. What is meant by event risk? Give several examples.
4. What is meant by operating risk? How might the volume of transactions in the origination of a particular type of loan impact operating risk?
5. What is meant by law of large numbers diversification?
6. How does diversification reduce the overall credit risk of an intermediary?
7. Why do smaller financial intermediaries have difficulty diversifying credit risk? What do they do about it?
8. What is loan participation and syndication? Why are they used?
9. What is reinsurance and what is it used for?
10. Explain the major factors that must be considered in a cash flow analysis of a company.
11. What is Altman's Z score designed to do?
12. What were Argenti's findings regarding failed companies? How did his analysis differ from the Altman approach?
13. What is a loan or security covenant?
14. What types of covenants would you expect to find in a consumer loan collateralized by a durable good such as an automobile?

15. What types of covenants would you expect to be written into a loan agreement on a corporate loan or corporate bond to a less than investment-grade borrower?
16. Discuss the major areas of credit losses for depositories in the last decade.
17. What are the primary factors that have given rise to losses on individual loans?
18. What are the major activities related to loan servicing that are designed to reduce the chance of credit loss?

Problems

Problem 20-1   Law of Large Numbers Diversification

Williams Bank wants to begin a regional credit card program for college students. It expects to open 4,000 accounts with an average credit balance of $500 each.

The national delinquency rate on student credit cards is 11 percent. The relationship between delinquency rate and credit losses as a percent of credit balance is shown in the following chart.

Delinquency Rate %	Credit Loss %
10%	4.0%
11	4.5
12	5.0
13	6.0
14	7.0
15	9.0

Williams is pricing the loans anticipating a 12 percent delinquency rate and 5 percent loss rate.

Will 4,000 cards ensure that William's delinquency rate will be at or below 12 percent with 99.9 percent confidence (3 SE)? If not, how many cards does Williams need to issue?

Problem 20-2   Law of Large Numbers Diversification

Safety National Bank will originate auto loans. It plans to originate 1,000 loans at $14,000 average loan size for a total of $14,000,000. The delinquency rate on loans similar to the ones Safety plans to originate is 6 percent.

What is the highest delinquency rate Safety can expect with 99.9 percent degree of confidence?

Problem 20-3   Law of Large Numbers Diversification

Nashville Bank is considering a regional recreational vehicle financing program. It has $30 million available for this program. The average loan size is $22,000 and the industry statistics indicate the loans have an 8 percent delinquency rate.

Nashville wants to know how large a program in dollars will be needed so that they can be 99.9 percent certain they will experience a delinquency rate no larger than 9.5 percent.

Covenants

project 20.1

One of the most important functions of professional financial experts is the origination of financial claims. Financial claims represent legal contracts evidencing ownership of a stream of income or assets under the control of a third party. All debt and equity are evidenced by a contract. Debt contracts are usually quite complicated.

It is not unusual for consumers who borrow money for a car or home purchase to sign a complicated contract without paying close attention to all the provisions. For a business, the contractual provisions are particularly important, since they normally constrain the activities of management and shareholders. These constraints are known as covenants. Covenants are contractual provisions that must be upheld by the borrower in order to meet the terms of the contract.

Obtain a legal note or prospectus of a debt, such as an offering statement that provides a discussion of the covenants. The following is a list of notes that could be used.

Auto loan

Recreational vehicle loan

Boat loan

Mortgage loan—residential property

Mortgage loan—apartment

Mortgage loan—commercial office building

Construction loan agreement

Corporate bond indenture (high or low grade)

Municipal bond indenture

Mobile home loan

Collateralized debt

Project:

After obtaining a copy of the loan agreement or offering material, analyze it and identify the covenants in the contract. Describe each covenant and explain why you think it was included in the contract.

Problem Loans and Investments

appendix

The competitive pressures on financial depository institutions to find new profitable lending markets have had a particularly unpleasant side effect on the depositories, their deposit insurance agencies, their financial regulators, and our financial system in general. These lending pressures have resulted in a substantial increase in nonperforming loans and represented the misallocation of significant investment dollars within the economy.

This Appendix will review the recent history of problem loans at depositories and then discuss how financial depositories go about the task of managing a problem loan portfolio. In the 1990s, this task is turning out to be a major issue for financial intermediaries as well as for the government agencies that insure depositories. The Resolution Trust Corporation, established by Congress in 1989 to manage and liquidate the assets of failed thrifts, is the largest single depository of problem loans. Its mandate is to manage these assets to retain as high a value as possible to reduce the losses to the American taxpayer.

Four Recent Waves of Problem Loans

The pressure on interest rate margins at depositories has resulted in these lenders expanding their lending operations into new markets and/or extending credit on more lenient terms than they have historically. Since the mid-1970s, this more aggressive lending posture has resulted in four major waves of increasing problem loans. Table A20.1 provides recent data on loan loss reserves established by commercial banks from 1985 to 1990. The table also relates the loss provisioning to net after-tax profits and return on stockholders' equity.

Table A20.1

**Commercial Bank Loss Reserves,
After-Tax Profits, and Return on Equity
1985–1990
(dollars in millions)**

Year	Loss Provisions	After-Tax Profits	Return on Equity
1985	$17,504	$17,802	11.18%
1986	21,538	17,202	9.97%
1987	36,534	3,181	1.80%
1988	15,825	24,777	13.52%
1989	28,702	15,730	7.94%
1990	30,296	16,175	7.77%

Source: Federal Reserve *Bulletin*. "Developments Affecting the Profitability of Commercial Banks." (July 1990): pp. 477–99 and Federal Reserve *Bulletin*. "Recent Developments Affecting the Profitability and Practices of Commercial Banks." (July 1991): pp. 505–27.

The first of these waves of loan losses related to the expansion of U.S. banks into the foreign lending markets, particularly in loans to developing countries. Countries eager to develop their economies were aggressive borrowers in the late 1960s and 1970s. They found an eager lender in the U.S. banking community, which was looking to new markets to escape the growing national competition. Many money centers, as well as large regional banks, opened up loan processing offices in foreign countries to obtain a share of the fast growing foreign-lending business.

Unfortunately, the economic shocks relating to the rise and fall of oil prices had an adverse effect on the performance of these borrowers. Many could not live up to the terms of the loans despite support from their respective governments. As a result, the loans to developing countries, known as LDC loans, became the first very large problem loan concerns of many large U.S. banks.

The second major wave of loan problems related to real estate in the oil producing states. Just as a number of developing countries used their oil reserves to support large loans, so did borrowers from Texas, Colorado, Oklahoma, and Louisiana. These states benefitted from the sharp run-up in oil prices and were able to directly or indirectly borrow off this increase in oil value to support large real estate developments and other investments.

As the value of the oil resource declined, however, the collateral value behind these loans fell drastically, causing loan problems like those experienced by Continental Bank and Trust of Chicago, an aggressive energy lender. This bank, as well as most other real estate and energy lending banks and thrifts in Texas and

Oklahoma, suffered greatly, creating a record number of failures. Continental, unlike many of the smaller local depositories, survived because it was able to work out a government financed bailout.

The third wave of problem loans again related to real estate. However, these problems were not driven by commodity prices such as oil, but rather by real estate speculation related to favorable local economic trends. Real estate loan problems became a serious concern in the late 1980s in the New England area, as the technology-driven economy began to slow down. Weak real estate loans on commercial offices were also a problem in most large urban areas. In the New York City area, the slowdown in the financial services industry in the late 1980s resulted in substantial loan losses on both residential and commercial real estate. Even real estate developer Donald Trump was not able to escape the real estate devaluations that took place.

The fourth problem loan wave also took place in the late 1980s. This wave related to the excessive financial leveraging that occurred throughout the 1980s. Stock repurchase programs, hostile and friendly leveraged buy-outs, corporate takeovers, and management buy-outs sharply increased overall corporate financial leverage. This wave manifested itself in the explosive growth of the high-yield bond market as well as the growth in highly leveraged corporate loans made by commercial banks.

Risk Versus Return in Lending

The most difficult credit decisions for a financial institution involve assessing the trade-off between the risk a loan will go into default and the return the institution receives in the form of fees and interest income.

Large portfolios of personal credit card receivables typically experience losses of 3 to 5 percent annually. This would be considered very high for many other types of loans. Yet, for a well-managed credit card portfolio, a loss rate of 4 percent could be extremely profitable. Loan losses at large commercial banks on credit cards have ranged from 2.57 percent to 3.29 percent from 1985 to 1990. These loans are profitable largely because the rate charged on the outstanding credit line at the time was 18 to 20 percent. At the same time, the bank may be charging a substantial annual membership fee.

Loans on leveraged buy-out transactions are also considered highly risky. However, this risk must be weighed against the fact that a leveraged buy-out loan made by a bank might earn a fee of 1 to 2 percent or more of the loan balance up front and be earning an interest rate tied at 1.5 to 2.0 percent above prime. The typical quality business loan would unlikely earn as much as the prime rate.

The trade-off between risk and return is at the heart of the asset management challenge facing intermediaries. Certainly the large portfolio losses facing banks have brought into question their credit risk judgments in the areas of real estate, foreign lending, and leveraged corporation transactions. The decline in overall bank profit margins makes better credit management more important than ever before.

What Makes a Bad Loan?

The causes of a bad loan do not require an exhaustive listing. Since the viability of a loan relates to cash flow, it is clear that loans go into default when the sources of the borrower's cash flow are interrupted or seriously impaired or when the value of the underlying collateral is materially impaired, making it impossible to sell at a value that will repay the debt. Many leveraged buy-out loans were made under the expectation that the firm would be divided into several operating units and sold at a certain multiple of cash flow. If conditions altered either the valuation multiple or the underlying cash flows, then the debt was a candidate for default.

The major causes of loan losses can be classified into two major categories. These include operating risk factors and financial risk. The operating risk factors include the following:

1. General economic conditions at both the national and regional levels
2. Technological obsolescence
3. Competitive forces at both the domestic and foreign levels
4. Management capabilities
5. Specific aspects of the product and its marketability in the case of a loan to a product producing company.

Problem Loan Management

The sharp increase in problem loans at financial institutions has resulted in a substantial increase in the time and attention being paid to the management of sour credits. While not a very glamorous field in the past, the problem loan workout is fast becoming a growing specialty in financial institutions.

Professional loan workout specialists are becoming more willing to take an equity interest in a problem loan to receive some or all of the upside should the loan be enhanced in value. Today, there are even investment limited partnerships that specialize in defaulted commercial loans of banks and thrifts as well as partnerships willing to buy defaulted high-yield bonds in anticipation that value can be enhanced despite a protracted period of Chapter 11 bankruptcy.

From a financial institution's perspective, problem loan management issues relate to several activities identified by Peter Clarke (1989). These activities include the following:

1. Loan monitoring and problem loan identification
2. Protecting collateral rights and value
3. Loan repossession and foreclosure
4. Bankruptcy
5. Loan loss provisions, charge-off, and recovery

Loan Monitoring and Problem Loan Identification

The servicing function within the intermediary is usually the staff responsible for determining whether a loan is performing against the agreed-upon terms and conditions. This includes whether the borrower is meeting all the loan covenants found in the agreement.

Problem loans come to the attention of the lending institution in a variety of ways. The borrower may default or financial reports may indicate the borrower is experiencing financial deterioration. A major event may take place that can be expected to adversely impact the borrower, such as the death of the owner-manager or an announcement that the firm's major customer has just filed bankruptcy. The lending institution may receive notification from the borrower that difficulties have emerged in their ability to meet the loan terms. Internal audits may disclose possible loan violations and/or fraud.

The loan servicing function must develop the appropriate policies and procedures to identify and respond as quickly as possible to a deterioration in credit. This involves the development of delinquency and problem loan tracking reports, late notice of payment notifications, periodic reviews of financial statements, collateral inventorying, and analyses of borrower information that may impact on the borrower.

Most often a problem loan is a loan in default. This occurs when a loan payment is past due or when the borrower does not meet a specified term or condition of the loan contract or fails to meet a covenant in the loan or security agreement. Once a loan goes into default a number of defensive activities begin with the objective of minimizing any loss to the institution. The basic question asked at this point is what is the prospect of repayment and what can be done to improve those prospects? This normally involves working with the borrower to identify the cause of the problem and the development of a strategy to solve the problem. If the problem cannot be solved in the opinion of the lender, then it is necessary to consider more immediate steps to ensure the best possible recovery.

If it is possible and desirable to work with the current management, then it is customary to develop a loan modification that assists the borrower in implementing a recovery plan. This loan modification may involve substantially altered terms and conditions and loan covenants. It might also rely on additional new collateral, if any is available. In return, the borrower may receive an extended loan repayment period or possibly even additional funds, if they are needed, to keep the firm viable and forestall bankruptcy.

Since a lender will almost always be better off responding to a problem loan earlier rather than later, it is crucial to the lending institution that it develop adequate loan servicing and monitoring capabilities.

Collateral Protection and Workout

Loans with the benefit of collateral are only less risky to the extent that the collateral retains value and can be legally and readily identified, recovered, and if necessary, sold. Making sure that collateral meets each of these conditions is no simple matter. In a problem loan situation, all stockholders and creditors will be looking to the collateral as a primary means of raising cash and paying the firm's obligation.

This means that the servicing function must develop an appropriate collateral strategy. This involves (1) assessing the documentation to ensure that the collateral meets the legal standard, (2) identifying the location of the collateral and completing an inventory, and (3) assessing what should be done with the collateral if repossession or foreclosure is considered an appropriate response.

Repossession and Foreclosure

Once a secured lender is reasonably certain that a workout will not result in repayment, the next step is to consider the process of repossession or foreclosure of the collateral underlying the loan. This process is not at all straightforward and can be made very complicated by a bankruptcy filing. Certainly, if the firm feels that repossession or foreclosure will make it impossible to return the firm to viability, it will choose the bankruptcy route.

If repossession or foreclosure can be accomplished without the threat or actuality of a bankruptcy filing, then the lender should handle all the necessary legal steps under the laws of the state. It must also determine how best to realize the highest value for the collateral. Not surprisingly, if the collateral value exceeded the loan principal, it is very likely the borrower would have sold it to avoid the default and repossession or foreclosure. Thus, the repossession and foreclosure alternative is unlikely to make the lender whole.

Another problem with the repossession and foreclosure alternative is that the lender must consider the rights of other creditors. They will do whatever is possible to encourage a situation that will enhance their position, despite that fact that a secured lender is in the picture. An unsecured lender may decide that a bankruptcy filing provides the greatest chance of recovery, while the secured lender will want to sell the collateral as quickly as possible to achieve maximum recovery.

Bankruptcy

Despite everyone's best efforts, resorting to bankruptcy is the inevitable course for many businesses and individuals. Bankruptcy is a long, costly, and technically difficult course for most businesses to follow. Yet, it provides certain protections for the stockholders and creditors, so that bankruptcy may come about at the request of the individual or business or involuntarily as a result of a petition by the creditors.

Once in bankruptcy, all parties lose considerable control, since a court-appointed judge will become the major decisionmaker. This means that even the most secure lenders will be subject to considerable loss of control and rights to their collateral. Bankruptcy proceedings can take a long time, which can serve to reduce the value of collateral or the business's franchise value. Also, decisions can be made in the bankruptcy proceedings that adversely affect the value of the remaining entity. In virtually all cases, however, bankruptcy results in a substantial increase in expenses for legal work. This reduces the value for stockholders and creditors alike. The legal aspects of bankruptcy for businesses and individuals contain many important features that should be part of planning any loan recovery strategy. They are beyond the scope of this book, however.

Loan Loss Provisions, Charge-Offs, and Recoveries

Problem loans take their toll on the income statement and can lead to insolvency of the lender. Financial institutions must anticipate the possibility of losses on loans in a number of ways. *Loan loss provisions* are established based on individual asset performance, or specific performance of designated portfolios of homogeneous assets. Commercial banks and thrifts use a loan classification system required by their examiners. This system places loans and investments into three classifications: substandard, doubtful, and loss. These classes are defined in Exhibit A20.1.

The definitions of these assets are subjective. As a result, the management of financial institutions, their independent auditors, and regulators frequently differ on how to classify a particular loan and on how much of a loss reserve to establish. Many financial institutions have been forced to establish additional loan loss reserves after the completion of an examination.

In the case of individual assets, such as commercial business loans or real estate loans, the performance of each loan is considered. GAAP regulatory standards and the institution's loss reserving policies will impact on how loan loss reserves are established and how charge-offs and recoveries are taken. Loan loss reserves are established prior to the actual recording of a loss. They serve to reduce current income for GAAP accounting purposes. A loan is charged off when it is recognized as a loss. Then it can be used to reduce income for tax purposes. Table A20.2 on page 589 shows loan charge-offs by commercial banks from 1986 to 1990 for several types of credit. It indicates the large losses on loans to foreign governments, businesses, and depositories and the rising loss experienced in real estate lending.

For individual assets, a default of 90 to 120 days will almost always trigger a loss provision. Other mediating factors may influence the extent of the writedown, however. For large homogeneous portfolios, the loss provision may be based on historical loss experience in the portfolio. For example, a portfolio of credit card receivables in which underwriting standards has remained largely unchanged may

Exhibit A20.1

Regulatory Asset Classification System

Substandard Assets: A substandard asset is inadequately protected by current sound worth and paying capacity of the obligator or the collateral pledged, if any.

Doubtful Assets: An asset classified doubtful has all the weakness inherent in a substandard asset, with the added characteristic that the weakness makes collection in full or liquidation highly improbable.

Loss Assets: Assets classified as a loss are considered uncollectible and of such little value that their continuance as bankable assets is not warranted.

Source: *Commercial Bank Examination Manual.* Federal Reserve Board of Governors, 1989.

Table A20.2

**Loan Charge-offs at Large Commercial Banks
1985–1990
(percent of average loans)**

Type of Loan	1986	1987	1988	1989	1990
Total loans	.89	.91	1.03	1.21	1.58
Commercial and Industrial	1.14	.96	.95	.93	1.31
U.S. addresses	1.10	.86	.82	.78	1.20
Foreign addresses	1.29	1.35	1.55	1.70	1.89
Consumer loans	1.58	1.58	1.52	1.63	1.86
Credit card	3.28	3.26	3.08	3.05	3.29
Other	.75	.74	.73	.90	1.09
Real estate	.38	.47	.42	.52	.92
Foreign government	.47	2.58	9.38	17.01	21.05
Depository Institutions	.36	.56	.98	1.35	2.43
U.S. depositories	.33	.11	.15	.19	.08
Foreign banks	.36	.96	1.83	2.52	5.41

Source: Federal Reserve *Bulletin*. "Recent Developments Affecting the Profitability and Practices of Commercial Banks." (July 1991): p. 505–27.

have experienced a historical loss of 3 percent per annum. The institution may then choose to use that experience in establishing a loss reserve of 3 percent of the outstanding receivables in this portfolio adjusted to reflect the net of actual charge-offs and recoveries.

Despite specific loan loss provisioning policies required by regulators and accountants, a number of academics have studied the behavior of banks that set up loan loss reserves to determine whether the timing of these provisions is influenced by factors other than the discovery of a problem loan. Several analysts have concluded that the managers of banks attempt to use the timing of loss reserves to smooth earnings.

GAAP and regulatory policies have become more consistent over time, but they are not always consistent. As already mentioned, loss reserves may not represent a tax deductible expense. This creates another inconsistency in the accounting system.

The large problem loan portfolios built up in the 1980s have raised numerous questions about the procedures for setting up appropriate and adequate loss reserves. Regulators have taken a leading role in this debate, since loss reserves provide another cushion before the capital of the institution is impaired. In the last decade, real estate appraisal practices were subject to regulations from the former thrift regulatory agency, the FHLBB. These regulators felt that appraisals provided overly inflated valuations of problem loans. There has also been controversy over what commercial bank regulatory agencies have been calling adequate reserving for loans to developing countries.

Loan loss reserving policies are very important issues for financial institution management, directors, accountants, and line managers. Proper security disclosure practices also rely on these policies. Many institutions have faced stockholder class action suits due to large accounting adjustments covering losses on problem loans. Consequently, today senior management and directors are spending considerable time reviewing the problem loan area.

Legal and Ethical Issues

Shareholder Class Action Lawsuits

The sharp rise in problem loans during the 1980s and early 1990s has created a growing legal specialty, the shareholder class action lawsuit. Many financial institutions announced large additions to loss reserves that have surprised investors, leading to sharp declines in share prices. Law firms specializing in this business represent classes of shareholders who purchased the stock prior to the announcement and suffered a financial loss due to the stock price decline.

A typical suit alleges that management and directors knew about the losses before they were announced or engaged in lending programs that were unwise, causing the large losses. In either case, suits calling for damages of many millions of dollars are filed. Most of these cases are settled out of court, resulting in large settlements and legal fees.

Performance Analysis for Financial Institutions

chapter 21

The reason for conducting performance analysis is to develop a data base of consistent and meaningful operating statistics for financial institutions. This chapter develops a number of financial measures that can be applied to depository and nondepository institutions. Depository institutions are sufficiently similar so that they can be evaluated using comparable criteria. The nondepository institutions include life insurance companies, finance companies, property and casualty companies, and pension funds.

Performance analysis is concerned with several major areas of operations, including profitability, capital adequacy, asset credit quality, degree of interest rate risk, liquidity, operating efficiency, funding risk, and off-balance sheet risks. These operational areas will be discussed with respect to depository institutions and several of the nondepository institutions. Many of the ratios that will be presented in this chapter are unique to a specific type of financial institution and particular examples of these ratios are taken from the financial reports of publicly traded companies.

First, however, it is necessary to determine how to present these data for meaningful performance analysis. This chapter offers two common approaches to presenting financial data, namely, time series analysis and cross-sectional analysis.

Time Series Analysis

Time series analysis is a technique that presents financial ratios calculated over a period of time. Using time series, it is possible to detect improving or deteriorating performance of an institution over time by comparing it to itself or to a peer group. Table 21.1 shows a hypothetical time series analysis of the one-year periodic *GAP* for an institution and its peer group.

Time series analysis allows us to track the performance of an institution over time under differing economic situations. Firms perform differently during rising and falling interest rate environments. In Table 21.1, it is clear that the periodic one-year *GAP* of First Federal has improved both with respect to itself and its peer group over the period covered by the analysis.

Cross-Sectional Analysis

Cross-sectional analysis is used when comparing the financial ratios of one institution with those of others at a point in time. This form of data presentation provides a snapshot of the institution's financial ratios in comparison to a peer group, or one or more competitors. Table 21.2 provides a cross-sectional financial ratio analysis of a hypothetical commercial bank and several of its competitors.

In Table 21.2, it is apparent that the Briggs Bank does not compare well on a financial performance basis with its primary competitors. The bank's profitability is below the competition, its capital position weaker, and its expenses higher. This may account for Briggs's weak common stock price in relation to book value. Cross-sectional analysis is frequently used by financial analysts for a wide variety of analyses.

Table 21.1

Time Series of One-Year *GAP* of First Federal Savings and Peer Group Quarterly 1990–1991

Institution	1990 I	II	III	IV	1991 I	II	III	IV
First Fed	19.1	13.4	9.8	8.9	7.6	7.8	5.5	4.5
Peer group	14.5	13.5	10.9	11.2	8.9	9.0	7.5	7.4

Table 21.2

Cross-Sectional Financial Ratio Analysis of Briggs Bank and Two Competitors
(dollars in millions)

Financial Ratio	Briggs Bank	First National Bank	State Bank
Total assets	$145	$201	$187
Net worth to total assets	6.70%	7.30%	8.10%
Market value of equity to book value of equity	95	109	112
Return on equity	8.50	11.20	12.50
One-year periodic *GAP*	12.30	−10.10	−5.40
Operating expenses to average assets	4.02	3.40	3.24

Financial Ratios for Depositories

This section reviews the primary financial ratios of depository institutions. The first area of analysis includes measures of general financial performance, specifically measures of profitability. Measures of performance related to profitability include return on shareholder's equity, (*ROE*), and return on average assets, (*ROA*). These measures must be augmented with measures of portfolio performance, which include the interest income on assets and interest cost of liabilities. Portfolio performance was discussed in Chapter 16. Profitability measures must be carefully used because they are significantly impacted by such factors as financial leverage and the level of interest rate and credit risks accepted by the institution.

The second group of financial ratios deals with the degree of capital adequacy of depositories. Here the analyst is concerned with the financial leverage of the firm. This is important for two reasons. First, the higher the financial leverage, the greater is the financial risk of the company. Generally, firms with high financial leverage will experience more volatile earnings behavior. Second, regulated financial firms with high financial leverage are normally subjected to greater supervisory scrutiny by their regulator. This may involve sanctions on permissible activities and on the freedom of the institution to implement its business strategy.

The next two groups of ratios concern measures of the firm's assumption of interest rate and credit risks. Since interest rate and credit risks are the two greatest areas of operating risks for most financial intermediaries, these analyses deserve special attention.

Operating efficiency is another area of analysis. The problem with most ratios of operating efficiency is that financial depositories differ significantly in the variety of financial activities they choose to perform. As discussed in Chapter 7, the functions performed by depositories can be easily unbundled for each of the financial claims that a firm chooses to originate, service, or invest. Adding an origination and servicing capability for a new claim can significantly affect operating efficiency measures. These operating cost differences may be more than offset by higher interest rate margins and produce higher profits. However, the firm may appear to be operating less efficiently than its competitors. For example, a commercial bank with a high percentage of assets in a credit card activity will generally experience higher operating expenses as a ratio of average assets compared to a bank with a lower level of assets in credit card receivables. Still, the bank with the higher credit card receivables may well have a much higher interest rate margin and greater overall profitability.

Our last two areas of review are funding risks and off-balance sheet risks. Funding risk is concerned with the relationship between retail and wholesale funding sources. As discussed in Chapter 17, it is expected that retail funding risks will be less than wholesale. That is, it is generally assumed that deposits attracted from locally placed branches will be less interest elastic and, therefore, more stable than deposits attracted from wholesale distribution channels, such as brokered insured deposits and institutionally sold negotiable CDs. The same is true for insurance policies sold to individuals as opposed to those sold to corporate clients by life insurance companies.

Off-balance sheet risks include the degree to which the depository extends commitments, engages in swap transactions, engages in forward transactions in security and foreign exchange trading, and all other transactions that impact credit, interest rate, and liquidity risks that are not reflected on the balance sheet.

Profitability: Overall Performance Measures

Profitability is one of the primary objectives of any firm. Profits depend on three primary structural aspects of the firm: financial leverage, net interest margin, and nonportfolio income sources. These measures were discussed fully in Chapter 16. The two most important measures of general financial performance are net income to beginning year equity, *ROE,* and net income to average assets, *ROA*. The *ROE* measure is used for virtually all shareholder-owned financial intermediaries. The *ROA* measure is applicable to all depositories, finance companies, and life insurance companies.

**Net Income to Average Assets and Equity
First Interstate Bancorp.
1986–1990**

Net Income to Average	1990	1989	1988	1987	1986
First Interstate					
Assets	.86%	−.22%	.23%	−1.17%	.64%
Equity	19.60%	−7.40%	6.00%	−23.80%	12.40%

Source: First Interstate Bancorp. *1990 Annual Report,* p. 49.

Capital Adequacy/Financial Leverage

Capital adequacy relates to the firm's overall use of financial leverage. It also measures the relationship between the firm's market value of assets and liabilities and the corresponding book value. Not all sources of capital show up on the firm's balance sheet. For example, a firm might have a large loan-servicing unit that has been built over many years and that has a market value substantially in excess of its book value. The reverse is also possible. A firm might have a portfolio of securities that, when marked-to-market, falls far below the firm's book value.

The adequacy of a firm's capital depends on many variables. For example, it would be considered appropriate for a financial firm to have more capital, everything else held constant, in the following circumstances:

1. The institution has a high percentage of risky assets.
2. The institution has a large unmatched interest rate risk position.
3. The institution employs a high percentage of wholesale funding sources.
4. The institution lacks diversification of assets by having a high concentration of assets in a few markets.

The net worth to total assets ratio tells us about the firm's overall financial leverage relating to those assets held on the balance sheet. The higher the ratio, the lower the financial risk of the company. The reciprocal of the net worth to total assets ratio is the equity multiplier *EM* discussed in Chapter 16.

Chapter 21 Performance Analysis for Financial Institutions

**Net Worth to Total Assets
Security Pacific Corporation
Year-end 1985–1990**

1990	1989	1988	1987	1986	1985
4.50%	4.83%	4.51%	4.16%	4.52%	4.50%

Source: Security Pacific Corporation. *1990 Annual Report*, p. 23.

Market Value of Common Stock Equity to Book Value of Equity

Shareholders are very sensitive to the overall performance and future prospects of a company. As a result, many analysts believe that the relationship between a firm's market value of shareholder's equity as reflected by common stock price and its book value reveals considerable information about the financial health of the firm. A sharp decline in the ratio typically is interpreted as a sign of financial distress.

**Market Value of Common Stock Equity to Book Value
First Interstate Bancorp.
End of Quarter 1989–1990**

1990				1989			
IV	III	II	I	IV	III	II	I
59.1%	57.1%	106.8%	98.8%	113.9%	141.5%	135.4%	105.4%

Source: First Interstate Bancorp. *1990 Annual Report*, p. 32.

Capital to Total Risk-Based Assets

The recent move by depository regulators to a risk-based capital requirement has made the capital to total risk-based assets a more frequently analyzed financial ratio. The higher this ratio, the more it is expected the company is financially stable.

Total Capital to Net Risk-Based Assets
First Interstate Bancorp.
Year-end 1990
(December 1992 capital requirements)

	First Interstate
Total qualifying capital/net risk-weighted assets	9.4%
Total regulatory required qualifying capital to net risk-weighted assets	8.0%

Source: First Interstate Bancorp. *1990 Annual Report,* p. 24.

Asset Credit Quality

Asset credit quality refers to the credit risks embodied in the institution's asset portfolio. An institution with a high percentage of agency, Treasury securities, and other high-quality short-term securities has much less credit risk exposure than a firm heavily engaged in construction lending on shopping centers.

Risk assets usually include the following:

1. Consumer loans, generally excluding single-family first mortgages
2. Commercial and industrial loans (loans to business)
3. Income property mortgages
4. Foreign loans
5. Acquisition, development, and construction loans

Another aspect of credit quality is the performance of loans on the books. Here the focus is on loan loss experience and delinquency rates of various loan portfolios.

The ratios that will be looked at in an analysis of credit risk include net loan charge-offs to average net loans. This analysis tells us the extent to which the firm has written off losses on loans and leases. Typically, the net loan charge-offs are divided by average net loans to form a ratio that can be compared to other institutions.

Net Loan Charge-offs (credit losses) to Average Net Loans and Leases
First Interstate Bancorp.
1986–1990

	1990	1989	1988	1987	1986
First Interstate	2.45%	2.45%	2.22%	1.71%	1.21%

Source: First Interstate Bancorp. *1990 Annual Report,* p. 28.

Allowance for Credit Losses to Total Loans

The credit loss provision tells us the extent to which financial firms used profits to establish reserves against anticipated future losses on loans and leases. These reserves are set up for losses that are not anticipated to be charge-offs until future periods.

Credit Loss Provision to Total Loans and Leases
Security Pacific Corporation
Year-end Balances
1986–1990

1990	1989	1988	1987	1986
2.2%	1.9%	2.1%	3.3%	1.6%

Source: Security Pacific Corporation. *1990 Annual Report,* p. 41.

Various Delinquency Ratios

Delinquency ratios provide timely information about the credit quality of specific asset categories held by the firm, such as mortgage loans, credit cards, and auto loans. These statistics can be compared to delinquency ratios of other firms and industry statistics.

Interest Rate Risk Position

Interest rate risk is today one of the most sophisticated areas of analysis within well-run financial firms. The development of computerized periodic *GAP,* mark-to-market, and duration *GAP* statistics have helped to substantially improve analysis of the interest rate position of firms.

Several measures of identifying the interest rate position of the firm were discussed fully in Chapter 18.

Periodic *GAP* Buckets for Various Periods
Security Pacific Corporation
December 31, 1990
(total assets $72.6 billion)

	0–30 Days	31–90 Days	91–365 Days	0–365 Days	Over 365
Earning assets	$31.6	$ 9.9	$9.6	$51.1	$21.5
Sources of funds	$31.1	$13.3	$7.7	$52.1	$20.5
GAP	$ 0.5	–$3.4	$1.9	–$1.0	$1.0
GAP to total earning assets	.6%	–4.5%	2.7%	–.4%	1.4%

Source: Security Pacific Corporation. *1990 Annual Report,* p. 35.

Mark-to-Market of Investment Securities Portfolio
Security Pacific Corporation
December 31, 1990
(dollars in millions)

Security	Book Value	Market Value
U.S. Treasury	$709	$711
Other U.S. government	682	675
State and municipal	465	451
Other bonds, notes, and debentures	698	643
Federal Reserve Bank and other securities	518	495
Total	$3,072	$2,975

Source: Security Pacific Corporation. *1990 Annual Report*, p. 34.

Operating Efficiency

Operating efficiency is one of the easiest of the comparative data to compute, but it is also one of the most difficult to interpret. This is because each financial firm operates in different markets with vastly different ratios of retail to wholesale asset and liability strategies. As a result, the most common measures of operating efficiency must be considered clues for additional questions to ask rather than taken as conclusive evidence of efficient or inefficient operations.

Operating expenses to average assets is the most frequently used measure of operating efficiency. This measure tends to be higher for highly diversified firms such as large commercial banks than it is for specialized firms such as thrifts. Also, firms that originate and service assets for others tend to have high operating to average assets ratios.

Operating Expenses to Average Assets
Security Pacific Corporation
1986–1990

1990	1989	1988	1987	1986
3.88%	3.80%	3.98%	3.96%	3.74%

Source: Security Pacific Corporation. *1990 Annual Report*, p. 24.

Some of the other most frequently used operating efficiency measures include average size of branch in deposits, personnel per $1 million of assets, and noninterest income to average assets.

Noninterest Income to Average Assets
Security Pacific Corporation
1986–1990

1990	1989	1988	1987	1986
2.10%	2.29%	2.36%	2.33%	2.27%

Source: Security Pacific Corporation. *1990 Annual Report*, p. 24.

Funding Risks

Funding risks refer to an institution's need to borrow money. Generally, funding risks are thought to be higher if the institution relies more on nonretail deposits. Retail deposits are sometimes referred to as *core deposits* and are thought to be less price elastic and more stable. Wholesale sources include negotiable certificates of deposit, brokered insured deposits, and other capital market sources like commercial paper.

Core Deposits to Total Funding Sources
Wells Fargo and Company
December 31, 1991
(dollars in millions)

Core Deposits		$41,840
Noninterest-bearing deposits	$8,130	
Interest-bearing checking	4,348	
Savings deposits	3,529	
Market rate savings	11,115	
Savings certificates	14,718	
Noncore Deposits		844
Certificates of deposit	412	
Other time deposits	176	
Interest-bearing foreign deposits	258	
Short-term Borrowings		6,723
Federal funds borrowed and repurchase agreements	4,861	
Commercial paper outstanding	1,753	
Other	109	
Acceptances outstanding		164
Accured interest payable		87
Senior debt		529
Other liabilities		763
Subordinated debt		1,887
Total		**$52,838**
Core deposits to total funding sources ($41,840/$52,838)		79.19%

Source: Wells Fargo and Company. *1990 Annual Report*. p. 20 and 26.

Funding risks can be measured by looking at core deposit sources to total funding sources and brokered deposits and other deposits over $100,000 to total deposits.

Off-Balance Sheet Risks

Today, many of the risks of financial institutions do not show up on the balance sheet. The institution may have sold assets with recourse, meaning that it is still liable for any credit losses on the assets. It may also have commitments outstanding that could result in both credit and interest rate exposure. Some of the most common off-balance sheet exposures include loan commitments, standby letters of credit, and loans sold with recourse.

One measure of off-balance sheet risk is loan commitments and standby letters of credit to total assets.

Commitments Outstanding
Security Pacific Corporation
Year-end 1989 and 1990

	1990	1989
Commitments to extend credit	$35.0	$33.2
Standby letters of credit and foreign office guarantees	7.4	7.2
Other letters of credit	.9	1.0
Total	**$43.3**	**$41.4**
Percent of Total Assets	**48.4%**	**49.8%**

Source: Security Pacific Corporation. *1990 Annual Report,* p. 61.

Performance Criteria for Finance Companies, Property and Casualty Companies, Insurance Companies, and Pension Funds

Performance measures for nondepository institutions have the same objective as that of depositories. However, because of the differences in the nature of the risks, asset and liability structures, and operations of these institutions, some new performance measures need to be devised. For example, property and casualty companies accept the risks of health and accident costs, fire, and other hazard liabilities, as well as personal liability. Life insurance companies accept mortality risk as do pension funds. Still, the major categories of performance and risk, namely, capital adequacy, profitability, asset quality, interest rate risk, funding risk, and operating efficiency, are still relevant. Consequently, many of the ratios found in the previous section can be used for these nondepository institutions.

The purpose of this section is to add to the list of performance measures some new measures that are particularly suitable for this new group of institutions.

Finance Companies

Since finance companies operate much like depository institutions, the analyst should feel free to use many of the same performance measures in their analysis. The main difference will be the peer group chosen, if any. The added measures relate primarily to the high concentration of consumer receivables (loans) on some of the finance company's books for those companies specializing in consumer finance.

Some measures for finance companies include credit risk (direct cash loans to gross receivables) and efficiency (operating expenses, ignoring loan losses, to average net receivables).

Property and Casualty Companies

Performance measures for property and casualty (P&C) companies must take into account the special risks they face that relate to the hazards they insure. The sharply rising costs of health care, legal civil liability, and repair of damaged goods have caused P&C companies to face enormous risks in their basic business. Many of the risks they attempt to insure are impacted by laws, social forces, weather, and other factors that are very difficult to forecast with confidence.

Many of the financial ratios used by P&C companies are the same as those used by depositories, such as return on equity, operating expenses to average assets, interest rate periodic and duration *GAP*s, and market value of equity to book value of equity. The unique performance measures relate to the special factors that impact casualty risks.

Profitability Ratios

The three most important special financial ratios for P&C companies are the underwriting loss, expense, and combined ratios. These ratios provide measures for the performance of the firm's property and casualty risk management function and operating efficiency.

The underwriting ratio indicates the relationship of property and casualty losses sustained by the P&C to the premium earned during a specified period. It reflects the adequacy of premium rates and/or the ability of the company to control for excessively risky customers.

The expense ratio is a measure of operating and administrative efficiency. P&C companies strive to have very low expense ratios.

The combined ratio provides the most comprehensive measure of performance. This measures the overall success of the company in covering its operating costs and property and casualty losses without relying on investment income sources.

Operating Ratios
TransAmerica Property and Casualty Insurance Subsidiaries
1988–1990
(percent of total)

	1990	1989	1988
Underwriting Loss Ratio Loss and loss adjustment expenses to premiums and other insurance income/premium and other insurance income	77.2%	74.3%	73.3%
Expense Ratio Commissions and other expenses/premium and other insurance income	35.1%	37.0%	36.6%
Combined Ratio Loss ratio + expense ratio	112.3%	111.3%	109.9%

Source: TransAmerica Corporation. *1990 Annual Report,* p. 60.

Life Insurance Companies

Life insurance companies use many of the same profitability, operating efficiency, and capital adequacy ratios used by depository institutions. These include return on equity, capital to total assets, market value of equity to book value of equity, operating expenses to average assets, and net interest spread. Again, the focus will be on the ratios that are unique to the life insurance business.

Funding Risk

The life insurance business has changed significantly in the last 20 years as policy purchasers have become much more sophisticated in purchasing insurance contracts. Many now favor term insurance over whole life and investment insurance products such as universal life, variable life, annuities, and variable universal life policies. As a result, life companies have much more interest-sensitive liabilities than in previous times. The new products are competed for on the basis of cost for the term policies and on the basis of yields on annuity products.

    Another product offered by the life company is the guaranteed investment contract (GIC). This is a liability of the insurance company that obligates the company to pay an agreed-upon return to the purchaser. GICs are sold to administrators of pension funds and employee tax-sheltered retirement programs, such as 401k programs, who are looking for a safe, high-yielding investment.

The ratios are designed to measure the percentage of a life company's total policy and contract reserves that are related to the less interest-sensitive whole life policies as compared to more interest rate sensitive policies. The other group of ratios relates to the sensitivity of the insurance company's customers to changing economic and competitive circumstances. The ratio of policy lapses to total policies is very important, since a high ratio of lapsed policies is very costly to insurance companies. This is because insurance companies have large policy acquisition and marketing costs to put new business on the books.

Policy loans are also undesirable to insurance companies, since they represent financial options held by the insured. Policy loans tend to get taken out only when market interest rates exceed the policy loan rate. This works to the insurance company's disadvantage, since they must sell high-earning assets to fund the policy loans.

Policy Life Insurance Reserves to Total
Life Policy Reserves and Policy Deposit Account Balances
USLIFE Corporation
December 31, 1989 and 1990
(dollars in millions)

	1990	1989
Life insurance reserves	$1,083	$1,097
Policyholder deposit accounts	$1,471	$1,267
Total reserves and deposit accounts	$2,554	$2,364
Ratio of life reserves to total reserves and deposit account	42.4%	46.4%

Source: USLIFE Corporation. *1990 Annual Report,* p. 37.

Policy Loans to Life Insurance Policy Reserves
USLIFE Corporation and Subsidiaries
December 31, 1989 and 1990
(dollars in millions)

	1990	1989
Policy loans	$286	$288
Life policy benefit reserves	$1,083	$1,097
Ratio of policy loans to benefit reserves	26.4%	26.3%

Source: USLIFE Corporation. *1990 Annual Report,* pp. 36–37.

Pension Funds

A primary financial ratio of concern to the pension fund manager is the relationship between the fund's market value of assets and its actuarially determined liabilities. Based on this performance ratio a pension fund may be underfunded or overfunded.

Pension Fund Market Value to Projected Benefit Obligation
Xerox Corporation
December 31, 1988–1990
(dollars in millions)

	1990	1989	1988
Pension benefit obligations	$3,579	$3,624	$3,047
Plan assets at fair value	$3,504	$3,769	$3,138
Ratio of asset value to benefit obligation	−2.1%	4.0%	3.0%
Funding	Underfunded	Overfunded	Overfunded

Source: Xerox Corporation. *1990 Annual Report,* p. 52.

Where to Obtain Financial Data

Data used for analyses of financial firms is quite easy to obtain for regulated commercial banks and most thrifts and more difficult for life insurance companies and other intermediaries. Typically, a firm's data comes from its published financial reports, such as its annual report, quarterly reports, and 10k filings. A number of private data collection firms publish comparative data for commercial banks and thrifts. These include Sheshunoff and Co. and SNL Securities, L.P. Insurance data are available from A. M. Best Co. Considerable help for publicly traded companies is available from security analysts.

Data for commercial banks, S&Ls, and SBs are available from regulators at the FDIC, OTS, and the Board of Governors of the Federal Reserve System. Performance measures for peer groups are available in the annual report *Uniform Bank Performance* published by the Federal Financial Institution Examination Council and in the report *Statistics on Banking* published annually by the FDIC.

The less-regulated firms require that the analyst use data filed with the Securities and Exchange Commission for publicly traded companies or from the many computer data banks that provide access to these data.

The best approach, however, is to use the company's financial reports and those of a small group of companies who compete with the firm.

Summary

Financial ratio analysis has been used by regulators, management, security analysts, rating agencies, and investors for years to evaluate the performance of financial companies. Industrial and commercial firms have a large number of ratios that they use for comparative analysis purposes. These are also an important subject of financial management. In the study of financial institutions, however, many of the ratios that have meaning in the context of industrial and commercial firms are of little value. As a result, a wide variety of financial ratios have been developed for financial intermediaries.

Most of these ratios are applicable to the majority of intermediaries. Some, however, apply only to specific institutions.

Financial ratios are presented for analysis using time series and cross-sectional exhibits. **Time series analysis** refers to the exposition of financial data with comparisons at discrete periods over time. Typically, a firm is compared to itself at different points in time using one or more ratios. **Cross-sectional analysis** refers to comparisons of financial data at one point in time compared with similar data of another company or peer group.

The primary sources of financial data are the firm's balance sheet, income statement, and supporting financial exhibits.

Profitability measures are used to assess the firm's profitability in relation to shareholders' equity and levels of earning assets and liabilities. Noninterest income and fee income are also an important focus of this analysis.

Capital adequacy or financial leverage ratios are used to determine the degree of financial risk of the institution. A number of these ratios are also used to compare a financial institution's capital position to that required by its regulator.

Interest rate risk measures are used to assess the extent to which the firm has a mismatch between the cash flow and repricing characteristics of its assets and its liabilities. These ratios are designed to measure the potential that interest rate volatility will adversely impact the firm's profitability and equity values.

Credit risk data are used to assess the quality of the firm's assets in terms of credit risk exposure.

Operating efficiency ratios are used to determine the relative efficiency of the financial firm in relation to some measure of activity.

Funding risk measures relate to how the financial firm generates its liabilities. Financial liabilities are typically attracted through retail and wholesale distribution channels. It is assumed that in most cases retail-generated liabilities will be less interest elastic and more stable. Several financial ratios are designed to measure the relative use of each of these funding strategies.

Off-balance sheet risks are measured using supplemental data that show the extent to which the firm incurs interest rate risks, liquidity risks, and credit risks related to financial transactions that are not reflected on the current balance sheet.

Questions

Chapter 21

1. Explain the difference between time series and cross-sectional data analysis. Can these two methods of data presentation be combined?
2. What characteristics of financial firms are financial ratios designed to analyze?
3. Which financial ratios are important for measuring capital adequacy?
4. What are some of the problems with using most measures of operating efficiency?
5. Are measures of interest rate risk suitable for all financial depository institutions? Why or why not?
6. What are some financial ratios that deal with funding risk? What are they designed to show?
7. Where do financial analysts obtain data to perform financial analyses of most financial institutions?
8. What special ratios are used by property and casualty companies?
9. What is meant by an overfunded and underfunded pension fund? Why should the trustees of a pension fund concern themselves with this measure of performance?
10. The credit quality of a financial institution is difficult to ascertain. Explain this statement. Do you agree or disagree?

Performance Evaluation: First Independent Bank of Boise

case 21.1

Introduction

The First Independent Bank of Boise was founded in 1918. It was owned by the Brown family until 1954, when the bank was sold in a secondary public offering. Currently, the majority of the bank is owned by local Boise residents.

William Bradford is now the chairman of the board and chief executive officer. He recently came back from a meeting in which a group of bank executives were discussing the performance of their respective institutions. They talked about capitalization, profitability, high credit risk assets, and a host of other subjects. What disturbed Mr. Bradford was the fact that these other executives had the ability to compare a variety of financial ratios with each other. Several of the banks belonged to an informal peer group that shared this type of financial information with one another. Mr. Bradford belonged to no such group.

Mr. Bradford came back from the meeting convinced that his bank was deficient in establishing a system for reporting and monitoring the financial position of his bank and in comparing his bank's performance to other banks like First Independent. Mr. Bradford wanted to develop a system that would be updated each quarter or annually depending on the ratio's importance.

The first thing that Mr. Bradford did was ask Bob Fine, the financial officer of the bank, to assemble the bank's latest balance sheets for 1993 and 1994 and its 1994 income statement. These are shown in Tables C21.1 and C21.2.

The Problem

With the information obtained from Mr. Fine, it was determined that you should develop a sources and uses of funds statement for the year 1994 using Exhibit C21.1. This year is considered

Table C21.1

**First Independent Bank of Boise Balance Sheet
December 31, 1993–1994**

	1993	1994
Cash and due from banks	$12,300	$11,690
U.S. Treasury securities	13,500	12,460
Agency securities	21,900	20,876
Municipal bonds	40,000	38,000
Mortgage pass-through securities	12,000	14,000
Short-term deposits, reserve repos, and federal funds sold	24,675	25,765
Loans*		
Residential first mortgage loans	34,509	38,990
Business loans	35,097	47,087
Consumer loans	12,765	23,456
Plant and equipment	7,879	8,543
Foreclosed and repossessed assets	3,453	5,765
Other assets	1,234	2,543
Total Assets	**$219,312**	**$249,175**
Demand deposits	$ 42,900	$ 45,789
Money market deposits	12,097	13,490
Savings deposits	54,070	47,768
Consumer certificates of deposit	81,647	90,097
Large-denomination CDs	8,098	22,601
Repurchase agreements	0	5,980
Other liabilities	1,000	2,620
Stockholder's equity (1,200,000 shares outstanding)	19,500	20,830
Total Liabilities and Shareholder's Equity	**$219,312**	**$249,175**

*Loan committments outstanding at December 31, 1994 were $12.0 million.

important because that was when the bank undertook a much more aggressive strategy. In particular, the company decided to increase its market share of the loan market while decreasing investments. It also chose to increase its reliance on wholesale funding sources. Mr. Bradford was interested in seeing how this

Table C21.2

**First Independent of Boise Income Statement 1994
(dollars in millions)**

Income	
Interest and fees on loans	$12.030
Interest on investments	7.975
Other income	2.750
Total Interest Income	**$22.755**
Interest Expense	
Interest on consumer deposits	$ 9.750
Interest on other	1.530
Borrowed funds	.400
Total Interest Expense	**$11.680**
Fee and Noninterest Income	$ 4.400
Noninterest Expense	
Salaries and employee benefits	$ 5.320
Net occupancy expenses	.800
Furniture and equipment	.920
Other operating expenses	3.890
Total Noninterest Expense	**$10.930**
Provision for loan losses	$ 1.315
Income before taxes	$ 3.230
Income tax expenses	1.100
Income before security transactions	2.130
Security gains (and losses)	0
Net Income	**$ 2.130**

affected the sources and uses of funds statement. Another aspect of the business strategy was to continue to originate mortgages for sale to the secondary market mortgage credit agencies. Over the years, the bank has built up a very large mortgage-servicing portfolio. This has been designed to increase the fee income of the bank. The bank now services over $600 million in mortgages for other investors. Mr. Bradford expects that this activity should improve the fee income of the bank.

    Mr. Fine indicated that he was concerned the new strategy to increase loans and decrease security investments had increased the credit risk exposure of the bank. Mr. Fine stated that risk assets were defined to be all loans, except residential first mortgages, plus foreclosed and repossessed assets. He also disclosed the need for additional space, since the bank now had grown to 125 employees. He further indicated that the company paid a cash dividend of $800,000 in 1994. The price of First Independent stock as listed over the counter was last traded at $14.875 per share.

Mr. Bradford also supplied you with Exhibit C21.2, a schedule of important financial ratios of a group of five similar banks whose management he met with at the meeting. These will provide you with a peer group to compare with First Independent Bank.

Exhibit C21.1

Sources and Uses Statement for 1994

	Sources	Uses
Cash and due from banks	_____	_____
U. S. Treasury securities	_____	_____
Agency Securities	_____	_____
Municipal bonds	_____	_____
Mortgage pass-through	_____	_____
Short term deposits, reverse repos, and federal funds	_____	_____
Loans	_____	_____
Plant and equipment	_____	_____
Foreclosed and repossessed assets	_____	_____
Other assets	_____	_____
Demand deposits	_____	_____
Money market deposits	_____	_____
Savings deposits	_____	_____
Consumer certificates of deposits	_____	_____
Large-denomination CDs	_____	_____
Repurchase agreements	_____	_____
Other liabilities	_____	_____
Retained earnings	_____	_____
Dividends paid	_____	_____
Total	_____	_____

Exhibit C21.2

First Independent and Peer Group Ratios for 1994

	First Independent	Peer Group
Capital Adequacy		
Equity to total assets	_____	8.10%
Market value of equity to book value of equity	_____	1.05%
Equity to total risk assets	_____	20.50%
Asset Quality		
Risk assets to total assets	_____	41.55%
Loan loss provision to average net loans	_____	.85%
Foreclosed and repossessed loans to net worth	_____	10.52%
Operating Efficiency		
Operating expenses to average assets	_____	3.35%
Personnel per $1 million in average assets	_____	.422%
Profitability		
Net income to beginning equity (ROE)	_____	8.75%
Net income to average assets	_____	.81%
Interest income to average assets	_____	9.42%
Interest expense to average assets	_____	4.75%
Interest expense to average interest-paying liabilities	_____	5.02%
Noninterest income to average assets	_____	.92%
Funding Risks		
Wholesale funding sources to total funding sources	_____	1.44%
Brokered and other large CDs to total deposits	_____	1.11%
Off-Balance Sheet Risks		
Loan commitments to total assets	_____	3.20%

Questions

Case

1. Using the information supplied above, develop a sources and uses of funds statement using Exhibit C21.1. Discuss how you would respond to Mr. Bradford's statement that the company tried in 1994 to increase its loan portfolio at the expense of investments and that it relied more on wholesale as compared to retail funding sources. Do you agree or disagree?

2. Mr. Bradford would like you to determine the ratios listed in Exhibit C21.2 on peer group ratios. He is concerned about how his bank compares in terms of these ratios. He would like you to comment on each of the ratios shown.

   Do you feel that First Independent Bank is correct in its effort to increase its loan market share using wholesale funding sources? Use financial ratios to support your answer. What other ideas do you have for the bank to improve its financial position?

   What do you think about the strategy to originate and sell loans in the secondary market? Does it seem to be working for the bank? Use financial ratios to support your answer.

Asset Management and Pricing

chapter 22

Asset management consists of three primary activities: the development of an overall asset strategy for the firm, the management of liquid assets, and the pricing of loans and the determination of the minimum required yield on asset acquisitions. These decisions are made by the portfolio management unit.

Asset management is one of the most dynamic activities within any financial firm because the expected returns and risk on assets change constantly. A manager's objective is to make only those loans and investments that will be profitable enough to provide shareholders with their target return on equity. However, the optimal asset structure can change from one week to the next. Asset management requires constant monitoring of the competition's actions, the economic environment, the conditions within financial markets, and the changes in the regulatory and legal environments.

Determining the Asset Structure

The development of the optimal asset structure is of critical importance for a financial institution. Since portfolio management income is the largest source of income for depositories, life insurance companies, and pension funds, the portfolio structure decision will impact profitability the most. The portfolio decision is constrained by a multitude of factors. These include the following:

1. Laws and regulations that constrain the asset portfolio options of management
2. Diversification options available
3. Local market supply and demand conditions and market pricing
4. Fixed costs that may affect the economic size needed to effectively operate in certain markets for particular types of claims

Laws and Regulations

Most financial intermediaries must accept certain constraints on the allowable assets they may hold. These constraints are usually incorporated in their charter and typically differ by type of institution, by whether a state or national authority grants the charter, and by state-issuing authority. Most other financial institutions have broader leeway in their asset portfolio management decisions.

On the surface, it may appear somewhat counterproductive that financial institutions have constraints on the types of assets they hold. Chapter 20 discussed the importance of diversification in reducing credit risk. Asset constraints such as those that apply to S&Ls and credit unions, for example, would appear to be inconsistent with the need to provide for prudent diversification of credit risk. This inconsistency is explained by the fact that the public policymakers that create the charters for these institutions have other objectives in addition to promoting risk-reducing diversification. One objective of the regulation of financial institutions includes allocating credit. S&Ls were chartered to increase access to home mortgages, and credit unions were chartered to add to the supply of consumer loans.

By constraining asset powers, the regulators of these institutions are able to simplify the supervision of these institutions. The rapid diversification of S&Ls in the 1980s convinced many in Congress that the risk of inadequate asset diversification was less than the risk of diversification combined with inadequate supervision and capital.

Diversification Options

Diversification of credit risk is a major concern of the portfolio manager. Unfortunately, achieving diversification is no simple matter. The average size or type of loan may make it impossible to achieve law of large numbers diversification. Diversification is also limited by the market demand in the area served by the financial institution. Commercial banks and thrifts in Texas, Oklahoma, and Colorado suffered as a result of their heavy concentration of real estate assets lent in those states in the 1980s. However, the strongest source of loan demand in the late 1970s and early 1980s in those states came from the real estate development business, and most of those institutions were too small to open lending offices outside of those markets.

Many smaller firms must invest a much higher percentage of the firm's assets in low-risk securities because of their inability to diversify. Consequently, small commercial banks, thrifts, and insurance companies usually have a much higher percentage of assets in low-risk, highly marketable securities.

Market Demand Limitations and Pricing

Local credit demand is also a major determinant of a depository's asset structure. Local markets can be categorized as capital surplus or capital deficit markets. *Capital surplus markets* are stable or declining areas that generate more savings than they borrow. *Capital deficit markets* are growing markets that must import capital. The intermediaries in capital surplus markets are forced to consider investments that were originated outside their market or were purchased in the secondary markets. Firms in capital deficit areas are likely to be sellers of loans to investors through secondary markets. The types of loans that are available will be influenced by the local economy. Fast-growing areas will experience strong demand for real estate loans. Rural areas will emphasize agricultural loans. Major cities will have a relatively larger demand for business lending.

Each financial firm must complete a thorough analysis of their local market. It cannot be assumed that, because an area is growing rapidly in population and employment, real estate lending will be profitable. Today, lenders have loan origination offices in markets outside their local areas. These offices can be opened and closed quickly and relatively inexpensively. As a result, a market that has strong demand can still face excess supply. Many financial institutions from the slow-growing agricultural states such as Kansas, Iowa, and Nebraska were major lenders in the Texas and Colorado markets during the mid-1980s. Remember too, it was Continental Illinois National Bank that was a major lender financing oil and gas exploration in Texas and Oklahoma in the early 1980s. Prices are determined by the interaction of supply and demand. Profitable pricing levels are not always found in markets experiencing strong demand.

Loan pricing and the relationship of pricing to alternative investments are major factors involved in achieving an optimal asset structure. The local markets in which financial institutions operate are dynamic, and most loans exhibit substantial pricing variations between local markets. Changes in macroeconomic policies, local economic conditions, competitive conditions, and financial conditions around the world have a way of impacting the asset structure decision.

The firm's asset structure is heavily influenced by changes in relative asset prices. Changes in the relative prices between two assets is called *basis*. The basis between two financial claims may change because of marketability, changes in the value of embedded options, credit risk expectations, taxation, laws and regulations, and other institutional factors. These same factors influence the expected returns on loans and investments. A primary responsibility of the portfolio management function is constantly monitoring the financial markets to track basis changes over time. By doing so, the firm can be positioned to make investments with the highest return for any given level of risk.

Economies of Scale

Many lenders would like to diversify to a greater extent, but find the costs of establishing new lending capacity to be prohibitively high. Each new lending program requires putting in place all the origination and servicing capabilities discussed in Chapter 7. There are high costs associated with each new type of loan that is added to the menu of the firm. These costs add up quickly as the firm grows and diversifies. Many of these activities are subject to economies of scale, which must be considered in order to be operationally competitive.

The risk and return characteristics of a particular type of loan also change rapidly. If the firm sets up a business loan origination group, for example, it may find that its competitors make the same choice. The result would be that this additional competition drives down loan rates and lowers volume per institution. The firm still has to pay the staff and service the business on the books, but it cannot achieve adequate scale economies.

Liquidity Management

Liquidity management represents the beginning of portfolio management activities for financial institutions. Financial institutions are the primary suppliers of liquid assets to government, business, and household sectors. On December 31, 1990, commercial banks and thrift institutions had transaction liabilities of $277 billion in demand deposits and another $294 billion in checkable deposits, including NOW accounts, automated transfer service balances, and credit union share drafts. The creation of these liquid liabilities is one of the basic transformation products that these institutions can offer. Providing this quantity of liquid liabilities necessitates managing the liquidity of the institution in an optimal fashion. This section will discuss the development of a liquidity management strategy and its implementation.

Liquidity, Profitability, and Regulatory Requirements

The management of liquidity is important to the profitability of the institution for two reasons. First, the need to hold highly liquid, low-credit risk short-term assets makes it difficult to show a suitable positive interest rate spread on this portion of the firm's assets. In this respect, regulatory liquidity requirements act as a form of tax on the institution by adversely affecting profitability. Certainly the reserves required by the Federal Reserve, which are held in a noninterest-bearing Federal Reserve account or vault cash, act as a major drag on profitability. Holding excess interest-earning liquid assets at a time when other investment opportunities provide higher returns also acts to reduce earnings.

The second reason liquidity requirements matter is because assets that are held to meet regulator requirements alter the overall investment strategy of the firm in such a way as to adversely impact on profitability. A minimum liquidity requirement ties up assets in liquid form that would otherwise be lent or invested in assets in higher yielding markets. Moreover, assets held to meet regulator requirements are not available to meet normal liquidity needs without penalty. This is because these assets are held primarily to avoid regulator sanctions and financial penalties, not to meet forecast cash flow or emergency cash needs. As a result, firms must hold liquid assets generally in excess of the regulatory minimums established.

The Liquidity Management Process

The process of liquidity management involves a number of financial activities. First, it involves completing a highly detailed pro-forma cash flow statement for the firm. Because most financial institutions have large and frequently volatile cash flow needs, the financial manager responsible for liquidity management usually must provide daily pro-forma cash flow statements for the firm.

Second, liquidity management requires determining the types of investments the liquidity portfolio will be invested in. Such factors as the liquidity of the investments held, credit risk, maturity, basis risk, and taxation are important in selecting a liquidity portfolio strategy.

Third, the financial manager must develop a separate liquidity strategy for each approach to raising cash. This strategy involves raising cash by identifying (1) assets that may be liquidated, (2) liabilities that may be issued quickly, and (3) assets that can be used as collateral. Each of these alternatives must be analyzed in some detail to determine the optimal liquidity raising strategy.

Developing Pro-Forma Cash Flow Statements

Developing pro-forma cash flow statements for the financial intermediary is the first step in the liquidity management process. The financial manager must identify all the items on the balance sheet, income statement, and off-balance sheet statements that impact on cash flow. A sample pro-forma cash flow statement is shown in Table 22.1 on page 618.

Table 22.1

**Commercial World Bank
Pro-Forma Cash Flow Statement
for March 1990**

Sources of Cash

Loan repayments	$ 34,000,000
Loan prepayments	5,000,000
Interest receipts	122,000,000
Net (+ −) demand deposits	23,000,000
Net (+ −) savings and time deposits	45,000,000
Sale of loans and investments	12,000,000
Maturing securities	22,000,000
Total	**$263,000,000**

Uses of Cash

Loans funded	$150,000,000
Investments purchased (settlements)	35,000,000
Operating expenses	14,000,000
Cash interest paid on liabilities	22,000,000
Lines-of-credit taken down	8,000,000
Non-deposit liabilities maturing	34,000,000
Total	**$263,000,000**

For an institution large enough to use it, a full-time cash management function is usually justified. This function is responsible for integrating with all the operating units to ensure that all asset and liability decisions that impact cash flow are identified. This function is also responsible for identifying ways to improve cash flow within the firm by making recommendations to alter operations in ways that will reduce float and increase the timing of cash flows and reduce outflows.

Out of these analyses frequently come ideas for changing bill-paying methods, changing the timing of sending out interest payments, improving payment processing, altering product design, and modifying funding methods.

Sources of Liquidity: Assets, Liabilities, and Collateral

One myth of liquidity management is that the primary source of liquidity or cash is the maturity or sale of the institution's liquid assets. This does not hold true for many institutions, because they have many other sources of cash that may be easier to access. Another reason is that a regulator may require a certain percentage of an institution's liquid assets to be held. As a result, these assets are not truly liquid.

Thus, the financial manager will want to look at the following alternatives to raise cash:

1. Saleable assets
2. Assets that can be pledged for borrowing purposes
3. Lines of credit
4. Wholesale deposit sources
5. Government sources, such as the Federal Reserve's discount window, the FHLBs, and the Credit Union Liquidity Fund

Saleable Assets

Most financial institutions hold assets other than assets that can be sold in highly liquid markets. Many banks hold Treasury securities, while many thrifts hold government agency mortgage-backed securities. The sale of these assets may be an effective way to generate cash.

Pledgeable Assets

Many institutions can easily raise cash by using assets on their books as collateral for a short-term loan. The repurchase agreement was designed as a way to use assets to raise cash quickly and inexpensively. There are very large repo markets in virtually all Treasury, agency, and agency guaranteed mortgage-backed securities. In addition, security dealers will provide repo programs for most other securities held by financial firms. Because collateral is so important to the ability of firms to generate cash, many financial institutions have someone responsible for keeping track of eligible assets that can qualify as collateral for borrowing.

Lines of Credit

Stronger financial institutions, primarily large well-capitalized commercial banks, establish lines of credit with other financial institutions. The most frequently used is the federal funds market. Many smaller banks and thrifts have excess liquidity they want to invest overnight or for a few days. The federal funds market is a good investment for these institutions also.

Wholesale Deposit Sources

The wholesale funds market has significantly increased in scope and activity over the last decade. While wholesale deposits have been available to large commercial banks for years through the negotiable CD market, it has only been the last decade in which smaller institutions have been able to participate through the brokered insured deposit market. The brokered insured deposit market will be less important in the future because the FDICIA of 1991 put restrictions on the types of institutions that can use this market and constraints on the rates that can be offered. The availability of negotiable CDs and brokered insured deposits provide another efficient way for financial institutions to raise cash quickly.

Government Sources

There are several government agencies available to financial institutions that need to raise cash quickly. The major programs include the Federal Reserve's discount window, the FHLB's advance window, and the Credit Union Liquidity Fund. Although each of these handle their lending differently, they are all in the business of lending to their member firms with acceptable collateral.

Liquidity and Regulatory Requirements

For a portion of the liquid assets held, the asset strategy is sometimes controlled by the regulator. The Federal Reserve requires the reserves held against transaction and other savings deposits be held in noninterest bearing deposits in the Federal Reserve and vault cash. For thrift institutions regulated by the OTS, the liquidity requirements dictate the percentage of specified liabilities that must be held in a specified group of eligible investments. These investments include U.S. government securities, agency securities, high-grade corporate investments, and deposits. The requirement also specifies that a certain percentage of these liquid assets be in short-term investments having maturities less than two years, while the remainder must be less than five years. *The National Credit Union Administration (NCUA)* also has the authority to require credit unions to hold a specified percentage of their assets in liquid form. Since credit unions now must hold reserves at the Federal Reserve, the NCUA does not now impose liquidity requirements.

This leaves many financial institutions in the perplexing situation that a certain portion of liquid assets are really not liquid after all. This makes liquidity management more difficult, since it is necessary to optimize liquidity management, subject to a number of regulatory constraints that act to reduce profitability for the institution. This objective of liquidity management is to reduce the negative drag on earnings caused by the regulator's imposed liquidity requirements.

Selecting the Liquidity Asset Portfolio

Developing a liquidity portfolio strategy requires identifying the following:

- Types of assets
- Maturities

- Credit risks
- Marketability
- Taxability

Types of Assets

Liquid assets fall into four classifications, namely, U.S. government and agency securities, short-term corporate securities, deposits in regulated institutions such as negotiable CDs, and short-term state and municipal securities of investment grade. Each of these can be represented in liquidity portfolios, depending on acceptance by the regulator and on the liquidity investment strategy chosen by management.

The development of this strategy relies on the four additional aspects of the portfolio. Investment strategies have also been designed around each of the following elements of the portfolio.

Maturity

The maturity structure of the liquidity portfolio impacts the interest rate risk position of the firm's entire asset portfolio. Consequently, the maturity structure of liquid assets should be an element of the interest rate risk strategy for the firm. A portfolio manager that attempts to minimize interest rate risk will concentrate on short-term investments, while one willing to accept greater interest rate risk exposure will do the opposite.

Two strategies that can be implemented as long as they are consistent with the firm's overall interest rate position are the *ladder of maturities* strategy and the *barbell liquidity* strategy. A ladder of maturities strategy would have the institution make an interest rate neutral forecast of future interest rates. In this example, the firm spaces the maturities of its liquid assets evenly over the liquidity portfolio's holding period, say, three years.

A barbell liquidity strategy, on the other hand, would have the liquidity manager invest a high percentage of all discretionary liquid funds in a particular maturity or risk class of liquid investments. Usually, the barbell would be between very short- and very long-term liquid assets. If the liquid asset holding period is two years, for example, the firm would alter the average maturity of its liquid asset portfolio between 6 and 18 months. The average maturity would depend on the firm's forecast of future interest rates. Another barbell strategy relating to credit risk would be between holding very low credit risk assets, such as U.S. Treasuries, and more risky liquid instruments such as corporate money market instruments. The liquidity investment manager would move between the two classes depending on the relative yield relationships, or basis, between the two groups of money market instruments. When the basis is wide, as measured by the yield differential between the two, the decision rule would be to sell the relatively high-priced asset and buy the relatively lower-priced asset.

Credit Risk

Credit risk impacts on liquidity management. Liquidity managers must make judgments about the risk versus return expectations for the allowable types of liquid investments. This assessment of credit risk uses the barbell strategy.

Marketability

During periods of financial stress, an institution is most concerned about the marketability of its liquid assets. Not all liquid assets are equally marketable. Marketability is a matter of degree. During stress periods, a high concentration of the most marketable U.S. government and agency securities is a common strategy. This may also be a good strategy for the institution that relies primarily on the sale of liquid assets as the optimal way to raise cash.

Taxability

Some institutions are able to invest their liquid assets in tax-exempt securities. They find that the after-tax equivalent yield on tax-exempt securities is higher than the taxable yields on other liquid investments. This means that tax-exempt securities might have a place in the institution's liquidity portfolio. As discussed in Chapter 4, however, the Tax Reform Act of 1986 has made tax-exempt state and local bonds less attractive to intermediaries.

Financial Depository Pricing of Loans

This section will develop a methodology for pricing loans at depository institutions. This methodology incorporates information about financial alternatives and all costs and financial risks that must be covered in order to ensure that a loan is profitable. To accomplish this, the financial intermediary must understand its capital structure, regulatory equity requirements, marginal cost of funds, credit risks, and servicing costs for each of its loan classes. Each of these elements is needed to complete the development of the pricing methodology.

Capital Structure and Regulatory Capital Requirements

Each financial institution must determine its appropriate capital structure. The capital structure decision is important, since it will determine the ratio of debt to equity that the firm commits to any financial investment. The capital structure decision for any financial institution is accomplished in the same manner as it is for all businesses. In the case of depository firms, however, the capital structure decision is complicated by the regulatory capital or equity requirements.

Like all firms, a financial firm's capital structure will be influenced by distress and agency costs. Generally, financial institutions that rely on unsecured and uninsured debt will be more concerned about maintaining a high credit rating and stronger capital structure, since the cost of these funding sources will rise as the firm deploys a more highly leveraged capital structure. These sources of funds are subject to greater agency costs.

On the other hand, firms that utilize only insured deposits and collateralized borrowings as their primary funding sources will be able to employ a more highly leveraged capital structure. That is because buyers of insured deposits and collateralized debt are less concerned about the safety and soundness of the institution. They rely on the guarantee of the insurance corporation or the value of the collateral to reduce credit risk.

A financial firm's optimal capital structure can be thought of as a function of several variables over which management has control. The firm's management probably would pursue a lower level of financial leverage (1) the greater its use of wholesale funding sources, (2) the greater its use of uninsured and uncollateralized funds sources, (3) the higher its asset portfolio credit risk, (4) the higher its portfolio interest rate risk, and (5) the lower its diversification of asset portfolio risk. Another factor that influences the capital structure decisions are regulatory equity requirements.

Regulatory Capital Requirements

Unlike manufacturing and commercial firms, financial depositories using insured deposits are able to leverage significantly without incurring the rising cost of liabilities associated with distress and agency costs. Indeed, the experience with thrift institutions in the 1980s showed that, if permitted by regulators, insured depositories can continue to issue debt in the form of insured deposits despite insolvency. This means that the regulatory system must step in to establish the minimum equity or capital standards for insured depositories. This process has become extremely important in recent years as regulators internationally developed a risk-based capital standard known as the *Basle agreements*.

Here in the United States, the bank and thrift regulators have struggled with the development of a separate set of risk-based capital standards. Congress also got into the act with the passage of the FIRREA of 1989, which established minimum capital standards for savings and loans and savings banks. The FDICIA of 1991 went even further in strengthening regulatory enforcement of capital standards. The concept of a risk-based capital system is not new in the United States. The Federal Reserve of New York and the Federal Reserve Board employed such a system in the 1950s. It was called the ABC formulas. Over time, the formulas became very complex and the system fell into disuse. Replacing it in the 1960s and 1970s was the CAMEL ratings. CAMEL stands for capital, assets, management, earnings, and liquidity. This approach to examination and supervision is still in use today. It is important since the risk-based capital requirements are tied to the CAMEL ratings in a few instances. The highest CAMEL rating is 1 and the lowest is 5. Only about 20 percent of all the commercial banks in the nation receive the highest rating. The CAMEL rating is a regulatory rating system and does not necessarily conform to shareholder objectives.

The reasons for the latest effort to develop a risk-based system include the following:

- A simple capital to asset ratio, or its reciprocal, the equity multiplier EM, was not sensitive to the broadening of on- and off-balance sheet risk exposures.
- Overall capital to assets ratios were declining for the banking system in the 1970s and 1980s.
- Regulators wanted to provide consistency with the international risk-based Basle systems.
- There was concern over the deregulation of deposit rates on bank costs and profitability.
- Bank activities expanded into new, more risky activities including securities and real estate development.
- Banks were allowed to include loss reserves as capital, which may have diminished the value of the capital account.

The final rules on the risk-based capital requirement were adopted by the three principle bank regulators in 1989. Thrifts regulated by the OTS must also adhere to capital requirements "no less stringent" than commercial banks as a result of the passage of FIRREA. However, the OTS has made several modifications of the requirements.

The risk-based capital standard involves the establishment of a risk weight for each asset on the balance sheet, a conversion factor for all off-balance sheet risk positions, and a minimum capital requirement, currently 8 percent. The risk weights determine the percentage of the minimum capital requirement that must be held against particular assets. A single family mortgage with a risk weight of 50 percent would be required to have a capital reserve of (50% × 8% =) 4 percent. The total capital requirement for the institution is determined by calculating the capital required under the standard for all on- and off-balance sheet assets and risk exposures and adding them up. Off-balance sheet risk exposures include, but are not limited to, the following:

1. Credit guarantees
2. Standby letters of credit
3. Forward currency transactions

4. Interest rate and currency swaps
5. Unused loan commitments over one year
6. Assets sold with recourse
7. Forward commitments to purchase assets

International Focus

Basle Committee Responds to New Bank Risks

The Basle committee is a group of central bank regulators from the world's richest nations. In 1988, they developed a set of risk-based capital standards for commercial banks involved in international banking. These standards will be fully implemented in 1992. The standards, however, focus primarily on the credit quality of commercial bank assets. They tend to ignore several other important risks.

The committee in 1992 went to work on two other risks, interest rate risk and trading or positioning risk. Interest rate risks relate to the potential that sharp changes in interest rates will reduce the value of bank assets more than liabilities, while positioning risk deals with unhedged commitments to buy and sell foreign currencies and securities. The Basle group is concerned that the rapid growth in commercial bank trading is not being addressed by the capital standards.

The capital guidelines call for an absolute minimum of 3 percent capital to assets, with a risk-based level of 8 percent by year-end 1992. Only commercial banks with a CAMEL rating of 1 can have a 3 percent capital level, while all others will be at 4 percent. An illustration of the proposed risk-based risk weights for a sampling of assets for commercial banks and thrifts regulated by the OTS are shown in Table 22.2 on page 626. These regulatory-based capital standards provide the minimum capital requirements for a depository. They establish the maximum leverage of the firm's equity, based on the regulator's estimates of an asset's riskiness.

Establishing a marginal capital requirement for each new asset is the first step in developing our pricing algorithm. *Marginal* means the dollar change in equity for a given dollar change in the asset or off-balance sheet factor. These marginal equity or capital percentages are determined by management for depository institutions. The regulator's risk-based minimum capital requirement may be considered an important factor in setting the level for each firm. Of course, depository institutions can use a higher or lower capital standard than the minimum imposed by the regulator. The objective, in either case, should be to minimize the firm's weighted cost of capital and still attain the selected capital minimum.

Table 22.2

Risk-Based Capital Requirement Risk Weights for Commercial Banks and Thrifts Regulated by the Office of Thrift Supervision

Investment Type	Risk Weight
Banks	
Cash	
U.S. Treasury securities	
U.S. agency securities (full faith and credit-backed) including GNMA-backed mortgage securities	0%
U.S. government sponsored agency securities (not full faith and credit) including FNMA-, FHLMC-backed mortgage securities	
CMOs backed by GNMA, FNMA, or FHLMC collateral (other than residual or stripped securities)	
State and municipal general obligation bonds	
Claims collateralized by U.S. Treasury agency and government sponsored agency securities	20%
One-to-four-family residential mortgage loans meeting typical secondary market tests	
CMOs backed by qualifying residential mortgages (other than residuals or stripped securities)	
State and municipal revenue bonds	50%
All other assets not specifically covered elsewhere, including multifamily residential mortgages, other income property loans, unsecured commercial loans, and third world debt	100%

Investment Type	Risk Weight
Thrifts	
Cash	
U.S. Treasury securities	
U.S. agency securities (excluding GNMA-backed mortgage securities)	0%
GNMA-, FNMA-, and FHLMC-backed mortgage securities and collateralized CMOs	
All secondary mortgage market (SMMEA)-qualified "mortgage related" securities including IOs and POs except residuals	
State and municipal general obligations	
Claims collateralized by the U.S. Treasury and government sponsored enterprises	20%
One-to-four-family residential mortgages	
Non-SMMEA mortgage-related securities backed by qualified residential mortgages	
State and municipal revenue bonds	50%

Table 22.2 continued

Risk-Based Capital Requirement Risk Weights for Commercial Banks and Thrifts Regulated by the Office of Thrift Supervision

Investment Type	Risk Weight
All assets not specifically covered elsewhere including residential construction loans, multifamily residential loans, income property loans, and other secured or unsecured loans	100%
Goodwill and other intangibles	
Real estate acquired by foreclosure	200%
Equity securities	
Real estate held for development	
Investment in subsidiaries	
High loan-to-value ratio and nonresidential construction loans	300%

Calculating the Weighted Average Cost of Capital

As discussed earlier, it is very likely that financial depositories will establish a capital structure that calls for higher equity levels than is required by the minimum risk-based standards. Once these are established, the firm is in a position to determine the relative ratio of debt and equity for the acquisition of each asset to be acquired on the margin. The cost of capital for the next asset acquired is defined as the *weighted average cost of capital, WACC,* and is shown in Equation 22.1. Notice that the before-tax cost of debt is used. This can be done as long as the before-tax cost of equity is used. Since financial asset yields are typically quoted on a before-tax or taxable equivalent basis, this approach greatly simplifies the computational process. It saves us from computing asset yields on an after-tax basis.

$$WACC = C_e(W_e) + \sum_{i=1}^{N} C_{di}(W_{di}) \qquad [22.1]$$

where:

N = number of liabilities

C_e = cost of equity before tax

W_e = equity percent of funding

C_{di} = cost of debt of type i before tax

W_{di} = weight of debt of type i

The relevant cost of equity, C_e, in the case of a new issue of common stock would be estimated from one of the three capital market equilibrium models: the capital asset pricing model, arbitrage pricing theory, or discounted cash flow models. Alternatively, the cost of equity, C_e, could be the firm's cost of retained earnings or newly issued preferred stock.

The relevant cost of debt for type i, C_{di}, should it be a deposit, must include the origination costs, the servicing costs, the Federal Reserve required reserves, required insurance of accounts premiums, and broker's commission, if any. The cost of debt should be for the least cost source of comparable duration as the asset intended to be purchased or originated.

The following is an example of three different assets being considered for investment by a depository institution. The differences for each asset relate to the financing sources used. Asset A will be financed with 6 percent equity and 94 percent deposits. Asset B will be financed with 8 percent equity and 92 percent deposits, while asset C will be financed with 6 percent equity, 50 percent collateralized debt, such as FHLB borrowings, and 44 percent deposits. Table 22.3 provides a schedule of the cost of each of these funding sources. Table 22.4 provides the *WACC* for each asset to be financed.

Breakeven Risk Adjusted Asset Yield

The calculation of the *WACC* provides only one-half of the pricing methodology. The other half is far more difficult to develop. This involves analyzing each type of asset to identify all the possible risks and costs that may serve to reduce the gross yield on the asset. The result of this analysis is the development of the *breakeven risk adjusted yield, BERAY*.

These risks and costs include credit risk premium, *crp*, marketability risk premium, *mrp*, call option premium, *cop*, delivery option premium, *dop*, and servicing cost, *sc*. The breakeven risk adjusted yield is equal to the *WACC* plus a yield estimate for each of these factors. The equation for the breakeven risk adjusted yield is shown in Equation 22.2 on page 629.

Table 22.3

Cost of Funding Source Alternatives*

Equity	16.00%
Collateralized debt	9.75%
Deposits	9.60%

*Includes origination, servicing, deposit insurance, reserve requirements, and brokerage costs where applicable.

Table 22.4

Weighted Average Cost of Capital*

Asset A = (.16)(.06) + (.096)(.94)	= 9.984%
Asset B = (.16)(.08) + (.096)(.92)	= 10.112%
Asset C = (.16)(.06) + (.096)(.44) + (.0975)(.50)	= 10.059%

*The rates shown in this example assume that the assets are financed with liabilities of comparable duration as the assets they finance.

$$BERAY = WACC + crp + mrp + cop + dop + sc \qquad [22.2]$$

Each of the factors affecting the breakeven risk adjusted yield will be discussed. With the exception of the delivery option premium, each of these factors was discussed in Chapter 2.

- *Credit Risk Premium, crp:* The credit risk premium relates to the average credit losses expected on any given portfolio of assets. Credit card portfolios might be expected to experience a 2.5 to 4 percent per annum loss of principal due to credit losses, while a portfolio of single-family home loans, with low loan-to-value ratios, might have an anticipated annual loss of principal of .25 percent per annum or less.

- *Marketability Risk Premium, mrp:* Some assets are inherently more marketable than others. The marketability risk premium could be measured as the difference between the asset's bid and ask prices. Home mortgages conforming to purchase standards of the FHLMC or FNMA are considered very marketable, while highly leveraged business loans have low marketability. The lender must be compensated for the lack of marketability.

- *Call Risk Premium, cop:* Many loans, such as auto loans and first and second mortgages, have embedded call options providing for prepayment. This presents a major funding risk for the financial firm. The value of this call option must be subtracted from the gross yield on the loan, since it represents nothing more than a premium paid by the borrower for the option, not a profit to the lender. In other words, if the gross yield on a loan is 10.25 percent and the option is valued at .75 percent, then the true yield to the lender is only 9.50 percent (10.25% − .75%). The .75 percent represents the option price as a percentage of the loan balance converted to a yield equivalent. These option values are estimated using sophisticated option pricing models.

- *Delivery Option Premium, dop:* Some loans are originated in terms that allow the borrower to have the advantage of fixing the rate on the loan before closing the transaction. On a mortgage, the rate might be set up to 60 days before the transaction is closed. For an auto loan, on the other hand, the rate might be set a week before the loan closes. In both cases the borrower can go to another lender or walk away from the transaction. This amounts to an option offered to the borrower by the lender that must be hedged. The cost of hedging this option risk could be charged directly to the borrower in the form of a commitment fee, but frequently it is not. When a fee isn't charged, the cost of hedging this risk should be netted out of the gross yield on the loan.

- *Servicing Costs, sc:* The cost of servicing the asset must be considered also. The appropriate cost of servicing will be the marginal cost of servicing the additional asset being analyzed. This involves all the activities of collection, document control, and other servicing activities, but not credit losses. This cost must be included in the gross yield.

Table 22.5 shows how, after considerable analysis, the various components of the cost and risk matrix might look for three types of loans: a single-family home mortgage, a low-risk auto loan, and a commercial business loan.

Table 22.5

Servicing Costs and Risk Matrix (estimated in basis points)

Cost and Risk Factors	First Home Mortgage (fixed rate)	High-Grade Auto Loan	Business
Credit risk	12	50	75
Marketability risk	5		10
Call risk	90	0	
Delivery option	15	5	0
Servicing cost	12	120	50
Total	**134**	**175**	**135**

The *BERAY* is a rate that allows the financial firm to earn its weighted cost of capital while covering the costs of servicing, credit, marketability, and option risks. The appropriate weighted cost of capital for each asset must provide funds with a duration that matches the asset. The duration match is important for pricing, but it does not obligate the firm to use a particular liability to fund an asset.

Table 22.3 compared the *BERAY* using the appropriate financing options for a single-family fixed-rate first mortgage under three financing alternatives. To these weighted cost of capital estimates, add the total of the column in Table 22.4, or 134 basis points. This produces a breakeven risk adjusted loan rate for Asset A of 11.324 percent (9.984% + 1.34%) assuming a financing mix of 96 percent deposits and 4 percent equity. Asset B produces 11.452 percent (10.112% + 1.34%) assuming a financing mix of 92 percent deposits and 8 percent equity, and Asset C produces 11.399% (10.059% + 1.34%) assuming a financing mix of 50 percent deposits, 44 percent collateralized debt and 6 percent equity.

Table 22.6 provides another example of the loan pricing matrix for several common loans made by depository institutions. In the table, the cost of debt and equity are calculated. This is done by first determining the cost of the debt and equity. Then the appropriate capital structure is determined

Table 22.6

BERAY for Four Types of Loans

Cost Factors	Single-Family 15-Year Fixed	Single-Family ARM 1-Year	Auto Loan 48-Month	Business Loan @ Prime
Cost of Debt and Equity				
Debt C_d	9.65%	8.25%	7.75%	6.80%
Equity C_e	15.00	15.00	15.00	15.00
Finance Weights				
Weight debt W_d	.94%	.94%	.92%	.92%
Weight equity W_e	.06	.06	.08	.08
Weighted Cost of Capital *WACC*				
$[(C_d \times W_d) + (C_e \times W_e)]$	9.671%	8.355%	8.33%	7.456%
Risk and Cost Factors				
Credit risk premium	.12%	.17%	.70%	1.25%
Marketability risk premium	.05	.05	.15	.20
Call option premium	.85	.05	.07	.00
Optional delivery premium	.20	.05	.02	.00
Servicing costs	.12	.20	1.30	.50
BERAY	**11.011%**	**8.875%**	**10.57%**	**9.406%**

for the loan from which *WACC* is calculated. Added to this are the various additional risk and cost factors mentioned previously. The result is the *BERAY* that the firm must earn in order to cover all costs, to be compensated for all risks, and to achieve the firm's targeted return on equity.

Although the example was for a depository, the analysis would be the same for an insurance company that sells guaranteed investment contracts and invests in bonds, mortgages, or other investments or a finance company that invests in installment paper or warehouse financing. Even though these firms would have different capital structures and costs of equity and debt, the basic pricing algorithm would remain the same.

Using the BERAY

The *BERAY* is used to determine which assets the firm should acquire that are expected to earn a profit. Loans whose yield exceeds the *BERAY* will have a positive net present value. For more complicated investments with volatile cash flows, the *BERAY* can be used to discount the cash flows to determine the asset's net present value. It is also necessary to compare the *BERAY* for each loan to the yield charged by the competition in the marketplace. Financial institutions typically take a survey to establish the market yields. For highly liquid assets, the yield would come from a security dealer. An example of such a comparison is shown in Table 22.7.

As indicated earlier in the chapter, supply and demand conditions within local and regional loan markets may have a significant influence on the pricing of particular types of loans. A financial firm attempting to build a large market share for a particular type of loan may price the loan below its *BERAY*. Other institutions in the market must know their *BERAY* to determine whether or not they want to meet the competition.

Table 22.7

BERAY of Four Loans Compared to Market Yields

BERAY and Market	Single-Family 15-Year Fixed	Single-Family ARM 1-Year	Auto Loan 48-Month	Business Loan @ Prime
BERAY	11.011%	8.875%	10.57%	9.406%
Yields derived from market survey	11.00	7.75	10.75	10.00
Expected profit (or loss) spread	−.011%	−.125%	.18%	.594%

Another reason that the *BERAY* for one institution may indicate the loan is profitable while for another unprofitable is that different institutions have different cost structures and they make different estimates of a loan's credit risk, marketability premium, and value of the options offered. Firms also have different *WACC*s. These differences are what makes a market.

In the late 1980s, for example, many institutions continued to make commercial real estate loans while others dropped out, thinking the market for new commercial properties was overbuilt. The latter institutions put a higher value on the credit risk premium than the former. They turned out to be right.

The Prime Rate

The *prime rate* is widely quoted in the financial press. It is frequently referred to in the press because many depository institution borrowers have loans whose interest rate is tied to the prime. The prime rate has the exalted reputation for being the interest rate that commercial banks charge their most creditworthy customers. Well, this characterization is not true. The opening of the capital markets to many more firms has put tremendous pressure on banks to be more competitive in their pricing. Today, a majority of commercial bank loans are tied to open-market interest rates that represent the marginal cost of funds to commercial banks. Two indices that are often used are the cost of new funds to the bank represented by the federal funds rate and the negotiable CD rate. Another frequently used index rate is LIBOR (the London interbank offered rate).

The prime rate has truly fallen from grace. A study of 48 large commercial banks completed by Brady (1985) using 1984 data indicated that approximately 90 percent of loans with maturities of less than one year were made at a rate below prime, while over 50 percent of loans with maturities over one year were priced below prime. With the domination of open-market indexed commercial bank pricing of business loans, the prime rate has become largely an "administered rate." This means it is a rate that is not very responsive to changes in open-market conditions. It is primarily used for loans to smaller and less creditworthy borrowers. This is because the prime rate is generally above the commercial bank rates tied to LIBOR, negotiable CDs, and federal funds.

Loan Participations and Syndications

The separation of the origination, servicing, and portfolio management functions at intermediaries has facilitated the growth of loan participations and syndications. *Loan participations* and *syndications* are the sale of a fixed percentage of the principal value of a loan to one or more investors or correspondents. Typically, the originating institution will maintain a portion of the loan in portfolio.

Participations and syndications are sold for several reasons. First, participation loan sales facilitate diversification of credit risk. Many loans are very large and present excessive credit risk exposure to one borrower. To reduce this large credit exposure, the originator sells a percentage interest in the loan to one or more other investors. Loan participation sales are also used to increase a firm's origination and servicing revenues. If the firm is particularly profitable in these functions, then the participation permits the firm to originate and service a volume of loans that far exceeds its portfolio capacity.

Loan participations also permit the firm to leverage the revenue from its investment in a loan by earning a spread between the yield it offers to the participation buyer and the yield it receives from the borrower. This process provides additional compensation for the origination and servicing units within the firm.

In addition, loan participations are sometimes easier to sell to other investors than whole loans because, since the originator is also an investor, the buyer has additional confidence in the credit underwriting of the loan. This situation translates into the ability of the seller to offer a lower yield to the buyer of the participation than if the seller had no investment.

Loan participation and syndication sales are used primarily in large real estate and commercial and industrial loan transactions. Many are large balance loans that would be quite risky if they were held by one institution. The financing of development and construction of large commercial real estate projects and large corporate loans used for restructuring, leveraged buy-outs, and hostile takeovers are frequent participation sale candidates.

Profiting from Loan Participations and Syndications

When a financial intermediary sells a participation, the main problem is to identify all the marginal costs and revenues that impact the firm. These involve the costs of origination, earned origination fees, the cost of servicing, and the revenue comprising the excess yield earned on the loan that is not distributed to the participation buyer.

Here is an example for consideration. A mortgage lender must decide whether to originate a $50 million mortgage on a regional shopping center. The loan will be made at a rate, r, of 10.5 percent. The originator will earn a fee of 3 percent of the loan principal from the borrower at the time the loan is closed.

One reason the originator expressed an interest in this loan is that several other portfolio lenders agreed to purchase up to $40 million, leaving the originator with an investment of $10 million. The $10 million is well below the board of directors' established maximum loan amount. The seller of the participation will offer a participation yield, r_p, of 10.25 percent and a 2 percent origination fee on the amount of their investment. The selling

Table 22.8

Participation Seller's Cash Flows from Origination and Sale of Participation in Loan*

Loan disbursement to borrower	−$50,000,000
Origination fees paid by borrower	
3% of $50 million principal	$1,500,000
Less cost of origination	
@ $550,000	−$550,000
Proceeds from participation sale	$40,000,000
Origination fees paid to participants	
@ 2% of $40 million	−$800,000
Net amount of investment	−$9,850,000
n (7 years × 12 months)	84
r (loan rate)	10.50%
r_p (participation rate)	10.25%

*Incorporates loan fees, origination costs, and investor fees paid.

institution is interested in estimating the yield on the retained portion of the loan.

The seller estimates that the servicing costs for remitting principal and interest payments to the four participation buyers will be $120 per month. The cost of origination is estimated to be $550,000. The loan has a balloon clause that makes it due and payable in seven years. The loan is nonamortizing and interest is charged monthly. Table 22.8 shows the cash flows representing the selling firm's investment in the loan after it sells the participation.

The present value equation for determining the participation seller's yield, *PSY*, on the selling firm's $10 million investment in the loan is shown in Equation 22.3.

$$\$9,850,000 = \left[\sum_{t=1}^{84} [\$16,666.67 + \$89,583.33 - \$120.00] / (1 + PSY)^t \right]$$

$$+ \$10,000,000 / (1 + PSY)^{84}$$

$$PSY = 13.06\% \qquad [22.3]$$

where:

The monthly interest earned on the

$40,000,000 sold is $16,666.67

(.005/12) × $40,000,000

The monthly interest earned on the $10,000,000 retained portion of the loan is	$89,583.33
$(.1075/12) \times \$10,000,000$	
The servicing cost per month is	$120.00
The balloon payment at the end of 7 years or 84 months is	$10,000,000

As can be seen by this example, the yield on the originating firm's investment of $9.85 million is 13.06 percent, when the additional cash flows received on the sold portion is factored into it. A rough approximation of *PSY* on the retained portion of a loan participation retained in the portfolio of the selling institution can be calculated using Equation 22.4. This approximation ignores origination fees, origination costs, and servicing costs.

Yield on retained portion of $PSY = r + \{(r - r_p) \times [\text{sold amount/retained amount}]\}$ [22.4]

where:

PSY = participation seller's yield
r = yield paid by borrower
r_p = yield paid to participant investor
retained amount = dollar amount of loan retained in seller's portfolio
sold amount = dollar amount of loan sold to participation investors

The following uses the equation for the previous example while ignoring both the fee income and servicing costs.

$$PSY = 10.50\% + [(10.50\% - 10.25\%) \times (\$40,000,000/\$10,000,000)]$$
$$= 10.50\% + (.25 \times 4)$$
$$PSY = 11.50\%$$

The yield on the retained $10 million investment is estimated to be 11.50 percent. This provides a good example of how a participation sale of a loan can substantially increase (or decrease if the yield on the sold portion is higher than the loan rate) the yield to the selling organization. Table 22.9 provides several examples of computations using Equation 22.4 for an original 8 percent loan.

Table 22.9

Yield to Seller on the Retained Portion of a Participation (coupon rate on loan, r: 8.00%)

Coupon Rate on Participation, r_p	\multicolumn{5}{c}{Percent of Loan Sold as Participation (in percent of original loan balance)}
	10.00	30.00	50.00	70.00	90.00
7.00	8.114	8.429	9.00	10.33	17.00
7.50	8.056	8.214	8.509	9.16	12.50
8.00	8.00	8.00	8.00	8.00	8.00
8.25	7.972	7.893	7.75	7.417	5.75
8.50	7.944	7.786	7.50	6.833	3.50

DEMONSTRATION PROBLEM: Example of Participation Yield

Situation: Wilderness Bank sells a $9 million participation in a $10 million loan. The yield on the loan, r, is 11 percent. The 90 percent participation is sold to yield, r_p, 10.75 percent. The following equation provides an estimate of the yield on the retained portion of the loan, *PSY*. This figure disregards origination fees, origination costs, and servicing costs.

Result:

$$PSY = 11.00\% + (11.00 - 10.75) \times (9{,}000{,}000/1{,}000{,}000)$$
$$= 11.00\% + (.25 \times 9) = 13.25\%$$

The yield on the retained $1 million investment is approximated to be 13.25 percent.

Accounting for Loan Sales

Generally, GAAP accounting rules permit an institution to take into income any excess yield derived from a loan sale. This excess income is determined by calculating the difference between the rate earned on the portion of the loan retained in portfolio and the yield to the participation buyer. The difference is in the form of an ordinary annuity that will be earned for the life of the loan. From this annuity, the cost of servicing must be subtracted. The remainder can be taken into income by calculating the present value of the excess income stream less servicing costs.

Consider the following example. A mortgage lender originates a $500,000 ten-year fixed-rate nonamortizing loan with a coupon rate of 11.75 percent. The lender is able to sell a 50 percent participation at a coupon rate of 11.25 percent. The accountants determine that a minimum of .25 percent is needed to cover the cost of servicing. This leaves a .25 percent excess yield. If the loan is expected to remain on the books for a loan life of seven years, then the firm can take into income the present value of Equation 22.5. This is the equation for the present value of an ordinary annuity. If the loan is an amortizing variety, the calculations would be far more difficult.

Present value of excess yield for

$$\text{participation sale} = (erm/m) \times (RL) \times [1 - (1/(1 + (k/m))^{nm}]/(k/m) \qquad [22.5]$$

where:

erm = annualized excess interest rate margin

m = number of periods per year payments are received

RL = retained loan amount

k = before-tax cost of capital

n = number of annual periods

The following solves for the previous example and uses a 15 percent cost of capital as the discount rate k.

Present value of excess yield

for participation sale = $(.25/12) \times$

$(\$250{,}000) \times \{[1 - (1/(1 + (.15/12))^{84})]/(.15/12)\} = \$1{,}348.27$

Once the firm has capitalized the income it will receive in the future, it must be concerned that the loan life is at least seven years. If it is shorter, the firm will not earn the profit that it had earlier recorded on its income statement at the time the participation was sold. This will require the firm to take a charge against income for the amount of the present value of the income stream it did not receive. This happens frequently when interest rates fall and mortgages prepay earlier than expected. The reverse can also take place as well. If the loan extends beyond seven years, the firm could earn more than the amount estimated.

Summary

Asset management is one of the most difficult tasks for the financial institution manager. Laws and regulations, credit risk diversification potential, market supply and demand conditions, and potential economies of scale impact on the asset structure decision.

Asset pricing is also crucial to determining the asset structure. It requires assembling a significant amount of information about the firm's optimal capital structure, its funding options, and its estimates of a financial asset's credit, marketability and option risks, and servicing costs. All this information is used to determine the interest rate that will permit the firm to fund a loan profitably. This is the expected minimum rate that will produce the firm's targeted return on the equity capital.

Selecting the firm's asset structure requires analyses of **laws and regulations** that determine the allowable investments of the firm, **diversification** impact on the firm's portfolio **expected risk and return,** asset **supply and demand conditions,** and asset market **pricing.**

Asset management begins with **liquidity management.** Financial firms must manage liquidity to meet any foreseen and unforeseen cash needs. Some regulated financial firms must also contend with liquidity requirements imposed on them by regulators.

Liquidity management begins with a detailed **cash flow analysis.** The next step is to identify all sources of raising cash. These include (1) **salable assets,** (2) **pledgable assets,** (3) **lines of credit,** (4) **wholesale deposit sources,** and (5) **government agencies** that provide liquidity.

The **selection of assets** depends critically on knowledge of the firm's **weighted cost of capital, WACC.** This is determined by estimating the cost of all the debt and equity financing mixes that can be used to finance a particular asset that are consistent with the firm's optimal capital structure.

The **optimal capital structure** for many financial firms is impacted by **regulatory capital requirements.** Commercial banks, SBs, and S&Ls must meet a set of **risk-based capital requirements** that are calculated as a weighted average of the firm's asset structure. This sets the minimum level of capital needed to finance a new asset. The firm can then establish higher capital levels.

The yield on a particular asset must be high enough to cover all the costs of financing it as well as the **credit risk premium, marketability risk premium, servicing costs,** and the **value of options for call and delivery.** This is calculated as the **breakeven risk adjusted yield, BERAY:**

$$BERAY = WACC + crp + mrp + cop + dop + sc$$

where:

$WACC$ = weighted cost of capital

crp = credit risk premium

mrp = marketability risk premium

cop = call option premium

dop = delivery option premium

sc = servicing costs

The *BERAY* is compared to market yields to determine which assets are expected to meet the return on equity target of the firm.

Financial institutions have become major sellers of loans through **participations** and **syndications.** These are sales of a fixed percentage of a loan's principal to one or more investors. The objectives of these sales are to (1) improve portfolio diversification, (2) increase origination and servicing volumes and profits, and (3) create a positive income stream by selling a portion of a loan at a yield lower than that paid by the borrower.

One way to determine the financial benefit from a loan participation sale is to calculate the yield, *PSY,* on the retained portion of a loan sale using the following formula:

Yield on retained portion of participation =

$$PSY = r + [(r - r_p) \times (\text{sold amount/retained amount})]$$

where:

r = yield on loan to borrower

r_p = yield paid to participant investor

retained amount = dollar amount of loan retained in seller's portfolio

sold amount = dollar amount of loan sold to participation investors

Questions

Chapter 22

1. Laws and regulations impact asset management by prescribing the types of loans and investments a financial firm can legally make. Provide some examples of how this actually impacts several institutions you have studied.
2. Why is it very hard for small financial intermediaries to diversify?
3. A specific local financial market for a certain type of claim may be experiencing a strong demand. Despite this fact, it may be very difficult to make a profit in this market. How can this be the case?
4. How do economies of scale influence the assets originated and held by a financial intermediary?
5. Why is holding a high percentage of liquid assets generally a negative influence on profitability?
6. What are the sources of liquidity for a large financial firm?
7. How does collateral fit into the liquidity management program?
8. What is meant by a ladder of maturities and barbell liquidity strategies?
9. What factors influence management's choice of a capital structure? List the factors and explain whether each calls for more or less capital in the capital structure.
10. What types of liabilities that financial firms originate are likely to be subject to high distress and agency costs?
11. How do regulatory risk-based asset reserve requirements impact the capital structure decision?
12. Explain what the weighted cost of capital is for a financial institution.
13. Would you expect an asset that is financed with a high percentage of equity as compared to another asset to have a higher or lower weighted cost of capital? Why?
14. What factors must be added to the weighted cost of capital before establishing the minimum price for a loan or investment acquisition?
15. How do you explain the delivery option premium? Give an example.
16. Why do financial firms use loan participations and syndications?
17. How do firms profit from loan participation and syndication loan sales?
18. The prime rate is held to be important because it is the rate charged by commercial banks to their most creditworthy customers. Is this belief justified?

Problems

Problem 22-1 Weighted Average Cost of Capital

You are considering funding a large new loan program with 5 percent equity at a cost of 21.5 percent, 50 percent collateralized borrowings at a cost of 7.25 percent, and 45 percent negotiable CDs at a cost of 9.5 percent.

1. What is the weighted average cost of capital for the loan program?
2. You have just learned that regulatory changes will require you to fund this program with 10 percent equity. What is the new cost of capital if you reduce collateralized borrowings to 45 percent?

3. Price competition for this type of asset is strong and you don't want to increase the overall cost of capital. What alternative mix of collateralized borrowings and negotiable CDs would bring the cost of capital back down to the result you obtain in number 1 above?

Problem 22-2 Weighted Average Cost of Capital

As portfolio manager for a small southeastern bank, you are analyzing the firm's cost of capital. Your staff has prepared the following list of available funding sources and their costs:

Funding Source	Current Weight	Cost	Servicing Costs
Equity	6.00%	18.00%	0.00%
Demand Deposits	15.00	0.00	2.75
Retail Time Deposits	65.00	6.50	1.25
Brokered Deposits	9.00	8.00	.50
Other	5.00	0.00	0.00

1. Compute the total cost of each funding source.
2. Compute the weighted cost of capital for a new loan program to be funded with 8 percent retained earnings (equity) and 92 percent retail time deposits.
3. Compute the weighted cost of capital for an asset that is funded 6 percent by retained earnings, 40 percent by retail time deposits, and the remaining 54 percent by brokered deposits.

Problem 22-3 Breakeven Risk Adjusted Yield, BERAY

Eastern Savings Bank is considering originating auto loans. The new risk-based asset equity requirements call for 8 percent equity for auto loans. Eastern estimates that these loans will experience .7 percent credit losses as a percent of outstanding balances annually. The loans cost 70 basis points per year to service based on outstanding balances. The loans are not liquid and management suggests that a marketability premium of 20 basis points is needed to cover this. The loans are originated with a one-week delivery option, which is estimated to be valued at 5 basis points. They can also be paid off without penalty. This call provision is valued at 15 basis points in yield.

Eastern is conservative and is considering holding 10 percent equity rather than the required 8 percent behind these loans.

1. Calculate the *BERAY* assuming its pre-tax cost of equity is 18 percent and deposits cost 7.25 percent.
2. A competitor of Eastern has estimated that all risks and costs of auto loans will be the same as those estimated by Eastern. This firm's cost of equity and debt are also the same as Eastern's. However, this competitor will use 8 percent equity rather than 10 percent. What is the competitor's *BERAY*?

Problem 22-4   Breakeven Risk Adjusted Yield,
Consider the following thrift institution assets:

Asset X: 25-year ARM
Asset Y: 60-month construction loan
Asset Z: 36-month unsecured consumer loan

The thrift's cost of equity is 18 percent. The cost of duration-matched debt, the appropriate financing weights, and other risk and cost factors for each asset are shown in the following table:

For each asset, compute the weighted cost of capital, *WACC*, and breakeven risk adjusted yield, *BERAY*.

Problem 22-5   Participation Seller's Yield,
You have been asked to determine a rough estimate of the yield on the portion of a loan that will be retained in portfolio after a participation is sold. The loan is $8,000,000. You can sell $7,000,000. The yield the borrower will pay is 8 percent. You promise the participation buyer a yield of 7.80 percent.
What is the *PSY* on the retained portion of the loan?

Problem 22-6   Participation Seller's Yield,
Security S&L originated a portfolio of $8,000,000 of home mortgages whose dollar balances exceed the purchase limits of the GSE. The mortgages have a coupon of 8.75 percent. Security has found a buyer for a 90 percent participation in the portfolio at 8.50 percent.

1. What yield will Security receive on the portion of the loans it retains?
2. Security estimates it will cost 12 basis points per year to service the outstanding balances of the loans. Given this information, what would you estimate the yield adjusted for servicing to be on the retained portion of the portfolio held by Security?

Liability Management and Pricing

chapter 23

Liability management concerns selection and pricing of funding sources. Liability management is a major issue for depositories, finance companies, and insurance companies because these firms have a great deal of freedom in the selection of liabilities and because the liabilities they sell are primary products, not simply funding sources. For pension funds, mutual funds, REITs, and limited partnerships the liability decision is not a major issue.

The liability management and pricing problems for depositories and insurance companies can be broken down into several parts. The first step is to determine which funding sources are available. Second, the marginal cost of each source in relation to the quantity that can be raised must be ascertained. Third, the appropriate mix of liabilities is selected by considering such issues as the firm's optimal capital structure and funding risks.

Identifying Funding Sources: Wholesale and Retail

Depository institutions and insurance companies have many funding sources. These are generally broken down into two primary types. *Retail funding sources* refer to the sale of liabilities in small denominations to consumers. Examples include demand and time deposit accounts and individual life policies. *Wholesale funding sources* include large dollar denominated liabilities sold primarily to institutions and very wealthy individuals. Wholesale funding sources are sometimes sold by third-party brokers.

Most institutions consider wholesale funding sources to be less dependable and more price sensitive or interest rate elastic than retail funding sources. Most wholesale sources are uninsured, causing investors to be very concerned about the institution's capital structure, profitability, and asset quality. Information that causes concern over the credit quality of the institution can quickly cause wholesale funding sources to dry up.

One exception to the general rule that wholesale funding sources carry higher funding risks than retail sources is the collateralized or asset-backed borrowing. Here the investor is secured by assets that normally provide more than adequate interest cash flow and collateral value to pay off interest and principal on the debt. Many firms with very weak credit ratings are able to issue asset-backed securities with investment-grade ratings.

The positive side of wholesale funding sources is that the firm can quickly attract funds in large quantities if it is willing to pay the marginal rate required of the wholesale market. A slightly higher rate paid in the wholesale market can usually attract funds in quantity. Moreover, the higher rate is paid only to new customers, whereas a higher rate paid to retail customers is also paid to existing customers, many of whom would likely roll over their deposits at a lower rate. It is necessary to identify the most important retail and wholesale funding sources for depositories and life companies.

Retail Funding Sources

Retail sources for depositories include virtually all liabilities attracted through branch offices. They include a variety of transaction-type accounts including demand deposits, money market demand accounts, negotiable order of withdrawal accounts, and debit-activated accounts. Retail savings and time deposits include savings and passbook accounts and small-denomination time accounts, such as certificates of deposit.

Insurance companies also have a variety of retail funding sources. These include retail consumer insurance programs that are sold through large sales forces using direct marketing, telemarketing, and direct mail. The most popular are whole life and single premium annuity policies.

Wholesale Funding Sources

Depository institutions have a variety of wholesale funding sources. Negotiable certificates of deposit, commercial paper, repurchase agreements, insured certificates of deposit sold by broker/dealers, collateralized deposits of government units, and federal funds are examples of wholesale sources.

Insurance companies also market liabilities in the wholesale markets. The primary liability they sell is the guaranteed investment contract (GIC). The GIC is an unsecured liability of the life company and is sold in large denominations primarily to pension funds and employee trusts. The GIC has many of the attributes of a certificate of deposit, except it is uninsured. Insurance companies also sell insurance policies to large corporations for group plans. These include lump sum purchases of annuities used to meet pension fund obligations.

Another major source of funds for depositories and finance companies is asset-backed securities. In the 1980s, the word *securitization* was coined. Securitization refers to the process of using loans and investments as collateral for a hybrid liability. During the last decade mortgages, both residential and commercial, mobile home loans, auto loans, corporate bonds, credit card receivables, leases, and trade receivables have been used as collateral for securities. This source of wholesale funds will be discussed more fully later in the chapter.

Table 23.1 provides a brief summary of the primary wholesale and retail funding sources of depositories, life companies, and finance companies.

Table 23.1

Primary Retail and Wholesale Funding Sources of Depositories, Life Companies, and Finance Companies

Type of Institution	Retail	Wholesale
Depositories	Demand deposits, NOW accounts, and money market demand accounts	Negotiable CDs, commercial paper, asset-based securities, brokered deposits
	Passbook and certificates of deposit	Collateralized borrowings such as repos and FHLB borrowings
		Guaranteed investment contracts
Insurance companies	Term, whole life, and annuities sold to individuals	Group insurance annuities sold to pension funds
Finance companies		Commercial paper, asset-backed securities, debentures

Costs of Alternative Depository Funding Sources

Determining the cost of each of the funding sources is not nearly as easy as it might appear at first glance. Each deposit source has its own unique set of cost factors. These costs vary from liability to liability and include such factors as deposit insurance premiums, opportunity costs associated with Federal Reserve Regulation D reserve requirements, servicing costs, commissions, compensating balances, and the cost of equity in which collateral is involved. The true marginal cost of each funding source can be computed only after each of the following cost factors are determined.

Deposit Insurance Cost

Depositories are required to pay insurance premiums to their respective deposit insurance corporations. For example, as a result of the Financial Institution Reform Recovery and Enforcement Act of 1989, the cost of deposit insurance has changed significantly. The cost of deposit insurance for commercial banks insured by the Bank Insurance Fund and thrifts insured by the Savings Association Insurance Fund in early 1992 was 23 basis points computed off of deposit balances.

Federal Reserve Regulation D Reserves

All insured depositories are now subject to holding reserves in noninterest earning accounts or vault cash at a Federal Reserve Bank for specified types of deposits. These reserve requirements were modified extensively in 1980 as a result of the passage by Congress of the Depository Institution Deregulation and Monetary Control Act. At that time, reserve requirements were also applied to thrift institutions. Table 23.2 shows the reserve requirements currently imposed.

The fact that depositories must hold reserves in noninterest bearing accounts or vault cash increases the true cost of these deposits. For example, a $100,000 demand deposit held by a large commercial bank would require a reserve of 10 percent. This means that the institution has use of 90 percent of the deposits raised. If the effective cost of processing these deposits is 3.85 percent, the reserve requirement would serve to increase the true cost to [(3.85%/.90) =] 4.27 percent, or roughly 42 basis points.

Servicing Costs

Each source of funds must be serviced. Since the servicing requirements are different for each source of funds, the firm must estimate the marginal servicing cost for each funding alternative. A 1985 Federal Reserve functional cost analysis indicated that the cost of servicing a savings account for one month ranged from $1.97 for small banks to $2.61 for medium-sized banks. The same study estimated the monthly cost of servicing a checking account to be $12.42 for small banks and $18.61 for medium-sized banks.

Table 23.2

**Regulation D Reserve Requirements
Effective February 18, 1992**

Type of Deposit	Reserve Requirement	Permissible Range Min.	Max.
Transaction deposits	3% < $41.1 million	3%	3%
	10% > $41.1 million	8	14
Nonpersonal time deposits maturing in less than 1/2 year	0	0	9
Nonpersonal time deposits maturing in over 1/2 year	0	0	9
Consumer savings deposits under $100,000	0		
Eurodollar deposits	0		

Source: Federal Reserve *Bulletin*.

Commissions Paid to a Distributor

Some wholesale funding sources, such as brokered insured deposits, necessitate paying the distributing broker/dealer a commission to sell the accounts. This commission is usually expressed as an additional interest cost.

Compensating Balances or Required Investments

Some types of borrowings require compensating balances or investments related to the size of the loan. A *compensating balance* is a percentage of the loan that remains on deposit at the lending institution as a condition for obtaining the loan. Institutions that borrow from the Federal Home Loan Bank, for example, are required to hold stock in a Federal Home Loan Bank up to 1 percent of the amount borrowed. Compensating balances are also a common feature of many business loans made by commercial banks. The compensating balance effectively increases the cost of the borrowing if the income earned on the compensating balance pays a lower interest rate than the borrowing rate.

Consider a loan that requires the borrower to maintain a compensating investment in a Federal Home Loan Bank equal to 1 percent of the loan balance. The investment pays a return equal to 5 percent below the cost of the loan. In this case, the effective rate, ER, of a loan made at a base rate, BR, of 9 percent would be equal to the base rate less the interest earned on the compensating balance, CBR, if any, times the amount of the compensating balance percentage, $CB\%$, all divided by 1.00 minus the compensating balance percentage. Equation 23.1 solves for ER as shown:

$$ER = [BR - [CB\% \times CBR]] / (1.00 - CB\%) \qquad [23.1]$$

where:

ER = effective rate

BR = base rate on loan

$CB\%$ = compensating balance as a percent of loan

CBR = interest rate paid on compensating balance

The example discussed previously is solved using the following equation:

$$ER = [9.00 - [.01 \times 5.00\%]] / (1.00 - .01)$$
$$[9.00\% - (.05\%)] / (1.00 - .01) = 9.04\%$$

In this case, the impact of the compensating balance is small. However, on many loans made by commercial banks to commercial customers there might be as high as a 10 percent compensating balance to be held in a noninterest-bearing account. If that were the case using a 9 percent loan, the effective cost would be $\{[((9.00\%) - (0))/.90] =\}$ 10.00%. Compensating balances result in firms having to borrow more than they need.

Cost of Equity for Collateralized Borrowing

The use of collateral to raise funds also entails a hidden cost. This is the cost of the equity that the institution must hold on the margin to have the collateral available. Say that the institution wants to use a government guaranteed mortgage-backed security as collateral behind a term reverse repurchase agreement. This would require a 3 percent equity holding under the risk-based reserve requirement.

Assuming the firm held 3 percent equity to support the investment in a mortgage security at a 25 percent pretax cost of capital, and the rest is financed at 7 percent, the weighted capital cost would be $[(.03) \times (.25\%) + (.97) \times (.07\%)] = 7.54\%$. Thus, the marginal cost of equity adds 54 basis points to the marginal cost of this borrowing alternative. This example, or course, assumes the firm has no excess capital. Management may decide to ignore the additional equity cost if it uses the collateral infrequently for borrowing purposes and has excess equity.

Chapter 23 Liability Management and Pricing 651

Determining the interest rate equivalent cost of each of these factors and adding them to the interest rate paid on the source of funds allows the firm to compare the costs of each funding source in a consistent manner. The result of this analysis is shown in Table 23.3, which shows the cost of alternative funding sources for a hypothetical commercial bank. This table also indicates the expected amount of funds that can be attracted at the rate specified.

Picking the Optimal Funding Mix: The Funding Alternatives Matrix

Once the alternative funding sources have been identified and the marginal cost of each determined, it is time to determine the optimal funding mix. This decision is made in conjunction with the determination of the optimal interest rate risk position of the firm and the extent to which the institution wants to use wholesale versus retail funding sources.

The result of this analysis is portrayed in the *funding alternatives matrix*. This matrix shows each alternative funding source, the quantity of funds that can be obtained, and the marginal cost of each. With the data from Table 23.3, it is possible to determine the lowest cost source of funds and the quantities of each that can be raised at each interest rate. Table 23.4 on page 652 shows the funding alternatives matrix. The table also

Table 23.3

Cost of Alternative Funding Sources
(dollars in millions)

Type of 6-Month Term Funding

Cost Factors	Retail CD < $100,000	Retail CD > $100,000	Collateralized CD	Brokered Insured CD
Base interest rate	7.23%	7.45%	7.45%	7.30%
Insurance premium	.21	.21	.21	.21
Brokerage fee				.60
Equity cost of holding collateral			.54	
Servicing cost	.55	.15	.07	.05
Federal Reserve Regulation D reserves			.15	
Total cost	7.99%	7.96%	8.27%	8.16%
Amount available at this rate	$2	$5	$10	$10

Table 23.4

Funding Alternatives Matrix
Costs and Quantities of Alternative Sources of Funds

	Rate and Quantity (millions of dollars)			
Source	$0–1	$1–3	$3–5	$5+
Retail CD < 100k	**7.99%**	**7.99%**	8.95%	9.05%
Retail CD > 100k	8.81	8.81	8.81	8.95
Collateralized CD	8.42	8.42	8.42	8.42
Brokered CD	8.16	8.16	**8.16**	**8.16**
Interest rate swap	9.05	9.05	9.05	9.05
Reverse repo (Mortgage-backed security)	8.65	8.65	8.65	8.60
Reverse repo (U.S. Treasury)	8.60	8.60	8.60	8.55
Term fed funds	9.10	9.10	9.10	9.20
Least cost	7.99	7.99	8.16	8.16
Treasury benchmark	7.60%	7.60%	7.60%	7.60%
Least cost source: spread over Treasury	.39	.39	.56	.56

shows the relationship of the cost of each funding source to the amount of funds that can be attracted at each specified interest rate.

With the funding alternatives matrix the asset and liability manager can make sound judgments about which of the alternative funding sources to utilize. This process is dynamic. Yield relationships among the various funding sources and their respective quantities change constantly. For a large institution with many sources of funds, maintaining a current funding alternatives matrix is a full-time activity.

The Marginal Cost of New Retail Deposits

One of the more difficult decisions faced by depositories concerns the pricing of retail deposits. A primary advantage of retail deposits is the fact that they are less interest elastic than wholesale. In order to profit from this alleged advantage, depositories frequently attempt to avoid paying as high an interest rate to existing customers as they do to attract new customers to the institution. In order to determine whether raising interest rates on retail deposit programs is cost effective, it is necessary to compute the *marginal cost of new funds*.

Consider a depository attempting to raise $10 million in additional funds. It can go to the negotiable CD market and pay the going rate. Alternatively, it can pay a higher rate in the retail market. However, in the retail market, the existing customers who have accounts maturing may be the major recipients of the higher rate paid, since they have accounts that will be automatically renewed at the higher rate.

In our example, the firm may end up paying a higher rate on $50 million of deposits to obtain only $10 million of new funds. This means that calculating the marginal cost of additional funds at the retail level requires making estimates of the amount of marginal new funds. The marginal new funds equals the dollar amount going into the higher rate account that is new to the institution and the amount that is renewed by current customers that would have been lost to competitors if the higher rate were not paid. In practice, these estimates are difficult to obtain and most firms must rely on their past experience as a guide.

The formula for calculating the marginal cost of new funds is shown by Equation 23.2.

$$MCNF = [(Rn \times \$New) + (Rn - Rnor) \times \$Roll)] / \$New \quad [23.2]$$

where:

$MCNF$ = marginal cost of new funds

Rn = proposed higher rate to attract new funds and increase market share

$Rnor$ = normal rate expected to maintain balances and market share

$\$New$ = new dollars attracted plus dollars rolled over by existing customers that were retained due to higher rate

$\$Roll$ = dollars rolled over by existing customers at the higher rate that would have been retained without paying the higher rate

DEMONSTRATION PROBLEM: Calculating Marginal Cost of New Funds

Situation: Honest Federal has been paying a rate, *Rnor*, of 7.50 percent on 18-month deposits. Since market conditions haven't changed, it feels it could continue to pay 7.50 percent and retain its existing market share. The liability manager has proposed a new rate of 7.75 percent, R_n, designed to attract new customers and increase market share. The savings department anticipates that $50 million will go into the higher rate account. Of that $50 million, $10 million will consist of new funds plus funds rolled over that would have left the institution if the higher rate had not been paid. The $40 million is estimated to be the amount rolled over into the new higher rate account that would otherwise have stayed with the firm at 7.50 percent, R_{nor}.

Data Input:

$MCNF$ = marginal cost of new funds

R_n = 7.75%

R_{nor} = 7.50%

$New = $10 million

$Roll = $40 million

Result:

$$\{(7.75\% \times \$10 \text{ million}) + [(7.75\% - 7.50\%) \times \$40 \text{ million}]\} / \$10 \text{ million} = 8.75\%.$$

This equation reveals that the cost of attracting the marginal new funds is 8.75 percent, or 1 percent higher than the old rate.

You might observe sometime that when depository institutions have a savings certificate promotion they will frequently promote a certificate with an unusual number of months to maturity, say, four months. They do this knowing that the most popular certificate maturities are three and six months. By offering a higher rate on a four-month account, the higher rate does not apply to accounts of existing customers, many of whom will automatically roll over their three- and six-month accounts.

Asset-Backed Financing

Asset-backed financing has become a major source of funding for financial institutions in the last decade. The growth in the use of asset-backed financing follows in the tracks of the successful issuance of asset mortgage-backed securities by GNMA, FHLMC, and FNMA. The growth in asset-backed financing continues to be rapid, with mortgage securities representing the largest share of this market. The primary types of collateral used in these securities include the following:

- Residential mortgages
- Multi-family mortgages
- Auto loans
- Credit card receivables
- Leases
- Other consumer loans
- Trade receivables
- Manufactured homes
- Corporate bonds

Reasons for Securitization

There are five primary reasons why financial institutions use securities and loans as collateral for asset-backed securities.

1. The ability to transfer interest rate risk
2. The ability to tap large volumes of funds in a single transaction
3. The ability to generate a larger volume of origination and servicing profits without commensurate growth in the asset portfolio
4. The ability of financial institutions with low credit ratings to borrow at the lower interest rates found on highly credit-rated securities
5. The rising cost of deposit liabilities due to increases in deposit insurance premiums

One of the most attractive uses of asset-backed securities is to transfer interest rate risk. This has become more important as the volatility of our financial markets has increased. Depositories do not have ready access to large sources of longer term liabilities because most deposits have short-term maturities. The asset-backed security represents an excellent way to finance longer term assets, such as mortgages and manufactured housing loans.

The use of the asset-backed security permits the borrowing of large volumes of funds in a single transaction. The typical asset-backed security is issued in a volume of $75 million or more. This is because the high fixed costs of underwriting and distribution must be spread over as large a quantity of borrowed funds as possible. The large size of asset-backed securities effectively denies this financing option for most small institutions.

The demand for asset-backed security financing has been matched by an increase in the supply of funds. The last several decades have witnessed a substantial institutionalization of savings through pension funds and mutual funds. These investors are attracted to asset-backed investments because they are standardized, rated, easy to service, and available in large amounts.

Asset-backed securities also allow the lender to maintain a large origination and servicing market presence without having to put all the loans originated in portfolio. As a result, firms with fairly small asset portfolios can operate large origination and servicing units. The best example of this is the mortgage banking business.

These securities allow financial firms that carry very low credit ratings to borrow using their collateral to obtain an investment-grade rating. Many financial institutions that carry a below investment-grade rating on their unsecured debt can borrow at investment-grade interest rates using asset-backed securities.

Depository institutions face rising costs of deposit liabilities due to rising deposit insurance premium costs and other factors. In some cases, asset-backed securities may be less expensive.

The relative cost of asset-backed financing has been reduced by the significant declines in transaction costs brought about by today's computer technologies. This has permitted a degree of financial sophistication in security design and information gathering and dissemination that was not possible several decades ago. Adding to the cost savings of these securities was the 1982 Securities and Exchange Commission's *shelf registration Rule 412*. This permits a firm to obtain permission to issue one or more similar securities under a shelf registration within a specified period of time and up to a specified amount. Shelf registration permits lower issuing costs and greater flexibility for issuers.

Types of Asset-Backed Securities

Asset-backed securities come in four primary structures. These include pass-through securities, asset-backed bonds, pay-through securities, and real estate mortgage investment conduits (REMICs). The main features of these four structures are shown in Exhibit 23.1.

Asset-Backed Collateral Attributes

One of the most important characteristics of the asset-backed bond is the type of collateral that is used. The type of collateral has a significant impact on the cost and ease of issuing these securities. The primary characteristics of the collateral that influence the cost of the securitization process are the following:

1. The complexity of the credit characteristics of the collateral
2. The predictability of the collateral's cash flow
3. The maturity of the collateral
4. The delinquency and default rate on the collateral
5. The degree of diversification of credit risk relating to the number of obligators
6. The servicing experience and reputation of the servicing organization
7. The liquidation value of the collateral

Exhibit 23.1

Primary Attributes of Asset-Backed Securities

Type of Asset-Backed Structure	Attributes of Security
Pass-Through	Security represents a pro-rata share of the assets in the pool.
	Assets are not shown on the originator's balance sheet, since they are treated as a sale of assets.
	Principal and interest payments are passed through to investors on a schedule similar to the assets.
Asset-Backed Bond	Security is a debt obligation.
	Assets remain on originator's balance sheet.
	Principal and interest payments are passed through to investors on a schedule that may differ from the asset.
Pay-Through	Security is a debt obligation.
	Assets remain on the originator's balance sheet.
	Payment of principal and interest are passed through to investors on a schedule that may differ from the asset.
Real Estate Mortgage Investment Conduit (REMIC)	Payment of principal and interest are passed through to one or more regular classes of securities and one residual class.
	Assets are transferred to the REMIC in a nontaxable transfer.
	Allows for creation of CMO type of multisecurity structure without having debt on the balance sheet.

It is clear from this list that most loans only score well with respect to a few of these characteristics. Mortgages, for example, which comprise the collateral in the largest volume of securities, do not score well on the criteria relating to predictability of cash flows and maturity. However, they score well on most of the other criteria. Despite these many criteria, investment bankers, issuers, and credit rating organizations have worked to find ways to use a wide variety of loans as collateral for these bonds.

Liability Management for Life Insurance Companies

Life insurance companies can be thought of as selling two primary products. The first is pure life insurance. The second is liabilities that provide retail and institutional investors investments that offer a variety of credit, return, and maturity options. One advantage of these investments is that the income they earn is deferred for federal and state income tax purposes. This advantage is heavily exploited in the marketing of certain types of life insurance policies.

The separation of the pure insurance cost component from the investment component is not always straightforward. First, many life policies have fixed premiums, which makes it difficult to determine what portion of a premium is being used to purchase insurance coverage and what portion is used to purchase the investment. Second, a number of life insurance companies are mutual companies that return a portion of the premium to the policyholder at the end of the policy year in the form of a dividend. Because this return of premium is not contractual, it is impossible for the policyholder to know what the true cost of the policy is going to be. The policyholder is forced to make assumptions about the size of the dividend, if any.

In recent years, life insurance companies have faced greater competition. Increasingly, term insurance has been sold as a cost-effective investment strategy when combined with sales of mutual fund shares and other investments. These factors have made it more difficult for life companies to attract liabilities. As a result, they have been forced to offer higher yielding annuities and GICs.

Liability Costs at Life Insurance Companies

Like the depository institution, the life insurance company has many different options to sell liabilities. Each of these options has different cost parameters that must be estimated by management. The most important parameters include the guaranteed rate of return on the liability, the cost of marketing and originating the liability, and the cost of servicing.

A simple example will serve to demonstrate the methodology. One of the most competitive policies marketed by life insurance companies in recent years is the single-premium annuity. This policy provides for a guaranteed interest return to the policyholder for a specified period of time, say one to three years. After the guarantee period, the rate is determined by whatever rate the insurance company feels it needs to pay to retain the policy.

These policies are generally marketed by a direct sales force. The commission on these policies might be as high as 8 percent of the principal invested by the policyholder. The insurance company also must service the policy and this is also a costly activity.

Table 23.5 provides a hypothetical example of how an insurance company might estimate the cost of raising funds from this type of policy, assuming it stays on the insurance company's books from one to seven years. A policy like this typically has an early redemption (put) feature so that the policyholder can redeem the policy in the early years of the policy's life, but at a discount from the stated policy value. The yield, y, for these funds is calculated using Equation 23.3:

$$PP = COM + [[PP(1+r)^n](1-d)]/(1+y)^n \qquad [23.3]$$

where:

PP = initial investment in policy and policy principal

COM = commission paid to sales person and issuance costs

n = number of periods policy is outstanding

r = rate of interest paid on policy

y = interest yield on policy to insurance company including payment of commissions

d = discount percentage at redemption

Consider a $25,000 policy. Assume that the redemption discount, d, ranges from 5 percent at the end of year 1 to 0 percent at the end of year 5. Assume also that the insurance company pays a premium of .25 percent over the seven-year Treasury bond rate, r, of 7 percent. In this example, r does not change from year to year. From these data, the yield for the number of years the policy is assumed to be outstanding is computed. A 30 basis point per annum cost for servicing has also been incorporated. The company pays a commission of 8 percent, or $2,000, to the sales person. The early redemption rate, d, at the end of year 3 is 3 percent. The cost of these funds to the life company is shown by solving the following equation:

$$\$25{,}000 = \$2{,}000 + [[\$25{,}000(1+.07)^3 \times (1.00-.03)]/(1+y)^3]$$

$$\$25{,}000 = \$2{,}000 + [\$30{,}626 \times (.97)]/(1+y)^3$$

$$y = 8.90\%$$

The 8.90 percent is the number shown on the three-year row in column 5 of Table 23.5. It represents the cost of the funds to the insurance company for three years without factoring the cost of servicing or the cost of providing pure insurance coverage. The cost of servicing is added in column 6 of the table.

The table shows the potentially high cost of these funds to the insurance company as a result of the large marketing costs and incurred at the time of sale and servicing expenses.

Another way life insurance companies raise funds is through the sale of GICs. GICs provide a fixed rate of return, and the cost to the life insurance

Table 23.5

Estimated Cost of Single-Premium Annuity Over Seven-Year Average Term

Amount of principal invested in the policy	$25,000
Commission paid @ 8%	2,000
Available for investment	23,000
Rate paid on annuity	7.00%

End of Policy Year (1)	Redemption Discount % (2)	Policy Value (3)	Redemption Value (4)	Cost to Insurance Company (5)	Cost with Servicing Added @ 30 bp (6)
1	5%	$26,750	$25,413	10.49%	10.79%
2	4	28,623	27,478	9.30	9.60
3	3	30,626	29,707	8.90	9.20
4	2	32,770	32,115	8.70	9.00
5	1	35,064	34,713	8.58	8.88
6	0	37,518	37,518	8.50	8.80
7	0	40,145	40,145	8.28	8.58

company depends largely on the credit quality of the life company selling the GIC. The yields offered by life insurance companies on GIC contracts are higher than comparable maturity Treasury security yields. The yields typically are 15 to 25 basis points higher for short-term Treasuries and 65 to 75 basis points higher for Treasuries of five-year maturities.

GICs have been used by pension funds to provide fixed-rate investments to meet funding requirements. The GIC's advantage to the investor is its higher rate of return as compared to Treasury securities. Another GIC advantage is that the investor can purchase the GIC in a maturity to meet its specific needs. The GIC has also been used as an investment for defined contribution retirement accounts, such as employee 401k programs. These programs allow employees to make contributions to investments in a trust account in before-tax dollars. The employer may also make contributions to the employee's account. The GIC is used to provide fixed-return investment options for the employee in the program.

The GIC came under increased scrutiny in the early 1990s when the First Executive Life Company of California, Mutual Benefit Life Company of New Jersey, and the First Capital Life Company of California ran into financial difficulties and were forced to cease operations for a period of time.

> **DEMONSTRATION PROBLEM:** Cost of Single Premium Annuity
>
> **Situation:** The life company you work for will issue a new single-premium annuity policy. It will pay 8.50 percent for the first two years on a simple interest basis. The insurance policy can be redeemed at 96 percent of its principal and accrued interest value in two years.
>
> The sales person is paid a 6 percent commission, and it costs 25 basis points per year to service the policy. Your supervisor would like to know the cost of funds received in this manner, disregarding the cost of insurance coverage provided, if the policy is redeemed in two years. This problem should be worked out for a $10,000 principal value policy.
>
> **Result:**
> $$\$10,000 = (.06 \times \$10,000) + \{[\$10,000(1+.085)]^2(.96)\}/(1+y)^2$$
> $$= \$600 + [(\$11,772.23)(.96)]/(1+y)^2$$
> $$(1+y)^2 = \$11,301.36/\$9,400.00$$
> $$y = [\$11,301.36/\$9,400]^{.5} - 1.0 = 9.65\%$$
> $$\text{Total Cost} = y + \text{Servicing Cost} = 9.65\% + .25\% = 9.90\%$$

The holders of the GIC contracts were unsecured creditors of these firms. Their unsecured position caused them to redeem their GICs and to seek out additional financial information about the safety and soundness of the insurance companies offering GICs.

The insurance companies that have issued GICs have also had to become more sophisticated in their interest rate risk management policies. Because the GIC is a fixed-return and fixed-term liability, the insurance company has to be sure it can find investments that provide a long-term fixed-rate return. In the early 1980s, a number of life companies issued a high volume of GIC contracts when interest rates were very high. When interest rates fell in the mid-1980s, these life companies found that they did not have sufficient high-yielding noncallable assets to cover the high interest costs of these GIC contracts. This resulted in a sharp squeeze on the interest margins for these firms.

Summary

Liability management involves the selection and pricing of the firm's liabilities. Depository and insurance institutions have the most complex liability management decisions because they issue a wide variety of liability products.

The pricing of liabilities is difficult because there are many factors that influence the true cost of liabilities. Each of these has to be taken into account. The result of a comprehensive liability management program is the development of a schedule that identifies the firm's lowest cost liabilities and the volumes that are available.

Funding sources are categorized as either retail or wholesale. **Retail funding sources** are liabilities that are sold to individuals. These include time and savings deposits, transactions accounts, and life insurance policies. Retail funding sources are thought to be less price sensitive, less elastic, than wholesale funding sources. **Wholesale funding sources** involve large sales of liabilities sold primarily to institutional clients. Wholesale sources include negotiable CDs, GICs, commercial paper, and repurchase agreements.

Liability cost includes such factors as deposit insurance cost, opportunity cost of Federal Reserve Regulation D reserves, servicing costs, commissions, compensating balances, and the cost of equity for collateralized borrowings. This is in addition to the cost of interest paid.

Compensating balances increase the effective cost of borrowing. The following equation allows the effective interest rate, ER, to be calculated when there is a compensating balance required.

$$ER = [BR - [CB\% \times CBR]] / (1.00 - CB\%)$$

where:

$$ER = \text{effective rate}$$

$$BR = \text{base rate on loan}$$

$$CB\% = \text{compensating balance as a percent of loan}$$

$$CBR = \text{interest rate paid on compensating balance}$$

The **funding alternatives matrix** serves to identify all sources of funds available to the institution, the full cost of issuing these liabilities, and the volume of funds that can be obtained at the costs specified. From this matrix, the firm can make intelligent choices about which liabilities to issue.

Asset-backed securities are increasingly used by financial intermediaries to raise funds. The advantages of asset-backed securities include transferring interest rate risk, borrowing in large volume, originating and servicing a large volume of loans without balance sheet growth, borrowing at investment-grade interest rates, and avoiding rising cost of retail funds. The primary types of asset-backed bonds include pass-through, asset-backed bonds, pay-through bonds, and REMICs. A wide variety of different loans and securities can be used as collateral in asset-backed financings.

Questions

Chapter 23

1. Explain what is meant by wholesale and retail funding sources. Give several examples of each.
2. Why are wholesale funding sources sometimes considered to be more risky than retail funding sources?
3. Discuss and describe the factors that should be considered in determining the cost of alternative funding sources.
4. What is the function of the funding alternatives matrix? Explain how it would be used.
5. What is asset-based financing? Give several examples. What are the reasons for the substantial growth in asset-based financing?
6. What is the primary difference between a pass-through and pay-through mortgage-backed bond?
7. What advantage does a REMIC have over a collateralized mortgage obligation?
8. Why is the cost of funds raised in annuity policies generally quite high if the policy is redeemed in early years?
9. How would you describe the overall objectives of liability management?
10. Do larger financial intermediaries tend to have more liability alternatives than smaller financial firms? If so, why?
11. What is a guaranteed investment contract? What has happened in this market as a result of the failure of several large insurance companies in the early 1990s?

Problems

Problem 23-1 Wholesale versus Retail Borrowing

A savings and loan association has a need for $35 million in new funds. It can issue brokered insured deposits at 8.95 percent plus 15 basis points commission, or it can attract additional deposits through its retail branches. The thrift figures that it can attract the $35 million by raising its CD rate from 7.65 percent to 7.95 percent. However, raising the rate will result in $80 million in deposits that will automatically rollover from the lower rate into the higher rate. These deposits have stayed with the institution despite the higher rate.

1. What is the marginal cost of each funding alternative?
2. Which alternative should the thrift choose?

Problem 23-2 Compensating Balance Yield Impact

You are about to borrow from the Federal Home Loan Bank. They will lend you $10 million at a rate of 6.40 percent. However, they expect you to purchase stock in the Federal Home Loan Bank that is fully redeemable at par when the loan matures. The stock will pay a dividend of 2 percent. You must buy stock equal to 4 percent of the loan balance. How does the stock purchase affect the cost of the loan?

Problem 23-3   Cost of Equity in Collateralized Borrowing
You are preparing a short-term collateralized borrowing for which you will pledge your portfolio of GNMA securities.

1. You are required to hold 3 percent equity against the collateral. Your firm's pretax cost of equity is 21.5 percent. What is the weighted marginal cost of equity for the collateral in basis points?
2. If the cost of the collateralized borrowing is 6.50 percent plus servicing and maintenance costs of 25 basis points, what is the marginal cost of the collateralized borrowing?

Problem 23-4   Cost of Annuity Funds
Banner Life will offer a single premium annuity. It pays 6.75 percent guaranteed for three years. The commission is 7 percent. The policy can be redeemed at 96 percent of principal and accrued interest value at any time. The company can sell guaranteed investment contracts at 7.10 percent. Ignoring the cost of insurance, if the annuity is redeemed in three years, will the cost of these funds be more or less than the GIC?

Foreign Exchange, Exchange Rates, and Managing Currency Risk

chapter **24**

Changes in exchange rates represent one of the most serious risks that differentiate international from domestic financial transactions. Other problems affecting international transactions include language, different legal structures, and institutional structures. The sharp growth in trade, together with the technological improvements in communication, has brought about an integration of financial markets worldwide. Today, virtually all companies have to consider the potential of international markets for both the sale and production of their goods and services and the impact of foreign competition.

This chapter provides a framework for understanding the foreign exchange system, the reasons why foreign exchange is a source of risk, and the tools for managing these risks. This is accomplished in three sections. First, foreign exchange and the changes in the foreign exchange markets since World War II are discussed. Second, the topic of exchange rates, what they are and how they are determined, is introduced. Finally, the risk associated with changes in exchange rates and the methods for managing that risk are covered.

Changing Structure of Foreign Exchange Markets: Bretton Woods to Floating Rates

This section covers the post–World War II international system for foreign exchange arrangements. This review begins with the signing of the Bretton Woods agreement in 1944 and ends with a discussion of our current floating rate system.

Bretton Woods

The discussion of foreign exchange begins in 1944. In this war environment, a number of forward-looking leaders from the United States and other developed countries began to concern themselves with the postwar environment. Many felt that both World War I and World War II were, in part, the result of a poorly functioning system of international trade and economic opportunity. The United States, in particular, pushed for expanded world trading opportunities.

Out of this concern came the *Bretton Woods Agreement* in 1944. This agreement, which represented primarily the negotiations of the United States and United Kingdom, was signed by 44 countries. The agreement set up a system of international foreign exchange that remained in place until the early 1970s. The following are the main points of the Bretton Woods Agreement:

- Established the U.S. dollar and British pound as the world's two reserve currencies. International settlements could be made in these currencies.
- Established the *International Monetary Fund (IMF)* as an organization to lend foreign exchange to countries that needed it.
- Established a U.S. agreement to buy and sell gold at $35 per ounce.
- Required member countries to establish a value for their currency in relation to the dollar and to agree to maintain that par value relationship.
- Required that the par values for each country's respective currency could only be changed with the acceptance of the IMF and only when a serious disequilibrium occurred. A disequilibrium was said to occur when the relationship of a country's par value was such that it resulted in a serious oversupply or shortage of a currency.
- Required that currencies of the member countries be convertible, which means that each country agreed to allow their currency to be converted into currencies of other member countries.

The establishment of the appropriate initial par value exchange rate was an important action. If a central bank set an exchange rate for its currency that was too high in relationship to the reserve currency, then the central bank would find that it would tend to lose foreign exchange. Consider the following example. If the equilibrium value of the Italian lira is 250L = $1.00 and the Italian authorities establish a value of 150L = $1.00, then the tendency will be for Italians to convert their lira into dollars and buy U.S. goods and services because they will be artificially cheaper than Italian goods and services. The result will be that the Italian monetary authorities will be constantly converting lira into dollars, until they run out of dollars. At that point, they will have to revalue or borrow more dollars to meet the demand.

The opposite will also occur. If the exchange rate is established at too low a level, say 350L = $1.00, the result will be that the demand for Italian goods and services will increase and the Italian monetary authorities will accumulate an excess supply of dollars.

Because of this phenomenon, the initial establishment of the exchange rates for a system as inflexible as Bretton Woods was very important. Setting exchange rates too high or too low would result in central bankers building up unwanted inventories of foreign currencies or having inadequate supplies to meet demand. Despite this potential problem, the Bretton Woods system was successful in bringing confidence to the foreign exchange markets and encouraging world trade. This was vitally important as Europe and Japan rebuilt after World War II. Adding to the encouragement in support of free trade was the U.S. push to create the 1947 General Agreement on Trade and Tariffs (GATT). This stipulated that each signing country agreed not to provide special treatment for one trading partner over another.

The Breakdown of Bretton Woods

Initially, the system under Bretton Woods worked quite well. From 1945 to 1959, the demand for dollars was strong in Europe, as these countries purchased U.S. goods to rebuild. By 1960, however, the European countries began to develop economically and the first evidence that the U.S. dollar might be overvalued began to appear. The evidence of this was that European central banks began to accumulate large reserves of dollars. Indeed, by the early 1960s, the dollar reserves held around the world exceeded the value of the U.S. gold stock valued at $35 per ounce.

This massive accumulation of dollars led the United States to stem the flow of dollars. In 1963, the Interest Equalization Tax was established. This was designed to decrease the demand of foreign borrowers who, when needing dollars, would issue dollar denominated securities in the United States. The Interest Equalization Tax would effectively increase the cost of those borrowings and reduce the demand. This action, plus several other events, led to a major innovation in international finance, the creation of the Eurodollar market. The Eurodollar market represented the first case in which banks of one country, namely European and British banks, took deposits in a foreign currency, namely U.S. dollars, and relent them. The large supply of dollar reserves held in Europe and the sanctions in the United States designed to arrest the flow of dollars out of the United States made the creation of the Eurodollar market a necessity.

The sharp increase in dollars held in Europe had other impacts as well. The French began to agitate about the need for a more stable exchange reserve. They promoted gold as the only sensible reserve asset and accumulated considerable gold rather than hold dollars. The result was that by 1968, the United States had to establish a two-tiered gold market. This provided for a private market for gold at one price and an official market at another price for country-to-country international settlements.

This change was short-lived. The sharp inflation registered in the United States during the late 1960s combined with the growth in the economies of Europe, the United Kingdom, and Japan resulted in the continued accumulation of dollars by central banks outside the United States. Germany and Japan, in particular, found it necessary to support the dollar by selling their currencies to meet the growing demand.

By 1971, the Smithsonian Agreement was developed. This agreement was a stopgap measure that modestly realigned currencies and increased the value of gold to $38 an ounce. Despite these efforts, during the 1973 to 1974 period, the system of fixed exchange rates fell apart. The era of *floating exchange rates* began. Under this sytem, supply and demand for various currencies would ultimately determine the value of one currency in relation to another.

Floating Exchange Rates to the Present

The system of floating exchange rates, begun in 1973, was not accomplished without considerable effort and concern. Nor is the system a truly floating system. Central banks will, from time to time, attempt to support the levels of their currency by selling foreign exchange to meet demand, as opposed to allowing their currency to fall in value relative to another.

Central bank intervention has caused some observers to call the floating system a managed or *dirty float*. In 1978, for example, the Carter administration pursued a policy of massive intervention to support the level of the dollar. Intervention on this scale has not occurred in the Reagan and Bush administrations, and as a result, the exchange rate system has been closer to a true floating system in recent years.

Another reason why the floating exchange rate is not a pure system is because most countries of lesser economic development do not float their currencies. Instead, they have established fixed exchange rates in relation to some other country's currency or in relation to some other index. Countries that have significant trading activities or political relationships with a particular country, for example, are likely to establish a fixed exchange rate with that country. A number of countries fix the value of their currency to the U.S. dollar and French franc, for example. Other countries fix the value of their currency to a basket of other currencies, a set of economic indicators, or they perform a managed float.

The system of floating exchange rates has prevailed despite major changes in foreign trade and international monetary affairs. The following recent events have put significant pressure on the floating exchange rate system:

1. The large and persistent deficit in the U.S. balance of trade
2. The occurrence of two massive cartel-induced increases in oil prices in 1973 to 1974 and in 1979
3. A major international debt crisis in developing countries
4. A change in the balance of trade that has made Japan the world's largest trading nation and creditor

Nevertheless, the system has shown remarkable durability. Because the U.S. currency does float in relation to other major currencies, it is important to investigate the nature of foreign exchange.

Foreign Exchange Markets, Trading, and Exchange Rates

This section explores the basics of foreign exchange. Which economic units have a need for foreign exchange? Much of the following discussion involves foreign exchange markets and trading and the concept of the foreign exchange rate. The discussion also covers both cash and forward foreign exchange markets, which draws on information from Chapter 6 involving forward and cash markets in domestic financial claims.

Who Uses Foreign Exchange?

Foreign exchange is simply the supply and demand for another country's currency. The exchange depends on several of the following economic activities:

Exporters and Importers: These firms supply goods to foreign buyers. In return, they either receive foreign currency directly, or they are paid in their domestic currency, which has been purchased by the overseas importer with a foreign currency. For example, U.S. exporters are associated with the supply of foreign currency into the United States, while U.S. importers are associated with the demand for foreign currency by the United States.

Foreign Investors: Foreign investors who invest in a foreign country's assets supply foreign currency to the country in which they are investing. A foreign investor in a U.S.-owned hotel supplies foreign currency that is subsequently converted into U.S. dollars. The Japanese, for example, have used a large portion of their balance of trade surpluses of foreign currencies to make major investments in the U.S. financial and real asset markets.

Speculators: A speculator or trader is regarded as an economic unit who operates in the foreign exchange markets so as to make a profit from the activity of buying and selling foreign exchange.

Tourists: Tourists are a type of importer of another country's goods and services. They are a major source of foreign exchange to a number of countries. Some countries earn most of their foreign exchange from tourism.

Foreign Exchange Trading

Foreign exchange trading has become a significant activity in the last ten years. Foreign exchange trading in the late 1980s ran as high as $400 billion per day. There is no organized exchange in foreign exchange. Rather, like the market for Treasury securities, the foreign exchange market is a dealer-to-dealer market. It is primarily made up of large international commercial banks and international investment banking firms. The primary currencies involved in foreign exchange trading are the German mark, Japanese yen, British pound, Swiss franc, and Canadian and U.S. dollars. Trading in the spot market is carried out between institutions with a two day settlement period.

Commercial banks active in foreign exchange trading also speculate on changes in exchange rates by taking positions on foreign bonds or by borrowing foreign currencies. A speculator will hold foreign denominated securities if they believe the value of the foreign currency will rise above its interest rate parity forward value. Alternatively, the bank could borrow foreign currencies from another bank to invest in U.S. securities in hopes that dollars will rise in value above their interest rate parity forward value. Remember, the interest rate parity forward value is the forward price of a currency that eliminates an arbitrage profit opportunity.

Foreign Exchange Rates

The most important relationship in foreign exchange trading is the *exchange rate*. The exchange rate is a price of foreign currencies measured in domestic prices. For an American, the exchange rate for the British pound would be expressed as $1.75 per pound. This is also known as the *American term*. The exchange rate could be expressed as the *European term* and would become the amount of a foreign country's currency needed to purchase one dollar, say, .5714 pounds equals $1.00.

It is important to note that the European term exchange rate is simply the reciprocal of the American term. For example, the Belgian franc was

Chapter 24 Foreign Exchange, Exchange Rates, and Managing Currency Risk 671

worth $.02773 on Friday June 7, 1991, as quoted on the American term. The European term was quoted at 36.06 Belgian francs per $1.00. Equation 24.1 shows the reciprocal relationship between the two terms.

$$\$.02773/\text{Belgian franc} = 1 / [36.06 \text{ Belgian francs}/ \$1.00]$$

$$\text{American term} = 1 / \text{European term} \qquad [24.1]$$

Table 24.1 shows the European term exchange rates for the U.S. dollar versus several major currencies over the last few years.

A currency is said to be appreciating in value if its price rises in relation to the domestic currency. In the table, the currencies of all the countries shown, except for Canada and Japan, depreciated in value relative to the U.S. dollar between 1987 and 1989. That is, the price of one U.S. dollar rose as measured in terms of the foreign currency. Table 24.1 shows that the cost of one dollar measured in terms of the Japanese yen dropped from 144.6 yen/$ in 1987 to 128.17 yen/$ in 1988. The yen appreciated in value. Several currencies that have experienced very pronounced changes in value between 1987 and 1988 are shown below.

Change in foreign exchange rates, ER_t: $[(ER_{1987} - ER_{1988})/(ER_{1987})]$

Canadian $[(1.3259 - 1.2306)/(1.3259)] = + 7.1876\%$

Japan $[(144.6 - 128.17)/(144.6)] = + 11.362\%$

United Kingdom $[(.6098 - .5614)/(.6098)] = + 7.9370\%$

Table 24.1

European Term Exchange Rates
Annual Average 1987–1989
(foreign exchange units per U.S. dollar)

Country	1987	1988	1989
Canada	1.3259	1.2306	1.1842
France	6.0122	5.9595	6.3802
Germany	1.7981	1.7570	1.8808
Japan	144.6	128.17	138.07
Switzerland	1.4918	1.4643	1.6369
United Kingdom	0.6098	0.5614	0.6109

Source: Federal Reserve *Bulletin*. February 1990.

Forward Foreign Exchange Market and Interest Rate Parity

There is a very active forward market in foreign exchange. This market allows users of foreign exchange to purchase or sell it for delivery in the future. The price of a currency in the forward market can be above or below the current or spot price. A foreign currency is said to be selling at a discount in the forward market if a dollar purchases more units of the foreign currency for forward delivery than its does for spot delivery. For example, if the dollar purchases 1.50 DM in the spot market and 1.51 DM in the 90-day forward market, the German mark is said to be selling at a discount in the forward market. If the German mark sold for 1.49 DM = $1 for forward delivery compared to 1.50 DM = $1 in the spot market, then it is said to be selling at a premium in the forward market. Table 24.2 shows the spot and forward exchange rates for several major currencies as they appear in the press.

Table 24.2

Reading the Financial Page

Spot and Forward Foreign Exchange Rates (typical listing)

	American $ per Foreign Currency Unit		European Foreign Currency Unit per $	
Country	Tuesday	Monday	Tuesday	Monday
Britain (pound)	1.7910	1.8160	.5583	.5507
30-day forward	1.7810	1.8059	.5615	.5537
90-day forward	1.7623	1.7868	.5674	.5597
180-day forward	1.7357	1.7602	.5761	.5681
Canada (dollar)	.8666	.8711	1.1540	1.1480
30-day forward	.8642	.8687	1.1572	1.1512
90-day forward	.8601	.8645	1.1627	1.1567
180-day forward	.8546	.8590	1.1701	1.1642
France (franc)	.18519	.18771	5.4000	5.3275
30-day forward	.18425	.18677	5.4275	5.3543
90-day forward	.18254	.18501	5.4783	5.4050
180-day forward	.18017	.18250	5.5503	5.4795
Germany (mark)	.6321	.6410	1.5820	1.5600
30-day forward	.6292	.6381	1.5892	1.5671
90-day forward	.6238	.6327	1.6032	1.5806

Chapter 24 Foreign Exchange, Exchange Rates, and Managing Currency Risk

180-day forward	.6161	.6248	1.6232	1.6005
SDR	1.41232	1.42828	.70805	.70014
ECU	1.30578	1.33538	.76583	.74885

This table shows the American and European term exchange rates based on trading among the largest U.S. foreign exchange dealers. The American term represents the cost of one unit of the foreign exchange priced in dollars. The European term is the price in foreign currency of one U.S. dollar. The table represents the exchange rates for transactions typically over $1 million. The cost to an international traveler would be considerably different, due to the higher transaction costs and lower volume represented by an individual transaction.

The table also shows the forward rates of exchange. These are the rates for forward delivery of the foreign exchange in question. In the table, the 180-day forward American term exchange rate for German marks on Tuesday was U.S. $.6161/DM. The table also shows the exchange rates for the Special Drawing Rights (SDR) and European Currency Unit (ECU). The SDR is an international reserve currency used for exchange settlements between countries. The SDR is a weighted average of the values of a number of major currencies. The ECU is similar to the SDR, except that it is comprised of a basket of currencies representing the European Economic Community. It is the forerunner of the unified Common Market currency that could be implemented in 1999.

The reason that currencies sell at different exchange rates in the spot and forward markets relates to the level of interest rates domestically and in the country of the foreign currency in question. *Interest rate parity* is an arbitrage pricing theory that explains the relationship between spot and forward prices of foreign exchange.

To understand interest rate parity, it is necessary to know the spot price of foreign exchange, ER_s, the interest rates for specific maturity deposits in the foreign currency, r_f, and the domestic currency, r_d, and the period over which the forward contract is drawn, t. Assume that r_f and r_d are periodic interest rates for the period of time t. Also assume, for simplicity, that foreign currency can be bought and sold at a bid and ask price that is the same. Arbitrage interest rate parity works in the following way:

A trader borrows dollars in the U.S. at an interest rate of r_d. The trader then turns around and purchases a foreign currency at a spot exchange rate (ER_s) or say, at a price of $.5 = 1.00$ DM. The trader then sells the DM and any interest earned in the forward cash market for delivery at the end of period t. During period t, the currency is invested in German deposits at an interest rate of r_f. The amount of German marks sold forward is 2.0 DM $\times$ (1 + r_f) per dollar exchanged for marks.

Two things about this transaction are known. First, the amount of borrowed dollars to be repaid is known. This will be $1.00 \times (1 + r_d)$ per dollar borrowed. Next, the amount of DM that will be sold at the end of period t to meet the forward sale of DM can also be calculated. It is 2.0 DM $\times (1 + r_f)$ per dollar converted into DM.

The effect of interest rate parity in action is to ensure that a risk-free or pure arbitrage profit cannot take place. Interest rate parity will ensure that the forward market exchange rate, ER_f, will be set at a value that would preclude an arbitrage profit. Consider the following example and assume the initial conditions:

Spot exchange rate ER_s is $.5 = 1$ DM (domestic price of foreign currency)

Domestic periodic interest rate is $r_d = .04$ for six months

German periodic interest rate is $r_f = .02$ for six months

Time period $t =$ six months

Under interest rate parity, the forward exchange rate will be Equation 24.2. This condition will hold to eliminate any possibility for an arbitrage profit.

Forward six-month exchange rate: $ER_6 = ER_s [(1 + r_d)/(1 + r_f)]$ [24.2]

In the example, the interest rate parity can be used to determine the expected foreign exchange price of German marks in six months. This is shown in the following calculation:

$$ER_6 = \$.5/\text{DM} \times [(1.04)/(1.02)] = \$.5098/\text{DM}$$

In the example, it would not pay to borrow in the United States at a higher interest rate than one can earn on the foreign investment unless the forward price of the foreign currency is higher than the spot price. As shown, the forward price of DM, $.5098 = 1.00$ DM, must be higher than the spot price of $.5 = 1$ DM, as measured by the American term. But, at $.5098 = 1$ DM, no profit can be made. If the forward price of the DM were higher than $.5098 / $ DM, however, the trader would continue to sell dollars for DM and buy DM bonds and sell the principal and interest to be received on these bond investments in the forward $/DM market. If the forward exchange rate for DM were below the interest parity level of $.5098 / DM, then it would pay to convert DM into dollars, invest in dollar securities, and sell dollars in the forward dollar market for DM.

These examples are overly simplistic. It is not possible to borrow and invest at the interest rates implied in the interest rate parity theory. Traders must use actual, not hypothetical, interest rates to set foreign exchange rates. The interest rates they generally use are the rates on eurocurrency deposits. Using these rates, the interest parity condition is usually a very close approximation of the relationship between spot and forward foreign exchange rates. The rates used by foreign exchange dealers will also differ from the interest rates that a private company or individual might pay to a borrower or earn on investments. As a result, the interest parity condition will differ for a private entity having a different set of borrowing and investing alternatives. Moreover, our example assumes no difference between the bid and ask prices for currencies or other transaction costs. Consequently the equation would need to be adjusted to conform to these realities.

Why Exchange Rates Change

Since the breakdown of Bretton Woods, there have been significant changes in exchange rates for many of the major developed countries. These changes add an element of risk to transactions that involve future settlements of purchases and sales of goods and services or investments in foreign economies.

Since 1973, many theories have been offered to explain changes in exchange rates. Most of these theories have been subjected to empirical analysis as well. Unfortunately, no theory, as yet, seems to explain the volatility that has been evident in the market.

The simplest place to begin an investigation of exchange rate movements is to review the concept of *purchasing power parity (PPP)*. If we think of currencies as representing purchasing power over a certain amount of a particular country's goods and services, then the exchange rate should represent the relationship of the cost of goods and services in one country versus that of another. This is manifested in the PPP concept of the law of one price. The *law of one price* simply states that a commodity should cost the same in two countries, adjusted by the exchange rate between the currencies of the countries and costs of transportation and importing.

Consider the following example. If an ounce of gold costs $300 in New York and 171.43 pounds in the United Kingdom, then the spot exchange rate using the American term must be as shown in Equation 24.3 if the law of one price holds:

$$\$300 = 171.43 \text{ pounds} \times ER_s$$
$$ER_s = \$300/171.43 \text{ pounds} = \$1.75/\text{pound} \qquad [24.3]$$

There are several simplifying assumptions built into the law of one price that must be met for it to strictly hold. These include the following:

1. There are no transaction costs. That is, gold bought in London can be transported to New York at no cost. The law also dictates that there be no difference between the bid and ask prices for the good or service.
2. There are no trade barriers. For the law of one price to hold, goods and services must be freely traded. Trade barriers such as import quotas, tariffs, import taxes, and other constraints will act to negate and frustrate the law of one price.
3. The good or service is of equal quality. The law of one price must be used to compare truly equal goods and services. Quality differences will certainly frustrate the law of one price.

In practice, the concept of purchasing power parity is difficult to measure since there are many different prices of goods and services. Quality differences exist, and the relative consumption of particular goods in any two economies differs significantly. The concept of relative purchasing power parity has been used to construct price indices for two economies and measure the relative changes in price levels as reflected by the indices. Consider the following formulation in Equation 24.4:

Percentage change in price level in country A = Percentage change in price level in country B × Percentage change in exchange rate (cost of country A's currency in terms of B's currency)

$$(PA_{t+1} / PA_t) = (PB_{t+1} / PB_t) \times (ER_{t+1} / ER_t) \qquad [24.4]$$

where:

PA = price index of country A at period t and $t+1$

PB = price index of country B at period t and $t+1$

ER = exchange rate of one unit of country A's currency priced in terms of country B at period t and $t+1$

In this equation, for relative purchasing price parity to hold, increases in general prices in country A of 10 percent accompanied by no change in prices in country B would result in a 10 percent decline in the cost of country A's currency relative to country B.

The following is a hypothetical example. In Japan (country B) in 1994, the general price level increases from 134 to 145. In the United States (country A), the comparable price index increases from 154 to 157. The beginning of the year exchange rate is $1.00 = 135$ yen. What is the exchange rate expected to be at the end of the year, (ER_{t+1})? This calculation is as follows:

$$145/135 = 157/154 \times [(ER_{t+1})/135 \text{ yen/\$}]$$

$$1.0741 = 1.0194 \times [ER_{t+1}] / 135 \text{ yen/\$}$$

$$ER_{t+1} = 135 \text{ yen/\$} \times 1.0741/1.0194 = 142.24 \text{ yen/\$}$$

$$ER_{t+1}/ER_t = 142.24/135 = 1.05363 : \text{Dollar appreciates } 5.363\%$$

PPP considers changes in exchange rates to be primarily a monetary phenomena. That is, changes in exchange rates under PPP largely reflect the changes in price levels in different countries induced by monetary policy's impact on inflation. Countries that experience rapid changes in prices relative to another country will also experience depreciating exchange rates in relation to countries with more modest changes in price levels.

Considerable empirical analysis has been carried out in an effort to confirm PPP. Unfortunately, little of this work has confirmed the expected relationships between changes in prices and exchange rates. The exception to this is countries experiencing rapid inflation. These countries experience offsetting depreciation of their currency values. However, much of the empirical work is flawed due to the inability to measure certain data. Bilson and Marson (1984) showed that short-term changes in exchange rates for two countries are quite volatile and largely unpredictable. A study by Frankel and Meese (1987) indicates that the variability of exchange rates is far greater than the variability of inflation rates between countries. This finding is similar to the excess volatility anomaly reported in Chapter 6. PPP calculations are used by monetary policymakers to estimate the potential that a certain currency may be undervalued or overvalued, according to some equilibrium valuation calculation of PPP.

Although differential inflation rates are the primary cause of changes in exchange rates, there are other factors as well. These include differential changes in interest rates between two countries, differential income levels, and differential expected returns on real investments between two countries.

Differential Interest Rates

An investor is able to convert dollars into francs in the spot or cash market and sell francs for dollars in the forward cash market. The proceeds of this transaction is then put into French bonds. This is the interest rate parity transaction we discussed earlier. Now consider what would happen if French monetary authorities pushed French interest rates up. This would increase the demand for French francs to buy French bonds. The result would be a higher price of French francs in terms of dollars. This is why the value of a country's currency will fall whenever its interest rates fall relative to other country's rates.

Differential Income Levels

Consider a situation in which the United States enters into a recession and the economy in Germany accelerates its growth. The result will be that United States importers will reduce purchases in Germany, while German importers will purchase more U.S. goods and services. This will decrease U.S. demand for German marks and increase German demand for dollars. The result will be a declining mark price measured in terms of dollars.

Differential Expected Returns on Investments

Chapter 2 hypothesized about a situation in which a small country discovers oil. Investors will seek investment opportunities in this country. As a result, the value of the currency with the higher expected returns on capital would experience an increase in the value of its currency relative to the other country's with lower expected returns on investment. Unfortunately, it is not easy to determine the expected returns on invested capital in various countries. One approach is to try to estimate real interest rates. Still, major measurement problems remain.

As plausible as these theories of exchange rate movement are, empirical work corroborating these hypotheses is not available. The studies that have been done tell very little about changes in exchange rates. Exchange rate speculation can be extremely risky, which makes managing currency risk that much more important.

Managing Currency Risk

Managing currency risk is very similar to managing other price risks. The primary tools for managing interest rate risk were discussed in Chapter 19. The forward market, options, futures market, and swaps are used to reduce the firm's sensitivity to price changes of financial claims. The same tools are available in the foreign exchange markets to manage the risks of changes in foreign exchange prices.

The Volatility of Foreign Exchange Markets

The volatility of exchange rates has increased significantly since the days of Bretton Woods. In fact, exchange rates have become so volatile that managing foreign exchange risk is a very important activity for financial and nonfinancial firms operating in foreign markets. Table 24.3 shows the number of six-month periods from 1973 to 1989 when the U.S. dollar exchange rate with the British pound, German mark, and Japanese yen changed by more than plus or minus 10 percent. These represent very large changes for such a short period of time. These large changes dramatically indicate the risks associated with foreign exchange transactions.

Table 24.3

Six-Month Percentage Changes in the Exchange Rate Between the Dollar, Pound, Mark, and Yen
June 1973–December 1989

Dollar to Pound*		Dollar to Mark*		Dollar to Yen*	
Ending Date	Percent Change	Ending Date	Percent Change	Ending Date	Percent Change
July 1981	25.1%	Feb. 1986	−22.6%	Feb. 1986	−27.8%
Aug. 1985	−25.0	June 1981	19.9	Oct. 1978	−23.6
Feb. 1985	18.4	Aug. 1985	−17.8	Apr. 1979	21.6
Sept. 1975	16.6	Oct. 1978	−17.4	Mar. 1978	−17.7
May 1989	16.0	Jan. 1974	16.8	Dec. 1987	−17.4
Dec. 1987	−15.1	Nov. 1986	−15.7	Oct. 1982	16.5
Oct. 1976	13.8	Sept. 1984	15.5	Sept. 1980	−16.3
Mar. 1983	13.5	Feb. 1975	−15.4	May 1989	15.9
July 1979	−13.4	Dec. 1987	−14.6	Apr. 1983	−15.7
Oct. 1978	−13.2	June 1988	14.1	July 1981	15.7
May 1987	−12.4	Dec. 1989	−14.0	Sept. 1986	−15.6
Jan. 1978	−11.6	May 1989	13.5	Apr. 1987	−14.6
Sept. 1988	10.9	Mar. 1978	−13.2	Jan. 1974	12.7
Dec. 1973	10.6	Sept. 1975	12.7	Feb. 1980	12.7
		Aug. 1983	11.2		
		Mar. 1980	10.8		

*Positive values indicate appreciation in the value of the dollar while negative values indicate depreciation in the value of the dollar relative to the other currencies shown.

Source: Joseph A. Whitt, Jr. "Flexible Exchange Rates: An Idea Whose Time Has Passed?" *Economic Review,* Federal Reserve Bank of Atlanta. (September/October 1990): Adapted from Tables 1, 2, and 3. pp. 9, 10, 11.

Forward Cash Markets

The market most frequently used to hedge the price volatility of exchange rates is the forward cash market in foreign exchange. This over-the-counter market is operated by commercial banks and investment bankers who manage large foreign exchange trading activities. The primary way in which international firms can hedge a foreign exchange position of relatively short maturity, say a week to 12 months, is by using the forward exchange market. A firm that finds itself owing an entity a foreign currency for future delivery or having an account receivable representing a claim on a certain amount of foreign currency for future delivery has exchange risk exposure.

Consider a firm that owes a foreign exchange. This firm faces the risk that the value of the currency it owes will increase in value relative to the currency it customarily uses in its day-to-day dealings. If it is owed a foreign currency, then the risk it faces is the possibility that the value of the currency it will receive will fall relative to the value that the firm anticipated when it consummated the transaction.

The forward cash market can be used to reduce the risk of currency fluctuation. If a firm owes a foreign currency, it can purchase the currency today in the forward market for delivery at a set date. This effectively eliminates the price volatility risk. Alternatively, if the firm is to receive a foreign currency at some near-term future date, it can eliminate price volatility by selling the currency in the forward exchange market on a date to coincide with the date it receives the foreign currency. These represent foreign currency hedges.

These transactions may require that the user provide collateral to cover the difference between the forward agreed-upon price and the current cash price, which protects the dealer should the market go against the hedger. This is a type of margin that the dealer will require to ensure that the transaction is settled as agreed.

The forward market has the disadvantage for some users that the transactions are typically quite large, generally in minimum $1 million amounts, or their foreign currency equivalent. Forward contracts are tradable, however, as dealers will broker outstanding contracts. The major advantage of the forward contract is that some users of this market can avoid putting up margin, which is always required in the futures markets. This may make the forward cash market a more cost-effective hedging alternative for some users.

Futures Markets in Foreign Currencies

A futures market in foreign currencies that permits hedging of foreign exchange price risk has developed during the last 20 years. The International Monetary Market (IMM), run by the Chicago Mercantile Exchange, and the London International Financial Futures Exchange (LIFFE) are the largest markets for foreign exchange futures. The primary currencies offered by the IMM in 1991 are shown in Table 24.4.

The IMM contracts are settled March, June, September, and December. Most of the activity is in the contracts of nine months or less. The IMM removed a daily price limit circuit breaker on its foreign exchange contracts in 1985. Table 24.5 shows hypothetical listings for British pound futures contracts as they would appear in the financial press.

Chapter 24 Foreign Exchange, Exchange Rates, and Managing Currency Risk

Table 24.4

Major Foreign Exchange Contracts on the IMM

Contract	Face Amount
Australian dollar	100,000 dollars
British pound	62,500 pounds
Canadian dollar	100,000 dollars
German mark	125,000 marks
Japanese yen	12,500,000 yen
Swiss franc	125,000 francs

Table 24.5

Reading the Financial Page

Exchange Futures Contracts (typical listing)

British pound (IMM) - 62,500 pounds - $ per pound

Contract Date	Open	High	Low	Settle	Change pt = $.0001	Open Interest	Contract High	Contract Low
Mar	1.7412	1.7414	1.7409	1.7410	-02	31,000	1.7612	1.7323
June	1.7134	1.7156	1.7133	1.7137	-03	23,000	1.7345	1.7087
Dec	1.6900	1.6913	1.6956	1.6943	-04	123	1.7123	1.6845

Estimated volume: 12,765
Yesterday's volume: 23,000

The table above shows the futures quotations for future contracts in British pounds. The contract is for 62,500 pounds. The table shows the open price, high, low, and settlement (close) price expressed in the American term exchange rate. The change in price is expressed at 1/100 of a cent or $.0001. The open interest shows the number of contracts outstanding. The high and low prices are for the contract's life. The volume of contracts purchased or sold are shown as estimated volume for the day shown and actual volume for the previous day.

The futures market is used in conceptually the same way as the forward cash market. If a firm is owed a foreign currency to be received in the future (a long position), it would go short on a futures contract in that currency or a currency traded on the exchange whose value is closely correlated to one being hedged. If a firm owes a foreign currency for future delivery (a short position) it would want to go long in the futures contract of that currency.

Like the examples discussed in Chapter 19, a firm would be required to put up margin to the extent that buying back the futures position (covering the position) would result in a loss. It is this requirement of margin that may require large cash outlays that makes the forward cash market more desirable for some users. It is also necessary to calculate the appropriate hedge ratio, which is the relationship between the price change of the currency being hedged and the currency used in the futures contract, to determine the number of futures contracts to use. This can sometimes be difficult. This approach is discussed in Chapter 19.

The relationship between forward cash prices and futures prices is very close. Indeed, the markets tend to move in tandem, which makes either market an equally efficient hedge for foreign exchange risk.

Options on Foreign Exchange

Options are also available for hedging foreign exchange risk. Over-the-counter options in foreign currencies are available through dealers and also provided by organized exchanges such as the Chicago Board Options Exchange (CBOE), the Philadelphia Stock Exchange (PHLX), and several foreign exchanges. The currencies used by the CBOE and PHLX are the same. There is a major difference in the nature of the contracts, however. The contracts traded on the CBOE are European options, which can only be exercised on a specific date, while the PHLX options are European and American options, the latter of which can be exercised anytime during the contract life. A hypothetical listing of several contracts listed on the PHLX as they would be shown in the financial press is shown in Table 24.6.

In options contracts, there are two parties. The buyer of the option can purchase a put, which is the right to sell at an agreed-upon price on (European option) or before (American option) a specified date. A call option is the right to purchase. The other party to an option contract is the *writer of the option*. The writer can be a pure speculator, who does not care about ever owning the currency being optioned (described as an *uncovered position* or *naked option*), or an owner of the foreign exchange (*covered option*).

Options can be considered a form of price insurance. If a person owns a call on a foreign currency at a specified price in U.S. dollars, then the person has insurance that if the value of the foreign currency rises significantly, relative to the dollar, the price is fixed. The maximum hedged price, FX_{xx}, for an xx day option, will be equal to the option strike price, $Option_{xx}$,

Chapter 24 Foreign Exchange, Exchange Rates, and Managing Currency Risk

Table 24.6

Reading the Financial Page

Exchange Options
(typical listing)

		Calls			Puts		
Option and Current Price	Strike Price	Dec	Jan	Mar	Dec	Jan	Mar
German mark - 62,500 marks - American style - cents per unit							
61.23	60	.80	1.23	r	.10	.60	r
61.23	60 1/2	.45	.83	1.30	.20	.83	1.67
61.23	61	.40	.67	r	.45	1.23	s
German mark - 62,500 marks - European style - cents per unit							
61.23	61	.33	.56	s	.41	.98	s

This table shows the prices of three contract exercise dates for call and put options on German marks. The table indicates the type of currency and the underlying spot price for the mark, 61.23 cents per mark. The prices of the options are based on cents per number of units in a contract. Thus, a call option at a strike price of 60 1/2 for January delivery would be .83 cents times 62,500 units in the contract or (.0083 × 62,500 =) $518.75. The trading in options is not that active, so that an *r* represents no trading that day and an *s* indicates that no option is outstanding. The PHLX exchange has both American and European options in the German mark.

plus the cost of the option call premium paid, *CP*. This is shown as Equation 24.5.

$$FX_{xx} = Option_{xx} + CP \qquad [24.5]$$

where:

FX_{xx} = maximum price of foreign exchange in *XX* days

$Option_{xx}$ = call contract option strike price for settlement in *XX* days

CP = call premium paid for option

XX = option period in days

Consider the following example. A firm will need 3,000,000 British pounds to settle a contract with a British firm. The settlement will be in 180 days, which expires on December 31, 1993. It is now June 30, 1993. The current price of pounds is $1.6909 per pound. A European-type call option is offered on the CBOE for December settlement at a strike price of 172.5 cents per pound. The maximum price is shown as:

		Strike Price$_{180}$		Call Premium
British pound$_{180}$	=	172.5 cents/pd	+	3.40 cents/pd

When viewed as insurance against adverse foreign exchange price changes, the hedged ceiling price, $FX_{Dec.\ 93}$, of the pound for December 1993 settlement will be as follows:

$$\text{Ceiling Price } FX_{Dec.\ 93} = 172.5 \text{ cents} + 3.40 \text{ cents/pd}$$
$$= 175.90 \text{ cents/pd}$$

In this case, the price of insurance is (175.9 cents − 169.90 =) 6.00 cents per pound. This represents a 3.531 percent premium over the current price of pounds.

The buyer of an option must be concerned about the credit risk related to the writer of an option. If the optioned currency turns out to be worth more than the strike price in the case of a call or less in the case of a put, then the writer of the option will have to deliver the currency, if a call, or purchase currency, if a put. This could be very costly for the writer of the option and it might encourage the writer to default. This is not a problem in the organized exchanges, because they require the writer to have sufficient margin in the form of optioned currency on deposit, an irrevocable letter of credit, or cash margin. In the case of over-the-counter option transactions, on the other hand, the buyer of the option must be very concerned about the credit quality of the option seller. Usually the dealer will put its credit behind these transactions.

Currency Swaps

A typical currency swap is an agreement between two parties to exchange two currencies at the spot or current exchange rate, with the agreement that they will reverse the exchange at some agreed-upon future date, at the same exchange rate that prevailed at the time of the initial exchange. The agreement also calls for the party that obtains the currency from the country with the higher interest rate to pay the difference between the interest rate in their country and the rate in the lower interest rate country. Like interest rate swaps, currency swaps are major off-balance sheet activities at large international commercial banks and investment banking firms. These firms act as brokers and intermediaries in swap transactions.

Consider the five-year currency swap with a commercial bank that provides German marks for U.S. dollars. The U.S. company has $50,000,000 which it would like to swap for marks at an exchange rate of $.5747/mark. This would involve a swap of ($50,000,000/.5747 =) 87,001,914 marks. If the U.S. interest rate on five-year money is 7.5 percent, and the German rate 5.5 percent, then the bank would pay the U.S. company swapping the $50,000,000 a rate of 2.0 percent per annum to cover the difference. At the end of five years, the bank would pay the company back $50,000,000 and the U.S. company would pay the bank 87,001,914 marks.

The credit risk to the bank in this situation would be that the mark increases in value relative to the dollar. If the mark rose to $.71/ mark, then the company would be required to pay back a U.S. dollar equivalent of ($.71/mark × 87,001,914 marks =) $61,771,359. If the company was not able to create a viable economic activity in Germany, or was unable to invest in German securities, which provided an inadequate return, it might have difficulty raising the dollars needed to close out the swap. This creates significant credit risk for the bank. Today, bank regulators require banks to hold capital against this off-balance sheet exposure. Commercial banks can reduce this credit exposure by requiring collateral or other credit enhancements.

Summary

The international system of floating foreign exchange rates has created the need to develop sophisticated techniques for managing foreign exchange price risk. Foreign exchange rates have been volatile since the breakdown of the Bretton Woods Agreement in 1973. This has necessitated the development and growth of a number of markets and instruments used to hedge the foreign exchange price risk. Most prominent of these techniques are the forward cash market in foreign exchange, the futures market in foreign exchange, options on foreign exchange, and currency swaps.

The **Bretton Woods Agreement of 1944** established a system of **fixed exchange rates** in which the U.S. dollar and the British pound served as reserve currencies. The United States also agreed to sell gold to international governments at a fixed price of $35 per ounce.

By the early 1960s, the fixed exchange system began to unravel as Western Europe and Japan developed economically and the United States experienced severe inflation. By 1973, the fixed exchange program was abandoned in favor of **floating exchange rates.**

Foreign exchange is demanded to settle international transactions for importing and exporting, investments, speculation, and tourism. Foreign exchange is quoted under the **American term,** which represents the number of dollars needed to purchase one unit of foreign exchange ($1.80 per British pound) or the **European term,** which expresses the number of foreign currency units needed to purchase one dollar (1.5 German marks per one U.S. dollar).

Interest rate parity represents an arbitrage condition that establishes the relationship between **spot** and **forward exchange rates.** The forward exchange rate is related to the spot exchange rate using the following interest parity equation:

$$\text{Forward exchange rate: } ER_f = ER_s[(1 + r_d)/(1 + r_f)]$$

where:

ER_s = spot exchange rate (domestic price of foreign currency)

ER_f = forward exchange rate

r_d = domestic periodic interest rate

r_f = foreign periodic interest rate

Exchange rate fluctuations have been subject to considerable research. One theory that attempts to explain why exchange rates change is that inflation rates differ between countries. **Purchasing power parity (PPP)** is a theory that states the exchange rate between two countries will change in relation to changes in their relative inflation rates. The **law of one price** is a condition that must hold for PPP to operate. It states that a commodity should cost the same in two countries, adjusted by the exchange rate between the two countries and the cost of transportation and importing.

Purchasing power parity holds if increases in the general price levels of two countries are reflected in offsetting changes in the exchange rates between those two countries as shown in the following relationship:

$$(PA_{t+1} / PA_t) = (PB_{t+1}/PB_t) \times (ER_{t+1}/ER_t)$$

where:

PA and PB = relative price levels in countries A and B at periods t and $t + 1$ as measured by a general price index, and

ER_t = exchange rate for one unit of country A's currency priced in terms of country B's at periods t and $t + 1$

Forward cash markets in foreign currencies are the most widely used technique for hedging currency risk. The forward cash markets, operated by foreign currency dealers, provide the ability to buy and sell foreign currency for future delivery.

The **foreign currency futures market** provides the ability to purchase futures contracts in foreign currencies. The futures market is an organized market with specific contracts, settlement dates, and margin requirements.

Options on foreign exchange are available on several organized exchanges. They provide the ability to purchase put and call options in foreign currencies. The XX day forward price of foreign exchange, FX_{xx}, which will cover the cost of the options premium, CP, is shown in the following equation:

$$FX_{xx} = Option_{xx} + CP$$

where:

FX_{xx} = maximum price of foreign exchange in XX days

$Option_{xx}$ = call contract option strike price for settlement in XX days

CP = call premium paid for option

Currency swaps allow two parties to exchange currency at the spot exchange rate with the agreement that they will reverse the exchange at some future point. A currency swap also requires the party receiving the currency with a higher interest rate in that country's currency to pay interest to the counter party at a rate that represents the interest rate differential between the two countries.

Questions

Chapter 24

1. Why is managing currency risk more important to financial institutions today than it was 20 years ago?
2. What did the Bretton Woods Agreement of 1944 do to reduce the concerns about currency risk management?
3. What were the major provisions of the Bretton Woods Agreement? What provisions of the agreement are still in effect today?
4. What is the Eurodollar market? Why did it become so important?
5. What caused floating exchange rates to replace the fixed exchange rate system established by Bretton Woods?
6. Who should be most concerned about currency price risk?
7. What is meant by the expressions *American term* and *European term* in the quoting of exchange rates?

8. Explain the forward exchange market in foreign currencies. Who are the major participants?
9. What is meant by interest rate parity? How does interest rate parity impact the relative exchange rates between spot and forward exchange prices for foreign currencies?
10. Why do foreign exchange rates change?
11. What is meant by *purchasing power parity*?
12. What is meant by the *law of one price*?
13. How does the inflation rate in one country affect the value of its currency in relation to another country's currency under the theory of purchasing power parity?
14. How well does the theory of purchasing power parity seem to explain the actual changes in exchange rates?
15. Since Bretton Woods, would you say that changes in exchange rates have been significant, representing high risks to international firms, or largely insignificant?
16. How is the forward cash market in foreign currencies used and who are the major players?
17. What is the advantage of using the futures market in foreign currencies as compared to the forward cash market?
18. How would you use an option contract in foreign currencies?
19. Who are the major players in the currency swap market?

Problems

Problem 24-1   Quoting Exchange Rates—American and European Term
The spot rate of Canadian dollars is quoted on the European term as follows:
Bid: C$1.3060/US$ Ask: C$1.3078/US$
What are the bid and ask prices quoted on the American term?

Problem 24-2   Purchasing Power Parity
The average price of a specific good in the United States is $5,000. The average price of the same good in Switzerland is 8,000 sf. If purchasing power parity holds, what is the exchange rate between the United States and Switzerland measured on the American term?

Problem 24-3   Forward Exchange Interest Parity
The spot exchange rate of U.S. dollars to Swiss francs is SF1.5085/US$. The Eurodollar interest rate is 8 percent for one year and the comparable Swiss rate is 4 percent. What would you expect the forward exchange rate to be for delivery in one year?

Chapter 24 Foreign Exchange, Exchange Rates, and Managing Currency Risk 689

Problem 24-4 Foreign Exchange Interest Parity

The spot foreign exchange rate (American term) between the United States and Japan is $.032 = 1$ yen. The six-month T-bill rate in the United States is 7 percent. The comparable six-month rate on Japanese bonds is 3 percent. If interest parity holds, what is the six-month forward exchange rate FX_{180} between the United States and Japan?

Problem 24-5 Exchange Rate Risk

You are evaluating a one-year equity investment in the U.S. or German stock markets. Your analysts expect an 11 percent return on U.S. equities and 9 percent on German equities. Your foreign exchange analysts expect the exchange rate between U.S. dollars and German marks to fall from 1.60 DM/$1 to 1.35 DM/$1 in the next year. Given these expectations, which country's equities would you buy and why?

Problem 24-6 Foreign Exchange Arbitrage

The spot foreign exchange rate (American term) between the United States and United Kingdom is $1.80 = 1$ pound. The six-month rate on Europound securities is 12 percent. The six-month Eurodollar rate is 6 percent. The six-month forward exchange rate is $1.75 = 1$ pd. An arbitrage consisting of borrowing U.S. dollars to purchase pounds, investing in British debt and buying dollars forward would cost $5,000 in transaction costs per $1 million of trading. Would such an arbitrage be profitable? What would be your gain or loss?

Financial Tables

Table I
Present Value of $1: $\dfrac{1}{(1+k)^n}$ $PVIF_{r,n}$

Period	1%	2%	3%	4%	5%	6%	7%	8%	9%	10%
1	0.990	0.980	0.970	0.962	0.952	0.943	0.935	0.926	0.917	0.909
2	0.980	0.961	0.943	0.925	0.907	0.890	0.873	0.857	0.842	0.826
3	0.971	0.942	0.915	0.889	0.864	0.840	0.816	0.794	0.772	0.751
4	0.961	0.924	0.888	0.855	0.823	0.792	0.763	0.735	0.708	0.683
5	0.951	0.906	0.863	0.822	0.784	0.747	0.713	0.681	0.650	0.621
6	0.942	0.888	0.837	0.790	0.746	0.705	0.666	0.630	0.596	0.564
7	0.933	0.871	0.813	0.760	0.711	0.665	0.623	0.583	0.547	0.513
8	0.923	0.853	0.789	0.731	0.677	0.627	0.582	0.540	0.502	0.467
9	0.914	0.837	0.766	0.703	0.645	0.592	0.544	0.500	0.460	0.424
10	0.905	0.820	0.744	0.676	0.614	0.558	0.508	0.463	0.422	0.386
11	0.896	0.804	0.722	0.650	0.585	0.527	0.475	0.429	0.388	0.350
12	0.887	0.788	0.701	0.625	0.557	0.497	0.444	0.397	0.356	0.319
13	0.879	0.773	0.681	0.601	0.530	0.469	0.415	0.368	0.326	0.290
14	0.870	0.758	0.661	0.577	0.505	0.442	0.388	0.340	0.299	0.263
15	0.861	0.743	0.642	0.555	0.481	0.417	0.362	0.315	0.275	0.239
16	0.853	0.728	0.623	0.534	0.458	0.394	0.339	0.299	0.252	0.218
17	0.844	0.714	0.605	0.513	0.436	0.371	0.317	0.270	0.231	0.198
18	0.836	0.700	0.587	0.494	0.416	0.350	0.296	0.250	0.212	0.180
19	0.828	0.686	0.570	0.475	0.396	0.331	0.277	0.232	0.194	0.164
20	0.820	0.673	0.554	0.456	0.377	0.312	0.258	0.215	0.178	0.149
21	0.811	0.660	0.538	0.439	0.359	0.294	0.242	0.199	0.164	0.135
22	0.803	0.647	0.522	0.422	0.342	0.278	0.226	0.184	0.150	0.123
23	0.795	0.634	0.507	0.406	0.326	0.262	0.211	0.170	0.138	0.112
24	0.788	0.622	0.492	0.390	0.310	0.247	0.197	0.158	0.126	0.102
25	0.780	0.610	0.478	0.375	0.295	0.233	0.184	0.146	0.116	0.092
30	0.742	0.522	0.412	0.308	0.231	0.174	0.131	0.099	0.075	0.057
35	0.706	0.500	0.355	0.253	0.181	0.130	0.094	0.068	0.049	0.036
40	0.672	0.453	0.307	0.208	0.142	0.097	0.067	0.046	0.032	0.022
45	0.639	0.410	0.264	0.171	0.111	0.073	0.048	0.031	0.021	0.014
50	0.608	0.372	0.228	0.141	0.087	0.054	0.034	0.021	0.013	0.009

Period	11%	12%	13%	14%	15%	16%	17%	18%	19%	20%
1	0.901	0.893	0.885	0.877	0.870	0.862	0.855	0.847	0.840	0.833
2	0.812	0.797	0.783	0.769	0.756	0.743	0.731	0.718	0.706	0.694
3	0.731	0.712	0.693	0.675	0.658	0.641	0.624	0.609	0.593	0.579
4	0.659	0.636	0.613	0.592	0.572	0.552	0.534	0.516	0.499	0.482
5	0.593	0.567	0.543	0.519	0.497	0.476	0.456	0.437	0.419	0.402
6	0.535	0.507	0.480	0.456	0.432	0.410	0.390	0.370	0.352	0.333
7	0.482	0.452	0.425	0.400	0.376	0.354	0.333	0.314	0.296	0.279
8	0.434	0.404	0.376	0.351	0.327	0.305	0.285	0.266	0.249	0.233
9	0.391	0.361	0.333	0.308	0.284	0.263	0.243	0.225	0.209	0.194
10	0.352	0.322	0.295	0.270	0.247	0.227	0.208	0.191	0.176	0.162
11	0.317	0.287	0.261	0.237	0.215	0.195	0.178	0.162	0.148	0.135
12	0.286	0.257	0.231	0.208	0.187	0.168	0.152	0.137	0.124	0.112
13	0.258	0.229	0.204	0.182	0.163	0.145	0.130	0.116	0.104	0.093
14	0.232	0.205	0.181	0.160	0.141	0.125	0.111	0.099	0.088	0.078
15	0.209	0.183	0.160	0.140	0.123	0.108	0.095	0.084	0.074	0.065
16	0.188	0.163	0.142	0.123	0.107	0.093	0.081	0.071	0.062	0.054
17	0.170	0.146	0.125	0.108	0.093	0.080	0.069	0.060	0.052	0.045
18	0.153	0.130	0.111	0.095	0.081	0.069	0.059	0.051	0.044	0.038
19	0.138	0.116	0.098	0.083	0.070	0.060	0.051	0.043	0.037	0.031
20	0.124	0.104	0.087	0.073	0.061	0.051	0.043	0.037	0.031	0.026
21	0.112	0.093	0.077	0.064	0.053	0.044	0.037	0.031	0.026	0.022
22	0.101	0.083	0.068	0.056	0.046	0.038	0.032	0.026	0.022	0.018
23	0.091	0.074	0.060	0.049	0.040	0.033	0.027	0.022	0.018	0.015
24	0.082	0.066	0.053	0.043	0.035	0.028	0.023	0.019	0.015	0.013
25	0.074	0.059	0.047	0.038	0.030	0.024	0.020	0.016	0.013	0.010
30	0.044	0.033	0.026	0.020	0.015	0.012	0.009	0.007	0.005	0.004
35	0.026	0.019	0.014	0.010	0.008	0.006	0.004	0.003	0.002	0.002
40	0.015	0.011	0.008	0.005	0.004	0.003	0.002	0.001	0.001	0.001
45	0.009	0.006	0.004	0.003	0.002	0.001	0.001	0.001	*	*
50	0.005	0.003	0.002	0.001	0.001	0.001	*	*	*	*

Table II
Present Value of an Annuity of $1 for n Periods: $\left[\sum_{t=1}^{n} \dfrac{1}{(1+k)^t} \right] PVIFA_{r,\,n}$

Number of Payments	1%	2%	3%	4%	5%	6%	7%	8%	9%	10%
1	0.990	0.980	0.971	0.962	0.952	0.943	0.935	0.926	0.917	0.909
2	1.790	1.942	1.914	1.886	1.859	1.833	1.808	1.783	1.759	1.736
3	2.941	2.884	2.829	2.775	2.723	2.673	2.624	2.577	2.531	2.487
4	3.902	3.808	3.717	3.630	3.546	3.465	3.387	3.312	3.240	3.170
5	4.854	4.713	4.580	4.452	4.330	4.212	4.100	3.993	3.890	3.791
6	5.796	5.601	5.417	5.242	5.076	4.917	4.767	4.623	4.486	4.355
7	6.728	6.472	6.230	6.002	5.786	5.582	5.389	5.206	5.033	4.868
8	7.652	7.325	7.020	6.733	6.463	6.210	5.971	5.747	5.535	5.335
9	8.566	8.162	7.786	7.435	7.108	6.802	6.515	6.247	5.985	5.759
10	9.471	8.983	8.530	8.111	7.722	7.360	7.024	6.710	6.418	6.145
11	10.368	9.787	9.253	8.760	8.036	7.887	7.499	7.139	6.805	6.495
12	11.255	10.575	9.954	9.385	8.863	8.384	7.943	7.536	7.161	6.814
13	12.134	11.348	10.635	9.986	9.394	8.853	8.358	7.904	7.487	7.103
14	13.004	12.106	11.296	10.563	9.899	9.295	8.745	8.244	7.786	7.367
15	13.865	12.849	11.938	11.118	10.380	9.712	9.108	8.560	8.061	7.606
16	14.718	13.578	12.561	11.652	10.838	10.106	9.447	8.851	8.313	7.824
17	15.562	14.292	13.166	12.166	11.274	10.477	9.763	9.122	8.544	8.022
18	16.398	14.992	13.753	12.659	11.690	10.828	10.059	9.372	8.756	8.201
19	17.226	15.678	14.324	13.134	12.085	11.158	10.336	9.604	8.950	8.365
20	18.046	16.351	14.877	13.590	12.462	11.470	10.594	9.818	9.129	8.514
21	18.857	17.011	15.415	14.029	12.821	11.764	10.836	10.017	9.292	8.649
22	19.661	17.658	15.937	14.451	13.163	12.042	11.061	10.201	9.442	8.772
23	20.456	18.292	16.444	14.857	13.489	12.303	11.272	10.371	9.580	8.883
24	21.244	18.914	16.936	15.247	13.799	12.550	11.469	10.529	9.707	8.985
25	22.023	19.523	17.413	15.622	14.094	12.783	11.654	10.675	9.823	9.077
30	25.808	22.396	19.600	17.292	15.372	13.765	12.409	11.258	10.274	9.427
35	29.409	24.999	21.487	18.665	16.374	14.498	12.948	11.655	10.567	9.644
40	32.835	27.355	23.115	19.793	17.159	15.046	13.332	11.925	10.757	9.779
45	36.095	29.490	24.519	20.720	17.774	15.456	13.606	12.108	10.881	9.863
50	39.196	31.424	25.730	21.482	18.256	15.762	13.801	12.233	10.962	9.915

Number of Payments	11%	12%	13%	14%	15%	16%	17%	18%	19%	20%
1	0.901	0.893	0.885	0.377	0.870	0.862	0.855	0.848	0.840	0.833
2	1.713	1.690	1.668	1.647	1.626	1.605	1.585	1.566	1.547	1.528
3	2.444	2.402	2.361	2.322	2.283	2.246	2.210	2.174	2.140	2.107
4	3.102	3.037	2.975	2.914	2.855	2.798	2.743	2.690	2.639	2.589
5	3.696	3.605	3.517	3.433	3.352	3.274	3.199	3.127	3.058	2.991
6	4.231	4.111	3.998	3.889	3.785	3.685	3.589	3.498	3.410	3.326
7	4.712	4.564	4.423	4.288	4.160	4.029	3.922	3.812	3.706	3.605
9	5.537	5.328	5.132	4.946	4.772	4.607	4.451	4.303	4.163	4.031
10	5.889	5.650	5.426	5.216	5.019	4.833	4.659	4.404	4.339	4.193
11	6.207	5.938	5.687	5.453	5.234	5.029	4.836	4.656	4.487	4.327
12	6.492	6.194	5.918	5.660	5.421	5.197	4.988	4.793	4.611	4.439
13	6.750	6.424	6.122	5.842	5.583	5.342	5.118	4.910	4.715	4.533
14	6.982	6.628	6.303	6.002	5.725	5.468	5.229	5.008	4.802	4.611
15	7.191	6.811	6.462	6.142	5.847	5.576	5.324	5.092	4.876	4.676
16	7.379	6.974	6.604	6.265	5.954	5.669	5.405	5.162	4.938	4.730
17	7.549	7.120	6.729	6.373	6.047	5.749	5.475	5.222	4.990	4.775
18	7.702	7.250	6.840	6.467	6.128	5.818	5.534	5.273	5.033	4.812
19	7.839	7.366	6.938	6.550	6.198	5.878	5.585	5.316	5.070	4.844
20	7.963	7.469	7.025	6.623	6.259	5.929	5.628	5.353	5.101	4.870
21	8.075	7.562	7.102	6.687	6.313	5.973	5.665	5.384	5.127	4.891
22	8.176	7.534	7.170	6.743	6.359	6.011	5.696	5.410	5.149	4.909
23	8.266	7.718	7.230	6.792	6.399	6.044	5.723	5.432	5.167	4.925
24	8.348	7.784	7.283	6.835	6.434	6.073	5.747	5.451	5.182	4.937
25	8.422	7.843	7.330	6.873	6.464	6.097	5.766	5.467	5.195	4.948
30	8.694	8.055	7.496	7.003	6.566	6.177	5.829	5.517	5.235	4.979
35	8.855	8.176	7.586	7.070	6.617	6.215	5.858	5.539	5.251	4.992
40	8.951	8.244	7.634	7.105	6.642	6.233	5.871	5.548	5.258	4.997
45	9.008	8.283	7.661	7.123	6.654	6.242	5.877	5.552	5.261	4.999
50	9.042	8.304	7.675	7.133	6.661	6.246	5.880	5.554	5.262	4.999

Table III
Future Value of $1: $(1 + r)^n$ $FVIF_{r,n}$

Period	1%	2%	3%	4%	5%	6%	7%	8%	9%	10%
1	1.010	1.020	1.030	1.040	1.050	1.060	1.070	1.080	1.090	1.100
2	1.020	1.040	1.061	1.082	1.103	1.124	1.145	1.166	1.188	1.210
3	1.030	1.061	1.093	1.125	1.158	1.191	1.225	1.260	1.295	1.331
4	1.041	1.082	1.126	1.170	1.216	1.263	1.311	1.361	1.417	1.464
5	1.051	1.104	1.159	1.217	1.276	1.338	1.403	1.469	1.539	1.611
6	1.062	1.126	1.194	1.265	1.340	1.519	1.501	1.587	1.677	1.772
7	1.072	1.149	1.230	1.316	1.407	1.504	1.606	1.714	1.828	1.949
8	1.083	1.172	1.267	1.369	1.478	1.594	1.718	1.851	1.993	2.144
9	1.094	1.195	1.305	1.423	1.551	1.690	1.839	1.999	2.172	2.358
10	1.105	1.219	1.344	1.480	1.629	1.791	1.967	2.159	2.367	2.594
11	1.116	1.243	1.384	1.540	1.710	1.898	2.105	2.332	2.580	2.853
12	1.127	1.268	1.426	1.602	1.796	2.012	2.252	2.518	2.813	3.138
13	1.138	1.294	1.469	1.665	1.886	2.133	2.410	2.720	3.066	3.452
14	1.150	1.320	1.513	1.732	1.980	2.261	2.579	2.927	3.342	3.798
15	1.161	1.346	1.558	1.801	2.079	2.397	2.759	3.172	3.643	4.177
16	1.173	1.373	1.605	1.873	2.183	2.540	2.952	3.426	3.970	4.595
17	1.184	1.400	1.653	1.948	2.292	2.693	3.159	3.700	4.328	5.054
18	1.196	1.428	1.702	2.026	2.407	2.854	3.380	3.996	4.717	5.560
19	1.208	1.457	1.754	2.107	2.527	3.026	3.617	4.316	5.142	6.116
20	1.220	1.486	1.806	2.191	2.653	3.207	3.870	4.661	5.604	6.728
21	1.232	1.516	1.860	2.279	2.786	3.400	4.141	5.034	6.109	7.400
22	1.245	1.546	1.916	2.370	2.925	3.604	4.430	5.437	6.659	8.140
23	1.257	1.577	1.974	2.465	3.072	3.820	4.741	5.871	7.258	8.954
24	1.270	1.608	2.033	2.563	3.225	4.049	5.072	6.341	7.911	9.850
25	1.282	1.641	2.094	2.666	3.386	4.292	5.427	6.849	8.623	10.835
30	1.348	1.811	2.427	3.243	4.322	5.743	7.612	10.063	13.268	17.449
35	1.417	2.000	2.813	3.946	5.516	7.686	10.677	14.785	20.414	28.102
40	1.489	2.208	3.262	4.801	7.040	10.286	14.974	21.725	31.409	45.259
45	1.565	2.438	3.782	5.841	8.985	13.765	21.002	31.920	48.327	72.890
50	1.645	2.692	4.384	7.107	11.467	18.420	29.457	46.902	74.347	117.391

Financial Tables

Period	11%	12%	13%	14%	15%	16%	17%	18%	19%	20%
1	1.110	1.120	1.130	1.140	1.150	1.160	1.170	1.180	1.190	1.200
2	1.232	1.254	1.277	1.300	1.323	1.346	1.369	1.392	1.416	1.440
3	1.368	1.405	1.443	1.482	1.521	1.561	1.602	1.643	1.685	1.728
4	1.518	1.574	1.631	1.689	1.749	1.811	1.874	1.939	2.005	2.074
5	1.685	1.762	1.842	1.925	2.011	2.100	2.193	2.288	2.386	2.488
6	1.870	1.974	2.082	2.195	2.313	2.436	2.565	2.700	2.840	2.986
7	2.076	2.211	2.353	2.502	2.660	2.826	3.001	3.186	3.379	3.583
8	2.305	2.476	2.658	2.853	3.059	3.278	3.512	3.759	4.021	4.300
9	2.558	2.773	3.004	3.252	3.518	3.803	4.108	4.436	4.786	5.160
10	2.839	3.106	3.395	3.707	4.046	4.411	4.807	5.234	5.695	6.192
11	3.152	3.479	3.836	4.226	4.652	5.117	5.624	6.176	6.777	7.430
12	3.499	3.896	4.335	4.818	5.350	5.936	6.580	7.288	8.064	8.916
13	3.883	4.364	4.898	5.492	6.153	6.886	7.669	8.599	9.597	10.699
14	4.310	4.887	5.535	6.262	7.076	7.988	9.008	10.147	11.420	12.839
15	4.785	5.474	6.254	7.138	8.137	9.266	10.539	11.974	13.590	15.407
16	5.311	6.130	7.067	8.137	9.358	10.748	12.330	14.129	16.172	18.488
17	5.895	6.866	7.986	9.277	10.761	12.468	14.427	16.672	19.244	22.186
18	6.544	7.690	9.024	10.575	12.376	14.463	16.879	19.673	22.901	26.623
19	7.263	8.613	10.107	12.056	14.232	16.777	19.748	23.214	27.525	31.948
20	8.062	9.646	11.523	13.744	16.367	19.461	23.106	27.393	32.429	38.338
21	8.949	10.804	13.021	15.668	18.822	22.575	27.034	32.324	38.591	46.005
22	9.934	12.100	14.714	17.861	21.645	26.186	31.629	38.142	45.923	55.206
23	11.026	13.552	16.627	20.362	24.892	30.376	37.006	45.008	54.649	66.247
24	12.239	15.179	18.788	23.212	28.625	35.236	43.297	53.109	65.032	79.497
25	13.586	17.000	21.232	26.462	32.919	40.874	50.658	62.669	77.388	95.396
30	22.892	29.960	39.116	50.590	66.212	85.850	111.065	143.371	184.675	237.376
35	38.575	52.780	72.069	98.100	133.176	180.314	243.503	327.997	440.701	590.688
40	65.001	93.051	132.781	188.884	267.864	378.721	533.869	750.378	1051.668	1469.772
45	109.530	163.988	244.641	363.679	538.769	795.444	1170.479	1716.684	2509.651	3657.262
50	184.565	289.002	450.736	700.233	1083.657	1670.704	2566.215	3927.357	5988.914	9100.438

Glossary

Add-on loan A loan in which the amount of interest computed over the life of the contract is added to the balance of the loan before the monthly payment is determined. **(12)**

Adjustable rate mortgage (ARM) A mortgage whose interest rate, maturity, and/or payments are subject to change based on the movement of an index. **(3)**

Adverse self-selection A condition in which the inability to discriminate results in a high percentage of customers whose characteristics are likely to result in a loss to the seller. An insurance program that charges the same price to high- and low-risk customers and does not discriminate will appeal to the highest risk class of customers. **(14)**

Agency costs Costs incurred in agency relationships to ensure that agents are performing in the principal's best interest. Such costs include reporting, auditing, shareholder meetings, and costs of maintaining a board of directors. **(1)**

Agency relationship The use of paid professionals to manage savings of individuals and assets held by institutions. Examples of agents are the managers and directors of publicly owned corporations. **(1)**

Agency theory A financial theory describing the relationship between owners of assets and those hired by the owners to manage the assets. **(1)**

Agent One who makes investment decisions for financial institutions. **(1)**

American depository receipts (ADRs) Financial claims issued by U.S. banks holding foreign securities in trust. **(3)**

American option An option that can be exercised any time before its expiration date. **(5)**

American term exchange rate The dollar price of one unit of a foreign currency. **(24)**

Amortizing loan A loan that combines interest and principal payments to pay off the principal by the end of the loan's term to maturity. **(3)**

Annuity An insurance contract paying the owner a specified sum of dollars for a specified period of time on a regular periodic basis, usually for life. **(4)**

Arbitrage A group of financial claims that allow the owner to invest no money and earn a risk-free return. Actual arbitrage transactions involve some risk. **(5)**

Arbitrageur The party involved in an arbitrage transaction. **(6)**

Ask price The price sellers are willing to accept to sell a financial claim. **(2)**

Asset and liability transformation The process of converting liabilities with one set of characteristics into assets that may have entirely different characteristics. **(7)**

Asset-backed claims Financial claims created by using other financial claims as collateral for a new claim. **(3)**

At-the-money option An outstanding option that has an exercise price equal to the cash market price. **(5)**

Automated clearing house An organization owned by a group of depositories to facilitate check clearance. **(A8)**

Bank discount yield (BDY) An interest rate calculation that is used for discounted bonds. **(4)**

Banker's acceptance A short-term obligation guaranteed by a commercial bank and used to assist corporations involved in international trade. **(3)**

Bank Insurance Fund (BIF) The deposit insurance fund for commercial banks created in 1989 and administered by the FDIC. **(8)**

Barter A system of exchange that involves trading real goods without the benefit of a medium of exchange such as money. **(1)**

Basis In the futures market, it is the cash market price less the futures price for a specified financial claim. If the cash price is higher (lower) than the futures price it is a positive (negative) basis. **(5)**

Basis point One one-hundredth of 1 percent, .001. **(4)**

Basis risk Financial risks created when the price changes of the futures contract and cash market position are not stable. **(19)**

Basle agreements A series of agreements among foreign central bankers regarding uniform regulation of banks internationally. **(22)**

Best efforts A contractual agreement between the issuer of a security and a security dealer in which the security dealer agrees to sell a newly issued security, but with no obligation of success in selling the entire issue. **(12)**

Bid price The price buyers are willing to pay to purchase a financial claim. **(2)**

Black-Scholes option pricing model A formula used to price various types of European and American call options. **(5)**

Breakeven risk adjusted yield (BERAY) The yield an asset must equal or exceed to cover the firm's weighted cost of capital and all risks and costs associated with the asset. **(22)**

Bretton Woods Agreement A major international agreement among the major nations to facilitate foreign trade and stabilize foreign exchange rates. **(24)**

Brokerage A service related to bringing buyers and sellers together. **(7)**

Business risks Conditions within a business that are unrelated to capital structure and that give rise to volatility in earnings. **(16)**

Call option An option to buy a financial claim at a specified price on or before a specified time. **(3)**

Call option premium *cop* An amount of interest charged by a lender to compensate for the reinvestment risk inherent in a callable or prepayable debt instrument. **(2)**

Call provision A contractual clause in a debt instrument allowing the borrower to pay off the debt before the maturity date. **(2)**

Call or prepayment risk The risk faced by the owner of a callable financial claim relating to the likelihood that the funds paid off before maturity can only be reinvested at a lower yield to maturity than prevailed on the bond at the time of purchase. **(2)**

CAMEL ratings A regulatory system of evaluating the safety and soundness of commercial banks. **(22)**

Cap The highest rate the index plus margin can rise to, regardless of the rise in the index. **(19)**

Capital Deficit Unit (CDU) An economic unit in need of loanable funds. **(1)**

Capital market The financial market for long-term debt and equity financial claims. **(6)**

Capital Structure The relationship between the amount of equity and debt used to finance a firm's assets. **(1)**

Capital Surplus Unit (CSU) An economic unit with loanable funds to invest. **(1)**

Cash flow schedule A table showing the amounts and dates of the cash inflows and outflows from a specified investment. **(4)**

Certificates of deposit Fixed-rate and fixed-term deposit account of depositories. **(3)**

Charge-offs Charges taken to the loan loss reserve account after evidence of a loss is made available and its dollar amount can be established. **(A20)**

Circuit breaker A provision in the operations of an organized market designed to limit the length of the trading period, limit the maximum price change during a given period, or correct an order imbalance. **(6)**

Collateral The asset that is transferred to the investor if the borrower defaults under the obligation. **(3)**

Collateral trust bond A secured bond using common stock as collateral. **(3)**

Collateralized bonds Bonds issued with assets that transfer to the holder in the event of default. **(3)**

Collateralized mortgage obligations (CMOs) A hybrid series of mortgage-backed bonds created by altering the cash flows on a mortgage pass-through security. They provide several classes of bonds with different expected repayment periods. **(3)**

Commercial banks The largest group of depositories with broad asset and liability powers. **(1)**

Commercial finance company A nondepository financial intermediary that specializes in loans to businesses primarily for financing inventory and equipment. **(12)**

Commingled trust A trust in which several beneficiaries own a pro-rata share of a common pool of assets. **(8)**

Community banks Banks of small to medium size servicing small to medium-sized cities or neighborhoods of large cities. **(9)**

Compensating balance An amount of funds or investments that must be held with the lender in relation to the size of a loan as a condition for receiving the loan. **(23)**

Compliance examination A regulatory exam, focusing on the extent to which the firm fulfills its reporting responsibilities and requirements under various social lending laws. **(14)**

Compounding 360 over 365 The equation that uses the interest factor for a 360-day year and compounds for 365 periods. **(4)**

Conforming mortgages Home mortgages that qualify for purchase by the FHLMC and FNMA. **(13)**

Consol A bond issued in the United Kingdom that pays a fixed interest rate and has no maturity. **(4)**

Constant prepayment rate (CPR) A rate that is based on the assumption that mortgages will prepay by some predetermined percentage each month based on the existing principal outstanding after the previous month's prepayment. **(4)**

Consumer finance company A nondepository financial intermediary that specializes in loans to individuals. **(12)**

Contingent claims Financial claims whose cash flows are dependent on those of other financial claims. **(5)**

Continuous or infinite compounding A method of compounding in which the compounding periods per year approach infinity. **(4)**

Contractual savings Savings that occur on a specified periodic basis, such as the payment of life insurance premiums and pension fund contributions. **(2)**

Convergence The economic process by which the price in the futures market and in the cash market eventually equalize at the maturity of a futures contract. **(5)**

Conversion privilege The right to convert a bond into stock. **(3)**

Convertible currency Currency that is permitted to be exchanged for currencies of other countries. **(1)**

Convertible debenture A bond issued by a corporation that has a provision allowing the owner to convert the bond into shares of stock. **(3)**

Core deposits Deposits in generally small denominations attracted from consumers and small businesses. **(22)**

Corporate bond A financial claim representing an obligation of a corporation. **(3)**

Coupon rate The interest rate on a financial debt claim used to calculate the interest payments. **(4)**

Coupon stripping The process of creating a group of hybrid financial claims by converting each interest and principal payment of a bond into a new financial claim. **(4)**

Countercyclical An economic activity that moves in the opposite direction of the general economy. **(2)**

Covenant A contractual provision of a financial debt claim designed to reduce the probability of loss. **(3)**

Credit or default risk The probability of loss of principal and interest on a financial debt claim. **(2)**

Credit or default risk premium (*crp*) An amount of interest charged by the lender to cover the expected loss of principal and interest on a portfolio of a specific type of loan. **(2)**

Credit scoring The use of a number of attributes to help determine the credit worthiness of potential borrowers. **(20)**

Cross-sectional analysis Presentation of specified financial ratios for two or more institutions for comparison purposes. **(21)**

Debenture An unsecured debt of a borrower. **(3)**

Dealer market A market for financial claims in which security dealers buy, sell, and broker without use of an organized exchange. **(6)**

Defined benefit pension plan A pension plan that has a contractually predetermined retirement payment regardless of the investment results of the pension plan. **(11)**

Defined contribution pension plan A pension plan that has a contractually predetermined contribution of the employee and employer in which the retirement payment is affected by the investment results of the plan. **(11)**

Delegated monitoring The monitoring of the intermediary's investments as a service to the owners of those investments. **(7)**

Demand deposit A transaction account issued by insured depository institutions that is used as a medium of exchange. **(3)**

Depository institutions A group of intermediaries whose principle activity is to issue financial claims against themselves in order to purchase financial claims of others. The principle depositories are commercial banks and thrift institutions. **(1)**

Derivative claims Financial claims whose value depends on another financial claim or commodity's value, such as a futures contract or option. **(3)**

Derivative financial claim A financial claim whose value is based on that of another claim. Futures and options are derivative claims. (5)

Dialectical process A process in which an action by one party results in a response by the other party that in turn produces an off-setting response by the first party, and so forth. (14)

Direct investment Investment in physical assets for purposes of generating future income. (1)

Dirty float Central bank intervention into the market for foreign exchange. (24)

Discount The amount by which the market price of a financial claim is valued at less than the par value of the claim. (4)

Discount broker A security broker dealer that offers limited services compared to full-commission brokers and charges lower commissions. (12)

Discount rate The rate changed by Federal Reserve district banks to their members for short-term loans. (2)

Discount Window The lending activity of regional Federal Reserve banks. (8)

Discriminate analysis A statistical methodology that establishes the strength of relationships between several independent attributes and two or more independent variable classifications. (20)

Disintermediation The action of intermediary depositors withdrawing funds to invest directly in money and capital market securities. (15)

Distress costs Increasing costs borne by a firm as financial leverage increases; estimated to be the probability of bankruptcy times the cost of bankruptcy. (16)

Downward-sloping yield curve A situation in which short-term interest rates are above long-term interest rates. (2)

Dual banking structure A system under which federal and state governments charter certain financial institutions. (9)

Due diligence A process designed to establish the veracity of information given to a lender or security buyer regarding financial conditions and prospects. (20)

Due-on-sale A clause in a mortgage calling for it to be paid in full upon sale of the property. (A10)

Duration A measure of maturity calculated by dividing the time-weighted discounted cash flows of an investment by the investment's nontime-weighted discounted cash flows using a market interest rate. (18)

Early withdrawal penalty A fee assessed by a depository institution on a customer that withdraws funds from a fixed-term certificate of deposit before its maturity. (5)

Economies of scale The relationship of cost per unit to the number of units produced. (9)

Economies of scope The relationship of cost per unit of a related group of financial products that share a common production system to the number of units produced. (9)

Elastic currency Quantity of currency that rises and falls due to economic activity. (8)

Electronic data interchange (EDI) An electronic system that provides information on inventories and prices, facilitates ordering, and allows for the transference of funds. (A8)

Electronic funds transfer systems (EFTS) A general classification for a wide variety of electronic systems that are able to complete monetary transactions. (17)

Employee Retirement Income Security Act Legislation designed to protect an employee from losing benefits if terminated after many years. (11)

Equipment trust certificate A bond secured by equipment, usually railroad rolling stock or aircraft, as collateral. **(3)**

Equity multiplier (EM) A measure of financial leverage defined as the ratio of total assets to shareholders' equity. **(16)**

Equivalent annual yield (*EAY*) The annual interest rate, assuming no compounding, an investment would have to earn to produce the same future value as the same investment earns when compounding takes place at a specified coupon rate. **(4)**

Eurodollar certificates of deposit Deposits issued by Commercial banks in Europe and denominated in U.S. dollars. **(3)**

Eurodollar Market The acceptance of dollar deposits and the offering of dollar denominated loans by European banks. **(6)**

Euromarkets Markets for loans and securities denominated in a currency different from that of the country in which the transactions take place. **(6)**

European option An option that can only be exercised on the expiration date. **(5)**

European term exchange rate The foreign exchange value of one U.S. dollar. **(24)**

Exchange rate The price of foreign currencies measured in domestic prices. **(24)**

Exchange rate risk The risk that investing or borrowing in foreign currencies could alter expected yields or costs due to adverse changes in exchange rates between the domestic country and the foreign country. **(2)**

Exercise date The date when an option matures. **(5)**

Expectations theory A theory that holds that long-term interest rates represent the market's expectation of what future short-term interest rates will be. **(2)**

Expense ratio The relationship of property and casualty operating expenses to premiums earned. **(12)**

Fallacy of composition A logic term that means what may be good for a small group is not necessarily good for a large group. **(15)**

Fallen angels Bonds of a corporation that hold a noninvestment grade rating that held an investment grade rating when they were issued. **(3)**

Farm Credit Banks A group of GSEs that lend to farmers for housing, equipment, land, and supplies. **(13)**

Federal Agricultural Mortgage Corporation A GSE that provides a secondary market for loans to farmers. **(13)**

Federal Deposit Insurance Corporation (FDIC) The regulator of state-chartered insured banks and savings banks, and administrator of the Bank Insurance Fund and Savings Association Insurance Fund. **(8)**

Federal Deposit Insurance Corporation Improvement Act of 1991 (FDICIA) Legislation designed to strengthen the authority of depository institution regulators. **(14)**

Fed funds A short-term loan of reserves held as a deposit in a Federal Reserve bank from one Fed member to another. **(3)**

Federal Home Loan Bank Board (FHLBB) The former regulatory agency for savings and loans. It was replaced in 1989 by the Office of Thrift Supervision. **(14)**

Federal Home Loan Banks (FHLBs) A system of twelve banks owned primarily by savings and loans that lend to savings and loans and commercial banks for mortgage investment. **(13)**

Federal Home Loan Mortgage Corporation (FHLMC) One of the two large secondary market mortgage finance GSEs. **(13)**

Federal Housing Administration (FHA) A department within the Department of Housing and Urban Development that provides an insurance program for single and multifamily mortgages. **(13)**

Federal National Mortgage Association (FNMA) One of the two large secondary market mortgage finance GSEs. It purchases mortgages by issuing guaranteed mortgage-backed securities. **(13)**

Federal Savings and Loan Insurance Corporation (FSLIC) The former deposit insurance fund for savings and loans. **(8)**

Fedwire system A major electronic system operated by the Federal Reserve System used for making monetary wire transfers. **(17)**

FHA prepayment experience A payoff schedule used to determine when mortgages in a pool are likely to pay off based on experience gathered by the Federal Housing Administration on insured mortgages. **(4)**

Finance companies A nondepository financial intermediary that lends to businesses and consumers. **(1)**

Financial claim A contract evidencing ownership of a stream of cash flows. Bonds, stocks, or deposits are examples of financial claims. **(1)**

Financial claim/function matrix A chart describing the financial claims that represent the assets and liabilities of an intermediary and their functions. **(7)**

Financial engineering A process by which financial experts alter the cash flow or credit risk characteristics of an existing financial claim in order to create new types of financial claims with different cash flow or credit characteristics. **(4)**

Financial futures contract A derivative financial claim obligating the party to buy or deliver a financial claim at a predetermined price and time. **(5)**

Financial Institution Reform, Recovery, and Enforcement Act of 1989 (FIRREA) Legislation designed to reform the regulatory structure of savings and loans and organize the Resolution Trust Corporation to sell and liquidate failure savings and loans and savings banks. **(14)**

Financial leverage The extent to which a firm uses debt in relation to equity in its capital structure. **(16)**

Fisher Effect The theory that the nominal interest rate is equal to the real interest rate plus market inflation expectations. **(2)**

Fixed-rate mortgage A fully amortizing fixed-payment mortgage. **(3)**

Flat yield curve A situation in which interest rates on all maturity bonds are nearly equal. **(2)**

Float Funds in a checking account, which are available until the check is cleared by the receiving depository. **(A8)**

Floating exchange rates The value of one country's currency in terms of another as determined by a currency's supply and demand. **(24)**

Floor A limit below which the interest rate on an adjustable rate financial claim is not permitted to fall. **(19)**

Flow of Funds Accounts A set of financial statistics produced by the Federal Reserve Board showing the borrowing, lending, and assets of the major economic units in the United States. **(1)**

Forward cash market The market for financial claims in which settlement occurs in the future. **(6)**

Forward cash-market transaction The purchase or sale of a financial claim with delivery occurring in the future. **(5)**

Forward rate The interest rate on a loan to be obtained at some future time. **(2)**

Fraud Willful deceit to obtain an advantage. **(20)**

Fractional reserve banking A system of banking requirements that limit lending to a multiple of a specified asset held by the banks that is acceptable to a central bank. (8)

Free banking An early system that allowed banks to be chartered simply by meeting a set of financial requirements. (8)

Futures option An option written to buy or deliver a specified futures contract. (19)

Future value The amount of dollars that will be received in the future if a certain sum of dollars is invested today for a specified period of time at a specified rate of interest. (4)

GAAP capital The capital of a financial institution computed using generally accepted accounting principles (GAAP). (10)

General obligation bonds Bonds of states and municipalities whose repayment depends on the taxing authority of these government units. (3)

Glass-Steagall Act A law prohibiting commercial banks from underwriting securities and investment banks from accepting deposits. (8)

Goodwill An asset account on the balance sheet of a financial institution created when it purchases an asset, such as another institution, at a price greater than its book value. (10)

Government National Mortgage Association (GNMA) A federal government department within the Department of Housing and Urban Development that provides a full faith and credit guarantee to securities issued by financial institutions that are collateralized by mortgages guaranteed and insured by FHA and VA. (13)

Government Sponsored Credit Enterprises (GSEs) A group of federally sponsored financial intermediaries specialized in lending markets deemed to have special social significance. (1)

Government Sponsored Enterprises (GSEs) Government chartered financial intermediaries that purchase or guarantee loans deemed to be worthy of government support. The largest GSEs are the Federal Home Loan Banks, Federal National Mortgage Association, Federal Home Loan Mortgage Corporation, Student Loan Marketing Association, and Farm Credit Banks. (13)

Graduated payment mortgage A mortgage with a rising payment feature that does not fully amortize the loan in the early years of its life. These are used to assist buyers with growing income prospects. (3)

Guaranteed investment contract (GIC) A unsecured liability of a life insurance company typically sold to pension funds. (11)

Hedge ratio In the futures market, the number of futures contracts needed to provide the highest offsetting price change to the cash market position. (19)

Hedging A financial transaction that is entered into to reduce risk of price change. (5)

Home mortgage A financial claim in which residential property serves as collateral. (3)

Home Owners Loan Act A law that provided a program to prevent many homeowners from experiencing a foreclosure on their house. It also created federally chartered savings and loans and the Federal Home Loan Bank Board. (8)

Hybrid claims Financial claims created by altering the cash flows and/or credit characteristics of an existing financial claim. (3)

Implied forward rate The interest rate that must prevail in the future, given any specified yield curve, for an investor to be indifferent toward investing for a specified period or alternatively investing for a lesser period and reinvesting the proceeds for the remainder of the initial specified period. (2)

Income simulation A model used to forecast changes in income and other financial measures based on specified financial strategies and economic environments. (18)

Indicative bid The price at which an investment banker expects a security to be sold. (12)

Indirect investment Investment in financial claims of intermediaries. (1)

Inelastic currency Quantity of currency that rises and falls due to external events unrelated to economic activity. (8)

Inflation A rise in the general price level of a country's goods and services. (2)

Inflation expectations The tendency of CDUs and CSUs to consider the prospects for future price changes of goods and services in their borrowing and savings decisions. (2)

Informational asymmetry A condition in which one party has more information than the other party. (6)

Informational efficiency The valuation characteristics of a market that describe the process of how prices are influenced by information. (6)

Insurance companies A financial intermediary that pools risks related to the probability of death, and health, property, and casualty losses. (1)

Interest-only security (IO) A hybrid financial claim created by using the interest payments from a mortgage pass-through security to create the cash flows on a newly issued security. (4)

Interest parity The arbitrage process that acts to bring about a specific relationship between the price of a financial debt claim in the spot market and its price in the forward cash market. (6)

Interest rate cap A contractual limit on the maximum level of an interest rate for an adjustable interest rate financial claim. (18)

Interest rate elasticity The relationship of the supply offered and demand for loanable funds to changes in interest rates. (2)

Interest rate risk The impact on earnings and solvency of a financial firm related to changes in open-market interest rates. (18)

Interest rate swap A derivative financial claim in which two parties agree to make interest payments to one another based on a stated amount of nominal principal and at specified fixed or adjustable interest rates. (19)

Intermediation The process of purchasing financial claims issued by firms that use the funds to make investments in other financial claims. (1)

International Monetary Fund A financial intermediary that lends foreign currencies to countries to facilitate foreign trade. (24)

Intertemporal A transfer of consumption from one time period to another. (3)

In-the-money option An outstanding option that has an exercise price above (below) the cash market price in the case of a call (put) option. (5)

Intrinsic value The positive difference, if any, between the value of an option exercised immediately less the cash price of the option. (5)

Investment banking firm A specialized financial intermediary that is primarily involved in issuing, brokering, and trading securities. **(1)**

Investment grade rating One of the top four highest ratings by the major private credit rating firms. **(3)**

Investment intermediaries A group of intermediaries that provide specialized investment services for individuals and institutions, including mutual funds, limited partnerships, and real estate investment trusts. **(1)**

Junk bond A bond granted a rating below one of the four top ratings by the major credit-rating firms. **(3)**

Law of large numbers diversification The probability that a specific lender's credit loss experience on a portfolio of a particular type of loan will deviate from the actual loss experience for the population of loans from which they are drawn. **(20)**

Law of one price An arbitrage process that states that, adjusted for exchange rates, goods will have the same price in different countries. **(24)**

Legally binding contracts The existence of a legal system upholding the rights of individuals to make agreements with one another to own and transfer real and financial assets. **(1)**

Lender of last resort A central bank with the authority to lend to financial institutions and others in order to prevent a disruptive withdrawal of funds. **(8)**

Life insurance annuities A life insurance policy that provides a fixed monthly payment to the beneficiary. **(11)**

Life-line banking The requirement that insured depositories provide a low-cost checking service to low-income households. **(14)**

Limited branching Branching of financial depositories that is limited to a certain geographic area within a state. **(9)**

Limited partnerships A group of investment intermediaries that invest funds in intensively managed investments primarily in the real estate and corporate markets. **(1)**

Limit orders An agreement to buy (sell) a specified quantity of a security at a specified price, but no higher (lower). **(6)**

Liquidity preference theory A theory to describe the term structure that holds that differences in interest rates for bonds of various maturities are caused by the fact that CSUs prefer less risky short-term investments. Thus, the yield curve tends to have an upward-sloping bias. **(2)**

Liquidity premium The high-interest return as compensation for accepting maturity substitution. **(2)**

Load funds Mutual funds that charge a fee upon sale or redemption of shares. **(12)**

Loan correspondent A financial intermediary that purchases a participation in a loan originated by another firm. **(20)**

Loan loss provisions Expenses taken against the current income of the firm based on estimated losses from default on loans held. **(A20)**

London interbank offer rate (LIBOR) The interest rate that European and British banks use to lend funds to each other. **(6)**

Long cash Owning or having an obligation to purchase a financial claim. **(19)**

Long futures The purchase of a futures contract obligating the owner to accept delivery. **(19)**

Loss ratio The relationship of property and casualty claims paid to premiums earned. **(12)**

Margin requirement Cash or marketable securities maintained in an account by the holder of a futures contract to ensure that the conditions of a futures contract will be fulfilled. **(5)**

Marketability risk The risk that financial claims will have to be sold in a market that has a large spread between prices offered and prices bid or in which a purchase or sale may influence the price. **(2)**

Marketability risk premium (*mrp*) An amount of interest charged by a lender to compensate for the probability that a financial claim may lose value due to the need to sell it at a low bid price in an inactive market. **(2)**

Marketable securities Securities that are easy to sell or buy as a result of an active secondary market. **(3)**

Market-making The purchases and sales of financial claims by market participants. **(7)**

Market structure Attributes of the market for financial services including distribution of assets, size, efficiency, and competition among financial intermediaries. **(9)**

Mark-to-market The periodic valuation of financial claims at their current market value. **(5)**

Maturity The date of the last cash-flow payment on a debt financial claim. **(2)**

McCarran-Ferguson Act of 1945 Legislation that gave states the regulatory and chartering authority for insurance companies. **(14)**

McFadden Act A law limiting nationally chartered banks from branching to a greater extent than state chartered banks. **(8)**

Medium-term notes (MTNs) Claims with maturities of one to thirty years and of varying interest rates. They are offered to investors on a daily basis. **(3)**

Money center and international banks Very large commercial banks with domestic and international operations. **(9)**

Money market The financial market for short-term highly marketable financial debt claims. **(6)**

Money market deposit account A depository account that provides limited access by negotiable draft and typically pays a floating market interest rate. **(3)**

Money market mutual fund A mutual fund that invests in short-term highly marketable money market investments. **(12)**

Monitoring The need for the principal in an agency relationship to collect and evaluate information about the actions of the agent. **(7)**

Moral hazard A condition in which a participant to a transaction does not have an economic incentive to avoid risk or doing business with firms that take exceptional high risks. **(14)**

Mortality risk The risk related to insuring the lives of people using life insurance. **(11)**

Mortality tables Statistical probability data about the number of deaths from a population of similarly aged people. **(11)**

Mortgage-backed securities Financial asset-backed claims using mortgages as collateral. **(3)**

Mortgage bond A secured bond using a mortgage on commercial property as collateral. **(3)**

Multibank holding companies A bank holding company that owns banks in more than one state. **(9)**

Mutual funds A group of investment intermediaries that invest funds of shareholders in a professionally managed diversified pool of securities in which the shareholders hold a pro rata share. **(1)**

Mutual-stock conversion The conversion of a mutually chartered financial institution to a stockholder owned firm. **(10)**

Naked option A writer of an option that agrees to delivery without owning the claim on which the option is written. **(24)**

National Association of Insurance Commissioners (NAIC) An organization made up of insurance regulators of the various states. **(14)**

National Bank Act Legislation that created nationally chartered banks and the office of comptroller of the currency. **(8)**

National Credit Union Administration (NCUA) Regulator of federally chartered and insured credit unions. **(22)**

Near monies A financial claim that performs most of the functions of a medium of exchange. **(7)**

Negotiable certificate of deposit A fixed-rate and fixed-term deposit account of depositories that may be sold in a secondary market and transferred to a new owner. **(3)**

Negotiated and competitive bid A contractual arrangement between the issuer of a security and a security dealer in which the security dealer is obligated to sell a newly issued security or own the amount that is not sold. **(12)**

New York Safety Fund An early fund to insure the safety and soundness of commercial banks. **(8)**

Nominal interest rate The interest rate observed in the market. It is composed of a real interest rate and a premium for market inflation expectations. **(2)**

Nominal principal The amount of funds used to determine the interest payments under an interest rate swap. **(19)**

Nondepository institutions All financial intermediaries that do not accept deposits, including insurance companies, investment companies, finance companies, and trust companies. **(1)**

Nonpecuniary rewards Rewards to management that are not monetary, such as short working hours or reduced stress. **(16)**

Normal or upward-sloping yield curve A yield curve in which interest rates on short-term maturity bonds are less than long-term maturity bonds. **(2)**

Off-balance sheet transactions Outstanding financial contracts that are not shown on a financial firm's balance sheet. **(20)**

Office of Thrift Supervision (OTS) The regulator of savings and loans created in 1989 as a department within the Treasury. **(14)**

Open end mutual fund An investment fund that sells shares with the proceeds used to purchase investments. This type of fund typically has no limit on the number of shares it will sell. **(12)**

Operational efficiency The characteristics of a market that describe how well the market functions in terms of maintaining price stability, and providing pricing information. **(6)**

Option A contract allowing the owner to buy or sell a specified quantity of a specified financial claim on or before a specified date at a specified price. **(2)**

Option premium The difference between the option exercise price and the current market value of the optioned financial claim. The difference between the option price and its intrinsic value. **(5)**

Option writer The party to an option contract that agrees to buy or sell the financial claim on which the option is written. **(5)**

Ordinary annuity A financial contract that pays the owner a specified sum of dollars for a specified period of time on a regular periodic basis with each payment occurring at the end of each period. **(4)**

Organized exchange A financial market in which financial claims are bought and sold using an organization that provides a central location and set of trading rules. **(6)**

Origination The creation of a new financial claim. **(7)**

Out-of-the-money option An outstanding option that has an exercise price below (above) the cash market price in the case of a call (put) option. **(5)**

Overnight repo A repurchase that takes place in one day. **(4)**

Over-the-counter market (OTC) A group of security dealers who buy, sell, and broker stocks without an organized exchange. **(6)**

Participation A portion of a loan sold to one or more financial intermediaries. **(20)**

Par value The amount of principal on a bond. **(4)**

Pass-through security A financial claim collateralized by assets that amortize in which the owner receives a pro-rata share of the principal and interest payments of the pool of collateral, usually mortgages. **(3)**

Pension Benefit Guarantee Corporation (PBGC) A guarantee fund to covering the assets held by private pension plan for beneficiaries. **(14)**

Pension funds Private and public organizations that provide professional management of assets maintained for the benefit of working members for purposes of supplementing retirement income. **(1) (8)**

Periodic *GAP* A measure of interest rate risk computed by taking the firm's dollar amount of maturing or repricing assets and subtracting its maturing or repricing liabilities for a specified period of time. **(18)**

Periodic rate The interest rate that applies for the portion of a year when compounding takes place. **(4)**

Perpetual preferred stock A corporate equity issue that has no maturity and pays a specified dividend return. **(4)**

Portfolio risk management The process of managing assets and liabilities. Includes credit risk, interest rate risk, and liquidity management. **(7)**

Preferred habitat theory of the term structure A theory to describe the term structure that holds that differences in interest rates for bonds of various maturities are based on supply-and-demand conditions for various maturities, but that interest rates on bonds of other maturities can be higher by an amount sufficient to induce shifts in maturities for CSUs and CDUs. **(2)**

Premium The amount by which the market price of a financial claim is valued at more than the par value of the claim. **(4)**

Prepayment option A contractual provision in a loan permitting the borrower to pay off the principal before maturity. **(4)**

Prepayment penalty A fee charged a mortgage borrower on a mortgage assessed when the mortgage is paid off before maturity. **(4)**

Prepayment provision A contractual clause in a debt instrument allowing the borrower to pay off the debt before the maturity date. It is a form of call provision and is commonly found in home mortgages and installment loans. **(2)**

Present value theory A methodology to convert dollars received in the future into their value measured in terms of today's dollars. **(4)**

Price continuity A financial market condition in which a large volume of transactions does not significantly affect the market price. **(6)**

Pricing anomalies An empirical condition in which the price behavior of a security or group of securities does not conform to a specified efficiency theory. **(6)**

Primary claims Financial claims written against economic units making direct investments. (3)

Primary dealers A group of security dealers used to help distribute newly issued U.S. government bonds. (4)

Primary market The market in which a financial claim is created or originated. (6)

Prime rate An interest rate depositories use as an index for many loans. (22)

Principal The owner in an agency relationship, such as a stockholder. (1)

Principal-only security (PO) A hybrid financial claim created by using the principal payments from a mortgage pass-through security to create the cash flows on a newly issued security. (4)

Property rights A governmentally granted opportunity for individuals to own and transfer property and other real goods. (1)

Prospectus A legal document describing a new security offered for sale and the organization issuing it. (12)

Public Security Association Standard Prepayment Model (PSA) A set of mortgage prepayment cash-flow assumptions in which the prepayments begin slowly in the early years and increase to 16 percent per year. (4)

Purchase asset accounting An accounting methodology under GAAP providing for the creation of goodwill when the purchase price of an acquired firm is greater than its book value. (A10)

Purchasing power parity An arbitrage process that determines the relationship between prices of goods and services between countries and their exchange rates. (24)

Put option A financial contract allowing the owner to sell a specified quantity of a financial claim on or before a specified date at a specified price. (5)

Qualified thrift lender test (QTLT) A law limiting the investment authority of savings and loan associations to primarily home mortgages and consumer loans. (14)

Random walk hypothesis A theory that states that the next price change for a financial claim is independent of the last price change. (6)

Real Estate Investment Trust (REIT) A trust organized to own or finance real estate that meets certain federal tax requirements. (12)

Real estate mortgage investment conduit A tax trust entity that permits the creation of collateralized mortgage obligations that are not required to be shown on the balance sheet of the issuer. (3) (4)

Real interest rates The rate of interest that reflects the interaction between the demand for loanable funds related to the productivity of savings used by CSDs and the supply of loanable funds relating to the time preferences of CSUs. It is an interest rate determined in the absence of inflationary expectations. (2)

Recourse The sale of assets with a provision allowing the buyer to sell them back if they do not perform as expected. (20)

Redemption fee A charge assessed at the time of redemption of the shares of a mutual fund. (12)

Regional banks Large banks servicing an entire state or large portion of a large state. (9)

Regulation Q A regulation of the Federal Reserve System that prohibits payment of interest on demand deposits formerly used to limit the interest paid on time and savings accounts. (14)

Regulatory capital The capital of a financial institution computed using a formula provided by the firm's regulator. (10)

Reinsurance The process whereby an insurance company transfers a portion of the insurance risk exposure and premiums to one or more insurance companies. **(20)**

Reinvestment risk The risk that cash flows received before the maturity of a debt claim cannot be reinvested at the yield to maturity as high as the yield to maturity of the claim that produced the cash flows. **(2)**

Repurchase agreement (repo) An agreement under which one party sells a financial claim to another party with the stipulation that the first party repurchase it at a specified price on a specified date in the future. **(3)**

Reserve requirements A percentage of certain deposit liabilities, or depositories, that must be kept in the form of vault cash and deposits in a Federal Reserve bank. **(2)**

Resolution Trust Corporation (RTC) An organization created by Congress in 1989 to manage and liquidate the assets of failed savings and loans that were insured by the former FSLIC. **(14)**

Restrictive covenants Provisions in debt contracts required by lenders that restrict the actions of management and shareholders and reduce the potential for financial loss. **(16)**

Revenue bonds Bonds issued by states and municipalities whose repayment is backed by a specified revenue fee base. Revenue bonds are used to finance revenue-producing investments such as toll roads, airports, and sea ports. **(3)**

Reverse repurchase agreement (reverse repo) The position of the purchaser of the security in a repurchase agreement. **(3)**

Risk-free rate A nominal interest rate on a bond, which is considered to have no chance of credit loss. Typically a U.S. government bond is considered credit-risk free. **(2)**

Risk pooling A process of aggregating many similar financial claims to increase the predictability of credit loss. **(3)**

Safety and soundness examination A regulatory exam focusing on the financial soundness of the firm. **(14)**

Savings Association Insurance Fund (SAIF) The deposit insurance fund for savings and loan associations created in 1989 and administered by the FDIC. **(8)**

Savings deposit An account of a depository that allows withdrawals at any time. **(3)**

Search costs The costs incurred by an economic unit in finding a buyer (if a seller) or a seller (if a buyer) and in determining market prices. **(6)**

Secondary claims Financial claims issued by intermediary financial institutions. **(3)**

Secondary market The market in which a financial claim is bought and sold after it has been originated. **(6)**

Secondary marketing The process of determining the best place to sell loans originated by a financial intermediary. **(12)**

Securities Investor Protection Corporation (SIPC) An insurance fund that insures funds and securities held in security broker dealer accounts. **(14)**

Securitization The use of loans to collateralize and issue securities. **(23)**

Segmentation theory of the term structure A theory that holds that the differences in interest rates for bonds of various maturities are based solely on supply-and-demand conditions prevailing in specific markets representing different bond maturities. **(2)**

Semistrong-form market efficiency A theory of the informational efficiency of a market in which current prices reflect all publicly available information. **(6)**

Senior-subordinated pass-through security A series of financial hybrid claims created using pass-through securities as collateral. It involves creating two securities, with the subordinated class experiencing loss of principal first before the senior class suffers loss. **(3)**

Senior-subordinated security A security that redistributes the credit risk on the collateral underlying the security. **(4)**

Sensitivity analysis A model of a financial firm used to determine changes in financial statistics and ratios from specified changes in certain economic variables. **(18)**

Serial bonds Bonds that have a specified principal amount of their par value come due at a predetermined date. **(3)**

Servicing The process of collecting payments, accounting, collateral management, and ensuring the adherence of all covenants by borrower. **(7)**

Servicing cost (*sc*) The cost expressed as an interest rate to cover the cost of performing the various functions of owning a financial claim. **(2)**

Servicing income contract A financial contract that compensates the organization that collects payments on primary financial claims and forwards them to the investors in the financial claims. **(4)**

Settlement date The date when cash is due in the case of a purchase, or financial claims are due in the case of a sale in order to settle a transaction. **(6)**

Shared ATM networks Automated teller machines and cash dispensing systems used jointly by financial institutions. **(17)**

Short cash The position of a firm that needs to acquire a financial claim in the future. **(19)**

Short futures The sale of a futures contract. **(19)**

Sinking fund provision A provision of a bond that provides that a specified percentage of the principal value of the bonds be redeemed or paid off prior to maturity. **(3)**

Small Business Administration A department within the Department of Commerce that provides guarantee programs for loans to businesses. **(13)**

Speculators Economic units that profit through the purchase of financial contracts on the basis that favorable price changes will occur within a short period of time. **(5)**

Spot market A market in which financial claims can be bought and sold for immediate delivery. Delivery is typically required in two to five business days. **(6)**

Statewide branching Branching of financial depositories anywhere in the state. **(9)**

Stimulative policy A macroeconomic policy designed to increase income and employment. **(2)**

Stripped Treasury security The process of creating new securities from the interest and principal payments of an existing Treasury security. **(4)**

Strong-form market efficiency A theory of the informational efficiency of a market in which current prices reflect all public and private information. **(6)**

Student Loan Marketing Association (SLMA) A GSE that specializes in purchasing and servicing federally guaranteed student loans. **(13)**

Subordinated debenture An unsecured debt of a borrower that in event of default will not be repaid until general and secured creditors are repaid. **(3)**

Suffolk System An early system of reserve requirements designed to insure the acceptability of checks drawn on the member commercial banks. **(8)**

Super-regional banks Large banks servicing an entire state or group of states. **(9)**

Syndication group A group of security broker dealers that jointly sell a newly issued security. **(12)**

Tangible equity The amount of equity in a financial institution that subtracts intangible assets such as goodwill from capital computed under GAAP. **(10)**

Taxable equivalent yield (*TEY*) The interest rate that would have to be earned to provide the same after-tax yield as a tax-exempt investment, assuming the interest were fully taxed. **(4)**

Tax-preferenced investment An investment whose income is not taxed at ordinary income tax rates. The income may be tax free or tax deferred. **(4)**

Teaser An adjustable-rate mortgage whose initial rate is below the index plus margin. **(19)**

Term insurance A life insurance policy with no cash value buildup. **(11)**

Term loans Loans with maturities of approximately two years or more. **(20)**

Term repo A repurchase that takes place over more than one day. **(4)**

Term structure of interest rates The relationship of the yields on a specific class of bonds of different maturities. **(2)**

Thrift institutions Specialized depository institutions including savings and loans, savings banks, and credit unions. **(1)**

Time preference An individual's trade-off between consumption today and consumption tomorrow. **(1)**

Time series analysis Presentation of specified financial ratios over time for comparison purposes. **(21)**

Time value The value of an option over and above its intrinsic value. **(19)**

Too big to fail policy A policy of depository regulators to support large financial institutions that experience financial distress. This policy is based on the idea that a failure of a large bank will create major economic dislocations and financial runs and panics. **(14)**

Trade date The date when an order to buy or sell financial claims is executed. **(6)**

Trade debt Loans extended by the seller of goods and services to its customers in order to induce sales. **(3)**

Traders Individuals involved in market-making that execute orders to buy, sell, and broker financial claims for a financial firm. **(6)**

Tranches The number of different securities created in a collateralized mortgage obligation or real estate mortgage investment conduit. **(4)**

Transaction account Any type of deposit used to make transactions, such as demand deposits, money market demand accounts, share drafts, and negotiable order of withdrawal accounts. **(3)**

Transaction costs All costs associated with buying or selling a financial claim, including search costs, brokerage costs, marketability costs, and safekeeping. **(6)**

Treasury bills Debts issued by the U.S. government with maturities less than one year and no interest payment. They are issued at a discount from par value. **(3)**

Treasury bonds Debts issued by the U.S. government with maturities of ten years or more that pay interest semiannually. **(3)**

Treasury notes Debts issued by the U.S. government with maturities of two to ten years that pay interest semiannually. **(3)**

Unit banking Single-office banks in accordance with state branching laws. **(9)**

Unit banks Banks with only one office. **(8)**

Vesting A contractual requirement that a pension plan provide a portion of the actuarially determined value of the pension plan to the beneficiary if the beneficiary leaves the employment of the firm sponsoring the plan. **(11)**

Veterans Administration (VA) An organization that provides a guarantee program for mortgages taken out by military veterans. **(13)**

Warrant A financial claim offered by a corporation permitting the holder of the option to buy the company's common stock. **(5)**

Weak-form market efficiency A theory of the informational efficiency of a market in which current prices reflect all information embedded in past prices. **(6)**

Weighted average cost of capital (WACC) The cost of debt and equity for a financial firm weighted by each source of capital's relative contribution to the firm's capital structure. **(22)**

Weighted average life (WAL) A calculation of when all the cash flows from a group of mortgages are expected, based on weighting the cash flows over the life of the mortgages. **(4)**

Wholesale funding sources Liabilities sold using public security markets and security dealers. **(9)**

Wire transfer An electronic system for transferring funds from one depository to another. **(A8)**

Yield curve A graph of the nominal interest rate on the vertical axis and maturity on the horizontal axis for specific bonds, usually U.S. government bonds, of different maturities on a specified date. **(2)**

Yield to maturity The interest rate that will cause the discounted future cash flow's value to equal the amount of the investment measured in current dollars. **(2)**

Zero coupon A bond that pays no periodic interest payments and whose market value is below par value. **(3)**

Z score The mathematical statistical relationship based on the output of a discriminate analysis. **(20)**

References

Chapter 1

Fisher, Irving. *The Theory of Interest*. New York: The Macmillan Co., 1930.

Friedman, Benjamin M. "Effects of Shifting Savings Patterns on Interest Rates and Economic Activity." *Journal of Finance* (March 1982): 37–62.

Henning, Charles, William Pigott, and Robert H. Haney. *Financial Markets and the Economy*. Englewood Cliffs, NJ: Prentice-Hall, 1988.

Kaufman, Henry. *Interest Rates, the Markets, and the New Financial World*. New York: Times Books, 1986.

Metzler, L. A. "Wealth, Saving, and the Rate of Interest." *Journal of Political Economy* (April 1951): 93–116.

Chapter 2

Boskin, Michael. "Taxation, Savings, and the Rate of Interest." *Journal of Political Economy* (April 1978): 3–27.

Campbell, John Y. "A Defense of Traditional Hypotheses About the Term Structure." *Journal of Finance* (March 1986): 183–94.

Fama, Eugene F. "Forward Rates as Predictors of Future Spot Rates." *Journal of Financial Economics* (October 1976): 361–77.

———. "Term Premiums in Bond Returns." *Journal of Financial Economics* (October 1976): 509–28.

Fisher, Irving. *The Theory of Interest*. New York: The Macmillan Co., 1930.

Hamburger, Michael J., and Elliot N. Platt. "The Expectations Hypothesis and the Efficiency of the Treasury Bill Market." *Review of Economics and Statistics* (May 1975): 190–99.

Homer, Sidney. *A History of Interest Rates*. New Brunswick, NJ: Rutgers University Press, 1963.

Kaufman, Henry. *Interest Rates, the Markets, and the New Financial World*. New York: Time Books, 1986.

Keynes, John Maynard. *The General Theory of Employment, Interest and Money*. New York: Harcourt Brace Jovanovich, 1936.

Meiselman, David. *The Term Structure of Interest Rates*. Englewood Cliffs, NJ: Prentice-Hall, 1962.

Modigliani, Franco. "Debt Management and the Term Structure of Interest Rates: An Empirical Analysis of Recent Experience." *Journal of Political Economy*, Supplement, (August 1967): 569–89.

Siegel, Andrew F., and Charles R. Nelson. "Long-Term Behavior of Yield Curves." *Journal of Financial and Quantitative Analysis* (March 1988): 105–10.

Taylor, Herbert. "Interest Rates: How Much Does Expected Inflation Matter?" *Business Review*, Federal Reserve Bank of Philadelphia (July–August 1982): 3–12.

Chapter 3

Fabozzi, Frank J., and Frank G. Zarb, eds. *Handbook of Financial Markets*. 2nd ed. Homewood, IL: Dow Jones-Irwin, 1986. Stigum, Marcia. *The Money Market*. Homewood, IL: Dow Jones-Irwin, 1983.

Flow of Funds Accounts. Board of Governors of the Federal Reserve System, Washington, DC.

Handbook of Securities of the United States Government and Federal Agencies. New York: The

First Boston Corporation, 1988. Published biennially.

Chapter 4

Becketti, Sean. "The Role of Stripped Securities in Portfolio Management." *Economic Review,* Federal Reserve Bank of Kansas City (May 1988): 20–31.

Fabozzi, Frank J., ed. *The Handbook of Mortgage-Backed Securities.* 2nd ed. Chicago: Probus Publishing, 1988.

———. *The Handbook of Treasury Securities.* Chicago: Probus Publishing, 1987.

Fabozzi, Frank J., and Frank G. Zarb. eds. *Handbook of Financial Markets.* 2nd ed. Homewood, IL: Dow Jones-Irwin, 1986.

Handbook of Securities of the United States Government and Federal Agencies. New York: The First Boston Corporation, 1988. Published biannually.

Hendershott, Patric, and Robert Van Order. "Pricing Mortgages: An Interpretation of the Models and Results." *Journal of Financial Services Research* (September 1987): 19–55.

Ingersoll, Jonathan E. "An Examination of Corporate Call Policies on Convertible Securities." *Journal of Finance* (May 1977): 463–78.

Livingston, Miles. *Money and Capital Markets: Financial Instruments and Their Uses.* Englewood Cliffs, NJ: Prentice-Hall, 1990.

Stigum, Marcia. *Money Market Calculations: Yields, Breakevens, and Arbitrage.* Homewood, IL: Dow Jones-Irwin, 1981.

Stigum, Marcia, and Frank J. Fabozzi. *The Dow Jones-Irwin Guide to Bond and Money Market Instruments.* Homewood, IL: Dow Jones-Irwin, 1987.

Thygerson, Kenneth J., and Dennis Jacobe. *Mortgage Portfolio Management.* Chicago: United States League of Savings Institutions, 1978.

Chapter 5

Black, Fisher, and Myron Scholes. "The Pricing of Options and Corporate Liabilities." *Journal of Political Economy* (May–June 1973): 637–59.

Bookstaber, Richard M. "The Option Pricing Formula." In Fabozzi, Frank J., ed. *Readings in Investment Management.* Homewood, IL: Richard D. Irwin, Inc., 1983, 267–81.

Dubofsky, David A. *Options and Financial Futures.* New York: McGraw-Hill, 1992.

Fabozzi, Frank J., and T. Dessa Fabozzi. *Bond Markets, Analysis and Strategies.* Englewood Cliffs, NJ: Prentice-Hall, 1989.

Goodman, Laurie. "New Options Markets." *Quarterly Review,* Federal Reserve Bank of New York (Autumn 1983): 35–47.

Ingersoll, Jonathan E. "An Examination of Corporate Call Policies on Convertible Securities." *Journal of Finance* (May 1977): 463–78.

Kolb, Robert W. *Understanding Futures Markets.* Glenview, IL: Scott, Foresman and Co., 1988.

Kopprasch, Robert W. "Early Redemption (Put) Options on Fixed Income Securities." In Fabozzi, Frank J. ed., *Readings in Investment Management.* Homewood IL: Richard D. Irwin, Inc., 1983, 97–110.

MacBeth, James D., and Larry J. Merville. "An Empirical Examination of the Black-Scholes Call Option Pricing Model." *Journal of Finance* (December 1979): 1173–86.

Merton, Robert C. "Theory of Rational Option Pricing." *Bell Journal of Economics and Management Science* (Spring 1973): 141–83.

Thygerson, Kenneth J. "Hedging Forward Mortgage Loan Commitments: The Option of Futures and the Future of Options." *Journal of the American Real Estate and Urban Economics Association* (Winter 1978): 357–69.

———. "Futures, Options and the Savings and Loan Business." In *Savings and Loan Asset Management Under Deregulation.* Proceedings of the Sixth Annual Conference of the Federal Home Loan Bank of San Francisco, December 8–9, 1980, 118–47.

Whaley, Robert E. "Valuation of American Futures Options: Theory and Empirical Tests." *Journal of Finance* (1986): 127–50.

Williams, Jeffrey. "Futures Markets: A Consequence of Risk Aversion or Transactions Costs?" *Journal of Political Economy* (October 1987): 1000–1023.

Chapter 6

Arbel, Avner. "Generic Stocks: The Key to Market Anomalies." *Journal of Portfolio Management* 11 (1984–85): 4, 13.

Basu, Sanjoy. "Investment Performance of Common Stocks in Relation to their Price–Earnings Ratios: A Test of the Efficient Market Hypothesis." *Journal of Finance* 32 (1977): 663–82.

Campbell, John Y. "Stock Prices, Earnings, and Expected Dividends." *Journal of Finance* 43 (1988): 661–76.

Campbell, John Y., and Robert J. Shiller. "The Dividend-Price Ratio and Expectations of Future Dividends and Discount Factors." *Review of Financial Studies* 1 (1988): 195–228.

DeBondt, Werner, and Richard Thaler. "Does the Stock Market Overreact?" *Journal of Finance* 40 (1985): 793–805.

DeBondt, Werner, and Richard Thaler. "Further Evidence of Investor Overreaction and Stock-market Seasonality." *Journal of Finance* 42 (1987): 557–81.

Fama, Eugene F. "Efficient Capital Markets: A Review of Theory and Empirical Work." *Journal of Finance* (May 1970): 383–417.

———. "Efficient Capital Markets: II." *Journal of Finance* (December 1991): 1575–1617.

Granger, Clive W. J., and Oskar Morgenstern. *Predictability of Stock Market Prices.* Lexington, MA: Heath Lexington Books, 1970.

Jensen, Michael. "Some Anomalous Evidence Regarding Market Efficiency." *Journal of Financial Economics* 6 (1978): 95–101.

Keim, Donald. "Size-Related Anomalies and Stock Return Seasonality." *Journal of Financial Economics* (June 1983): 13–32.

LeRoy, Stephen F. "Capital Market Efficiency: An Update." *Economic Review,* Federal Reserve Bank of San Francisco (Spring 1990): 29–40.

Moser, James T. "Circuit Breakers." *Economic Perspectives,* Federal Reserve Bank of Chicago (September–October 1990): 2–13.

Reilly, Frank K. "Secondary Markets." In Fabozzi, Frank J., and Frank G. Zarb, eds. *Handbook of Financial Markets.* 2nd ed. Homewood, IL: Dow Jones-Irwin, 1986, 151–52.

Rozeff, Michael S., and William R. Kinney. "Capital Market Seasonality: The Case of Stock Returns." *Journal of Financial Economics* 3 (1976): 379–402.

Shiller, Robert. "The Volatility of Long-Term Interest Rates and Expectations Models of the Term Structure." *Journal of Political Economy* 87 (1979): 1190–1209.

———. "Do Stock Prices Move Too Much to Be Justified by Subsequent Changes in Dividends?" *American Economic Review* 17 (1981): 421–36.

Chapter 7

Allan, Franklin. "Information Contracting in Financial Markets." In Bhattacharya, Sudipto, and George M. Constantinides, eds. *Financial Markets and Incomplete Information.* Savage, MD: Rowman and Littlefield, 1989.

Benston, George J., and Clifford W. Smith, Jr. "The Transaction Cost Approach to the Theory of Financial Intermediation." *Journal of Finance* (May 1976): 215–33.

Baron, D. P. "A Model of the Demand for Investment Banking, Advising, and Distributions Services for New Issues." *Journal of Finance* 37(1982): 955–76.

Baron, D. P., and B. Holmstrom. "The Investment Banking Contract for New Issues Under Asymmetric Information: Delegation and the Incentive Problem." *Journal of Finance* (December 1980): 1115–58.

Campbell, T. "Optimal Corporate Financing Decisions and the Value of Confidentiality." *Journal of Financial and Quantitative Analysis* (1979): 913–25.

Campbell, T., and M. Kracow. "Information Production, Market Signalling and the Theory of Financial Intermediation." *Journal of Finance* 35(1980): 863–82.

Chan, Y. "On the Positive Role of Financial Intermediaries in Allocation of Venture Capital in a Market with Imperfect Information." *Journal of Finance* 38(1983): 1543–68.

Deshmukh, Sudhakar D., Stuart I. Greenbaum, and George Kanatas. "Lending Policies of Financial Intermediaries Facing Credit and Funding Risk." *Journal of Finance* (June 1983): 873–86.

Diamond, Douglas. "Financial Intermediation and Delegated Monitoring." *Review of Economic Studies* 51(1984): 393–414.

Diamond, Douglas W. "Asset Services and Financial Intermediation." In Bhattacharya, Sudipto, and George M. Constantinides, eds. *Financial Markets and Incomplete Information*. Savage, MD: Rowman and Littlefield, 1989.

Fama, Eugene. "Banking in the Theory of Finance." *Journal of Monetary Economics* (1980): 39–57.

Greenbaum, Stuart I., and Bryon Higgins. "Financial Innovation." In *Financial Services: The Changing Institutions and Government Policy*. Englewood Cliffs, NJ: Prentice-Hall, American Assembly, Columbia University, 1983.

Gurley, J. G., and E. S. Shaw. *Money in a Theory of Finance*. Washington, DC: Brookings Institution, 1960.

Leland, H., and D. Pyle. "Information Asymmetries, Financial Structure and Financial Intermediation." *Journal of Finance* 32 (1977): 371–87.

Pesek, Boris P. "Bank's Supply Function and the Equilibrium Quantity of Money." *Canadian Journal of Economics* (August 1970): 357–83.

Pyle, David. "Descriptive Theories of Financial Institutions." *Journal of Financial and Quantitative Analysis*. (December 1972): 2009–29.

Ross, Stephan A. "Institutional Markets, Financial Marketing, and Financial Innovation." *Journal of Finance* (July 1989): 541–56.

Sealey, C. W., Jr. "Valuation, Capital Structure, and Shareholder Unanimity for Depository Financial Intermediaries." *Journal of Finance* (June 1983): 857–71.

Tobin, J. "Commercial Banks and Creators of Money." In D. Carson, ed. *Banking and Monetary Studies*. Homewood, IL: Richard D. Irwin, Inc., 1963.

Tobin, J., and W. Brainard. "Financial Intermediaries and the Effectiveness of Monetary Control." *American Economic Review* 53 (1963): 383–400.

Towey, Richard E. "Money Creation and the Theory of the Banking Firm." *Journal of Finance*. (March 1974): 57–72.

Chapter 8

Commission on Money and Credit. *Money and Credit: Their Influence on Jobs, Prices and Growth*. Englewood Cliffs, NJ: Prentice-Hall, 1961.

Estabrook, Susan. *The Banking Crisis of 1933*. University Press of Kentucky, 1973.

Glassman, Cynthia, L. Pierce, and S. Karmel. *Regulating the New Financial Service Industry*. Washington, DC: Center for National Policy Press, 1988.

Grunewald, Alan E. "Rethinking Glass-Steagall." *Business and Society* (Spring 1987): 19–25.

Hammond, Bray. *Banks and Politics in America from the Revolution to the Civil War*. Princeton, NJ: Princeton University Press, 1957.

Hester, Donald. "Special Interests: The FINE Situation." *Journal of Money, Credit and Banking*. (November 1977): 652–61.

Huertas, Thomas F. "An Economist's Brief Against Glass-Steagall Act." *Journal of Bank Research* (1984), 148–59.

Kross, Herman E., and Paul Studenski. *Financial History of the United States*. 2nd ed. New York: McGraw-Hill, 1963.

Pecora, Ferdinand. *Wall Street Under Oath*. New York: Simon and Schuster, 1939.

Saunders, Anthony. "Securities Activities of Commercial Banks: The Problem of Conflicts of Interest." *Economic Review*, Federal Reserve Bank of Philadelphia (July–August 1985): 16–26.

U.S. President's Commission on Financial Structure and Regulation. *Report of the Hunt Commission*. Washington, DC: USGPO, 1972.

U.S. President's Commission on Housing. *Report of the President's Commission on Housing*. Washington, DC: USGPO, 1982.

Chapter 9

Benston, George J., ed. *Financial Services: The Changing Institutions and Government Policy*. Englewood Cliffs, NJ: Prentice-Hall, 1983.

———. "U.S. Banking in an Increasingly Integrated and Competitive World Economy." *Journal of *Financial Services Research* (December 1990): 311–39.

Goudreau, Robert E., and B. Frank King. "Recovering Bank Profitability: Spoiled Again by Large Banks' Loan Problems." *Economic Review,* Federal Reserve Bank of Atlanta (May/June 1990): 30–43.

Haraf, William S., and Rose Marie Kushmeider, eds. *Restructuring Banking and Financial Services in America*. Washington, DC: American Enterprise Institute for Public Policy Research, 1988.

Jesse, Michael A., and Stephen A. Seelig. *Bank Holding Companies and the Public Interest: An Economic Analysis*. Lexington, MA: D. C. Heath, 1977.

Kaufman, George G., and Roger C. Kormendi, eds. *Deregulating Financial Services: Public Policy in Flux*. Cambridge, MA: Ballinger, 1986.

Keeley, Michael C. "Deposit Insurance, Risk, and Market Poser in Banking." *American Economic Review* (December 1990): 1183–1200.

Mengle, David L. "The Case for Interstate Branch Banking." *Economic Review,* Federal Reserve Bank of Richmond (November–December 1990): 3–17.

Rose, Peter S. *The Interstate Banking Revolution*. New York: Quorum Books, 1989.

———. *The Changing Structure of American Banking*. New York: Columbia University Press, 1987.

Zimmer, Steven A., and Robert N. McCauley. "Bank Cost of Capital and International Competition." *Quarterly Review,* Federal Reserve Bank of New York (Winter 1991): 33–59.

Chapter 10

Barth, James R., and Philip R. Wiest. "Consolidation and Restructuring of the U.S. Thrift Industry Under the Financial Institutions Reform, Recovery, and Enforcement Act." Office of Thrift Supervision, Research Paper #89-01 (October 1989).

The Credit Union Report. Credit Union National Association.

Flannery, Mark J. "Credit Unions as Consumer Lenders in the United States." *New England Economic Review,* Federal Reserve Bank of Boston (July/August 1974): 3–12.

Furlong, Frederick T. "Savings and Loan Asset Composition and the Mortgage Market." *Economic Review,* Federal Reserve Bank of San Francisco (Summer 1985): 14–24.

Heaton, Gary G., and Constance R. Dunham. "The Growing Competitiveness of Credit Unions." *New England Economic Review,* Federal Reserve Bank of Boston (May/June 1985): 19–34.

LeCompte, Richard L. B., and Stephen Smith. "Changes in the Cost of Intermediation." *The Journal of Finance* (September 1990): 1337–46.

Masulis, Ronald. "Changes in Ownership Structure: Conversions of Mutual Savings and Loans to Stock Charter." *Journal of Financial Economics* (March 1987): 29–54.

Neely, Walter, and David Rochester. "Operating Performance and Merger Benefits: The Savings and Loan Experience." *Financial Review* (February 1987): 111–30.

Pearce, Douglas K. "Recent Developments in the Credit Union Industry." *Economic Review,* Federal Reserve Bank of Kansas City (June 1984).

Thygerson, Kenneth J., and Josephine McElhone. "Thrift Institutions: Savings and Loan Associations, Savings Banks, and Credit Unions." In Fabozzi, Frank J., and Frank G. Zarb, eds. *Handbook of Financial Markets*. 2nd ed. Homewood, IL: Dow Jones-Irwin, 1986, 462–84.

Appendix

Barth, James R., and Michael G. Bradley. "Thrift Deregulation and Federal Deposit Insurance." *Journal of Financial Services Research* (forthcoming).

Barth, James R., R. Dan Brumbaugh, Jr., Daniel Sauerhaft, and George H. K. Wang. "Thrift-Institution Failures: Causes and Policy Issues." *Proceedings: Bank Structure and Competition,* Federal Reserve Bank of Chicago 184–216.

Benston, George J. "An Analysis of the Causes of Savings and Loan Association Failures." *Mon-*

ograph Series in Finance and Economics. New York: Salomon Brothers Center for the Study of Financial Institutions, and Graduate School of Business Administration, New York University, 1985.

Benston, George J., Robert A. Eisenbeis, Paul M. Horvitz, Edward J. Kane, and George G. Kaufman. *Perspectives on Safe and Sound Banking: Past, Present, and Future*. Cambridge, MA: MIT Press and the American Banking Association, 1986.

Bernard, Victor L., Roger C. Kormendi, S. Craig Pirrong, and Edward A. Snyder. *Crisis Resolution in the Thrift Industry*. Boston: Kluwer Academic Publishers, 1989.

Brumbaugh, R. Dan, Jr. *Thrifts Under Siege*. Cambridge, MA: Ballinger Publishing Company, 1988.

Carron, Andrew S. *The Rescue of the Thrift Industry. Studies in the Regulation of Economic Activity*. Washington, DC: The Brookings Institution, 1983.

Eichler, Ned. *The Thrift Debacle*. Berkeley, CA: University of California Press, 1989.

Hendershott, Patric, and James D. Shilling. "The Impact of the Agencies on Conventional Fixed-Rate Mortgage Yields. *Journal of Real Estate Finance and Economics* (June 1989a): 101–15.

———. "Reforming Conforming Loan Limits: The Impact on Thrift Earnings and Taxpayer Outlays." *Journal of Financial Services Research* (December 1989b): 311–31.

Horvitz, Paul M. "The Case Against Risk-Related Deposit Insurance Premiums." *Housing Finance Review* (July 1983): 253–63.

Kane, Edward J., and Chester Foster. "Valuing Conjectural Guarantees of FNMA Liabilities." In *1986 Proceedings of a Conference on Bank Structure and Competition,* Federal Reserve Bank of Chicago (1986): 347–68.

Kane, Edward J. *The S & L Mess: How Did It Happen?* (Washington, DC: The Urban Institute Press, 1989.

———. "No Room for Weak Links in the Chain of Deposit-Insurance Reform." *Journal of Financial Services Research* (September 1987): 77–111.

———. *The Gathering Crisis in Federal Deposit Insurance*. Cambridge, MA: MIT Press, 1985.

Kaufman, George G. "Framework for the Future: Resurrecting and Legitimizing the Thrift Industry." In *The Future of the Thrift Industry*. Federal Home Loan Bank of San Francisco (1988).

———. "Public Policies Toward Failing Institutions: The Lessons from the Thrift Industry." *Proceedings: Conference on Bank Structure and Competition,* Federal Reserve Bank of Chicago, 267–71.

Meltzer, Allan H. "Major Issues in the Regulation of Financial Institutions." *Journal of Political Economy,* Supplement 75(August 1967): 482–501.

Pyle, David H. "Capital Regulation and Deposit Insurance." *Journal of Banking and Finance* (June 1986): 189–201.

Stigler, George J. "The Theory of Economic Regulation." *Bell Journal of Economics and Management Science* (Spring 1971): 3–21.

Chapter 11

Arnott, Robert, and Peter L. Bernstein. "The Right Way to Manage Your Pension Fund." *Harvard Business Review* (January–February 1988): 95–102.

Allen, Everett, J. Melone, J. Rosenbloom, and J. Vanderhei. *Pension Planning*. Homewood, IL: Richard D. Irwin, Inc., 1988.

Babble, David F. "The Price Elasticity of Demand for Whole Life Insurance." *The Journal of Finance* (March 1985): 225–39.

Baldwin, Ben G., and William G. Droms. *The Life Insurance Investment Advisor*. Chicago: Probus Publishing, 1988.

Leibowitz, Martin L. "Total Portfolio Duration: A New Perspective on Asset Allocation." *Financial Analysts Journal* (September/October 1986): 18–29.

The Service 500. *Fortune*. Vol. 123, No. 11 (June 3, 1991): 272–73.

Warshawsky, Mark J. "The Funding of Private Pension Funds." Federal Reserve *Bulletin* (November 1987): 853–54.

Chapter 12

Bernstein, B. Jay. *The Professional Syndicator: A Guide for Creating Limited Partnerships.* Iowa: Kendall/Hunt Publishing, 1981.

Bloch, Ernest. *Inside Investment Banking.* Homewood, IL: Dow Jones-Irwin, 1986.

Haight, G. Timothy, and Deborah Ann Ford. *REITs: New Opportunities in Real Estate Investment Trust Securities.* Chicago: Probus Publishing, 1986.

Industry Outlook on Property/Casualty Insurance. New York: Standard & Poor's Corporation, 1990.

Kaufman, George G. "Security Activities of Commercial Banks: Recent Changes in Economic and Legal Environments." *Midland Corporate Finance Journal* (Winter 1988): 14–23.

Neihengen, Raymond, Jr., and Mark L. McClure. "Analysis of Finance Company Ratios in 1984." *Journal of Commercial Bank Lending* (September 1985): 40–49.

Trust Assets of Financial Institutions, 1988. Federal Financial Institutions Examination Council, Federal Deposit Insurance Corporation. Washington, DC, 1989.

Williamson, J. Peter. *The Investment Banking Handbook.* New York: John Wiley & Sons, 1988.

Chapter 13

Hendershott P. H., and J. D. Shilling. "The Impact of the Agencies on Conventional Fixed-Rate Mortgage Yields." *Journal of Real Estate Finance and Economics* (June 1989): 101–15.

———. "Reforming Conforming Loan Limits: The Impact on Thrift Earnings and Taxpayer Outlays." *Journal of Financial Services Research* (December 1989): 311–31.

Kane, E., and C. Foster. "Valuing Conjectural Government Guarantees of FNMA Liabilities." *Proceedings of the Conference on Bank Structure and Competition* (May 1986): 347–68.

Kaufman, H. M. "FNMA's Role in Deregulated Markets: Implications for Past Behavior." *Journal of Money, Credit and Banking* (November 1988): 673–83.

McGee, Robert T. "The Cycle in Property/Casualty Insurance." *Quarterly Review,* Federal Reserve Bank of New York (Autumn 1986): 22–30.

President's Commission on Housing. *The Report of the President's Commission on Housing,* U.S. Government Printing Office. 1982.

Thygerson, Kenneth J. "Privately Owned Federally Sponsored Credit Agencies Impact Depositories." *Journal of the School of Business,* San Francisco State University (June 1992): 33–38.

Chapter 14

Benston, George J. "Federal Regulation of Banking: Analysis and Policy Recommendations." *Journal of Bank Research* (Winter 1983): 216–44.

———. "Mortgage Redlining Research: A Review and Critical Analysis." In *The Regulation of Financial Institutions,* Conference Series No. 21, Federal Reserve Bank of Boston (October 1979): 144–95.

Benston, George J., and George G. Kaufman. "Risk and Solvency Regulation of Depository Institutions: Past Policies and Current Options." Staff Memoranda, Federal Reserve Bank of Chicago, SM 88-1. 1988.

Buser, Stephen, Andrew H. Chen, and Edward J. Kane. "Federal Deposit Insurance Regulatory Policy, and Optimal Bank Capital." *Journal of Finance* (March 1981): 512–60.

Flannery, Mark J. "Deposit Insurance Creates a Need for Bank Regulation." *Business Review,* Federal Reserve Bank of Philadelphia (January/February 1982): 17–27.

Horvitz, Paul M. "Reorganization of the Financial Regulatory Agencies." *Journal of Bank Research* (Winter 1983): 245–63.

Kane, Edward J. "Good Intentions and Unintended Evil: The Case Against Selective Credit Allocation." *Journal of Money, Credit and Banking* (February 1977): 55–69.

———. "Accelerating Inflation, Technological Innovation, and the Decreasing Effectiveness of Banking Regulation." *Journal of Finance* (May 1981): 355–67.

———. "Principal-Agent Problems in S&L Salvage." *Journal of Finance* (July 1990): 755–64.

Keeley, Michael C. "Deposit Insurance, Risk, and Market Power in Banking." *American Economic Review* (December 1990): 1183–200.

Maisal, Sherman J., ed. *Risk and Capital Adequacy in Commercial Banks*. Chicago: University of Chicago Press, 1981.

McDowell, Banks. *Deregulation and Competition in the Insurance Industry*. New York: Quorum Books, 1989.

Meier, Kenneth J. *The Political Economy of Regulation: The Case of Insurance*. Albany, NY: State University of New York Press, 1988.

Peterson, Manferd O. "Regulatory Objectives and Conflicts." In Aspinwall, Richard C., and Robert A. Eisenbeis, eds. *Handbook for Banking Strategy*. New York: John Wiley and Sons, 1985.

Stigler, George J. "The Theory of Economic Regulation." *Bell Journal of Economics and Management* (Spring 1971): 3–21.

Chapter 15

Benston, George J., Robert A. Eisenbeis, Paul M. Horvitz, Edward J. Kane, and George G. Kaufman. *Perspectives on Safe and Sound Banking: Past, Present, and Future*. Cambridge, MA: MIT Press and American Banking Association, 1986.

Bernard, Victor L., Roger C. Kormendi, S. Craig Pirrong, and Edward A. Snyder. *Crisis Revolution in the Thrift Industry*. Boston: Kluwer Academic Publishers, 1989.

Cargill, Thomas F., and Gillian C. Garcia. *Financial Reform in the 1980s*. Stanford, CA: Hoover Institution Press, 1985.

Carron, Andrew S. *The Rescue of the Thrift Industry*. Studies in Regulation of Economic Activity. Washington, DC: The Brookings Institution, 1983.

Hendershott, Patric, and J. D. Shilling. "The Impact of the Agencies on Conventional Fixed-Rate Mortgage Yields." *Journal of Real Estate Finance and Economics* (June 1989a): 101–15.

———. "Reforming Conforming Loan Limits: The Impact on Thrift Earnings and Taxpayer Outlays." *Journal of Financial Services Research* (December 1989b): 311–31.

Kane, Edward J. "Accelerating Inflation, Technological Innovation, and the Decreasing Effectiveness of Banking Regulation." *Journal of Finance* (May 1981): 355–67.

———. "Deregulation and Changes in the Financial Services Industry." *Journal of Finance* (July 1984): 759–72.

———. *The Gathering Crisis in Deposit Insurance*. Cambridge, MA: MIT Press, 1985.

Taylor, Jeremy F. *The Banking System in Troubled Times*. New York: Quorum Books, 1989.

Walker, David A. "Effects of Deregulation on the Savings and Loan Industry." *Financial Review* (Spring 1983): 94–110.

Chapter 16

Brewer, Elijah, III, and Cheng Few Lee. "How the Market Judges Bank Risk." *Economic Perspectives,* Federal Reserve Bank of Chicago (November/December 1986): 25–31.

Buser, Stephen A., Andrew H. Chen, and Edward J. Kane. "Federal Deposit Insurance, Regulatory Policy, and Optimal Bank Capital." *Journal of Finance* (March 1981): 51–60.

Keeton, William R. "The New Risk-Based Plan for Commercial Banks." *Economic Review,* Federal Reserve Bank of Kansas City (December 1989): 40–60.

Marcus, Alan J. "The Bank Capital Decision: A Time Series-Cross Section Analysis." *Journal of Finance* (September 1983): 1217–32.

Thomson, James B. "Using Market Incentives to Reform Bank Regulation and Federal Deposit Insurance." *Economic Review,* Federal Reserve Bank of Cleveland (1990–1991): 28–40.

Appendix

Ben-Horim, M., and W. Silber. "Financial Innovation: A Linear Programming Approach." *Journal of Banking and Finance* (1977): 277–96.

Cooper, Ian A. "Financial Innovation." In Aliber, Robert, ed. *The Handbook of International*

Financial Management. Homewood, IL: Dow Jones-Irwin, 1989.

Finnerty, John D. "Financial Engineering in Corporate Finance: An Overview." *Financial Management* (Winter 1988): 62–79.

Greenbaum, Stuart I., and Bryon Higgins. "Financial Innovation." In *Financial Services: The Changing Institutions and Government Policy*. Englewood Cliffs, NJ: Prentice-Hall, 1983.

Kane, Edward J. "Accelerating Inflation, Technological Innovation, and the Decreasing Effectiveness of Banking Regulation." *Journal of Finance*, No. 2 (1981): 355–67

———. "Microeconomic and Macroeconomic Origins of Financial Innovation." In *Financial Innovations*, Federal Reserve Bank of St. Louis. Boston: Kluwer Nijhoff Publishing, 1984.

Merton, Robert C. "The Financial System and Economic Performance." *Journal of Financial Services Research* (December 1990): 263, 300.

Miller, Merton H. "Financial Innovation: The Last Twenty Years and the Next." *Journal of Financial and Quantitative Analysis* (December 1986): 459–71.

Podolski, T. M. *Financial Innovation and the Money Supply*. Oxford: Basil Blackwell Inc., 1986.

Ross, Stephen A. "Institutional Markets, Financial Marketing, and Financial Innovation." *Journal of Finance* (July 1989): 541–56.

Silber, William L. "Towards a Theory of Financial Innovation." In Silber, William L., ed. *Financial Innovation*. Farnborough, Hants: Lexington Books/D.C. Heath, 1975.

———. "The Process of Financial Innovation." *American Economic Review* (May 1983): 89–94.

Van Horne, J. "Of Financial Innovation and Excesses." *Journal of Finance* (July 1985): 621–31.

Chapter 17

Bradley, M. D., and D. W. Jansen. "Deposit Market Deregulation and Interest Rates." *Southern Economic Journal* (October 1986): 478–89.

Brewer, E., III. "The Impact of Deregulation on the True Cost of Savings Deposits: Evidence for Illinois and Wisconsin Savings and Loan Associations." *Journal of Economics and Business* (February 1988): 79–95.

Cherin, A. C., and R. W. Melicher. "Branch Banking and Loan Portfolio Risk Relationships." *Review of Business and Economic Research* (September 1987): 1–13.

Davenport, T. O., and H. D. Sherman. "Measuring Branch Profitability." *Banker's Magazine* (September–October 1987): 34–38.

Davis, R., L. Korobow, and J. Wenninger. "Bankers on Pricing Consumer Deposits." *Quarterly Review,* Federal Reserve Bank of New York (Winter 1987): 6–13.

Davis, R., and L. Korobow. "The Pricing of Consumer Deposit Products—The Non-Rate Dimensions." *Quarterly Review,* Federal Reserve Bank of New York (Winter 1987): 14–18.

Faust, W. H. "The Branch as a Retail Outlet." *Bankers Magazine,* (January–February 1990): 30–35.

Jilk, L. T. "Strategies for Pricing Core Loans and Deposits." *Bankers Magazine* (November–December 1988): 47–52.

Thygerson, Kenneth J. "Modeling Branch Profitability." *Journal of Retail Banking* (Fall 1991): 19–24.

Chapter 18

Bierwag, Gerald O. *Duration Analysis*. Cambridge, MA: Ballinger Publishing, 1987.

Flannery, Mark J., and Christopher M. James. "The Effect of Interest Rate Changes on the Common Stock Returns of Financial Institutions." *Journal of Finance* (September 1984): 1141–53.

Kaufman, George. "Measuring and Managing Interest Rate Risk: A Primer." *Economic Perspectives,* Federal Reserve Bank of Chicago (January–February 1984): 16–29.

Macaulay, Frederick. *Some Theoretical Problems Suggested by the Movement of Interest Rates, Bond Yields, and Stock Prices in the U.S. Since 1856*. National Bureau of Economic Research, 1938.

Samuelson, Paul A. "The Effect of Interest Rate Increases on the Banking System." *American Economic Review* (March 1945): 16–27.

Weil, Roman L. "Macaulay's Duration: An Appreciation." *Journal of Business* (October 1973): 589–92.

Chapter 19

Arak, M., A. Estrella, L. Goodmand, and A. Silver. "Interest Rate Swaps: An Alternative Explanation." *Financial Management* (1988): 12–18.

Brewer, Elijah. "Bank GAP Management and the Use of Financial Futures." *Economic Perspectives,* Federal Reserve Bank of Chicago (March/April 1985): 12–22.

Goodman, John L., Jr., and Charles A. Luckett. "Adjustable-Rate Financing in Mortgage and Consumer Credit Markets." *Federal Reserve Bulletin* (November 1985): 823–35.

Haley, Charles W. "Interest Rate Risk in Financial Intermediaries: Prospects for Immunization." In *Proceedings of a Conference on Bank Structure and Competition.* Chicago: Federal Reserve Bank of Chicago, 1982. 309–17.

Kolb, Robert W., Stephen G. Timme, and Gerald D. Gay. "Macro versus Micro Futures Hedges at Commercial Banks." *Journal of the Futures Markets* (1984): 47–54.

Marshall, John F., and Kenneth R. Kapner. *Understanding Swap Finance.* Cincinnati, OH: South-Western Publishing Co., 1990.

Smith, Clifford W., Jr., Charles W. Smithson, and Lee Macdonald Wakeman. "The Evolving Market for Swaps." *Midland Corporate Finance Journal* (Winter 1986): 20–32.

Whittader, J. Gregg. "Interest Rate Swaps: Risk and Regulation." *Economic Review,* Federal Reserve Bank of St. Louis (March 1987): 3–13.

Chapter 20

Altman, Edward. "Financial Ratios, Discriminant Analysis and the Prediction of Corporate Bankruptcy." *Journal of Finance* (September 1968).

———. *Corporate Financial Distress: A Complete Guide on How to Understand, Predict, and Deal with Bankruptcy.* New York: John Wiley & Sons, 1983.

Altman, Edward, R. G. Haldeman, and P. Narayanan. "Zeta Analysis: A New Model to Identify Bankruptcy Risk of Corporations." *Journal of Banking and Finance* (1977).

Argenti, John. *Corporate Collapse.* New York: McGraw-Hill, Inc., 1976.

Beaver, W. H. "Financial Ratios as Predictors of Failure." *Journal of Accounting Research,* Supplement (1968): 71–127.

Donaldson, T. H. *Credit Risk and Exposure in Securitization and Transactions.* New York: St. Martin's Press, 1989.

Hale, Roger H. *Credit Analysis: A Complete Guide.* New York: John Wiley & Sons, 1983.

Appendix

Clarke, Peter S., *Managing Problem Loans.* Homewood, IL: Dow Jones-Irwin, Inc., 1989.

Greenawalt, Mary Brady, and Joseph F. Sinkey, Jr. "Bank Loan-Loss Provisions and the Income-Smoothing Hypothesis: An Empirical Analysis, 1976–1984." *Journal of Financial Services Research* (1988): 301–18.

King, Arnold. "The Rise in Bank Failures from a Macroeconomic Perspective." *Journal of Financial Services Research* (1988): 353–64.

Scheiner, J. H. "Income Smoothing: An Analysis in the Banking Industry." *Journal of Bank Research* (Summer 1981): 119–23.

Chapter 21

Aggregated Thrift Financial Report. Office of Thrift Supervision. Annual.

Annual Statistical Digest. Board of Governors of the Federal Reserve System, Washington, DC.

Brunner, Allan D., John V. Duca, and Mary M. McLaughlin. "Recent Developments Affecting the Profitability and Practices of Commercial Banks." Federal Reserve *Bulletin,* Board of Governors of the Federal Reserve System (July 1991): 505–27.

Finance Facts Yearbook. American Financial Services Association, Washington, DC.

Life Insurance Fact Book. American Council of Life Insurance, Washington, DC.

Mutual Fund Fact Book. Investment Company Institute, Washington, DC.

REIT Fact Book. National Association of Real Estate Investment Trusts, Inc., Washington, DC.

Statistics on Banking. Federal Deposit Insurance Corporation, Washington, DC. Annual.

Year-end Statistical Report. National Credit Union Administration, Washington, DC. Annual.

Chapter 22

Haraf, William S., and Rose Marie Kushneider. *Restructuring Banking & Financial Services in America*. Washington, DC: American Enterprise Institute for Public Policy Research, 1988.

Mahoney, Patrick I., Alice P. White, Paul F. O'Brien, and Mary M. McLaughlin. "Responses to Deregulation: Retail Deposit Pricing from 1983 through 1985." Working Paper of the Board of Governors of the Federal Reserve System (January 1987).

Napoli, Janet, and Herbert L. Baer. "Disintermediation Marches On." *Chicago Fedletter,* Federal Reserve Bank of Chicago (January 1991).

Pavel, Christine. *Securitization*. Chicago: Probus Publishing Company, 1989.

Chapter 23

Bailey, John M. "Regulating Capital Adequacy." *Bank Management* (February 1990): 3–33.

Bardos, Jeffrey. "Risk-Based Capital Agreement: A Further Step Towards Policy Convergences." *Quarterly Review,* Federal Reserve Bank of New York (Winter 1987/1988): 26–34.

Brady, Thomas F. "The Role of the Prime Rate in the Pricing of Business Loans by Commercial Banks, 1977–1984." Staff Paper No. 146. Board of Governors of the Federal Reserve System (November 1985).

Cole, G. Alexander. "Risk Based Capital: A Loan and Credit Officer's Primer." *Journal of Commercial Bank Lending* (August 1988): 4–20.

Crowley, Donald. "The Impact of Risk-Based Capital on U.S. Banking." *Bank Administration* (November 1988): 16–20.

Graddy, Duane B., and Austin H. Spencer. *Managing Commercial Banks*. Englewood Cliffs, NJ: Prentice-Hall, 1990.

Kane, Edward J. "Incentive Conflict in the International Risk-Based Capital Agreement." *Economic Perspectives,* Federal Reserve Bank of Chicago (May/June 1990): 40–50.

Kelly, J. Robert. "Risk-Based Capital Guidelines for Banks." *Journal of Accountancy* (January 1990): 115–18.

Nadler, Paul S. "Risk-Based Capital Standards and the Cash Manager." *Journal of Cash Management* (July/August 1988): 54–60.

Wall, Larry D. "Capital Requirements for Interest-Rate and Foreign-Exchange Hedges." *Economic Review,* Federal Reserve Bank of Atlanta (May/June 1990): 14–27.

Chapter 24

Bilson, John F. O., and Richard C. Marson, eds. "Exchange Rate Dynamics." In *Exchange Rate Theory and Practice*. Chicago: University of Chicago Press, 1984.

Frankel, Jeffrey A., and Richard Meese. "Are Exchange Rates Excessively Variable?" In *NBER Macroeconometrics Annual 1987*. National Bureau of Economic Research, 1987, 117–62.

Grabbe, J. Orlin. *International Financial Markets*. New York: Elsevier Science Publishing Co., 1986.

International Monetary Fund. *Annual Report*. Various issues.

Marrinan, Jane. "Exchange Rate Determination: Sorting Out Theory and Evidence." *New England Economic Review,* Federal Reserve Bank of Boston (November/December 1989): 39–51.

Pavel, Christine, and John N. McElravey. "Globalization in the Financial Services Industry." *Economic Perspectives,* Federal Reserve Bank of Chicago (May/June 1990): 3–18.

Index

Italicized references indicate material contained in tables and exhibits. Institutions, companies, and government acts are generally listed under their full titles rather than their acronyms.

Aetna Insurance Company, *319*
Agency for International Development, 333, 334
Agency theory, 10–11
Altman, Edward, 562–63
A. M. Best Co., 604
American Bond Exchange, *145*
American Continental Corporation, 262–64
American Depository Receipts (ADRs), 64
American Express Company, 196, *319*
American General Corporation, *319*
American options, 121–24, 129–34
American Savings and Loan Association, 360
American Stock Exchange, *145*
Annuities, 77, 288–92, *289, 647*
Arbitrage, 117, 146–50
Argenti, John, 563
Armco, *319*
Asset/Liability Committees (ALCOs), 413, *414,* 415
Assets, 5–6, *5,* 10
   and asset-backed securities, 56, 654–57, *657*
   as collateral, 52, 56, 59, 70, 87
   of commercial banks, 215–20, *216, 219*
   diversification of, 551–60, *553, 556, 557, 558, 559,* 614–15
   and duration, 482–90
   and *GAP,* 474–81, *477*
   and income simulation, 499–501
   and liquidity, 616–22, *618*
   management of, 613–39, *618, 626–27, 628, 629, 630, 631, 632, 635, 637*
   and mark-to-market, 490–99, *495*
   of nondepository institutions, 292–93, *292,* 297–99, *298,* 309–10, *310,* 315, *315,* 322, *322,* 326, *327*
   of thrift institutions, 255–56, *255,* 266, *266,* 269–70, *269*
   See also Liabilities
Automated clearing houses (ACHs), 212–13, 452
Automation. *See* Technological innovations

Balance of trade, 21–23, 152–53
Banc One, *405*
BankAmerica, *405*
Banker's acceptances (BAs), 69–70, 143
Bankers Trust, *405*
Bank for International Settlements, 551
Bank holding companies (BHCs), 215, 233, 236–38, *237, 240,* 422
Bank Holding Company Act (1956), 237
Banking Act (1933). *See* Glass-Steagall Act
Bank Insurance Fund (BIF), 199, 205–6, 266, 358, 360, 369, 382–86, 398, 648
Bank of America, 351
Bank of Credit and Commerce International (BCCI), 368, 550
Bank of New England, 360
Bank of New York, *405*
Bank of North America, 191
Bank of the United States, 191–92
Bankruptcy, 567–69, 586
Bankruptcy Reform Act (1984), 567–69, *568, 569*
Banks. *See* Commercial banks; Investment banks; Savings banks; *individual banks by name*
Banks for Cooperatives (BCs), 339
Barter system, 9–10

727

728   Index

Basle agreements, 623, 625
Beneficial Corporation, *319*
Benston, George J., 355
Berger, Allen N., 211–12
Biddle, Nicholas, 192, 193
Bilson, John F. O., 677
Black, Fisher, 129–30
Black-Scholes option pricing method, 129–34, *132, 133*
Boesky, Ivan, 161–62, 305
Bonds
   in business sector, *5, 58,* 59–60, 143, *145, 266, 292, 298, 323,* 565–66
   in government sector, 57–58, 62–63, 104–5, 143, *145, 323,* 565
   yield, 79–82, 104–5
   See also Options
Borg-Warner Corporation, *319*
Brady, Thomas F., 633
Bretton Woods Agreement (1944), 666–67
Brokerage, 171, 174–76, 425–26, 435
Bush, George, 206
Business cycle, 22–28, 32–33, 481, *482*
Business sector, 60
   financial claims issued by, 53–54, *53,* 58–60, *58*
   and loanable funds, 22–24, *25*

Capital deficit units (CDUs), 4, 6–7, 20–22, 30–37
Capital surplus units (CSUs), 4–7, 20–22, 30–37
Cash flow schedules, 82–83, *82*
Centrust Savings Bank, 442
Certificates of Accrual on Treasury Securities (CATS), 89
Certificates of deposit (CDs), 67, 124, 143, 218, *218,* 257, *257,* 458, 460, 500, 501, 647, 652
Chemical Bank, *405*
Chicago Board of Trade (CBOT), 115–16, *115,* 120, 122, 144, *145,* 156, *157,* 528
Chicago Board Options Exchange (CBOE), 122, *145,* 528, 682
Chicago Mercantile Exchange, 122, *145,* 680
Chrysler Corporation, *319,* 333
Circuit breakers, 120–21, 158–59
Citicorp, 204, 229, *405*
Clarke, Peter, 584
Clay, Henry, 193
Collateral. *See* Assets
Collateralized mortgage obligations (CMOs). *See* Mortgages

College Savings Bank, 442
Commercial banks, 10, *16,* 145
   asset and liability structure of, *66,* 215–20, *216, 218, 221, 251, 396*
   history of, 191–94, 198–206
   and international banking, 238–47, *240, 242, 243, 245, 246,* 400–401
   market structure of, 229–38, *230, 231–32*
   performance of during 1980s, 222–29, *225, 227, 228,* 236, 393, *394*
   regulation of, 218–22, *367. See also* regulatory institutions by name
   and thrift institutions, 228–29
   types of, 215, 219–20, *219,* 225–26
   See also Depository institutions
Commercial paper, *58,* 143, *316,* 647
Commissioners 1980 Standard Ordinary, 286, *287*
Commission on Financial Structure and Regulation (1970), 202
Commission on Housing (1981), 202, 345
Commission on Money and Credit (1958), 202
Commodity Credit Corporation, 334
Commodity Futures Trading Commission (CFTC), *367,* 370
Community Reinvestment Act (1977), *352,* 365
Competitive Equality Act (1987), 204
Computers. *See* Technological innovations
Consols, 87–88
Constant Prepayment Rate (CPR), 95, 98, 101
Consumer Credit Protection Act (1968), 352, *352*
Continental National Bank of Illinois, 357, 360, 582, 615
Contingent claims. *See* Futures; Options
Covenants, 52, 564–67
Credit risk
   and credit analysis, 560–63
   management of, 415, *416,* 429–30, 551–74, *553, 556, 557, 558, 559, 568, 569, 572, 574,* 581–89, *582, 587, 589*
   trends in, 547–48
   types of, 548–51
Credit Union Liquidity Fund, 173, 620
Credit Union National Association (CUNA), 268
Credit unions, 251, *251,* 267–71, *268, 269, 270. See also* Thrift institutions
Currency, 11, 191, 193, 194
   and exchange rates, 7, 41–43, 152–53, 173, 444, 665–78, *671*
   risks, 678–85, *679, 681*

Demand deposits. *See* Transaction deposits
Department of Defense, 68
Department of Housing and Urban Development (HUD), 340, 344, 345, *367,* 372, 381
Department of Labor, *367,* 370, 373
Department of the Treasury, 194
Depository institutions, 10, 396–97, *396,* 647
  and Federal Reserve System, 70, 173, 200, 218, 220–21, *222,* 367–68, *367,* 385, 537, 604, 620, 623–25, 649
  financial claims issued by, 64–67, *66*
  performance criteria for, 455–63, *458, 459, 460, 461, 462,* 591–600, *594, 595, 596, 597, 598, 599, 600*
  and problem loans and investments, 581–89, *582, 587, 589*
  regulation of, 358–63, 376–86, *381, 383–84*
  See also Commercial banks; Thrift institutions
Depository Institutions Deregulation and Monetary Control Act (DIDMCA) (1980), 202–4, 211, 274, 392–93, 648
Derivative claims. *See* Futures; Options; Swaps
DIA. *See* Garn-St. Germain Depository Institutions Act (DIA)
Discount rate. *See* Federal Reserve System
Diversification. *See* Assets
Donaldson, T. H., 549
Douglas Amendment. *See* Glass-Steagall Act
Dow Jones Industrial Average, 244
Drexel Burnham Lambert, 153, 161–62, 305
Duration, 482–90, *484, 488*

Edge Act (1919), *240,* 241, 242
Efficiency, types of
  allocational, 341
  and economies of scale and scope, 233–36, *234*
  informational, 155, 159–63
  operational, 155–58
Electronic Funds Transfer Act (1979), *353*
Employee Retirement Income Security Act (ERISA) (1974), 289, 299–300, 328, 370, 372
Equal Credit Opportunity Act (1974), *352*
Equitable Life Assurance Society, 293, *319*
Eurodollar markets, *9,* 152–53, 667
Europe, markets in, 3, 7, *63, 151,* 152, *152,* 238–39, 241–47, *243,* 246, 666–68, *671,* 678, *679*
European Currency Unit (ECU), 673
European Economic Community (EEC), 673
European options, 121, 123, 129–34

Exchange rates. *See* Currency; Global markets
Executive Life Insurance Company, 124
Export-Import Bank, *68,* 333

Fair Credit Billing Act (1974), *352*
Fair Credit Reporting Act (1970), *352*
Fama, Eugene F., 154, 162
Farm Credit Assistance Corporation, *68*
Farm Credit Banks (FCBs), *68,* 333, *336,* 338–39, 395
Farmers Home Administration, 334
Federal Agricultural Mortgage Corporation, *337,* 338, 342
Federal Asset Disposition Association, 204, 380
Federal Credit Union Act (1934), 199
Federal Deposit Insurance Corporation (FDIC), 199, 203–4, 206, 220, *222,* 253, 266, 281–82, 357, 360–61, *367,* 369, 376–86, 418–19, 604
Federal Deposit Insurance Corporation Improvement Act (FDICIA) (1991), 206, 282, 356, 360–62, 364, 368, 382–86, *383–84,* 403–4, 623
Federal Financial Institution Examination Council, 604
Federal Financing Banks (FFBs), *68,* 380, *381*
Federal Home Loan Banks (FHLBs), *68,* 78, 173, 199, 204, 205, 252–58, *257,* 276, 328, *336,* 341, 363, 369, 376–81, *381,* 394, 491, 588, 649
Federal Home Loan Mortgage Corporation (FHLMC), *68, 69,* 71, *71,* 94, 97–98, 144, 256, 279, 315, 333, *336, 337,* 338, 340, 341, 346, 355, 394, 517, *626,* 654
Federal Housing Administration (FHA), *68,* 94, 98, 99, 101, 201, 317, 334, *337,* 339, 340, *367,* 372
Federal Intermediate Credit Banks (FICBs), 339
Federal Land Banks (FLBs), 339
Federal National Mortgage Association (FNMA), *38, 68, 69,* 71, *71,* 144, 201, 256, 279, 315, *336, 337,* 338–40, 341, 345, 346, 355, 394, *405,* 517, *626,* 654
Federal Open Market Committee (FOMC), 197, 198
Federal Reserve Act (1913), 196
Federal Reserve System, 5, 11, 235, 237, 241, 338, 452
  and depository institutions, 70, 173, 200, 218, 220–21, *222,* 367–68, *367,* 385, 537, 604, 620, 623–25, 649
  effects of on interest rates, 26–28, *27,* 78, 391

730 Index

Federal Reserve System (cont'd)
  functions of, 196–98
  and monetary policy, 197–98, 211, 354
  and Treasury securities, 83, 143
Federal Savings and Loan Insurance Corporation (FSLIC), 199, 203–4, 254, 262, 276, 345, 356, 358, 369, 376–81, *396, 397*
Fidelity Investments, 333–34
Finance companies, 10, 314–15, *316,* 601, *647*
Financial Accounting Standards Board (FASB), 282, 299, 491
Financial claim/function matrices, 177–81, *178, 179, 180, 181, 182,* 221–22, *223–24,* 264, *265*
Financial claims, characteristics of, 7, 51–72. See also types of claims by name
Financial engineering, 88–102, 444–46
Financial futures contracts. See Futures
Financial institutions. See Financial management; Intermediaries; institutions by name
Financial Institutions Act (1975), 202
Financial Institutions and the Nation's Economy (FINE) (House Committee on Banking, Currency, and Housing), 202
Financial Institutions Reform, Recovery, and Enforcement Act (FIRREA) (1989), 205, 256, 258, 259, 262, 282, 338, 345, 356, 360–61, 364, 369, 376–81, *381,* 397, 398, 403–4, 418–19, 455, 623, 648
Financial management, 8, 15, *16*
  of assets, 426–32, 613–39, *618, 626–27, 628, 629, 630, 631, 632, 635, 637*
  and channels of distribution, 448–63, *451, 458, 459, 460, 461, 462*
  of commercial banks, 225–26
  of credit risks, 551–74, *553, 556, 557, 558, 559, 568, 569, 572, 574,* 581–89, *582, 587, 589*
  duties of, 412–16, *414, 416*
  and financial leverage, 417–23, *419, 421, 422*
  and innovations, 440–47
  of interest rate risk, 514–42, *516, 520, 524, 526, 527, 531, 534, 535, 536, 538, 540*
  of liabilities, 645–61, *647, 649, 651, 652, 657, 660*
  of mutual institutions, 435–37
  and profitability, 423–35, *427, 430, 431,* 455–63, *458, 459, 460, 461, 462*
  of property and casualty insurance companies, 314
  and regulation, 418–19, 423

  of thrift institutions, 258, 270–71
  and types of analysis, 590–91, *591, 592,* 604
Financial markets, characteristics of, 141–63, 171. See also Global markets; *institutions and aspects of markets by name*
Financial sector, 9–10, 64–72, *65.* See also Intermediaries
Financial service companies, 318–19, *319*
First Capitol Life Insurance Company, 124
First Chicago Bank, *405*
First Interstate Bank, *405*
1st National Bank of Cedar Falls, Iowa, 179–80, *180, 181*
First Wachovia, *405*
Fisher, Irving, 28
Fisher Effect, 28–29
Fitch rating service, 60
Fleet/Norstar Financial Group, *405*
Ford Motor Credit Corporation, 315, *319*
Forward cash markets, 119, 145–46, 516–17, 679–80
Frankel, Jeffrey A., 677
Futures, 8–9, *9,* 55–56, 114–17, *145*
  and foreign exchange, 680–82, *681*
  hedges, 516–28, *520, 524, 526, 527*
  illegal trading of, 120
  and options, 526–33, *527, 531*
  requirements of, 119–21
  valuation of, 117–18, *118*

GAP, 474–81, *476, 477, 478, 479, 482,* 528
Garn-St. Germain Depository Institutions Act (DIA) (1982), 203–5, 256, 264, 392–93
General Agreement on Trade and Tariffs (GATT) (1947), 667
General Electric Capital Corporation, 315, *319*
Generally accepted accounting principles (GAAP), 259, 278, 282, 383, 423, 427, 491, 499, 527–28, 587–88, 638
General Motors Acceptance Corporation, 315, 318, *319*
Glass-Steagall Act (1933), 199, 200, 202, 206, 274, 356, 362, 382, 392
Global markets, 444, 445
  and automation, 146, 156
  and Basle agreements, 623, 625
  and Eurodollar markets, 152–53, 667
  exchange rates and currency risk in, 665–85, *671, 679, 681*

and financial claims, 67, 69–70, 122
    growth of, 2–4, 7–9, *8, 9,* 64, 150–51, *151, 152*
    and influence peddling, 368
    and international banking, 238–47, *240, 242, 243, 245, 246,* 400–401
    and problem loans, 581–82
Globex, 122
Government, role of, 6, 11–13, 332–33
    changes in during 1980s, 392–99, *394, 396*
    and financial innovations, 443–46
    history of, 191–206
    and private financial institutions, 220–21, *222,* 336–38, *337,* 342–46, *344,* 358–63, 376–86
    and public good theory, 350–58
    in savings and loan debacle of 1980s, 262–64, *263,* 273–82, 376–81, 392–93
    and structure of regulatory system, 363–73, *367*
    and types of lending programs, 333–41, *335*
    See also Federal Reserve System; *regulatory institutions by name*
Government National Mortgage Association (GNMA), 71, *71,* 94, 97–99, 115, 144, 315, 333, *333, 337,* 338, 339, 355, *367,* 372, 394, *626,* 654
Government sector
    financial claims issued by, 53–54, *53,* 57–58, *57,* 62–63
    and loanable funds, 21–24, *25*
Government sponsored credit enterprises (GSEs), 10, 67–72, *68, 69, 71,* 334–46, *336, 337,* 394–95, 403–4. *See also institutions by name*
Great Depression (1930s), 78, 198–202, 226–27, 349, 356, 358
Guaranteed investment contracts (GICs), 285, 646–47, *647*

Hamilton, Alexander, 191
Hedging, 114–15, 118–21, 125–28, 155, 158–59, 308, 516–33, *520, 524, 526, 527*
Hendershott, P. H., 345
Home Mortgage Disclosure Act (1975), *353,* 364
Home Owner's Loan Act (1933), 199, 201
Home Owner's Loan Corporation (HOLC), 201
Household Finance Corporation, *319*
Household sector, *5,* 35
    financial claims issued by, 53–56, *53, 54,* 61–62, *61*
    and loanable funds, 21–23, 24, *25*
Housing Act (1968), 333

HUD. *See* Department of Housing and Urban Development (HUD)
Humphrey, David B., 211–12
Hunt Commission (1970), 202
Hybrid claims, 56, 89–105

Income simulation model, 499–501, *500, 501*
Inflation, rate of, 28–29, 279, 390–91, 668
Informational asymmetry, 141–42, 351–52
Insider trading, 161–62, 355
Insurance companies. *See* Life insurance companies; Property and casualty insurance companies (P&Cs)
Insurance Company of North America, 194
Interest Equalization Tax, 667
Interest Rate Control Act (1966), 202
Interest rate risk, 472–74, *472, 473*
    and duration, 482–90, *484, 488*
    and *GAP,* 474–81, *476, 477, 478, 479, 482*
    and income simulation, 499–501, *500, 501*
    management of, 317–18, 413–15, *414,* 430–31, 514–42, *516, 520, 524, 526, 527, 531, 534, 535, 536, 538, 540*
    and mark-to-market, 490–99, *494, 495, 496, 497, 498*
    types of, 37–46, *44, 45, 46*
Interest rates, 6, *26,* 28
    compounding of, 77–79
    on different types of financial claims, 37–46, *38. See also types of claims by name*
    and effects of inflation, 28–29
    elasticity of, 23, *24,* 485–86
    and Federal Reserve policies, 26–28, *27,* 78, 391
    implied forward rate, 31, 33–34
    real and nominal, 20, *21,* 28–29
    term structure of, 29–37, 497
    See also Regulation Q; Yield, types of
Intermediaries, 5
    functions of, 172, 174–81
    history of, *190,* 191–206
    profitability of, 423–35, *427, 430, 431*
    rationales for, 170–73
    See also institutions by name
International banking facilities (IBFs), 241, *242*
International Business Machines Corporation (IBM), 154–56
International Monetary Fund (IMF), 666
International Monetary Market (IMM), 115, *115,* 680

International sector
  financial claims issued by, 53–54, *53*, 63–64, *63*
  and loanable funds, 21–24, *25*
Investment. *See* Savings and investment process
Investment banks, 10, *145*, 304–10, *310*
Investment intermediaries, 10, 319–28. *See also institutions by name*
ITT, *319*

Jackson, Andrew, 193
Japan, markets in, *5*, 22, *63*, *151*, 152, *152*, 244, 307, 445, 666–68, *671*, 678, *679*
  and international banking, 238–39, 241–47, *243*, *245*, *246*, 400–401
J. C. Penney, 318, *319*
Jensen, Michael, 154
John Hancock Mutual Life Insurance Company, 293
J. P. Morgan & Company, 305, *405*
Junk bonds, 60, 153–55, 256, 400

Kane, Edward, 363–64, 441, 444
Kapner, Kenneth R., 533
Kaufman, George G., 355, 359
Keating, Charles, 262–64
Keeley, Michael C., 229
Kohlberg, Kravis, and Roberts (KKR), 308, 325

Liabilities
  of commercial banks, 217–20, *218*, *221*
  and duration, 482–90
  and *GAP*, 474–81, *478*
  and income simulation, 499–501
  management of, 645–61, *647*, *649*, *651*, *652*, *657*, *660*
  and mark-to-market, 490–99, *495*
  of nondepository institutions, 309–10, *310*, 315, *315*
  of thrift institutions, 257–58, *257*, 266–67, *267*, 270, *270*
  See also Assets
Life insurance companies, *5*, 10, *65*, 194–95, 284–86, *287*, *367*, *647*
  asset structure of, *54*, 292–93, *292*, *422*
  liability management of, 657–61, *660*
  and options, 124–25
  and pension funds, 296–97, *297*
  performance criteria for, 602–3, *603*
  types of, 293–94, *293*, *294*

and types of policies, 287–92, *288*, *289*, *291*
Limited partnerships, 10, 324–25
Lincoln Savings and Loan, 262–64
Loans, 216–17, *216*, *219*, *255*, 256, *266*, 269, *269*, *292*, *316*, *335*, 336–37, *337*, 432–34, *495*, *497*, 564–65, 571–72
  participations and syndications of, 633–39, *635*, *637*
  problems with during 1980s, 581–89, *582*, *587*, *589*
Lockheed Corporation, 333
London interbank offered rate (LIBOR), 153, 633
London International Financial Futures Exchange (LIFFE), 680

Macaulay, Frederick, 482
Manufacturers Hanover Trust, *405*
Market-making, 174, 176, 308
Markowitz, Harry, 555
Mark-to-market, 119–20, 282, 490–99, *494*, *495*, *496*, *497*, *498*
Marshall, John F., 533
Marson, Richard C., 677
McCarran-Ferguson Act (1945), 371
McCauley, Robert N., 245–47
McFadden Act (1927), 198–99, 230, 241, 362
Meese, Richard, 677
Mellon Bank, *405*
Merrill Lynch & Company, 89, *319*, 442, 443
Merton, Robert, 441–42
Metropolitan Life Insurance Company, 293
Milken, Michael, 60, 153–54, 305
Miller, Merton, 441
Mission Insurance Company, 180–81, *182*, 183
Monetary Control Act. *See* Depository Institutions Deregulation and Monetary Control Act (DIDMCA)
Monetary policy, 197–98, 279, 354, 376, 391, 440, 446–47
Money market deposit accounts (MMDAs), 66–67, *66*, *221*, *270*, *460*, *461*, *461*, *500*, *501*, *647*
Money market mutual funds. *See* Mutual funds
Moody's rating service, 60
Morris, Robert, 191
Mortgage banking companies, 315–18, *367*
Mortgages, *5*, 56, *58*, *61*, 143, 255, *266*, 275, *292*, *298*, *495*, *497*, *626*
  adjustable-rate mortgages (ARMs), 62, 539–42, *540*

and collateralized mortgage obligations (CMOs), *69,* 100–102, 445, *626*
and depository institutions, 217, 252, 255–56, 266
fixed-rate mortgages (FRMs), 61, 92–100, *94, 95, 96,* 274–75
graduated payment mortgages (GPMs), 62
and mortgage-backed securities, 56, 71–72, *71,* 92–102, *94, 95, 96, 99, 102, 104,* 144, *145,* 255, 266, *495, 497*
options on, 92–98, 123
stripping of, 98–100
See also government sponsored credit enterprises by name
Mutual Benefit Life Insurance Company, 124
Mutual funds, 10, 171, 196, 320–24, *321, 322, 323, 367,* 389–90, 444
Mutual institutions, 252–54, *253,* 264, 293, 435–37. *See also institutions by name*

National Association of Insurance Commissioners (NAIC), 371
National Association of Securities Dealers Automatic Quotations (NASDAQ), 144
National Bank Act (1863), 194, 200
National Credit Union Administration (NCUA), 268, 338, *367,* 369, 620
National Credit Union Share Insurance Fund (NCUSIF), 199, 268, 369, *495, 497*
National Housing Act (1934), 201
National Mortgage Association of Washington, 201
NCNB, *405*
Negotiable order of withdrawal accounts (NOW), 66, 202, 203, 257, *257,* 444, *460,* 461, *461, 647*
Net interest margin and spread, 428–32, *430, 431*
New York Bond Exchange, *145*
New York Futures Exchange, *145*
New York Life Insurance Company, 293
New York Safety Fund, 192, 358n
New York Stock Exchange (NYSE), 144, *145,* 146, 150, 154, 156–58, 339
Nikkei average, 244
1983 Individual Annuity Table, 286, *287*
Nondepository institutions, 10, 600–604, *602, 603,* 604. *See also institutions by name*
Nonmarket economy, 7
Northwestern Mutual Life Insurance Company, 293
Norwest Bank, *405*

Off-balance sheet transactions (OBSTs), 571–74, *572, 574*
Office of Management and Budget (OMB), 345–46
Office of the Comptroller of the Currency (OCC), 220–21, *222,* 236, 253, 367, *367*
Office of Thrift Supervision (OTS), 205, 253, 256, *367,* 369, 418–19, 491, 604, 620, 624
Options, 8–9, *9,* 55–56, 114–15, *145*
call and prepayment provisions, 39, 86, 92–98, 121–23
on foreign exchange, 682–84
and futures, 526–33, *527, 531*
mechanisms of, 125–28, *127*
types of, 121–27
valuation of, 128–34, *132, 133*
Organization of Petroleum Exporting Countries (OPEC), *63,* 238
Origination function, 174–75, 317, 336, 424–25, 432–33, 456–57

Pacific Stock Exchange (PSE), *145*
Pacific Telephone and Telegraph, 37–39, *38*
Parker Pen Corporation, *319*
Passbook accounts. *See* Savings deposits
Payment system, 9, 171, 211–13
Pension Benefit Guarantee Corporation (PBGC), 299, *367,* 370, 372–73
Pension funds, *5,* 10, *54, 65,* 196, 284, 294–97, *298, 367,* 604, *604*
Philadelphia Stock Exchange (PHLX), *145,* 682
Portfolio management, 174, 176–77, 426–32, *427, 430, 431,* 474, 555–59, *556, 557, 558, 559. See also* Assets; Financial management; Liabilities
Portfolio Selection—Efficient Diversification of Investments (Markowitz), 555
Present value (PV), theory of, 76–83
Prime rate, 633
Property and casualty insurance companies (P&Cs), 311–14, *313, 422,* 601, *602*
Prudential Insurance Company of America, 293, *319*
Public Security Association Standard Prepayment Model (PSA), 95, 98, 101

Qualified thrift lender test (QTLT), 378–79, 385

Random walk hypothesis, 159–60, *160*
Real estate investment trusts (REITs), 10, 325–26

Real estate mortgage investment conduits (REMICs), 69, 100–102, 445, 657
Real Estate Settlements and Procedures Act, 352
Recruit Company, 307
Regulation. See Government, role of; regulatory institutions by name
Regulation Q, 78, 201–3, 252, 274, 362, 377, 390–93, 399, 453, 455
Reliance Electric, 38
Repurchase agreements (repos), 65, 70, 87, 143, 221, 257, 267
Resolution Trust Corporation (RTC), 68, 100, 153–54, 205, 251, 262, 369, 376, 380–81, 381, 398, 404, 455, 581
Reverse repurchase agreements (reverse repos), 87, 219, 295, 497, 652
RJR Nabisco, Inc., 308
Roosevelt, Franklin Delano, 201
Rose, Peter S., 235
Rural Electrification Administration, 333, 334

Salomon Brothers, Inc., 89, 309, 351
Savings and investment process
  basic mechanisms of, 4–11, 13, 14
  and interest rates, 20–46, 21, 24, 25, 26, 27
  and loanable funds, 20–28
Savings and loan associations (S&Ls), 251, 252–58, 253, 254, 255, 257
  debacle during 1980s, 252, 259–64, 259, 260, 261, 263, 273–82, 376–81, 392–93
  See also Thrift institutions
Savings Association Insurance Fund (SAIF), 199, 205, 253–54, 360, 369, 376–81, 398, 648
Savings banks (SBs), 251, 264, 266–67, 266, 267
Savings deposits, 65, 66, 217–18, 218, 257, 257, 267, 270, 458, 495, 497, 647, 649
Scholes, Myron, 129–30
Sears, Roebuck and Company, 318, 319
Second Bank of the United States, 192–93
Securities. See types of securities by name
Securities and Exchange Commission (SEC), 161, 282, 334, 367, 371, 420, 491, 604, 656
Securities Investor Protection Corporation (SIPC), 372
Security Pacific Bank, 351, 405
Senior-subordinated securities, 102–4, 573
Servicing function, 40–41, 174, 175, 317, 337, 425, 433–35, 456–57
Sheshunoff and Co., 604

Shilling, J. D., 345
Signet Bank, 405
Silber, William, 441
Small Business Administration, 333–34, 337, 341
Smithsonian Agreement (1971), 668
SNL Securities, L.P., 604
Soviet Union, former, markets in, 3, 6, 7
Special Drawing Rights (SDR), 673
Standard and Poor's rating service, 60, 158
Statistics on Banking (Federal Deposit Insurance Corporation), 604
Stigler, George, 274, 363
Stock
  common, 122–23, 143–45, 145, 266, 292, 323
  preferred, 87–88, 143
Student Loan Marketing Association (SLMA), 68, 336, 337, 338, 340, 341, 355, 533
Suffolk System, 192
Swaps, 55–56, 533–38, 534, 535, 536, 538, 573, 652, 684–85

Taxation, 12, 22, 252
  on different types of securities, 43, 104–5
  and financial innovations, 445–46
Tax Reform Act (1986), 100–101, 104–5, 215, 289, 312, 325, 389
Technological innovations, 389–90
  automation, 8, 443
  computerized trading, 120, 122, 144, 146, 156
  and economies of scale and scope, 235–36
  electronic banking, 65, 175, 211–13, 451–54
  telemarketing, 449–50
Tennessee Valley Authority, 68
Theory of Interest, The (Fisher), 28
Thrift institutions, 10, 16, 66, 367
  and commercial banks, 228–29, 282
  history of, 195, 199–200, 203–6, 250–51, 251
  See also Depository institutions; Resolution Trust Corporation (RTC); individual thrift institutions by name
Time deposits, 67, 124, 143, 218, 218, 257, 257, 267, 270, 298, 649
Too big to fail policy (TBTF), 359–60, 385
Transaction deposits, 65–66, 66, 211–13, 217–18, 218, 221, 257, 257, 267, 270, 298, 434–35, 451–53, 458, 460, 461, 467, 647, 649
Transamerica Insurance Company, 319
Treasury Income Growth Receipts (TIGRs), 89

Treasury securities, *5*, 26, *30*, *38*, 83–85, *85*, 88, 142, 143, *145*, *151*, 156, *157*, *219*, *298*, 309, *626*
  and coupon stripping, 89–92, *89, 90, 91–92*
  and futures, *9*, 115–16, *115*, 119, 528
  risks and benefits of, 38, 39, 41, 43, 67–68
  types of, 57–58, *57*, 88
Trump, Donald, 583
Trust companies, 195, 326–28, *327*
Truth-in-Savings Act, *353*

Uniform Bank Performance (Federal Financial Institution Examination Council), 604
United States, markets in during 1980s, 2–3, 204–6, 388–92, *388–89*, 440–47
  automation and computerization. *See* Technological innovations
  changes in government role, 392–99, *394, 396*, 406–7
  and channels of distribution, 448–63, *451, 458, 459, 460, 461, 462*
  commercial banks, 78, 222–29, *225, 227, 228*, 233, 236, 243–46, 393, *394*, 397–99
  competition and overcapacity, 399–402
  credit risk trends, 547–48, 570–71
  financial engineering, 88–89, 444–46
  impact assessment of, 402–5, *403, 405*
  life insurance companies, 291–92
  problem loans and investments, 581–89, *582, 587, 589*

thrift institutions, 250–51, 259–64, *259, 260, 261, 263*, 273–82, 376–81, 392–94, 397–98
  See also Tax Reform Act
USAA Insurance Company, *319*

Valuation
  of financial claims, 83–105, 117–18, 128–34, 413
  and present value theory, 76–83
  and pricing anomalies, 161–62
Vernon Savings and Loan Association, 277–78, 329
Veterans Administration, 316, 334, *337, 367*
Volcker, Paul, 391

Westinghouse Corporation, *319*

Xerox Corporation, *319*

Yield, types of, 29, 30–37, *30, 32, 35, 37*
  bank discount yield (BDY), 84–85, *85*
  break-even risk adjusted asset yield (BERAY), 343–44, *344*, 628–33, *631, 632*
  equivalent annual yield (EAY), 81–82
  taxable equivalent yield (TEY), 104–5
  yield to maturity, 44, 79–80, 86–88

Zero coupon bonds, 56, 88–92, *89, 90, 91–92*, 445
Zimmer, Steven A., 245–47
Z score, 562–63